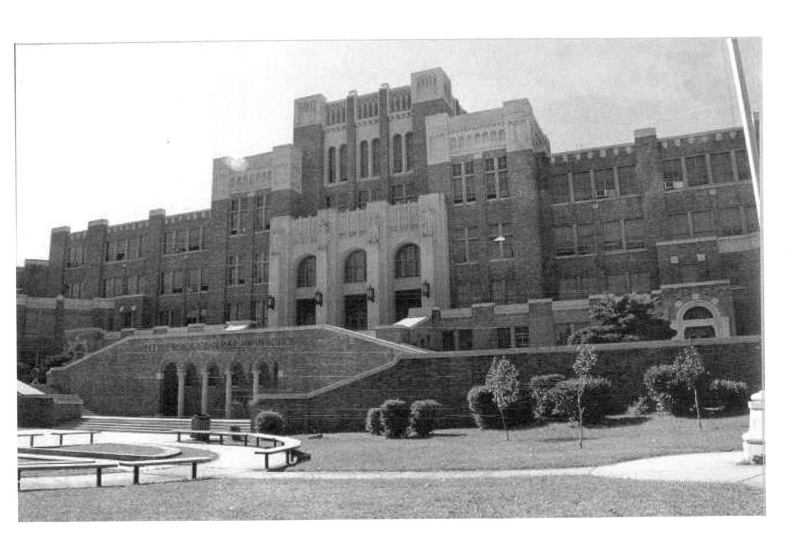

LITTLE ROCK CENTRAL HIGH SCHOOL
TIGER FOOTBALL

749-276-48

2 NATIONAL CHAMPIONSHIPS

32 STATE CHAMPIONSHIPS

43 CONFERENCE CHAMPIONSHIPS

15 UNDEFEATED SEASONS

347 SHUTOUTS

3 NATIONAL PLAYERS OF THE YEAR

16 ALL-AMERICANS

28 ALL-SOUTHERN

TIGER PRIDE

TIGER PRIDE

100 YEARS OF LITTLE ROCK CENTRAL HIGH FOOTBALL

by Brian Cox

Arkansas Business Ventures
Little Rock, AR
2005

EDITOR: Robert Yates
COVER DESIGN: Heather Alexander
PRINTER: Alexander Printing

FRONT COVER: Photographed and designed by Heather Alexander. Helmet provided by Marty Lubinsky, Past Time Sports.

BACK COVER: Photographed and designed by Heather Alexander. Helmet provided by Bernie Cox, Central High School.

TEAM PHOTOS PROVIDED BY CENTRAL HIGH SCHOOL: 1904, 1905, 1906, 1907, 1908, 1909, 1910, 1911, 1912, 1913, 1914, 1915, 1916, 1917, 1918, 1919, 1920, 1921, 1955, 1956, 1959, 1963, 1964, 1966, 1967, 1968, 1969, 1970, 1974
TEAM PHOTOS PROVIDED BY THE ARKANSAS HISTORY COMMISSION: 1925, 1926, 1927, 1928, 1930, 1931, 1934, 1937
TEAM PHOTO PROVIDED BY MARY STAFFORD: 1929
TEAM PHOTOS PROVIDED BY HARRY DONALDSON: 1932, 1933, 1938, 1939, 1940
TEAM PHOTOS PROVIDED BY BUDDY NICHOLS: 1936, 1941
TEAM PHOTOS PROVIDED BY LOUIS SCHAUFELE: 1942, 1943, 1944, 1945, 1946
TEAM PHOTO PROVIDED BY JOHNNY WALKER: 1949
TEAM PHOTO PROVIDED BY CURTIS FINCH: 1948, 1950
TEAM PHOTO PROVIDED BY HENRY MOORE: 1951
TEAM PHOTO PROVIDED BY MRS. JOHN MCCARTY: 1957
TEAM PHOTO PROVIDED BY GENE HALL: 1960
TEAM PHOTO PROVIDED BY DICKIE HEIEN: 1965
TEAM PHOTO PROVIDED BY RON COLLAR: 1971
TEAM PHOTO PROVIDED BY JEFF BEMBERG: 1972
TEAM PHOTO PROVIDED BY DON PERKINS: 1973
TEAM PHOTOS PROVIDED BY BERNIE COX: 1975, 1976, 1977, 1978, 1979, 1980, 1981, 1982, 1983, 1984, 1985, 1986, 1987, 1988, 1989, 1990, 1991, 1992, 1993, 1994, 1995, 1996, 1998, 1999
TEAM PHOTOS PROVIDED BY BRIAN COX: 1922, 2000, 2001, 2002, 2003, 2004

Published in 2005 by Arkansas Business Ventures, Little Rock

For information about permission to reproduce selections from this book, write to Arkansas Business Ventures, P.O. Box 241351, Little Rock, AR 72223-0006 or email info@arkansasbusinessventures.com.

Library of Congress Control Number: 2005902641
ISBN 0-9765425-0-1

Printed in the United States of America

10 9 8 7 6 5 4 3 2 1

 Arkansas Business Ventures
P.O. Box 241351
Little Rock, AR 72223-0006
info@arkansasbusinessventures.com

vi

The following provided photos, information, time or support in the creation of this book. I am grateful to each and every one listed.

Arkansas Democrat-Gazette
Arkansas History Commission
Central Arkansas Library System
Little Rock Central High School
Sitler and Henry Design
University of Arkansas at Little Rock Library
PastTimeSports.biz – Marty Lubinsky

Jimmy Albright (c/o 1947)
Heather Alexander
Jeff Bemberg (c/o 1975)
Sterling Cockrill
Ron Collar (c/o 1972)
Bernie Cox, assistant football coach 1972-1974, head football coach 1975-present
Harry Donaldson (c/o 1941)
DeWain Duncan
Curtis Finch (c/o 1951)
Gene Hall, c/o 1947, assistant football coach 1955-1957, head football coach 1958-1969
Dickie Heien (c/o 1967)
Clyde Horton, c/o 1947, assistant football coach 1960-1986, volunteer coach 2003-2004
Clark Irwin (c/o 2005)
Bill Jones (c/o 1955)
William (B.J.) Maack III, grandson of Billy Maack (c/o 1940)
Travis Mann, assistant football coach 1994-1998
Joyce A. McCarty, wife of John McCarty (c/o 1960)
Billy Moore (c/o 1958)
Henry Moore (c/o 1952)
Buddy Nichols
Houston Nutt (c/o 1976)
Don Perkins (c/o 1974)
Joe Reynolds (c/o 1951)
Nancy Rousseau, Central High principal
Louis Schaufele (c/o 1947)
Mary Stafford, wife of Ned Stafford (c/o 1930)
Johnny Walker (c/o 1950)
Jane Welch, Central High registrar
Robert Yates (c/o 1982)

Stacey:
Thank you for believing in this project and for being so patient every step of the way.
I love you.

DEDICATION

This book is dedicated to a man who has worked the past 33 years of his life to instill discipline, respect, commitment, competitiveness and pride in every young man who has donned a jersey with the word "TIGERS" boldly printed across the chest.

This is a man who has earned the respect of his players and peers. This admiration, though, does not come from the numerous games and championships he has won, but for his genuine care for each and every person associated with his program. This is clearly evident when he leads a prayer for an injured athlete or encourages athletes to make good grades and good classroom behavior a priority. Normally when he speaks to his players after practice, his words aren't always about football, but about living a good life and having pride in themselves and their actions.

Success, however, has not passed this man by. He took over a football program in 1975, one that now packs a 110-year history, and has become its most successful coach. His 250 victories are a school record and fifth among all high school football coaches in Arkansas history. In addition, his seven state championships rank third in Arkansas history behind Central's own Wilson Matthews and Barton High School's Frank McClellan.

This is a man who remains humble after his successes and a man who does not bring his disappointments into the home. He has been a leader for his players, for his assistant coaches, but most important, for his family. While he works in a career that demands an inordinate amount of time, his loved ones have never once failed to receive his attention or devotion.

This is a man I look up to.

This is a man I want to be like.

This is a man I call my hero.

This is a man I proudly call dad.

This book is dedicated to Bernie Cox.

Photo provided by Brian Cox
Watching game film, 1975

Photo provided by Central High School
Football practice, 1989

Photo provided by DeWain Duncan
2003 football season

Photo provided by DeWain Duncan
2004 state championship game

IN MEMORY OF

This book is in memory of Dr. Wells Farrin Smith and Dr. John McCollough Smith.

Dr. Wells Farrin Smith operated his own private practice and was division surgeon for the Missouri Pacific Railroad. In 1914, he volunteered as the team physician for Little Rock High School. He attended every major athletic event for 22 years until his death in 1936.

Following Smith's death, his partner, Dr. Theo Freedman, took over as team physician. Dr. Freedman was team physician for seven years until Dr. Smith's son, John, assumed the same role.

Dr. John McCollough Smith played football and ran track at Little Rock High School from 1921-1924. He then attended Chicago University for one year before transferring to Hendrix College where he ran track and boxed. He attended medical school and eventually went to World War II as a field surgeon.

In 1944, he set up a private practice in Little Rock and followed in his father's footsteps by becoming the Little Rock High School team physician. Affectionately known as "Mr. Tiger," he attended every major athletic event for 43 years until his retirement following the 1986 football season. He died the following year.

This father and son team provided sports medicine care at Central High for 65 years.

FOREWORD:

Pouring over nearly 500 pages on the history of Little Rock Central football during the spring of 2005, it was ironic that I stumbled across a little piece of my history with the program.

Surprisingly, the gray cutoff-style T-shirt, which the small faded tag read is 38 percent cotton, was in good condition when it was unexpectedly pulled from a bedroom closet.

Even with a frayed edge at the bottom of the right sleeve, the T-shirt, circa 1980, could pass for the latest model the school awards today.

Whether I could make the Tiger "800 LB. CLUB" now is another story. But a lot like the T-shirt, football at Little Rock Central has had some frayed edges (a 1-9 season as recently as 1993), yet, for the most part, has held up remarkably well for a century.

Because of my job as a sports writer with the Arkansas Democrat-Gazette newspaper, I had a front-row seat when the school authored the latest chapters in its glorious history - state championships in 2003 and 2004.

Because of this book, I have a much greater understanding of how that glorious past evolved.

I now wish I could have seen Howard Hughes, Jimmy Albright, Henry Moore and Bruce Fullerton play. I wish I could have seen Wilson Matthews coach.

Fortunately for me, personally and professionally, Dedrick Poole, Mickey Dean, Clark Irwin and Kevin Thornton also wore black and gold. Fortunately for me, Bernie Cox is still coaching.

As a player in the late 1970s and early 1980s, I was lucky enough to play on two state championship teams coached by Cox, a man whose blueprint for success hasn't wavered.

Discipline, defensive ferocity and a workhorse tailback helped produce the same top-shelf results in 2003 and 2004 as 1980 and 1981.

It was approximately 25 years ago that Cox presented a then-undersized tight end/defensive end with a T-shirt for meeting a goal of becoming stronger in the off-season.

I don't know why I still have that 800 LB CLUB shirt, its scripted letters, still bright red, framing a barbell. But I'll hang it back in the same closet and let it continue to age gracefully. Probably like the second century of football at Little Rock Central no doubt will.

Robert Yates
June 14, 2005

TABLE OF CONTENTS:

INTRODUCTION

Little Rock Central High School – A Brief History

The territory of Arkansas began educating its youth in 1816 when Caleb Lindsey met with a group of children in a cave in Ravenden (Lawrence County). The first school law, however, was not enacted by the Territorial Legislature until 1829. The law was meant to set aside land in each township strictly for educational purposes, but very few of these townships were able to establish schools due to lack of resources or funding.

The first official school building in the

**Little Rock's Sherman High School
7th and Sherman streets**

Arkansas' first school building

Arkansas Territory was located at Little Piney Creek in Pope County. The school, which was only a log house, opened in 1833.

The first public school in the city of Little Rock did not open until 1853, and it was not until 1869 that the city opened its first high school. This school, which was named Sherman High School, was located at the corner of 7th and Sherman streets and was only a small wooden building.

In 1885, the high school moved to 14th and Scott streets and was renamed Scott Street High School, although it was usually called "City High School." Five years later, the high school moved to West Capitol and Gaines streets and was renamed Peabody High School. The name change honored

philanthropist George Peabody, who donated nearly $200,000 to the city of Little Rock for construction of a new high school.

In 1905, the high school changed location once again, this time moving back to 14th and Scott streets. This new school building, which was renamed Little Rock Senior High School, had a telephone connection in each room, an extensive science laboratory, a shop class, modern heating and ventilation systems, electric lighting and the most modern plumbing, which included water fountains throughout and shower baths in the gymnasium. At the time of its opening, the school was considered

**Little Rock Senior High School
14th and Scott streets**

Photo provided by Central High School

Little Rock High School and Kavanaugh Field
14th Street and Park Avenue

one of the most modern high schools in the country.

The school remained at this location until 1927 when it was moved 22 blocks west to 14th and Park streets. At the time, this location was the site of Little Rock's largest city park, formerly known as West End Park. Kavanaugh Field, located on the south end of the park, was where the high school athletic events took place. It was also home to the Travelers baseball team.

Photo provided by Central High School

Greek Goddesses representing Ambition, Personality, Opportunity and Preparation

16

The new school building was positioned on the east end of the park, facing east on Park Avenue.

The new school was designed by an association of five local architects and built for $1.5 million. The immaculate architectural design has four Greek goddess statues at the entrance. These statues represent Ambition, Personality, Opportunity and Preparation.

As its predecessor, this new school was built with the most modern conveniences available. Measuring 564 feet long and 365 feet wide, the facility can accommodate 3,000 students. It houses 100 classrooms, an auditorium with seats for 2,000 and a cafeteria to feed approximately 1,000 at a time. All this space was used immediately as students of both Little Rock High School and Little Rock Junior College were housed in the new building.

At the time of its formal dedication, Nov. 17, 1927, the building was recognized as an incredible architectural achievement. The American Institute of Architects labeled the new structure as the "The Most Beautiful High School in America."

After this fourth and final move, the high school retained the name Little Rock High School for another 26 years. The Little Rock School Board, though, voted in 1953 to rename the school Little Rock Central High. This change was made once plans were finalized for construction of a second high school in west Little Rock.

Athletic Prowess At Little Rock Central

Little Rock Central High School was the focal point of the world's attention during its integration in 1957. Members of local, state, national and international media camped out on the school's lawn to get breaking news to their viewers, listeners and readers. Because of this monumental event, Gov. Orval Faubus, Daisy Bates, the "Little Rock Nine" and the school itself will forever be etched in America's history books.

What few people realize is that prior to the news of integration, the school had already made a name for itself in the country's athletic circles. Sports at Little Rock High School had been nationally renowned since approximately 1920.

Coach Earl Quigley and his track teams were featured in *Ripley's Believe It Or Not* on three occasions. Through *Ripley*'s publishings, the nation learned that the Tigers were victorious in 50 consecutive meets, competed for 15 years without a defeat and won 97 consecutive meets, including 18 consecutive state championships.

By the time the United States Supreme Court's ruling of Brown vs. Board of Education of Topeka was enacted in Little Rock in 1957, the Tiger track team had already won 38 state championships. The basketball and baseball teams combined for 24 state titles, while the football team had won one national championship (1946), one Southern championship (1921), one regional championship (1922) and 23 state championships.

Coach Wilson Matthews and his powerful football squad overcame the obstacles and negative attention the school was receiving in the fall of 1957 to post a 12-0-0 record. So respected throughout America's football society, it was honored with the title of national champion.

This tribute, though, was overshadowed by the news taking place on the school's front lawn and the decisions being made inside political offices.

To date (1904-2004), Central's athletic teams have won 11 state championships in baseball, 21 in basketball, 32 in football and 53 in track. The theme of this book, however, focuses only on one subject - the 100-year history of the Tiger football program.

Football at Central High School was chosen for two reasons. First, as Arkansas' most historic program, it is already noted throughout the country for the number of victories and championships. Because of this, the names, faces, games, rivalries and traditions associated with it have become legendary and should be both documented and celebrated.

The second, and main reason, is because football at Little Rock Central has been a part of this author's life since birth. As the son of one of its head coaches, Bernie Cox, I grew up in his office, in the locker room, on the sideline and on the field itself.

Officially, my name has been stamped in the chronicles of this storied program as both a letterman and the team's certified athletic trainer. For this, I am extremely proud.

To be mentioned in the same book as Ivan Williams, John Hoffman, Henry Moore, Houston Nutt and Riley "Doc" Johns is a tremendous honor and privilege. The pride that goes along with being a Tiger can only be realized by those who have been a Tiger.

The names listed in this book not only represent Central High School, they are also the roots of this city's athletic beginnings. As Little Rock's only high school, these names were ambassadors, playing, not for school pride, but for city pride.

As is chanted by current Tiger teams, and running through the veins of former Tiger players, this book has been titled *TIGER PRIDE*.

High School Football in Little Rock

Peabody High School fielded Little Rock's first high school football team in 1894. The inaugural event took place at West End Park on Thanksgiving Day (Nov. 29) and pitted the high school boys against Little Rock Academy. The game was documented in the Nov. 30 edition of the *Arkansas Gazette* by an unknown reporter. The game account was as follows:

LITTLE ROCK ACADEMY DEFEATES PEABODY ELEVEN

Football game yesterday between the elevens of Little Rock Academy and Peabody High School developed the fact that there is a great deal of latent football enthusiasm in Little Rock which is wasting away for an opportunity to turn loose and yell itself hoarse.

The teams and their maids of honor arrived in vans shortly after 3 o'clock and were driven around the field several times to arouse enthusiasm. Play was begun at 3:45 after fifteen minutes had been wasted getting Newton's nerve up to the playing point.

The Academy team began by a place kick and after seventeen minutes of hard play, mostly in Peabody's territory, Bates went around the right end for the first touchdown. Waters kicking goal. Peabody then braced up and kept the ball in the Academy's territory the remainder of the first half, but could not score. Score at the end of the half, Peabody, 0; Little Rock Academy, 6.

In the beginning of the second half the Peabody team went through the Academy line like water, King was slightly hurt and Christian took his place, the Academy team in the meantime regaining their form. Peabody several times worked the ball well up the field and lost it on flukes just as they were expected to score. With the ball in the Academy's possession near their own goal, Waters punted well into Peabody's territory, Newton falling on it. On the next play Bates again went around the end for a touchdown and Waters kicked the goal.

After a few minutes of play O'Hair got around the end for a good gain, but was interfered with by spectators and a possible touchdown missed. Score 12-0.

Waters, Bates, and Professor Hall were the particular stars for the Academy, and O'Hair, Moss and Professor Rhoten played the best game for Peabody.

The only other recorded game for Peabody High School during the 1894 season was a Dec. 22 battle against Brinkley. The following article in the Dec. 23 edition of the *Arkansas Gazette* recounts Little Rock's first victory.

BRINKLEY BEATEN

The Peabody Eleven Wins a Football Game Hands Down

The game of football between Brinkley and the Peabody High School yesterday afternoon resulted in a victory for the latter by a score of 38-0. Milton Loeb, Joe and Martin McNeil did the best work for Peabody, and Captain Kelly, Ware and McCollough for Brinkley. Wright Linsey, Captain of the great A.I.U. team, played with Brinkley in the last half and saved many points for the visitors.

Joe McNeil made a run of seventy-five yards for the first touch down after four minutes of play. The Peabody interference was good. If the Brinkley boys had more training they would play good ball.

If the Peabody's want another game from the working boys' team they will be accommodated and are requested to answer through the Gazette.

Complete documentation of games, coaches and complete season records cannot be found from 1894 through 1903. There are partial reports of games played during this era, but research cannot locate entire season records, scores, etc. Therefore, all information regarding football at Little Rock Central High School will begin with the 1904 season.

All information for this book was researched from the *Arkansas Democrat, Arkansas Gazette, Arkansas Democrat-Gazette* and the annuals at Central High School. Information on lettermen was researched through the same publications and statistical records kept by current and former coaches.

All photos were provided by the above publications or donated by former team members or their widows. Many of these photos are exceptionally old and copied as best as technically possible.

A HISTORY OF COACHES

Coach O.D. Longstreth

Bengals Coach 1904 – 1907

11 wins 11 losses 1 ties

1 state championship (1907)

Photo provided by Central High School

Due to the lack of school records prior to 1904, it is unknown when Coach O. D. Longstreth began his coaching career at Little Rock High School. Research does show that he was the coach from 1904 until 1907, compiling a record of 11-11-1. Longstreth's 1907 state championship was the first recorded for the Bengal Tigers.

Longstreth resigned at Little Rock High School to take a similar position at the newly opened State Normal School (now the University of Central Arkansas) in Conway. He came back to Little Rock in 1909 after he became president of Little Rock's Athletic Association, which was established in the fall of 1905. This association included the management and support of the school's literary interscholastic contests and all activities of the school. From the treasury of this association came the money to buy supplies, equipment, athletic goods, pay expenses of visiting teams and rent for fields and buildings used for contests. This association also allowed all students to take part in athletics without a participation fee.

Coach H.J. Bischoff

Bengals Coach 1908

8 wins 0 losses 0 ties

1 state championship (1908)

Photo provided by Central High School

When Coach O.D. Longstreth resigned as head coach before the 1908 season, Coach H.J. Bischoff took over Little Rock High School's football team. In his only season as Little Rock's head coach, Bischoff guided the Bengals to an 8-0-0 record and the state championship. They were scored on only twice, one field goal and one touchdown.

Coach G.J. Van Buren

Bengals Coach 1909

7 wins 0 losses 0 ties

1 state championship (1909)

Photo provided by Central High School

    An instructor of science, Coach G.J. Van Buren took control of the Little Rock football team for the 1909 season. In his first year, his team was undefeated and won the state championship. Coach "Van" was not only popular in the classroom, he was especially admired by the boys on the athletic teams that he coached successfully. He put all his energy into his work, never losing patience with any young student or athlete.

    On March 21, 1910, Van Buren announced his resignation to the students and left that night with his family for their home in New Auburn, Wis. Poor health was reason for his departure.

Coach E.E. Tarr

Bengals Coach 1910

3 wins 2 losses 2 ties

Photo provided by Central High School

No information available.

Coach Floyd H. Wingo

Bengals Coach 1911 – 1913

12 wins 7 losses 1 tie

Photo provided by Central High School

    Coach Floyd Wingo, a graduate of the University of Mississippi, became head coach in 1911. He was admired and respected by the athletes who played for him. More players tried out for football than for any other coach before him. He had total knowledge of the sport, was able to develop faultless teamwork and perfected many trick formations to outwitt opponents.

    Wingo preached to his players that clean athletics and good sportsmanship were much more important than winning. During Wingo's tenure, Little Rock High School became known throughout the state for good sportsmanship and well-behaved athletes.

Coach J.G. Pipkin

Bengals Coach 1914 – 1915

13 wins 2 losses 2 ties

2 state championships (1914, 1915)

Photo provided by Central High School

John G. Pipkin, a graduate of the University of Mississippi and assistant to Coach Floyd Wingo, became head coach in 1914. Like Coach Wingo, Coach Pipkin stressed clean athletics to his players. When Coach Pipkin became head coach of the athletic teams, he hired a young man named Earl Quigley to assist him.

Coach Earl F. Quigley

Bengals Coach 1916 – 1917, 1919 – 1935

134 wins 52 losses 9 ties

5 state championships (1917, 1919, 1920, 1921, 1923)

Photo provided by Central High School

Coach Earl F. Quigley began coaching the Tigers in 1914 as an assistant to Coach John G. Pipkin. After Pipkin took on other duties, Quigley became head coach in 1916. Quigley had a losing season his first year, 2-5-2, but his Tigers won the state championship the next year with a 7-2-0 record.

The following year, he was called away to Artillery Officers Training School at Camp Zachary Taylor in Louisville, Ky., and Coach G.H. Wittenberg was named interim head coach.

Quigley returned in 1919 and coached 17 more seasons before becoming Little Rock High School's full-time athletic director. With a constantly growing athletic program, Quigley began to take on more responsibility. He was promoted to athletic director in 1936, enabling him to turn over his football duties to a younger man, Coach Clyde Van Sickle. Quigley compiled a record of 134-52-9 and was the winngest coach in school history before Bernie Cox won his 135th game in 1990. Coach Quigley won five state championships.

Quigley's many accomplishments as coach and athletic director were recognized in 1957 with the renaming of Tiger Stadium in his honor. In a formal ceremony prior to homecoming festivities, Tiger Stadium officially became Earl Quigley Stadium.

Coach George H. Wittenberg

Bengals Coach 1918

1 win 2 losses 0 ties

1 state championship (1918)

Photo provided by Central High School

When Coach Earl Quigley was called to Artillery Officers Training School during the summer and fall of 1918, G.H. Wittenberg became interim head coach. Because of World War I, many high schools were unable to field athletic teams, and the Bengal Tigers were only able to find three opponents to compete against during the season. Wittenberg, one of the high school's professors and a football letterman in 1909, only managed a 1-2-0 record. But it was good enough to capture the state championship. Wittenberg became the first graduate of Little Rock High School to lead the school's football team.

Although Wittenberg was only an interim head coach during 1918, he was the only coach the Bengals had during the season. Therefore, he was credited with winning a state championship.

Coach Clyde Van Sickle

Bengals Coach 1936 – 1940

41 wins 9 losses 5 ties

1 state championship (1938)

Photo provided by Central High School

After the legendary Earl Quigley resigned to become athletic director for Little Rock High School, Clyde Van Sickle became coach in 1936. Van Sickle came to Little Rock from Cisco, Texas, where he had been head coach at Cisco High School. He originally moved to Texas from Green Bay, Wis., where he played for the Green Bay Packers. Van Sickle was also a standout collegiate player at the University of Arkansas.

In his first season as Little Rock's coach, the Tigers christened their new stadium. After only five seasons, Van Sickle accepted another coaching position and returned to Texas. He ended his career at Little Rock with a 41-9-5 record and one state championship.

Coach Clarence Geis

Bengals Coach 1941 – 1943

17 wins 12 losses 4 ties

Photo provided by Central High School

Clarence Geis became head coach following Clyde Van Sickle's resignation. Geis came to Little Rock from Jonesboro, where he was the head coach at Jonesboro High. He led the Tigers for three years, winning 17 games.

Following the 1942-1943 school year, Geis was called on by the Navy to help aid in World War II. Given a leave of absence by the Little Rock School District, he was stationed in Corpus Christi, Texas, as athletic instructor for the Navy. Following the war, he went back to Jonesboro as the school's head football coach.

Coach Raymond Burnett

Bengals Coach 1944 – 1946

32 wins 2 losses 2 ties

1 national championship (1946)

2 state championships (1944, 1946)

Photo provided by Central High School

Raymond Burnett graduated from Atkins High School before becoming a star collegiate quarterback at Arkansas Tech University, where he was All-Conference in 1935. He returned to Atkins in 1940 and led the Red Devils to an 11-3-1 record in two seasons.

In 1944, he accepted the head coaching position at Little Rock High School. During his three-year stint, Burnett was 32-2-2 and won state championships in 1944 and 1946 and a national championship in 1946.

After only three years in Little Rock, Burnett returned to Russellville to work as an assistant coach at Arkansas Tech. One year later, he was promoted to head coach and led the Wonder Boys for six years, compiling a record of 31-24-4.

Coach Wilson Matthews

Tigers Coach 1947 – 1957

109 wins 17 losses 3 ties

1 national championship (1957)

10 state championships (1947, 1948, 1949, 1950, 1952, 1953, 1954, 1955, 1956, 1957)

Photo provided by Central High School

Wilson Matthews' football ability at Atkins High School landed him a scholarship to Arkansas Tech University and then the University of Arkansas. He starred as a linebacker for the Razorbacks. After receiving both a bachelor's and master's degree from Arkansas, he began his career in 1944 as head coach at Rogers High School. After one year and a 7-3-0 record, he left Rogers to become an assistant coach under Raymond Burnett at Little Rock High School.

When Burnett left for Arkansas Tech following the 1946 season, Matthews took over Little Rock's program. At 25, he was the youngest head football coach at Little Rock High School since Earl Quigley. During his 11-season tenure with the Tigers, Matthews was 109-17-3 and won 10 state championships and a national championship. He left Little Rock after the 1957 season to become an assistant coach at the University of Arkansas under Coach Frank Broyles.

Matthews was the head football coach during the 1957 integration crisis at Central High school. He was able to keep his team focused on football rather than what was happening on the school's lawn and in the halls. He practiced around the tents, trucks and men of the 101st Airborne Division, which set up camp on his practice field. Despite the life-changing events and attention focused on the school, Matthews was able to lead the Tigers to an undefeated season, along with state and national championships.

Coach Gene Hall

Tigers Coach 1958 – 1969

82 wins 45 losses 7 ties

1 state championship (1960)

Photo provided by Central High School

Gene Hall was no stranger to football at Little Rock Central when he was promoted to head coach following the resignation of Coach Wilson Matthews. Hall was a three-year letterman and an All-State player at Little Rock High School from 1944-1946 under Coach Raymond Burnett. Hall was a standout athlete each year and played a significant role in the state championships of 1944 and 1946, as well as the national championship of 1946.

His coaching career began in Mountain Home, where he led the Bombers for one year before moving to Conway to work with the Wampus Cats. He finally returned to Little Rock in 1955 as an assistant to Matthews.

Following Matthews' departure in 1957, Hall was promoted to head coach for the 1958 season. Two years later, his team went undefeated and won the state championship. He retired from coaching in 1969 and began working for Spaulding Athletics. He ended his Central coaching career with an 82-45-7 record.

Coach Jerry Welch

Tigers Coach 1970 – 1971

6 wins 14 losses 1 tie

Photo provided by Central High School

After an All-State performance on Gene Hall's 1960 state championship team, Jerry Welch attended college only to return to his alma mater nine years later as an assistant coach. When Hall retired from coaching one year later, Welch was a unanimous choice to lead the Tigers into the 1970s.

Welch's team finished 1-8-1 in 1970, the school's worst season since an 0-5-0 record in 1905. Welch's 1971 team improved to 5-6-0, highlighted by an impressive 21-0 victory over ancient nemesis Pine Bluff.

Welch left Central after the 1971 season to continue his education. He later received his doctorate from Northwestern (La.) State University. Coach Welch is currently the athletic director for the Pulaski County Special School District in Arkansas.

Coach Joe Fred Young

Tigers Coach 1972 – 1974

23 wins 8 losses 3 ties

Photo provided by Central High School

Coach Joe Fred Young became head football coach at Conway High School in 1971 after being an assistant there the previous seven years. After leading Conway for one season, Young accepted the top position at Central High School. He coached the Tigers from 1972 until 1974 and finished with a 23-8-3 record. Young left Central after the 1974 season to become an assistant coach at the University of Arkansas under Coach Frank Broyles.

After coaching the Razorbacks for two years, Young accepted the head coaching position at Fayetteville High School. In 1981, he became head coach at Fort Smith Northside and coached the Grizzlies for 18 years before his retirement in 1999. Young retired as one of the most successful high school football coaches in Arkansas, guiding his teams to the state championship game eight times, winning once. He ended his career with an overall record of 194-107-5.

Coach Bernie Cox

Tiger Coach 1975 –

250 wins 93 losses 8 ties

7 state championships (1975, 1978, 1980, 1981, 1986, 2003, 2004)

Photo provided by DeWain Duncan

Bernie Cox, a 1966 graduate of Harding University, began his coaching career as an assistant at Searcy High School before accepting a similar position at Conway High School in 1968. When Conway assistant Joe Fred Young was promoted to head coach in 1971, Cox was elevated to assistant head coach and offensive coordinator. One year later, Young was named head coach at Little Rock Central and brought Cox with him as assistant head coach and offensive coordinator. In January 1975, just two months after Young left Central, Cox became the new head coach at Little Rock Central High School.

Cox's Tigers were undefeated and won the state championship in his first year as head coach. That 1975 team is still believed to be the best Arkansas high school football team in the latter part of the 20th century. Cox, who has won seven state championships, became the winningest coach in school history in 1990, passing the legendary Earl Quigley, who was 134-52-9. An 18-10 victory over Conway on Sept. 22, 2000, marked Cox's 200th career victory.

Cox's 1993 team finished 1-9-0, the second-worst record in school history. Cox, though, rebuilt the program in just a few years. The Tigers won conference championships in 1996, 2000, 2002, 2003 and 2004 and placed second in 1998 and 1999. Cox led his 2003 and 2004 teams to consecutive state championships and ended Central's first fully recorded century of football as Arkansas' No. 1 team.

The accomplishments during Cox's 30 years as head coach have not gone unnoticed. In honor of his success and love for his athletes, the Little Rock School Board voted unanimously Feb. 24, 2005, to name the field at Quigley Stadium after Bernie Cox. The athletic complex officially became known as Bernie Cox Field at Earl Quigley Stadium.

COACHING LOG

(1904 – 1907)	O.D. Longstreth	11 – 11 – 01	1 State Championship
(1908)	H.J. Bischoff	08 – 00 – 00	1 State Championship
(1909)	G.J. Van Buren	07 – 00 – 00	1 State Championship
(1910)	E.E. Tarr	03 – 02 – 02	
(1911 - 1913)	Floyd Wingo	12 – 07 – 01	
(1914 – 1915)	J.G. Pipkin	13 – 02 – 02	2 State Championships
(1916 – 1917)	Earl F. Quigley	09 – 07 – 02	1 State Championship
(1918)	G.H. Wittenberg	01 – 02 – 00	1 State Championship
(1919 – 1935)	Earl F. Quigley	125 – 45 – 07	4 State Championships
(1936 – 1940)	Clyde Van Sickle	41 – 09 – 05	1 State Championship
(1941 – 1943)	Clarence Geis	17 – 12 – 04	
(1944 – 1946)	Raymond Burnett	32 – 02 – 02	2 State Championships 1 National Championship
(1947 – 1957)	Wilson Matthews	109 – 17 – 03	10 State Championships 1 National Championship
(1958 – 1969)	Gene Hall	82 – 45 – 07	1 State Championship
(1970 – 1971)	Jerry Welch	06 – 14 – 01	
(1972 – 1974)	Joe Fred Young	23 – 08 – 03	
(1975 –)	Bernie Cox	250 – 93 – 08	7 State Championships

OVERALL RECORD (1904 – 2004)   749 – 276 – 48
72% winning percentage

2 national championships
32 state championships

"The [1946] team was made up of a great group of seniors and juniors and a few outstanding veterans that returned [from World War II] for their senior year. Just about any [offensive play] you called would make yardage. You could not tell much difference between the first and the second team."

Jimmy Albright
1946 quarterback, 14-0-0
national championship, state championship

"I have great memories of the Central High players, coaches, students and teachers. We were all one great big team that couldn't be beaten."

Billy Moore
1957 quarterback, 12-0-0
national championship, state championship

"My three years at Little Rock Central High were some of the greatest days of my life. The school is a beautiful national landmark filled with history. I loved my teachers, classmates and coaches. We had the prettiest cheerleaders and the greatest high steppers. We won championships in basketball and football. I look back on my high school days with such pride!"

Houston Nutt
1975 quarterback, 12-0-0
state championship

"The coaching staff at Central will always be a part of my life. A lot of what they taught will help me in the real world, long after my football career is over."

Clark Irwin
2003 quarterback, 14-0-0
state championship
2004 quarterback, 13-1-0
state championship

"I know no other game which does what football does. It is a game which gives courage to the young man who plays it and certainly courage is a virtue which we all need in the battle of life."

Rev. Frank James
volunteer coach at Little Rock High School, 1913

THE FIRST RECORDED SEASON

1904   0-1-1

Head Coach: O.D. Longstreth

1904 PLAYERS

Henry Bacon	Morris Farrell	Philip McNemer	John Sherrill
Noland Blass	Hugh Hull	Dean Morley	
Charles Collins	Curtis Jones	Graham Penick	
Russell Doyne	Scott McGehee	Albert Price	

1904 MANAGERS
Unknown

Peabody High School, which is now known as Little Rock Central High School, practiced at 16th and Main streets and played its home games at West End Park. The park was located off Park Avenue in the western section of the city.

Peabody's mascot was the Bengal Tiger and its first fully recorded season began Oct. 29 at West End Park.

The Bengals, who were eventually known only as the Tigers, were coached by one of the school's professors, O.D. Longstreth. His Tigers wore school colored orange and black sweaters and faced Arkansas Military Academy in the first game. AMA beat Peabody 10-0.

The second and final game found Peabody at Hot Springs to play the local high school from that city. A scoreless tie gave the Tigers something to build on for the 1905 season.

1904 TIGER SCHEDULE

Arkansas Military Academy 10	Peabody 0
Hot Springs 0	Peabody 0

STILL SEARCHING FOR VICTORY

1905   0-5-0

Head Coach: O.D. Longstreth

1905 PLAYERS

- Abbott	Charles Collins	- Guthrie	Scott McGehee	John Sherrill
- Beach	- Dabbs	Hugh Hull	Phillip McNemer	Harold Young
Noland Blass	Russell Fields	- Hutchins	- Parker	

1905 MANAGERS
Unknown

Prior to the 1905 school year, Peabody High School moved from West Capitol and Gaines streets to 14th and Scott streets. The new school, still Little Rock's only public high school, became known as Little Rock High School.

At the request of head coach O.D. Longstreth, 30 players reported to 16th and Main streets for the season's first practice. During preseason practice,

Coach Longstreth formed a first team that averaged 135 pounds per player.

The team then began preparing for Arkansas Military Academy, its first opponent and cross-town rival.

The contest was considered one of the most exciting games in Little Rock during the entire season. A large crowd showed up at muddy West End Park to

Little Rock's new high school at 14th and Scott streets

watch the two schools battle for city bragging rights.

The Military Academy scored first when it took possession after a punt and marched down the field for a touchdown. Little Rock almost answered late in the first half when Noland Blass returned a punt 50 yards to the 10. The half, however, ended just before the Tigers could score.

Early in the second half, AMA drove to the Tigers 20 before fumbling to Little Rock. On the Tigers' first offensive play, Phillip McNemer ran 80 yards for a touchdown to tie the score.

With three minutes remaining in the game, AMA scored another touchdown to beat Little Rock 11-5.

An Oct. 11 game with Christian Brothers College of Memphis was next for Little Rock. But an automobile accident in Wynne, 40 miles west of Memphis, kept the college team from arriving on time.

The game was rescheduled for Oct. 16 and Christian Brothers made the trip safely to West End Park to battle the Tigers.

The Memphis team scored 20 points in the first half by running through and around the Little Rock defense. The second half was much more successful for the home team. Little Rock held Christian Brothers to only one touchdown, but the costly first half resulted in a 25-0 loss for the Tigers.

Little Rock's next game was 10 days later and again against Christian Brothers College. The Tigers traveled to Memphis and were beaten 45-0.

After losing 5-0 to Hot Springs the following week, Little Rock traveled to Fort Smith for a Thanksgiving Day game against the Grizzlies. Because of sub-freezing temperatures, few spectators attended.

Fort Smith, which outweighed Little Rock 10 pounds per man, scored on several long runs to win 38-0 and claim the state championship.

1905 TIGER SCHEDULE

Arkansas Military Academy 11	LRHS 5
Christian Brothers College of Memphis, TN 25	LRHS 0
Christian Brothers College of Memphis, TN 45	LRHS 0
Hot Springs 5	LRHS 0
Fort Smith 38	LRHS 0

GREATEST SEASON IN HISTORY

1906   4-3-0

Head Coach: O.D. Longstreth

1906 PLAYERS

Robert Doyle	Harry Holmes	Warren King	George Naylor
Thomas Doyle	B. Holt	Billy Letson	Graham Penick
Russell Doyne	Cecil Holt	Clay "Sonny" Martin	Sibley Ward

1906 MANAGERS
Unknown

With no victories during the previous two years, Little Rock opened the 1906 season without three starters because of poor grades. The talent of this young team would be tested early as it opened against the Pine Bluff Zebras.

The Tigers were impressive, holding Pine Bluff scoreless in the first half. The Zebras, though, could not be controlled in the second half, scoring two touchdowns to take a 10-0 lead.

In the opening minutes of the second half, Little Rock's Thomas Doyle was knocked unconscious. Play was stopped for 20 minutes as Doyle was attended to on the field. Several minutes later, Doyle returned to the game and scored Little Rock's only touchdown.

One touchdown would not be enough to defeat the Zebras, who held on for a 10-5 victory. According to the *Arkansas Gazette*, the crowd was considered one of the most enthusiastic to ever watch Little Rock High School play.

The Tigers took on Henderson College's second team next. Little Rock's Robert Doyle scored the game's first touchdown on a 60-yard reverse in the first half.

Russell Doyne gave the Tigers another touchdown when he scored on a short run around left end for a 10-0 halftime lead. Doyne added another touchdown in the second half when he scored on a 33-yard run.

Henderson scored on a short run and dropped-kicked a field goal, but it was not enough as Little Rock won 15-7, its first victory in at least three years.

The Tigers lost to their next college opponent, the first team from Hendrix College. The squads were evenly matched throughout the game, but Hendrix scored a safety after tackling a Little Rock player in the end zone. The Tigers were unable to score and suffered their second loss of the season.

More than 200 fans were on hand the following week as Billy Letson scored on a 60-yard run, and Thomas Doyle scored on a 55-yard run to help Little Rock dominate the Benton Panthers 52-0.

The emotional high and excitement of the easy victory did not carry over to the Tigers' next game. Five days later, Arkadelphia High School beat Little Rock 11-0.

On Thanksgiving Day, West End Park was the site of a holiday battle between the Tigers and the Fort Smith Grizzlies. During the first minute of play, Fort Smith picked up a Little Rock fumble and returned it for a touchdown. The Grizzlies converted the extra-point attempt for a 6-0 lead.

Doyne and Clay Martin brought the Tigers back by each scoring a touchdown. Both extra-point attempts were good in a 12-6 victory.

West End Park was again the site of Little Rock's next game, a rematch with Pine Bluff. The Tigers scored just before halftime as Doyne passed 12 yards to Letson for a 5-0 lead.

Little Rock's next big offensive play came when a pass was batted away from the intended receiver. Little Rock's Warren King caught the tipped ball and ran an additional 20 yards for a touchdown to increase the lead to 10-0.

Just before the game ended, Doyne blocked a punt and returned it 30 yards for the Tigers' third and final touchdown. Pine Bluff never threatened to score, and Little Rock's 16-0 victory was its fourth of the year.

The 1906 season was the most successful in Little Rock's brief recorded history.

1906 TIGER SCHEDULE

Pine Bluff 10	LRHS 5
Henderson College (second team) 7	LRHS 15
Hendrix College 2	LRHS 0
Benton 0	LRHS 52
Arkadelphia 11	LRHS 0
Fort Smith 6	LRHS 12
Pine Bluff 0	LRHS 16

THE FIRST CHAMPIONSHIP

1907   7-2-0

Head Coach: O.D. Longstreth
Assistants: Wallace Townsend, A.O. Andrew

1907 LETTERMEN

Lawson Deloney   Thomas Doyle   Curtis Jones   Sibley Ward   Lynn Wassell

1907 MANAGERS
Unknown

Prior to the 1907 season, the city of Little Rock took possession of West End Park and planned to remodel it into a state-of-the-art sports complex. When the renovation was completed, the new park featured a track, baseball and football field, four tennis courts, two basketball courts and a pool.

Little Rock High School's first practice was Sept. 19. Practices were held at 29th and Scott streets and games were played at the new West End Park facility.

Four days into practice, Thomas Doyle was elected team captain. His leadership would be tested three weeks later when the Tigers were dealt their first blow of the season. Starting fullback Russell Fields was injured during practice and missed the remainder of the year. The captain was faced with keeping the team focused and its spirit high after Fields' loss.

Little Rock, wearing its orange and black colors, opened against Hot Springs High School. A crowd of more than 3,000 packed West End Park to watch both teams fight for their first victory.

The Trojans scored first when they returned a fumble 25 yards into the end zone.

They missed the extra-point attempt, an error that would come back to haunt them.

Trailing 5-0 with two minutes left in the game, Doyle passed to Sibley Ward for a 26-yard touchdown. Doyle also converted the extra-point kick to seal Little Rock's victory.

The Tigers' first loss of the season came to Arkansas Military Academy. With five players out with injuries, Little Rock was outweighed and outplayed. The Cadets dominated the line of scrimmage and beat the Tigers 21-6.

Little Rock's next game was against Pine Bluff. Little Rock scored 22 points in the first half and its second team, playing the entire second half, scored 16 points. Doyle drop-kicked two field goals, which were worth four points each, in the first half of the 38-0 victory.

On Oct. 22, Coach O.D. Longstreth split his squad into two first teams for games four days later. One team traveled to Arkadelphia to take on Henderson College, while the other traveled to Pine Bluff for a rematch with the Zebras.

The Tigers held Henderson scoreless, beating the college team 17-0. Robert Doyle highlighted the game with a 60-yard touchdown run.

The game in Pine Bluff ended in a Little Rock victory as well. Even with penalties totaling more than 100 yards, the Tigers were too much for the Zebras.

Little Rock scored twice against Pine Bluff with less than four minutes remaining in the game. The first score occurred on a 40-yard drop-kick for a field goal and the second when a blocked punt was recovered in the end zone for a touchdown. The 9-0 victory marked the second time the Tigers had beaten the Zebras in 1907.

Following a 13-0 victory over Clary Training School in Fordyce, Little Rock suffered its next loss against Christian Brothers College in Memphis. Heavy rain and mud hampered Little Rock's quick end runs and forward passes. Christian Brothers relied on the weight of its offensive line and the power of its running backs to run up the middle.

The Tigers led 6-5 at halftime, but the college team dominated the second half in a 15-6 victory.

Ward scored three touchdowns during Little Rock's next game against Hendrix College. The largest crowd of the season watched Hendrix drive 87 yards for first-and-goal at the 3. But a goal-line stand forced the college team to turn the ball over on downs.

On the Tigers' first play after gaining possession, Robert Doyle pitched the ball to Ward. Once he received the ball, Ward sprinted 97 yards for a touchdown. He also scored on runs of 35 yards and 26 yards in leading Little Rock to a 28-5 victory over Hendrix.

West End Park was the site of the Tigers' Thanksgiving Day game with the Fort Smith Grizzlies. Since both teams were undefeated against high school competition in Arkansas, the game would determine the 1907 state championship.

The game was a hard-fought defensive battle. Defensive ends from both teams were able to stop end runs, the strength of both offenses. Little Rock managed to score the game's only points on a field goal by Thomas Doyle. The 4-0 victory and 7-2-0 record gave the Tigers their first state championship.

The 1907 season was the first year that monograms were awarded by Little Rock High School. Ward, Lawson Deloney, Thomas Doyle, Curtis Jones and Lynn Wassell were the first players to officially letter for the Tigers.

1907 TIGER SCHEDULE

Hot Springs 5	LRHS 6
Arkansas Military Academy 21	LRHS 6
Pine Bluff 0	LRHS 38
Henderson College (second team) 0	LRHS 17
Pine Bluff 0	LRHS 9
Clary Training School 0	LRHS 13
Christian Brothers College of Memphis, TN 15	LRHS 6
Hendrix College (second team) 5	LRHS 28
Fort Smith 0	LRHS 4

LITTLE ROCK'S FIRST UNDEFEATED SEASON

1908   8-0-0

Head Coach: H.J. Bischoff
Assistants: C.E. Chambers, W.C. Bryant

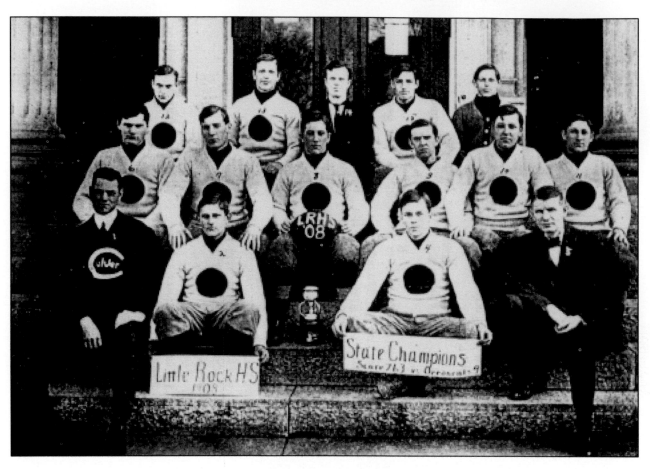

1908 LETTERMEN

Curtis Boydston	Robert Doyle	Russell May	Harold Young
Lawson Deloney	Will Hodgins	George Naylor	
John Dickinson	Billy Letson	Sibley Ward	

1908 MANAGERS
Unknown

On Sept. 24, 30 prospects turned out at Glenwood Park for Little Rock's first practice of the new season. Seven were returning players from Little Rock's first state championship team.

The Tigers' coach in 1908 was H.J. Bischoff, who took over after O.D. Longstreth became head coach at the new State Normal School in Conway.

Longstreth's State Normal School was Little Rock's first opponent of the season.

"Beat Coach Longstreth" was the cry from students of Little Rock High School.

Even though quarterback Sibley Ward was sick and unable to play, the Tigers still passed their way to victory. Robert Doyle passed to Billy Letson for a 25-yard touchdown, and Robert Martin passed to Lawson Deloney for a 25-yard touchdown. John Dickinson converted one of the two extra-point attempts for an 11-0 lead in the first half.

In the third quarter, Curtis Boydston increased the lead when he scored on a 15-yard run.

Late in the fourth quarter, Doyle set up Little Rock's next touchdown when he returned a punt 60 yards to the 10. Martin then passed to Deloney for the Tigers' fourth touchdown. Dickinson's extra-point kick failed as time ran out in Little Rock's 22-0 victory over the college team.

After the Tigers defeated Henderson College's second team 23-0, the Tigers traveled to Arkadelphia.

Arkadelphia High School was befuddled by Little Rock's passing attack. The Tigers scored touchdowns on a short run by Russell May, a 60-yard pass reception by Letson, a 40-yard pass reception by Doyle, a 30-yard run by May and a fumble return by Dickinson.

Doyle added a 35-yard field goal, helping Little Rock to a 33-0 victory.

The Tigers hosted Hot Springs High School the following week. Little Rock kept the ball between the tackles most of the first half, but opened up the offense late in the second quarter to score its first touchdown. Doyle passed to May for a 10-yard touchdown and a 5-0 lead. Just minutes later, May scored again on a short run for a 10-0 halftime lead.

Midway through the third quarter, Ward faked a pass and ran 20 yards around right end for another touchdown. Dickinson converted the extra point for a 16-0 lead.

Midway through the fourth quarter, Boydston ended the scoring on a short run up the middle. Little Rock beat the Trojans 21-0.

After a 56-0 victory over Clary Training School in Fordyce, the Tigers hosted the Memphis High School Warriors. The game pitted the largest school from Arkansas against the largest school from Tennessee. Both were unbeaten and among the best teams in each state.

Doyle and Martin didn't play because of injuries. But even in their absence, Little Rock played hard and played well.

The Tigers scored first in the opening quarter when Ward passed to Deloney. Once Deloney caught the pass, he sprinted the 30 yards needed for the touchdown. Little Rock struck again in the second quarter when Boydston scored from the 1. Dickinson converted both extra-point attempts for a 12-0 halftime lead.

Early in the second half, a short drive ended with a 35-yard touchdown run by Ward. Dickinson converted the extra-point attempt to increase the lead to 18-0.

Memphis fumbled the ensuing kickoff and Ward recovered for Little Rock. The fumble allowed the Tigers to score again, this time on a short run by Harold Young. Dickinson's extra-point attempt failed, but the Tigers led 23-0.

Little Rock scored three more times late in the game. May scored twice from the 15, and Walter Terry scored on a short run up the middle. Dickinson converted all three extra-point attempts in a 41-0 victory.

On Thanksgiving Day, Little Rock traveled to Fort Smith to play what was considered the most exciting game of the season. A record crowd of 2,500 packed Fort Smith's League Park to watch two of the state's top schools battle for the state championship.

A 35-yard field goal by Fort Smith early in the first quarter marked the first points Little Rock had allowed all season. The disappointment faded after Ward returned a punt for a touchdown. Dickinson kicked the extra point for a 6-4 lead.

One play after Young was ejected from the game for fighting, May ran around left end for a 15-yard touchdown. Dickinson's extra-point attempt was good to help Little Rock to a 12-4 victory.

Undefeated Camden High School challenged the Tigers to a postseason game to crown a true state champion. Little Rock agreed to the game and then crushed its opponent 54-5. The Tigers were proclaimed state champions for the second consecutive year.

1908 TIGER SCHEDULE

State Normal School 0	LRHS 22
Henderson College (second team) 0	LRHS 23
Arkadelphia 0	LRHS 33
Hot Springs 0	LRHS 21
Clary Training School 0	LRHS 56
Memphis, TN 0	LRHS 41
Fort Smith 4	LRHS 12
Camden 5	LRHS 54

THIRD STRAIGHT CHAMPIONSHIP

1909   7-0-0

Head Coach: G.J. Van Buren
Assistant: W.C. Bryant

1909 LETTERMEN

Robert Brown	Harry Holmes	Harry Weidemeyer	Harold Young
William Christian	Russell May	Jesse Weidemeyer	
Harper Harb	Walter Terry	G.H. Wittenberg	

1909 MANAGERS
Unknown

Replacing H.J. Bischoff in 1909 as head coach was G.J. Van Buren, also the high school's science teacher. Coach Van Buren began practice with 20 prospects and only seven were returning veterans.

Playing two 20-minute halves, the season's first game was against Arkadelphia High School. The game was scoreless at halftime. Arkadelphia outplayed the Tigers during the half, but was unable to cross the goal line.

On Arkadelphia's first possession of the second half, Little Rock's Walter Terry blocked a drop-kick and returned it 75 yards for a touchdown. The Tigers sealed the victory with just a few seconds remaining in the game when Russell May scored from the 2. Terry converted the extra point as time ran out to give Little Rock an 11-0 victory.

The Tigers played another scoreless first half the next week when they met Little Rock College. The college's only score

41

came early in the third quarter when Cass Coffman, a former Little Rock High School player, drop-kicked a 25-yard field goal for a 3-0 lead.

Trailing 3-0 with just under one minute to play in the game, May capped an 80-yard drive with a 3-yard run for a touchdown. Terry kicked the extra point as Little Rock High School defeated Little Rock College 6-3. It was considered by some the most exciting football game ever played in Little Rock.

After defeating the Hot Springs Trojans 11-0, the Tigers traveled to Conway for a game against State Normal School's varsity team. The varsity team, however, scrimmaged the previous night and the college coach decided to use the second team to play against Little Rock.

During 35 minutes of play, the Tigers scored at will and dominated the college team 80-0. Coach Van Buren was upset at the college coach for not allowing his varsity squad to compete. Coach Van Buren felt Little Rock could not only have improved from playing tougher competition, it could have defeated the varsity team as well.

The Tigers traveled to Red Elm Park in Memphis the next week. They met the Memphis High School Warriors in the second game of the city's doubleheader. In the first game, Christian Brothers College of Memphis beat Memphis Hospital Medical College 17-0.

The high school game began when Little Rock kicked off to Memphis. The Tigers gained possession two minutes later and eventually scored when May ran into the end zone from the 2. The conversion attempt failed and Little Rock led 5-0.

Six minutes later, the Tigers scored again when May went over from the 1 to increase the lead to 10-0. They padded their lead when May connected with G.H. Wittenberg for a 12-yard touchdown and Harold Young scored from the 6 with only two minutes remaining in the game.

Just before time was called, Little Rock scored again when Terry picked up a Memphis fumble and returned it 20 yards for another touchdown. Terry made only one of the five extra-point attempts, but Little Rock beat Memphis 32-0.

With two games left to play, quarterback Harry Holmes was diagnosed with typhoid and team captain Young was also sick. Both players missed the remainder of the season.

Without two top players, the Tigers pressed on and faced Clary Training School in Fordyce. In the rain and mud, both teams fumbled numerous times. May, though, had no problems in the rain. He averaged 8 yards each time he ran or caught the ball.

May passed to Frank Letzig for a 4-yard touchdown in the first half, and Little Rock scored again in the second half when William Christian dove over the goal line from the 1. Terry missed both extra-point attempts, but the Tigers put Clary Training School out of the running for the state title with a 10-0 victory.

On Thanksgiving Day, Little Rock's West End Park was the site of a holiday doubleheader featuring Little Rock High School against Fort Smith High School and the University of Arkansas against Washington University. The first game between Little Rock and Fort Smith began at 10 a.m.

Both teams were undefeated, giving the matchup a championship billing. More than 1,500 fans watched the Tigers and Grizzlies fight through a scoreless first half.

The second half, though, belonged to Little Rock. May scored twice, both on 12-yard runs, and Terry connected with Letzig for a 15-yard touchdown pass. This 18-5 victory over Fort Smith gave the Tigers their third consecutive state championship.

In the second game of the day, the undefeated Arkansas Razorbacks beat Washington University 34-0.

On March 21, 1910, Coach Van Buren informed Little Rock High School students of his resignation and left that night with his family for their home in New Auburn, Wis. Illness was the reason for his resignation.

1909 TIGER SCHEDULE

Arkadelphia 0	LRHS 11
Little Rock College 3	LRHS 6
Hot Springs 0	LRHS 11
State Normal School (second team) 0	LRHS 80
Memphis, TN 0	LRHS 32
Clary Training School 0	LRHS 10
Fort Smith 5	LRHS 18

NEW COACH, NEW RULES, NEW CHAMPION

1910   3-2-2

Head Coach: E.E. Tarr

1910 LETTERMEN

J. Gilroy Cox	Winnifred Harb	William Moore	Ernest Stansbury
Homer Hammonds	Dudley Jones	Menefee Moose	Walter Terry
Harper Harb	Robert Martin	-- Muller	Jesse Weidemeyer

1910 MANAGER
Unknown

Coach E.E. Tarr took over Little Rock in 1910, but the Tigers were not quite as successful as previous years. Many players reported for practice, and through long hours of hard work in the park on 17th and Main streets, the first team was rounded into shape.

This first team consisted of only four returning players from 1909. Coach Tarr filled the vacancies with newcomers and hoped the team would come together to win Little Rock's fourth consecutive state championship.

There were several rule changes for 1910, including switching from two, 25-minute quarters to four, 15-minute quarters. The allotted time for these quarters could be shortened or lengthened with the agreement of each coach prior to the game.

A ban on flying tackles was introduced to reduce the risk of serious injuries to the offensive player carrying the ball. This rule stated that a defensive player had to have one foot on the ground when he made contact with the runner.

Another rule banning pass interference was also instituted. This rule stated that the defensive player could not touch the intended receiver until the receiver caught the pass.

Walter Terry

Also new in 1910, at least at Little Rock High School, was the requirement of a physical for all athletes prior to sports participation. The physical began with athletes at the YMCA and then slowly spread into the state's school systems.

The season opened Oct. 1 at West End Park against Morrilton High School. Less than five minutes after the opening kickoff, Walter Terry scored on a 40-yard run and converted the extra-point attempt for a 6-0 lead.

Just before the first quarter ended, Winnifred Harb scored from the 20 and Terry converted the extra-point attempt for a 12-0 lead.

After a short run by Terry in the second quarter gave the Tigers an 18-0 halftime lead, Little Rock came out in the third quarter and quickly scored again. The score was set up by a fumble recovery at the Morrilton 10.

The Tigers' Dudley Jones picked up the loose ball and returned it the distance for a touchdown. Terry again kicked the extra point for a 24-0 lead.

Little Rock scored its last touchdown in the fourth quarter when Robert Martin had a 30-yard touchdown reception. Terry's extra-point attempt failed, but the Tigers beat Morrilton 34-0.

The second game and second victory for Little Rock was against Ouachita College. The Tigers were outweighed and outclassed, but still beat the college team 6-5.

As the score indicated, the victory was not easy. Ouachita scored the game's first touchdown just before halftime. The score was set up by a 20-yard interception return.

Two plays later, the college team was at the Little Rock 7 and then scored on an off-tackle play. The extra-point attempt failed, but Ouachita took a 5-0 lead into halftime.

Nine minutes into the fourth quarter, the Tigers' Harper Harb blocked a punt at the 12 and Little Rock recovered at the 8.

On the Tigers' first play, Winnifred Harb went through the left side of the line for the score. The extra-point attempt was good for the 6-5 victory.

After tying Physicians and Surgeons College 0-0, Little Rock again tried its luck against a college team, traveling to Conway to face Hendrix College.

The game was dominated by the college team and reinforced that the Tigers were playing out of their classification in a 27-0 loss.

Little Rock traveled to Fordyce for its next game. The Redbugs put up a good fight but were no match for the Tigers, who won 18-0.

Terry kicked field goals of 30 yards and 25 yards and returned an interception 10 yards for a touchdown. Jones scored Little Rock's only other touchdown on a short run.

The most anticipated and exciting game of the season was between Little Rock High School and Little Rock College at West End Park. Both teams were backed by a large crowd of loyal fans.

Those fans, though, did not expect the type of game that was played. The contest was a defensive battle and ended in a 3-3 tie. Followers of the high school team quickly forgot about the tie and turned their attention to the next game.

The final battle of the season was a Thanksgiving Day contest in Fort Smith. In a hard-fought affair, favored Fort Smith High School beat the Tigers 17-0.

Fort Smith's success was largely due to superior speed, size and spirit noticeable to spectators. Following Fort Smith's first touchdown, Little Rock fought harder to keep the score down, rather than to win.

The loss in Fort Smith eliminated the Tigers from the state championship race, the first time in three years the title did not belong to Little Rock High School.

1910 TIGER SCHEDULE

Morrilton 0	LRHS 34
Ouachita College 5	LRHS 6
Physicians And Surgeons College 0	LRHS 0
Hendrix College 27	LRHS 0
Fordyce 0	LRHS 18
Little Rock College 3	LRHS 3
Fort Smith 17	LRHS 0

TRAINING FOR TOUGH COMPETITON

1911   5-2-0

Head Coach: Floyd H. Wingo

1911 LETTERMEN

Ludovic Alexander	Foy Hammons	Robert Martin	Miller Silliman
Kuhl Brown	Harper Harb	William Moore	Mack Steele
Alfred Craig	Hickey Himsteadt	James Murrey	Jesse Weidemeyer
John Curran	Frank Kavanaugh	Joe Murrey	
Randall Falk	Nick Kupferle	Alex Rogoski	

1911 MANAGER
Menefee Moose

While Little Rock High School was building a $100,000 addition for an auditorium, pool and gymnasium, new head coach Floyd Wingo began preparation for the 1911 season with only seven returning players.

Of those seven players, two were dismissed from the team for unknown technicalities, one was hurt during preseason practice and played the year injured, one missed five games because of illness and one moved from the line to running back.

Special praise, though, was given to the 1911 team for its unprecedented record of training. At the beginning of the season, the players realized they were not as heavy as previous teams. They decided to overcome this handicap with serious training. Players eliminated smoking and other bad habits, a practice noticed by the student body and school ad-

Photo provided by Central High School
Little Rock's new auditorium and gymnasium

1911 Little Rock High School game photo at West End Park

ministration. Athletic department heads commended the players for their self-imposed training regimen.

Following a dominating 65-0 victory of Morrilton High School to open the season, the Tigers hosted the Zebras of Pine Bluff at West End Park. The field was covered with 2 inches of mud, and a steady drizzle soaked players and spectators.

Three minutes into the game, William Moore intercepted a pass and returned it 30 yards for a Little Rock touchdown. Moore converted the extra-point attempt for a 6-0 lead.

Just minutes later, Moore received a pass from Foy Hammons and the play resulted in a 60-yard touchdown. Moore failed to convert the extra-point attempt, but the Tigers led 11-0.

Following a scoreless second quarter, Ludovic Alexander scored from the 10 early in the third quarter. Moore converted the extra-point attempt for a 17-0 lead.

Five minutes into the fourth period, Pine Bluff lined up to punt, but the kick was blocked by Joe Murrey. Moore recovered the blocked punt and returned it 40 yards for a touchdown. He also converted the extra-point attempt to increase the lead to 23-0.

The Tigers' final touchdown came on a short run by Randall Falk. Moore's extra point ended the scoring and gave Little Rock its second victory, 29-0.

The Tigers traveled to Fordyce the following week to take on Clary Training

School. The Fordyce school proved to be too much for Little Rock to handle. After winning the toss prior to the game, Clary elected to kick off to the Tigers.

Little Rock's John Curran received the kickoff, but he fumbled to Clary. It took just two minutes for Clary to score and take an early lead.

The Tigers received the ensuing kickoff but could not gain any yard-age. In punt formation, Hammons fumbled before the kick. Little Rock recovered, but the player was tackled in the end zone for a safety and Clary led 7-0 at halftime.

Early in the third quarter, Clary returned a punt to the Tigers 25. On the first offensive play, a Clary receiver made a finger-tip catch to score on a 25-yard pass.

In the fourth quarter, Clary scored on a 10-yard run and a fumble return. Little Rock never threatened to score in a 23-0 loss.

Following the loss, the team realized it was not invincible and began to settle down and practice more seriously. This paid off the following week as the Tigers beat Arkadelphia 9-0.

Little Rock hosted Memphis High School the next week without Alexander, a starting right halfback, and team captain Harper Harb.

Even without these players, the Tigers were able to keep a tough Memphis team scoreless for the first three quarters. The Warriors finally scored with 11 minutes left to play in the game.

The score occurred after several players handled the ball in the backfield before it ended up in the hands of the Memphis tight end. Forty yards later, the Warriors were ahead by one touchdown and the extra point increased the lead to 6-0.

Just minutes later, Memphis scored again on a 30-yard field goal. The Warriors handed Little Rock its second loss of the season, 9-0.

After an easy 36-0 victory over Hot Springs, the Tigers prepared for a Thanksgiving Day game with Fort Smith.

The holiday game began with the Grizzlies scoring first on a 65-yard touchdown pass in the first quarter. Little Rock answered immediately when Hammons connected with Frank Kavanaugh for a 65-yard touchdown pass. Moore kicked the extra point to give the Tigers a 6-5 lead.

Fort Smith regained the lead in the second quarter when it returned a blocked punt for a touchdown. The extra-point attempt failed, but the Grizzlies took a 10-6 halftime lead.

Following a halftime speech by Coach Wingo, Little Rock came out in the second half and played tough defense. While the Tigers kept Fort Smith out of the end zone, the Little Rock offense was able to score three more touchdowns.

Early in the third quarter, Miller Silliman caught a short pass and took it 65 yards for a touchdown to put the Tigers up 11-10. On the first play of the fourth quarter, Hammons connected with Kavanaugh for another 65-yard touchdown.

Kavanaugh caught another pass on Little Rock's next possession and ran 50 yards before being brought down at the 5. Falk scored from there and the extra point extended the lead to 22-10. The Tigers went on to record their fifth victory of the season.

1911 TIGER SCHEDULE

Morrilton 0	LRHS 65
Pine Bluff 0	LRHS 29
Clary Training School 23	LRHS 0
Arkadelphia 0	LRHS 9
Memphis, TN 9	LRHS 0
Hot Springs 0	LRHS 36
Fort Smith 10	LRHS 22

LIGHT, FAST AND CLEAN

1912   3-3-0

Head Coach: Floyd H. Wingo
Assistants: John G. Pipkin, John A. Larson

1912 LETTERMEN

Ludovic Alexander	Oliver Johnson	Robert Martin	Alex Rogoski
Alvin Blass	Dudley Jones	James Murrey	Marshall Shackleford
Fred Hoeltzel	George Keopple	Rex O'Neal	Miller Silliman
Walter Jackson	Harrell Lenow	Leo Robbins	Charles Sommers

1912 MANAGER
Unknown

Fielding only five veterans, Little Rock played a fast and consistent brand of football in 1912, but was too light to compete against some opponents. Although the first-team players were blessed with speed, they averaged only 135 or 140 pounds.

The 1912 season was the first that allowed substitutions without a time out or switching players between quarters. Coach Floyd Wingo substituted many times in the opener against Portland High School at Little Rock's West End Park. The substitutions were beneficial during the hot and humid contest, which the Tigers easily won 41-0.

After defeating Conway 45-0, Little Rock traveled to Pine Bluff to take on the

Little Rock vs. Conway

Little Rock vs. Conway

Zebras. The Tigers, outweighed by an average of 15 pounds per man, entered somewhat overconfident and were quickly humbled.

Little Rock fell behind 13-0 at halftime and lost all control in the second half as Pine Bluff dominated the Tigers 38-0. The loss virtually eliminated Little Rock from the state championship race.

The game did give the Tigers a better idea of what they had to contend with for the remainder of the season. From that point, they played good football.

The next week against Central High of Memphis, Little Rock showed its true ability when it kept the strong Tennessee team out of the end zone. The battle proved to be the most fiercely contested game of the season. Neither team was able to score a touchdown, although Memphis advanced several times within a few yards of the goal line, only to be held on downs by the tough Little Rock defense.

Memphis, however, was able to score twice in the third quarter when it converted two 30-yard field goals. The Tigers were beaten 6-0, their second consecutive loss.

Little Rock, though, bounced back the following week, using the forward pass and end runs to beat Hot Springs 12-0.

The Tigers closed the season by traveling to Fort Smith to play the Grizzlies on Thanksgiving Day. More than 3,500 fans filled the stands at Fort Smith's League Park to watch the eighth annual holiday game between the teams.

The Grizzlies scored a touchdown three plays into the second quarter on a short run to cap a drive from midfield. They then converted the extra-point attempt to take a 7-0 lead.

Little Rock completed 8 of 18 passes, but had three interceptions. Fort Smith also stopped the Tigers' ground game and held on for a 7-0 victory.

Even though Little Rock ended the season with three losses and did not win the state championship, it earned a reputation of being one of the cleanest playing teams in Arkansas because of Coach Wingo, who stressed sportsmanship whether winning or losing.

1912 TIGER SCHEDULE

Portland 0	LRHS 41
Conway 0	LRHS 45
Pine Bluff 38	LRHS 0
Central of Memphis, TN 6	LRHS 0
Hot Springs 0	LRHS 12
Fort Smith 7	LRHS 0

THE CHAMPIONSHIP THAT WAS GIVEN AWAY

1913   4-2-1

Head Coach: Floyd H. Wingo
Assistant: John G. Pipkin

1913 LETTERMEN

William Anderson	Tom Harris	Harrell Lenow	Jesse Scroggins
Earle Bowman	Fred Hoeltzel	Rex O'Neal	Marshall Shackleford
Callan England	Walter Jackson	Terrence Pfaff	Edwin Weist
Lee Hampel	Scott Julian	Leo Robbins	

1913 MANAGERS
Unknown

1913 ALL-STATE
Lee Hampel
Fred Hoeltzel
Jesse Scroggins

The year 1913 brought out so many excellent football players that Coach Floyd Wingo was able to select a first team from 50 men.

Little Rock, one of the lightest but hardest fighting teams in the state, opened the season against Augusta High School.

The Red Devils' only score came in the third quarter when they intercepted a pass and returned it for a touchdown.

This was the only mistake made by the Tigers the entire game. Little Rock scored 21 touchdowns, and Callan England converted 11 extra-point attempts to defeat

Augusta 137-6. The Tigers took a 65-0 lead into halftime.

The Red Devils, a much weaker and inexperienced team, were unable to give Little Rock a hard fight. The Tigers could have benefited from a more challenging game prior to traveling to Texarkana, Texas, the following week.

Little Rock opened the game by kicking off and allowed the Texas team to return the ball to the Tigers 1. Unable to get into the end zone in three plays, Texarkana attempted a field goal. The kick was low and Little Rock escaped the scoring threat.

Four minutes into the second quarter, the Tigers' luck ran out as Texas scored on a short run after driving from midfield. Texarkana added another score when it returned a fumble for a touchdown. The extra-point attempt kick increased the lead to 13-0.

On its next possession, the Texas team drove to the Little Rock 20, where a 20-yard field goal ended the scoring at 16-0. This game gave the Tigers their first loss of the season.

Prior to Little Rock's next game, against Fordyce, Coach Wingo announced that nine of the 18 players on the first team were injured, sick or dismissed from the squad because of grades.

The coach was quoted in the *Arkansas Gazette* as saying, "One thing I can't seem to impress upon the boys is the importance of keeping up in their studies. They don't seem to realize that all their practice is useless if they fall down in their classroom work, and are barred by the faculty."

Even without these players, the Tigers scored twice against Fordyce early in the first quarter. Robert Martin scored both of these touchdowns, giving Little Rock a 13-0 lead.

On their third possession of the game, the Tigers took control at midfield and picked up 25 yards from Walter Jackson. Jackson's next carry resulted in a touchdown and added six more points to Little Rock's lead.

During the second quarter, the Tigers scored two more touchdowns. The first oc-

curred when Martin broke free for a long run, the second was on a short run by Rex O'Neal. These scores gave Little Rock a 31-0 halftime lead.

On their first offensive play of the third quarter, the Tigers ran a trick play and O'Neal easily scored to increase the lead to 37-0.

Moments later, a 20-yard pass from Jackson to Fred Hoeltzel was good for another touchdown. Little Rock rounded out its scoring when O'Neal and Leo Robbins each crossed the goal line late in the game in a 57-0 victory over the Redbugs.

The Tigers had their work cut out for them the next week when they hosted one of the best teams in the South, Central High School of Memphis. One of the largest crowds thought to have assembled for a high school athletic contest packed West End Park and watched Little Rock turn in one of its best performances in several years.

Memphis netted 27 first-half points when it scored on three short runs and a punt return. The Tigers, however, shut down the Warriors during the second half.

Little Rock was able to avoid a shutout with a touchdown late in the fourth quarter. Robbins set up the score when he recovered a Central fumble at the 13. On the next play, Martin bulled his way for the 13 yards needed to get the Tigers on the scoreboard. Although beaten 27-6 by the Warriors, Little Rock fought valiantly against the great team.

When Pine Bluff walked off the field victorious against the Tigers in 1912, Little Rock vowed revenge in 1913. It carried out the threat, beating the Zebras 6-0.

After producing three goal-line stands in the third quarter, the Tigers began their scoring drive on their first possession of the fourth quarter.

O'Neal began the drive when he passed to Jackson for 15 yards. A running play picked up 5 yards and two more passes gained 35 yards to the 15. A triple pass, ending in the hands of Tom Harris, accounted for the game's lone score.

The Monday following the Pine Bluff game, not enough players showed up to conduct a practice. Coach Wingo stated that "… the trouble is that the boys are all swelled up over defeating Pine Bluff Friday. They think they can win games without practicing now, I suppose. Well, unless they change their views radically Hot Springs will wipe up West End Park with them Saturday. I have the utmost respect for the Hot Springs aggregation and I wish I could instill some of it into the boys. It might save them from the beating that they are in line for now unless they wake up."

Little Rock entered the game against Hot Springs without two main starters. Martin and Jackson both sat out because of injuries. These injuries and some overconfidence did not hinder the play of the Tigers.

Robbins accounted for seven touchdowns in a nine-touchdown performance by Little Rock. Robbins scored four touchdowns and set up three more on long runs in the 55-0 victory over the Trojans.

The defeat of Hot Springs gave the Tigers four victories against in-state competition. Since the Memphis Central and Texarkana, Texas, games did not count for the Arkansas high school championship, Little Rock only had to defeat Fort Smith to be named champion.

Fortune had been with the Tigers all season, and the whole city was anxiously awaiting a bright and victorious Thanksgiving Day when the decisive championship game would be played. Along with hundreds of spectators, the teams were greeted by heavy rain.

Both schools consistently turned the ball over because of the field conditions, but fought through the rain and mud until the game ended in a scoreless tie. Each coach praised his own players for the effort, and each thought his respective team would have come out ahead if the conditions were more favorable.

Even though it was unbeaten and had not been scored on all season, the tie with Little Rock questioned whether Fort Smith was the most dominate team in the state. The Tigers had posted an unbeaten record against in-state competition as well, and had also held the tough Grizzly team scoreless. Therefore, the Arkansas Athletic Association's Executive Board was met with the challenge of determining the 1913 state champion.

A.B. Hill, principal of Little Rock High School, addressed the members of the Executive Board during its meeting. Mr. Hill stated that he was not going to make a claim for the high school football championship. He never intended to claim a share of the title after watching Fort Smith and Little Rock battle on Thanksgiving Day.

Mr. Hill went on to state that he believed Fort Smith deserved the championship.

1913 TIGER SCHEDULE

Augusta 6	LRHS 137
Texarkana, TX 16	LRHS 0
Fordyce 0	LRHS 57
Central of Memphis, TN 27	LRHS 6
Pine Bluff 0	LRHS 6
Hot Springs 0	LRHS 55
Fort Smith 0	LRHS 0

A COMMITTEE APPOINTED CHAMPIONSHIP

1914   8-1-0

Head Coach: John G. Pipkin
Assistant: Earl F. Quigley
Team Physician: Dr. Wells Farrin Smith

1914 LETTERMEN

William Anderson	Fred Hoeltzel	Terrence Pfaff	Edwin Weist
Linwood Brickhouse	Floyd Kavanaugh	Jack Pitcock	Otto Wells
Harold Harris	Campbell Marshall	Marshall Shackleford	
Tom Harris	Earnest Peckham	Miller Silliman	

1914 MANAGER
H. Hanley

1914 ALL-STATE
Tom Harris
Fred Hoeltzel
Marshall Shackleford
Miller Silliman

Forty players reported to West End Park for preseason practice under the leadership of new head coach John G. Pipkin. Coach Pipkin's highest priority, though, was to hire an assistant. He filled the opening with a young man from Wisconsin named Earl F. Quigley.

Little Rock opened the season at West End Park against Benton High School. The Tigers struck just three minutes into the game when Tom Harris scored his first of three touchdowns on a short run, putting Little Rock up 6-0.

After Miller Silliman scored on a 77-yard run early in the second quarter, Coach Pipkin put in the second team and 23 Tigers saw action in a 40-0 victory.

The following week, Little Rock hosted Lonoke High School. The 1914 season marked the first time Lonoke fielded a team. The Tigers took advantage of Lonoke's inexperience and were able to dominate almost immediately after the opening kickoff. They scored their first touchdown less than two minutes into the game.

Edwin Weist scored six touchdowns, including a 65-yard run, and Harris scored two touchdowns, one on a 40-yard run. Silliman and Floyd Kavanaugh didn't play after skipping a practice during the week, but Little Rock still easily beat Lonoke 64-0.

Arkadelphia, the Tigers' next opponent, was much bigger and stronger, outweighing Little Rock 8 pounds per man. The Tigers countered with speed and quickness.

The first half was a defensive battle with each team trading punts after every possession. Little Rock was the only team to convert a first down during the first half. It also managed the only score after an Arkadelphia snap sailed through the end zone giving the Tigers a safety.

As the fourth quarter began, Little Rock drove the length of the field and Silliman scored from the 2 to increase the lead to 8-0. Minutes later, Silliman scored on a 40-yard run to put the game away and give the Tigers a 14-0 victory.

The Little Rock defense posted its third shutout and kept Arkadelphia from converting a first down. Silliman finished the game with 172 yards rushing and two touchdowns.

The Tigers hosted Central High School of Memphis the following week. The contest was close and two plays decided the outcome.

Just before the end of the first half, Little Rock punted and the Warriors took possession at their 45. On the first play, Central's left halfback went 55 yards for a touchdown. The kick was good to give the Tennessee school a 7-0 lead.

Midway through the fourth quarter, Memphis scored again on a 10-yard pass. The extra point gave the Warriors a 14-0 victory over the previously unbeaten Tigers.

Little Rock traveled to Hot Springs the next week to meet a strong team. The Trojans were undefeated and eying a state championship. Little Rock, however, was believed to have its best team since 1909 and was not going to be intimidated.

The battle began with Silliman scoring twice in the first quarter. The first touchdown occurred on the Tigers' first possession when Silliman caught a long pass and ran an additional 30 yards for the score. Five minutes later, he scored again on a short run. He also converted both extra-point attempts to put Little Rock ahead 14-0.

Hot Springs' only score came on an 84-yard fumble return. Silliman added another score in the fourth quarter to give the Tigers a 21-6 advantage and eventually the victory.

Little Rock was scheduled to meet Fort Smith High School the following week. The Tigers, though, were set on winning the state title and feared a loss to the Grizzlies would end any hope of a championship. Little Rock cancelled the game with Fort Smith and scheduled Augusta High School in its place.

Augusta was undefeated, but the Tigers beat the Red Devils 137-6 the previous season. Because of that romp, Little Rock players apparently believed the game would be easy and its in-state winning record would remain intact.

Five players did not make the trip to Augusta after breaking team rules. Two of those players were starters, Silliman and William Anderson, who skipped practice during the week.

In their absence, Weist led his team to victory. He scored three touchdowns while Kavanaugh added another on a 50-yard punt return. The 25-6 victory over the Red

Devils helped the Tigers remain undefeated against Arkansas competition.

Little Rock overcame 140 yards in penalties the following week against Russellville High School. Russellville's only threat to score ended on downs after driving to the 2.

In a 69-0 victory, Silliman scored six touchdowns, Kavanaugh scored three touchdowns and Weist and Harris each scored once for the Tigers. The game was highlighted by Silliman's 88-yard punt return for a touchdown in the third quarter.

The celebration ended two days later when the Arkansas Athletic Association suspended Rex O'Neal from all high school athletic teams. The suspension came after the Association found that O'Neal used an assumed name while playing in the Little Rock City Baseball League the previous summer.

Since his parents did not want him to play baseball on Sunday, O'Neal played under an assumed name to keep his real name out of the newspaper box scores.

The Athletic Association passed the rule to keep high school athletes from receiving money under assumed names. Both the Little Rock City Baseball League and O'Neal appealed that money was neither offered nor accepted, but the Athletic Association would not drop its case since O'Neal did play under an assumed name.

After beating Prescott 34-7, Coach Pipkin's team prepared for a Thanksgiving battle against Texarkana, Ark. More than 1,500 fans turned out at West End Park for a doubleheader, which featured Little Rock and Texarkana followed by Little Rock College and Arkansas College.

Weist scored the game's first touchdown on a 15-yard run to give the Tigers a 6-0 lead. But Texarkana answered with a 30-yard touchdown pass to make it 6-6. Texarkana then took the lead, 12-6, on a 50-yard interception return for a touchdown.

Little Rock's Harris tied the score when he ran for a 35-yard touchdown. The extra point was converted, putting the Tigers in front 13-12. Another touchdown by Little Rock, this time a 15-yard run by Silliman, then put the Tigers ahead for good.

After Little Rock defeated Texarkana 20-12, it then proclaimed itself state champion. However, Fort Smith and Arkadelphia also staked a claim to the 1914 state title.

The Arkansas Athletic Association's Executive Board met to discuss the matter and declare a champion. Both Fort Smith and Arkadelphia believed that Little Rock avoided tough opponents and used an ineligible player during the year. After a five-hour discussion by the committee, it awarded the state championship title to Little Rock High School.

1914 TIGER SCHEDULE

Benton 0	LRHS 40
Lonoke 0	LRHS 64
Arkadelphia 0	LRHS 14
Central High of Memphis, TN 14	LRHS 0
Hot Springs 6	LRHS 21
Augusta 6	LRHS 25
Russellville 0	LRHS 69
Prescott 7	LRHS 34
Texarkana, AR 12	LRHS 20

INEXPERIENCED TO A CHAMPION

1915   5-1-2

Head Coach: John G. Pipkin
Assistant: Earl F. Quigley
Team Physician: Dr. Wells Farrin Smith

1915 LETTERMEN

Linwood Brickhouse	Joe Harb	James Milliken	Bob Sloan
Marshall Campbell	Todd Harris	Gordon Murray	Ardis Smith
Archie Capel	Ben Isgrig	Earnest Peckham	Edwin Weist
Elbert Dowell	Lee Lindsey	Terrence Pfaff	
Norman Hall	Van Manning	Jack Pitcock	

1915 MANAGERS
Unknown

1915 ALL-STATE
Linwood Brickhouse
Terrence Pfaff
Edwin Weist

Since the 1915 season opened with few returning starters, Coach John G. Pipkin had to rebuild the team from raw material and the outlook for a winning season was not good.

Even though there were more players on this team than in any previous year at Little Rock High School, most were new or members of the previous season's second team.

In the season opener against Lonoke High School, the Tigers were outplayed by a better team. The better team, however, did not win the game. Little Rock caught a break in the third quarter on a costly Lonoke penalty to turn the tide in its direction.

Tied 7-7 near the end of the quarter, Lonoke gained possession at its 35. The Lonoke quarterback faked a pass and handed the ball off for a 40-yard gain.

Two plays later from the Tigers 15, Lonoke faked to the left and the defense followed. This left the right side of the field open and the Lonoke quarterback walked across the goal line for a touchdown. The referee, however, called a penalty against Lonoke and the touchdown was taken away.

This penalty shifted the momentum back to Little Rock. On Lonoke's next possession, Archie Capel intercepted a pass and returned it 25 yards for a touchdown. Edwin Weist converted the extra point for the 14-7 lead. The Tigers went on to score again in the fourth quarter when Weist scored on a short run.

Even with the 21-13 victory over Lonoke, the coaches were discouraged, stating the game was won by luck and not by playing good football.

Little Rock was not sluggish for its next contest, coming out against Benton High School with an incredible amount of fight and spirit.

Little Rock scored its first touchdown in the second quarter on a short run. Weist converted the extra point for a 7-0 lead.

Capel recovered a fumble at the Benton 25 to end the Panthers' next possession. Two plays after gaining possession, Todd Harris scored and the extra point by Weist increased the lead to 14-0.

Weist scored two touchdowns on short runs, and Lee Lindsey added another score in a 33-0 victory over Benton.

Another home game the following week had the Tigers against Hot Springs High School. Leading 14-0, Little Rock increased the advantage on a short touchdown run by Lindsey. Weist converted the extra point to take a 21-0 halftime lead.

The Trojans' next possession ended when Capel picked up a fumble at the 50. Lindsey and Harris took turns rushing during a drive that ended on a short touchdown run by Weist. Another score just before the game ended gave Little Rock a 35-0 victory.

Little Rock hosted Pine Bluff the next week in a game to decide the state championship. Unfortunately, the Tigers seemed to lose their punch at a critical time.

Driving into Pine Bluff territory on almost every possession, once getting inside the 1, Little Rock was unable to score. Pine Bluff, on the other hand, rarely got inside the Tigers 40.

The showdown ended in a 0-0 tie.

Little Rock played its first road game when it traveled to Central High School in Memphis. Memphis Central was considered to have one of the best high school teams in the South. More than 1,200 fans attended the game at Russwood Park to watch the Tennessee team, which outweighed the Tigers by almost 20 pounds per man, take on its Arkansas rival.

Runs of 50 and 40 yards, along with a 65-yard punt return, highlighted a game dominated by the powerful Memphis team. The Warriors scored at will and shut down the Little Rock offense in a 52-0 victory.

The Tigers were at home for their next game against Texarkana, Texas.

Texarkana forced Little Rock to kick on its opening possession and Weist's punt was downed at the Texas 5. On the first play, Bob Sloan broke through the line and tackled the Texas ball carrier behind the goal line for a safety.

Lindsey stopped Texarkana's next drive when he intercepted a pass and returned it to the Texas 10. Gordon Murray picked up 4 yards and Lindsey finished the 10-yard drive with a 6-yard touchdown run. Weist missed the extra-point attempt, but the Tigers led 8-0.

After opening the fourth quarter with an 8-yard touchdown run by Harris, Little Rock scored again just minutes later. With

Texarkana attempting a punt from its 20, Linwood Brickhouse broke through the line and blocked the kick. Brickhouse then fell on the ball in the end zone for a touchdown. Weist's extra point put the Tigers up 22-0.

Murray added another touchdown late in the game to help Little Rock to a 29-0 victory over Texarkana, Texas.

After another 0-0 tie, this time against Arkadelphia High School, the Tigers hosted Muskogee, Okla. This game proved to be Little Rock's best showing of the season.

The game was played on Thanksgiving Day and attended by more than 1,000 at Kavanaugh Field.

Muskogee was bigger, stronger and faster than the Tigers, but Little Rock played with perfection.

Four players scored for the Tigers. Murray and Harris each scored twice, while Lindsey and Weist scored once to give Little Rock a 40-0 victory.

The Tigers were undefeated against Arkansas opponents and awarded the state title for the fifth time in school history.

1915 TIGER SCHEDULE

Lonoke 13	LRHS 21
Benton 0	LRHS 33
Hot Springs 0	LRHS 35
Pine Bluff 0	LRHS 0
Central High of Memphis, TN 52	LRHS 0
Texarkana, TX 0	LRHS 29
Arkadelphia 0	LRHS 0
Muskogee, OK 0	LRHS 40

EARL QUIGLEY TAKES CONTROL

1916   2-5-2

Head Coach: Earl F. Quigley
Assistant: John G. Pipkin
Team Physician: Dr. Wells Farrin Smith

1916 LETTERMEN

Burdette Beals	Harold Harris	Neal McDermott	Ray Scott
Alvin Bell	Ben Isgrig	James Milliken	Ardis Smith
James DeMent	Charles Julian	William Powell	
Norman Hall	Van Manning	Clare Rudisill	

1916 MANAGER
R. Stevenson

1916 ALL-STATE
Ben Isgrig
Van Manning

Earl Quigley took over as head coach for the 1916 season after John G. Pipkin stepped down to become an assistant coach. In reality, neither coach was considered superior to the other. Both coaches worked together, striving to form a competitive team that would vie for a championship.

At the request of the coaches for tryouts, between 40 and 50 players responded. Out of the many responses, only one letterman and three substitutes from the 1915 team reported.

The one letterman was captain Harold Harris, and the three substitutes were Ardis Smith, Norman Hall and James Milliken.

Little Rock's first game was against the Benton Panthers. This game proved to be a great disappointment for the Tigers, marking the first time in almost four years that

61

Little Rock High School had lost to another Arkansas school.

After Milliken recovered a fumble in the first quarter, the Tigers took over at the Benton 20. A 10-yard loss caused Little Rock to settle for a 30-yard field goal by Burdette Beals.

A punt to Benton in the third quarter gave the Panthers possession at their 20. Three plays netted 33 yards, and after a 3-yard loss, they were at midfield. A pass play resulted in a 49-yard gain before Smith made the tackle at the 1.

The Panthers scored on the next play to narrowly defeat the Tigers 6-3.

The next two weeks saw Little Rock record scoreless ties with Arkadelphia and Fordyce. Neither team deserved to win the games, which were littered with fumbles, penalties and mistakes.

The Tigers' next opponent was Central High of Memphis. Played at Little Rock's Kavanaugh Field, the game pitted the Tigers against one the South's best high school teams.

Memphis jumped all over Little Rock, scoring 56 points by running straight through the defensive line. The Warriors ran away with the game 56-0.

After another loss, this time 39-0 to Texarkana, Texas, Little Rock High School played a game with its familiar rival, Little Rock College. The Tigers went in determined to win this contest, even though the college team was heavily favored.

The only points were scored during the third quarter when the Tigers' Clare Rudisill passed to James DeMent for a 30-yard touchdown. The extra-point attempt put the high school in front 7-0.

Little Rock's next possession resulted in a punt, and the college team fielded it at the 1. The college offense was unable to move and was forced to punt. Hall blocked the kick and it rolled out of the end zone to give the Tigers a safety.

This was all the scoring Little Rock needed in a 9-0 victory.

One of the most interesting moments of the game occurred at halftime. Several students from the high school led a goat, the stolen mascot of the college, on the field and began chanting and gloating around the animal. Outraged college students then rushed the field and a fight ensued for several minutes.

After school officials were unable to control the situation, police were called and the free-for-all was finally brought under control. Many students, as well as the goat, were injured during the halftime brawl.

As the season continued, the Tigers went on to lose the next week against Pine Bluff (19-0) and Fort Smith the following week (10-6). Little Rock, though, came alive for its last game of the season, a Thanksgiving Day battle with Van Buren.

The Tigers scored seven touchdowns and tallied 20 first downs in a 47-0 blowout of Van Buren.

1916 TIGER SCHEDULE

Benton 6	LRHS 3
Arkadelphia 0	LRHS 0
Fordyce 0	LRHS 0
Central High of Memphis, TN 56	LRHS 0
Texarkana, TX 39	LRHS 0
Little Rock College 0	LRHS 9
Pine Bluff 19	LRHS 0
Fort Smith 10	LRHS 6
Van Buren 0	LRHS 47

BACK ON TOP

1917   7-2-0

Head Coach: Earl F. Quigley

1917 LETTERMEN

Julian Adams	Asa Burroughs	Emmett Hoffman	James Milliken
Burdette Beals	James DeMent	Ben Isgrig	Willie Mitchell
Alvin Bell	Earle Elrod	Edward Kruger	William Powell
Ulysses Bratton	Harold Harris	Neal McDermott	

1917 MANAGER
Clyde Gay

1917 ALL-STATE
Burdette Beals
Alvin Bell
Harold Harris
Ben Isgrig
James Milliken

The Tigers opened the season with a 38-0 victory over Benton High School. A week later, Lonoke High School beat Little Rock, a 19-18 upset in which the Tigers made many mistakes, including uncountable penalties and several lost fumbles.

Little Rock got back on track the following week with a 14-0 victory over Russellville High School, but fell again a week later when Central High of Memphis handed the Tigers their second loss.

The Memphis game, which became known in the city of Little Rock as "the annual defeat," ended in a 27-0 shutout. This marked the only game of the year that the Tigers did not score at least two touchdowns.

Little Rock again challenged Benton High School for its next game. After easily defeating the Panthers earlier in the season, the Tigers entered the second meeting a little overconfident. This overconfidence almost cost Little Rock as Benton outplayed the Tigers during the first half.

Late in the first quarter, the Panthers recovered a Little Rock fumble and took possession deep inside their territory. Benton's quarterback then ran 18 yards on a run around the end.

After making three first downs, a completed forward pass moved the Panthers to the Tigers 18. The quarter ended at that point, 0-0.

Two plays into the second quarter, Benton converted another first down and then scored on a short run. The extra point put Benton on top 7-0.

After a series of punts, Little Rock took possession at its 38 and two first downs put it at the Panthers 35. James DeMent then received a pass from Burdette Beals behind the line of scrimmage and ran 35 yards for the Tigers' first touchdown. Ben Isgrig's extra-point kick made it 7-7.

Little Rock kicked off to open the second half, but quickly took possession after holding Benton on downs. Alvin Bell made 3 yards on the first play, and another long pass play from Beals to DeMent put the ball at the Panthers 13.

Beals and Harold Harris each carried to the 8. Bell scored from there; Isgrig's extra point extended the lead to 14-7.

The Tigers ended the scoring when Emmett Hoffman added a touchdown run from the 14. Isgrig kicked the conversion point for a 21-7 lead.

The game was called midway through the fourth quarter because of darkness as Little Rock once again defeated the Benton Panthers.

The Tigers hosted Texarkana, Texas, the following week and the teams were scoreless after the first quarter. Little Rock, though, began the second quarter with a Bell to DeMent pass completion to the Texas 15. Little Rock moved to the 5 in

three plays before Harris scored on a run. Isgrig's conversion was good for a 7-0 lead.

A fumble recovery and three running plays gave the Tigers control at the Texas 40 just before the end of the half. DeMent gained 30 yards on a pass play, then Bell scored immediately after that on a 10-yard run. The half ended 13-0.

Little Rock recovered a fumble early in the third period to take over at midfield. With first down at the Texas 18, Harris went into the end zone to put the Tigers up 20-0.

Hoffman added another score early in the fourth quarter in a 26-0 victory.

Little Rock jumped all over rival Pine Bluff the next week. Harris scored four touchdowns, and Beals' punts averaged 55 yards to keep the Zebras out of Little Rock territory. Little Rock dealt Pine Bluff its first loss of the season, 24-7.

Following the upset over the Zebras, the Tigers played Stuttgart High School at Kavanaugh Field. The Tigers continued their strong play, scoring 17 touchdowns in a 111-0 domination of the Ricebirds.

Little Rock's Bell accounted for 11 of these touchdowns. He scored six touchdowns on short runs and returned one fumble for a score. He also passed for four touchdowns, including a 40-yard connection with Willie Mitchell and a 60-yard connection with Isgrig.

Isgrig also starred at kicker with nine extra points.

Kavanaugh Field was the site of Little Rock's final game against State Normal College.

A gloomy day and soggy field kept many spectators away. One of the smallest crowds of the season turned out as the Tigers defeated the Conway school 45-0.

Hoffman began the game's scoring when he scored on a short run early in the first quarter. Bell added to the score in the second quarter with an 8-yard run for a 12-0 halftime lead.

Hoffman added to his points when he ran around right end for a third-quarter touchdown. With State Normal in Little Rock territory later in the third quarter,

Beals returned an interception 70 yards for another touchdown.

The college received the ensuing kick-off and took possession on its 30. On its first play, the center made a bad snap and the ball rolled back to the 8. State Normal was then forced to punt; Mitchell returned the kick to the 4 just prior to the end of the quarter.

On the Tigers' first play of the fourth quarter, Bell scored again. Isgrig failed to convert the extra-point attempt, but Little Rock had a commanding 32-0 lead.

James Milliken blocked a State Normal punt midway through the fourth quarter and it was recovered by DeMent, who returned it for a touchdown.

Just moments later, Asa Burroughs recovered a State Normal fumble on the 40. It took the Tigers five plays before Harris scored Little Rock's last touchdown on a short run.

The Tigers ended the year with a 45-0 victory over State Normal College of Conway.

From many viewpoints, the 1917 season was a notable one for Little Rock, a season highlighted by another state championship.

1917 TIGER SCHEDULE

Benton 0	LRHS 38
Lonoke 19	LRHS 18
Russellville 0	LRHS 14
Central High of Memphis, TN 27	LRHS 0
Benton 7	LRHS 21
Texarkana, TX 0	LRHS 26
Pine Bluff 7	LRHS 24
Stuttgart 0	LRHS 111
State Normal College 0	LRHS 45

WAR TOUCHES FOOTBALL IN LITTLE ROCK

1918   1-2-0

Head Coach: George H. Wittenberg
Assistant: Nick Kupferle
Team Physician: Dr. Wells Farrin Smith

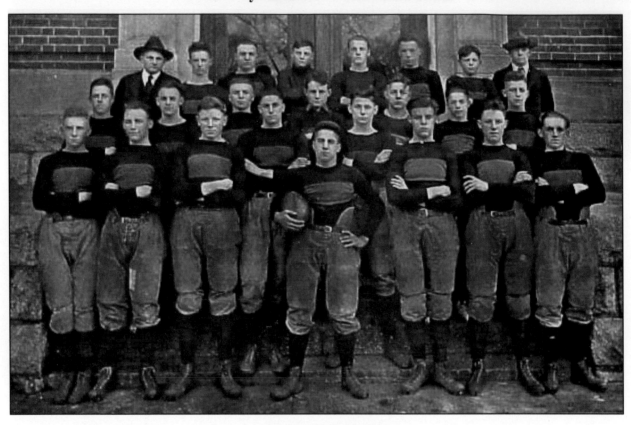

1918 LETTERMEN

Julian Adams	Roy Biggadike	Edward Kruger	Charles Stewart
Hubert Adkins	Darrell Crook	Neal McDermott	John Ward
Edward Barbee	Clarence Howard	Robert Powell	Charles Welch
Alvin Bell	Allen Isgrig	Hershell Riffel	

1918 MANAGER
Byron Niemeyer

1918 ALL-STATE
None

During the summer of 1918, Coach Earl Quigley was called to Artillery Officers Training School at Camp Zachary Taylor in Louisville, Ky. After completion of the training school, Quigley was stationed at Camp Jackson in Columbia, S.C., as an instructor.

When it was time for Little Rock High School to begin practice, a coach had not yet been named. A teacher at the high school, George H. Wittenberg, volunteered to help coach the team.

Nick Kupferle joined Wittenberg as assistant coach. Neither coach was new to Little Rock's football program since Coach Wittenberg lettered for the Tigers in 1909 and Coach Kupferle in 1911.

As in previous years, Little Rock was represented by some great athletes on the team. The 1918 team worked under difficult circumstances throughout the season and was not as successful on the field as some past teams. This team, however, accomplished much more by showing the spirit and determination needed to succeed in high school athletics.

The season was hard hit by an influenza epidemic and gas shortage and games were hard to schedule because all eyes were turned to a bigger battle – World War I.

During the second week of practice, team captain Alvin Bell was injured and unable to return to full participation for several weeks. A few weeks after Bell's injury, there was an influenza quarantine put on the city of Little Rock. The quarantine closed school and suspended football practice for one week.

Almost every city and school in the state was quarantined at one point during the year, placing a heavy burden on teams across the state. Games were postponed, rescheduled and finally cancelled.

When school finally opened again and football practice resumed, fallout from the influenza epidemic was easy to see. Two returning lettermen were too sick to return to school.

The Tigers played only three games, yet the two-month season was the longest ever in Little Rock. The Tigers were outplayed in every game and won just once.

The three games played were against Henderson-Brown College, Fort Smith High School and the 13th Training Battalion of Camp Pike.

The first game with Henderson-Brown College was close, but Little Rock was beaten because of its lack of weight and experience.

In front of 300 fans in Arkadelphia, the game was one of the hardest fought at the college campus.

The only score came early in the fourth quarter after the Tigers turned the ball over on downs at their 40. The Reddies scored just a few plays later from the 5. The extra point made it 7-0.

Little Rock was inside the Henderson-Brown 10 three times, but turned the ball over each time. The Tigers never found the goal line, losing the opener by a touchdown.

Little Rock's second game was against Fort Smith High School. Approximately 500 fans watched Bell and Julian Adams score in the first quarter for a 12-0 lead.

The Tigers scored their first touchdown on their second series of the game after taking possession at the Grizzlies 40 following a Fort Smith punt. Bell ended the 40-yard drive with a 12-yard touchdown run.

Little Rock's second touchdown came almost immediately after its first score.

Fort Smith took the ensuing kickoff and drove close to the goal line. But Adams intercepted a pass and returned it 98 yards for the score.

Fort Smith scored twice, but each was negated by a penalty. The Grizzlies did score in the fourth quarter when they were awarded a safety. This was the only score Fort Smith could manage in a 12-2 loss to the Tigers.

Little Rock's third and final game was played on Thanksgiving Day against the 13th Training Battalion of Camp Pike. More than 1,000 fans filled Little Rock's Kavanaugh Field to watch the holiday game.

Outweighed 20 pounds per man by the Camp Pike team, and without John Ward and Adams because of injuries, the Tigers put up a good fight but were unable to keep the soldiers out of the end zone.

The Training Battalion was in control of the game from the start, scoring three touchdowns in the first quarter, two touchdowns in the second quarter and one touchdown in the third and fourth quarters.

The Camp Pike team beat Little Rock 42-0.

The Tigers were scheduled to play Pine Bluff High School on Dec. 14 in Pine Bluff, a game that would decide the state championship. Pine Bluff city officials, however, cancelled the game when five Zebras came down with influenza.

Little Rock ended the season as the only team in Arkansas unbeaten against high school competition. Therefore, the Tigers were awarded their seventh state title.

1918 TIGER SCHEDULE

Henderson-Brown College 7	LRHS 0
Fort Smith 2	LRHS 12
13th Training Battalion of Camp Pike 42	LRHS 0

STATEWIDE DOMINATION

1919   9-0-1

Head Coach: Earl F. Quigley
Team Physician: Dr. Wells Farrin Smith

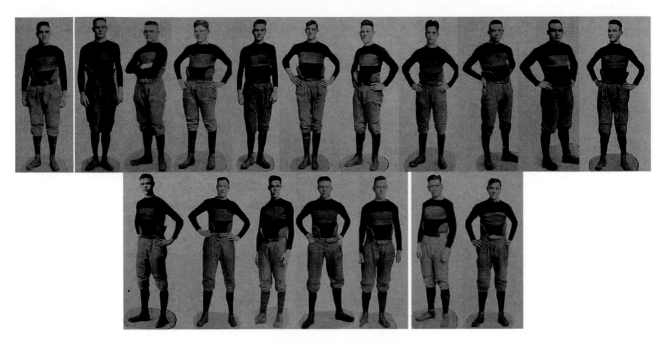

1919 LETTERMEN

Shy Anderson	Earle Elrod	Neal McDermott	Charles Welch
Edward Barbee	Emmett Hoffman	James Mills	Ivan Williams
Alvin Bell	Allen Isgrig	Robert Powell	Orval Williams
Darrell Crook	Edward Kruger	Charles Stewart	

1919 MANAGERS
Virgil Owen
Benjamine Eugene Smith

1919 ALL-STATE

Alvin Bell	James Mills
Darrell Crook	Ivan Williams
Allen Isgrig	Orval Williams
Neal McDermott	

The 1919 season was the most successful in Little Rock's brief football history. Little Rock had nine victories and dominated most teams it faced during the year.

Coach Earl Quigley, who returned from military service during the spring, began the season with an unusual amount of experience. Almost every player who reported for practice had been trained in the past by Coach Quigley and knew the system he used.

Kavanaugh Field was the site of the Tigers' opening game against Russellville High School. Little Rock outweighed its opponent by 15 pounds per man and used its speed and power to dominate the Cyclones.

The Tigers set a state record for points, 174, while quarterback Alvin Bell set an individual state record by scoring eight touchdowns.

Charles Stewart added seven touchdowns. Ivan Williams had five touchdowns, including a punt return the length of the field for one of his scores.

Little Rock usually needed only two plays to score, returning a punt half the distance and then scoring on its first offensive play of the series.

Coach Quigley put in the second team during the second quarter and closed the first half with 26 points to give the Tigers a 73-0 halftime lead.

The first team returned in the second half and scored 101 points in the 174-0 victory. The previous state scoring record also belonged to Little Rock, which beat Augusta 137-6 in 1913.

The Tigers beat Hendrix College's second team the following week, but the game disappointed many fans when Little Rock only scored 12 points.

The game was played at Kavanaugh Field, which was covered in mud and mostly under water.

Midway through the second quarter, Edward Barbee received a punt on the Hendrix 30 and returned it to the 8. Bell scored on the next play giving the Tigers a 6-0 lead.

James Mills recovered a Hendrix fumble early in the third quarter to set up Little Rock's second touchdown. After taking over on the Hendrix 25, three plays moved the ball within 1 yard of the goal line. Bell scored from there to put the Tigers up 12-0, helping Little Rock to its second consecutive victory of the season.

Two victories later, including 50-7 over Arkadelphia, the Tigers next met old nemesis Central High of Memphis.

Defenses dominated most of the game.

With only 1 yard to go for a touchdown, Little Rock held the powerful Memphis team for four downs. The Tigers then took over and drove to the 3 with six consecutive first downs. A fumble on second down halted the march and neither team came close to scoring again.

The game ended scoreless, and Little Rock was given much acclaim since Memphis Central was considered among the top teams in the South.

The Tigers traveled to Texarkana, Texas, for its next game. A 21-0 victory marked the first time Texarkana had lost to Little Rock at home.

The following week, however, was the toughest game of the season against in-state high school competition. The game was against Pine Bluff, and Little Rock escaped 13-0.

A first-quarter fumble recovery by the Tigers gave them possession on the Pine Bluff 20 and set up their first score. Bell passed to Darrell Crook for the touchdown. Bell kicked the extra point for a 7-0 lead. Bell scored again on a short run in the fourth quarter to end the scoring and beat Little Rock's biggest enemy.

The Tigers traveled to Fort Smith for their next game, which was played on a 92-yard field.

The Grizzlies got the best of Little Rock in the first quarter and led 13-0. The Tigers, however, came out in the second quarter and mounted a comeback when Bell scored on a 60-yard run and Williams scored on a 15-yard run. After the extra points, Little Rock led 14-13.

Fort Smith quickly regained the lead after Bell fumbled the Grizzlies' next punt. A Fort Smith player recovered the fumble and returned it for a touchdown and a 20-14 lead.

The Tigers were able to tie the score just as quickly. Little Rock's Orval Williams intercepted a pass on the Grizzlies' next possession and returned it 50 yards for a touchdown. Bell missed the extra-point attempt and the score remained 20-20.

Ivan Williams scored from the 5 on the Tigers' next possession for a 26-20 lead. Little Rock never relinquished the advantage and scored five more times to defeat the Grizzlies 59-20.

On Thanksgiving Day, the Tigers played Benton High School for the state championship.

The Panthers were undefeated through a nine-game schedule and considered Little Rock's most dangerous in-state opponent of the season. Benton, though, proved to be no match for the Tigers as they won 52-0.

Past football seasons usually ended on Thanksgiving Day, but there was an exception in 1919.

Paragould High School finished undefeated in seven games and challenged Little Rock for the overall championship. The Tigers accepted the challenge and Paragould's title hopes faded quickly.

Behind a four-touchdown performance by Ivan Williams, Little Rock dominated Paragould 90-0.

Robert Powell added three touchdowns, Bell and Douglas Wycoff each scored twice and one touchdown was scored by both Mills and Emmett Hoffman.

Powell scored his third touchdown with 15 seconds left in the game on a 37-yard run, giving the Tigers 505 points for the season.

It was unusual for teams to score 500 points during the early part of the century. Little Rock's total was among the highest scored by a high school, college or professional team during season.

1919 TIGER SCHEDULE

Russellville 0	LRHS 174
Hendrix College (second team) 0	LRHS 12
Lonoke 0	LRHS 34
Arkadelphia 7	LRHS 50
Central High of Memphis, TN 0	LRHS 0
Texarkana, TX 0	LRHS 21
Pine Bluff 0	LRHS 13
Fort Smith 20	LRHS 59
Benton 0	LRHS 52
Paragould 0	LRHS 90

ROARING TWENTIES BEGIN WITH CHAMPIONSHIP

1920   8-1-0

Head Coach: Earl F. Quigley
Team Physician: Dr. Wells Farrin Smith

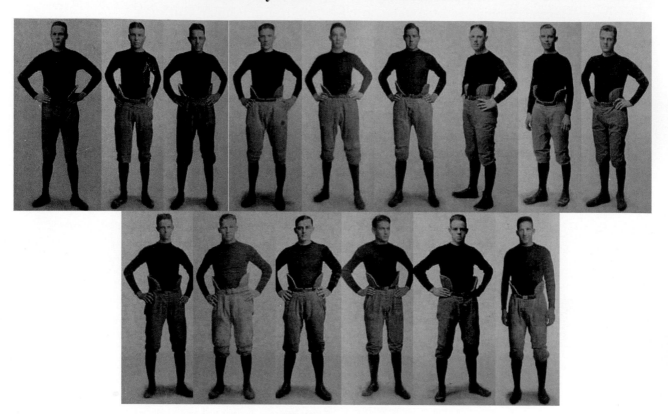

1920 LETTERMEN

Elbert Allen	Haco Boyd	Nick Nicholson	Ivan Williams
John Arendt	Vernon Felix	Jack Patterson	Orval Williams
Eugene Bale	Harold Mabbitt	Herbert Rule	Douglas Wycoff
Roy Biggadike	Lewis Mashburn	Charles Welch	

1920 MANAGERS
Earnest J. Field
Claude Thompson

1920 ALL-STATE
Charles Welch
Ivan Williams
Orval Williams
Douglas Wycoff

Only six out of the 70 players who reported to Coach Earl Quigley had previous football experience. The six veteran players included three first-team members and three second-team members from 1919.

The 48 who played the entire season represented the highest number to ever finish a football season at Little Rock High School.

After defeating their first three opponents by a combined score of 150-13, the

Tigers took on Hendrix College's second team. Little Rock entered the game without four starters because of injuries: Elbert Allen, Charles Welch, Haco Boyd and Nick Nicholson.

The Tigers scored a touchdown midway through the first quarter when Douglas Wycoff passed to Jack Patterson.

Little Rock scored again in the second quarter when Vernon Felix blocked a Hendrix punt and recovered it in the end zone. The Tigers ended their scoring in the third quarter with a Wycoff to Lewis Mashburn touchdown pass.

Little Rock led 20-14 going into the fourth quarter, but Hendrix scored early in the period for a 20-20 tie. The extra-point attempt was good to give the college team a 21-20 lead.

The Tigers had one last chance after recovering a fumble on their 30 with only four minutes remaining in the game. On the next play, Wycoff gained 10 yards around left end and Roy Biggadike then passed to Felix.

As the pass was about to land in the arms of Felix, a Hendrix defender jumped to intercept. The defensive player was only able to tip the pass, and Felix made the catch to complete an apparent 60-yard touchdown.

An official, however, blew his whistle after the tip because he thought the pass was going to hit the ground and did not expect Felix to make the catch.

A rule stated that any time an official blew the whistle, even if it was inadvertent, the ball was dead. The winning touchdown was negated and Little Rock suffered its first loss since 1918.

The Tigers next traveled to Memphis to take on Central High School, a team they had not beaten in 11 years.

After a scoreless first quarter, a Memphis punt gave Little Rock possession at the 50. From here, the Tigers began their first scoring drive.

Ivan Williams went 25 yards on the first play, and then Mashburn added 10 yards when he passed to Patterson. A second pass from Mashburn to Patterson was complete for a 15-yard touchdown.

To open the fourth quarter, Little Rock blocked a Central punt that Welch recovered at the Warriors 20. Memphis, though, intercepted a pass on the next play to end another threat by the Tigers. The Warriors couldn't move and were forced to punt back to Little Rock, giving the Tigers possession at their 30.

Eugene Bale capped a 70-yard drive with a 7-yard touchdown run. Ivan Williams converted the extra-point attempt to put Little Rock up 13-0.

Following the ensuing kickoff, Felix intercepted a pass at the Tigers 40 and returned it 60 yards for Little Rock's last touchdown. The extra-point attempt failed, but the Tigers had a 19-0 victory.

The next game put Little Rock against El Dorado, a battle that had the potential to determine the state championship. Both teams were undefeated and the Wildcats hadn't allowed a point.

Williams scored three touchdowns and converted six extra-point attempts, while Patterson and Bale each scored two touchdowns. Felix scored once and converted four extra-point attempts. The Tigers scored at will and the defense had no problem in a 70-0 victory.

The next week, Little Rock played in-state rival Pine Bluff. Williams and Mashburn scored two touchdowns each to help the Tigers to a 35-0 victory over the Zebras. The game ended with 10 minutes left on the clock due to excessive injuries for Pine Bluff.

In a spontaneous ceremony at the end of the game, the Pine Bluff team presented Williams, Little Rock's team captain, with the game ball.

The Tigers hosted Fort Smith at Kavanaugh Field the following week. With both teams undefeated against high school competition in Arkansas, the game would decide the state championship.

The contest was a defensive battle until the fourth quarter. Mashburn scored on a short run and Williams kicked the extra point for a 7-0 lead.

With only a few minutes remaining in the game, Little Rock's Harold Mabbitt intercepted a pass at the Fort Smith 20 and went into the end zone. The touchdown put the game out of reach, 14-0, and gave the Tigers the state championship.

Little Rock's last game was a Thanksgiving Day battle with Tupelo Military Institute of Mississippi. The Tupelo team, riding its third consecutive undefeated season, was the reigning champion in Mississippi.

The game was a defensive battle, with each team having only one opportunity to score. The Tigers took advantage of their chance with a 1-yard touchdown run in the second quarter. The Military Institute scored on a 22-yard field goal in the third quarter, but it would not be enough as Little Rock came away with a hard-fought 6-3 victory.

1920 TIGER SCHEDULE

Henderson College (second team) 0	LRHS 48
Lonoke 6	LRHS 74
Arkadelphia 7	LRHS 28
Hendrix College (second team) 21	LRHS 20
Central High of Memphis, TN 0	LRHS 19
El Dorado 0	LRHS 70
Pine Bluff 0	LRHS 35
Fort Smith 0	LRHS 14
Tupelo Military Institute of MS 3	LRHS 6

SOUTHERN CHAMPION

1921 8-0-1

Head Coach: Earl F. Quigley
Assistant: Terrence Pfaff
Team Physician: Dr. Wells Farrin Smith

1921 LETTERMEN

Eugene Bale	Nate Ginsberg	Dawson Mills	Ivan Williams
Richard Bright	Frank Kirkpatrick	S.B. Nickelson	Douglas Wycoff
Ashley Cockrill	George Ladd	Herbert Rule	
Vernon Felix	Lewis McCarthy	Bert Salley	

1921 MANAGER
Earnest J. Field

1921 ALL-STATE

Richard Bright	Herbert Rule
Nate Ginsberg	Ivan Williams
George Ladd	Douglas Wycoff
Lewis McCarthy	

There were 72 hopefuls awaiting Coach Earl Quigley's return from Oshkosh, Wis., where he was vacationing for the summer. The group included only five returning players from the 1920 team, but Quigley was anxious to begin practice.

Among the new faces were several good athletes who had transferred from out of state. Richard Bright transferred from Kentucky, where he had earned "All-Kentucky" honors in 1919 as a fullback and in 1920 as a lineman. Nate Ginsberg transferred from Iowa, where he had earned "All-Iowa" honors as a lineman and 160-pound halfback Jack Hodges transferred from Texas.

The 1921 team was the heaviest that Coach Quigley had coached. Bright was the largest and fastest player, weighing 194 pounds and running the 100-yard dash in just under 10 seconds.

Without an assistant, Coach Quigley was coaching all the players and decided to cut the team down to 50. He then separated these players into a first, second and third team and relied on team captains Ivan Williams and Douglas Wycoff to help teach the younger players.

On Oct. 4, however, Terrence Pfaff was hired by the school to assist Coach Quigley with the team. Coach Pfaff was a Little Rock football letterman in 1913, 1914 and 1915, as well as All-State in 1915.

After a crushing 75-0 season-opening victory over Camden, the Tigers played the second team from Hendrix College in Conway. Williams scored the game's first touchdown on a short run for Little Rock. He also kicked the extra point for a 7-0 lead in the third quarter.

Hendrix waited until late in the fourth quarter to score its touchdown. A short pass to Ross Williams for six points and an extra point tied the score, 7-7. Neither team threatened to score again, resulting in a tie.

The Tigers traveled to Texarkana, Ark., the following week. Bright scored on a short run up the middle to give Little Rock a 7-0 lead at halftime.

Texarkana drove to the Tigers 1 on its first possession of the second half. Little Rock held for three downs before the Razorbacks finally pushed into the end zone.

Just as the scoring play began, several hundred Texarkana fans stormed the field. Coach Quigley protested to the officials, stating they could not see whether the ball crossed the goal line because of the mass of people. He also argued that if the runner did get into the end zone, he may have been aided by the crowd.

The touchdown stood, but Coach Quigley pulled his team off the field until the officials removed the crowd from the sidelines and forced them into the bleachers. When play resumed, the Tigers went on to score twice during the quarter. Both touchdowns occurred on short runs following long sustained drives.

After playing the entire fourth quarter in the dark, Little Rock was victorious 21-13.

Instead of practicing at their usual location, City Park, Coach Quigley and the Tigers practiced in privacy the following week at Kavanaugh Field, where there was a privacy fence surrounding the complex.

Out of respect for the upcoming opponent, Arkadelphia High School, Coach Quigley did not want anyone to note his play changes. He did not want to enter the game with one team having an advantage over the other. Following the contest, however, the *Arkansas Gazette* labeled the game as "… the poorest game of football that a Little Rock High School team ever played for Earl F. Quigley. …"

The only bright spot for the Tigers was a 10-yard touchdown run by Williams in the first quarter. Williams also converted the extra point, giving Little Rock the only points of the game.

After giving up the touchdown, Arkadelphia's defense shut down the Tigers. This included a goal-line stand from the 1, where Little Rock was stopped on four consecutive downs.

Arkadelphia had problems moving, too. Unable to penetrate the Tigers' defense, it was held scoreless and Little Rock posted a 7-0 victory.

After defeating Central High School of Memphis 34-0, the Tigers traveled to Muskogee (Okla.) Central High. Muskogee was defeated by Little Rock 14-7. Central High had only suffered one other loss against a high school team in three years.

The Tigers scored first midway through the first quarter when Bright capped an 80-yard drive with a 15-yard touchdown run. Williams added the extra-point attempt for a 7-0 lead.

The lead increased late in the second quarter when Williams scored on a short run and also converted the extra-point attempt for a 14-0 lead.

Midway through the third quarter, Muskogee took possession on its 25 after recovering a fumble. On its second play, an Oklahoma substitute ran 65 yards for a touchdown. The extra point brought Muskogee within one touchdown, but Little Rock held on for the victory.

After a 49-7 domination of Central High School in Springfield, Mo., the Tigers traveled to Fort Smith. Williams scored two touchdowns and George Ladd received a 25-yard touchdown pass in the 21-0 victory over the Grizzlies.

With the defeat of Fort Smith, Little Rock was declared state champion.

The Tigers were scheduled to play Warren Easton High School of New Orleans on Thanksgiving Day to decide the Southern championship.

Warren Easton, the Louisiana state champion, was undefeated and hadn't allowed a point all season. The New Orleans school had not been beaten by another high school team in several years and was quite confident of winning the holiday game.

At Kavanaugh Field, Little Rock was held scoreless for three quarters. New Orleans, however, led by only three points the majority of the game after a 30-yard field goal midway through the first quarter.

In the fourth quarter, a Warren Easton punt was blocked by Wycoff and recovered by Ginsberg at the 4. On first down, Williams went through the right side of the line for a touchdown. He also converted the extra point to give the Tigers a 7-3 lead.

Williams scored again on Little Rock's next possession after a 60-yard drive was capped by a 1-yard run. The extra point increased the lead to 14-3.

New Orleans was forced to punt on its next possession. Williams returned it 60 yards for a touchdown. His extra point put the Tigers up 21-3.

As a result of the successful season, Little Rock received many offers for postseason games. Steele High of Dayton, Ohio, East and West Technical high schools of Cleveland and Stamford, Conn., asked for games to be played in Little Rock.

Peabody, Mass.; Toledo, Ohio; Waco, Texas; and Madisonville, Ky., each wanted a game to be played in their respective cities.

According to the 1922 Little Rock high school yearbook, *The Cage*, a battle with Peabody, Mass., was being organized until a heavy snowstorm in Massachusetts cancelled any hope of a game.

The Cage went on to say that the Tigers then began discussing a game with Waite High in Toledo, Ohio, until it insisted on using a "Negro" in its lineup. Little Rock objected to this and negotiations were terminated.

The only negative mark on the Tigers' season was sharing the state championship title with rival Pine Bluff.

To accommodate out-of-state opponents, Little Rock had to postpone its scheduled game with the Zebras. The two teams were unable to agree upon another date and decided to end discussions until the following season.

1921 TIGER SCHEDULE

Camden 0	LRHS 75
Hendrix College (second team) 7	LRHS 7
Texarkana, AR 13	LRHS 21
Arkadelphia 0	LRHS 7
Central High of Memphis, TN 0	LRHS 34
Central High of Muskogee, OK 7	LRHS 14
Central High of Springfield, MO 7	LRHS 49
Fort Smith 0	LRHS 21
Warren Easton High of New Orleans, LA 3	LRHS 21

RULING A NEW CONFERENCE

1922   8-2-0

Head Coach: Earl F. Quigley
Assistants: Thomas Landers, J.R. Bullington, Earnest Gold
Team Physician: Dr. Wells Farrin Smith

1922 LETTERMEN

Robert Avinger	Choice Elliott	George Hogshed	Bert Salley
Eugene Bale	Vernon Felix	Marvin Johnson	John Smith
Bill Brasher	Carl Hall	Bruce Morris	George Sprick
Richard Bright	J.H. Hodges	Vernon Moult	Gerald Vinsant

1922 MANAGERS
Dorothy Snapp
Tom Wood

1922 ALL-STATE
Richard Bright
Vernon Felix

On Dec. 13, 1921, a meeting was held in Fort Smith to discuss the formation of a high school conference that would include two high schools from four states.

These schools were: Little Rock and Fort Smith from Arkansas, Muskogee and Tulsa from Oklahoma, Springfield and Joplin from Missouri, and Central High (Fort Worth) and Bryan High (Dallas) from Texas.

The conference, the largest in the country, was named the Southwest Interscholastic Conference.

Before returning to Little Rock from his summer home in Oshkosh, Wis., Coach Earl Quigley informed 110 players to meet him at 8:30 a.m. Sept. 11 at City Park. Coach Quigley, though, arrived two days before the meeting to prepare the equipment and the practice facility for the upcoming season.

Little Rock's line was devastated by the graduation of five starters and further weakened when Nate Ginsberg withdrew from school for unknown reasons. Another 1921 letterman, Dawson Mills, was hospitalized with pneumonia and was considered doubtful for the entire season.

Coach Quigley welcomed 83 hopefuls to the practice field for the season's first practice. Only four of these were returning lettermen from an 8-0-1 team crowned state and Southern champion.

Coach Quigley also welcomed three new assistants: Thomas Landers, J.R. Bullington and Earnest Gold. All were new to the school, but each had coaching experience.

The new staff rounded a first team into shape for the opener against England High School.

With 1921 captain and halfback Ivan "The Terrible" Williams lost to graduation, the city of Little Rock was concerned with how his replacement would perform.

Bruce Morris scored only one touchdown, but he gave fans in the city hope by performing in much the same manner as Williams.

A foot shorter and 20 pounds lighter, Morris was not the powerful runner Williams was, but Morris was quick and elusive once he broke the line of scrimmage.

In addition to Morris' touchdown, George Sprick scored four times, including two runs of 51 yards.

England was no match for the Tigers, who recorded a 62-0 victory.

The five-time defending state champions may have been a bit too overconfident when they met Prescott High School the next week.

On Little Rock's first play from scrimmage, Eugene Bale fumbled on the Tigers 10, and a Prescott lineman scooped up the ball and ran into the end zone for a touchdown.

On the ensuing kickoff, Morris fumbled to Prescott at the Little Rock 20. The Curley Wolves had to settle for a field goal, but a 10-0 margin in the first five minutes rattled the Tigers, who could not recover.

A lighter and less experienced line was evident on both sides of the ball. Prescott used this advantage in a 22-14 victory.

A 33-point first half helped Little Rock beat Texarkana, Ark., the following week.

The Tigers were shut down in the second half, only scoring two points. The game, though, gave Little Rock its second victory of the season and set the stage for its next opponent, Pine Bluff.

The Tigers and the Zebras could not agree on a playing date in 1921, and Coach Quigley refused to play them in a post-season game that would have decided the outright state champion. The teams instead shared the state title.

Pine Bluff had a great team in 1921 and had supposedly built an even greater power in 1922. To try and help his team gain an advantage, Coach Quigley held secret practices during the week leading up to the contest.

The largest crowd ever to watch a game at Kavanaugh Field, more than 4,000, entered the stadium as the teams went through pregame routines.

Once the game began, the light and inexperienced Little Rock line began to wear down against its opponent. Although the Tigers only gave up two scores, Pine Bluff's line proved too much for Little Rock on both sides of the ball.

A 30-yard field goal by Pine Bluff's Victor Bullock in the second quarter and a 48-yard run by Bullock in the fourth quarter were the game's only scores. Following the 10-0 loss, Coach Quigley publicly praised his team for its tough play and for holding the Zebras to only 10 points.

A trip to Memphis followed the Pine Bluff game, and Vernon "Red" Felix single-handedly outscored the Warriors. Felix's first score occurred after he received a Memphis punt that sailed straight up into the air. He was standing on the Warriors 20 when he caught the punt and easily went the distance for the score.

A third-quarter touchdown pass from Dick Bright to Felix put the Tigers up 12-10. After holding Memphis on downs, Little Rock regained possession on the Warriors 40. Three passes by Bright were incomplete, but on fourth down he completed a pass to Felix, who ran to the 10. Felix scored on the next play. Bright converted the extra point for a 19-10 lead.

Memphis opened the fourth quarter with a short touchdown run to cap a 70-yard drive. The conversion attempt was good, but the Tigers held on a for a 19-17 victory.

Muskogee (Okla.) Central, billed as the best team in the conference, had a tremendous weight and experience advantage over Little Rock. The game was expected to be a blowout in favor of Muskogee.

Bright, the team captain and quarterback, proved the predictions wrong when he scored five touchdowns. Bright scored on a 40-yard interception return and runs of 31, 22, 12 and 11 yards. Defensive lineman George Hogshed also intercepted a pass and returned it 55 yards for a touchdown. Little Rock won its first conference game 47-7.

The Tigers' next opponent was Warren Easton High School of New Orleans. Warren Easton was the team Little Rock beat the previous season to win the Southern championship.

New Orleans took the opening kickoff and used 6:30 to drive 75 yards for a score. The Tigers did not answer until the second quarter when Bright passed to Felix. Felix caught the pass for a 20-yard gain, but took it an additional 40 yards for a touchdown. Bright failed on the conversion attempt and Little Rock trailed 7-6.

The Tigers scored their go-ahead touchdown in the third quarter. The drive began when Felix received a pass and was tackled at the 23. Bright then passed 15 yards to Robert Avinger, who carried three defenders to the 3. Bright ran to the 1 on the next play, with Gerald Vinsant covering the remaining distance for the touchdown. Bright converted the extra-point attempt for a 13-7 lead.

Warren Easton had a chance to tie the score when it had possession on the Little Rock 10 with 45 seconds remaining in the game. On third down, Bill Brasher broke through the New Orleans line and tackled the runner for a 10-yard loss. On fourth-and-goal, Easton went for the tie with a pass into the end zone. Bert Salley, though, was there to knock the pass away and clinch the victory for the Tigers.

After a 7-3 victory over Fort Smith, Little Rock won by forfeiture on its ninth playing date. A coaching change at Springfield (Mo.) Central High School caused some confusion regarding its scheduled opponents. The new coach refused to honor the commitments scheduled the previous year and was forced to forfeit any games not played. Coach Quigley gladly accepted the forfeit and used the extra week to prepare for the Tigers' Thanksgiving meeting with Bryan Street High School of Dallas.

When the holiday arrived, more than 4,000 fans showed up at Kavanaugh Field to watch Little Rock play the Texas high school. Both teams were undefeated in conference play, and Dallas had only been scored on once during the season.

The game was a defensive battle, with neither team crossing the 20 until late in the game.

With nine minutes to play in a scoreless game, the Tigers had possession on their 35. On fourth down, they lined up in punt formation with Bright back to kick. Once he received the snap, however, he faked a kick and threw a perfect pass to Felix, who was just across the line of scrimmage. Felix broke two tackles and then raced 60 yards for a touchdown. Bright converted the extra-point attempt for a 7-0 victory.

Little Rock was the only undefeated team in the conference and captured the

1922 Little Rock High School starting offense

81

championship. Even though the Tigers won the Southwest Interscholastic Conference title, it was the first time in five years that Little Rock was not home to the Arkansas state champion. That honor belonged to the city of Pine Bluff in 1922.

1922 TIGER SCHEDULE

England 0	LRHS 62
Prescott 22	LRHS 14
Texarkana, AR 0	LRHS 35
Pine Bluff 10	LRHS 0
Central High of Memphis, TN 17	LRHS 19
*Central High of Muskogee, OK 7	LRHS 47
Warren Easton High of New Orleans, LA 7	LRHS 13
*Fort Smith 3	LRHS 7
*Central High of Springfield, MO 0	LRHS 2 (forfeit)
*Bryan Street High of Dallas, TX 0	LRHS 7

CONFERENCE CHAMPION VIA FORFEITURE

1923   11-0-0

Head Coach: Earl F. Quigley
Assistant: John G. Pipkin
Team Physician: Dr. Wells Farrin Smith

[1923 TEAM PHOTO NOT AVAILABLE]

1923 LETTERMEN

George Arendt	Pat Couch	Carl Hall	Bert Salley
Robert Avinger	Choice Elliott	Marvin Johnson	James Sharp
Bill Brasher	Rench Galloway	Dawson Mills	George Sprick
Miles Bright	Nate Ginsberg	Vernon Moult	Gerald Vinsant

1923 MANAGERS
Nat Hughes
Milton Karcher
William Mitchell

1923 ALL-STATE

Robert Avinger	Nate Ginsberg
Pat Couch	Marvin Johnson
Choice Elliott	George Sprick

Yandell Rogers

Robert Avinger

George Sprick

Photos provided by the Arkansas Democrat-Gazette

Coach Earl Quigley trimmed 99 candidates to a first team of 18 for the first game of the season, which was at home against Batesville High School.

Kavanaugh Field, with a new press box, was the site of a scoreless first half. Little Rock, however, had come within 5 yards of the goal line twice during the second quarter.

James Sharp did score for the Tigers during the third quarter when he burst up the middle for a short touchdown run. Sharp again scored in the fourth quarter on another short run up the middle to increase Little Rock's lead to 13-0.

George Sprick ended the game's scoring when he ran around right end for the Tigers' third touchdown. The final touchdown put Little Rock up 19-0 late in the fourth quarter. The Tigers had 27 first downs, while not allowing the Mountain Rams a first-down conversion.

The only score during Little Rock's second game against Texarkana, Ark., occurred during the second quarter. After a 75-yard drive, the Tigers' Nate Ginsberg dropped back to pass from the 20 and connected with Robert Avinger.

Avinger then raced to the goal line to put Little Rock in the lead. Sharp converted the extra point and the Tigers defeated the Razorbacks 7-0.

Kavanaugh Field was again the site of Little Rock's next game when it hosted Prescott High School, which returned six veterans from a team that defeated the Tigers 22-14 the previous season.

Little Rock quarterback Dawson Mills didn't play because of a bad knee and was replaced by Gerald Vinsant. Vinsant, who scored three touchdowns, turned out to be the star of the game. Avinger caught a pass for another touchdown in a 27-0 victory over Prescott.

Following a week of private practice behind the gates of Kavanaugh Field, the Tigers traveled to Athletic Field in Pine Bluff. Little Rock fans who wanted to make the trip could ride a private train. A round-trip ticket cost $2.08. Approximately 1,500

Photo provided by the Arkansas Democrat-Gazette
Bill Brasher

loyal followers took advantage of the promotion and were among the 4,000 who packed the stadium's bleachers.

With the exception of quarterback, Coach Foy Hammons returned every member from his 1922 team that beat the Tigers 10-0. The odds favored Pine Bluff, which hoped to again shut out Little Rock.

With the score tied 0-0, a Ginsberg to Carl Hall pass gained 30 yards and put the Tigers on the Zebras 9. Two plays and a penalty moved Little Rock back to the Pine Bluff 14. Marvin Johnson then dropped back on the next play and kicked a field goal from the 25, putting the Tigers in front 3-0.

Late in the fourth quarter, the tough Little Rock defense posted a goal-line stand at the 4. The Zebras were held on four consecutive downs, opting for a victory rather

Photo provided by the Arkansas Democrat-Gazette
Earl Quigley (1), Choice Elliott (2), Pine Bluff's Atkinson (3), and Zebras Coach Foy Hammons (4)

for three quarters before Memphis kicked a 30-yard field goal in the opening minutes of the fourth quarter to take a 3-0 lead.

It was the first points Little Rock had allowed during the season.

The Tigers punted on their ensuing possession and missed a 30-yard field-goal attempt on their next series.

Another series of punts put the Warriors back at their 10. Three runs didn't gain any yards. On the fourth-down punt attempt, Memphis fumbled the wet ball.

Little Rock downed the punter at the 5, where the Tigers gained control.

With one minute to play, Rench Galloway, a left halfback, bulled through the line for 3 yards. Sprick failed to gain any yards on the next play, but Sharp pushed through the defense for the score. Johnson converted the extra point for a 7-3 victory.

Little Rock traveled to New Orleans the following week to play Warren Easton High School. The game, played at Heinemann Park, was the New Orleans Prep Classic of 1923.

Warren Easton started strong as team captain Eugene McCarroll broke free for a 77-yard touchdown run on the first play from scrimmage.

Bill Brasher answered for the Tigers in the second half when he scored three touchdowns. Sharp added another score to help Little Rock to a 27-6 victory over the Louisiana team.

After a 48-14 victory over East St. Louis (Ill.) High School and a 73-0 homecoming victory over Springfield (Mo.) Central, the Tigers defeated Fort Smith High School 20-0.

The victory over the Grizzlies guaranteed Little Rock the state championship. The Tigers had beaten every Arkansas team they faced, and their last two games were against out-of-state competition.

There was no time to celebrate another state title, though, as Little Rock prepared for its next opponent, Ensley High School of Birmingham, Ala.. Ensley had recorded only one loss and a tie, which was against Central High of Memphis. The Alabama

than a field goal-goal attempt and a tie. The Tigers held on for a 3-0 victory.

The city of Pine Bluff declared the 1923 contest against Little Rock one of the best games ever played in the city.

The schedule did not get any easier the following week when Little Rock played Central High School of Memphis.

The week before the game, Coach Quigley learned Pete Moult, a reserve player, would be lost for the remainder of the season because of diphtheria.

Coach Charlie Jamerson, a former end for the Arkansas Razorbacks, brought his Central High Warriors to cold and rainy Kavanaugh Field. The game was scoreless

school was considered to be one of the toughest secondary teams in the South.

The Tigers received the opening kick-off. After six first downs, Avinger received a pass and scored Little Rock's first touchdown.

Ensley answered in the second quarter when a 17-yard pass reached the Tigers 20. Just seconds later, another pass gave the Jackets their only score of the game.

After a scoreless third quarter, Little Rock opened the fourth quarter with possession on the Ensley 25. Two first downs moved the Tigers to the 2, and Sharp then went over for the score. Johnson's extra-point attempt failed, but Little Rock still led 13-7.

Sharp intercepted a pass to end Ensley's next possession, giving the Tigers possession at midfield. Little Rock went on to convert four first downs before Mills ran up the middle for the score in a 20-7 victory.

The Tigers were hoping to keep their unbeaten record intact the next week when they traveled to Texas to meet Bryan Street High School of Dallas. Since both were the only unbeaten teams in league play, the game was to decide the Southwest Interscholastic Conference championship.

Just days before the game, the principal of Bryan Street High School informed Little Rock High School that the team was too badly beat up and sore to play.

The conference committee awarded Little Rock a forfeit, which was documented as a 2-0 victory.

The forfeiture gave the Tigers the Southwest Interscholastic Conference championship to go along with their 11th state championship.

1923 TIGER SCHEDULE

Batesville 0	LRHS 19
Texarkana, AR 0	LRHS 7
Prescott 0	LRHS 27
Pine Bluff 0	LRHS 3
Central High of Memphis, TN 3	LRHS 7
Warren Easton High of New Orleans, LA 6	LRHS 27
East St. Louis High of East St. Louis, IL 14	LRHS 48
*Central High of Springfield, MO 0	LRHS 73
*Fort Smith 0	LRHS 20
Ensley High of Birmingham, AL 7	LRHS 20
*Bryan Street High of Dallas, TX 0	LRHS 2 (forfeit)

The first half ended in a scoreless tie, but the third quarter began with a 60-yard touchdown run by Fort Smith's "Nig" Brutton for a 7-0 lead.

Midway through the fourth quarter, the Grizzlies intercepted a pass at the 20. Fort Smith was held on downs, but the Tigers were forced to punt back to the Grizzlies. Fort Smith took possession at the Little Rock 18. A pass on first down resulted in another touchdown for the Grizzlies.

Fort Smith beat the Tigers 14-0, marking the first time in 12 years that the Grizzlies defeated the Tigers.

Little Rock finally got another victory the next week when it defeated Springfield (Mo.) Central 21-0. However, times got tough again the following week when it met Tech High School of Atlanta on Thanksgiving Day at Kavanaugh Field.

Tech High was considered the best team in the South, but the Tigers were able to force a 7-7 halftime score.

The Atlanta team, however, took control in the second half when "Stumpy" Thomason scored touchdowns on runs of 70, 65 and 60 yards.

He also converted five extra-point attempts, while Tech's fullback scored twice in a 35-7 holiday victory over Little Rock.

1924 TIGER SCHEDULE

Dermott 0	LRHS 47
Texarkana, AR 0	LRHS 6
Prescott 3	LRHS 23
Wichita, KN 36	LRHS 6
Central High of Memphis, TN 0	LRHS 2 (forfeit)
Pine Bluff 33	LRHS 0
DuPont Manuel High of Louisville, KY 20	LRHS 0
Fort Smith 14	LRHS 0
Central High of Springfield, MO 0	LRHS 21
Tech High of Atlanta, GA 35	LRHS 7

PINE BLUFF LEADS THE NATION

1925   5-5-0

Head Coach: Earl F. Quigley
Assistants: J.R. Bullington, W.B. Ivy, B. Brown
Team Physician: Dr. Wells Farrin Smith

1925 LETTERMEN

Page Bledsoe	Joe Lacky	William Poppenheimer	Mackey Whitten
Harry Coonley	J.T. Lipe	Clifford Shaw	Stuart Williams
Harold Faisst	Julian Masters	Harry Smith	
Guy Gunn	Mitchell McCowan	Armil Snow	
Fred Holt	Melvin Miller	Paul Wage	

1925 MANAGERS
Daniel Autry
Thad Felton
Jack Smith

1925 ALL-STATE
Page Bledsoe
Harold Faisst
Harry Smith
Mackey Whitten

Coach Earl Quigley narrowed 105 candidates to a 20-member first team and planned to begin the season with an extra week of practice because of an open date. This occurred when a school from Louisville, Ky., notified Coach Quigley that no field was available for their Oct. 24 game in Kentucky because of a scheduling mistake.

Coach Quigley, however, rearranged Little Rock's schedule and added Helena High School in place of Louisville.

The first playing date, though, would be against England High School. The Tigers prepared for a tough game, as the Lions were thought to be a contender for the state championship.

Coach Homer Berry brought England to Kavanaugh Field and opened the season with a 7-0 upset over Little Rock. England's line averaged 200 pounds per man and shut down Little Rock's offense and defense.

More than 3,000 fans packed Kavanaugh Field the next week to see the first meeting between Little Rock and North Little Rock high schools.

The Tigers appeared to be in control of the game early as they drove down the field after the opening kickoff. Clifford Shaw scored on a short run just 4:20 into the opening quarter, and William Poppenheimer converted the extra-point attempt for a 7-0 lead over the Wildcats.

Just minutes later, though, North Little Rock completed a pass for a touchdown. The extra-point failed and the score remained 7-6 the remainder of the half.

Midway through the third quarter, Shaw fumbled a North Little Rock kick at the Little Rock 12. The ball was recovered by the Wildcats and taken the 12 yards needed for the score. The extra point was converted for a 13-7 lead.

Little Rock opened up its passing attack to get back into the game. But two minutes into the fourth quarter, North Little Rock intercepted a pass and returned it 50 yards for another touchdown.

North Little Rock missed the extra-point attempt, but the game ended in favor of the Wildcats, 19-7.

A 7-0 loss to Prescott the next week dropped the Tigers to 0-3-0. But Coach Quigley regrouped his team and prepared for a trip to Fort Smith and a showdown with the Grizzlies.

Fort Smith fumbled on its opening possession and Little Rock recovered at midfield.

A pass from Shaw to Poppenheimer gained 20 yards, and another pass from Shaw to Mackey Whitten picked up another 15 yards. Poppenheimer then ran up the middle to score the Tigers' first touchdown.

Little Rock's next score came at the end of the first quarter. Shaw passed to Whitten for 25 yards, Harold Faisst ran for 6 yards and Shaw carried the remaining 4 yards for the score. Poppenheimer kicked his second extra point and the Tigers led 14-0 after the first quarter.

After a scoreless second quarter, the Grizzlies opened the second half with a passing attack. Shaw, however, intercepted

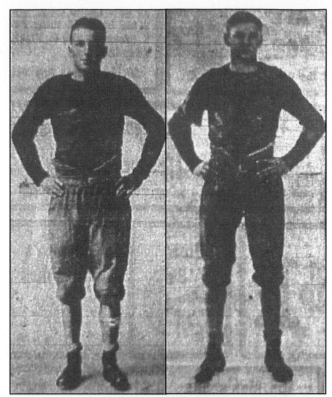

Photo provided by the Arkansas Democrat-Gazette
Harold Faisst (left) **and Mackey Whitten**

a pass on Fort Smith's second play and returned it for a touchdown.

Poppenheimer missed the extra-point attempt, but he made up for it later in the quarter when he drop-kicked a 25-yard field goal.

Poppenheimer extended Little Rock's lead in the fourth quarter when he drop-kicked a 38-yard field goal. This helped pad the lead as the Tigers defeated Fort Smith 26-0.

Prior to its game with Helena High School, Little Rock found out it would be without Shaw, Whitten and J. T. Lipe.

The Executive Committee of the Arkansas Athletic Association suspended the players 30 days for allegedly playing professional baseball during the summer.

It was alleged the three Tigers received payment for playing summer league baseball, which was against the Athletic Association's rules for high school athletes.

Even without these athletes, Little Rock scored four touchdowns and Poppenheimer kicked a 35-yard field goal to defeat Helena in the first matchup between the schools.

Two consecutive decisive victories gave the Tigers the confidence they needed for their next game against rival Pine Bluff.

More than 4,000 people packed Pine Bluff's stadium to see if the undefeated Zebras could continue their winning streak and bid for the 1925 state championship.

Pine Bluff played like a championship team, yet only had a 7-0 halftime lead. This one-touchdown lead after the first period of play left many Pine Bluff fans worried during the break.

Midway through the third quarter, though, Pine Bluff recorded five consecutive first downs on its way to a second touchdown. The extra-point attempt failed and the Zebras led 13-0.

Late in the same quarter, Poppenheimer fumbled deep inside Little Rock territory. A Pine Bluff lineman scooped up the ball and took it across the goal line for the Zebras' third touchdown.

A 30-yard field goal by Pine Bluff set the final at 23-0. The game marked the Tigers' fourth loss of the season.

A rain soaked and muddy Kavanaugh Field was the site of Little Rock's next game against Joplin, Mo. The Tigers scored an apparent touchdown just two minutes into the game, but a holding call negated the score and moved the ball back 15 yards.

Little Rock waited until the second quarter to officially get on the scoreboard. Quarterback Julian Masters scored on a short run up the middle, and Page Bledsoe caught a pass from Shaw to record the Tigers' first-half touchdowns.

As the fourth quarter opened, a 15-yard penalty and a 5-yard penalty by Little Rock gave Joplin possession on the Tigers 5. Joplin then scored three plays later to make it 12-7.

Late in the game, Joplin attempted to punt, but a Little Rock lineman blocked the kick and Harry Smith made the recovery in the end zone for the Tigers' last score in an 18-7 victory.

Central High of Memphis visited Little Rock the following week and one of the best teams in the South returned home with a 7-6 loss.

The Tigers' touchdown, just 4:25 into the game, came after forcing the Warriors to end their first possession with a punt. The kick gave Little Rock control at midfield.

Faisst carried 20 yards around right end, but on the next play the Tigers were penalized 5 yards for being offside.

Poppenheimer failed to gain through the line, but a pass, Masters to Faisst, netted 15 yards.

Masters gained 7 yards around right end, and on the following play Faisst took a reverse and ran around right end for a 15-yard touchdown. Poppenheimer converted the extra-point attempt, which proved to be the game-winning point.

Memphis completed a drive for a touchdown just as the second quarter began, but a missed extra-point attempt proved costly for the visiting team.

Little Rock suffered another loss the next week, this time against Ensley High School of Birmingham, Ala.

The Alabama team beat the Tigers 13-0, giving Little Rock its fifth loss of the season.

Coach Quigley and the Tigers hoped their Thanksgiving holiday would produce another victory for the school. Warren Easton High School from New Orleans was their opponent.

After two scoreless quarters, Shaw passed to Whitten for 9 yards and Faisst added several yards to the 10. Faisst then passed to Bledsoe for the game's only score, giving Little Rock its fifth victory of the season. The Tigers finished the season 5-5-0.

Pine Bluff, on the other hand, ended with a record of 15-0-0. The Arkansas champion then trained for a postseason game with Stivers High School of Dayton, Ohio. Coach Foy Hammons and his Zebras played host to the Ohio school with the national championship on the line.

Billed as the country's most important high school football game during the 1925 season, the Pathe Motion Picture Company of New Orleans announced that moving pictures of the game would be taken and shown throughout the country.

Stivers High School, undefeated for the past four years, met its match in Pine Bluff.

More than 7,000 fans watched the Zebras score 61 points against the best team the North had to offer.

Pine Bluff dominated the game and its defense shut out the Ohio school. The Zebras won the 1925 national championship with a 61-0 victory over Stivers High. Pine Bluff also placed eight players on the 11-man All-State Team.

1925 TIGER SCHEDULE

England 7	LRHS 0
North Little Rock 19	LRHS 7
Prescott 7	LRHS 0
Fort Smith 0	LRHS 26
Helena 6	LRHS 29
Pine Bluff 23	LRHS 0
Joplin, MO 7	LRHS 18
Central High of Memphis, TN 6	LRHS 7
Ensley High of Birmingham, AL 13	LRHS 0
Warren Easton High of New Orleans, LA 0	LRHS 6

A SEASON SPOILED BY PINE BLUFF ... AGAIN

1926   7-2-1

Head Coach: Earl F. Quigley
Assistant: W.B. Ivy
Team Physician: Dr. Wells Farrin Smith

1926 LETTERMEN

Charles Avinger	John Estrada	Fred Holt	Harry Smith
Allen Bradley	Douglas Graydon	Mitchell McCowan	Paul Wage
Edward Clark	Guy Gunn	Corbin Neblett	Mackey Whitten
O.B. Clark	W. D. Harris	Paul Parks	
Harry Coonley	Russell Hawn	Clifford Shaw	

1926 MANAGERS
Robinson Campbell
W. D. Harris
John Hodges
McMillan Jackson
John Smith

1926 ALL-STATE
Harry Coonley
Fred Holt
Clifford Shaw
Mackey Whitten

Seventy-two candidates vying for a spot on the team filled the high school's gymnasium on Sept. 1 to discuss the upcoming season with Coach Earl Quigley.

Coach Quigley's first remark to the players was encouragement to keep their grades up during the season. He reminded them that the team lost 11 players because of poor grades the previous year.

One week into practice, 83 hopefuls were trying out for the team and that number increased to 105 when school began. Nine of these players were returning lettermen, and there were also several returning substitutes from previous seasons.

One of these returning lettermen was Clifford Shaw. Shaw alone dominated Stuttgart High School in the season opener by scoring 37 points. He scored five touchdowns and converted seven extra-point attempts in a 68-0 victory.

Clifford Shaw runs around left end for the Tigers

Shaw's first touchdown came in the first quarter on a broken play. Little Rock had driven to the Stuttgart 1 when Shaw attempted to hand off to one of his halfbacks, but he found himself alone in the backfield.

He then ran toward the line of scrimmage and leaped over the pile for the first score of the game.

Douglas Graydon and Ralph LaForge added to the game's excitement when each scored on runs of 55 yards.

The Tigers didn't allow a first down and converted 32.

After defeating Little Rock the previous season, Coach Homer Berry's England High School Lions visited Kavanaugh Field to try and upset the Tigers once again. Little Rock, however, was in charge from the start. The Tigers scored an average of once every three minutes in a 110-0 victory over the Lions.

Once again, Shaw starred for the offense. He scored 41 points on six touchdowns and five extra points.

After dominating its first two opponents, Little Rock was expecting another easy victory the next week when it was scheduled to play Benton High School.

Panthers Coach Henry Finkbiner's game plan was to use a powerful defense to hold the Tigers scoreless and hope his team could score once or twice.

Coach Finkbiner's philosophy worked much of the game.

In the first quarter, a 15-yard penalty against Little Rock backed the Tigers up to their 1. They fumbled on the next play.

Benton recovered in the end zone for the game's first score.

It wasn't until the end of the second quarter that Little Rock was able to score. A 5-yard offside penalty against Benton gave the Tigers possession inside the Panthers 3.

John Estrada went the 3 yards needed for the touchdown, and Shaw converted the extra-point attempt to make it 7-7.

Another penalty against Benton, this time in the third quarter, gave Little Rock the ball inside the Panthers 2. The Tigers, however, were penalized for offside and the ball was moved back 5 yards.

On the next play, Charles Avinger ran into the end zone for a touchdown to give Little Rock the lead. Shaw converted his 14th extra point of the season to make it 14-7.

The Tigers padded their lead in the fourth quarter when Shaw scored on a short run. He failed to convert the extra-point attempt, but Little Rock escaped with a 20-7 victory.

Following a 27-11 loss to DuPont Manuel High School in Louisville, Ky., an angry group of Tigers and a muddy Kavanaugh Field awaited Central High of Tulsa.

Little Rock struck first in the opening quarter when Shaw connected with Fred Holt. Russell Hawn, the intended receiver, tipped the ball and it fell into the hands of

Mitchell McCowan punts for the Tigers

Holt. Shaw's extra-point attempt was blocked, but the Tigers led 6-0.

Tulsa answered in the second quarter after a Little Rock punt was returned 55 yards for a touchdown. The extra-point attempt failed and the half ended in a 6-6 tie.

After a scoreless third quarter, Tulsa struck again in the fourth quarter after a 26-yard run around right end moved the visitors to the Tigers 20. The run set up a 20-yard field goal and the Oklahoma team went in front 9-6.

With only four minutes remaining in the game, a passing attack moved Little Rock down the field. The Tigers, however, ran out of downs and Tulsa took over on its 42. It could not make a first down and was forced to punt.

Little Rock took over at its 46 and Shaw threw three consecutive incompletions. On fourth down, Hawn faked a punt, ran toward the right end and heaved the ball to Shaw.

A Tulsa defender knocked Shaw off balance as he caught the ball, but Shaw stayed on his feet and was able to avoid three more defenders for the 51-yard game-winning touchdown.

The stands went wild with enthusiasm and fans spilled onto the field to congratulate the home team. It took several minutes for police and game officials to remove everyone from the playing surface to complete the game.

Graydon kicked off to Tulsa, and three plays later the game ended. Little Rock once again escaped, this time with a 13-9 victory over Central High of Tulsa.

Photo provided by the Arkansas Democrat-Gazette

Mackey Whitten (left) and Mitchell McCowan

The Tigers then traveled to Fargason Field in Memphis to take on Central High School. The fierce battle, played in the rain and mud, ended in a 0-0 tie.

During the week leading up to Little Rock's annual battle with Pine Bluff, Coach Quigley held secrete practices behind the walls at Kavanaugh Field. The privacy was taken as precaution while the team devised a special defense to stop the Zebras' passing attack.

Coach Allen Dunaway and his Pine Bluff Zebras had a lot riding on the game. They could claim a state championship with a victory and also be rewarded with a postseason game in Dayton, Ohio.

The big game attracted the largest crowd to ever see a football game at Kavanaugh Field. The grandstand and bleachers were filled and the overflow on the field

Photo provided by the Arkansas Democrat-Gazette

Little Rock attempts to run a play against Pine Bluff

numbered approximately 2,500. The record crowd was estimated between 7,500 and 8,000.

Following a series of passes and running plays, the only touchdown came during the fourth quarter

The Tigers kicked to the Pine Bluff 40 early in the quarter, and the Zebras returned the kick for a nice gain. Two plays netted 6 yards before Pine Bluff converted a first down on the next play.

A pass gained 12 yards and another first down. Five plays later, a short pass resulted in a Pine Bluff touchdown. The extra point gave Pine Bluff a 7-0 victory.

Little Rock traveled to New Orleans the next week and played Warren Easton High School in Tulane Stadium.

More than 3,000 fans watched as the Tigers beat Warren Easton for the fifth consecutive time, 18-6.

Coach Ben Mayo brought his Fort Smith Grizzlies to Little Rock for a battle with the Tigers the following week.

Little Rock's first touchdown came in the first quarter on a 35-yard pass from Shaw to Estrada. The Tigers scored again just as the second quarter opened when Shaw passed to Allen Bradley for a 34-yard touchdown. Shaw converted both extra-point attempts to give Little Rock a 14-0 lead.

The Grizzlies answered quickly with a

Photo provided by the Arkansas Democrat-Gazette
Little Rock's Clifford Shaw

50-yard touchdown pass. Their extra point made it 14-7. The Tigers, however, added to their lead in the fourth quarter when Shaw scored on a 9-yard run.

The Little Rock defense held Fort Smith scoreless in the second half and added to its lead with just one second remaining in the game. Hawn threw a 20-yard pass to Shaw, who ran another 20 yards for a touchdown. Time elapsed as Shaw caught the pass, but the score counted.

Another pass, this time from Shaw to Avinger, added the extra point and gave the Tigers a 27-7 victory.

A game with Ensley High School of Birmingham, Ala., on Thanksgiving Day ended the season for Little Rock. Several thousand people turned out for the holiday game as the Tigers used their passing attack for the victory.

Photo provided by the Arkansas Democrat-Gazette
Pine Bluff's "Buster" Brannon catches a pass

Little Rock, though, couldn't score its first touchdown until the second quarter.

Paul Wage broke through the Ensley line to block a punt. Holt recovered in the end zone to give the Tigers a 6-0 lead.

Ensley responded in the third quarter when a defender intercepted a Shaw pass and returned it 43 yards for the score and a 6-6 tie. Little Rock quickly regained the lead, though.

Early in the fourth quarter, the Tigers drove 65 yards to the Ensley 1. Hawn then scored to put Little Rock up 12-6.

Following the kickoff, the teams exchanged punts and Shaw eventually completed a pass to keep a drive alive. The pass was caught by Cy Whitten, a substitute end, for a gain of 30 yards to the 5.

The Tigers were penalized, however, and the ball was placed at the 10. On the next play, Shaw passed to Whitten for the final touchdown of the game.

Neither team was able to convert an extra-point attempt in Little Rock's 18-6 victory.

The Tigers ended 7-2-1, losing only once to an in-state opponent. That loss, only by a single touchdown, came to their long-time rival Pine Bluff, the defending national and state champion.

1926 TIGER SCHEDULE

Stuttgart 0	LRHS 68
England 0	LRHS 110
Benton 7	LRHS 20
DuPont Manuel High of Louisville, KY 27	LRHS 11
Central High of Tulsa, OK 9	LRHS 13
Central High of Memphis, TN 0	LRHS 0
Pine Bluff 7	LRHS 0
Warren Easton High of New Orleans, LA 6	LRHS 18
Fort Smith 7	LRHS 27
Ensley High of Birmingham, AL 6	LRHS 18

ANOTHER FINISH BEHIND PINE BLUFF

1927   7-2-1

Head Coach: Earl F. Quigley
Assistants: Homer Berry, LeRoy Scott
Team Physician: Dr. Wells Farrin Smith

1927 LETTERMEN

Allan Avinger	John Estrada	Edward Hooper	Robert Tubbs
Charles Avinger	Douglas Graydon	Charles LaForge	Clyde Williams
Bill Benard	Randall Grimmett	Corbin Neblett	
Francis Bennett	Russell Hawn	Robert Satterwhite	
Arnold Castleberry	Claude Heath	Homer Stalnaker	

1927 MANAGERS
Unknown

1927 ALL-STATE
John Estrada
Douglas Graydon
Corbin Neblett
Homer Stalnaker

Coach Earl Quigley returned to Little Rock from his summer home in Oshkosh, Wis., earlier than usual to move all the athletic equipment from the old gymnasium to the city's new high school at 14th and Park streets. The new athletic dressing rooms, which included a shower area, were considered top of the line.

Coach Quigley hired two new assistants for the 1927 season. Homer Berry, a University of Arkansas football star and former head coach at England High School, assisted Coach Quigley with the first team. LeRoy Scott assisted with the second team.

The coaches got the team into shape and the Tigers opened with a 32-0 victory over Morrilton High School.

The second game, against Searcy High School, began at 10:30 a.m. because the Lindberg Day parade was scheduled to take place downtown during the afternoon.

John Estrada struck first for Little Rock when he scored on a short run in the first quarter. The Tigers struck again in the second quarter after Estrada gained 38 yards

Robert Satterwhite (left) and Homer Stalnaker

on four carries to move Little Rock into scoring position. Robert Tubbs went into the end zone on the next play. Douglas Graydon added the extra point to put his team up 13-0.

This was just the beginning as the Tigers rolled to a 57-0 victory over the Lions.

A 0-0 tie with Arkadelphia the next week was followed by Little Rock's first out-of-state game against Tulsa Central.

A scoreless first half proved that the Little Rock defense was tough. Even from the 1, the Oklahoma team could not score in four downs.

The third quarter, however, proved costly for Little Rock with a fumble that was recovered at midfield by Whitey Brown. Don Bailey ran 45 yards for a touchdown and converted the extra-point attempt to give Tulsa a 7-0 victory.

More than 4,500 fans watched the Braves hand Little Rock its first loss of the season.

The Tigers traveled to Fort Smith the following week to take on the Grizzlies. Little Rock stuck to running plays in the first half and used its line shifts to puzzle Fort Smith throughout the first quarter. The

Grizzlies, though, were able to hold the Tigers scoreless each time they were in striking distance.

Fort Smith scored first when a 20-yard pass ended in a 50-yard touchdown play. The extra-point attempt snap was fumbled, but the Grizzlies led 6-0.

Early in the third quarter, a Fort Smith running back fumbled and Graydon recovered, giving Little Rock possession at the Fort Smith 37.

After two plays, Graydon had an 18-yard pass reception to the 19. Robert Satterwhite then caught an 11-yard pass before Graydon added 6 yards to set up Charles LaForge's 2-yard touchdown run. Graydon converted the extra-point attempt for a 7-6 lead.

The Tigers' second touchdown came in the fourth quarter when Arnold Castleberry caught a pass and raced 40 yards for the score. Graydon again added the extra point to increase the lead to 14-6.

Little Rock was able to hold the Grizzlies scoreless the remainder of the game to take the victory.

The Tigers hosted their Memphis rival, Central High, the following week. The story of the game took place in the second

(Left to Right) Homer Berry, Earl Quigley and LeRoy Scott

quarter when Little Rock scored three touchdowns and held the Tennessee team scoreless in a 20-0 victory.

The first score was set up when Charles Avinger returned a punt 10 yards to the Warriors 20.

A pass from Leroy Brinkley to Russell Hawn moved the Tigers to the 5, and Estrada passed to Avinger two plays later for the score. Graydon converted the extra-point attempt for a 7-0 lead.

Little Rock received another punt after Central's next possession, and it only took a few plays for the Tigers to strike again. Avinger scored from the 2 to increase the lead to 13-0.

Avinger once again fielded a punt, but this time he was tackled at his 25. He then ran 9 yards around right end on first down.

Claude Heath ran through a hole in the left side of the line to the Memphis 33. After one failed pass, Little Rock completed its next attempt when Tubbs passed to Graydon, who covered enough ground for the Tigers' third touchdown.

Avinger converted the extra-point attempt for a 20-0 lead and the defense held the Warriors scoreless.

Photo provided by the Arkansas Democrat-Gazette
Paul Parks (left) **and Arnold Castleberry**

More than 6,000 fans packed the stadium in Pine Bluff the following week to see the rivals battle for bragging rights.

Little Rock kicked off and the Zebras began their first series at their 35.

Whiskery Perry took the first snap, stepped through a gap in the right side of the line, found a clearing through the secondary and ran untouched for a 65-yard touchdown. The extra point put Pine Bluff up 7-0 just seconds into the game.

Late in the second quarter, the Tigers were within scoring distance, but a bad pass was intercepted by Warren Duncan on the 5. Duncan outran the Little Rock team for a 95-yard touchdown. The extra-point attempt failed, but the Zebras led 13-2.

Pine Bluff scored twice in the second half as well, once on a short pass and once on a 10-yard run by Bill Perry. The Tigers' only score occurred in the second quarter when the Pine Bluff punter stepped out of his end zone while fielding a bad snap.

In the 26-2 victory over Little Rock, the Zebras completed 12 passes for 183 yards.

Following a 40-0 victory over Poplar Bluff, Mo., a team that had not lost a game

Photo provided by the Arkansas Democrat-Gazette
Randall Grimmett (left) **and Allan Avinger**

in two years, the Tigers played Memphis University High of Tennessee.

Little Rock scored once in the first quarter, twice in the second quarter, three times in the third quarter and five times in the fourth quarter. The scoring included a 47-yard touchdown run by LaForge and a 35-yard interception return by Ralph La-Forge. The Tigers defeated the Memphis school 70-0.

Little Rock's final game was Thanksgiving Day against Central High of Wichita, Kan. Central had lost only one game during the year and was considered one of the premier teams in Kansas.

The Tigers worked from their 45 to within a yard of end zone, only to lose possession on downs.

Little Rock stopped Wichita's offense, and when the Kansas team attempted to punt, Homer Stalnaker blocked it and the ball rolled out of the end zone to give the Tigers a safety.

Nine plays after the second quarter opened, Little Rock got on the scoreboard again.

Taking over at the 50, Avinger picked up 9 yards and Hawn gained 5 yards around right end for a first down.

After two plays and a 15-yard pass from Avinger to Hawn, the Tigers were 19 yards from the goal line. It took three plays, but Little Rock scored when Estrada ran off tackle for the touchdown. Graydon converted the extra-point attempt for a 9-0 half-time lead. The Tigers went on to score four more touchdowns in the second half for a 37-0 victory over Wichita.

The victory gave Little Rock a 7-2-1 record and second place in the state's final standings. The runner-up finish was once again behind Pine Bluff, which won its third consecutive state championship.

Photo provided by the Arkansas Democrat-Gazette
(Left to Right) Corbin Neblett, Charles Avinger and Robert Satterwhite

1927 TIGER SCHEDULE

Morrilton 0	LRHS 32
Searcy 0	LRHS 57
Arkadelphia 0	LRHS 0
Central High of Tulsa, OK 7	LRHS 0
Fort Smith 6	LRHS 14
Central High of Memphis, TN 0	LRHS 20
Pine Bluff 26	LRHS 2
Poplar Bluff, MO 0	LRHS 40
University High of Memphis, TN 0	LRHS 70
Central High of Wichita, KN 0	LRHS 37

"DOC" BECOMES A TIGER

1928   7-3-1

Head Coach: Earl F. Quigley
Assistants: Homer Berry, Leroy Scott
Team Trainer: Riley "Doc" Johns
Team Physician: Dr. Wells Farrin Smith

1928 LETTERMEN

Allan Avinger	Clyde Buchanan	Edward Hooper	Paul Parks
Charles Avinger	Arnold Castleberry	Ralph LaForge	Robert Satterwhite
Francis Bennett	John Fulton	Steele Lipe	Homer Stalnaker
Joe Biddle	Hampton Hall	J.J. McLeod	Robert Tubbs
Leroy Brinkley	William Haynes	Corbin Neblett	Clyde Williams

1928 MANAGERS
Howard Gladden
Lon Heffington
Sammy Miles

1928 ALL-STATE
J.J. McLeod
Corbin Neblett
Homer Stalnaker

Coach Earl Quigley was met by 120 players on Sept. 1, the largest turnout in the history of the school's football program.

The number continued to grow. By the second week of practice, there were 150 hopefuls out for the team.

The first team was narrowed to 50 and these players would wear new equipment during the 1928 season. The new head gear, which was the latest model, was lined with light sponge shock absorbers and weighed considerably less than past years.

Black and gold stripes covered the head gear, while the new jerseys and pants were the same style as 1927.

A new member joined Little Rock's staff in 1928. Riley Johns was a black groundskeeper and trainer for the Little Rock Baseball Club. He helped care for the Arkansas Travelers as well as Kavanaugh

Field, where both the Travelers and Tigers played their games.

Coach Quigley was able to employ Johns for the Little Rock High School athletic department during the baseball team's off-season. He began working with the Tigers as their first full-time medical trainer and soon became know affectionately as "Doc."

Little Rock opened at Kavanaugh Field against McGehee High School. The Tigers scored two touchdowns early in the game to take control. They went on to score 10 more times and didn't allow a first down.

Charles Avinger and Arnold Castleberry did not play after breaking team rules in the preseason.

Ralph LaForge emerged as the offensive star with four touchdowns, including a 55-yard run, in the 77-0 victory.

Little Rock again dominated the next two weeks with it hosted Hot Springs and Benton high schools.

The Tigers beat Hot Springs 76-0. Benton became their third consecutive shutout victim, 27-0.

The domination continued the following week when Little Rock traveled to Arkadelphia to meet the Badgers.

Little Rock had 14 first downs and didn't allow any.

The Tigers controlled the game from the start, leading 21-0 after the first quarter and 33-0 at halftime.

Coach Quigley's second team was only to score once during the second half, a short run by Paul Parks in the third quarter of a 39-0 victory.

The Tigers did not run rampant the next week whey they met Central High of Tulsa. Little Rock put together only one decent series, which occurred midway through the fourth quarter.

Avinger returned a punt from his 5 to the 25, then gained an additional 30 yards on first down by going around right end. Castleberry, though, lost 4 yards on the next play.

Two successive passes, Avinger to Castleberry and Castleberry to Leroy Brinkley, both gained 7 yards to give the Tigers a first down. Avinger gained another 8 yards before Clyde Buchanan then picked up 13 yards around left end.

From the 13, Buchanan failed to gain any yards on first down, then ran 7 yards on the next play.

An Avinger to Brinkley pass resulted in a touchdown. Avinger converted the extra point for a 7-0 victory.

The victory marked Little Rock's fifth consecutive shutout.

A trip to Memphis and a battle with Central High awaited the Tigers the following week. A crowd of more than 1,200 at Hodges Field watched Little Rock's first loss of the season.

The Tigers scored early when Avinger ran 60 yards for a touchdown in the first quarter. The Warriors answered in the second quarter when they blocked punt and recovered it in the end zone.

The extra-point attempt failed, leaving it 6-6.

Moments later, Central again blocked a Little Rock punt and it was recovered at the Tigers 12. Two plays later, the Warriors scored the go-ahead touchdown for a 12-6 victory.

For the first time, seats completely surrounded Kavanaugh Field to accommodate a capacity crowd for the Pine Bluff game.

The matchup was another defensive battle, scoreless until late in the fourth

Photo provided by the Arkansas Democrat-Gazette

Paul Parks, Edward Hooper, Allan Avinger, Joe Biddle, Clyde Buchanan

quarter when the Tigers began their final drive for possible victory.

The drive began at the Little Rock 26. After a first down and 16-yard pass from Avinger to John Fulton, the Tigers were at the Pine Bluff 45. The next two plays gained no yardage before the game was decided on third down.

Avinger took the snap, and, going for victory, threw a deep pass that was intended for Corbin Neblett. Pine Bluff's Billy Sisco, however, took the pass out of the air and returned it almost the length of the field for a touchdown.

Wade Harrell's extra point put the Zebras up 7-0. The game ended just after the ensuing kickoff.

Little Rock rebounded the following week with a comeback victory.

Trailing Poplar Bluff, Mo., 7-6 in the third quarter, the Tigers scored three touchdowns to beat the Mules 26-7.

Following a scoreless tie with Fort Smith, Little Rock lost again, this time 18-13 to Central High of Wichita, Kan.

The Tigers ran up a two-touchdown lead in the first quarter after J.J. McLeod blocked a punt and recovered it in the end zone and Neblett returned a fumble 15 yards for another score.

The Kansas team fought hard in the second quarter to come within one point. After returning an interception 30 yards for a touchdown, it quickly scored again on a 32-yard run to narrow the deficit to 13-12.

Photo provided by the Arkansas Democrat-Gazette
Robert Tubbs, Francis Bennett, Homer Stalnaker, Unknown, Robert Satterwhite

A short scoring pass in the fourth quarter put Wichita in front 18-13 and Little Rock never threatened again. The game marked the third loss for the Tigers.

Little Rock's final game was against Lindblom High School of Chicago. Lindblom was the 1928 Chicago city champion and had won the title four of the past five seasons.

Although Coach E.L. Moore's team was undefeated, it was hundreds of miles away from home and playing the Tigers on Thanksgiving Day at Kavanaugh Field.

The holiday game was one that Little Rock rarely lost, and the 13 seniors playing their last high school game proved they were a tough team to beat.

The Tigers ended the season with an 18-7 victory over the powerful Chicago team to finish 7-3-1.

Photo provided by the Arkansas Democrat-Gazette
Little Rock's Arnold Castleberry runs downfield

1928 TIGER SCHEDULE

McGehee 0	LRHS 77
Hot Springs 0	LRHS 76
Benton 0	LRHS 27
Arkadelphia 0	LRHS 39
Central High of Tulsa, OK 0	LRHS 7
Central High of Memphis, TN 12	LRHS 6
Pine Bluff 7	LRHS 0
Popular Bluff, MO. 7	LRHS 26
Fort Smith 0	LRHS 0
Central High of Wichita, KN 18	LRHS 13
Lindblom High of Chicago, IL 7	LRHS 18

A REBUILDING YEAR

1929   5-5-1

Head Coach: Earl F. Quigley
Assistants: Homer Berry, J.A. Bigbee
Team Trainer: Riley "Doc" Johns
Team Physicians: Dr. Wells Farrin Smith, Dr. Theo Freedman

1929 LETTERMEN

Coy Adams	Hampton Hall	Ralph LaForge	Norman Withee
Tilburn Baily	Joe Harlan	Lancaster	
Joe Biddle	Roy Keith	Ned Stafford	
Arnold Castleberry	Troy Keith	Clyde Williams	

1929 MANAGERS
Alton Elkins
Lon Heffington
John Odgen

1929 ALL-STATE
Clyde Williams

Although 150 players reported for two-a-day practices, the Little Rock Tigers returned only six lettermen from the previous season. Coach Earl Quigley had to essentially put together a new Little Rock 11, and build it around returning halfbacks Ralph LaForge and Arnold Castleberry.

The Tigers opened the season against Batesville High School, and midway through the first quarter Little Rock took possession on the Batesville 25.

LaForge ran around right end for a 15-yard gain, and Roy Keith scored three plays later on a short run up the middle. Keith's extra-point attempt failed, but the Tigers led 6-0.

On their next possession, they took control at the Batesville 47. Castleberry capped a 53-yard touchdown drive by going around left end for the score. Keith's extra-point attempt was blocked.

Batesville punted to Little Rock on its next possession. Tigers took over at the 32.

On first down, LaForge raced around right end for the third touchdown. The extra-point attempt was good for a 19-0 lead at the end of the first quarter.

In the second quarter, reserve lineman Hugh Smith recovered a blocked Batesville punt in the end zone for Little Rock's sixth touchdown. Joe Harlan converted the extra-point attempt for a 39-0 halftime lead.

The Tigers continued to dominate Batesville during the second half, scoring four more touchdowns and a safety to win the opener 68-0.

Keith scored four touchdowns, while Castleberry added three. On top of a great offensive performance, the Little Rock defense did not allow a first down.

It was not quite as easy for the Tigers the following week when they battled Clarksville High School.

With the score 0-0 midway through the third quarter, LaForge returned a punt 5 yards to the Clarksville 25.

On first down, LaForge gained 4 yards around left end and Castleberry gained 6 yards on the next play. LaForge then went 14 yards to the 1. Keith then scored and kicked the extra point to give Little Rock a 7-0 lead.

The defense played tough, keeping Clarksville out of the end zone. The one Little Rock touchdown was enough to give the Tigers their second victory of the season.

After squeaking by Clarksville, Little Rock hosted Fordyce High School. Another defensive battle was fought the entire game, the only breakdown coming at the end of the fourth quarter.

With just one minute remaining to play, the Tigers had possession inside their 20. Little Rock's quarterback, Ned Stafford, punted to Fordyce's Clark Jordan at midfield.

Photo provided by the Arkansas Democrat-Gazette
(Left to Right) Clyde Williams, Coy Adams and Ralph LaForge

Jordan returned the punt to the Tigers 42. On the Redbugs' first offensive play, Jordan ran 24 yards to the 18. Fullback Le'Moyne Martin then ran up the middle and gained 14 yards to the 4.

With 10 seconds left to play, Jordan received the pitch and went around right end for the game-winning touchdown.

The Redbugs not only gave Little Rock its first defeat, they posted a 6-0 shutout.

Another close game was played the next week when the Tigers traveled to Chicago to meet Lindblom High School. The Chicago high school gave the Arkansas team its second consecutive 6-0 loss.

More than 7,000 fans watched a defensive battle turn sour for the visiting school when its punt team allowed Lindblom to return a kick for the game's only score.

The following week, Little Rock again traveled out of state, this time to play the Tulsa Central Braves.

This game marked the first time that a Little Rock high school football team played a night game.

Although it took the Tigers time to adjust playing under the lights, they were able to avoid their third consecutive loss with a 6-6 tie.

LaForge fumbled a punt and Tulsa recovered on the Tigers 20. Three plays later, Tulsa scored its only touchdown.

Photo provided by the Arkansas Democrat-Gazette
Ned Stafford (center) chases a Memphis running back

108

Referee Alvin Bell, a former Tiger, signals touchdown

LaForge went on to score Little Rock's lone touchdown after the Tigers recovered a fumble inside the Tulsa 20. Neither team was able to successfully kick its extra-point attempt.

Little Rock played Tennessee power Central High of Memphis the next week. The Warriors passed for 108 yards, but 13 yards passing by the Tigers were enough for a touchdown and the victory. Coy Adams caught the pass in the end zone for a 13-yard touchdown.

Joe Biddle scored the first touchdown on a short run up the middle as Little Rock defeated the Memphis team 13-7 for its third victory of the season.

Following the victory over Memphis, the Tigers lost three consecutive games.

The first was to Fort Smith. In a 14-0 victory, Billy Pansze scored on a 25-yard touchdown pass and a 20-yard run.

Capitol Hill High School of Oklahoma City then beat Little Rock the next week, 13-0.

In-state rival Pine Bluff gave the Tigers their third consecutive loss, 2-0.

The Zebras scored their safety when Little Rock was in punt formation and the snap sailed over the head of LaForge and into the end zone. LaForge fell on the ball to keep Pine Bluff from recovering it for a touchdown.

The Tigers traveled to Joplin, Mo., for their next victory. The Joplin Miners were playing their second game in two days.

After defeating Carthage, Mo., the day before, the Miners entered the game against Little Rock with tired and sore players, several of whom had broken noses. The Tigers capitalized, winning 38-0.

Soldan High School of St. Louis won the St. Louis city championship and was rewarded with a trip to Little Rock for a Thanksgiving battle with the Tigers.

Soldan (9-0-0) was a heavy favorite to win the holiday game.

Little Rock, though, was able to drive down the field several times to score. LaForge scored twice, Castleberry scored once and Keith scored once and kicked two extra points.

The 26-6 upset by the Tigers was Soldan's only loss of the season. Little Rock finished the season 5-5-1.

1929 TIGER SCHEDULE

Batesville 0	LRHS 68
Clarksville 0	LRHS 7
Fordyce 6	LRHS 0
Lindblom High of Chicago, IL 6	LRHS 0
Central High of Tulsa, OK 6	LRHS 6
Central High of Memphis, TN 7	LRHS 13
Fort Smith 14	LRHS 0
Capitol Hill High of Oklahoma City, OK 13	LRHS 0
Pine Bluff 2	LRHS 0
Joplin, MO 0	LRHS 38
Soldan High of St. Louis, MO 6	LRHS 26

LITTLE ROCK BEGINS NIGHT PLAY

1930   9-2-0

Head Coach: Earl F. Quigley
Assistants: Homer Berry, LeRoy Scott
Team Trainer: Riley "Doc" Johns
Team Physician: Dr. Wells Farrin Smith

1930 LETTERMEN

Coy Adams
Tom Anderson
John Bell
Arnold Castleberry
Percy Davidson

Harry Haynes
Ralph LaForge
Carl McConnell
Sterling Miller
John Patterson

Billy Smith
Ned Stafford
Carl Stewart
Clifford Stalnaker
Harry Walden

Clyde Williams
Norman Withee

1930 MANAGERS
T. Roy Reid
Gus Remmell
William Sims
W.S. Thomas

1930 ALL-STATE
Ralph LaForge
Clyde Williams

On Sept. 1, one week before the beginning of school, 132 football candidates met Coach Earl Quigley at Kavanaugh Field. Among these candidates were 27 returning lettermen or reserve players from the 1929 team.

Little Rock High School's first game against Clarksville made history for the Tigers and the city. It was the first football game played at night in Little Rock.

The Tigers played their first night game in 1929, when they traveled to Tulsa.

Playing under portable floodlights, used by the Arkansas Travelers baseball team, Little Rock used a white football to defeat Clarksville 45-0 in front of 3,500 fans.

Senior halfback Ralph LaForge scored on touchdown runs of 1, 21 and 15 yards and had two more scoring runs negated because of penalties. The Tigers scored seven touchdowns, but only converted three extra-point attempts.

Little Rock played its next game under the lights as well when Jonesboro Coach Clarence Geis brought his Golden Hurricane to Kavanaugh Field to take on a group of ill Tigers.

Coach Quigley was without seven starters because of severe side pains. The team physician believed the illnesses were due to swallowing too much dust practicing on Kavanaugh Field.

But the game went on, and midway through the first quarter Tom Anderson intercepted a Jonesboro pass and returned it to the Little Rock 37. LaForge then ran 63 yards for a touchdown on the first play from scrimmage. LaForge passed to Coy Adams for the two-point conversion.

During the second quarter, Jonesboro punted and LaForge returned it 15 yards to the Tigers 37.

Arnold Castleberry took a handoff and ran 55 yards before being tackled at the Jonesboro 7. LaForge then carried the rest of the way to give Little Rock a 14-0 lead.

The Hurricane immediately scored two touchdowns to pull within one point, 14-13, at halftime.

After a strong second quarter, Jonesboro could not make a first down during the third quarter.

The Tigers, though, scored again when Anderson ran for a 1-yard touchdown. The extra-point attempt was blocked and Little Rock held a 20-13 lead.

The fourth quarter was a defensive battle with each team having several stalled drives that resulted in punts. The Tigers would eventually sustain a short drive that would prove fatal to the Hurricane.

LaForge would end all hope for Jonesboro when he ran off tackle for a 25-yard touchdown. The two-point conversion failed, but Little Rock was victorious 26-13.

Twenty-six players made the trip to C.E. Byrd Stadium in Shreveport for the Tigers' third game.

In the first meeting between Shreveport Byrd and Little Rock, the Tigers were ahead 13-0 five minutes into the game.

LaForge ran for a 30-yard touchdown and Castleberry returned a kick 90 yards for the two-touchdown lead.

The Yellow Jackets didn't seem shaken, as their defense controlled Little Rock and their offense sustained two scoring drives to come within one point at the end of the first quarter.

The score remained the same until midway through the third quarter when the Byrd quarterback threw a short pass to

Photo provided by the Arkansas Democrat-Gazette
Clyde Williams (left) and Johnny Patterson

Buck Bryant, who broke several tackles for a 30-yard touchdown. The extra-point attempt failed and Shreveport Byrd led 18-13.

With just moments remaining in the game, the Tigers used an aerial attack to drive 53 yards to the Yellow Jackets 2. On third-and-goal from the 2, the gun sounded and Little Rock suffered its first loss of the season.

The Tigers were scheduled to play Camden High School next. Camden, however, refused to reschedule the game from Saturday to Friday night in order to play under the lights at Kavanaugh Field.

The El Dorado Wildcats, though, happened to have an open date and were willing to play on Friday night. The game was scheduled and another night game would be played in Little Rock.

Playing for El Dorado was Linwood "Schoolboy" Rowe, the standout quarterback, kicker and play caller. Rowe played an outstanding game, but he failed to find the goal line against the Tigers.

Twice, Rowe threw into the end zone and the receiver dropped the ball. A third scoring opportunity failed when Rowe and the Wildcats drove inside the 10, but were stopped short by a tough defense.

After two long drives, Little Rock's LaForge scored on a short run in the third quarter and Clifford Stalnaker scored on a short run in the fourth quarter.

The Tigers beat El Dorado 13-0.

Central High School of Joplin, Mo., was no match for Little Rock the next week when the visiting Tigers handed the defending Missouri state champion its worst home defeat in several years.

The Little Rock defense once again showed its strength when it held the Miners scoreless in a 20-0 victory.

The following week found the Tigers again traveling, this time just across the eastern border to play their Tennessee rival, Central High of Memphis.

LaForge, Little Rock's star halfback, rushed for four touchdowns. His first carry of the game was a run around right end for a 79-yard gain to the 1. Anderson crossed the goal line on the next play to put the Tigers up 6-0.

Little Rock dominated the game 57-6.

For several days after the contest, the Tennessee newspapers hailed the Tigers as "... one of the best prep teams to play in Tennessee in several years, if not ever."

Photo provided by the Arkansas Democrat-Gazette
Carl Stewart (left) and Johnny Bell

The papers also touted 140-pound LaForge as one of the best backs ever to carry the ball in Tennessee.

With attendance expected to exceed 9,000 for the following game, Little Rock erected two additional sets of bleachers to accommodate the crowd.

The largest crowd to watch an athletic event in Arkansas (more than 10,000) packed Kavanaugh Field to see the highly anticipated game with the Fordyce Redbugs.

The game featured two of the state's top teams and was expected to decide the state championship. Fordyce brought three of the state's premier players to play against the Tigers, twins Clark and George Jordan and Paul "Bear" Bryant.

Clark Jordan set up the Redbugs' first score when he returned a punt 85 yards to the 10 where he was tackled by Little Rock's punter, LaForge. George Jordan then ran into the end zone for a 6-0 lead.

Later in the first quarter, LaForge fumbled and Bryant recovered at the Tigers 28. After a short drive, Clark Jordan scored on third down from the 1 to increase the Fordyce lead.

The Redbugs came out in the second half and played even harder.

Midway through the third quarter, Clark Jordan completed a short pass to Bryant, who ran 65 yards for a touchdown.

Clark Jordan accounted for another score in the fourth quarter when he threw a 55-yard touchdown pass.

Fordyce completed 2 of 7 passes for 120 yards and two touchdowns. Little Rock completed 5 of 21 passes for 86 yards and had two interceptions.

The Redbugs used only 11 players, with no substitutions, and still dominated the Tigers.

The *Arkansas Gazette* dubbed the game as "... one of the most convincing demonstrations of football power and football superiority that has ever been shown on the local gridiron where some great teams of the past have performed."

Fordyce defeated Little Rock 34-0.

Four touchdowns by LaForge and two touchdowns by Castleberry were more than enough to defeat Capitol Hill High School of Oklahoma City the following week. The 38-7 victory, though, would prove only a warm-up since rival Pine Bluff came to town the following week.

The Tigers had not scored a touchdown against the Zebras since 1920. This year, though, LaForge and Castleberry ran through and around the Pine Bluff defense. LaForge rushed for three touchdowns and Castleberry rushed for two.

Pine Bluff's Don Hutson scored the Zebras' lone touchdown on a short pass, which he took into the end zone from the 1.

With a 32-7 victory, Little Rock defeated the Zebras for the first time since 1923.

After another three-touchdown performance by LaForge in a 47-0 victory over Fort Smith, the Tigers prepared for their Thanksgiving game against Lindblom High School of Chicago.

Lindblom had given up only 25 points during the year and no team had scored more than one touchdown against it.

After consistently outplaying Little Rock in the first half, Lindblom took a 13-0

Photo provided by the Arkansas Democrat-Gazette
(Top) Clifford Stalnaker, Ned Stafford, Sterling Miller, (bottom) Tom Anderson, Ralph LaForge, Arnold Castleberry

lead into halftime. However, the Tigers took the lead in the third quarter after La-Forge scored on a 30-yard touchdown pass and 4-yard run. Both extra-point attempts were good and Little Rock led 14-13.

After a Lindblom punt, the Tigers marched to the Chicago 37. LaForge ran around left end to score and increase Little Rock's lead to 20-13.

After an interception in the fourth quarter, the Tigers drove to the Lindblom 13 and Stalnaker ran in for the score. The kick was good to make it 27-13.

After the ensuing kickoff, Lindblom fumbled on the first play and Little Rock recovered at the Chicago 22. Three plays netted 11 yards before LaForge covered the remaining distance for the Tigers' final score in a 33-13 victory.

In his last high school game, LaForge rushed 34 times for 173 yards and scored four of Little Rock's five touchdowns.

Photo provided by Central High School
Riley "Doc" Johns

1930 TIGER SCHEDULE

Clarksville 0	LRHS 45
Jonesboro 13	LRHS 26
Byrd High of Shreveport, LA 18	LRHS 13
El Dorado 0	LRHS 13
Central High of Joplin, MO 0	LRHS 20
Central High of Memphis, TN 6	LRHS 57
Fordyce 34	LRHS 0
Capitol Hill High of Oklahoma City, OK 7	LRHS 38
Pine Bluff 7	LRHS 32
Fort Smith 0	LRHS 47
Lindblom High of Chicago, IL 13	LRHS 33

LITTLE ROCK BUYS KAVANAUGH FIELD

1931   8-3-0

Head Coach: Earl F. Quigley
Assistants: Homer Berry, LeRoy Scott
Team Trainer: Riley "Doc" Johns
Team Physicians: Dr. Wells Farrin Smith, Dr. Theo Freedman

1931 LETTERMEN

Coy Adams	Jack Herbert	Sterling Miller	Clifford Thorpe
Bill Dalrymple	Robert Holcomb	Jack Newby	Gene Walden
Kelly Ellington	Bob Johnson	Eugene Pool	
Clay Fulford	Lorayne King	Herman Ray	
Melville Gamblin	Woodrow McMurray	Clifford Stalnaker	

1931 MANAGERS
Unknown

1931 ALL-STATE
Herman Ray

The 1931 Tigers met for the first time Sept. 4 to receive their equipment and instruction from Coach Earl Quigley. The following day marked the first day of two-a-day practices. Little Rock practiced at 9 a.m. and 2 p.m.

Many of the 1930 stars graduated, and Coach Quigley believed that a majority of the 1931 first-team players would be newcomers from the city's junior high schools.

On Sept. 12, the Arkansas Travelers defeated the Nashville Volunteers 7-1. This marked the last time the Travelers played at historic Kavanaugh Field.

The team purchased land on the southeast corner of Fair Park to build a new baseball stadium. In return, the Little Rock School District bought Kavanaugh Field from the city of Little Rock with plans to build an outdoor athletic complex in the near future.

For their first game of the season, the Tigers hosted the Malvern Leopards under the lights at Kavanaugh Field. More than 3,500 fans braved extreme heat and humidity to watch a first half full of offense and a second half filled with defense.

Malvern fumbled on its first possession and Little Rock recovered. The Tigers eventually capitalized on the fumble recovery when Clifford Stalnaker scored from the 6 for Little Rock's first touchdown.

The Tigers punted on their next possession. But the Malvern safety fumbled and

(Left to Right) Sterling Miller, Bob Johnson, Clifford Stalnaker and Kelly Ellington

After traveling to Blytheville to take a 26-6 victory over the Chickasaws, the Tigers were at home the next week against North Little Rock High School. This marked the first meeting between the schools since 1925, when the Wildcats won 19-7.

More than 7,000 fans were the first to hear a loud speaker at a Little Rock High School football game.

The new loud speaker was used to announce names, penalties, etc. J.C. Conway served as Little Rock's first football announcer.

After a scoreless first half, the Tigers scored late in the third quarter on a 31-yard pass from Herman Ray to Bob Johnson. After the ensuing kickoff, North Little Rock marched 62 yards to tie the score at 6-6.

Late in the fourth quarter, the Wildcats were backed up on their 10 and set to punt. Eugene Smith, Little Rock's left end, broke through the line and blocked the punt, which Clay Fulford recovered on the North Little Rock 6.

On the Tigers' first play, Ray passed to Coy Adams for a touchdown. Stalnaker kicked the extra point for a 13-6 lead.

Two minutes later, the game ended. The Wildcats passed for 119 yards, Little Rock passed for 105 yards.

Little Rock recovered on the Leopards 10. Four plays later, Stalnaker scored again.

The Leopards' points came on a short run in the second quarter, but the Tigers held on for a 12-6 victory.

Jonesboro High School was next on the schedule for Little Rock. Coach Quigley believed this would be one of the toughest games of the season. The Golden Hurricane was a veteran team that had only lost three players from the previous year.

Just less than 2,500 fans watched a series of punts during the first quarter until Jonesboro gained possession on the Tigers 35.

On its first play, "Roachy" Smith ran through the defensive line for a touchdown. The Hurricane converted the extra-point attempt to lead 7-0.

A 50-yard drive by Little Rock in the second quarter netted the Tigers their first touchdown, a 9-yard run by Stalnaker. Little Rock failed to convert the extra-point attempt and trailed 7-6.

Jonesboro kicked off to open the second half. On the Tigers' first play from scrimmage, Robert Holcomb ran off left tackle for a 75-yard touchdown.

Little Rock led 12-7 and held the Golden Hurricane scoreless in the second half to win the game.

Springfield's Bill Downing scores a touchdown

The Tigers lost their first game of the season the next week, 18-7, to Byrd High School of Shreveport. Little Rock, though, rebounded the following week when it traveled to Fordyce to take on the rebuilding Redbugs.

Fordyce had beaten the Tigers the past two years, but only returned one experienced player in 1931. This was evident as Little Rock's second team played most of the second half in a 32-0 victory.

Central High of Memphis traveled to Little Rock for the Tigers' last night game of the season. Little Rock had only lost to Memphis one time in the past 11 years.

The Warriors, however, entered the game undefeated and with hopes of breaking their losing streak against the Tigers.

Little Rock scored first after recovering a fumble on the Memphis 15. Holcomb passed to Adams for a 15-yard touchdown. Stalnaker kicked the extra point for a 7-0 lead.

The Warriors took the ensuing kickoff and drove down the field, scoring on a 7-yard run. Memphis failed to convert the extra-point attempt, allowing the Tigers to maintain a 7-6 advantage.

Little Rock then began to dominate the game, scoring twice more during the first half. Ray passed to Lorayne King for a 40-yard touchdown; Holcomb returned an interception 45 yards for a touchdown.

During the second half, Ray passed to Adams for a 5-yard touchdown. Kelly Ellington added a 23-yard run to give the Tigers a 32-6 victory over the Warriors. Coach Quigley used 40 players during the game, with the third team playing the entire fourth quarter.

Little Rock hosted unbeaten Springfield (Mo.) Central the following week. Springfield had not been scored on all season.

Midway through the first quarter, Ray punted from the Tigers 4 and Springfield took possession at the Little Rock 45.

On the first play, the Missouri quarterback passed to Bill Downing. Downing zigzagged down the field, breaking several tackles before finally being downed at the 5.

Three plays later, Springfield's line opened a hole big enough that Downing jogged through for a touchdown. Missouri converted the extra-point attempt for a 7-0 halftime lead.

The Tigers kicked off to open the second half and forced Springfield to punt after its first four plays. Little Rock then drove 75 yards for a touchdown, with Jack Herbert scoring on a 1-yard run. The extra-point attempt was converted to make it 7-7.

The Tigers began their next possession on their 14. Herbert and Ray each gained 8 yards, and Sterling Miller ran 64 yards on a reverse before being brought down at the Missouri 6. After Ellington gained 5 yards, Herbert scored to give Little Rock the lead.

Downing, Springdale's star halfback, was injured on Miller's long run, and the Missouri team's offense was never able to get back into stride. The Tigers scored once more on a Ray to King touchdown pass in a 19-7 victory.

Following a 19-0 loss to Pine Bluff and a 20-7 loss to Fort Smith, Little Rock's hopes of winning a state championship were lost as well.

The Tigers continued the season, though, when they hosted

Photo provided by the Arkansas Democrat-Gazette
(Left to Right) Ben Russell, Jack Herbert, Lorayne King and Robert Holcomb

Woodrow Wilson High of Dallas on Thanksgiving Day. Woodrow Wilson, losing only in the Dallas city championship game, had one of the most talented quarterbacks in the country in "Red" Webb. Webb, though, did not prove to be a factor in a steady downpour of rain and several inches of mud.

During the first minute of play, Holcomb ran for a 70-yard touchdown, then Miller ran for a short touchdown just before the end of the first quarter.

Other Little Rock scores came when Woodrow McMurray blocked a Dallas punt and recovered it in the end zone and two short runs by Holcomb.

The Tigers dominated Woodrow Wilson High, allowing only one first down in a 31-0 victory.

1931 TIGER SCHEDULE

Malvern 6	LRHS 12
Jonesboro 7	LRHS 12
Blytheville 6	LRHS 26
North Little Rock 6	LRHS 13
Byrd High of Shreveport, LA 18	LRHS 7
Fordyce 0	LRHS 32
Central High of Memphis, TN 6	LRHS 32
Central High of Springfield, MO 7	LRHS 19
Pine Bluff 19	LRHS 0
Fort Smith 20	LRHS 7
Woodrow Wilson High of Dallas, TX 0	LRHS 31

A DEFENSIVE SEASON

1932   7-4-0

Head Coach: Earl F. Quigley
Assistants: Homer Berry, LeRoy Scott
Team Trainer: Riley "Doc" Johns
Team Physicians: Dr. Wells Farrin Smith, Dr. Theo Freedman

1932 LETTERMEN

Williard Dickey	Bob Johnson	Ernest Miller	Eugene Smith
John Donaldson	Bill Jones	James Phillips	J.D. Turner
Kelly Ellington	Howard Link	Eugene Pool	Gene Walden
Melville Gamblin	Woodrow McMurray	Jack Robbins	Harry Walden

1932 MANAGERS
Erp Jennings
W.J. Jernigan
H. Remmell
Fred Watkins

1932 ALL-STATE
John Donaldson
Kelly Ellington
Melville Gamblin

Prior to the 1932 season, a new drainage system and new turf were added to Kavanaugh Field. With the Arkansas Travelers no longer calling Kavanaugh Field home and Little Rock High School owning all rights to the facility, the Tigers were able to apply grass on the base paths of the old baseball diamond.

This marked the first season that the field was completely covered in grass. Additional bleachers were also added to the field, increasing the capacity to 9,000.

Sixty players reported for two-a-day workouts. Soon, Coach Earl Quigley cut the team to 36 prior to its first game. The game took place under the lights at Kavanaugh Field and was against Morrilton High School.

Little Rock kicked off, and after three plays Morrilton was forced to punt. Bob Johnson returned the punt to the Morrilton 38.

On Little Rock's first play from scrimmage, Kelly Ellington ran around right end for a 62-yard touchdown.

With the Tigers' second team playing early in the second quarter, Little Rock blocked a punt and recovered it on the Morrilton 11. Jack Robbins then carried around right end for another touchdown.

The rout continued on the Tigers' next possession when Robbins ran 35 yards for a third touchdown.

Little Rock scored only once in the third quarter when Troy Holiman went in from the 1.

After John Donaldson intercepted a Morrilton pass and returned it deep into enemy territory in the fourth quarter, Lorayne King scored the Tigers' fifth touchdown. Shortly after that, they added a sixth touchdown when Eugene Smith scored on a 35-yard run.

Little Rock's defense played a great game, holding Morrilton to three first downs in a 38-0 victory.

Coach Ed Dunaway and his Texarkana Razorbacks would be the next battle for the Tigers. This was the first meeting between the schools since 1924. The game was a defensive battle played mostly in Little Rock territory.

The Tigers, however, were able to score in the third quarter when Robbins scored from the 5. Williard Dickey converted the extra point and the defense posted its second shutout, 7-0.

The following week, 23 players traveled to Shreveport to meet Byrd High School.

The game's only exciting minutes came when Little Rock's Melville Gamblin

Photo provided by the Arkansas Democrat-Gazette
Melville Gamblin (left) and Bob Johnson

punted from his 45 to the Byrd 14. The Tigers held the Yellow Jackets on downs, forcing the Shreveport team to punt.

Gamblin and James Phillips broke through the line to block the punt. Phillips recovered it in the end zone for the only touchdown of the game.

Little Rock's defense kept its opponent scoreless in a 7-0 victory.

Just two days prior to the Tigers' next game, the Arkansas Athletic Association ruled Little Rock's starting end, Coy Adams, ineligible due to being older than 21. Association President O.G. Holmes of Harrison stated: "The ruling is no reflection on any officials or coaches of the Little Rock school, but is merely an enforcement of one of the Association's rules."

More than 5,000 fans were at Kavanaugh Field for the Tigers' game against North Little Rock High School.

Early in the first quarter, Little Rock drove 50 yards for its first touchdown, a 5-yard run by Ernest Miller. The remainder of the first quarter and all of the second and third quarters became a punting duel.

Late in the fourth quarter, North Little Rock was at its 22 and attempted a pass. Donaldson intercepted and returned it to the 10.

It took the Tigers three plays to score. Miller scored when he went around left end

Photo provided by the Arkansas Democrat-Gazette
The Tigers stop Pine Bluff

Little Rock's Eugene Smith (79)

for a 4-yard touchdown. Smith converted the extra point and the game ended just minutes later.

Little Rock recorded its fourth victory and fourth shutout.

The Tigers met their match the following week when they were beaten by one of the state's toughest teams, El Dorado.

The Wildcats, thought to have their best team in school history, were good enough to claim a 19-6 victory over the Tigers.

Little Rock, though, came back the next week to dominate Fordyce 31-0. The game's offensive highlight was an 85-yard touchdown run by Ellington.

The defense played another spectacular game, allowing the Redbugs only 12 possessions and recording their fifth shutout of the season.

Little Rock was victorious the next week when it defeated old rival Central High of Memphis. The Tigers kept a tough offense scoreless in the fourth quarter and held on for a 19-13 victory.

Coach Quigley, however, voiced his disgust over the play of his linemen and benched four players for the following game. This disciplinary action may have cost his team a victory when it traveled to Tulsa the following week.

On a rain soaked and muddy field, Little Rock lost to Central High 12-7 for its second loss of the season.

The fans, though, still turned out the next week as more than 6,000 entered Kavanaugh Field for the annual battle with Pine Bluff.

Coach Allen Dunaway's Zebras upset the Tigers late in the fourth quarter when quarterback LeRoy Goldberg scored on a 13-yard run. The touchdown broke a scoreless tie, allowing Pine Bluff to defeat Little Rock 7-0.

Fort Smith and the Tigers battled to a 0-0 first-half tie at Kavanaugh Field the following week. The Grizzlies, though, came out in the second half and took the lead on their first possession.

Fort Smith's drive began at its 10 and was capped with a 28-yard touchdown run by Van Brown.

With six minutes left in the game, Ellington intercepted a pass and returned it 75 yards for a touchdown. However, the touchdown was called back because of a clipping penalty.

The Fort Smith defense was able to keep the Tigers at bay and the Grizzlies were victorious 6-0.

Little Rock lost more than the game when Johnson was injured in the first quarter. He was rushed to St. Vincent's Infir-

Little Rock stops Pine Bluff's LeRoy Goldberg

mary and remained in the hospital under observation for six days before being released. It was determined that he only had bruising to his ribs and abdomen.

Grover Cleveland High School, St. Louis city champion, met the Tigers on Thanksgiving Day at Kavanaugh Field.

Marred with several fumbles by each team, the game appeared to favor Little Rock when Donaldson blocked two punts to twice give his team possession inside the St. Louis 10. The Tigers, however, were unable to score, turning the ball over on downs each time.

The game's only score occurred midway through the third quarter when Miller ran for a 50-yard touchdown. This gave Little Rock a 6-0 victory and its sixth shutout of the season.

During the defensive battle, the Tigers had only six first downs. St. Louis converted only four.

1932 TIGER SCHEDULE

Morrilton 0	LRHS 38
Texarkana, AR 0	LRHS 7
Byrd High of Shreveport, LA 0	LRHS 7
North Little Rock 0	LRHS 13
El Dorado 19	LRHS 6
Fordyce 0	LRHS 31
Central High of Memphis, TN 13	LRHS 19
Central High of Tulsa, OK 12	LRHS 7
Pine Bluff 7	LRHS 0
Fort Smith 6	LRHS 0
Grover Cleveland High of St. Louis, MO 0	LRHS 6

A HIGH SCORING YEAR

1933   9-2-0

Head Coach: Earl F. Quigley
Assistants: Homer Berry, LeRoy Scott
Team Trainer: Riley "Doc" Johns
Team Physicians: Dr. Wells Farrin Smith, Dr. Theo Freedman

1933 LETTERMEN

Joe Dangston	Billy Glover	Howard Link	John Stillman
John Donaldson	Billy Hunter	Jack Robbins	Gene Walden
Phillip Farrell	Bob Johnson	Brooks Robinson	Harry Walden
Dan Futrell	Kenneth Kavanaugh	Ben Russell	
Melville Gamblin	Gaughan Lewis	Eugene Smith	

1933 MANAGERS
Alston Jennings
Jimmy Moses
Jesse Scott
George Wittenburg

1933 ALL-STATE
John Donaldson
Melville Gamblin
Jack Robbins

Forty-five candidates attended two-a-day workouts in early September. Of these 45 candidates, nine were returning lettermen from a 7-4-0 team in 1932.

These veterans and their coach, Earl Quigley, wasted no time in showing the state that Little Rock High School was a contender for the state championship.

The Tigers hosted Arkadelphia to open the season. Little Rock sent a message to every remaining team on its schedule with a 105-0 victory over the Badgers. The Tigers hadn't scored 100 points since a 110-0 victory over England High School in 1926.

Coach Quigley used 40 players, with the second and third teams playing most of the game.

Bob Johnson, Ben Russell, Billy Glover and Brooks Robinson each scored three touchdowns. John Stillman and Dan Futrell scored two touchdowns and Jack Robbins scored one.

The Tigers had 32 first downs and didn't allow any.

Coach H.M. Knilans brought 30 players from Byrd High School in Shreveport to meet the Tigers at Kavanaugh Field. The Yellow Jackets returned 11 lettermen from a team that Little Rock beat 7-0 the previous season.

Johnson started the scoring in the first quarter when he ran for a 50-yard touchdown. In the third quarter, Eugene Smith passed to Billy Hunter for a 25-yard touchdown.

Photo provided by the Arkansas Democrat-Gazette
John Stillman scores against Van Buren

Gene Walden intercepted a pass in the fourth quarter and returned it 15 yards for a touchdown. Johnson then scored again on a short run to give the Tigers a 26-0 victory.

Coach Quigley and 24 players made the trip to Fordyce for their next game.

Little Rock began the second quarter on the Redbugs 30. The Tigers marched 70 yards, with Walden capping the drive on a 1-yard plunge to put Little Rock up 6-0.

The remainder of the first half was a defensive battle.

Fordyce opened the second half with a fumble that Hunter recovered at midfield. It took eight plays, but Little Rock scored when Johnson ran into the end zone from the 2.

The Redbugs took the ensuing kickoff and marched to the Tigers 6. This marked the first time during the game that Fordyce crossed the Little Rock 40. However, Fordyce could not overcome a penalty and a tough defense. The scoring threat ended when the Redbugs were forced to punt.

On Little Rock's next possession, Johnson fumbled a snap at the 20 and Fordyce recovered. Four plays later, Carrol Wood went around left end for a touchdown. The Redbugs converted the extra-point attempt to cut the Tigers' lead to 12-7.

Little Rock struck again after the ensuing kickoff fell into the arms of Johnson at the Tigers 10. Johnson returned the kick 90

yards for another Little Rock touchdown. The extra-point attempt failed, but the Tigers still led 18-7.

Fordyce's Jim Benton scored on a short run midway through the fourth quarter to cut Little Rock's lead to 18-13.

The Redbugs again drove deep into Little Rock territory, but Johnson intercepted a pass to end the scoring threat. Johnson, however, was injured on the next play trying to break through the Fordyce defense.

Unable to move without Johnson, Little Rock lined up to punt on fourth down. The Redbugs, however, broke through the line and blocked the kick. The ball was recovered in the Little Rock end zone by Benton for a Fordyce touchdown.

The touchdown gave Fordyce a 19-18 victory, handing the Tigers their first loss of the season.

Four players missed practice the following week because of malaria. However, all but one of these players was healthy enough to play in Little Rock's next game. Johnson, who was nursing an injury as well as his illness, couldn't play, however.

Van Buren High School traveled to Little Rock for the first meeting between the schools since 1916, a game that the Tigers won 47-0.

Van Buren had lost only once the previous three years and hoped to continue this winning streak when it met the Little Rock

Tigers. Little Rock, though, was not impressed with Van Buren's previous triumphs and dominated the Pointers from the opening kickoff until the game's end.

The Tigers blocked three punts, one that resulted in a safety, and also scored 11 touchdowns.

Robbins led Little Rock in scoring with three touchdowns, while Stillman, Russell and Glover each scored two touchdowns.

One of Glover's touchdowns was a breathtaking 80-yard run from scrimmage. Hunter and Futrell each added one touchdown for the Tigers in a 73-0 romp over the Pointers.

Central High of Tulsa, defending Oklahoma champion, returned 11 veterans and battled Little Rock the following week at Kavanaugh Field.

Coach Art Griffith's hard-fighting Braves never gave up, but the Tigers were the superior team and defeated Tulsa 19-6. More than 3,000 fans watched as Johnson averaged more than 9 yards per carry to avenge a five-point loss to the Braves the previous year.

Little Rock hosted undefeated Central High of Memphis the next week and narrowly escaped with a 19-12 victory. Johnson and Harry Walden each scored touchdowns in the fourth quarter for the comeback victory.

The Tigers traveled to south Arkansas to take on Texarkana High School the next week. Little Rock dominated the game, scoring more than 100 points for the second time during the season.

Johnson scored five touchdowns to lead the Tigers in scoring. The touchdowns included punt returns of 70 yards and 60 yards and a pass reception for 50 yards.

Glover scored four touchdowns, runs of 80 yards and 47 yards, a pass reception of 59 yards and an interception return of 80 yards.

Other Little Rock highlights included touchdowns on a 54-yard run by Russell and interception returns of 40 and 25 yards by Kenneth Kavanaugh.

The Tigers scored a season-high 107 points in the victory over the Razorbacks.

After a 19-0 victory over the North Little Rock Wildcats, Little Rock found itself in Pine Bluff battling the Zebras.

Scoreless late in the fourth quarter, a bad punt by Melville Gamblin gave Pine Bluff possession at the Tigers 37.

More than 7,000 fans watched as Little Rock threw Ed Craven for a 3-yard loss, backing up the Zebras to the 40.

Photo provided by the Arkansas Democrat-Gazette

Eight of Little Rock's nine returning lettermen
(Top) Howard Link, John Donaldson, Melville Gamblin, Gene Walden
(Bottom) Woodrow McMurray, Jack Robbins, Harry Walden, Bob Johnson

Photo provided by the Arkansas Democrat-Gazette
Howard Link (92) returns an interception 50 yards

As Halbert Hughes dropped back to pass on the next play, Little Rock's Smith attempted to sack him for a 5-yard loss. Hughes, though, broke Smith's grasp and completed a pass to offensive tackle "Dutch" King.

King, an eligible receiver because he was the widest man on his side of the line, ran untouched into the end zone. The score gave Pine Bluff a 6-0 victory over the Tigers.

Little Rock defeated Fort Smith 20-6 before hosting Hot Springs for the Tigers' annual Thanksgiving Day game.

Since Coach Quigley decided to no longer invite out-of-state teams for the annual holiday event, a new tradition would begin the next season. It would showcase an annual matchup between Little Rock and North Little Rock in the holiday game.

The Tigers, however, needed to concentrate on the 1933 Thanksgiving game against the Hot Springs Trojans.

Coach Merving Perry brought his Trojans to Little Rock for the first meeting between the schools since 1928.

Early in the first quarter, Hot Springs punted to the Tigers. Russell fielded the kick and returned it to the Trojans 30.

Robbins ran 28 yards around right end, and then scored on the following play. He also kicked the extra point to give Little Rock a 7-0 lead.

Midway through the third quarter, the Tigers drove 60 yards, with Robbins and Hunter capping the drive by connecting for a 15-yard touchdown pass.

Paul Longinotti eventually passed for a fourth-quarter Hot Springs touchdown. However, one touchdown would not be enough as Little Rock defeated the Trojans 13-6.

1933 TIGER SCHEDULE

Arkadelphia 0	LRHS 105
Byrd High of Shreveport, LA 0	LRHS 26
Fordyce 19	LRHS 18
Van Buren 0	LRHS 73
Central High of Tulsa, OK 6	LRHS 19
Central High of Memphis, TN 12	LRHS 19
Texarkana, AR 0	LRHS 107
North Little Rock 0	LRHS 19
Pine Bluff 6	LRHS 0
Fort Smith 6	LRHS 20
Hot Springs 6	LRHS 13

A HOLIDAY RIVALRY BEGINS

1934 7-4-0

Head Coach: Earl F. Quigley
Assistants: Homer Berry, LeRoy Scott
Team Trainer: Riley "Doc" Johns
Team Physicians: Dr. Wells Farrin Smith, Dr. Theo Freedman

1934 LETTERMEN

William Anderson	Charles Hinton	Ed McCully	Wilfred Thorpe
Clark Beavers	P.D. Huff	Elbert Milner	Halliburton Ware
Bill Dalrymple	Kenneth Kavanaugh	Bert Roberts	Art Withers
Charles Driver	Joe Langston	Ben Russell	
Billy Glover	Gaughan Lewis	John Stillman	

1934 MANAGERS
Billy Burr
J.D. Chester

1934 ALL-STATE
Bill Dalrymple

Since all but two of the 11 starters graduated, 1934 appeared to be a rebuilding year for Coach Earl Quigley and his assistants.

Coach Quigley was able to choose new starters from a group of 65 players who showed up for preseason workouts. On Sept. 9, Coach Quigley cut the team from 65 players to 49 players.

Little Rock opened against Forrest City High School at Kavanaugh Field. The Thoroughbreds were big winners the past three years, posting a 29-2-0 record. They returned 11 veterans from the previous season.

The Tigers' first two touchdowns came on long drives, 71 yards and 63 yards, and consisted of pounding the middle for yardage.

In the third quarter, John Stillman intercepted a Forrest City pass and returned it 30 yards to the Thoroughbreds 7. Wilfred Thorpe scored on the second play for Little Rock's third touchdown.

Forrest City's next possession ended with Kenneth Kavanaugh's interception at the Thoroughbreds 44.

Thorpe then took a handoff on the first offensive play and ran 26 yards. Clark

Beavers, a transfer from Nebraska, then scored.

The Tigers scored three more times, the last on a 55-yard pass from Beavers to Thorpe. This helped Little Rock beat Forrest City 42-7.

The Tigers challenged Russellville High School the following week. The Cyclones, who claimed a share of the 1933 state championship, returned eight starters and were primed for a battle with Little Rock.

More than 4,000 fans watched the first meeting between the schools since 1919, a 174-0 victory by the Tigers. Little Rock entered without Thorpe, who broke his finger during the week's practice.

Late in the first quarter, the Tigers drove 89 yards to the Russellville 1. This resulted in the Cyclones' only excitement of the game.

Russellville put together a goal-line stand, but Little Rock scored on its next possession when Art Withers kicked a 30-yard field goal.

Capping a 25-yard drive in the second quarter, Stillman scored from the 2 for Little Rock's first touchdown.

Halliburton Ware went on to score twice for the Tigers in the fourth quarter. He ended an 80-yard drive with a short run and later ran for a 41-yard touchdown.

Little Rock shut out the defending state champion Cyclones 21-0.

Photo provided by the Arkansas Democrat-Gazette
Bill Dalrymple (left) and **Clark Beavers**

The Tigers received a blow when Woodrow McMurray, who didn't attend school in 1933 because of an illness, was forced to withdraw again after his father became sick.

Without McMurray and Thorpe, still out with a broken finger, Little Rock traveled to Louisiana only to lose its first game of the season to Byrd High School of Shreveport.

The Tigers tallied only 40 yards of total offense in a 14-0 loss to the Yellow Jackets.

Little Rock, however, recorded another victory by beating Fordyce the next week, 20-0.

On the first play of the second quarter, Ware ran 91 yards for a touchdown.

Little Rock kicked off to the Redbugs, but Fordyce was forced to punt on fourth down.

On the first play of the possession, Ware ran for a touchdown. He went over right tackle only to meet the defense. But Ware then reversed field and raced for a 75-yard touchdown.

Beavers intercepted a Fordyce pass in the third quarter and returned it 65 yards for Little Rock's third and final score.

More than 6,500 fans, the largest crowd in Hot Springs history, packed Rix Stadium to watch the Tigers battle the Trojans.

Paul Longinotti, considered the best passer in Arkansas, intercepted a Little Rock pass and returned it to the Tigers 45. On the next play, Longinotti passed to Wilbur

Photo provided by the Arkansas Democrat-Gazette
Joe Langston (left) and **Kenneth Kavanaugh**

Photo provided by the Arkansas Democrat-Gazette
(Left to Right) Art Withers, Woodrow McMurray, P.D. Huff and Kenneth Kavanaugh

Green for a 45-yard touchdown to put Hot Springs up 7-0.

With just seconds remaining in the game, Little Rock was deep in Hot Springs territory and threatened to tie the score. Green, though, intercepted a pass and returned it 90 yards for a touchdown. This put the game out of reach and Hot Springs won 13-0.

This marked the first time that Little Rock had ever lost to the Trojans.

A four-touchdown performance by Victor Bradford of Memphis Central was more than enough to topple the Tigers the follow-ing week. The Tennessee team dominated Little Rock 44-0 in Memphis.

Fort Smith, which only had ties with Pine Bluff and Fayetteville, met the Tigers at Kavanaugh Field for Little Rock's homecoming game.

More than 3,500 were on hand during pregame ceremonies as Martha Langhorne was crowned homecoming queen.

Midway through the first quarter, the Grizzlies punted. Ed McCully received the kick and returned it 30 yards to the Fort Smith 20. On the next play, Beavers went 20 yards around right end for the score.

Photo provided by the Arkansas Democrat-Gazette
(Left to Right) Halliburton Ware, Ben Russell and Billy Glover

Photo provided by the Arkansas Democrat-Gazette
(Left to Right) Francis Harrison, Wilfred Thorpe and Clark Beavers

129

Little Rock's first series of the second quarter ended with a 23-yard touchdown pass from McCully to Thorpe.

The Tigers scored twice in the fourth quarter, a 4-yard run by Beavers and a 3-yard run by Thorpe. Thorpe's 3-yard score was set up by Kavanaugh's interception return to the Grizzlies 3.

Little Rock was victorious on homecoming night, 25-0.

Searcy High School, another team that claimed a share of the 1933 state championship, was unbeaten and had hopes of winning the championship for the second consecutive year.

Searcy running back Roy Fisher, the "Blonde Blizzard," was one of the best offensive players in Arkansas. Fisher scored 181 points in 1933, leading the Lions to the state title.

While their defense stopped Fisher, the Tigers gained 448 total yards. Thorpe scored three touchdowns in an easy 49-7 victory.

Little Rock's next game was not only important because it was against rival Pine Bluff, a share of the 1934 state championship was also on the line. The Tigers and Hot Springs had only one loss to Arkansas competition. The Zebras were unbeaten against Arkansas teams, however, they did post a 6-6 tie with Fort Smith.

A Little Rock victory over Pine Bluff would give the three teams one loss each and guarantee each at least a share of the 1934 championship.

The Zebras struck first after recovering a fumble on the Little Rock 30. They immediately scored when Ed Craven completed a 30-yard pass for a touchdown. Later, Pine Bluff recovered another fumble at the Little Rock 32. Craven eventually scored on a 10-yard run to give the Zebras a 12-0 lead.

The Tigers finally scored in the fourth quarter after a 90-yard drive. They converted the extra-point attempt to cut the lead to 12-7.

Pine Bluff answered when it took the ensuing kickoff and drove 83 yards for its third touchdown, putting the game out of reach at 18-7.

Photo provided by the Arkansas Democrat-Gazette
Charles Driver

Photo provided by the Arkansas Democrat-Gazette
Kenneth Kavanaugh (left) **and Robert Majors**

Craven finished with 135 yards rushing and three touchdowns. Little Rock accounted for only 110 yards rushing.

Hope High School and Coach Foy Hammons, former coach at Pine Bluff, hosted the Tigers the following week.

Withers kicked a 33-yard field goal to put the Tigers up 3-0. Stillman ran for a 1-yard touchdown in the 10-0 victory over the Bobcats.

Stillman's touchdown marked the first time that an Earl Quigley-coached team had ever scored a touchdown against a team coached by Hammons.

A tradition began on Thanksgiving Day when Little Rock High School and North Little Rock High School began scheduling their annual battle on the holiday. The inaugural event was dampened by heavy rain and thick mud, which hampered the performance of both offenses.

The game's only points were scored when the Wildcats tried to punt from their 20. Kavanaugh was able to break through the line and block the punt into the end zone. The North Little Rock punter chased the ball into the end zone and fell on it for a safety, rather than allowing Tigers a chance to recover the ball for a touchdown.

Little Rock only needed those two points to defeat the Wildcats. Thorpe carried 25 times for 144 yards in the 2-0 victory.

1934 TIGER SCHEDULE

Forrest City 7	LRHS 42
Russellville 0	LRHS 21
Byrd High of Shreveport, LA 14	LRHS 0
Fordyce 0	LRHS 20
Hot Springs 13	LRHS 0
Central High of Memphis, TN 44	LRHS 0
Fort Smith 0	LRHS 25
Searcy 7	LRHS 49
Pine Bluff 18	LRHS 7
Hope 0	LRHS 10
North Little Rock 0	LRHS 2

QUIGLEY'S LAST SEASON AS HEAD COACH

1935   5-5-1

Head Coach: Earl F. Quigley
Assistants: Homer Berry, LeRoy Scott
Team Trainer: Riley "Doc" Johns
Team Physicians: Dr. Wells Farrin Smith, Dr. Theo Freedman

[1935 TEAM PHOTO NOT AVAILABLE]

1935 LETTERMEN

Leo Ambort	Billy Glover	Kenneth Kavanaugh	Seth McElvaney
William Anderson	Lloyd Heitman	Gaughan Lewis	Howard Pearce
James Biddle	Max Holiman	Robert Majors	Wilfred Thorpe
Billy Edwards	Leon Hoffman	Owen Marrow	Halliburton Ware
J.B. Evans	P.D. Huff	Lowell Martindale	Eugene Wayman

1935 MANAGERS
Ellis Gardener
Billy Lusby
Joe Stanley
Clarence Young

1935 ALL-STATE
Kenneth Kavanaugh
Howard Pearce

On Sept. 2, seven returning lettermen reported to Kavanaugh Field for practice. Among the lettermen not returning was quarterback Charles Driver, who transferred to a military academy. Finding a replacement at quarterback was the highest priority for Coach Earl Quigley, who was extremely anxious about the situation.

Little Rock opened the season with a surprising upset to the Clarksville Panthers. The Tigers crossed into Clarksville territory only once during a 10-0 loss.

Little Rock also had a tough game the following week when Coach Lee Dobson and his Shreveport Byrd High Yellow Jackets traveled to Kavanaugh Field.

Byrd High had won the Louisiana state championship four out of the last five years and returned 11 lettermen from the previous season.

The Tigers put up a good fight, highlighted by touchdown passes of 53 and 45 yards from Billy Glover to Kenneth Kavanaugh.

Two touchdowns, however, were not enough in a 22-13 loss to the powerful Shreveport team.

After another loss to an out-of-state team, Central High of Oklahoma City, Little Rock returned to in-state competition when it traveled to Fordyce.

The Tigers were without Glover because of a leg injury and Wilfred Thorpe, who had contracted malaria.

Photo provided by the Arkansas Democrat-Gazette
Little Rock's 1935 starting offense

Owen Marrow (78) with Kenneth Kavanaugh

The game was scoreless until midway through the third quarter when Lloyd Heitman scored on a 1-yard run. Kavanaugh added a score when he intercepted a pass and returned it 80 yards for a touchdown in the fourth quarter. Little Rock's last score came when Halliburton Ware passed to Kavanaugh for a 30-yard touchdown.

The Tigers defeated the Redbugs 18-0 for their first victory of the season.

Hot Springs claimed a share of the state title in 1934 and returned six starters from its championship team. The Trojans were strong contenders to win the championship for a second consecutive year when they met Little Rock with a 4-0-0 record.

More than 4,000 fans showed up at Kavanaugh Field and watched Hot Springs score first when Paul Longinotti ran 56 yards for a touchdown late in the first quarter.

From the Hot Springs 36 on Little Rock's next possession, Ware faked a punt on fourth down and completed a pass to Kavanaugh, who was brought down at the 2. Thorpe ran the 2 yards for a touchdown and a 6-6 tie.

Early in the second half, Hot Springs regained the lead when Longinotti ran 32 yards for another score.

Late in the third quarter, Little Rock fielded a punt at the Hot Springs 35. During the ensuing series, Ware passed to Thorpe for a touchdown. Lowell Martindale kicked the game-winning extra point to put the Tigers up 13-12.

But the Tigers padded their lead when Max Holiman scored on a 10-yard run, Ware scored on a 68-yard run and Martindale ran 4 yards for a touchdown.

Longinotti finished with 147 yards rushing. Ware rushed for 140 yards and passed for 142 yards. The Tigers were able to upset the favored Trojans 33-12.

The following week, Coach Quigley started four sophomores against Central High of Memphis. Even with this inexperience, Little Rock scored first following a drive of 66 yards, highlighted by a 35-yard run by Ware.

After receiving the ensuing kickoff, the Warriors used an aerial display to drive more than 60 yards and score on a 35-yard pass from Billy Barnes to Bill Venn.

With the score tied 6-6 late in the second quarter, Martindale recovered a Memphis fumble at the Warriors 21. On Little Rock's next play, Martindale passed to Kavanaugh. Kavanaugh immediately pitched the ball to Ware, who then ran across the goal line for another touchdown.

The half ended just after Martindale missed the extra-point attempt.

Little Rock still had the momentum when Thorpe scored on a 55-yard run to increase its lead to 18-6 midway through the third quarter.

Venn returned the ensuing kickoff 70 yards for a touchdown. The extra point cut the Tigers' lead to 18-13.

Wilfred Thorpe (right)

Little Rock scored once more, this time in the fourth quarter after recovering another Memphis fumble.

Glover passed to William Anderson for a 15-yard touchdown. Glover also converted the extra point to give the Tigers a 25-13 victory.

At Andrews Field in Fort Smith, the Grizzlies and Little Rock ended the first half scoreless.

The second half, though, found the teams combining to score five touchdowns. However, the final did not favor the Tigers.

Fort Smith completed nine passes for 140 yards and two touchdowns to beat Little Rock 20-12.

After a 79-yard drive, the Tigers scored first on a 1-yard run by Martindale. Fort Smith then tied the score on its next possession with a 29-yard touchdown pass.

Early in the fourth quarter, Little Rock scored again on a short plunge by Holiman. The Grizzlies tied the score again on a 3-yard pass. One minute later, Fort Smith recovered a fumble and drove the field to score again. The game-winning score occurred when quarterback Grover Fuller ran up the middle for a 3-yard touchdown.

After passing for 179 yards the following week to defeat Benton High School, the Tigers prepared for their annual battle with the Zebras of Pine Bluff.

Pine Bluff was building a new stadium and set up temporary bleachers for the

Photo provided by the Arkansas Democrat-Gazette
Halliburton Ware (far right) intercepts a Benton pass

Little Rock fans. As fans were waiting for the game to begin, two women injured their ankles and one man broke his leg when one set of temporary bleachers collapsed. The injuries required the three fans to be hospitalized, but they were released later in the day.

The game went on as scheduled and did not go as well as the Tigers had hoped. The Zebras rushed for 295 yards, with the bulk gained by Eddie Craven.

Craven, "Dub" McGibbony and Frank Reed each scored one touchdown to beat Little Rock 20-0. The Tigers passed for 101 yards, but also threw seven interceptions, two that set up Pine Bluff's touchdowns.

With their fifth consecutive victory over Little Rock, the Zebras were guaranteed at least a share of the 1935 state championship.

The next week, the Tigers twice had possession inside the Russellville 4 but were unable to score.

As a result of a sloppy offensive performance, Little Rock came away with a disappointing 0-0 tie against the Cyclones.

More than 5,000 fans filled Kavanaugh Field for the second Thanksgiving Day game with North Little Rock High School.

After a scoreless first quarter, the Tigers received a punt at the Wildcats 49. Little Rock drove the 49 yards, capped by Martindale's 1-yard run to put the Tigers up 6-0.

In the fourth quarter, North Little Rock's Freddy Goss, from the 4, fumbled into the end zone. An offensive lineman jumped on the ball to tie the score at 6-6.

Photo provided by the Arkansas Democrat-Gazette
Kenneth Kavanaugh catching a pass

134

Little Rock later received a punt on its 35. Ware then passed for 36 yards to the North Little Rock 29.

Ware passed again, this time to Kavanaugh, for a 29-yard touchdown. Martindale kicked the extra point and the Tigers defeated the Wildcats 13-6.

With the continuing growth of Little Rock's athletic programs, Coach Quigley's duties were increasing as well. Because of this increased responsibility, Coach Quigley accepted a promotion to full-time athletic director of the Little Rock School District. This enabled him to turn his football program over to a younger man.

Coach Quigley ended his career with a record of 134-52-9, leading Little Rock to five state championships.

Quigley left after winning more football games than any other coach in Little Rock history. He did, however, remain the school's head track coach.

1935 TIGER SCHEDULE

Clarksville 10	LRHS 0
Byrd High of Shreveport, LA 22	LRHS 13
Central High of Oklahoma City, OK 25	LRHS 7
Fordyce 0	LRHS 18
Hot Springs 12	LRHS 33
Central High of Memphis, TN 13	LRHS 25
Fort Smith 20	LRHS 12
Benton 6	LRHS 20
Pine Bluff 20	LRHS 0
Russellville 0	LRHS 0
North Little Rock 6	LRHS 13

A NEW COACH IN A NEW STADIUM

1936   6-3-2

Head Coach: Clyde Van Sickle
Assistants: Homer Berry, LeRoy Scott
Team Trainer: Riley "Doc" Johns
Team Physicians: Dr. Wells Farrin Smith, Dr. Theo Freedman

1936 LETTERMEN

Leo Ambort	Hamilton Gunn	Robert Majors	Norman Schmuck
Billy Edwards	Lloyd Heitman	Lowell Martindale	Eugene Wayman
J.B. Evans	Leon Hoffman	Don McConnell	
Richard Gardiol	Albert Kopert	Seth McElvaney	
Joe Green	Gaughan Lewis	John Russell	

1936 MANAGERS
Robert Eubanks
John Hunt
Jack Miller
Herbert Reiman

1936 ALL-STATE
Leo Ambort
Lowell Martindale

For the first time in 17 years, a new head football coach met the Tigers as they arrived for workouts Sept. 1.

Clyde Van Sickle, a star offensive lineman for the University of Arkansas and the Green Bay Packers, left as head coach at Cisco High School in Cisco, Texas, to take over for Coach Earl Quigley.

A new stadium was built just behind historic

Photo provided by the Arkansas Democrat-Gazette
The east stands at Tiger Stadium still under construction

Photo provided by the Arkansas Democrat-Gazette
Robert Majors (79)

Kavanaugh Field and was dedicated to Little Rock High School prior to the Sept. 18 season opener.

But construction on the east stands, permanent lighting and a concrete wall around the new athletic facility were still unfinished.

The east stands would house the coaching offices, training room and the home and visiting dressing rooms.

Because of the ongoing construction, temporary lighting was used and both visiting and home fans had to share the west stands.

While Little Rock played in the new stadium, it began practicing on Kavanaugh Field.

The first opponent in new Tiger Stadium was Little Rock Catholic. The first meeting between the schools pitted former Arkansas Razorback stars against each other, Van Sickle and Rockets Coach Tom Murphy. Coach Murphy, the Southwest Conference MVP in 1933, was in his second year as head coach of the Rockets.

More than 5,000 fans watched Catholic High outplay Little Rock most of the game. The Rockets struck first on their opening possession when they drove 77 yards and scored on a 6-yard run. Tunnis Bishop kicked the extra point for a 7-0 lead.

A second-quarter fumble recovery by Little Rock on the Catholic 22 set up Lowell Martindale's 1-yard touchdown run.

The extra-point attempt failed and the Rockets still led 7-6.

In the second quarter, the Rockets drove 40 yards for a touchdown. Bishop scored from the 2 and kicked the extra point to put Catholic up 14-6.

Midway through the third quarter, Catholic ran out of downs at its 30. Little Rock then reached the 3, with Martindale scoring from there and kicking the extra point to make it 14-13.

The Tigers caught a break late in the fourth quarter after running out of downs at the Catholic 18. The Rockets received a 15-yard penalty, and from the 3, quarterback H.A. Mayer dropped to pass and was tackled in the end zone by Little Rock's Billy Edwards for a safety. This allowed the Tigers to escape with a 15-14 victory.

It wasn't long until Little Rock suffered its first loss in the new stadium.

The following week, Central High of Oklahoma City dominated the Tigers. Little Rock crossed midfield only once, and three fumbles resulted in touchdowns for the visiting team. Little Rock was beaten 38-0.

It didn't get any better the next week when the Tigers traveled to Shreveport, only to lose to Byrd High 26-7.

Following two consecutive losses, Little Rock's fortunes didn't appear any brighter when it met Fordyce High School at Tiger Stadium. The Redbugs, who returned 13 lettermen, were undefeated and boasted one of their strongest teams in years.

Little Rock's luck did change, though, when Martindale scored four touchdowns and kicked four extra points to defeat the strong Fordyce team 28-0.

Little Rock's Hamilton Gunn intercepted a pass at the Fordyce 21 to set up Martindale's first score, a 1-yard run in the second quarter. On the Tigers' next possession, Binks Bushmaier passed to Norman Schmuck for a 34-yard gain to the Fordyce 5. Martindale scored two plays later and kicked his second extra point to make it 14-0.

In the fourth quarter, Little Rock's Leo Ambort returned an interception to the Redbugs 17. Martindale eventually scored from the 2 and converted the extra point to extend the lead to 21-0.

Martindale's last touchdown came on a 53-yard interception return.

An overflow crowd of more than 6,000 at Rix Stadium in Hot Springs watched Little Rock's next game. The Hot Springs High School Trojans, who returned 15 veterans, were undefeated and considered one of the state's best teams.

Hot Springs played most of the game without star quarterback Paul Longinotti, who was nursing an injury suffered the previous week. He was taken out of the game against the Tigers when the injury became worse.

After the game ended in a 0-0 tie, the *Arkansas Democrat* labeled each team's defense "outstanding."

The game was highlighted by Bushmaier's three punts, all more than 60 yards, and the Little Rock defense, which held the Trojans to two first downs. The Hot Springs defense recorded seven interceptions, the Tigers had six.

Little Rock had its second consecutive tie the following week, 6-6, the result of a missed extra-point attempt against Central High of Memphis.

The week after a 45-0 homecoming victory over Fort Smith, Little Rock received some bad news when the Arkansas Athletic Association ruled Bushmaier ineligible because he was not a resident of Little Rock.

His father was a resident of Van Buren and his mother was living in an apartment in Little Rock. Since his parents were neither separated nor divorced, the Association ruled that Bushmaier temporarily lived in Little Rock only to play football. This was a violation of an Association rule and Bushmaier was ruled ineligible.

Melvin White, Bushmaier's replacement, led the Tigers against Clarksville High School during the next game.

White took advantage of his playing time, throwing to Howard Hughes for a 24-yard touchdown and to Gunn for another 24-yard touchdown.

Lloyd Heitman scored Little Rock's final touchdown on a 9-yard run in a 20-7 victory over Clarksville.

Even with ticket prices raised to $1.50 for the Pine Bluff game, an overflow crowd of more than 9,000 resulted in the gates being closed 15 minutes prior to kickoff.

Pine Bluff scored first when "Dub" McGibbony passed to Virgil Benson for a 22-yard touchdown. The extra-point attempt was blocked, but the Zebras led 6-0 in the first quarter.

Little Rock scored in the third quarter when Gunn returned a punt 70 yards for a touchdown. Martindale converted the extra point for a 7-6 lead. Pine Bluff, though, scored on its next possession when McGibbony again passed to Benson, this time for a 10-yard touchdown. The extra-point kick was again blocked and the Zebras led 12-6.

To open the fourth quarter, McGibbony punted to the Tigers. Gunn received the kick and returned it 5 yards to the Little Rock 43. On third down, White passed to Hughes, who immediately pitched the ball to Schmuck.

Schmuck broke two tackles before being brought down at the Pine Bluff 1. Martindale scored on the next play to give Little Rock a 13-12 victory.

The Tigers beat the Zebras for the first time since 1930, and for only the second time since 1923. Following the game, the *Arkansas Gazette* quoted former Coach

Photo provided by the Arkansas Democrat-Gazette
Howard Hughes (62)

138

Photo provided by the Arkansas Democrat-Gazette
Robert Majors (72)

Quigley as saying: "God has moved back to Little Rock."

Little Rock and Blytheville were the only major high schools undefeated against Arkansas competition, and the Tigers needed to win their next two games to claim the championship. Little Rock's next game, though, would end that chance.

The Russellville Cyclones dominated the Tigers. Little Rock passed for 180 yards but threw eight interceptions and had no rushing yards.

Russellville's two touchdowns and James Keeton's 113 yards rushing were enough to beat the Tigers 14-7 and end any hope of a championship season for Little Rock.

The Tigers may have played with overconfidence against the Cyclones, but they played with extreme determination the next week against North Little Rock.

More than 5,000 fans at Tiger Stadium on Thanksgiving Day saw White, Martindale and Robert Majors each score touchdowns in a 21-0 victory over the Wildcats. Little Rock outclassed North Little Rock with a powerful running game to record its sixth consecutive victory over the Wildcats.

On Dec. 3, the Arkansas Razorbacks and the Texas Longhorns christened Little Rock's new Tiger Stadium with the first college football game. More than 8,000 fans braved the rain to watch the Razorbacks battle for the Southwest Conference championship.

Arkansas defeated the Longhorns 6-0, ending the season with a 5-1-1 conference record and the championship.

1936 TIGER SCHEDULE

Little Rock Catholic 14	LRHS 15
Central High of Oklahoma City, OK 38	LRHS 0
Byrd High of Shreveport, LA 26	LRHS 7
Fordyce 0	LRHS 28
Hot Springs 0	LRHS 0
Central High of Memphis, TN 6	LRHS 6
Fort Smith 0	LRHS 45
Clarksville 7	LRHS 20
Pine Bluff 12	LRHS 13
Russellville 14	LRHS 7
North Little Rock 0	LRHS 21

139

A MISSED EXTRA-POINT ATTEMPT PROVES COSTLY

1937   9-1-1

Head Coach: Clyde Van Sickle
Assistants: Homer Berry, LeRoy Scott
Team Trainer: Riley "Doc" Johns
Team Physicians: Dr. Wells Farrin Smith, Dr. Theo Freedman

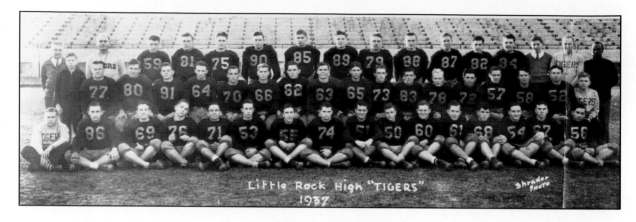

1937 LETTERMEN

Leo Ambort	Terry Fields	Albert Kopert	Norman Schmuck
Tom Burrows	Estes Freeland	Billy Maack	Tom Spaulding
Binks Bushmaier	Richard Gardiol	Lowell Martindale	Wallace Stalnaker
Harry Carter	Joe Green	Don McConnell	Robert Thomas
Walter Crowson	Lloyd Heitman	Rex Mize	Louis Walters
Bill Donham	Leon Hoffman	Leland Pritchard	Melvin White
Billy Edwards	Howard Hughes	John Russell	

1937 MANAGERS
Robert Pettus
Linden Rainwater

1937 ALL-STATE
Leon Hoffman
Lowell Martindale
Don McConnell

Eleven lettermen returned to Little Rock High School for the 1937 season. The campaign saw the Tigers in the newly formed Arkansas High School Athletic Conference, which included Benton, Blytheville, Camden, Clarksville, El Dorado, Fordyce, Forrest City, Fort Smith, Hope, Hot Springs, Jonesboro, North Little Rock, Pine Bluff and Russellville.

Little Rock opened the season with a nonconference home game against Little Rock Catholic. The Tigers tallied 23 first downs and held the Rockets to only two.

Little Rock's Binks Bushmaier and Howard Hughes each scored two touchdowns. Melvin White, Lowell Martindale, Wallace Stalnaker and Leon Hoffman each had one score in a 50-0 victory.

The victory came with a price, however. Quarterback Hamilton Gunn was lost for the season when he injured his knee during the game.

Without their starting quarterback, the Tigers headed to Muskogee, Okla., to take on powerful Central High School.

After an uneventful first half, Little Rock kicked off to open the second half. Muskogee's Jack Jacobs fielded the kick and returned it for a touchdown. The extra-point attempt failed, but the Oklahoma team led 6-0.

Late in the fourth quarter, White passed to Hughes to reach the Muskogee 11. Three plays later from the 1, Hughes ran between the center and right guard to tie the score. Martindale kicked the game-winning extra point in a 7-6 victory.

The following week, the Tigers hosted Byrd High of Shreveport. The Yellow Jackets returned several lettermen from a team that defeated Little Rock the previous season and finished 8-1.

Memories of this beating came rushing back to the Tigers when Byrd High recovered Lloyd Heitman's fumble at the Little Rock 15 on the opening kickoff. On Byrd's fifth play, it scored on a reverse and converted the extra point for a 7-0 lead.

A punt by the Yellow Jackets late in the fourth quarter backed up the Tigers to their 18. On the next play, White dropped back and passed to Hughes, who sprinted 82 yards for a touchdown. Martindale kicked the extra point to make it 7-7.

Defenses for both teams kept the remainder of the game scoreless in a 7-7 tie.

Coach Sam Coleman brought his Camden Panthers to Tiger Stadium the following week, the first conference game of the season for the Tigers.

More than 7,000 fans watched Martindale provide the only points of the first half on a 36-yard field goal in the second quarter.

A Camden punt ended the third quarter and gave Little Rock possession on its 34. On the first play, White passed to Hughes for a 66-yard touchdown.

Photo provided by the Arkansas Democrat-Gazette
Don McConnell (left) and Wallace Stalnaker

White set up the second touchdown after he intercepted a Camden pass and returned it to the Little Rock 47.

White was sacked for a 15-yard loss on the first play, but gained it back when he passed to Leo Ambort for 17 yards on the next play. White then passed to Martindale, who pitched to Don McConnell for a 7-yard gain and a first down.

White ran for 17 yards on the next play to the Camden 27. He then picked up another yard before Bushmaier gained 7 yards. White passed to Martindale for 10 yards. Hughes ran the final 9 yards for the score. Martindale converted the extra point to complete the Tigers' 16-0 victory.

Little Rock played at home again the next week, and more than 6,000 fans watched the Tigers total 337 yards of offense against the Hot Springs Trojans.

On the first play of the second quarter, J.R. Smith scored on a 62-yard run to put Hot Springs up 6-0. Little Rock answered two possessions later when it drove 63 yards with Bushmaier scoring on a 4-yard run. Martindale missed the extra-point attempt and the score was tied 6-6.

In the third quarter, White capped a 67-yard drive with a 10-yard touchdown run. Midway through the fourth quarter, Martindale scored from the 1 to end a 60-yard drive and put the Tigers up 19-6.

Homecoming queen Betty Hewitt with Lowell Martindale

Reserve Louis Walters sealed the victory when he intercepted a Smith pass and returned it 25 yards for Little Rock's fourth touchdown. Hughes kicked the extra point to put the Tigers up 26-6.

Following 195 yards passing in a 32-0 victory over Fort Smith, Little Rock hosted Central High of Memphis.

A small homecoming crowd of approximately 3,000 watched Miss Betty Hewitt crowned homecoming queen during pregame ceremonies.

The celebration continued as Coach Clyde Van Sickle used 42 players. Eleven scored touchdowns, including a 70-yard punt return by Hughes and a 40-yard interception return by defensive lineman McConnell.

The Tigers finished with 370 yards passing in an 85-6 domination of the Warriors.

After a 40-0 victory over Jonesboro, Little Rock traveled to Pine Bluff for its annual matchup with the Zebras. At stake for both teams was a chance to win the conference and state championship.

Pine Bluff was looking for its eighth conference victory and the title. If the Tigers won, they would have to win their two remaining conference games to be named champions.

More than 10,500 fans, the largest crowd ever to watch a high school or college football game in Arkansas, packed Pine Bluff's Jordan Stadium.

The game began with the Zebras recovering a fumble on the opening kickoff. Little Rock, however, held Pine Bluff on downs to gain possession at its 20.

From the 45, Stalnaker went over the right tackle, cut to his left, stiff-armed the first Zebra who met him and sprinted through the secondary for a 55-yard touchdown. Martindale missed the extra-point attempt, but Pine Bluff was offside. Martindale also missed his second attempt and the Tigers led 6-0.

The Zebras returned the ensuing kickoff to their 42. Bill Phillips passed to Ed Carey on a screen play for 28 yards to Little Rock's 30. Pine Bluff gained 2 yards on a short run, and then Phillips passed to Ogden Bolin for a 28-yard touchdown. Bolin converted the extra point for a 7-6 Pine Bluff lead.

The defense for each team battled hard the remainder of the game, but Pine Bluff's extra point gave it the victory.

The *Arkansas Gazette* labeled the game as "one of the most sensational games in the history of the [Pine Bluff–Little Rock] series."

Stalnaker fractured his right ankle in the game and missed the remainder of the season.

Pine Bluff's Ogden Bolin (left) intercepts a pass intended for Leon Hoffman

Hughes was the hero against a rebuilding Fordyce team the following week. He capped Little Rock's first possession with a 20-yard touchdown run, scored again just before halftime on a 42-yard pass reception and recorded a 70-yard punt.

Fordyce Coach Russell Charles saw his team suffer a 43-0 defeat in front of a homecoming crowd of only 400.

Photo provided by the Arkansas Democrat-Gazette

Little Rock vs. North Little Rock on Thanksgiving Day

The fourth annual Thanksgiving Day game with North Little Rock was played at Tiger Stadium in front of 8,500 fans. The Wildcats were 8-2-0, the Tigers 8-1-1.

North Little Rock took the opening kickoff and kept possession most of the first quarter, scoring just before the period ended to take a 7-0 lead. Hughes, however, took the ensuing kickoff and returned it 63 yards for a touchdown. Little Rock missed the extra-point attempt and the Wildcats held their lead.

Martindale capped a 59-yard drive in the second quarter with a 1-yard touchdown run. The extra point was good and the Tigers took a 13-7 lead.

Little Rock threatened to score again, moving to the Wildcats 9. But a goal-line stand forced the Tigers to turn the ball over on downs.

On North Little Rock's ensuing possession, Lester Stinson took the ball from Mike Gross on an end-around play. The ball, though, bounced out of Stinson's hands and into the end zone. Both teams dove for the ball, but it rolled out of the end zone for a Little Rock safety.

The Tigers won their seventh consecutive game over North Little Rock since renewing the rivalry in 1931.

1937 TIGER SCHEDULE

LR Catholic 0	LRHS 50
Central High of Muskogee, OK 6	LRHS 7
Byrd High of Shreveport, LA 7	LRHS 7
*Camden 0	LRHS 16
*Hot Springs 6	LRHS 26
*Fort Smith 0	LRHS 32
Central High of Memphis, TN 6	LRHS 85
*Jonesboro 0	LRHS 40
*Pine Bluff 7	LRHS 6
*Fordyce 0	LRHS 43
*North Little Rock 7	LRHS 15

THE CHAMPIONSHIP RETURNS TO LITTLE ROCK

1938   10-0-1

Head Coach: Clyde Van Sickle
Assistants: Homer Berry, LeRoy Scott
Team Trainer: Riley "Doc" Johns
Team Physician: Dr. Theo Freedman

1938 LETTERMEN

Leo Ambort	Walter Crowson	Howard Hughes	Byron Spaulding
Bill Atkinson	Billy Edwards	Albert Kopert	Tom Spaulding
Carl Baer	Estes Freeland	Billy Maack	Robert Thomas
Wesley Bernard	Richard Gardiol	Rex Mize	Louis Walters
Kelton Brown	Joe Green	Louie Nickell	Melvin White
Harry Carter	A.C. Hinton	John Russell	

1938 MANAGERS
Warren Brown
Harry Cooke
John McDowell
Rose Richardson
George Wittenberg

1938 ALL-STATE
Leo Ambort
Harry Carter
Howard Hughes
Albert Kopert

144

Fifty-three players reported to Coach Clyde Van Sickle for preseason practice. For the first several weeks of practice, however, the Tigers were without star running back Howard Hughes.

Hughes was in Chicago playing in the National Softball Championship. Hughes' team, International Harvester, advanced to the championship game, but was defeated by Cincinnati 2-1. Hughes would not return to Little Rock until after the Tigers' opener against Malvern High School.

In front of 5,000 fans at Tiger Stadium, Bill Atkinson replaced Hughes at halfback and helped Little Rock to a 37-6 season-opening victory. Little Rock was again the site of the Tigers' next game against Central High of Muskogee, Okla.

Central was a highly regarded team in Oklahoma and favored to win the state championship. Little Rock, however, had no problems with the Oklahoma power-house in a 39-6 victory.

The Tigers' first road game was against Byrd High in Shreveport.

More than 6,000 fans watched as Little Rock took a 13-0 first-half lead. The Tigers added to the lead when Billy Edwards blocked a Jerry Mize punt at the Byrd 23. The ball bounced to the 5, where Billy Maack scooped it up and ran into the end zone for a 19-0 lead.

Early in the second half, Edwards blocked another punt by Mize at the Byrd 25. After Little Rock recovered, Melvin White ran off right tackle for an 8-yard gain on first down.

On the next play, White pitched to Leo Ambort, who ran for the touchdown. White kicked the extra point for a 26-0 lead.

Albert Kopert then recovered a fumble for the Tigers at the Byrd 36. White and Atkinson each picked up yards to move the ball to the 3. Raymond Rolf ran for a touchdown and a 32-0 lead.

Reserves scored when Byron Spaulding passed to Bedford Smith for a 42-yard touchdown late in the fourth quarter of a 38-0 victory.

The Louisiana newspapers declared the 1938 Little Rock team as "the best team to ever invade Shreveport." The Tigers handed Byrd High School its worst defeat in 10 years.

Little Rock was back home the next week to face Blytheville. Blytheville was undefeated the previous three seasons, but came into this game having lost to Pine Bluff two weeks earlier.

More than 9,000 fans at Tiger Stadium watched both teams battle for contention in the state championship race.

Midway through the first quarter, a short 33-yard drive was capped by Harry Carter's 2-yard touchdown run. The extra-point attempt failed, but Little Rock still took a 6-0 lead.

Blytheville scored early in the second quarter when White punted to Russell Mosley, who returned it 60 yards for a touchdown. The Chicks converted the extra point to take a 7-6 lead.

The Tigers took the ensuing kickoff and drove 60 yards for a touchdown. White scored on a 2-yard

Photo provided by Harry Donaldson

Pine Bluff attempts an extra point

145

run, then Spaulding converted the extra point for a 13-7 lead.

Blytheville took possession on its 37 after the kickoff. Two runs and a 17-yard pass got the Chicks to the Tigers 34. Mosley then passed for a 34-yard touchdown. The extra point was converted for a 14-13 Blytheville lead at halftime.

Little Rock kicked off to Blytheville to open the second half and the Chicks took possession at their 33. The drive stalled when John Russell intercepted a Mosley pass and returned it to the Blytheville 31.

Carter eventually pounded his way into the end zone from the 1 to put the Tigers up 19-14.

Late in the third quarter, Bill Goodwin intercepted an Atkinson pass at the Blytheville 45. Mosley then passed 47 yards to the Little Rock 8. He threw a touchdown pass on the next play. The extra point was good as Chicks regained the lead 21-19.

As the fourth quarter opened, Carter capped an 89-yard drive with a 3-yard run. The extra point gave the Tigers a 26-21 lead.

Russell recovered a Mosley fumble on Blytheville's next possession, resulting in another touchdown for Little Rock. Tom Spaulding accounted for the tally when he scored on a short run. The extra point put the Tigers up 33-21.

Hughes rushed for 115 yards in Little Rock's victory.

Hot Springs High School was the site of the Tigers' next game. More than 4,000 fans watched Little Rock take the lead early in the first quarter on a 50-yard touchdown pass from White to Maack.

A Trojan defender missed the interception attempt and knocked the ball backward into the hands of Maack, who then turned and stepped into the end zone.

The Tigers drove 63 yards on their next posses-

146

sion, with Hughes scoring on a short run to increase Little Rock's lead.

The Tigers ended their scoring after a Tom Spaulding interception set up a 35-yard drive and a 5-yard touchdown run by Carter.

With just seconds remaining in the game, an unsportsmanlike penalty was called against a player from each team. As a result, the two players involved began exchanging blows as soon as the gun sounded to end the game.

A brawl immediately erupted between the teams and many spectators soon joined in the scuffle. Police were unprepared for such an event and remained helpless throughout the fight. The situation, though, soon settled itself and no one was seriously injured.

Homecoming and a game against Fort Smith awaited Little Rock the following week.

Prior to the game, more than 6,000 fans cheered when Miss Virginia Lou Treischman was named homecoming queen.

Coach Ben Mayo's Grizzlies included seven two-year lettermen, but Fort Smith would not spoil Little Rock's night. Hughes got the night off to a good start when he took the opening kickoff from the end zone and returned it to the Little Rock 29. A 71-yard drive ended with a 1-yard dive by Carter.

After trading punts, the Tigers took possession at the Fort Smith 18 and moved to

Photo provided by Harry Donaldson

Little Rock throws an incomplete pass against Pine Bluff

the 7 with three running plays. Hughes then ran to the 3 before Carter scored from there to extend Little Rock's lead to 12-0. Carl Baer's extra point made it 13-0.

Midway through the fourth quarter, Fort Smith's night got even worse when team captain Claude DeShazo left the game by ambulance because of a fractured skull.

Later in the quarter, the lead grew when A.C. Hinton returned an interception 40 yards for a touchdown.

Little Rock was victorious over the Grizzlies 19-0.

The Tigers defeated Tennessee rival Central High School of Memphis before taking on the Fordyce Redbugs. Little Rock's defense forced Fordyce to punt on its first possession. Hughes fielded the punt at the 50 and returned it 20 yards to the 30. On the Tigers' fifth offensive play, Carter ran 20 yards for a touchdown.

Hughes returned the Redbugs' next punt 38 yards to the Fordyce 27. Three plays later, he scored on a 12-yard run around right end. The extra-point attempt was missed and Little Rock led 13-0.

Later in the first quarter, Richard Gardiol recovered a fumble at the Fordyce 35. Tom Spaulding gained 20 yards up the middle before Atkinson ran to the 6. It took Carter three plays to reach the end zone, but the score gave the Tigers a 19-0 advantage. After a Hughes touchdown run in the third quarter, reserves played the remainder of the game and scored once more to give Little Rock a 39-7 victory.

A state-record crowd of 13,000 packed Tiger Stadium to watch Little Rock and Pine Bluff in their annual battle. Coach Allen Dunaway stated during the week leading up to the game that his Zebras "should get whipped by at least 30 points." The game, though, would be anything but a runaway for either team.

After a scoreless first half, Pine Bluff struck first when Hughes was intercepted by W.S. Lafitte, who returned it 45 yards for a Pine Bluff touchdown. The extra point gave the Zebras a 7-0 lead.

Later in the first quarter, a punt by Ray Hutson netted only 11 yards and gave the

Photo provided by the Arkansas Democrat-Gazette
Billy Edwards (left) **and Albert Kopert**

Tigers possession on the Zebras 35. On the Tigers' first play, Hughes went through the right side of the line, cut to his left and went untouched for a touchdown. Baer kicked the extra point to make it 7-7.

In the third quarter, Pine Bluff's Everett Payne punted to Hughes, who returned it 9 yards to the Zebras 34. Five plays later, Hughes ran around right end for a 6-yard touchdown. Baer again converted the extra point to give Little Rock a 14-7 lead.

On Pine Bluff's next series, Payne connected with Hutson for a 45-yard pass completion to the Tigers 5. After a 2-yard loss on the next play, Payne dropped back to pass on third down, but was sacked by Wesley Bernard for a 13-yard loss. Little Rock, however, was penalized for holding and the ball was moved forward. The Zebras scored a fourth-quarter touchdown. Payne's extra point made it 14-14.

The Tigers had two more possessions but could not move against the Zebras. Little Rock's last play was an incomplete pass into the end zone by Byron Spaulding.

The game ended in a tie, but the statistics heavily favored the Tigers. Little Rock had 234 total offensive yards compared to 69 total yards by Pine Bluff. Hughes stood out for Little Rock with 28 carries for 122 yards.

Following a victory over the Camden Panthers, more than 12,000 fans began their

Photo provided by the Arkansas Democrat-Gazette
Pine Bluff's Ray Hutson and two Little Rock defenders

Thanksgiving Day by watching the annual Little Rock-North Little Rock game.

On the Wildcats' third possession, Dale Duckworth fumbled a snap from center and Kopert recovered for the Tigers on the North Little Rock 9. On Little Rock's first play, Atkinson ran off left tackle for the score. Baer kicked the extra point for a 7-0 lead.

A Hughes punt from his end zone gave the Wildcats possession at the Little Rock 40. A holding penalty against the Tigers moved North Little Rock closer, then Duckworth ran for a first down to the 10. George Zawislak passed to Duckworth for a North Little Rock touchdown. Duckworth converted the extra point for a 7-7 tie.

Following an exchange of punts to begin the third quarter, the Tigers were held on downs at the Wildcats 23. On North Little Rock's second play, Zawislak was intercepted by Carter, who took it to the Wildcats 17. Hughes ran around right end for the go-ahead touchdown. Baer's extra-point kick was wide and Little Rock led 13-7.

With just seconds remaining in the game, North Little Rock faced fourth down at the Tigers 4. The Wildcats' Bill Fortner was stopped at the 2, giving Little Rock possession. The Tigers let time expire to take a 13-7 victory over North Little Rock and claim their 12th state championship.

1938 TIGER SCHEDULE

Malvern 6	LRHS 37
Central High of Muskogee, OK 6	LRHS 39
Byrd High of Shreveport, LA 0	LRHS 38
*Blytheville 21	LRHS 33
*Hot Springs 6	LRHS 25
*Fort Smith 0	LRHS 19
Central High of Memphis, TN 6	LRHS 14
*Fordyce 7	LRHS 39
*Pine Bluff 14	LRHS 14
*Camden 0	LRHS 26
*North Little Rock 7	LRHS 13

A GREAT YEAR FOR THE ZEBRAS

1939   9-1-1

Head Coach: Clyde Van Sickle
Assistants: Homer Berry, LeRoy Scott
Team Trainer: Riley "Doc" Johns
Team Physician: Dr. Theo Freedman

1939 LETTERMEN

Kelton Brown	Estes Freeland	Billy Maack	Charles Steed
Harry Carter	Richard Gardiol	Wayne Marshall	Robert Thomas
Jack Chaney	A.C. Hinton	Osborne McMurry	Benjy Waddle
Walter Crowson	Howard Hughes	Raymond Rolf	
Harry Donaldson	Homer Kinney	Beford Smith	

1939 MANAGERS
G. Blass
T.A. Booth
C.C. Collie
L.C. Steiner
J. Strom

1939 ALL-STATE
Howard Hughes
Billy Maack

Photo provided by Harry Donaldson

Howard Hughes vs. North Little Rock

Little Rock lost six great players to graduation the previous spring, and 40 candidates reported to preseason practice hoping to fill the vacancies.

Coming off a state championship, the Tigers were a heavy favorite to repeat as champions. Another team that was thought to have a great chance of dominating the state was Little Rock's old rival, Pine Bluff.

A.C. Hinton tackles Pine Bluff's Ray Hutson

The Tigers opened against the Benton Panthers. After an exchange of punts to begin the game, Little Rock took possession and used three plays and a penalty to advance to the Benton 20.

The Tigers moved 19 yards in three plays before Harry Carter took it the remaining yard for the score. Howard Hughes converted the extra-point attempt for a 7-0 lead.

Robert Thomas scored for Little Rock in the second quarter when he plunged in from the 1. Carter converted the extra point to increase the lead to 14-0.

An interception in the third quarter set up the Tigers' next score, a 37-yard run around left end by Wayne Marshall.

Another interception in the third quarter resulted in a touchdown for Little Rock as

well. A.C. Hinton intercepted a pass at the Tigers 15 and returned it 85 yards for Little Rock's final score.

The Tigers earned a 28-6 season-opening victory.

Little Rock hosted Shreveport's Byrd High School the following week.

Hinton kicked off to start the game and the ball rolled past Byrd's deep man and into the end zone. Hinton was the first man down the field and fell on the ball for a touchdown.

There would not be another score until the opening minutes of the second half.

The Tigers forced Byrd to punt on its first possession of the third quarter. Shreveport kicked from its 20 and Hughes fielded

Howard Hughes (75) vs. Camden

the ball at the Little Rock 40. He returned the punt 60 yards for the Tigers' second touchdown.

Later in the quarter, Little Rock's Kelton Brown recovered a fumble at the Byrd 20. This set the stage for a 2-yard scoring plunge by Carter.

The Tigers finished their scoring midway through the fourth quarter when Charles Steed returned a punt 50 yards for another touchdown.

Little Rock went on to defeat the Louisiana team 26-0 for its second victory of the season.

Blytheville High School was the site of a defensive battle the next week when the Tigers won a close game against the Chicks. Each team scored a touchdown in the first quarter, but a missed extra-point attempt by Blytheville would cost it the game.

Benjy Waddle's extra point for the Tigers proved to be the game-winning play as both defenses took over the game. Little Rock escaped 7-6.

Richard Gardiol, the Tigers' three-year starter at guard, broke his leg during the game and missed the remainder of the season.

The week prior to playing the Hot Springs Trojans, Little Rock temporarily lost another player. Hughes, the Tigers' star halfback, lost a finger during an accident in the school's wood-working class.

As he was working at the jointer saw during his manual training period, someone called to him. He turned to answer and his left hand came in contact with the blade, cutting off his second finger and the tip of his index finger.

Physicians were able to repair his index finger, but his middle finger was lost. He was required to sit out three weeks for the wounds to heal.

Without Hughes or Gardiol, Little Rock narrowly escaped Hot Springs. A third-quarter safety was the only scoring, a 2-0 outcome that kept the Tigers unbeaten in their last 17 games.

The celebration, however, ended the next week when Little Rock traveled to Fort Smith. The Grizzlies scored twice to defeat the Tigers 12-0 and snap their unbeaten streak.

For homecoming the following week, Little Rock hosted Central High of Memphis.

The homecoming queen, Miss Sidney Stiff, watched Memphis Central's Kenney Holland return a punt 87 yards in the third quarter for the game's first score.

Little Rock answered in the fourth quarter when a 50-yard drive ended with a 22-yard touchdown run by Steed on an end-around play.

On its next possession, Memphis turned the ball over on downs, giving the Tigers control on the Warriors 18. Little Rock moved to the 4 on its first-down play, and Steed covered the remaining distance on the next play to put the Tigers in front.

Little Rock scored once more when Marshall passed to Jack Chaney for a 40-yard touchdown in a 25-6 victory.

Following a 22-7 victory over Jonesboro, Little Rock traveled to Fordyce to take on the Redbugs.

Howard Hughes (75) vs. Pine Bluff

151

With Hughes back in the lineup, the Tigers moved at will. Hughes rushed for 55 yards on nine carries in the first quarter alone. Little Rock's initial score came early in the first quarter when a short drive resulted in an 8-yard touchdown run by Hughes.

Carter capped a 70-yard second-quarter drive with a short run for the Tigers' second touchdown. Hughes scored in the third quarter before Little Rock reserves played the remainder of the game.

The Tigers beat Fordyce 26-0.

Two inches of rain fell just before kick-off the next week in Pine Bluff. Still, more than 8,000 fans sat through the rain to watch Arkansas' annual high school football classic.

There was not much excitement as each team was hampered by the rain and mud, resulting in a defensive battle. The teams combined for only 10 first downs and 169 yards of total offense in a 0-0 tie.

It marked only the third tie since the series began in 1906.

A 26-7 victory over Camden brought Little Rock to the final game of the season, the annual Thanksgiving Day showdown with North Little Rock.

More than 5,000 fans braved a cold and rainy morning to see the Tigers once again involved in a defensive battle.

After a scoreless first quarter, the second quarter opened with Hughes punting from his 35. North Little Rock's Dale Duckworth backed up cautiously and let the ball fall near the Wildcats 15. The punt bounced and grazed Duckworth's foot. Little Rock's Billy Maack recovered at the Wildcats 11.

On the next play, Hughes took the handoff and went through the line, cut to his right and crossed into the end zone. The extra-point attempt was low, but the 6-0 lead for the Tigers was enough to win the game.

The Pine Bluff Zebras, 1939 Arkansas state champions, were invited to play for the high school national championship in Baton Rouge, La. The Zebras, whose record was marred only by a 0-0 tie to Little Rock, played Baton Rouge High School and represented Arkansas well.

Pine Bluff beat Baton Rouge 26-0 and won the national title for the second time in its football history.

1939 TIGER SCHEDULE

Benton 6	LRHS 28
Byrd High of Shreveport, LA 0	LRHS 26
*Blytheville 6	LRHS 7
*Hot Springs 0	LRHS 2
*Fort Smith 12	LRHS 0
Central High of Memphis, TN 6	LRHS 25
*Jonesboro 7	LRHS 22
*Fordyce 0	LRHS 26
*Pine Bluff 0	LRHS 0
*Camden 7	LRHS 26
*North Little Rock 0	LRHS 6

SLOW START TURNS INTO A WINNING RECORD

1940   7-4-0

Head Coach: Clyde Van Sickle
Assistants: Homer Berry, LeRoy Scott
Team Trainer: Riley "Doc" Johns
Team Physician: Dr. Theo Freedman

1940 LETTERMEN

Randall Atkinson	Harry Donaldson	Wayne Marshall	Billy Sims
Thomas Barksdale	Bill Fitzgibbons	Gerald McKinney	Bowman Starnes
Sam Coots	Clinton Fritts	Jimmy Morgan	Charles Vestal
Jimmy Crafton	Don Hudson	Raymond Rolf	

1940 MANAGERS
Bill Gulley
Phil Haskins
William McCombs
Curtis McGowan
Jack McKenzie

1940 ALL-STATE
Wayne Marshall
Jimmy Morgan

On Sept. 1, Coach Clyde Van Sickle and 53 hopefuls met at historic Kavanaugh Field to begin two-a-day practices. Only five of the 53 players, three running backs and two linemen, were returning lettermen.

After two weeks of practice, the Tigers opened the season by hosting the Malvern Leopards.

Malvern received the opening kickoff, but fumbled on its second play. Little Rock recovered at the Leopards 38.

A short pass and a run by Wayne Marshall moved the Tigers to the 27. Raymond Rolf gained 5 yards, then Clinton Fritts caught a 9-yard pass from Marshall.

Marshall gained 10 yards and finally scored on the next play. The extra-point attempt was wide and the Tigers led 6-0.

Malvern scored a touchdown in the second quarter when Rolf, attempting a pass from his 33, was intercepted by W.J. Hodges, who returned it for the score. The extra-point attempt hit the crossbar and the score remained 6-6.

Facing fourth down on the Leopards 30 late in the fourth quarter, Little Rock chose

153

Photo provided by Harry Donaldson

Wayne Marshall

to run instead of punting. The result was a 9-yard loss, forcing the Tigers to turn the ball over on downs.

After a 5-yard penalty, Malvern took over on its 34. A 13-yard pass from Hodges to Clint Fuller and a 21-yard pass completion from Eugene Rowe gave Malvern a first down on the Little Rock 32.

Rowe gained 12 yards for another first down at the 20. The Leopards then moved to the 2 following gains of 11 yards and 7 yards.

With 1:30 remaining in the game, Rowe picked up the remaining 2 yards for a 12-6 lead. The touchdown gave Coach Clyde Koon and his Leopards an upset victory over Little Rock in front of 4,000 fans at Tiger Stadium.

Little Rock went on to lose to Jonesboro (13-6) and Blytheville (21-0) before traveling to Rix Stadium in Hot Springs.

More than 6,000 fans cheered after J.C. Childs passed to Messers Dugan for an 18-yard touchdown for Hot Springs. Later, Dugan passed to Childs for a 9-yard touchdown, sealing a 13-0 victory over the Tigers. The loss dropped Little Rock to 0-4-0.

The Tigers' homecoming game brought Fort Smith to Tiger Stadium, where more than 5,000 fans watched winless Little Rock High School take on the undefeated Grizzlies.

After Little Rock turned the ball over on downs at the Fort Smith 34, a short pass and two runs moved the Grizzlies to the

Little Rock 45. A pass to Buddy Jaber then gained 32 yards.

After two plays netted a first-and-goal from the 3, it took the Grizzlies four plays to score. Jaber went in from the 1 for a 6-0 lead.

Rolf returned the ensuing kickoff to his 37. An offside penalty moved the ball to the 32, but Marshall broke loose on the first play and ran 40 yards to the Fort Smith 28.

Rolf went through the right side of the line on the next play and was tackled at the 4. Bowman Starnes then scored, with Marshall adding the extra point for a 7-6 lead.

Rolf returned the second-half kickoff to the Tigers 24. Marshall, Rolf and Starnes took the ball to the 35 before Rolf set up another Little Rock touchdown with a 46-yard run to the Grizzlies 19.

Marshall gained 9 yards in two plays and Starnes scored from the 10. The extra-point attempt failed, but the Tigers led 13-6. Fort Smith returned the ensuing kickoff to its 34. But on its first offensive play, Jimmy Crafton intercepted a pass to give Little Rock possession on the 26.

On Little Rock's sixth play, Marshall scored from the 5. Harry Donaldson kicked the extra point for a 20-6 lead.

Photo provided by the Arkansas Democrat-Gazette
Clinton Fritts (74)

With only two minutes remaining in the third quarter, the Grizzlies responded with a 40-yard touchdown run by Sterling Ramey. The extra-point attempt failed, but Fort Smith narrowed the deficit to 20-12.

On the Grizzlies' next possession, Jaber ran 82 yards for a touchdown on first down. The extra-point conversion was good to bring the Grizzlies within 20-19.

Fort Smith threatened to score again late in the game, driving to the Tigers 17. Little Rock's defense held the Grizzlies on downs and kept Fort Smith out of the end zone, enabling the Tigers to win their first game of the season.

The University of Arkansas and the University of Mississippi met at Crump Stadium in Memphis, where the Razorbacks beat the Rebels 21-20.

Just hours later, the Little Rock Tigers and the Memphis Central Warriors took the same field and played scoreless football for the first three quarters.

Midway through the fourth quarter, the Tigers took control on their 37. Five pass completions put Little Rock on the Warriors 2. Starnes scored from there for the game's only touchdown.

On the last play of the game, Marshall intercepted a pass at the Tigers 24 to end

Jimmy Morgan (left) and Jimmy Crafton

any hope of a Memphis touchdown. Little Rock beat the Warriors 6-0.

In another game as a heavy underdog, Little Rock hosted El Dorado High School the following week.

After an exchange of punts early in the game, the Wildcats took control at the Tigers 45. Ed Batchelor gained 12 yards on first down, then Kenny Reese picked up 2 more yards to the 31.

On the next play, Batchelor was knocked out of bounds at the 10 on a reverse. Reese gained 6 yards and then scored on a 4-yard run. Reese's extra-point attempt was wide and the Wildcats led 6-0.

Little Rock answered on the second play of the second quarter when Charles Vestal blocked Sam Lyle's punt at the 3. Marshall scored from the 1, but Donaldson's extra-point attempt failed to leave the score tied.

An interception by Rolf set up El Dorado's second touchdown.

The Wildcats took over at their 37 and moved to the Little Rock 45 in three plays. Lyle then caught a pass at the 20 and scored for a 12-6 lead.

In the third quarter, Donaldson blocked a Lyle punt and it was recovered by Bill Fitzgibbons at the El Dorado 23.

On fourth down, Rolf connected with Marshall for a 10-yard touchdown pass to tie the score. Marshall put the Tigers up for good, 13-12, with the extra point.

Little Rock scored once more on a 25-yard run by Marshall. He also added the extra point in a 20-12 victory.

After the upset over El Dorado, the Tigers barely defeated Fordyce.

With the Tigers leading 7-6, Fordyce kicker Bill Johnson attempted a field goal on the last play of the game. The kick, though, was short and Little Rock recorded its fourth victory of the season.

The Tigers then prepared for their next game against rival Pine Bluff. The Zebras scored two touchdowns during the second quarter, but failed on both extra-point attempts. Regardless, Pine Bluff had a 12-0 lead at halftime.

The Tigers received the second-half kickoff and began a scoring drive with a 32-yard run by Marshall. A pass netted 6 yards and Vestal picked up a first down at the Zebras 29.

Rolf passed to Jimmy Morgan, who pitched to Fritts for a 9-yard gain. Marshall gained 2 more yards for a first down on the 18.

Three plays later, Fritts caught a pitch from Morgan for an 18-yard touchdown. The conversion attempt was good to narrow the deficit to 12-7.

With two minutes remaining in the game, Vestal capped a 64-yard drive with a 2-yard touchdown run to give Little Rock a 13-12 advantage. The extra point put the Tigers up 14-12, a lead they maintained during the final minute of play.

Marshall rushed for 196 yards and his two extra points proved to be the difference in the 14-12 victory, Little Rock's first over Pine Bluff since 1936.

The Tigers defeated the Camden Panthers 30-12 before their annual Thanksgiving Day battle with North Little Rock.

More than 6,000 fans watched as Little Rock's Don Hudson blocked Leonard Bauman's punt early in the second quarter to set up the Tigers' first score.

Photo provided by the Arkansas Democrat-Gazette

The 1940 Little Rock offensive line

Sam Coots recovered for Little Rock on the Wildcats 5. Vestal covered the needed distance to give the Tigers a 6-0 lead. North Little Rock, however, took a 7-6 lead at halftime following a 1-yard touchdown run by Carol Griffith.

The Wildcats fumbled the second-half kickoff and Little Rock recovered on the North Little Rock 40.

It took eight plays, but the Tigers scored on a 15-yard touchdown pass. Rolf connected with Morgan, who pitched to Marshall, who then crossed the goal line for a 13-7 Little Rock lead.

Little Rock's Gerald McKinney intercepted a pass on the Tigers 30 in the closing minute of the game to seal a 13-7 holiday victory.

After four consecutive losses to open the season, the Tigers won seven consecutive games and finished runner-up in the conference.

1940 TIGER SCHEDULE

Malvern 12	LRHS 6
*Jonesboro 13	LRHS 6
*Blytheville 21	LRHS 0
*Hot Springs 13	LRHS 0
*Fort Smith 19	LRHS 20
Central High of Memphis, TN 0	LRHS 6
*El Dorado 12	LRHS 20
*Fordyce 6	LRHS 7
*Pine Bluff 12	LRHS 14
*Camden 12	LRHS 30
*North Little Rock 7	LRHS 13

A THANKSGIVING DAY LOSS

1941   5-5-1

Head Coach: Clarence Geis
Assistants: Homer Berry, LeRoy Scott
Team Trainer: Riley "Doc" Johns
Team Physician: Dr. Theo Freedman

1941 LETTERMEN

Frankie Birch	Gene Cork	Clinton Fritts	Harold Pevia
Earl Bowman	Jimmy Crafton	Don Hudson	Billy Sims
Otis Cathey	Alfred Craig	Billy Nicholas	Jimmy Stanton
Sam Coots	Charles Dillon	Bill Nichols	Alan Stevenson

1941 MANAGERS
Earl Fuqua
James Gammill
Bill Henker
John Larson
Frank Schay

1941 ALL-STATE
Jimmy Crafton

Clinton Fritts

Pine Bluff's Finis Buckner scores

157

Clarence Geis took over the reigns of the Tigers after Coach Clyde Van Sickle resigned following the 1940 season. Coach Geis, who led the Jonesboro Hurricane prior to taking the Little Rock position, was a standout football player at the University of Arkansas.

Coach Geis opened his first season at Little Rock High School with 45 candidates vying for starting positions. Of the 45 players out for the team, only five were returning lettermen. Clinton Fritts, Little Rock's quarterback, was the only experienced back returning.

The Tigers showcased their new uniforms, including gold helmets, black jerseys and gold pants, for their opening game against Malvern.

The Leopards scored first when Clint Fuller ran for a 4-yard touchdown. The extra-point attempt failed, leaving Malvern with a 6-0 lead.

With just under two minutes remaining in the game, Little Rock took possession on its 41. Fritts passed to Earl Bowman at midfield, and Bowman ran 50 yards to tie the score at 6-6. Fritts converted the extra-point attempt to win the game 7-6.

Photo provided by the Arkansas Democrat-Gazette
Little Rock's 1941 starting offense

The Tigers crossed the Leopards 40-yard line six times, but failed to score each time following fumbles or being held on downs.

Illness swept through the Little Rock team during the next week, causing several players to miss practice. Only Harold Pevia, though, missed the next game against Jonesboro High School.

Coach Geis' former team held the Tigers scoreless with the help of a goal-line stand. Little Rock put together two defensive stands to keep the Hurricane scoreless.

More than 5,000 fans in Tiger Stadium watched Little Rock tie its first conference game, 0-0.

The Tigers lost their next conference game the following week when the Blytheville Chicks defeated them 20-13.

Little Rock scored early in the second quarter after receiving a punt at the Blytheville 35. Fritts passed to Bowman for a first down on the Chicks 20. Fritts then picked up 6 yards. Alan Stevenson ran 4 yards for a first down at the 10.

Two plays later, Frankie Birch went off tackle for a 9-yard touchdown run. Birch converted the extra-point attempt for a 7-0 lead.

Photo provided by the Arkansas Democrat-Gazette
Little Rock's 1941 starting seniors

158

Earl Bowman (78) and Earnest Medlin (70)

Following an 87-yard touchdown run by Alfred Craig that was nullified by a clipping penalty, the Tigers punted. Blytheville's Sonny Lloyd returned it 14 yards to the Little Rock 16.

Two plays picked up a first down at the 6. After Lloyd gained 3 yards, the Chicks scored on a 3-yard run. Lloyd's extra-point attempt was good, tying the score at 7-7.

One minute after Lloyd scored on a 57-yard run late in the third quarter, Blytheville found itself within scoring distance again.

The Chicks drove from midfield for a first down on the Tigers 10. On the next play, Lloyd went the 10 yards for the score. A bad snap ended the chance for an extra point, but Blytheville increased a lead that it never relinquished.

Little Rock lost its next game as well. Charles "Stuff" Dugan scored on a 53-yard run to give the Hot Springs Trojans a 6-0 victory.

More than 7,000 fans watched Hot Springs rush for 122 yards and hand the Tigers their second loss of the season.

The following week, Little Rock traveled to Fort Smith to take on the Grizzlies.

More than 3,600 fans saw the Tigers rush for 241 yards and four players score touchdowns.

After a scoreless first quarter, Craig sparked Little Rock's offense on the second play of the second quarter with a 14-yard run to the Fort Smith 31. Stevenson, Fritts and Craig combined on runs to the 4. Fritts went the final 4 yards for the touchdown.

Late in the second quarter, an 8-yard pass from Fritts to Craig capped a 65-yard drive by the Tigers. The extra-point attempt increased the lead to 13-0.

Little Rock scored again when Pevia ended a 66-yard drive with a 16-yard scoring run in the fourth quarter.

Fort Smith received the ensuing kickoff and took possession at its 30. But James Mosley was intercepted by Stevenson at the line of scrimmage to set up the Tigers' final score.

On the first play, Fritts passed 25 yards to Bowman, who ran the remaining 5 yards for a touchdown. Stevenson's extra-point attempt was good to make it 25-0.

Fort Smith's only touchdown came late in the fourth quarter on a 28-yard run by Mosley. Mosley's extra point made the final 25-7. Little Rock returned home with its first conference victory.

In their longest rivalry, one that spanned more than 30 years, the Tigers hosted the Central High Warriors of Memphis the following week.

The Warriors, who were ranked No. 3 in Tennessee, rushed for 304 yards and scored the game's first touchdown when "Rambling" Robert Love ran untouched for 66 yards.

Billy Nicholas was the only player to score for Little Rock, recovering his own team's fumble and running 5 yards for a touchdown. Memphis, however, scored two more times in a 19-6 victory.

After victories over El Dorado and Camden, the Tigers lost to another longtime rival, Pine Bluff, 33-0.

Little Rock went into the game with only a mathematical chance of winning the championship. The loss meant the Tigers would play the remainder of their schedule only for pride.

Only a handful of spectators braved cold and rain the next week when Little Rock hosted Fordyce.

After their second series, Harry Ledbetter punted for the Redbugs. Birch received the punt on the Fordyce 38 and a 19-yard return gave the Tigers possession on the 19. After two incomplete passes and a fumbled snap, Little Rock faced fourth down.

Fritts threw toward the east sideline, near the 10-yard marker. Birch and the Redbugs' James Flowers both went up for the catch. The pass bounced off the hands of both players. Birch grabbed it out of the air and went across the goal line for the game's only touchdown. Fritts converted the extra-point attempt to give the Tigers a 7-0 victory.

During its annual Thanksgiving Day game against North Little Rock, Little Rock dressed 13 seniors for their last high school game. The Tigers had won 25 of 26 games played on Thanksgiving Day, the only loss 35-7 to Atlanta Tech in 1924.

After a scoreless first half, North Little Rock dominated the second half by scoring four touchdowns.

Leonard Bauman connected with Bill Wano for touchdown passes of 21 and 12 yards. Bauman also connected with Don Young for a 42-yard touchdown pass.

Sonny Howard intercepted a Fritts pass and raced 40 yards for another touchdown, helping North Little Rock to a 26-0 victory.

More than 7,000 fans packed Tiger Stadium and watched Little Rock throw five interceptions, three that led to touchdowns for the Wildcats.

The Tigers, who finished eighth in the Arkansas High School Conference, lost a game on Thanksgiving Day for only the second time since 1914.

1941 TIGER SCHEDULE

Malvern 6	LRHS 7
*Jonesboro 0	LRHS 0
*Blytheville 20	LRHS 13
*Hot Springs 6	LRHS 0
*Fort Smith 7	LRHS 25
Central High of Memphis, TN 19	LRHS 6
*El Dorado 0	LRHS 6
*Camden 14	LRHS 34
*Pine Bluff 33	LRHS 0
*Fordyce 0	LRHS 7
*North Little Rock 26	LRHS 0

TIGERS SUFFER WORST RECORD IN 24 YEARS

1942   4-6-1

Head Coach: Clarence Geis
Assistant: Harold Brotherton
Trainer: Riley "Doc" Johns
Team Physician: Dr. Theo Freedman

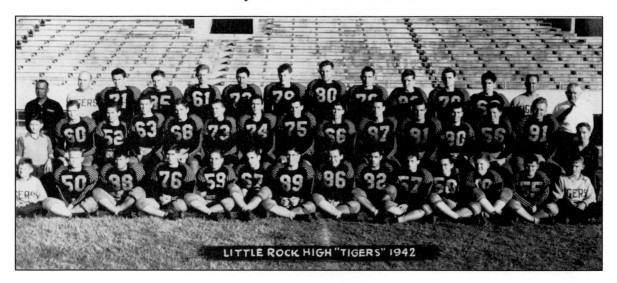

LITTLE ROCK HIGH "TIGERS" 1942

1942 LETTERMEN

Drexel Atkinson	Sam Coots	J.T. Long	Neill Robins
George Bailey	Charles Dillon	Earnest Medlin	Sam Stathakis
Walter Barksdale	John Hoffman	Billy Nichols	Morris Williams
Don Burnett	Paul Horton	Harold Pevia	
Otis Cathey	Don Hudson	Roy Reagan	

1942 MANAGERS
Marion Boggs
Robert Fair
Ransom Jackson
Sam Kuykendall
Edwin Stitt

1942 ALL-STATE
Otis Cathey
Sam Coots

When former assistant coach Homer Berry joined the Army at the end of the 1941-1942 school year, it left Coach Clarence Geis without an assistant. Harold Brotherton, a faculty member at the high school, agreed to help Coach Geis with the football team until a formal assistant could be hired. Longtime assistant LeRoy Scott also left the staff.

With only six returning lettermen, Coach Geis and Coach Brotherton began getting the team into shape during preseason practice.

Little Rock opened against the Fordyce Redbugs. The game began when Paul Horton received the Fordyce kickoff at the Tigers 19 and returned it to the 35.

Horton and Don Burnett each had a carry to move to the 45. Harold Pevia then

Drexel Atkinson

ran 26 yards on a reverse to the Redbugs 29. Burnett then went up the middle for a 29-yard touchdown. Sam Stathakis' extra-point attempt was wide, but Little Rock took a 6-0 lead with only 2:30 off the clock.

Fordyce had a chance to tie the score late in the second quarter when Tommy Crossett recovered a fumble at the Tigers 23. Jess Flowers and Willis Leslie picked up 13 yards for a first down at the 10.

The Little Rock defense, however, only allowed the Redbugs 1 yard on the next four plays. Fordyce ran out of downs at the 9. The Tigers were unable to move the remainder of the period and led 6-0 at halftime.

Late in the third quarter, Pevia returned a Redbugs punt to the Fordyce 22. Little Rock was unable to move and a punt was partially blocked by a Fordyce lineman and recovered by the Tigers on the 43.

Three plays later, the third quarter ended with Little Rock at the Fordyce 20. Walter Barksdale eventually scored from the 3 to give the Tigers a 12-0 lead.

Little Rock held the Redbugs scoreless and was victorious.

After a victory over Jonesboro, the Tigers' third game was a battle of unbeaten teams when Blytheville visited Tiger Stadium.

The Blytheville Chicks won the conference championship in 1940 and 1941 and were favored to win the title again in 1942.

Blytheville running back J.T. Victory ran over and around the Little Rock defense, leading the Chicks to a 12-6 victory.

Blytheville quarterback Billy Eldridge scrambled 29 yards for a touchdown, and the Chicks later scored again on a 50-yard pass play. Sam Coots scored the Tigers' only touchdown on a 14-yard pass reception.

Little Rock traveled to Hot Springs for the next game. During pregame interviews, both Coach Geis and Hot Springs Coach Milan Creighton stated that their teams would lose the game.

They both were right since neither team would win.

Both teams were stalled by great defensive efforts. The Tigers gained 84 yards rushing and 47 yards passing, while the Trojans gained 92 yards rushing and 41 yards passing. The game ended in a scoreless tie.

After a 6-0 loss to Fort Smith, Little Rock traveled to Memphis to play its annual game against the Central High Warriors.

The game's first score came in the first half on a 45-yard reverse by Horton, who put the Tigers up 6-0.

The Warriors, however, scored twice during the third quarter. Slick Williams returned a punt 42 yards for a touchdown. The extra point put Central High up 7-6.

Late in the game, Jack Ham ran 28 yards to put the game out of reach for Little Rock. The Memphis school defeated the Tigers 14-6.

Little Rock hosted El Dorado the following week in a game played in the mud. It began with the Tigers fumbling the opening kickoff.

The Wildcats recovered the fumble at the Little Rock 40. A 5-yard penalty by the Tigers aided El Dorado prior to its first snap. Jacky Myers went off tackle for 13 yards on first down. He bulled his way through the Little Rock line on the next three downs to give the Wildcats a first down at the Tigers 10.

Veldon McKnight picked up 3 yards on the first play and then went over tackle once more for a 7-yard touchdown. He then kicked the extra point to give El Dorado a 7-0 lead.

The Wildcats' Nolen Harris recovered another Little Rock fumble to set up El Dorado's second touchdown.

After taking over at the Tigers 40, McKnight passed to Melvin Lyle for 30 yards. Myers ran 10 yards for a touchdown and a 13-0 lead.

Late in the second quarter, the Wildcats shanked a punt and gave Little Rock possession on the El Dorado 20.

Burnett picked up 2 yards on the first play. John Hoffman then went around the end to score the Tigers' first touchdown.

In the fourth quarter, an El Dorado punt from its 2 was blocked. Little Rock's Barksdale grabbed the ball out of the air and crossed the goal line for the Tigers' second touchdown.

With El Dorado leading 13-12 late in the game, Myers sealed the victory for the Wildcats when he intercepted a pass and returned it for a touchdown. The 20-12 loss marked the Tigers' fourth of the season and pushed them farther down in the conference standings.

After a 45-0 domination of Camden, the Tigers hosted Pine Bluff.

Backup quarterback Ernie Medlin led Little Rock during the Pine Bluff game after Barksdale broke his arm in a tackling drill during practice.

After a scoreless first quarter, the second quarter opened with Pine Bluff's quarterback being sacked on fourth down to give the Tigers possession on the Zebras 26.

Hoffman ran 3 yards off left tackle and the same play on second down netted the same result.

Hoffman then took the next snap from center before the Zebras were at the line of scrimmage. This enabled him to go the remaining 20 yards untouched for a touchdown. The extra-point attempt failed and Little Rock had a 6-0 lead.

Hoffman scored again on a 5-yard run to give the Tigers a 12-0 halftime lead.

After Pine Bluff's Valensino "Shorty" Turchi scored on a 1-yard run in the fourth quarter, the Zebras lined up for their extra-point attempt. The attempt failed, but there was a penalty against Pine Bluff.

Instead of declining the penalty and accepting the missed extra-point attempt, Coach Geis elected to have the Zebras kick again following the 5-yard penalty.

Pine Bluff took advantage of Coach Geis' generosity by converting the extra-point and narrowing the deficit to 12-7.

Turchi went on to score another touchdown from the 1. The extra-point attempt was good and gave the Zebras a 14-12 lead.

The score remained the same, and Little Rock's loss to Pine Bluff was its fifth of the season.

The Tigers defeated the Russellville Cyclones 27-6 the next week, then played North Little Rock in their annual Thanksgiving Day game.

The Wildcats' Carol Griffith received the opening kickoff at the North Little Rock 5 and returned it to the Little Rock 39.

Jack Presley and Jim Lee Plant took turns carrying to the Tigers 20. Griffith ran to the 14 on the next play and then went into the end zone from there for a 6-0 lead.

Later in the first quarter, the Wildcats took over at the Little Rock 44 and sustained a drive to score their second touchdown.

Griffith passed 9 yards to Plant, Presley picked up 8 yards off left tackle, Griffith failed to gain and Presley then made only 1

Photo provided by the Arkansas Democrat-Gazette
John Hoffman (left)

163

yard. On fourth down, Plant bulled his way over center for 4 yards and a first down.

Three plays later, North Little Rock had a first down at the Tigers 4. Griffith scored his second touchdown when he went over the goal line on the next play. The Wildcats scored once more prior to halftime to take a 19-0 lead into the break.

North Little Rock opened the third quarter with another touchdown on its first possession.

Griffith returned a Little Rock punt to the Tigers 36. The Wildcats covered the short distance in just five plays, scoring on a 2-yard run by Presley.

North Little Rock's last touchdown came less than a minute later.

Little Rock could not move after the ensuing kickoff and proceeded to punt on fourth down. The Wildcats broke through to block Hoffman's punt, which North Little Rock's left guard scooped up and took 25 yards for a touchdown. The Wildcats then led 31-0.

The Tigers returned the ensuing kickoff to midfield. On second down, Horton passed to Coots for Little Rock's first touchdown.

The Tigers scored again on their next possession when they marched 80 yards. The drive included two 20-yard pass receptions by Coots and a 23-yard run by Horton to reach the Wildcats 22.

On a quick play without a huddle, Hoffman went the remaining 22 yards needed to score. The conversion attempt failed and time ran out, spoiling a Little Rock comeback.

The Tigers suffered their first losing season since a 1-2-1 record in 1918. Little Rock finished 11th in the conference standings.

1942 TIGER SHEDULE

*Fordyce 0	LRHS 12
*Jonesboro 6	LRHS 15
*Blytheville 12	LRHS 6
*Hot Springs 0	LRHS 0
*Fort Smith 6	LRHS 0
Central High of Memphis, TN 14	LRHS 6
*El Dorado 20	LRHS 12
*Camden 0	LRHS 45
*Pine Bluff 14	LRHS 12
*Russellville 6	LRHS 27
*North Little Rock 31	LRHS 12

FORT SMITH ENDS HOPE FOR CHAMPIONSHIP

1943   8-1-2

Head Coach: Clarence Geis
Assistants: Unknown
Trainer: Riley "Doc" Johns
Team Physician: Dr. Theo Freedman

1943 TIGER LETTERMEN

Chester Almond	Bobby Cook	Mike Kumpuris	Sammy Sanders
Drexel Atkinson	Gene Crafton	G.H. Lackey	Fletcher Sullards
Walker Barksdale	Frank Harris	J.T. Long	Billy Woodiel
Albert Benight	Basil Hodges	Charles Parker	
Wayne Berry	John Hoffman	Harold Pevia	
Buddy Coleman	C.W. Keopple	Neill Robins	

1943 MANAGERS
Walter Ahring
Guy Amsler
Dolf May
Joe Norbury
Roy Rhen

1943 ALL-STATE
Drexel Atkinson
John Hoffman
Neill Robins

Photo provided by the Arkansas Democrat-Gazette
John Hoffman

The Tigers opened against the Fordyce Redbugs and combined a crushing ground attack with a superb aerial display.

On Fordyce's first possession, John Hoffman intercepted a pass and returned it to the Redbugs 39. On Little Rock's second play from scrimmage, Hoffman ran 38 yards for a touchdown.

The Tigers' second touchdown came soon after the first when Little Rock took over on downs at the Fordyce 40.

On first down, Hoffman passed to Walter Barksdale, who immediately pitched to Harold Pevia to move to the 6. Barksdale picked up 3 yards before Hoffman scored on the next play. Hoffman also converted the extra-point attempt to give the Tigers a 14-0 lead.

Little Rock was only able to score one time in the second quarter, but scored three times in the third quarter. Substitutes Basil Hodges and C.W. Keopple each added a score for the Tigers in the fourth quarter.

Hoffman finished with four touchdowns and was almost unstoppable running off tackle. He was protected by an offensive line that consistently won the battle at the line of scrimmage.

Little Rock gained 96 yards passing and 310 yards rushing in a 57-0 rout of the Redbugs.

The Tigers turned on the power in the second half to defeat Jonesboro 36-6 the following week.

Hoffman scored Little Rock's first touchdown on a 1-yard run. His second score capped a 13-play, 45-yard drive.

Pevia's touchdown run early in the third quarter was the highlight of the game.

Pevia took the handoff through the line, reversed field and ran 52 yards for a score to give the Tigers an 18-0 lead.

Late in the third quarter, a series of runs by Hoffman and Barksdale carried Little Rock from its 21 to the Jonesboro 4. Barksdale scored from there to increase the Tigers' lead.

In the fourth quarter, Keopple intercepted a pass and returned it 55 yards for a touchdown.

An interception ended Jonesboro's next possession and set up another score for Little Rock. Buddy Coleman passed to Keopple for 18 yards. On the next play, Keopple broke through the line and ran for the touchdown.

With only 10 seconds to play in the game, the Hurricane scored its only touchdown when Billy Price completed a long pass to Tom Burres.

Hoffman finished with 133 yards rushing and two touchdowns.

Photo provided by the Arkansas Democrat-Gazette
Neill Robins

Coach Clarence Geis' Tigers then won their third consecutive conference game by crushing the Blytheville Chicks 38-0.

At Haley Field in Blytheville, Little Rock's dominance began on its first possession.

From the 24, Hoffman ran 13 yards to the 37 on the first play. Barksdale then went over right tackle and ran for a 63-yard touchdown.

The Tigers blocked a punt on the Chicks' first possession of the game and recovered at the Blytheville 28. Pevia took the handoff on first down and went the 28 yards needed for another Little Rock touchdown.

On Little Rock's next possession, Pevia again scored when he took a reverse 51 yards for his second touchdown. This touchdown gave Little Rock a 19-0 lead.

Hoffman then ended the Chicks' next series when he intercepted a pass at the Blytheville 18. Barksdale scored on a draw play to increase the lead to 25-0.

Pevia set up another touchdown late in the fourth quarter with a 34-yard gain to the Chicks 13. A pass to Hoffman gained 2 yards, then Hoffman received another pass for a touchdown.

The Tigers needed just two minutes to score again after Blytheville was held on downs at its 31.

On the first play, Coleman swept 31 yards for a touchdown. Keopple converted the extra-point attempt to put Little Rock up 38-0.

In the featured game of the week, the Tigers hosted the Hot Springs Trojans. The Trojans held the Tigers scoreless for the fourth consecutive season.

A crowd of more than 6,000 hoped to see Little Rock beat a lightweight Hot Springs team, but the Tigers were outplayed from the opening whistle. The Trojans gained 243 yards rushing compared to Little Rock's 152 yards rushing.

A mistake giving the Tigers five downs was still not enough to get the momentum started as Little Rock ended the possession with a punt.

Photo provided by the Arkansas Democrat-Gazette
John Hoffman

The defensive battle ended in a scoreless tie.

The Tigers, who were ranked first in the conference, traveled to Fort Smith for their next game.

Late in the fourth quarter, Coleman capped a 75-yard drive when he scored Little Rock's only touchdown on a 1-yard run. The touchdown drive marked the only time the Tigers crossed midfield, and it came against Fort Smith's second team.

Led by Tommy Donoho and Done Bowers, Fort Smith scored in every quarter.

The Grizzlies overwhelmed Little Rock 41-7 to give the Tigers their first loss of the season. The loss, combined with the tie against Hot Springs, all but eliminated Little Rock from the state title race.

The Tigers' homecoming game was played the next week against Central High of Memphis. The Warriors, highly re-

Photo provided by the Arkansas Democrat-Gazette
Arkansas Gazette cartoon

spected throughout the South, were undefeated and had only allowed two touchdowns during the season.

Miss Geraldine Canby reigned as queen while Little Rock capitalized on several breaks to come away with a stunning upset over the highly touted Memphis team.

Both teams scored touchdowns in the third quarter. The Warriors took possession at their 17 after a punt and sustained an 83-yard drive that was capped by a 27-yard pass from Bill Wright to John Trent. The extra-point attempt failed and the Memphis team led 6-0.

Hoffman returned the ensuing kickoff to the Little Rock 44, and a 25-yard penalty against the Warriors for unsportsmanlike conduct moved the ball to the Memphis 31.

Pevia broke a 29-yard run on the first play and was brought down at the 2. Hoffman scored on the next play, exactly two minutes after Memphis scored its touchdown. Hoffman also converted the extra-point attempt to give the Tigers a 7-6 edge.

The Warriors sealed their doom with a series of fumbles and interceptions. Little Rock took advantage of these opportunities,

168

intercepting four passes and recovering seven fumbles to end 11 scoring threats by the Memphis team.

After a 20-6 victory over Little Rock Catholic and a 35-7 victory over El Dorado, the Tigers traveled to Jordan Stadium in Pine Bluff to take on the Zebras.

A Little Rock victory would put it back in the hunt for a conference title. A Pine Bluff victory would clinch the conference title for the Zebras.

After a scoreless first half, the Tigers scored the game's first touchdown on Hoffman's 77-yard run. He failed to convert the extra-point attempt, but Little Rock led 6-0.

Pine Bluff answered immediately, driving from its 46 to score on a 21-yard pass. Pine Bluff failed to convert the extra-point attempt, meaning one of the fiercest battles between the two schools ended in a 6-6 tie.

A 25-0 victory over Russellville brought the Tigers to their annual Thanksgiving Day matchup with North Little Rock. The game was a battle for pride since both teams were eliminated from the conference race.

Taking advantage of a blocked punt in the first quarter, the Wildcats scored their only touchdown on an 18-yard run by Jackie Baker. North Little Rock was able to hold its lead most of the game by playing great defense and keeping Little Rock out of the end zone.

Midway through the fourth quarter, though, Hoffman broke through the tough defense and ran off tackle 40 yards for a touchdown and a 7-7 tie. Pevia's 26-yard touchdown run a few minutes later put the Tigers ahead and eventually gave them a 13-7 victory.

Hoffman finished the day with 217 of Little Rock's 290 yards rushing.

The Tigers finished third in the conference standings.

Following the school year, Coach Geis was called by the Navy to aid his country during World War II. Given a leave of absence by the Little Rock School District, Coach Geis was stationed in Corpus Christi, Texas, as the Navy's athletic instructor.

1943 TIGER SCHEDULE

*Fordyce 0	LRHS 57
*Jonesboro 6	LRHS 36
*Blytheville 0	LRHS 38
*Hot Springs 0	LRHS 0
*Fort Smith 41	LRHS 7
Central High of Memphis, TN 6	LRHS 7
Little Rock Catholic 6	LRHS 20
*El Dorado 7	LRHS 35
*Pine Bluff 6	LRHS 6
*Russellville 0	LRHS 25
*North Little Rock 7	LRHS 13

A NEW COACH RETURNS LITTLE ROCK TO GLORY

1944   10-1-0

Head Coach: Raymond Burnett
Assistant: Everett Barnes
Trainer: Riley "Doc" Johns
Team Physician: Dr. John McCollough Smith

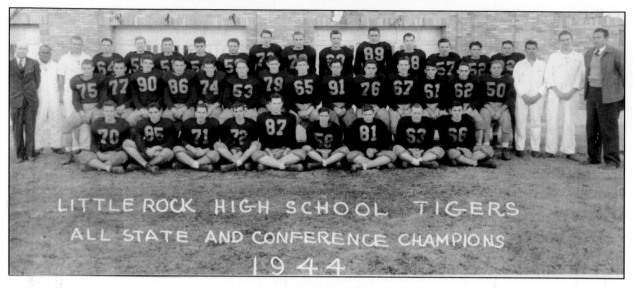

1944 LETTERMEN

Jimmy Albright	Buddy Coleman	John Hoffman	Jack Rushing
Wayne Berry	Gene Hall	Clyde Horton	Sammy Sanders
Alfred Bracy	Earl Harvey	Mike Kumpuris	Billy Woodiel
Kit Carson	Johnny Hestir	Neill Robins	

1944 MANAGERS
Unknown

1944 ALL-SOUTHERN
John Hoffman
Billy Woodiel

1944 ALL-STATE

Alfred Bracy	Neill Robins
John Hoffman	Sammy Sanders
Mike Kumpuris	Billy Woodiel

Raymond "Rabbit" Burnett took over the Tigers for the 1944 season. Burnett, a star collegiate player at Arkansas Tech University, inherited the program after the Navy called on Coach Clarence Geis.

Sixty players reported for preseason workouts, but only seven were returning starters. Among the starters was All-State running back John Hoffman.

More than 7,000 fans turned out at Tiger Stadium to watch Burnett's Tigers open the season against Fordyce. The game-time temperature was tremendously high and coaches for both teams had to substitute often because of fatigue.

Hoffman scored 31 points against the Redbugs, including four touchdowns and three extra points. He scored on runs of 1, 1 and 43 yards and returned an interception 27 yards for another score. Johnny Hestir scored on a 40-yard run and a 52-yard punt return. Jimmy Albright scored on a 4-yard run. Little Rock beat Fordyce 49-0.

The Tigers beat Jonesboro 39-0 the next week and then took on Blytheville at Tiger Stadium. More than 6,000 fans watched as Hestir scored Little Rock's first two touchdowns on runs of 20 yards and 8 yards. Hoffman then added three touchdowns on a 38-yard run, 18-yard run and an 85-yard kickoff return.

Gene Hall intercepted a pass and returned it 48 yards to the 2. Jimmy Eberts

Photo provided by the Arkansas Democrat-Gazette
Sammy Sanders

then scored on a 2-yard run and later scored on a 20-yard pass reception from Hall.

Little Rock gained 249 yards rushing, intercepted four passes and held the Chicks to 32 yards of total offense in a 48-0 victory.

In its fourth consecutive conference game, Little Rock traveled to Hot Springs to play the Trojans. More than 7,000 fans had packed Rix Stadium 45 minutes before kickoff to watch the Tigers go for their first victory over Hot Springs in five years.

Little Rock used power to bull its way through the Trojans for 14 first downs. A tough defense allowed the Trojans only three first downs. The Tigers rushed for 397 yards behind Hoffman and Hestir.

Hoffman scored touchdowns on runs of 47 yards and

Photo provided by the Arkansas Democrat-Gazette
John Hoffman scores a touchdown for the Tigers

171

10 yards. Wayne Berry intercepted a pass and returned it 35 yards for a touchdown. Sammy Sanders scored on a 20-yard pass reception from Buddy Coleman.

Other scores came on short runs by Hestir and Albright in a 40-0 victory.

The next week, Patty Carson was crowned homecoming queen in front of 8,500 fans at Tiger Stadium. Miss Carson reigned proudly over the homecoming game against the powerful Fort Smith Grizzlies.

Little Rock relied on Hoffman to provide all the offense. He rushed for 271 of Little Rock's 284 yards and scored on runs of 57, 38 and 17 yards. He converted two extra-point attempts and accounted for a safety when he tackled a Fort Smith player in the end zone.

Hoffman and the unbeaten Tigers beat Fort Smith 22-0 and posted their fifth consecutive shutout.

The Tigers played their first nonconference game against Central High of Memphis. Coach Burnett and 26 players crossed

Photo provided by the Arkansas Democrat-Gazette
John Hoffman

the Mississippi River by train to take on the Warriors of Central High.

More than 3,500 fans watched Little Rock take to the air to beat Memphis 7-0. Little Rock's running game, led by Hoffman, was shut down. Hoffman did break several long runs, but was never able to score.

Just before halftime, Albright passed to Berry for a 13-yard touchdown and the game's only score.

The game was full of defense, including a goal-line stand by Little Rock to stop the Warriors' only scoring threat. With first down on the Tigers 3, Memphis was stopped on four consecutive plays. The 7-0 victory marked the sixth consecutive shutout by the Tigers.

A capacity crowd filled Tiger Stadium the next week to see Little Rock take on the El Dorado Wildcats, a game predicted to be the Tigers' toughest battle of the season.

Little Rock, which didn't make a first down during a scoreless first half, was able to spread out the Wildcats in the second half with a passing attack. Once the Tigers stung El Dorado passing, they scored with their powerful running game.

In the third quarter, Hoffman scored on a 2-yard run and Hestir added a 32-yard touchdown run. Albright scored Little Rock's final touchdown on a 2-yard run.

The Wildcats drove 62 yards late in the fourth quarter to score on a 1-yard run, ending the Tigers' streak of six consecutive shutouts.

Following a 35-13 victory over the Russellville Cyclones, the Tigers hosted the Pine Bluff Zebras in one of the most anticipated games of the season. The 35th meeting between the schools was played on a Saturday afternoon at Tiger Stadium.

More than 10,000 fans watched Pine Bluff score the game's first touchdown to lead 7-0. Hoffman started Little Rock's barrage of scoring when he returned the ensuing kickoff 88 yards for a touchdown.

The Zebras could not move on their next possession and were forced to punt. Alfred Bracy broke through the Pine Bluff line to block the kick. He then scooped up the ball and returned it 25 yards for a touchdown.

On the Tigers' next possession, Hoffman scored on a 32-yard pass reception from Albright. Two possessions later, Albright went over left tackle, cut to the sideline and ran 76 yards for another touchdown.

The Tigers scored twice more to embarrass their rival 40-7. Albright finished with 141 of Little Rock's 281 yards rushing.

In a steady downpour the following week, the Tigers defeated Greenville, Miss., 32-0. This nonconference game was used to prepare Little Rock for its annual Thanksgiving Day battle with North Little Rock.

In front of a large crowd at Tiger Stadium, Little Rock drove 87 yards in the second quarter for its only score. Hoffman ran 3 yards and converted the extra-point attempt for a 7-0 lead.

The Wildcats' Raymond Combee scored on a 14-yard run in the third quarter. The Tigers still led after the extra-point attempt failed. Combee, though, scored again on a 7-yard run to give North Little Rock a 13-7 victory in front of 8,000 fans.

The Wildcats finished with 42 yards passing and 204 yards rushing. Combee rushed for 121 yards on 21 carries.

Little Rock finished with 154 yards passing and 114 yards rushing. Hoffman rushed for only 36 yards on 12 carries.

Photo provided by the Arkansas Democrat Gazette
Mike Kumpuris

With its victory over Pine Bluff, Little Rock was guaranteed the conference and state championship for the first time since 1938.

Senior John Hoffman, who was selected to the All-Southern and All-State teams, led the conference with 181 points, including 24 touchdowns.

1944 TIGER SCHEDULE

*Fordyce 0	LRHS 49
*Jonesboro 0	LRHS 39
*Blytheville 0	LRHS 48
*Hot Springs 0	LRHS 40
*Fort Smith 0	LRHS 22
Central High of Memphis, TN 0	LRHS 7
*El Dorado 7	LRHS 20
*Russellville 13	LRHS 35
*Pine Bluff 7	LRHS 40
Greenville, MS 0	LRHS 32
*North Little Rock 13	LRHS 7

A TURKEY DAY TIE ENDS CHAMPIONSHIP BID

1945   8-1-2

Head Coach: Raymond Burnett
Assistant: Wilson Matthews
Team Trainer: Riley "Doc" Johns
Team Physician: Dr. John McCollough Smith

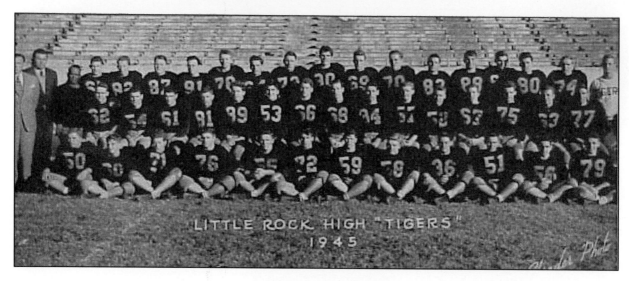

1945 LETTERMEN

Jimmy Albright	Jimmy Eberts	Earl Harvey	Jack Rushing
Wayne Berry	Dick Finch	Jack Mitchell	Louis Waldron
Kit Carson	Tom Floyd	Bill Neely	Carl Williams
Buddy Coleman	Don Fuqua	Bill Powell	Fred Williams
Gene Eberle	Gene Hall	Bill Rule	Bill Wright

1945 MANAGERS

Bill Diffee	Frederic Rice
Jack Guenther	Louie Schaufele
Charles Hill	Darwin Spencer
Owen Lyons	

1945 ALL-STATE
Jimmy Albright
Wayne Berry

Coach Raymond Burnett entered his second season as head coach, hoping to lead his 61 players to a second consecutive state championship. During preseason interviews, Coach Burnett said Little Rock's backfield and secondary would be strengths, but the offensive and defensive lines would need a lot of work.

Two days before the Tigers' season opener against Fordyce, starting halfback

Clyde Horton was replaced by Gene Hall after Horton broke his fibula during practice.

The game against Fordyce proved to be disappointing for the Tigers after poor blocking and missed tackles led to a 6-6 tie. Little Rock's only touchdown came on a short run by Bill Rule.

Following a 20-0 rout of Jonesboro and squeaking past the Blytheville Chicks 6-0, the Tigers hosted the Hot Springs Trojans. More than 9,000 fans packed Tiger Stadium to watch the skill of Little Rock's Jimmy Albright and Hot Springs' Dewey Thomason.

Albright rushed 28 times for 261 yards and two touchdowns. Thomason scored both Hot Springs touchdowns on runs of 44 and 14 yards. With the score tied 13-13 and under two minutes to play in the game, Albright scored his second touchdown on a 12-yard run. The touchdown gave the Tigers a 20-13 victory.

Little Rock's next game was considered by the *Arkansas Democrat* to be "one of the most stunning upsets in prep school history." The Fort Smith Grizzlies were the top-ranked team in the state and highly favored to win the state championship.

Both teams scored within five minutes after the opening kickoff. Albright completed a 27-yard touchdown pass to Wayne Berry for the Tigers' first score. Fort Smith answered on its next possession when Jack Simpson ran 61 yards for a touchdown.

Simpson scored two more times on runs of 99 and 10 yards. Albright rushed for two

Photo provided by the Arkansas Democrat-Gazette
Jimmy Albright scores

touchdowns on runs of 1 and 2 yards.

The game was decided by extra points. Little Rock made all three of its kicks, but Fort Smith missed one attempt. The Tigers capitalized on the Grizzlies' miscue and won 21-20.

For its annual homecoming game the following week, Little Rock hosted the Warriors of Memphis Central High. A crowd of more than 8,000 watched Miss Ruth Ann Daniels crowned homecoming queen in pregame activities. Miss Daniels reigned over a close but brutal game for the Tigers.

With five minutes remaining in the first half, Central's Nelson Burton intercepted one of Albright's passes at the Little Rock 40 and returned it for a touchdown. The extra-point attempt failed and Memphis led 6-0 at halftime.

The Warriors scored again three minutes into the second half when a 33-yard pass was good for another six points. The extra-point attempt was good and Memphis led 13-0. The Tigers answered midway through the third quarter when Albright pitched to Hall, who ran to the 6 to set up a touchdown. Albright then went off right tackle to score Little Rock's first touchdown. The extra-point attempt failed, but the Tigers narrowed the deficit to 13-6.

Photo provided by the Arkansas Democrat-Gazette
North Little Rock's Harold Waggoner scores

On Central's next series, Hall intercepted a pass to give Little Rock possession at the Warriors 35. An unnecessary roughness penalty by Central and several running plays moved Little Rock to the 10. Buddy Coleman scored from there, but the Tigers still trailed 13-12 after a missed extra-point attempt.

Midway through the fourth quarter, the Tigers recovered a blocked Memphis punt at the Warriors 13. Little Rock scored the winning touchdown when Albright passed to Rule in the end zone. Albright's extra-point attempt was wide, but the Tigers won 18-13.

Several Little Rock players were injured during the game. Berry suffered a broken arm during the third quarter and missed the remainder of the season.

Fred Williams, a sophomore tackle, lost four teeth and received several bad facial injuries when three Warriors ganged up on him in front of the Memphis bench. A Little Rock fan even came out of the stands to aid Williams, and one of the Memphis coaches began fighting with the fan.

The unsportsmanlike conduct by Memphis, which amassed 110 yards in penalties, forced Coach Burnett to send all reserve players to the locker room prior to the game's end. This was done to avoid any retaliation or situation that may have erupted between the teams after the game.

Following a disappointing 35-7 loss to El Dorado, Little Rock hoped to bounce back against Russellville. More than 2,000 fans braved the rain at Tiger Stadium to see the Tigers and Cyclones battle.

Russellville dominated Little Rock during the first half, holding the Tigers to 34 yards of total offense. The Tigers turned the ball over on downs at their 2 early in the first quarter

The Cyclones scored on the first play after taking possession and led 6-0. Russellville scored again in the second quarter. From its 17, Russellville moved to the 48 in four plays. Several plays later, the Cyclones scored on a 25-yard run to take a 12-0 lead into halftime.

Photo provided by the Arkansas Democrat-Gazette
Jimmy Albright

Little Rock began a third-quarter drive from its 44 and scored in less than three minutes. After a 20-yard run by Albright to the 2, he then went 2 more yards for the score. He also kicked the extra point to cut Russellville's lead to 12-7.

Less than five minutes elapsed before the Tigers scored again. The touchdown came on a 23-yard pass from Albright to Hall. Albright again kicked the extra point and Little Rock led 14-12.

The Tigers scored twice more during the fourth quarter, dominating both sides of the ball. Don Fuqua scored early in the quarter on a 15-yard reverse. Albright scored the last touchdown on a 23-yard run to seal a 26-12 victory over the Cyclones. Little Rock finished with 272 yards rushing.

The Tigers traveled to Jordan Stadium in Pine Bluff the next week to take on the Zebras. More than 6,000 fans watched as Little Rock humiliated Pine Bluff during their annual battle.

The Tigers scored their first touchdown after receiving a punt at their 41. A running play and 32-yard pass from Albright to Hall

176

moved Little Rock to the Pine Bluff 21. Albright went up the middle for 3 more yards and then passed to Bucky Carson for the score. Albright converted the extra point for a 7-0 lead.

On the first play of the second quarter, Coleman recovered a fumble at the Pine Bluff 25. A pass from Coleman to Carson capped the short drive, and Albright's kick gave Little Rock a 14-0 lead.

A few minutes later, Albright intercepted a pass at the Pine Bluff 23 to set up the Tigers' next score. A 16-yard pass from Albright to Hall was good to the 8. Albright and Hall connected again, this time for the touchdown. Coleman converted the extra-point attempt.

Little Rock's final touchdown came with less than three minutes left in the game. Dick Finch recovered a fumble at the Pine Bluff 5. A penalty against the Tigers moved them back to the 10. On the first play, Albright passed to Bill Powell for the touchdown. The extra-point attempt failed, but Little Rock beat its old rival 27-0.

The victory over the Zebras moved the Tigers into a tie with El Dorado for the conference lead. Each team had one loss and one tie. Little Rock needed to win its remaining games for at least a share of the state title.

After defeating the Batesville Pioneers 48-6, the Tigers entered their 16th meeting with North Little Rock High School. The 13,336 fans who packed Tiger Stadium marked the largest crowd to witness a Thanksgiving Day game in Little Rock.

The Tigers scored five minutes into the game when Albright passed to Hall for a 59-yard touchdown. Albright's extra-point attempt was wide right. The touchdown play was set up after Little Rock took possession on its 36. Rule ran to the 41 before Albright passed 18 yards to Hall, who weaved his way through the defense for the remaining yardage and the score.

North Little Rock took the ensuing kickoff and drove 73 yards to score on a 1-yard run by Harold Waggoner. The extra-point attempt was good and the Wildcats took a 7-6 lead into halftime. The Tigers regained the lead early in the third quarter when Albright passed to Hall.

With 43 seconds remaining in the game and Little Rock leading 13-7, North Little Rock tied the score when a 1-yard touchdown run by Waggoner capped a 50-yard drive. Tommy Russell's extra-point attempt would have given the Wildcats the victory, but it was blocked when the entire Little Rock defensive line broke through the North Little Rock line.

The tie proved costly for the Tigers. A victory would have guaranteed Little Rock the conference championship. Instead, the Tigers finished second behind state champion El Dorado.

The 1945 Tiger offense

177

1945 TIGER SCHEDULE

*Fordyce 6	LRCH 6
*Jonesboro 0	LRCH 20
*Blytheville 0	LRCH 6
*Hot Springs 13	LRCH 20
*Fort Smith 20	LRCH 21
Central High of Memphis, TN 13	LRCH 18
*El Dorado 35	LRCH 7
*Russellville 12	LRCH 26
*Pine Bluff 0	LRCH 27
Batesville 6	LRCH 48
*North Little Rock 13	LRCH 13

NATIONAL CHAMPION

1946   14-0-0

Head Coach: Raymond Burnett
Assistants: Wilson Matthews, George Haynie
Team Trainer: Riley "Doc" Johns
Team Physician: Dr. John McCollough Smith

1946 LETTERMEN

Jimmy Albright	Gene Hall	Charles Parker	Armour Wayman
Albert Benight	Earl Harvey	Jack Rushing	John Webb
Bucky Carson	Johnny Hestir	Louie Schaufele	Jack Wilkins
Gene Eberle	Clyde Horton	Richard Shell	Carl Williams
Dick Finch	C.W. Keopple	Tucker Smith	Fred Williams
Don Fuqua	Ray Melton	Kermit Tracy	Bill Wright
Stanley Goldberg	Jack Mitchell	Louis Waldron	

1946 MANAGERS

Robert Chowning	Earnest Funk	Darwin Spencer
Dale Diffee	Morrow Graham	Gene Wells
Bill Floyd	Ashley Ross	Leonard White

1946 ALL-SOUTHERN
Jimmy Albright
Bucky Carson
Jack Rushing
Louie Schaufele

1946 ALL-STATE

Jimmy Albright   Gene Hall
Bucky Carson   Jack Rushing
Dick Finch   Louie Schaufele

1946 ALL-DISTRICT
Jimmy Albright
Bucky Carson
Dick Finch
Jack Rushing
Louie Schaufele

Photo provided by the Arkansas Democrat-Gazette
Gene Hall

Little Rock returned 18 starters from an 8-1-2 campaign in 1945. Four of those starters lettered in 1943 or 1944 and had just returned to the team after serving their country in World War II.

To win the 1946 state championship, the Tigers would have to survive a new playoff system. The playoffs consisted of champions from each classification (or district) playing each other for an outright and overall state champion.

More than 9,000 fans packed Tiger Stadium for Little Rock's season opener against the Fordyce Redbugs. The Tigers tallied 422 yards of total offense, but were also penalized 125 yards on 13 penalties.

Little Rock's scoring highlights included a 40-yard touchdown pass from Jimmy Albright to Gene Hall and a 45-yard touchdown run by Clyde Horton. The Ti-

gers went on to score two more times in a 31-6 victory over the Redbugs.

Former Little Rock head coach Clarence Geis, who came to Little Rock from Jonesboro, had returned to Jonesboro for his second stint as the Hurricane head coach. Geis' team put up a hard fight against the Tigers, but Little Rock's speed and power were too much to handle.

Albright led the Tigers with three touchdowns and four extra-point conversions. He scored the game's first touchdown on a 38-yard run in the first quarter and added another score in the third quarter with a 12-yard run.

Louie Schaufele capped a second-quarter drive with a 4-yard touchdown run, and Stanley Goldberg recovered a blocked punt in the end zone for a fourth-quarter touchdown in Little Rock's 36-0 victory.

Eight Little Rock players, including Horton, Hall, Schaufele, Earl Harvey, Johnny Hestir, Bill Wright and Don Fuqua, scored the following week against Blythe-

Photo provided by the Arkansas Democrat-Gazette
Johnny Hestir

180

Clyde Horton

ville. Albright added six extra points and also completed 13 passes for 161 yards. More than 8,000 fans watched the 48-0 victory over the Chicks.

In a game against Hot Springs the next week, Albright scored 21 points, three touchdowns and three extra points. His first score came on a 23-yard run in the first quarter. His 5-yard run capped the Tigers' next drive to put them up 14-0.

Horton set up Little Rock's next score when he ran 70 yards to the 10. Schaufele went in from there and Albright converted his third extra-point attempt. Late in the second quarter, Albright passed to Hall for a 27-0 halftime lead.

Horton began the second-half scoring with a 33-yard touchdown early in the third quarter. Later in the quarter, Wright passed to Albright for a 38-yard gain to the 1. Albright scored on the next play to increase the Tigers' lead.

Little Rock added to the lead when Albright passed to Hall for a 34-yard touchdown. The last Little Rock score was on a 28-yard run by Hall late in the fourth quarter. The Little Rock defense held the Trojans to one touchdown in a 52-6 victory.

Three weeks later, El Dorado traveled to Little Rock for what was considered the state's high school game of the year. Both teams entered 6-0-0 and were tied for the lead in the Big 6 Conference.

More than 15,000 were expected to fill Tiger Stadium for a game that would decide the Big 6 Conference and state championship for the largest classification. However, only 11,000 were in attendance because of heavy rain.

After Little Rock received a punt early in the first quarter, it took only three plays to score. Albright was stopped at the line of scrimmage on the first play, but Schaufele broke free for a 33-yard gain to the 3. Schaufele scored on the following play. Albright's extra-point kick was low, but Little Rock led 6-0.

El Dorado punted again on its next series and Hall returned it to the Tigers 32. Schaufele made a first down at midfield, then Horton ran 10 yards to the Wildcats 34. After a bad snap from center lost 15

1946 Tiger offense

yards, Albright completed passes to Bucky Carson and Hall to the 7.

Horton lost 3 yards on the next play, but Hall gained it back, and more, as he went around left end for the touchdown. Albright's extra-point attempt was blocked and Little Rock led 12-0.

Carl Williams recovered a fumble for the Tigers during the second quarter and Little Rock took possession at its 25.

Hall began the scoring drive with a 28-yard run around right end and Schaufele added 12 yards on two plays. Schaufele then passed to Fuqua to the El Dorado 27. A 7-yard run by Schaufele, a pass from Wright to Hall and a short gain by Horton set up a 3-yard touchdown run by Schaufele.

The fourth quarter opened with the Tigers taking over at their 24. Schaufele gained 45 yards on the first play, Horton picked up 11 yards and Albright added another 11 yards. Schaufele covered the 9 remaining yards for the score. Albright added the last score on the next series when he capped an 85-yard drive with a 3-yard run. Little Rock totaled 427 yards of offense, including 156 yards rushing by Schaufele, in a 32-0 victory.

During a 53-0 victory over Russellville, Schaufele scored three touchdowns, including an interception return of 55 yards. Hall also added a touchdown by returning a kick 63 yards.

More than 5,000 fans braved rain and threatening weather to watch the annual battle between Little Rock and Pine Bluff. The Zebras could not move on their first possession and were forced to punt. Horton returned the kick to the 42. A gain of 4 yards was pushed back to the 43 after an offside penalty on the Tigers. Schaufele then passed to Fuqua for a 43-yard touchdown. Albright converted the extra-point attempt for a 7-0 lead.

After Harvey tackled a Pine Bluff back on a fake punt, Little Rock took over at the Zebras 48. Albright gained 3 yards and Schaufele picked up 21 yards when he went around right end to the 24. Horton went off tackle, stiff-armed a Pine Bluff defender

and outran the secondary for the Tigers' second score. Albright converted his second extra-point attempt to put Little Rock up 14-0 as the first quarter ended.

The Tigers scored again on their next possession when Hestir went over from the 4. C.W. Keopple's extra-point attempt failed, but Little Rock still led 20-0. Just before halftime, Hall capped a 55-yard drive with a 5-yard run for a 26-0 halftime lead.

Early in the third quarter, Hestir scored from the 1 to end a 70-yard drive and put the Tigers up 32-0. Little Rock's last score came just before the game ended when Schaufele pitched to Hall for a 16-yard touchdown run. The extra-point attempt failed, but the Tigers won 38-0.

The game marked Little Rock's third consecutive victory over Pine Bluff.

Little Rock entered the first round of the playoffs the following week by hosting Catholic High School. The Rockets proved no match for the Tigers, who scored a dominating 61-0 victory.

Little Rock continued its regular-season schedule the following Thursday when it hosted North Little Rock High School for the annual Thanksgiving Day battle. The Wildcats were not much of a challenge for the Tigers. Little Rock ruined North Little Rock's holiday with a 41-7 victory.

The Tigers continued playoff action a week later when they met Magnolia High School. Hall highlighted the game with an

Johnny Hestir

88-yard punt return for a touchdown. Little Rock went on to win 34-6 and earn a date with Helena-West Helena High School for the overall state championship.

The District 5 champion Indians received the opening kickoff. Lee Williams returned it to his 26. Williams, though, was thrown back to his 10 after two offensive plays. The Tigers scored their first touchdown six plays later when Albright passed to Harvey for a 17-yard score.

Hall set up Little Rock's second touchdown when he returned a punt 46 yards in the second quarter. This set up a 3-yard touchdown run by Schaufele to make it 13-0. Another score came less than two minutes later when Hall ran 30 yards to give the Tigers a 19-0 halftime lead.

Helena-West Helena kicked off to Little Rock to begin the second half. Hall received the kick at his 5, sprinted down the west sideline and broke into open field at the 50. The run ended when Hall crossed into the end zone to complete a 95-yard kickoff return.

The Tigers went on to dominate the smaller high school, amassing 413 total yards and defeating the Indians 45-6. The victory made Little Rock High School Arkansas' first official high school football state champion.

As a result of their outstanding play, the Tigers (13-0) were invited to play in the 14th annual *New Orleans Times-Picayune* Doll and Toy Fund game known as the Toy Bowl. The Arkansas Athletic Association waived a rule banning competition after the scheduled end of the season and allowed the Tigers to participate in the Toy Bowl on Dec. 22 in Baton Rouge, La.

The Toy Bowl matched Little Rock against Warren Easton High School of New Orleans. Little Rock had beaten the Louisiana school five consecutives times after they regularly began meeting in 1921.

Photo provided by Louie Schaufele

The 1946 Tiger defense makes an interception

The game was played at City Park, and more than 8,000 fans watched Little Rock beat Warren Easton again, 21-7.

Hall ended an early Warren Easton threat when he intercepted a pass at the Tigers 5 and returned it 63 yards to the Eagles 32 to set up Little Rock's first score.

The 32-yard drive began when Schaufele gained 7 yards. Albright then picked up 10 yards, Hall went 5 yards and Albright got 1 yard for a first down at the 9.

Three more plays reached the 3 before Albright scored from there. He also converted the extra-point attempt to put the Tigers up 7-0.

Little Rock scored again midway through the second quarter after it took possession at the 20 following a punt. Schaufele went 11 yards to the 31. Hall then went through the left side of the line, reversed field and ran 53 yards before being pushed out of bounds at the Eagles 16.

Schaufele gained 11 yards to the 5. Albright spun his way through would-be tacklers to score the Tigers' second touchdown. He again converted the extra-point attempt for a 14-0 halftime lead.

After an uneventful third quarter, Goldberg recovered a fumble at the Little Rock 8 to set up Little Rock's final score.

Two running plays by Albright and one by Schaufele only netted 4 yards. On fourth down, Schaufele dropped into his end zone to punt. But instead of kicking, he lobbed a screen pass to Hall, who was untouched as he sprinted down the middle of the field for an 88-yard touchdown. Albright converted his third extra-point attempt to increase the lead to 21-0.

Warren Easton scored its only touchdown after the ensuing kickoff. The Eagles drove 60 yards and scored on a 10-yard pass. The New Orleans team threatened to score on four other possessions when it drove inside the Tigers 10. But each series ended when the Eagles ran out of downs or fumbled to Little Rock.

The Tigers were now Southern champions and named "mythical" national champions for the first time.

1946 TIGER SCHEDULE

Fordyce 6	LRHS 31
Jonesboro 0	LRHS 36
Blytheville 0	LRHS 48
*Hot Springs 6	LRHS 52
*Fort Smith 0	LRHS 52
Malvern 0	LRHS 33
*El Dorado 0	LRHS 32
Russellville 0	LRHS 53
*Pine Bluff 0	LRHS 38
LR Catholic 0	LRHS 61 (state playoffs)
*North Little Rock 7	LRHS 41
Magnolia 6	LRHS 34 (state playoffs)
Helena-West Helena 6	LRHS 45 (state playoff final)
Warren Easton of New Orleans, LA 7	LRHS 21 (Toy Bowl)

Bucky Carson

Louie Schaufele

Jack Rushing

Photos provided by the Arkansas Democrat-Gazette

WILSON MATTHEWS TAKES CONTROL

1947   12-0-1

Head Coach: Wilson Matthews
Assistants: Howard Pearce, Charles Gray
Team Trainer: Riley "Doc" Johns
Team Physician: Dr. John McCollough Smith

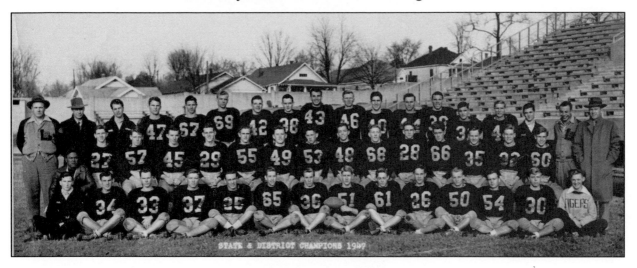

1947 LETTERMEN

Floyd Almond	Edward Eschweiler	David Hunter	John Webb
Bill Barnard	Glen Evans	Henry Johnson	Jack Wilkins
Kenneth Carter	Henry Fitzgibbons	Roger Knight	Fred Williams
David Conrad	Don Fuqua	George Oliver	Bill Wright
Don Countryman	Charles Gildehaus	Edgar Rowe	Luther Young
David Donoho	Bill Hollis	Kermit Tracy	
Tommy Dunaway	John Hunt	Jack Tucker	

1947 MANAGERS

Marion Burton	Jimmy Henderson
Bill Floyd	Jack Thompson
Skipper Graham	Jimmy Wilson
Dale Harris	

1947 ALL-STATE

Kermit Tracy
Jack Wilkins
Fred Williams

To find a replacement for Raymond "Rabbit" Burnett, who left Little Rock for an assistant coaching position at Arkansas Tech University, the Little Rock School District began a statewide search. Little Rock students, athletes, parents and media wondered why the district would look any farther than Wilson Matthews, an assistant to Burnett for the past two years.

Matthews did receive the job, but inherited only six returning lettermen from a senior-laden team that won the state and national championship. It was believed Matthews would face a rebuilding job in his first season.

While waiting for their new plastic helmets to arrive, the Tigers wore their new black and gold jerseys, new whip-cord pants and old leather helmets in the opener against the Fordyce Redbugs.

Little Rock wasted no time scoring. Kenneth Carter set up the first touchdown when he returned the opening kickoff 38 yards to the Tigers 47. John Hart picked up 23 yards, Carter gained 11 yards and Luther Young added 5 yards on a run around end to the Redbugs 24.

After Young picked up 1 yard, Carter ran over right guard for Little Rock's first touchdown. Floyd Almond kicked the extra point and the Tigers led 7-0 only three minutes into the game.

Houston Nutt, Fordyce's first-year quarterback, took the Redbugs to the Little Rock 2 in the fourth quarter. But a loss on fourth down cost Fordyce possession. The Redbugs gained 174 yards rushing, but the Tigers' 159 yards rushing produced three touchdowns in a 20-0 victory.

Quarterback Bill Wright starred for Little Rock the following week, completing seven passes for 127 yards and four touchdowns. Springfield, Mo., succumbed to the aerial attack after the Tigers lost possession

Photo provided by the Arkansas Democrat-Gazette
Don Fuqua scores for Little Rock

on the 13 following a run-sustained drive.

Wright's first touchdown pass was caught by John Webb, a 31-yard play during the first minute of the second quarter. Four minutes later, a pass to Young was worth 11 yards and another touchdown.

Even with a 12-0 lead at halftime, Little Rock came out passing in the third quarter. Wright connected with Don Fuqua for a 23-yard touchdown, and then Jack Wilkins caught a 16-yard touchdown pass to give the Tigers a 26-0 lead.

Photo provided by Central High School
Little Rock's 1947 starting offensive line

186

Bill Wright tackles Subiaco's Norman Jones

Wilkins also scored the fifth touchdown when he went 43 yards on an end-around at the end of the third quarter. The score put Little Rock up 33-0 as it went on to win its second game of the season.

The Tigers traveled to Blytheville for their third game. Little Rock scored early in the first quarter when Wilkins recovered a blocked punt in the end zone to put the Tigers up 7-0. Wright caught a 29-yard touchdown pass from Kermit Tracy, and Fuqua ran 6 yards around right end to give Little Rock an 18-0 victory over the Chicks.

After a 39-0 victory over Hot Springs, the Tigers visited Fort Smith for a battle with the Grizzlies. Played in a thunderstorm, the game began with Little Rock receiving the kickoff and driving 76 yards in nine plays for the opening score.

Fort Smith's Ben Lee Scanlon fumbled on the first play following the Tigers' kickoff. Henry Fitzgibbons recovered for Little Rock at the 20. Young's touchdown gave the Tigers a 14-0 lead before the Grizzlies ran their second play.

Little Rock scored again in the second quarter after Wilkins recovered a fumble on the 16. On the third play, Wright passed to Wilkins for a 1-yard touchdown. Wright converted the extra-point attempt to give the Tigers a 21-0 lead.

Fort Smith scored just minutes later when a broken play turned into a big play. Scanlon was back to punt and a fumbled snap kept him from getting off a kick. He picked up the ball and ran 85 yards for a touchdown. The extra-point attempt failed, but the touchdown pulled Fort Smith within 21-6.

Little Rock's defense held the Grizzlies the remainder of the game and also came up with the Tigers' final points. Little Rock blocked a punt late in the fourth quarter. Scanlon recovered in the end zone for a safety that gave the Tigers a 23-6 victory.

After breezing by Jonesboro 33-6, Little Rock faced the El Dorado Wildcats. Both undefeated teams met to possibly determine the Arkansas District AA championship. The last time the Tigers were beaten was by El Dorado in 1945.

The most anticipated game in Arkansas was believed to be one of the best and most exciting in many years. A defensive battle ensued, with the Wildcats turning the ball over on downs twice inside the 2. Little Rock did not fare any better, threatening to score just once. The game ended in a 0-0 tie.

A 36-0 victory over Russellville and a 33-6 victory over Pine Bluff set the Tigers up with a first-round playoff date with Blytheville High School. The second meet-

Henry Johnson scores on a 41-yard run

ing of the season between the schools took place at Tiger Stadium and remained close until the end of the third quarter. Jack Tucker's 30-yard field goal broke a 6-6 tie as the Tigers went on to win the playoff battle 16-6.

Little Rock resumed regular-season play the following week with its annual Thanksgiving Day game against North Little Rock High School. The only blemish for either team was a tie with El Dorado.

A crowd of 14,542 watched the Tigers slip by the Wildcats 13-0 to win the District 5 AA championship. Little Rock's 13 points came from an interception by defensive tackle Fred Williams, who ran 45 yards for the score, and a Tracy to Wilkins touchdown pass.

The playoffs continued the next week as the Tigers traveled to El Dorado for a rematch.

Tracy threw touchdown passes of 36 and 51 yards to Carter. Wright returned an interception 35 yards for the final Little Rock score. The Tigers beat the Wildcats 19-6 and advanced to the final of the state playoffs.

Little Rock hosted Subiaco Academy for the state championship game. More than 7,000 fans watched Little Rock's Edgar Rowe return the opening kickoff 47 yards.

On the Tigers' first play from scrimmage, Wright faked a bootleg and ran around right end. Guard Henry Johnson,

Photo provided by the Arkansas Democrat-Gazette
Kermit Tracy

who had taken the handoff, went 41 yards for the touchdown. Tucker kicked the extra point and the Tigers were up 7-0, only 20 seconds into the game.

Wright passed to John Webb, who pitched to Wilkins for Little Rock's second touchdown. The Tigers scored again in the fourth quarter on a short run by Rowe. The touchdown gave Little Rock a 19-0 victory, its second consecutive state title and an unbeaten streak of 31 games.

1947 TIGER SCHEDULE

Fordyce 0	LRHS 20
Central High of Springfield, MO 0	LRHS 33
Blytheville 0	LRHS 18
*Hot Springs 0	LRHS 39
*Fort Smith 6	LRHS 23
Jonesboro 6	LRHS 33
*El Dorado 0	LRHS 0
Russellville 0	LRHS 36
*Pine Bluff 6	LRHS 33
**Blytheville 6	LRHS 16 (state playoffs)
*North Little Rock 0	LRHS 13
**El Dorado 6	LRHS 19 (state playoffs)
**Subiaco Academy 0	LRHS 19 (state playoff final)

THE UNBEATEN STREAK ENDS

1948   9-1-1

Head Coach: Wilson Matthews
Assistants: Howard Pearce, Charles Gray
Team Trainer: Riley "Doc" Johns
Team Physician: Dr. John McCollough Smith

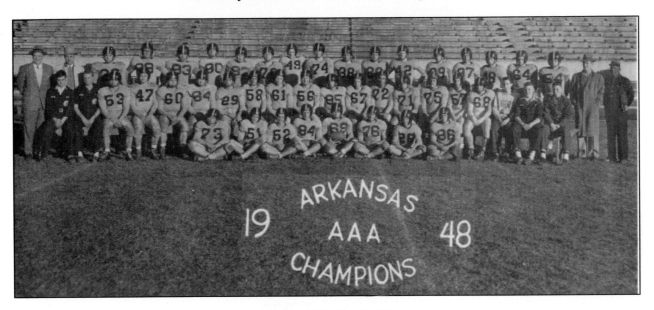

1948 LETTERMEN

John Armstrong	Charles DeViney	Robey Irwin	Bob Updegraff
Bill Barnard	David Donoho	G.W. McVay	Allen Venner
Warren Carpenter	Charles Dugan	George Oliver	Johnny Walker
Kenneth Carter	Tommy Dunaway	Joe Peterson	Billy Walthall
Fred Clark	Marlin Edgin	Oley Rooker	Luther Young
Don Countryman	Henry Fitzgibbons	Preston Saunders	
Bill Demmer	Charles Gildehaus	Bobby Spann	

1948 MANAGERS

Richard Burt	Ernest Gephardt
Fred Cazort	Warren Graham
Wayne Eskridge	Buddy Herndon
Curtis Finch	Raymond Huff
Bill Floyd	Bobby Langston
Sonny Fulk	

1948 STUDENT COACH
Edgar Rowe

1948 NATIONAL LINEMAN OF THE YEAR
Henry Fitzgibbons

1948 ALL-AMERICAN
Henry Fitzgibbons

1948 ALL-SOUTHERN
Henry Fitzgibbons

1948 ALL-STATE
Kenneth Carter
Don Countryman
Henry Fitzgibbons
George Oliver

Coach Wilson Matthews and the Tigers entered 1948 with a 31-game unbeaten streak. Little Rock was also the two-time defending state champion.

More than 8,000 fans at Tiger Stadium watched Little Rock open defense of its state championship against Russellville High School. The Cyclones shut down Little Rock's running game, forcing the Tigers to go to the air.

Russellville struck first. The score was set up after a punt and a Little Rock penalty forced the Tigers to start from their 1. Kenneth Carter attempted a sweep, but never made it out of the end zone. Russellville was awarded a safety and led 2-0 just minutes into the game.

After two possessions and two punts, the Cyclones took over at the Little Rock 46. Fullback Doy Fox went up the middle for 20 yards, then Harry Wilson passed to John Rye to the 15. Three plays later, Rye ran around left end untouched for a touch-down. Raymond Dacus converted the extra-point attempt and the Cyclones were up 9-0.

The Tigers began their comeback during the second quarter when Bobby Spann passed to Carter for a 22-yard touchdown.

Carter took Russellville's next punt and returned it 59 yards to the Cyclones 6. It took three plays, but Spann passed to Johnny Walker for another score. Carter failed to convert the extra-point attempt, but the Tigers led 13-9.

Early in the fourth quarter, Carter had the play of the game as he returned a punt 80 yards for a touchdown. The extra point gave Little Rock a 20-9 victory. The unimpressive victory still ran Little Rock's unbeaten streak to 32 games.

David Donoho's 45-yard run for a touchdown early in the first period set the tone for the Tigers' next game against Fordyce High School. Little Rock was stung only once during the game as quarterback

Don Countryman carries the ball

Houston Nutt led his Redbugs on a 55-yard scoring drive. Johnnie Green scored Fordyce's only touchdown as the Tigers easily defeated the Redbugs 34-6.

Following a 19-0 victory over Oklahoma power, Classen High of Oklahoma City, Little Rock hosted Blytheville High School. More than 10,000 fans filled Tiger Stadium to watch two powerful teams battle.

The Tigers scored early in the first quarter when George Oliver recovered a Blytheville fumble in the end zone. Warren Carpenter failed to convert the extra-point attempt and Little Rock led 6-0.

The Chicks answered in the second quarter after taking possession at the Tigers 41. They moved to the 16 in three plays, but a penalty pushed the Chicks to the 23. On the next play, Jack Elliot dropped to the 40 and fired a perfect pass to Danny Gentry in the end zone for a touchdown. The extra-point attempt failed.

A perfectly executed "Statue of Liberty" play by Blytheville gained 15 yards to give the Chicks possession at the 20 late in

Photo provided by the Arkansas Democrat-Gazette
Kenneth Carter

the game. Two pass plays moved to the 2, and James Donner needed two plays to score. It gave Blytheville a 12-6 lead and eventually the victory.

The loss ended a 34-game unbeaten streak. It was Little Rock's first loss since a 35-7 upset by El Dorado in 1945. The loss was also the first for a Wilson Matthews-coached team.

Little Rock rebounded with a 19-0 victory over Hot Springs High School. The momentum continued when approximately 7,000 fans watched the Tigers overcome 110 yards in penalties to defeat Fort Smith 7-0.

G.W. "Jiggs" McVay stopped Fort Smith's first series when he intercepted a pass at the Little Rock 35. Carter carried to the 42 on a short run up the middle, then Spann dropped back, rolled to his right and threw a beautiful pass to McVay. McVay caught the pass during his sprint down the field and added another 30 yards before being brought down at the 1 by Donnell Wells.

Carter then ran through the left side of the line for the Tigers' first and only touchdown. Carpenter converted the extra-point

Photo provided by the Arkansas Democrat-Gazette
Henry Fitzgibbons with homecoming queen Norma Krekorian

Photo provided by the Arkansas Democrat-Gazette

G.W. McVay (left) intercepts a pass

Just seven minutes later, the same pair connected again for another touchdown. Carpenter again converted the extra-point attempt, and the Tigers held on for their sixth victory of the season.

After a tie with El Dorado the following week, Little Rock traveled to Hope High School to take on the top-ranked and undefeated Bobcats.

Hope started strong as halfback Buddy Sutton ran 90 yards for a touchdown on the Bobcats' first possession. Bobby Lee kicked the extra point for a 7-0 lead.

Little Rock scored in the second quarter when a 40-yard drive ended with a 15-yard pass from Spann to Carter. Carpenter's kick was blocked and Hope retained the lead.

The Tigers struck again in the fourth quarter when an 85-yard drive was capped by a 12-yard "Statue of Liberty" play. Carpenter's kick again failed, but Little Rock took the lead and held on for a 12-7 upset over the state's No. 1 team.

The Tigers went into their annual Thanksgiving Day game with North Little Rock after a 39-6 victory over rival Pine Bluff. The holiday battle was for the Big 6 Conference title. More than 11,000 fans spent their morning at Tiger Stadium and watched Little Rock hand the Wildcats their worst defeat in series history.

The Tigers dominated the game, with every running back scoring at least one touchdown. Both teams lost two players, the result of ejections for fighting. But Little Rock's 46-7 victory gave the Tigers their third consecutive state championship.

attempt for a 7-0 lead. The Little Rock defense then held the Grizzlies scoreless the remainder of the game and came away with the victory.

Prior to the Tigers' homecoming game against Male High of Louisville, Ky., Norma Krekorian was named queen. Miss Krekorian reigned over more than 9,000 fans who watched the Little Rock offense shine during the first quarter.

Male could not move during its first possession and punted to the Tigers 41. Spann passed to McVay for Little Rock's first touchdown. Carpenter converted the extra point for a 7-0 lead.

1948 TIGER SCHEDULE

Russellville 9	LRHS 20
Fordyce 6	LRHS 34
Classen High of Oklahoma City, OK 0	LRHS 19
Blytheville 12	LRHS 6
*Hot Springs 0	LRHS 19
*Fort Smith 0	LRHS 7
Male High of Louisville, KY 6	LRHS 14
*El Dorado 6	LRHS 6
Hope 7	LRHS 12
*Pine Bluff 6	LRHS 39
*North Little Rock 7	LRHS 46

STATE CHAMPION ... AGAIN
1949   10-1-0

Head Coach: Wilson Matthews
Assistants: Raymond Daugherty, Howard Pearce
Team Trainer: Riley "Doc" Johns
Team Physician: Dr. John McCollough Smith

1949 LETTERMEN

Bill Barnard	Drew Clements	Bob Marlin	Clyde Tracy
Joe Bates	Charles DeViney	G.W. McVay	Allen Venner
Bill Beavers	Phil Dixon	George Plaster	Johnny Walker
Eddie Bradford	Bob Gosser	Wayland Roberts	Billy Walthall
S.M. Brooks	Robey Irwin	Oley Rooker	Don Wardlaw
Kenneth Carter	Larry Jones	James Sewell	Hardy Winburn
Jim Cauthron	Tom Lane	Bobby Spann	
Fred Clark	Frank Maley	Harold Tilley	

1949 MANAGERS

Eddie Barron	Ray Middleton
Jack Burney	Jimmy Shumate
Scott Glover	Ronald Short
Ted Kell	

1949 ALL-SOUTHERN
Kenneth Carter

1949 ALL-STATE
Kenneth Carter
Fred Clark
G.W. McVay
Bobby Spann
Johnny Walker

Photo provided by Central High School
G.W. "Jiggs" McVay (33)

The season-opening game against Fordyce High School showed that the Tigers had not lost much of their power and speed from the previous year. Little Rock's running backs ran free in a 65-6 victory over the Redbugs.

Tiger Stadium was the site of the Tigers' next game against Classen High of Oklahoma City. Little Rock's second possession began on its 44. Hardy Winburn crossed midfield on an off-tackle running play to the 46. G.W. McVay ran around left end for 26 yards, then picked up another 13 yards on the next play. It took Kenneth Carter two carries to go the 7 yards needed for a 6-0 lead.

After an exchange of punts to open the third quarter, a Classen fumble gave Little Rock possession on its 37. McVay and Carter carried for 7 yards and 15 yards, respectively, to move to the Classen 40. McVay added 2 more yards and Bobby Spann then handed off to Carter, who faded back and passed to Spann on the 14. Spann, though, was not brought down until he reached the 9.

McVay carried off tackle to the 4, and Carter finished the drive for the Tigers' second touchdown in a 12-0 victory over the Oklahoma team.

In 1948, the Tigers' only upset was against Blytheville High School. Little

194

Rock was prepared for revenge when it traveled to the northeast Arkansas town for its next game. Behind a powerful offensive line and a five-touchdown performance by McVay, the Tigers were victorious. Carter and Winburn each scored once in the 49-19 victory over the Chicks.

After a scoreless first quarter the next week against Hot Springs, Little Rock center Jimmy Cauthron blocked a punt. Little Rock recovered at the 6 and McVay carried twice, scoring from the 5 to give the Tigers a 6-0 lead.

Hot Springs could not move after the ensuing kickoff and punted from its end zone. Little Rock took possession at the Trojans 17, and Billy Walthall ran around end on first down for a touchdown to increase lead to 12-0.

An exchange of punts gave the Tigers possession on their 20. Spann passed to Carter, who cut off tackle and outran the defense for an 80-yard touchdown.

The half ended with Little Rock up 20-0. The domination continued throughout the second half in a 46-7 victory.

A trip to Fort Smith awaited Little Rock the following week. Even though they were highly favored over the Grizzlies, the Tigers had to come from behind twice to overtake them.

Fort Smith returned a punt to the 24 early in the first quarter. On third down,

Photo provided by Central High School
Billy Walthall (13)

Hubert Henry handed off to Buddy Moore for a touchdown. Moore's conversion attempt was no good, but the Grizzlies took a 6-0 lead into halftime.

Little Rock answered in the third quarter with a Spann to Johnny Walker touchdown pass. Carter converted the extra-point attempt for a 7-6 lead. Fort Smith took the ensuing kickoff and Charlie Nations capped a long drive with a quarterback sneak for a touchdown. Moore's conversion was good for a 13-7 Fort Smith lead.

The Tigers regained possession following a punt late in the fourth quarter and began a drive from their 20. McVay had two long runs to the Grizzlies 42.

Spann passed to Phil Dixon to reach the 12, and McVay ran the remaining distance for the score. Carter converted the extra-point attempt with four minutes left in the game for a 14-13 victory.

Little Rock's next road trip wasn't as successful against Male High School of Louisville, Ky.

The Tigers scored first on their initial possession when Spann connected with Bill Beavers for a 70-yard touchdown to put Little Rock up 6-0. Carter's conversion made it 7-0.

Photo provided by the Arkansas Democrat-Gazette
Little Rock's 1949 starting offense

With the score tied 7-7 midway through the fourth quarter, a Spann pass was intercepted by Paul Grider. Grider raced 62 yards to put the Purples on top and hand the Tigers their first loss of the season, 14-7.

Homecoming queen Louise Heiman was among the 8,500 fans at Tiger Stadium who watched McVay run 52 yards against El Dorado High School to set up the Tigers' game-winning touchdown.

Seven plays after McVay's long run, Carter scored from the 1 and kicked the extra point for a 13-7 lead. Little Rock was able to hold the Wildcats out of the end zone and end their hopes of a Big 6 Conference championship.

Behind 145 yards rushing by Carter, the Tigers ran over Hope High School 35-7. The highly anticipated matchup with Pine Bluff followed, and the game was one of the most exciting in years.

More than 10,000 filled Pine Bluff's Jordan Stadium and watched a scoreless first half. The Zebras, though, scored in the third quarter after they blocked a McVay punt. J. Holmes recovered for Pine Bluff and returned it to the 20. Don Wilson twisted his way the remaining 20 yards on the first play for a 6-0 Pine Bluff lead.

Photo provided by the Arkansas Democrat-Gazette
Little Rock celebrates a state championship

195

Little Rock took the ensuing kickoff and marched 68 yards to score on a 38-yard run by Carter.

Charles DeViney intercepted a pass in the fourth quarter and returned it 21 yards to set up the Tigers' winning touchdown.

On fourth down, Carter scored from the 1 to give Little Rock the victory.

Following a thrilling 21-20 victory over Tupelo, Miss., the Tigers celebrated Thanksgiving by meeting North Little Rock High School at Tiger Stadium. With more than 9,000 fans looking on, Carter and McVay led a four-touchdown performance by Little Rock to give Coach Wilson Mat-thews his second Big 6 title in as many years.

McVay scored two touchdowns and Carter scored once to give the Tigers their fourth consecutive victory over the Wildcats. Carter's touchdown came on the most spectacular play of the game.

He took a North Little Rock punt on his 8 and ran 92 yards for Little Rock's second score. This touchdown came within two minutes of the Tigers' first score. Little Rock was named the 1949 state champion following a 28-0 victory over the Wildcats.

1949 TIGER SCHEDULE

Fordyce 6	LRHS 65
Classen High of Oklahoma City, OK 0	LRHS 12
Blytheville 19	LRHS 49
*Hot Springs 7	LRHS 46
*Fort Smith 13	LRHS 14
Male High of Louisville, KY 14	LRHS 7
*El Dorado 7	LRHS 13
Hope 7	LRHS 35
*Pine Bluff 6	LRHS 13
Tupelo, MS 20	LRHS 21
*North Little Rock 0	LRHS 28

A FIFTH CONSECUTIVE STATE CHAMPIONSHIP

1950   10-2-0

Head Coach: Wilson Matthews
Assistants: Raymond Daugherty, Steed White
Team Physician: Dr. John McCollough Smith

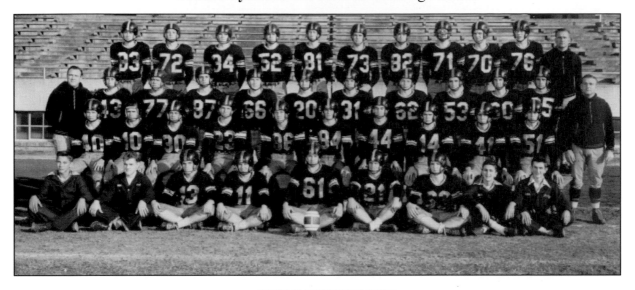

1950 LETTERMEN

Jay Barron	Don Garner	Danny Holman	Jodie Parker
Ted Bellingrath	Bobby Glover	Dub Johnson	Winston Porter
Thomas Blagg	Paul Goad	Larry Jones	Joe Reynolds
Eddie Bradford	Ed Goldman	Harold Meeks	Wayland Roberts
Jim Cauthron	Bob Gosser	Marvin Miracle	James Sewell
Drew Clements	Bill Hastings	Henry Moore	Clark Shelton
Bob Duncan	Carol Henry	Larry Mullens	Carl Slaughter

1950 MANAGERS

Jack Burney	Curtis Finch	Paul Searcy
David Burton	Jim Guenther	Ronald Short
Jerry Dhonau	Ben Piazza	Jimmy Shumate

1950 ALL-AMERICAN
Eddie Bradford

1950 ALL-SOUTHERN
Eddie Bradford

1950 ALL-STATE
Eddie Bradford
Jim Cauthron
Carol Henry
Henry Moore
Wayland Roberts

Henry Moore (34)

The 1950 season was the first time in many years that Riley "Doc" Johns was not on the Little Rock High School sideline. Riley was diagnosed with cancer in early 1949 and died Oct. 22, 1950.

More than 9,000 attended the funeral service held in Tiger Stadium. Johns was survived by his wife, Hazel Johns, and his brother, Percy Johns. "Doc" spent 22 years caring for the Tigers.

Little Rock opened a week earlier than other schools, and more than 6,000 fans filled Tiger Stadium for the first game. Coach Wilson Matthews began his fourth season as head coach when Little Rock met Central High School of Knoxville, Tenn. The Tigers hoped to win the first of many games en route to a fifth consecutive state championship.

Little Rock scored first in the opening quarter after a Knoxville fumble gave the Tigers possession on the Bobcats 36. Paul Goad ran up the middle for 5 yards, and Dub Johnson then gained 10 yards when he ran off right guard. On the following play, Henry Moore put Little Rock on the scoreboard when he went 21 yards around right end. Johnson converted the extra point for a 7-0 lead with only 3:40 gone in the first quarter.

Knoxville's answer was set up two possessions later after Little Rock's punter was tackled for a 19-yard loss, giving the Bobcats possession at midfield. It took four plays, but a short touchdown run gave the Tennessee team hope. The extra-point attempt was blocked with one minute remaining in the first quarter.

The Tigers countered quickly, scoring four plays later. Carol Henry took the ensuing kickoff 45 yards to the Knoxville 40. Ed Goldman picked up 6 yards on first down and Moore did the rest.

Moore rushed 13 yards, 21 yards and then 15 yards around end to reach the Knoxville 6. He then went off tackle for the remaining yardage and the score. Goldman's kick increased Little Rock's lead to 14-6 only 40 seconds into the second quarter.

Little Rock's defense allowed Knoxville to score again, but the Tigers were almost unstoppable offensively as Goad rushed for 120 yards and Moore rushed for 145 yards in the 34-13 season-opening victory.

A 22-yard touchdown run by Moore in the first quarter and a 22-yard touchdown run by Henry in the second quarter were all the Tigers needed for their next game against Subiaco Academy. The Trojans did give the 6,000 fans in Tiger Stadium a scare late in the third quarter when they scored on a 47-yard pass play. Little Rock, however, stopped the conversion as Jay Barron intercepted the pass in the end zone.

Clark Shelton (14)

The Tigers were able to control Subiaco the remainder of the game and came away with a 12-6 victory.

Classen High of Oklahoma City was no match for Little Rock the following week. The Tigers scored eight touchdowns, including a 99-yard touchdown run, in a 52-13 victory over the Indians. The next week was a little tougher when the Tigers played host to Texarkana, Texas.

Texarkana's Kerby Carter intercepted a pass midway through the second quarter to give the Texas team possession at the Little Rock 43. On the next play, Bobby Barnes went through the right side of the line for a 43-yard touchdown. Carter added the extra point for a 7-0 lead.

The Tigers scored as the second half opened. Goad received the opening kickoff and ran toward the sideline. He then handed off to Moore, who ran 85 yards for a touchdown. Drew Clements attempted the extra point, but the kick was wide. This mistake would prove costly as Little Rock lost its first game of the season, 7-6.

Little Rock rebounded the next week when it opened conference play at Rix Stadium in Hot Springs. Moore, Goldman and Ted Bellingrath each scored in an 18-6 victory over the Trojans.

Little Rock then beat Fort Smith 52-0 in front of a homecoming crowd of more than 8,000 at Tiger Stadium. Jean Hackett was crowned homecoming queen, and she watched eight Tigers score in the easy victory over the Grizzlies.

Jean Hackett, homecoming queen

One of the roughest games in many years was played the next week at Tiger Stadium when Little Rock hosted Gadsden, Ala. There were numerous penalties and injuries after many fights broke out during the game. Bellingrath, however, was able to concentrate long enough to complete three touchdown passes in a 45-14 romp over the Alabama team.

The Tigers traveled to El Dorado next and returned home with their first victory in that city since 1943. They withstood a fierce fourth-quarter comeback in front of a homecoming crowd of more than 10,000. The 27-21 victory maintained Little Rock's conference lead and all but eliminated El Dorado from the race.

Following a loss to Tilghman High of Paducah, Ky., the Tigers prepared for their annual game with Pine Bluff. Billed as a battle for the conference and state championship, the game was seen by more than 10,000 fans at Tiger Stadium.

Little Rock dominated the game, rushing for 402 yards, passing for 199 yards and scoring eight touchdowns in a 53-6 victory over the Zebras. The only black mark for the Tigers was 121 yards in penalties, ne-

Eddie Bradford is tackled during a scrimmage game

gating two additional touchdowns. It was the most lopsided outcome in series history and sealed the championship for Little Rock.

The following week, University of Oklahoma head coach Bud Wilkinson watched the Tigers beat Norman, Okla., 65-7. In an interview after the game, Coach Wilkinson said Little Rock was the best-coached team he had ever seen.

The Tigers ended the season by pounding North Little Rock 64-7 on Thanksgiving Day. This victory gave the Tigers (10-2-0) their fifth consecutive state championship.

1950 TIGER SCHEDULE

Central High of Knoxville, TN 13	LRCH 34
Subiaco Academy 6	LRCH 12
Classen High of Oklahoma City, OK 13	LRCH 52
Texarkana, TX 7	LRCH 6
*Hot Springs 6	LRCH 18
*Fort Smith 0	LRCH 52
Gadsden, AL 14	LRCH 45
*El Dorado 21	LRCH 27
Tilghman High of Paducah, KY 12	LRCH 9
*Pine Bluff 6	LRCH 53
Norman, OK 7	LRCH 65
*North Little Rock 7	LRCH 64

Photo provided by Central High School

Henry Moore carries the ball against Texarkana, Texas

200

FALLING FROM NO. 1

1951   9-3-0

Head Coach: Wilson Matthews
Assistants: Raymond Daugherty, Steed White
Team Physician: Dr. John McCollough Smith

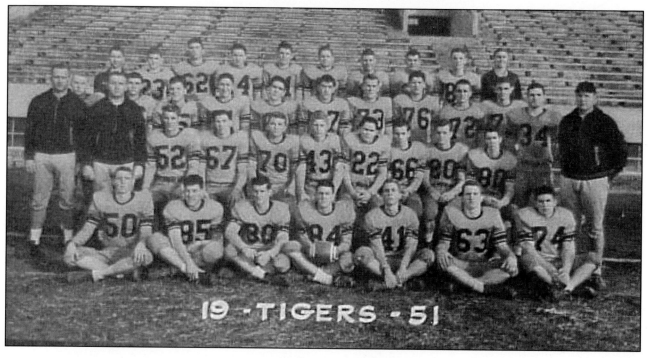

1951 LETTERMEN

Joe Allen
Bill Barnhouse
Ted Bellingrath
Thomas Blagg
Frank Caple
George Cate
John Cochran

Lacy Frazer
Bobby Glover
Paul Goad
Bobby Hannon
Bill Hastings
Dub Johnson
Bill Jones

Billy Kumpuris
Bob McFarlin
Harold Meeks
Henry Moore
Larry Mullins
John Nutt
Bob Oberle

Jodie Parker
Winston Porter
Charles Reed
M.L. Stevens
Ronald Underwood
Jim Wallace
Milton Williams

1951 MANAGERS

Allan Bradley
Jack Burney
Walter Faust

Benny Goad
Pete Jump
Charles Miller

Bob Norrish
Charles Rea
Fred Warner

1951 ALL-SOUTHERN
Henry Moore

1951 ALL-STATE
Henry Moore
Winston Porter

Photo provided by Central High School
Little Rock's Bill Hastings

The Tigers opened the season against the highly rated Adamson High School Leopards of Dallas. For several days prior to the game, Little Rock newspapers published articles praising the Texas squad.

Adamson was picked to win the overall Texas championship and considered one of the premier teams in the South in 1951.

All this fanfare, though, ceased once the game began. The Tigers scored almost at will against Adamson. The game was highlighted by an 80-yard touchdown run by Henry Moore and four touchdown passes by quarterback Bobby Hannon. Little Rock dominated the Leopards 53-20.

The Tigers' second game was against defending Louisiana champion Istrouma High School. The Baton Rouge school had Little Rock fans at Tiger Stadium on the edge of their seats until a last-minute drive put the home team on top for good.

Trailing 12-7 with 1:30 left in the game, Paul Goad returned a punt to the Tigers 14 to set up an amazing 86-yard game-winning drive.

Ted Bellingrath passed to Jodie Parker for 15 yards and then to Bill Hastings, who ran to the Baton Rouge 25. On the next play, Bellingrath connected with Ronald Underwood to reach the 3.

Moore took a handoff with 13 seconds remaining in the game and stepped through a hole in the left side of the line for the go-ahead touchdown. Dub Johnson's extra-point attempt failed, but time elapsed after the ensuing kickoff and Little Rock escaped 13-12.

Classen High of Oklahoma City, the Tigers' third opponent, did not put up much of a fight. Moore began the scoring in the first quarter with a 74-yard run. The second touchdown came on the final play of the quarter when Bellingrath completed a pass to Underwood at the Classen 10.

Underwood, who made the reception on the run, easily made it into the end zone. Johnson converted the extra point for a 13-0 lead.

Little Rock struck again in the third quarter when Hastings scored on a 46-yard run. Johnson then converted his second extra point for a 20-0 lead. The Tigers were able to hold on for their fourth consecutive victory over the Oklahoma team.

Photo provided by Central High School
Henry Moore

Within five minutes after the start of the next game, Little Rock's opponent began a drive that resulted in the game's first touchdown. Texarkana, Texas, took possession on the Tigers 35, and a pass from Jimmy Williams to Earl Johnson placed the ball on the 1.

The Little Rock line held Texarkana three times, but on fourth down Marvin Lay scored for a 6-0 lead.

Later in the same quarter, Texarkana took control at its 35. A deep pass from Williams to Johnson resulted in an interference penalty against the Tigers. Texarkana was awarded possession on the Little Rock 5, and three plays later Sam Buchmeyer scored to increase the lead to 13-0.

The Tigers scored early in the second quarter when Bellingrath passed to Winston Porter for a 60-yard touchdown. Johnson added the extra point and Little Rock trailed 13-7 at the half.

Texarkana scored on its first possession of the second half. Kenneth Sutton went up the middle for a 50-yard gain before being pulled down at the 10. He carried two more times to the 1 before Williams slipped

Photo provided by Central High School
The Little Rock bench

around right end for the score. Williams added the extra point for a 20-7 lead.

Texarkana guard Dick Clem recovered a fumble on the Little Rock 23 to set up the final score of the game. Williams passed to Johnson to reach the 6, then Buchmeyer passed to Billy Fairchild for the touchdown. Williams again converted the extra point to increase the lead to 27-7.

Coach Watty Myers' team upset the Tigers for the second consecutive year, 27-7, in front of approximately 7,000 fans in Texarkana, Texas.

After two commanding victories over conference opponents Hot Springs (46-6) and Fort Smith (45-12), Little Rock met another out-of-state opponent. The Tigers traveled 400 miles to Murphree Stadium in Gadsden, Ala., to take on a tough Alabama team for homecoming.

More than 8,500 fans watched Little Rock take the opening kickoff and drive 63 yards in eight plays for a touchdown. Goad started the drive with a 21-yard run. Moore ran 19 yards a few plays later.

On fourth down from the 9, Goad went around left end for the touchdown. Johnson converted the extra point for a 7-0 lead after only four minutes of play.

Gadsden began to move just before the close of the first quarter. A 49-yard drive ended as the second quarter opened, and Don Conner capped the march when he went up the middle for a 3-yard touchdown

Photo provided by Central High School
Deborah Nelson, homecoming queen

run. The conversion was good to make it 7-7.

Later in the second quarter, the Tigers held the Alabama team on downs and took over on their 20. They proceeded to cover 80 yards for another score.

Goad carried eight times during the drive and gained 40 yards. On first down from the Gadsden 37, Bellingrath passed to Porter, who made the reception at the 3. He was tackled there, but fell into the end zone for the touchdown. Johnson converted his second extra point as Little Rock held on for 14-7 victory.

After dominating victories over El Dorado (59-14) and Tilghman High of Paducah, Ky. (46-7), the Tigers traveled to Pine Bluff for their annual battle with the Zebras.

More than 9,000 fans at Jordan Stadium were stunned when Pine Bluff jumped to a 21-0 lead in the first three quarters. Little Rock began its comeback early in the last period when Bellingrath passed to Hastings on the first play of the fourth quarter for a 70-yard touchdown.

On their next possession, Bellingrath passed the Tigers from their 3 to the Zebras 14. Moore scored from there, but Johnson missed his second extra-point attempt of the game.

After holding Pine Bluff on downs and forcing a punt, Little Rock took possession on the Zebras 47. A pass fell incomplete on first down. But on the next play, Bellingrath handed to Moore, who easily covered the 47 yards for the score. Johnson's extra point pulled Little Rock within 21-19.

The Tigers, however, were unable to score again and lost to Pine Bluff 21-19. It marked Little Rock's first conference loss since an upset by El Dorado in 1945.

The Tigers won a wild one the following week in Clarksdale, Miss., to complete their out-of-state schedule. Ronnie Bennett ran 88 yards for a touchdown on the opening kickoff to put Clarksdale ahead. Jim Jones converted the extra point to make it 7-0.

The Tigers countered on their first possession when Moore capped a 69-yard drive with a 3-yard run. The Wildcats regained the lead when Stan Schwartz passed 16 yards to Bennett for a touchdown. Little Rock, however, tied it again when Bellingrath passed to Parker for a 12-yard touchdown.

A 62-yard run by Moore and another 12-yard touchdown pass, this time from Bellingrath to Porter, put the Tigers up 27-13.

Little Rock's final score of the first half occurred when Jim Wallace intercepted a Schwartz pass and returned it for a touchdown to give the Tigers a 34-13 advantage at the break.

Coach Wilson Matthews is presented a car on Thanksgiving Day

Clarksdale rallied with four touchdowns in the third quarter, but Little Rock scored two of its own to edge the Wildcats 48-45. Bennett led his Mississippi team with four touchdown receptions to go along with his kickoff return.

Bellingrath completed 13 of 17 passes, three for touchdowns, and Moore rushed for 156 yards and two touchdowns to lead the Tigers.

Before Little Rock's Thanksgiving Day matchup with North Little Rock, Coach Wilson Matthews was presented with a new Dodge vehicle by Little Rock fans. Assistants Raymond Daugherty and Steed White were each awarded a certificate for a new suit.

The Little Rock team did not fare as well. The Wildcats converted one more extra point, which was enough for the holiday victory. More than 9,000 fans watched North Little Rock beat Little Rock for only the fifth time in 22 meetings.

Following the game, North Little Rock fans tore down the goal posts at Tiger Stadium. This resulted in a melee between spectators from each school. Police were able to control the situation before much damage was done.

In the Big 6 Conference standings, North Little Rock's victory pushed it into second behind conference and state champion Pine Bluff. The loss dropped the Tigers into third place, the first year since 1945 that Little Rock was not crowned conference and state champion.

1951 TIGER SCHEDULE

Adamson High of Dallas, TX 20	LRHS 53
Istrouma High of Baton Rouge, LA 12	LRHS 13
Classen High of Oklahoma City, OK 0	LRHS 20
Texarkana, TX 27	LRHS 7
*Hot Springs 6	LRHS 46
*Fort Smith 12	LRHS 45
Gadsden, AL 7	LRHS 14
*El Dorado 14	LRHS 59
Tilghman High of Paducah, KY 7	LRHS 46
*Pine Bluff 21	LRHS 19
Clarksdale, MS 45	LRHS 48
*North Little Rock 14	LRHS 13

RECLAIMING THE TOP SPOT

1952   9-2-0

Head Coach: Wilson Matthews
Assistants: Winston Faulkner, Steed White
Team Physician: Dr. John McCollough Smith

[1952 TEAM PHOTO NOT AVAILABLE]

1952 LETTERMEN

Joe Allen	Lacy Fraiser	Bill Jones	Harold Stone
Harold Bagby	Ralph Goldman	Don Manes	Sonny Teddar
Richard Bennett	Carl Habig	Elwood Mosley	Ronald Underwood
Jimmy Clark	Lee Hammer	Reggie Nalls	John Venable
Lee Curry	Bobby Hannon	John Nutt	Ronnie Weeks
John Cusick	Darryl Herbert	Stuart Perry	Jim Wetherington
Andy Davis	Don Jolly	Joe Reese	Scott Woodmansee

1952 MANAGERS

Bruce Barnes	Fred Palmer
Holland Brown	Charles Rea
John Joyce	Fred Warner
Charles Miller	Robert White

1952 ALL-SOUTHERN
Bobby Hannon

1952 ALL-STATE
Richard Bennett
Bobby Hannon
Don Jolly
Stuart Perry
Ronald Underwood

Photo provided by the Arkansas Democrat-Gazette

Andy Davis

Coach Wilson Matthews' Tigers opened 1952 with a 40-20 victory over Norman, Okla. A heartbreaker, though, occurred the next week with a 19-14 loss to Texarkana, Texas. This marked the third consecutive year that the Texas team upset Little Rock.

The following week at Baton Rouge, La., the Tigers suffered their worst defeat since 1945. Istrouma High School quarterback Win Turner passed for 220 yards in the first half and finished the game with eight completions for 270 yards in a 34-9 rout.

The Tigers began conference play the next week when they traveled to Hot Springs for a showdown with the Trojans. Little Rock performed well, finishing with 240 yards rushing and 206 yards passing and holding Hot Springs to 36 yards rushing and 29 yards passing.

Bobby Hannon converted seven extra-point attempts and completed two touchdown passes. Six other players scored for the Tigers, including a 60-yard touchdown reception by Ronald Underwood. Little Rock dominated Hot Springs 55-0.

Another domination occurred a week later when the Tigers played their home-

Photo provided by the Arkansas Democrat-Gazette
Sonny Teddar (44) intercepts a pass

coming game against Fort Smith High School. Little Rock received the opening kickoff and returned the ball to its 29. From there, halfback Bill Jones ran off right tackle, cut to his left and covered the 71 yards for the touchdown. The score put the Tigers up 6-0 just 35 seconds into the game.

Midway through the second period, Hannon passed to Scott Woodmansee for a 63-yard scoring play. This touchdown gave Little Rock a 41-0 halftime lead.

Coach Matthews played his second and third teams during the second half, but the Tigers kept scoring. Behind an unstoppable offense and a strong defense that intercepted five passes, Little Rock won 61-0 in front of more than 6,000 fans.

The Tigers and Texarkana High School met in Texar-

Photo provided by the Arkansas Democrat-Gazette
Elwood Mosley returns an interception

kana, Ark., for a matchup between unbeaten Big 6 Conference foes. Following a scoreless first quarter, Little Rock received a punt at its 48. On the first play, Woodmansee burst over left tackle and was in the clear for a 52-yard touchdown run. The conversion gave the Tigers a 7-0 halftime lead.

Little Rock scored twice more in the second half while rushing for 302 yards. The Razorbacks were unable to score against the tough defense and Texarkana received its first conference loss of the season, 21-0.

Another long trip awaited the Tigers the following week against El Dorado. Another dominating loss was in store for Little Rock's opponent as the Tigers posted their fourth conference shutout, 50-0.

Highlighting the game was a 57-yard run by John Venable, a 55-yard touchdown pass from Venable to Don Jolly and 208 yards passing. The victory spoiled the Wildcats' homecoming and put the Tigers atop the conference standings.

Little Rock took a break from conference action and took a trip to Paducah, Ky., to play Tilghman High School at Keiler Field. Hannon completed 10 passes for 171 yards, Venable scored twice and Jones scored once in a 21-6 victory over the Tornadoes. The Tigers handed Tilghman, the No. 2 team in Kentucky, its first loss of the season.

Finally, the week that all of central Arkansas waited for had arrived. The Pine Bluff Zebras arrived at Tiger Stadium, as well as more than 13,000 fans to watch the annual rivalry.

With possession on his 33 early in the second quarter, Hannon gave Andy Davis a pitchout for 9 yards and later sent him up the middle for another 10 yards to the Pine Bluff 43. Hannon dropped back on the next play and passed to Jimmy Clark. Clark caught the ball over his shoulder and made it to the 1 before being tackled. Hannon

208

then scored on the next play, but a penalty moved the ball back to the 6. Hannon pitched to Venable for the short touchdown run and a 6-0 lead.

Little Rock scored again on its next possession, a 39-yard pass from Hannon to Clark. This score would be all the Tigers needed for the victory, but Little Rock went on to score six more touchdowns in a 53-7 victory. The Tigers finished the night with 471 yards of total offense.

With Pine Bluff now out of the title race, the only team standing in the way of an outright title for Little Rock was North Little Rock High School. The Tigers were guaranteed at least a share of the championship, regardless of the outcome against the Wildcats. North Little Rock could only share the championship with a victory over Little Rock.

Before the game against the Wildcats, the Tigers defeated Clarksdale, Miss., 49-13 to finish their nonconference schedule. The next Thursday, Thanksgiving Day, was the matchup with North Little Rock.

Jones began the scoring when he ran more than 50 yards for a Little Rock touchdown on the first play from scrimmage. Just minutes later, Venable scored on a short run to increase the lead to 12-0.

Late in the second quarter, Venable took a handoff up the middle, and behind two great blocks by Jolly, ran 24 yards for

Photo provided by the Arkansas Democrat-Gazette
Little Rock's 1952 starting defense

another score to give the Tigers an 18-0 lead. Hannon converted the extra-point attempt for a 19-0 lead.

A 58-yard drive by Little Rock in the fourth quarter ended the scoring. A 21-yard pass from Hannon to Jolly moved Little Rock to the 4. Hannon then went off left guard for the touchdown. His conversion attempt was blocked, but the Tigers held on for a 25-6 victory and an outright state championship.

Little Rock won five consecutive state championships before three losses in 1951 set it back in the rankings. The 1952 championship, though, put the Tigers back on top.

1952 TIGER SCHEDULE

Norman, OK 20	LRHS 40
Texarkana, TX 19	LRHS 14
Istrouma High of Baton Rouge, LA 34	LRHS 9
*Hot Springs 0	LRHS 55
*Fort Smith 0	LRHS 61
*Texarkana, AR 0	LRHS 21
*El Dorado 0	LRHS 50
Tilghman High of Paducah, KY 6	LRHS 21
*Pine Bluff 7	LRHS 53
Clarksdale, MS 13	LRHS 49
*North Little Rock 6	LRHS 25

PREPARING TO WIN UNDER A NEW NAME
1953   8-2-1

Head Coach: Wilson Matthews
Assistants: Steed White, Winston Faulkner, Don Sparks
Team Trainer: Don Sparks
Team Physician: Dr. John McCollough Smith

[1953 TEAM PHOTO NOT AVAILABLE]

1953 LETTERMEN

Richard Bell	Troy Green	Stuart Perry	John Trieschmann
Richard Bennett	Lee Hammer	Frank Plegge	Ben Tubb
Kenneth Brown	Darryl Herbert	Brinton Ramoly	Freddie Tubbs
Robert Brown	Robert Lemmer	Joe Reese	Ronnie Weeks
Jimmy Clark	Igor Malczycki	Herb Rule	Jim Wetherington
Eddie Copeland	Don Manes	Benny Scroggins	Scott Woodmansee
Bob Dugger	H.N. Means	Ralph Sewell	
Don Elkins	Buddy Milligan	Tommy Taylor	
Ralph Goldman	Charles Patterson	Sonny Teddar	

1953 MANAGERS

Bruce Barnes	Danny Mobley
Bobby DeBin	Robert Murray
John Gill	Robert Nosari
Leslie Grady	Fred Palmer
Peter Hartstein	Robert Sullards
Pete Haydon	Terry Watson
Robin Jones	Robert White

1953 ALL-AMERICAN
Stuart Perry

1953 ALL-SOUTHERN
Richard Bennett
Jimmy Clark
Stuart Perry

1953 ALL-STATE

Richard Bennett	Don Manes
Jimmy Clark	Stuart Perry
Darryl Herbert	Joe Reese

In the spring of 1953, the Little Rock School Board decided to build another high school in western Little Rock to accommodate the growing population. The school was to be built on the corner of Hayes Street and Highway 10.

Since both schools could not be known as "Little Rock High School," each would assume another name. Little Rock High School would become Little Rock Central, but the planned school had yet to a receive a name.

The Little Rock Tigers opened against Southside High School of Memphis. On its second possession, Little Rock took over at the Scrappers 42. Two running plays positioned Little Rock at the 30, and then Ronnie Weeks passed to Joe Reese at the 5. Reese kept his feet and crossed the goal line for a 6-0 lead.

Photo provided by Central High School

Jim Wetherington

Southside came charging back with the next kickoff as Bob Rose returned it to the Tigers 38. The Scrappers moved to the 25 in two plays before John Hunter bulled his way through the defense for a touchdown. The Scrappers converted the extra point and led 7-6.

Sonny Teddar returned a second-quarter punt 25 yards to the Southside 27 to set up the Tigers' next score. Darryl Herbert ran through the right side of the line to the 5 and gained 4 more yards on the following play. Freddie Tubbs finished the drive with a 1-yard run. Igor Malczycki's conversion was good and Little Rock led 13-7 at half-time.

Teddar scored on a 2-yard run in the third quarter to end the scoring in a 19-7 victory over Southside. Little Rock spent the next week preparing for a trip to Texarkana, Texas, to play a team that had beaten it the previous three years.

The teams combined for seven first-quarter turnovers before the Tigers began a scoring drive late in the period. After receiving a punt, Ralph Goldman ran to the Little Rock 48. A Teddar to Jimmy Clark pass moved Little Rock to the Texas 42.

Teddar, Jim Wetherington and Herbert each carried once to move the Tigers to the 25. Wetherington went another 12 yards for

Photo provided by Central High School

Joe Reese (86) catches a pass against Pine Bluff

211

Photo provided by the Arkansas Democrat-Gazette
Richard Bennett tips a punt.

a first down. Teddar carried to the 10, then passed to Reese for the touchdown. Malczycki converted the extra point for a 7-0 lead.

After the ensuing kickoff, the Tigers recovered a fumble on the Texas 37. On the first play, Teddar passed to Reese at the 10. Reese ran untouched for the touchdown.

Little Rock's defense held strong until midway through the fourth quarter when Texarkana's Bill Gresham capped a 63-yard drive with a 2-yard touchdown run. James Moffatt converted the extra point, but the Tigers went on to win 13-7.

In a wild battle with Istrouma High School of Baton Rouge, La., Little Rock began the scoring frenzy midway through the first quarter. A poor punt gave the Tigers possession at the Istrouma 31, but a penalty and a loss on first down sent Little Rock back to the 34. Teddar connected with Clark at the 10, and he was pushed out of bounds at the 1. Herbert failed to gain the yard on the next play, but Teddar then ran a bootleg to the right for the score and Malczycki converted the extra-point attempt for a 7-0 lead.

Just moments later, Clark scored from the 1 on an end-around. Malczycki's kick increased the lead to 14-0. The Tigers went up 21-0 after a 68-yard drive in the third quarter ended with a 51-yard pass from Teddar to Wetherington. Malczycki again converted the extra point.

Little Rock went on to score two more times and held off a Baton Rouge rally in the second half to narrowly escape with a 34-28 victory. The loss was Istrouma's first of the season.

The defending Big 7 champion Tigers opened conference play the next week with a 61-0 victory over Hot Springs. They continued the dominance a week later with a 39-9 victory over Fort Smith.

A game with Texarkana, Ark., resulted in another victory for Little Rock. Although the Tigers did not play up to their potential, they raced to a 26-0 lead and withstood a fourth-quarter rally to beat the Razorbacks.

Little Rock's first drive ended when Wetherington fumbled on the Texarkana 5. The Tigers, though, forced a punt and began another drive from their 34.

On first down, a Weeks to Clark pass resulted in an apparent 66-yard touchdown. A clipping penalty, though, negated the score. The next play, also a Weeks to Clark pass, moved Little Rock to the Texarkana 22. Two running plays moved the Tigers to

Photo provided by the Arkansas Democrat-Gazette
Little Rock's Stuart Perry

212

1953 Tiger seniors

the touchdown. The Pounders scored again in the second quarter when Bill Heaton passed to Cantrell for a 41-yard touchdown.

Following a scoreless third quarter, Tennessee began a 54-yard drive that ended in a 12-yard touchdown run by Heaton. Gene Etter converted his third extra-point attempt for a 26-0 lead.

The Tigers' only score was set up by a 33-yard pass from Weeks to Clark to the 5. With three seconds left in the game, Teddar passed to Reese for the touchdown, but Little Rock suffered its first loss of the season.

The following week, a 73-yard punt return for a touchdown by Clark helped the Tigers to a 13-7 halftime lead against Paducah (Ky.) Tilghman High School. Another touchdown late in the fourth quarter was no help because of the Kentucky school's second-half rally. The Tornadoes struck three times, two scores set up by turnovers. Tilghman handed Little Rock its second consecutive loss, 27-19.

The Tigers were favored to win the next game against rival Pine Bluff. More than 7,000 fans at Jordan Stadium in Pine Bluff watched penalties and fumbles plague Little

the 19, and a "Statue of Liberty" play was good to the 10. Four plays later, Herbert scored on a 1-yard run to take an early lead.

A 25-yard touchdown pass from Weeks to Reese, a 7-yard run by Clark, a 25-yard run by Goldman and an 11-yard run by Clark completed Little Rock's scoring in a 32-12 victory.

El Dorado was the team to beat during the Tigers' homecoming game. The contest started well for Little Rock with a 7-0 lead before its offense took the field.

Teddar received a punt at his 33 and handed to Clark, who ran down the west sideline for a touchdown. Wetherington converted the extra-point attempt.

Weeks, playing quarterback, passed for 103 yards and one touchdown, while Teddar added another scoring pass in a 48-7 victory. It was Little Rock's fourth conference victory and seventh overall.

The undefeated Tigers were outrushed, outpaced and outscored the next week at Chattanooga (Tenn.) Central High School. Chattanooga totaled 250 yards rushing and 84 yards passing, while holding Little Rock to only 93 yards rushing and 60 yards passing.

The Purple Pounders scored late in the first quarter when halfback Bob Tate ran around left end for a 4-yard touchdown. The extra-point attempt failed and the Tigers trailed 6-0.

Little Rock fumbled on its 46 and Chattanooga recovered. Charles Cantrell passed to W.H. Geren, who went the distance for

Little Rock's Ralph Goldman

Rock during the first half. Two first-half touchdowns by the Tigers were nullified by penalties.

Little Rock was only able to post one first-half score. This occurred when it took the opening kickoff and drove 58 yards to take the lead. Goldman capped the drive on a 21-yard run. Malczycki's extra-point attempt put the Tigers up 7-0.

Late in the second quarter, Teddar fumbled while being sacked. A Pine Bluff player picked up the loose ball and ran 55 yards for a touchdown. Jerry Hopkins converted the extra point to make it 7-7.

As the second half opened, Wetherington fumbled on his 49. Pine Bluff's Ralph Cloar recovered at the 40 and returned it 56 yards to the Little Rock 4. The Zebras scored four plays later and the extra-point conversion gave them a 14-7 lead.

The Tigers tied the score in the fourth quarter when Wetherington capped a 98-yard drive with a 2-yard run. Malczycki's extra point made it 14-14. Each team scored once more and the game ended in a 21-21 tie. It was a stunning upset for Little Rock, which was without a victory for three consecutive weeks.

An idle week allowed additional time for the Tigers to prepare for their Thanksgiving Day game with North Little Rock High School.

More than 8,000 fans began their holiday at Tiger Stadium, where defense dominated a scoreless first quarter.

Little Rock scored early in the second quarter when Reese leaped over two Wildcats to catch a Weeks pass at the 21. Reese then ran the remaining yards to complete a 47-yard pass play. Malczycki's conversion attempt was good for a 7-0 lead.

On the Tigers' next possession, Weeks again completed a long pass to Reese. The play covered 50 yards to the 6. Wetherington ran to the 1 before Herbert dove over for the touchdown.

On its opening possession of the second half, Little Rock drove 80 yards for another score. A 41-yard pass from Teddar to Reese highlighted the drive, capped by a short lateral to Teddar for the score. Malczycki's extra point ended the scoring.

The Tigers kept North Little Rock out of the end zone in a 20-0 victory. The fifth conference victory resulted in another conference and state championship for Little Rock.

1953 TIGER SCHEDULE

Southside High of Memphis, TN 7	LRCH 19
Texarkana, TX 7	LRCH 13
Istrouma High of Baton Rouge, LA 28	LRCH 34
*Hot Springs 0	LRCH 61
*Fort Smith 9	LRCH 39
*Texarkana, AR 12	LRCH 32
*El Dorado 7	LRCH 48
Central High of Chattanooga, TN 26	LRCH 7
Tilghman High of Paducah, KY 27	LRCH 19
*Pine Bluff 21	LRCH 21
*North Little Rock 0	LRCH 20

KEPT HUMBLE BY OUT-OF-STATE FOES

1954   9-3-0

Head Coach: Wilson Matthews
Assistants: Ray Peters, Winston Faulkner, Don Sparks, Lawrence Mobley
Team Trainer: Don Sparks
Team Physician: Dr. John McCollough Smith

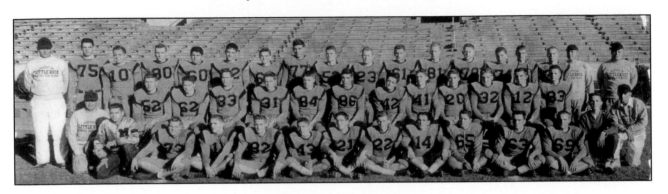

1954 LETTERMEN

Lewis Barnard	Doug Francisco	Richard Maxwell	Hammond Satterfield
Gene Barnett	Ralph Goldman	Buddy Milligan	Charles Smith
Richard Bell	Troy Green	Calvin Moore	Warner St. John
Charles Carter	Bill Harmon	Fred Morgan	Jim Wetherington
Robert Castleberry	Darryl Herbert	Larry Nahlen	Scott Woodmansee
Eddie Copeland	Michael Johns	Frank Plegge	Jimmy Wood
Bob Darling	Bill Jones	Brinton Ramoly	
Joe Day	Jimmy Martin	Herb Rule	

1954 MANAGERS

James Byrd	Joel Hicks	Robin Meadows
Hal Gentry	Connie Jackson	Bob Smith
John Geyer	Robin Jones	Terry Watson
Peter Hartstein	Rodney Jones	
Robert Hendrix	John Lile	

1954 ALL-STATE

Eddie Copeland	Frank Plegge
Darryl Herbert	Warner St. John
Richard Maxwell	Jim Wetherington

Coach Wilson Matthews entered the preseason needing to replace almost every lineman. This caused the coaching staff to focus more on fundamentals rather than drilling inexperienced players with schemes and advanced mechanics.

In addition to the loss of lettermen, the majority of the players reported out of shape. The extra time it took to condition the players put the team about one week behind schedule. The season, however, began whether Little Rock was ready or not.

The opener against Treadwell High of Memphis was played in front of more than 7,000 fans at Tiger Stadium. Little Rock's Darryl Herbert, Jim Wetherington and Ralph Goldman were too much for Treadwell, giving fans confidence in the offense. The Tigers opened with a 34-13 victory.

Little Rock's confidence may have been shaken a bit the next week after the offense gained only 76 yards rushing. The Tigers hosted Texarkana, Texas, on a rainy night and only 5,000 fans were in attendance. The Texas team upset Little Rock 2-0, shutting down the Little Rock offense.

The game's lone score came midway through the first quarter after Little Rock stopped a Texas drive on the Tigers 40. Don Carroll punted for Texarkana and Jimmy Martin received it at the 5. Martin was immediately knocked back into his end zone for a safety by Texarkana's Kenneth Green.

The remainder of the game was a defensive battle. It marked the first time the Tigers failed to score since a 0-0 tie with El Dorado in 1947.

Another disappointing loss occurred a week later when Istrouma High of Baton Rouge, La., defeated Little Rock 46-20. More than 8,000 fans at Baton Rouge's 22,500-seat Memorial Stadium watched Istrouma excel with almost every offensive play it ran. The game was highlighted by Johnny Yaun's 91-yard touchdown run for Baton Rouge.

The Tigers began to dominate the next couple of weeks, beating Hot Springs (52-0) and Fort Smith (28-6).

Photo provided by the Arkansas Democrat-Gazette
Darryl Herbert (left)

In front of a homecoming crowd of more than 9,000, Little Rock's ground attack piled up 305 yards and held the Grizzlies to only 124 yards rushing.

Little Rock traveled to Texarkana the following week to play Texarkana, Ark. The Razorbacks shocked the Tigers on the opening kickoff when Kenneth Vanderslice returned it 90 yards for a touchdown. The extra point put Texarkana up 7-0 just seconds into the game.

The Tigers answered on their first possession with an eight-play, 66-yard drive. They scored on a 34-yard pass from Martin to Scott Woodmansee. The extra-point attempt failed and Little Rock trailed 7-6.

The Tigers sealed a victory in the second half when Martin received a punt on his 5, faked a handoff on a crisscross and followed the sideline for a 95-yard touchdown. Wetherington converted the extra point and Little Rock won 25-7.

A 7-7 halftime tie in El Dorado was broken early in the third quarter when Herbert recovered a fumble at the 43 and re-

1954 Tiger linemen

turned it 57 yards for a touchdown. The Tigers spoiled El Dorado's homecoming 21-7. The loss was the Wildcats' first of the season and the victory moved Little Rock into the conference lead.

After a scoreless first half against Central High of Memphis, Martin set up the Tigers' first score. Midway through the third quarter, Martin returned a punt 32 yards to the Memphis 40. Wetherington completed three consecutive passes for 31 yards, then Goldman added a 5-yard run to the 4. Goldman scored on the next play to give Little Rock a 7-0 lead.

Later in the same quarter, Brinton Ramoly intercepted a pass on his 11 and took it 9 yards to the 20. Seven plays later, Hammond Satterfield went through the left side of the line, cut back to the right and outran the Memphis defense to the end zone. Wetherington's extra point put the Tigers up 14-0.

A 52-yard touchdown run by Bill Jones was called back because of clipping in the fourth quarter, but two touchdowns were all that was needed in a 14-0 victory over the Tennessee team. Several of the Little Rock running backs were badly bruised and sore because of pounding they received by the tough Warriors. An estimated 3,000 attended the game at Tiger Stadium.

The Tigers were in Paducah Ky., the following week to play Tilghman High School. After receiving the opening kickoff, Tilghman's first play ended when Frank Plegge stripped the ball from Glen Shaw to give Little Rock possession at the 27. Satterfield took advantage of the opportunity and put the Tigers ahead with a 6-yard touchdown run just five plays later.

Paducah began a 77-yard drive late in the first quarter. The drive came to an end on the second play of the second quarter when Shaw ran 52 yards for a touchdown. The conversion attempt failed, but Little retained a 7-6 lead.

The Tigers added another score with just two minutes remaining in the half. Goldman raced 14 yards on a sweep to cap a 78-yard drive for a 14-6 halftime lead.

Little Rock opened the second half with a 36-yard run by Goldman, a 21-yard run by Calvin Moore and a 1-yard touchdown run by Satterfield. Coach Matthews put his second and third teams in the game and they scored another touchdown to give the Tigers a 28-12 victory.

Darryl Herbert (32)

Just under 4,000 fans at Tiger Stadium watched Little Rock battle Pine Bluff the next week. The attendance was the smallest since the teams began scheduling their game at night. Wetherington gave Little Rock fans something to cheer about early in the first quarter when he broke through the defense for a 58-yard touchdown run. Moments later, though, Pine Bluff fans were just as excited when Royce White broke free for a 44-yard touchdown run. After the Zebras failed on the extra-point attempt, Little Rock began to control the game.

Goldman added a touchdown in the second quarter, then Woodmansee scored on a 42-yard touchdown run in the third quarter. Wetherington struck again the fourth quarter when he scored on a 51-yard run. Satterfield ended the touchdown parade with a short burst up the middle. Wetherington converted his fourth extra point to give the Tigers a 34-12 victory.

It marked Pine Bluff's seventh consecutive loss and led to a record-equaling worst season in school history. The victory was Little Rock's eighth of the season and fifth consecutive over Big 7 opposition.

Little Rock jumped ahead early the next week against Bessemer, Ala. A 61-yard drive was capped by a 1-yard dive from Satterfield. Bessemer, though, answered in the second quarter with two scores.

Alabama's Tommy Lorino passed to Lawrence Dollar for a 20-yard touchdown to end an 81-yard drive. On the next possession, Lorino capped a 50-yard drive with an 8-yard run around right end to put the Purple Tigers up 13-7.

Bessemer sealed the victory late in the fourth quarter when Pete Curren scored on a 20-yard run. The conversion gave the Alabama team a 20-7 victory over the Tigers.

The annual Thanksgiving Day game against North Little Rock High School began with a scoreless first quarter. But a scoring frenzy began as the second quarter opened. Little Rock started the second period with a 12-yard touchdown pass from Satterfield to Goldman to finish a 53-yard drive that began in the first quarter.

The Wildcats' Tommy Worrell received the ensuing kickoff at his 9. He cut to his left and followed the sideline to the 2, where he was knocked out of bounds by Fred Morgan. Worrell took the handoff on the next play and dove into the end zone for a 6-6 tie.

The Tigers broke the tie in six plays after Moore returned the kickoff to his 37. Woodmansee caught a third-down pass and took it 25 yards to the North Little Rock 29. Herbert gained 2 yards and Satterfield then went the remaining 27 yards for the score. The conversion kick was blocked, but Little Rock would not relinquish its 12-6 lead.

After scoring their fifth touchdown, early in the third quarter, the Tigers were up 32-6 and Coach Matthews put the second and third teams in the game. The reserves gave up a few touchdowns, but were still able to hold on for the victory, 38-26.

More than 8,000 watched the Tigers capture the Big 7 Conference and the state championship, losing only to out-of-state teams.

1954 TIGER SCHEDULE

Treadwell High of Memphis, TN 13	LRCH 34
Texarkana, TX 2	LRCH 0
Istrouma High of Baton Rouge, LA 46	LRCH 20
*Hot Springs 0	LRCH 52
*Fort Smith 6	LRCH 28
*Texarkana, AR 7	LRCH 25
*El Dorado 7	LRCH 21
Central High of Memphis, TN 0	LRCH 14
Tilghman High of Paducah, KY 12	LRCH 28
*Pine Bluff 12	LRCH 34
Bessemer, AL 20	LRCH 7
*North Little Rock 26	LRCH 38

THE STREAK BEGINS

1955   9-3-0

Head Coach: Wilson Matthews
Assistants: Ray Peters, Don Sparks, Lawrence Mobley, Gene Hall
Team Trainer: Don Sparks
Team Physician: Dr. John McCollough Smith

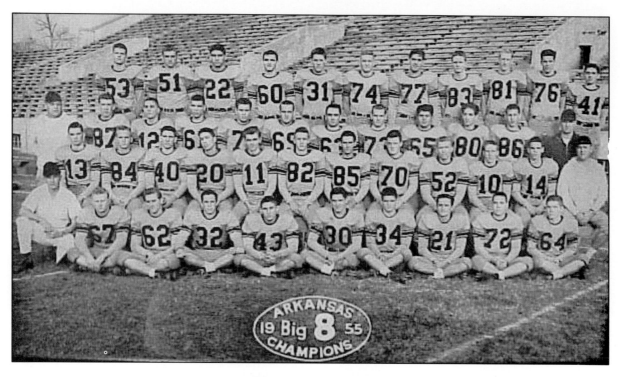

1955 LETTERMEN

Lewis Barnard	Doug Francisco	Boris Malczycki	Lamar Riggs
Gene Barnett	Bruce Fullerton	Jimmy Martin	Bill Roth
Charles Carter	Bill Glasscock	Bill McMurray	Hammond Satterfield
George Clark	Bill Harmon	Buddy Milligan	Charles Smith
Leroy Danner	Carl Harris	Calvin Moore	Warner St. John
Bob Darling	Bill Hicks	Billy Moore	Jimmy Wood
Joe Day	Bob Hollaway	Fred Morgan	
George Edwards	Michael Johns	Frank Plegge	

1955 MANAGERS

George Barnwell	Rodney Jones	Jesse South
Fred Blazer	Kenneth Koonce	Bill Spencer
Hal Gentry	Henry Mahan	Terry Watson
John Hatley	Danny Mobley	
Andy Johnson	Gordon Rather	

1955 ALL-AMERICAN
Frank Plegge

1955 ALL-STATE
Bill Hicks
Frank Plegge

1955 ALL-STAR TEAM
None

Little Rock began another championship campaign when it hosted Treadwell High School of Memphis in the season opener.

The Tigers scored first, just after Jimmy Martin broke free for a first down on the Treadwell 36. Jimmy Wood then pulled in a screen pass and fought his way to the 6. Hammond Satterfield picked up 5 yards and Wood ran the remaining yard for the score. Doug Francisco's extra-point attempt was wide right, but Little Rock took a 6-0 lead.

Treadwell didn't answer until its first possession of the second half. The scoring drive began when the Eagles intercepted a Satterfield pass to give them control at their 34. A Teddy Steele extra point followed a 5-yard touchdown run and ended up being the game-winning play as Treadwell defeated the Tigers 7-6. Little Rock hadn't lost a season opener in 15 years.

A road trip to Texarkana, Texas, proved too much for Little Rock the next week. The tough Texarkana team jumped out in front 14-0 in the first quarter. The Texas team scored on a 30-yard pass from George McKinney to Bill Erie and a 1-yard run by Wade Fowler. With 4:44 left in the first half, Little Rock scored its first touchdown when Wood ended a 63-yard drive with a 1-yard run over right tackle.

The Tigers opened the second half by taking the lead on a 32-yard scramble by Satterfield. The conversion put Little Rock in front 14-13.

The lead only lasted two plays. Texarkana returned the ensuing kickoff to its 34, and McKinney then dropped to throw toward Erie. Erie caught the pass over his shoulder at the 25 and easily made it to the end zone for a 19-14 lead.

Trying to run out the clock late in the fourth quarter, the Texas team scored its last touchdown when Fowler capped a 51-yard drive with a 6-yard run. Fowler converted the extra-point attempt to give Texarkana a 26-14 victory.

Approximately 6,500 fans gathered the following week at Tiger Stadium to witness one of the best played high school games in years.

Istrouma High School of Baton Rouge, La., received the opening kickoff and a first-down run by Billy Cannon moved the visitors to the 33. George Guidry broke free over right tackle and ran untouched for a 67-yard touchdown. Cannon added the extra point for a 7-0 lead.

Photo provided by Central High School
Calvin Moore (31)

221

Little Rock was forced to punt after its first possession. Cannon returned the kick to his 14. He then capped an 86-yard drive with a 2-yard dive. The extra-point attempt was wide, but Baton Rouge led 13-0 with 10:05 remaining in the first quarter.

Little Rock's only score came after Satterfield returned a punt 70 yards for an apparent touchdown. Satterfield, though, stepped out of bounds at the Istrouma 39. On the next offensive play, Little Rock got to the 4 after a Satterfield to Joe Day pass. Three plays later, Martin scored from the 1 and converted the extra-point attempt to pull the Tigers within 13-7.

Baton Rouge took over at its 40 late in the fourth quarter, and it took 11 plays to put Istrouma at the 1. Guidry scored Baton Rouge's third touchdown to end the game at 19-7.

Cannon finished the game with 142 rushing yards on 25 carries. He and Guidry combined for 296 yards rushing in Istrouma's victory.

Little Rock finally won the following week when it opened conference play against Hot Springs High School. After celebrating the 41-0 victory, the Tigers prepared for a trip to Fort Smith and a battle with the Grizzlies. The game's first score was set up when Little Rock recovered a Fort Smith fumble at its 47. Wood capped

Photo provided by Central High School

Calvin Moore against Pine Bluff

the 53-yard drive with a 6-yard run. The conversion failed, giving the Tigers a 6-0 lead at the half.

Coach Steed White's Grizzlies were recharged during the break and able to put together a 63-yard drive after receiving the second-half kickoff. Paul Alberty, Darrell Williams and Tommy Boch led Fort Smith down the field, with Boch going over from the 10 for the score. Eddie Walker's conversion kick was good and the Grizzlies led 7-6.

It wasn't until the fourth quarter that Little Rock could put another drive together. Following a punt, the Tigers took possession at the Fort Smith 39. A 10-yard run by Bruce Fullerton was good to the 29. From there, Satterfield fired a pass to Day at the 2. Day fought his way into the end zone to put Little Rock back in front. The extra point made it 13-7, a lead the Tigers held the remainder of the game.

Little Rock evened its record, 3-3-0, following a 31-0 victory over Texarkana, Ark. It hoped to continue its short winning streak the next week against El Dorado. The homecoming crowd at Tiger Stadium cheered as Dewena Price was crowned queen during pregame festivities.

After a scoreless first half, the Tigers scored in the third quarter when Francisco and Bill Harmon broke through the line to block an El Dorado punt. Frank Plegge scooped up the ball and ran the 5 yards

Photo provided by the Arkansas Democrat-Gazette

(Left to Right) Warner St. John, Louis Barnard, Gene Barnett and Bob Darling

Photo provided by the Arkansas Democrat-Gazette
Bruce Fullerton

needed for the score. The extra point gave the Tigers a 7-0 lead, and they struck again with one minute remaining in the game.

Warren St. John recovered an El Dorado fumble at the 31, and it took five plays for Little Rock to cover the distance. The late drive sealed its fourth consecutive victory, 13-0.

The Tigers again met an out-of-state team when they traveled to Memphis to take on the Central High Warriors. Three plays after the opening kickoff, the Warriors fumbled and Little Rock recovered. Three plays later, Satterfield threw a pass into the end zone. The ball bounced off the shoulder of a Memphis player and was caught by Day for a touchdown. The conversion gave the Tigers a 7-0 lead.

Midway through the second quarter, Memphis' David White intercepted a Satterfield pass and returned it to the Little Rock 37. Several plays later from the 26, Bobby Vollmer broke through the Little Rock line for the score. The extra-point attempt failed as Little Rock held on for a one-point victory.

Behind 331 yards rushing, including 143 on 13 carries by Calvin Moore, and 139 yards passing, the Tigers beat another out-of-state opponent the following week. The 38-12 victory over Tilghman High of Paducah, Ky., was highlighted by a 60-yard touchdown run by Moore and an interception returned 67 yards for a touchdown by Billy Moore. The victory gave Little Rock the confidence needed heading into its next game against Pine Bluff.

A tie against Fort Smith was the only blemish on the Zebras' record. Their powerful offense had scored at least four touchdowns in each of the previous five games, and their defense was anxious to get a shot at the highly touted Tiger running backs.

Early in the game, Pine Bluff's Royce White fumbled and Boris Malczycki recovered for Little Rock at the Zebras 29. When the Tigers reached the 11, Satterfield passed to Charles Smith in the end zone for the score. Martin's conversion put Little Rock up 7-0.

The Tigers went on to score three more times in the second half and held Pine Bluff scoreless. The Zebras managed only four first downs, two the result of Little Rock penalties. The victory clinched the third consecutive Big 7 championship for the Tigers.

Little Rock narrowly escaped Bessemer, Ala., the following week. The Tigers were only able to score twice, but the defense was perfect.

The first score came in the second quarter when Fullerton, a sophomore, caught a Satterfield pass and took it to the end zone to complete a 93-yard play.

The second touchdown came on a 70-yard punt return by Martin. Fullerton fumbled the punt on the 30, picked it up and handed to Martin, who sprinted down the sideline for the score. The extra-point attempt failed, but the conversion was good after the initial touchdown and the Tigers took a 13-0 victory over the Alabama team.

A Thanksgiving Day game with North Little Rock High School was played with only pride on the line. Little Rock had already clinched the championship and the Wildcats entered 5-4-1.

Approximately 6,000 fans were in the stands at Tiger Stadium to watch the Tigers defeat North Little Rock 27-0 for their ninth consecutive victory.

The first Arkansas High School All-Star football game was played the summer following the school year. The game was to showcase the state's best senior players, as well as coaches.

The game was scheduled in conjunction with the Arkansas High School Coaches Association Clinic. No Little Rock players were chosen for the inaugural event.

For the first time in four decades, Little Rock Central was without Athletic Director Earl Quigley, who retired shortly before the school year began. Coach Quigley served as

Photo provided by the Arkansas Democrat-Gazette

The Tigers celebrate their victory over Pine Bluff

athletic director from 1936-1955 and coached the Little Rock football team from 1916-1917 and 1919-1935.

1955 TIGER SCHEDULE

Treadwell High of Memphis, TN 7	LRCH 6
Texarkana, TX 26	LRCH 14
Istrouma High of Baton Rouge, LA 19	LRCH 7
*Hot Springs 0	LRCH 41
*Fort Smith 7	LRCH 13
*Texarkana, AR 0	LRCH 31
*El Dorado 0	LRCH 13
Central High of Memphis, TN 6	LRCH 7
Tilghman High of Paducah, KY 12	LRCH 38
*Pine Bluff 0	LRCH 27
Bessemer, AL 0	LRCH 13
*North Little Rock 0	LRCH 27

Photo provided by Central High School

Joe Day catches a pass against Central High of Memphis

224

THE DOMINATION CONTINUES
1956   12-0-0

Head Coach: Wilson Matthews
Assistants: Ray Peters, Don Sparks, Gene Hall, Lawrence Mobley
Team Trainer: Don Sparks
Team Physician: Dr. John McCollough Smith

1956 LETTERMEN

Richard Almond	George Edwards	Nelson Laing	John Rath
Warren Argo	Charles Ferriter	Joe Matthews	Howard Riley
Gilbert Arnold	Bruce Fullerton	Bill May	Gregory Robertson
Ted Blagg	Gilroy Garner	Mike McGibbony	Bill Sims
Ralph Brodie	Frank Grant	Bob McWilliams	Cecil Tackett
George Clark	Bob Gutheridge	Billy Moore	Jack Tucker
Bill Collier	Jerry Hammonds	Calvin Moore	Jimmy Wood
Clarence Crist	Steve Hathcote	Arthur Pearrow	Kenneth Zini
Ladd Davies	Bill Hicks	Sammy Peters	

1956 MANAGERS

George Barnwell	Andy Johnson	Ronnie Moore
Dan Chisholm	Aubrey Knight	Wendell Ross
Jimmy Gee	Kurn Kruger	Bill Spencer
John Hatley	Henry Mahan	Jerry Williams
Jay Heflin	Tony Minick	Ray Wilson

1956 ALL-SOUTHERN
Bill Hicks

1956 ALL-STATE

George Clark	Bill Hicks
George Edwards	Billy Moore
Bruce Fullerton	Jimmy Wood
Frank Grant	

Photo provided by the Arkansas Democrat-Gazette

Little Rock's 1956 offense

After an incredible 1955 season, winning nine consecutive games after opening with three consecutive losses, Coach Wilson Matthews had to replace 17 lettermen lost to graduation. There was a pool of more than 100 players to choose from, but most had little or no experience. Because of this, die-hard Tiger fans and even the coaching staff expected a rebuilding year.

There was one change in Little Rock Central's schedule for the 1956 season. Bessemer, Ala., was taken off the schedule and replaced with Blytheville High School, a new conference game. With the addition of the Chicks, the Big 7 Conference became the Big 8 Conference.

The Tigers opened with a nonconference game against Christian Brothers College High School of Memphis. Bruce Fullerton was the scoring hero for Central with touchdown runs of 40 and 7 yards and a punt return of 62 yards. The halfback finished with 122 yards on six carries. Calvin Moore, a 200-pound fullback, added 127 yards on 13 carries. Little Rock used the second and third quarters to post a 33-0 decision over Christian Brothers High.

A battle with Texarkana, Texas, awaited the Tigers the following week.

Moore broke a scoreless tie in the third quarter with a 1-yard touchdown run. Central added to its lead in the fourth quarter after Bill Hicks intercepted a Texas pass and returned it to the Texarkana 18. Expecting a running play, the Texas defense crowded the line of scrimmage. Bill Sims took advantage of the open passing lanes and connected with Jimmy Wood in the back of the end zone for Little Rock's second touchdown.

The Tigers held Texarkana scoreless in a 13-0 victory. The victory was only Coach Matthews' second against the Tigers of Texarkana, Texas.

A third consecutive game against out-of-state competition was on the schedule the following week. A game in Baton Rouge, La., put Little Rock Central against Istrouma High School.

Moore starred for the Tigers as he rushed for 131 yards on nine carries. Fullerton added 111 yards on 14 carries and scored one touchdown in a 32-0 victory over the Indians, only the second time in seven years Istrouma had been shut out and its worst loss since 1949.

Following a 41-0 victory over Hot Springs to open Big 8 Conference play, Little Rock hosted the Fort Smith Grizzlies. Fort Smith Coach Steed White, a former assistant coach at Little Rock High School, was pleased with his team's performance. The Grizzlies were outweighed approximately 30 pounds per man, yet put up a great fight against the Tigers.

Fort Smith scored early in the first quarter after Little Rock fumbled the opening kickoff. Montey Boley recovered at the Tigers 34 and successive penalties moved Fort Smith to the 8. Jarrell Williams broke through on the first play to put Fort Smith up 6-0.

Little Rock took the lead with one second remaining in the first quarter when Moore scored on a short run and Hicks converted the extra point.

Williams scored again for the Grizzlies in the third quarter, taking a pass 58 yards for a touchdown. The Tigers, though, were too tough for Fort Smith as Little Rock went on to win 28-12. The Grizzlies' two touchdowns were the first scored against the Tigers in 1956.

Photo provided by the Arkansas Democrat-Gazette
Bruce Fullerton (22)

Little Rock's defense recorded another shutout the next week, this time against Texarkana, Ark. The 33-0 victory gave the Tigers a 6-0-0 record heading into a road trip to El Dorado.

Little Rock scored on its first possession as Sims connected with George Edwards for a 6-yard touchdown pass. The conversion was good for a 7-0 lead. The lead, though, did not last long as El Dorado tailback Larkus Pesnell slipped through the defense for a 57-yard touchdown run. Pesnell also kicked the extra point, tying the score at 7-7.

Little Rock's next score followed an El Dorado punt. Sims passed for most of the yardage and his 14-yard toss to Jerry Hammonds resulted in the touchdown. The conversion failed, but the Tigers led 13-7 at the half.

El Dorado controlled the game in the third quarter and was able to once again tie the score. Pesnell took the Wildcats to the Little Rock 4, and fullback Warren Taylor scored from there to make it 13-13.

Photo provided by the Arkansas Democrat-Gazette
Bill Hicks (left) and **Calvin Moore**

227

The Tigers, though, answered after the ensuing kickoff. Quick passes by Sims and short runs by Wood took Little Rock to the 15. Fullerton powered his way through the line for the third touchdown and the Tigers took the lead for good. Fullerton scored again in the fourth quarter to set the score at 27-13.

A battle with Central High of Memphis the following week left Little Rock with an 8-0-0 record and its 17th consecutive victory. The game's scoring began the first time Memphis had possession.

Starting from its 26, Memphis moved to the Tigers 42 after a pass interference penalty. Quarterback Byron Green hit Jerry Martin at the 29. Billy Orick then went off left tackle for a 29-yard touchdown run. The conversion attempt failed, but the Warriors had a 6-0 lead.

The second quarter was halfway over before Little Rock scored. Sims completed a pass to Hammonds, who pitched to Wood for a 50-yard gain. Billy Moore received a Sims pass at the 8, and four plays later Nelson Laing scored on a short run. Hicks converted the extra point for a 7-6 halftime lead.

The second half was dominated by the Tigers. Memphis never threatened to score, and Little Rock added four more touch-

Photo provided by the Arkansas Democrat-Gazette
Jimmy Wood

downs, including a blocked punt by Arthur Pearrow that was picked up and returned 12 yards for a score by Hicks. The Tigers defeated Memphis Central 33-6.

Little Rock Central amassed 630 total yards against Tilghman High School of Paducah, Ky., the following week. Sims passed for three touchdowns, Fullerton rushed for 180 yards and Laing rushed for 109 yards. The Tigers rushed for 350 yards and passed for 280 yards in the 45-13 domination of the Tornadoes.

The next week wasn't quite as easy for Little Rock when it took on the Zebras of Pine Bluff. The Tigers scored on their opening possession when Fullerton broke through the right side of the line, cut back toward the east sideline and outran the defense for a 61-yard touchdown.

It wasn't until midway through the fourth quarter that Little Rock scored again. With the score still 6-0, Billy Moore intercepted a Pine Bluff pass and returned it to

Photo provided by the Arkansas Democrat-Gazette
Bruce Fullerton (22)

The 1956 defense gave up only 56 points in 12 games

the Zebras 42. The Tigers advanced to the 7 before Hicks kicked a field goal for a 9-0 lead.

After the ensuing kickoff, Pine Bluff's Bubba Ferguson tried another pass and it was once again intercepted. George Clark made the interception at the 30 and outran Ferguson to the corner of the end zone for another touchdown.

Little Rock was able to score twice more late in the game in a 28-0 victory over the Zebras. Fullerton carried the load for the Tigers by rushing for 199 yards on 22 carries and scoring three touchdowns. Pine Bluff was a young team, starting four 15-year-old sophomores, yet still held Little Rock in check for three quarters.

The 1-7-0 Blytheville Chicks were new to the conference and having a hard time adjusting to the competition. The once powerful program from Blytheville suffered another loss when it met Little Rock.

The Tigers scored on their first two possessions as Fullerton ran for a 36-yard touchdown and Calvin Moore ran for a 51-yard touchdown. Several minutes later, Sims passed to Fullerton for a 76-yard touchdown. Hicks converted three extra points and Little Rock led 21-0 after 11 minutes of play. The Tigers went on to defeat the Chicks 59-0.

The Little Rock Central Tigers entered their annual holiday game against North Little Rock High School 11-0-0 and guaranteed at least a share of the conference and state championship, regardless of the outcome.

Led by former Tigers Coach Raymond Burnett, the Wildcats entered 9-1-0. A victory would guarantee them a share of the conference and state title, but a loss would keep them second in the final standings.

A Thanksgiving Day crowd of more than 9,000 packed Tiger Stadium and witnessed an offensive display by Little Rock. Central's big plays included Fullerton's 38-yard touchdown run and his 40-yard punt return for a touchdown. The 45-12 victory was not only highlighted by the offense, but by the defense as well. The Tigers held North Little Rock to 76 total yards of offense.

The rout over the Wildcats gave Little Rock a 12-0-0 record, the first undefeated season since 1946 when the Tigers were 14-0-0 and named national champions. The victory also extended Little Rock's winning streak to 21 games.

George Edwards (left) and Jerry Hammonds

1956 TIGER SCHEDULE

Christian Brothers College High of Memphis, TN 0	LRCH 33
Texarkana, TX 0	LRCH 13
Istrouma High of Baton Rouge, LA 0	LRCH 32
*Hot Springs 0	LRCH 41
*Fort Smith 12	LRCH 28
*Texarkana, AR 0	LRCH 33
*El Dorado 13	LRCH 27
Central High of Memphis, TN 6	LRCH 33
Tilghman High of Paducah, KY 13	LRCH 45
*Pine Bluff 0	LRCH 28
*Blytheville 0	LRCH 59
*North Little Rock 12	LRCH 45

MAKING HISTORY ON AND OFF THE FIELD

1957   12-0-0

Head Coach: Wilson Matthews
Assistants: Don Sparks, Gene Hall, Lawrence Mobley, Ralph Holland, Clyde Hart
Team Trainer: Clyde Hart
Team Physician: Dr. John McCollough Smith

1957 LETTERMEN

Gilbert Arnold	Fallon Davis	Bill Hicks	Sammy Peters
Buford Blackwell	Jim Davis	Joe Matthews	Jerry Pickens
Ted Blagg	Daney Duggar	Bill May	John Rath
Ralph Brodie	Alton Fausette	Jack McClain	Bob Shepherd
Bill Collier	Bruce Fullerton	Billy Moore	Buddy Tackett
Alvin Crawford	Sam Gill	Charles Patterson	Charles Teague
Clarence Crist	Bill Hathcote	Arthur Pearrow	Edward Thorne
Ladd Davies	Steve Hathcote	Jim Penn	Kenneth Zini

1957 MANAGERS

Paul Frith	J.W. Lewis	Jon Tate
Roel Garber	Henry Mahan	Harper Thomason
Jim Garrison	Jerry McKenney	Bill Tidmore
Jim Gee	Jerry McNabb	
Jay Heflin	Jim Shepherd	

1957 NATIONAL PLAYER OF THE YEAR
Bruce Fullerton

1957 ALL-AMERICAN
Bruce Fullerton
Bill Hicks

1957 ALL-STATE

Gilbert Arnold	Bruce Fullerton	Billy Moore
Ted Blagg	Bill Hicks	Sammy Peters
Jim Davis	Bill May	Buddy Tackett

1957 ALL-STAR TEAM
Bill Hicks
Bill May

Before the 1957 season, the Little Rock School Board voted unanimously to rename Tiger Stadium after Earl F. Quigley, Little Rock's legendary coach and athletic director. Quigley retired as athletic director in 1955 and left as head football coach after the 1935 season. During 20 years as Little Rock's football coach, he was 134-52-9 and won five state championships.

Coach Wilson Matthews and his staff were excited about the upcoming campaign since they lost few starters from the 12-0-0 team in 1956. The coaches were about to endure an extremely tough season, though. The coaching staff had to keep each player focused on the game rather than the life-changing events in the halls of Little Rock Central High School.

The 1957 school year, which should have started like any other, began in utter chaos.

Photo provided by Central High School

The Arkansas National Guard was to keep nine black students from entering Central High School

Little Rock and Central High School became the focal point of the entire world. Gov. Orval Faubus ordered the Arkansas National Guard to block the entrance of Central High School to keep out nine black students.

The all-white school was to be integrated by the black students as a result of an order of the United States Supreme Court. Mornings were anything but normal as more than 250 people filled Park Avenue in front of the school to protest the integration. Each morning, the National Guard turned away the black students.

On Sept. 24, President Dwight D. Eisenhower sent 1,200 Army troops from Kentucky's 101st Airborne Division to Little Rock to enforce law and order. The troops were not only to escort the nine black students into the building, but walk them to each of their classes throughout the day. For nine months, federal troops and the national media occupied the Central High campus.

Photo provided by the Arkansas Democrat-Gazette

A crowd protests outside Central High

232

The Tigers had to practice around the 101st Airborne Division's helicopters, tents and vehicles, which were housed on the practice field behind the school. Even the office for coaches was overtaken by the Airborne Division's commanding officers.

Despite all the distractions, Coach Matthews and the Tigers were able to prepare for the season and opened against Christian Brothers College High School of Memphis. An incredible display of defense helped Little Rock to a 20-0 victory.

The 101st Airborne Division occupies Central's practice field

The Tigers scored on their first possession, driving 77 yards in 11 plays. Bruce Fullerton capped the drive with an 11-yard touchdown run. Bill Hicks converted the extra point for a 7-0 lead.

Little Rock fumbled the next three times it had possession, giving Christian Brothers the ball on the Tigers 41, 22 and 21. The tough Little Rock defense did not even allow a first down during these three possessions. For the night, it only allowed 103 total yards.

Fullerton gained 130 yards and scored all three touchdowns. Little Rock scored its first two touchdowns in the fourth quarter on two short runs by Fullerton. The final score was set up by a 64-yard punt return by Billy Moore.

Against Watty Myers' Texarkana, Texas, team, the Tigers rushed for 319 yards, passed for 106 yards and returned two punts for touchdowns. Fullerton gained 178 yards on 18 carries and scored three touchdowns, including a 50-yard pass reception and a 70-yard run. Moore passed for 106 yards, threw two touchdowns and also scored on a 55-yard punt return.

Ed Thorne blocked a Texas punt and returned it 46 yards for a touchdown to help Little Rock to a 54-13 victory. It was the worst loss in Meyers' 19 years as a coach.

Hosting Istrouma High School of Baton Rouge, the defending Louisiana state champion, proved to be a tough task. The Tigers

Central High's 1957 offensive line

Bruce Fullerton (22)

scored first after a 40-yard drive. Fullerton picked up most of the yardage on running plays, but a Moore to Hicks pass placed Little Rock at the 3. Sammy Peters then scored with 6:05 left in the second quarter for a 6-0 lead.

Istrouma answered with a 12-play, 68-yard drive that took six minutes off the clock. An interference call against the Tigers helped the Louisiana team move to the 1 before Don Smith broke through the line for the score. The conversion attempt failed and it was 6-6 at halftime.

The 6,000 in attendance at Quigley Stadium, many of whom were Army troops, watched as Little Rock came out strong in the second half. It wasn't until the fourth quarter, though, that the Tigers scored again. Fullerton sprinted toward the right sideline and cut upfield for a 42-yard touchdown run.

Later in the quarter, Hicks kicked a 31-yard field goal against the wind to help Little Rock defeat Baton Rouge 15-6 for its 24th consecutive victory.

The Tigers added a 46-6 victory over Hot Springs the following week as Fullerton rushed for 115 yards. Fullerton provided the spark again the next week against Fort Smith when he rushed for 228 yards and scored two touchdowns.

Little Rock won the toss and elected to receive the kickoff. Fort Smith's kicker, Jim Grizzle, caught the Tigers off guard with an onside kick. The ball bounced off the leg of Arthur Pearrow and David Wassen of Fort Smith recovered on the Little Rock 46.

Thirteen plays later, Fort Smith was facing fourth down at the 3. The Tigers stuffed the fourth-down play and took over at their 3. This was the only time that the Grizzlies crossed Little Rock's 20.

The game's first score came midway through the second quarter when Fullerton went over right tackle for a 73-yard touchdown run. The Tigers scored three more times in the second half during a 28-0 victory over 1-4-1 Fort Smith.

Little Rock expected a hard battle against Texarkana, Ark., the next week, but did not receive one. Fullerton scored three touchdowns in the first quarter before the second and third teams entered the game. The Tigers easily handled the Razorbacks 47-7.

Next on the schedule was unbeaten El Dorado. Before the game, Barbara Barnes was crowned Little Rock's homecoming queen. Quigley was also formally honored for his work with Little Rock High School and its athletic programs. It was during this

Bill Hicks

ceremony that Tiger Stadium was officially renamed Earl Quigley Stadium.

Little Rock's first score was set up when Eddie Thorne blocked a punt to give the Tigers possession at the 36. Eight plays later, Fullerton scored from the 6. Hicks kicked the extra point for a 7-0 lead.

It again only took eight plays for Little Rock to score on its next possession. Fullerton's 25-yard run to the 2 was followed by a Moore touchdown.

Following an El Dorado punt, Fullerton broke loose for a 41-yard gain to the 23. Two penalties set the Tigers back before Moore connected with Hicks in the end zone for the third touchdown. Hicks converted his third extra point for a 21-0 lead at the half.

Fullerton scored again in the second half on an 11-yard run to help Little Rock to a 28-0 victory. The win virtually wrapped up the Big 8 Conference championship for the Tigers.

Little Rock defeated Central High of Memphis 34-0 before hosting Tilghman High of Paducah, Ky. Tilghman was the No. 1 team in Kentucky, but was no real match for the Tigers.

Fullerton returned the opening kickoff 76 yards for a touchdown and quickly added two more scores on a 16-yard run and a punt return of 68 yards. Peters, Moore and Bob Shepherd each scored in the second quarter for a 40-0 lead.

Photo provided by Central High School
Steve Hathcote

Photo provided by Central High School
Billy Moore

Little Rock's second and third teams played the entire second half in the Tigers' 30th consecutive victory, 46-13.

Tilghman Coach Ralph McRight, who had coached high school football for 20 years, called Little Rock Central High School "the greatest high school football team I've ever seen."

After a 33-0 victory over Pine Bluff and a 53-12 victory over Blytheville, the Tigers prepared for the Thanksgiving Day game with North Little Rock High School. A new coach replaced Raymond Burnett for the 1957 season and it was Jimmy Albright, a former Little Rock player under both Burnett and Wilson Matthews.

The 1957 matchup against North Little Rock marked the last time the two teams would play on Thanksgiving Day. The Tigers' new holiday foe would be Little Rock's Hall High School.

Little Rock struck first when Moore scored on runs of 4 yards and 2 yards. Fullerton scored on a 68-yard run and a 4-yard pass reception from Moore. Peters added to the lead with a 1-yard run, and Hicks scored on a pass reception from Moore. Hicks also converted four extra-point attempts in the 40-7 victory.

Following the game, Coach Matthews stated that this 1957 squad was "the finest bunch of boys I've ever coached."

The final victory of the season extended the Tigers' winning streak to 33 games. Little Rock scored 444 points and allowed only 64 points during the 12-game schedule.

When the season ended, the National Sports News Service of Minneapolis named Little Rock Central High School the No. 1 high school team in the country.

With this honor came an invitation to play in the "Best of the Rest" game against a Miami high school. The game, which was to be played in Miami's Orange Bowl Stadium, did not feature the Tigers because of an Arkansas Activities Association rule that didn't allow postseason play.

Along with its second national championship, Little Rock boasted two All-Americans in Fullerton and Hicks.

Fullerton, 17, who was named National Player of the Year by *The Sporting News*, scored 27 touchdowns to break the single-season school record previously held by John Hoffman, who scored 26 in 1944. Fullerton, a 185-pound halfback, rushed for 228 yards and two touchdowns against Fort Smith in his best performance of the season.

Hicks, a 187-pound end, was honored by *Teen* magazine. Hicks was named an All-State linebacker in 10th grade, an All-State tackle in 11th grade and an All-State end in 12th grade. He and Fullerton were two of the most highly recruited players in the country during the 1957 season.

Following the season, Coach Wilson Matthews resigned at Little Rock Central High School to become an assistant at the University of Arkansas. Coach Frank Broyles was hired as the new head football coach and asked Matthews, a longtime friend, to join his staff.

Coach Matthews left Little Rock with a 109-17-3 record, 10 state championships and one national championship in 11 seasons.

1957 TIGER SCHEDULE

Christian Brothers College High of Memphis, TN 0	LRCH 20
Texarkana, TX 13	LRCH 54
Istrouma High of Baton Rouge, LA 6	LRCH 15
*Hot Springs 6	LRCH 46
*Fort Smith 0	LRCH 28
*Texarkana, AR 7	LRCH 47
*El Dorado 0	LRCH 28
Central High of Memphis, TN 0	LRCH 34
Tilghman High Paducah, KY 13	LRCH 46
*Pine Bluff 0	LRCH 33
*Blytheville 12	LRCH 53
*North Little Rock 7	LRCH 40

SCHOOLS CLOSE, STREAK ENDS

1958   8-3-1

Head Coach: Gene Hall
Assistants: Ralph Holland, Allen Howard, V.E. Baber, Clyde Hart
Team Trainer: Clyde Hart
Team Physician: Dr. John McCollough Smith

[1958 TEAM PHOTO NOT AVAILABLE]

1958 LETTERMEN

Buford Blackwell	Charles Dodd	Jim Kinderman	Ronnie Spann
Bob Brazzell	Larry Dum	Tom King	Buddy Tackett
Richard Carpenter	Claude Fulton	John McCarty	Gayle Voth
John Coggins	Gary Hackney	Jack McClain	Gary Wahlquist
Bill Collier	Steve Hathcote	Charles Patterson	Kenneth Zini
Darrell Collier	Bob Head	John Rath	
Alvin Crawford	Ronnie Holmes	Gary Robinson	

1958 MANAGERS
Jerry McKinney
Jerry McNab
Jon Tate

1958 ALL-STATE
Steve Hathcote
Charles Patterson
Buddy Tackett
Kenneth Zini

1958 ALL-STAR TEAM
Steve Hathcote
Buddy Tackett

Following Coach Wilson Matthews' resignation to become an assistant coach under Frank Broyles at the University of Arkansas, assistant Gene Hall was promoted to Little Rock Central's head coach.

Coach Hall began his career as head coach by inheriting a program that had just won a national championship, six consecutive state championships and riding a 33-game winning streak.

In addition to the pressure of taking over a nationally renowned football program, Coach Hall had to deal with the loss of several players because of mandatory transfer to the city's new school, Hall High, which opened the previous year. Coach Hall lost one senior because of a voluntary transfer, but lost numerous sophomores and juniors due to mandatory transfers ordered by the Little Rock School Board.

One other obstacle for the new head coach to overcome was the threat of another integration crisis for the opening of the 1958 school year.

Federal District Judge Harry J. Lemley of Hope granted the Little Rock School District and Central

Photo provided by the
Arkansas Democrat-Gazette
Coach Gene Hall

237

High School a 2 ½-year delay in integration. Judge Lemley stated the ruling was "in the public's best interest, including the interest of both white and Negro students." Judge Lemley believed that a peaceful delay was needed for a smoothly functioning educational system. However, on Sept. 11, 1958, the United States Supreme Court denied the request for a delay of integration and ruled that Little Rock must continue with its desegregation plan.

Photo provided by the Arkansas Democrat-Gazette

Coach Hall leads his team off the field after the school district ordered all extracurricular activities to stop

The United States Justice Department then prepared the U.S. Marshals Service to send agents to Little Rock to enforce both integration and the safety of the black students.

On Sept. 12, 1958, Gov. Orval Faubus ordered all Little Rock high schools closed. This included Central High, Hall High, Horace Mann High and the city's Technical High School. The schools would remain closed until a special election could be held for the citizens of Little Rock to vote "yes" or "no" to integration.

On Sept. 15, the Little Rock School Board ordered all extracurricular activities in the high schools to cease. Central High, Hall High and Horace Mann were to stop

football practice immediately and notify each of its opponents that Little Rock would not field any football teams during the 1958 season.

Gov. Faubus held a press conference and publicly ridiculed the school board for its ruling against extracurricular activities. Gov. Faubus called the ruling a "cruel and unnecessary blow to the children."

The superintendent of the Little Rock School District, Virgil T. Blossom, stated the next day that the ruling was in conjunction with the closing of the schools. However, more consideration and discussion with the Arkansas Activities Association revised the board's decision. The superintendent announced that football and other extracurricular activities would continue.

The result of the Sept. 27 special election found that 19,470 voted against integration and 7,561 voted for integration.

With this in mind, Faubus ordered the high schools to remain closed. The teachers and staff reported to empty school buildings each day and students had to either transfer to a county school or take correspondence courses. Most athletes in the city took classes via correspondence to remain eligible for athletics.

Just as Coach Matthews had the previous season, Coach Hall worked to keep his players focused on football

Photo provided by the Arkansas Democrat-Gazette

Doyne Davis (12)

238

(Left to Right) Buddy Tackett, Kenneth Zini, John Rath

rather than the political issues around them. The Tigers, preseason favorites to again win the Big 9 Conference, continued preparation for the season despite no school.

With only nine returning lettermen, Central's weaknesses were in the secondary and offensive backfield. The entire secondary graduated, as did many experienced offensive backs. The team's strengths, however, were in both the offensive and defensive fronts as eight of the returning lettermen were linemen.

The Tigers looked to continue their winning streak when they opened the season against West Monroe High School of Louisiana. Central scored in the first quarter when a 10-yard pass from Fallon Davis to Charles Patterson capped a nine-play, 71-yard drive. Steve Hathcote converted the extra-point attempt for a 7-0 lead.

West Monroe answered after fullback Dwaine Johnston sprinted 72 yards before being brought down at the Central 8. Halfback Jerry Stovall scored from there and also converted the extra-point attempt to tie the score at 7-7.

Stovall scored the Rebels' next touchdown with 6:30 left in the third quarter when he intercepted a Davis pass in the flats and outran the Tigers for 68 yards. He converted his second extra-point attempt for a 14-7 lead.

Late in the same quarter, the Tigers tied the score on a 10-yard run by Doyne Davis. After stopping West Monroe on its next series and forcing a punt, Doyne Davis returned the kick 28 yards to the Rebels 22. Hathcote carried five times during the drive, finally scoring from the 1 for the game-winning touchdown.

Hathcote finished with a game-high 112 yards on 20 carries. The 20-14 outcome was Central's 34th consecutive victory, its toughest contest since the streak began in 1955.

Although the score was relatively close, 25-14, Central's next game was not much of a struggle. Tilghman High School of Paducah, Ky., was only able to gain 75 yards rushing. The defense manhandled the Tornadoes most of the night, and only one of Tilghman's touchdowns came against Central's starters.

An improved offense drove 75 yards for a score on its first possession. Hathcote, who finished with 119 yards rushing, ran 25 yards for the touchdown. The Kentucky team answered immediately when Freddy Lookofsky passed to Craig Stubblefield for a 91-yard touchdown. Ken Hurley converted the extra-point attempt for a 7-6 lead.

Central broke the game open in the second half when it scored twice within two minutes. Patterson returned a punt 31 yards for a touchdown, and Bob Shepherd intercepted a pass and returned it 46 yards for another score. Hathcote's extra point put the Tigers up 19-7.

A 30-yard touchdown pass from Fallon Davis to Patterson in the fourth quarter gave Central a 25-7 lead. Coach Hall then put his second team in the game, which eventually allowed Paducah to score its second touchdown when S.W. Stamper scored on a short run. The Tigers defeated Tilghman for their 35th consecutive victory.

Central met its match during the third week of the season when it traveled to Baton Rouge, La., to face Istrouma High School. Istrouma, the last team to defeat the Tigers in September 1955, would become the team that ended the nation's longest high school winning streak.

More than 14,000 fans were at Memorial Stadium in Baton Rouge to watch the No. 1 team in Louisiana meet the No. 1 team in Arkansas.

Once the game began, the Louisiana team simply did as it wished against Central. Baton Rouge scored just two minutes into the game when Steve Ward returned an interception 40 yards for a touchdown.

The Tigers didn't have a first down in the first half and only three during the game. They never threatened to score and only had one possession inside the 40, that coming after a fumble recovery at the Indians 32. Istrouma's domination ended in a 42-0 loss for Little Rock Central.

The Tigers opened conference play the next week by traveling to Rix Stadium in Hot Springs to battle the Trojans. The 3,000 fans who filled the stadium witnessed the closest game between the two schools since they tied 0-0 in 1943.

It wasn't until the second-half kickoff that Central began to look like itself. Halfback Doyne Davis cut to the outside for a 29-yard gain before being run out of bounds by Hot Springs' Hal Melton.

Patterson then caught a Fallon Davis pass to move to the 10. Hathcote eventually

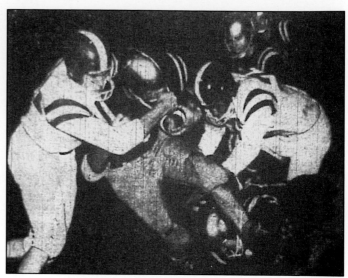
Photo provided by the Arkansas Democrat-Gazette
Steve Hathcote carries against North Little Rock

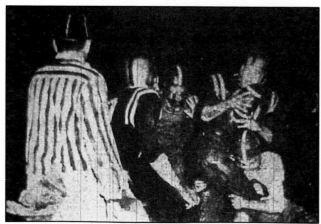
Photo provided by the Arkansas Democrat-Gazette
Buddy Tackett returns an interception

ran over left tackle for a 4-yard touchdown. The extra-point attempt failed, but the Tigers led 6-0.

With quarterback Franklin Francis out with an injured knee, the Trojans were unable to find an offensive spark. They only managed 36 yards of total offense, while Central had 220 yards rushing and 60 yards passing. Doyne Davis rushed for 98 yards to lead all rushers in the 6-0 victory.

Fort Smith head coach Bill Stancil labeled the game against Central the following week as "the biggest game of my career, either as a player or coach." This statement was made just minutes after the Grizzlies became the first Arkansas team to defeat the Tigers since North Little Rock in 1951.

Just more than 2,000 fans showed up at Quigley Stadium to watch Fort Smith capitalize on a Central fumble and score its first touchdown within the first six minutes of the game. Just as the first quarter was ending, Fort Smith's Jim Grizzle blocked a punt. Robert Parker recovered and advanced 5 yards for the Grizzlies' second touchdown. The extra-point attempt failed for the second time, but Fort Smith led 12-0.

The Grizzlies scored their final touchdown with 6:40 remaining in the fourth quarter. Jim Bob Weir ran the final 2 yards following Fallon Davis' 7-yard punt that went out of bounds at the Central 20. The extra-point attempt was good to give the Grizzlies a 19-6 victory.

Following the Tigers' first loss to an in-state team in seven years, 26 players transferred to other schools to formally continue their education. Only six of these players, however, would have played enough to letter.

These six transfers were quarterback Fallon Davis, backup quarterback Gary Mobley, halfback Archie Dumas, tackle Clarence Crist, tackle Charles Cusick and defensive lineman Bob McWilliams. Coach Hall and his staff were forced to fill those positions with young and inexperienced players.

When Central traveled to Texarkana, Ark., for its next game, sophomore Claude Fulton had been named starting quarterback. He made the most of the opportunity as he completed a 15-yard pass to Patterson to take the lead late in the game.

After a scoreless first quarter, Hathcote returned a punt 43 yards to set up a 3-yard touchdown run by Ronnie Holmes. Texarkana answered when Charles Jacobs returned a punt 73 yards for a touchdown and again when David Potter scored from the 10. Jacobs converted both extra-point attempts for a 14-6 lead.

Jack McClain started things off for Central in the second half when he returned a Texarkana fumble 80 yards for a touchdown. Buddy Tackett blocked a Texarkana punt on its next possession, and John McCarty returned it 36 yards for a touchdown. Hathcote's conversion put the Tigers in front 19-14.

Gary Brown, the Big 9 Conference's sprint champion, scored on a 69-yard run for Texarkana to put it ahead 20-19. Fulton then threw his touchdown pass to regain the lead, and Hathcote later clinched the victory with touchdown runs of 41 yards and 37 yards. The 38-21 victory gave Central a 2-1-0 conference record going into its matchup with conference leader El Dorado the next week.

It was homecoming night at Memorial Stadium in El Dorado and more than 7,000 fans cheered as the heavily favored Wildcats struck first. Herbert Ray Martin returned a punt 19 yards to the Central 15. Tommy Brasher eventually scored from the 2 with only 47 seconds left in the first quarter.

Fulton began to loosen up in the second quarter. With 3:40 left in the half, he passed 43 yards to Patterson to reach the 25. He then connected with Bill Collier for a 25-yard touchdown to tie the score at 7-7.

An El Dorado punt return again set up its next score as Martin returned a kick to the Tigers 32. Nine plays moved the Wildcats to the 5, with Martin scoring from there. The conversion was good for a 14-7 lead over Central.

The Tigers were given another scoring opportunity late in the game after Alvin Crawford recovered a fumble on the Central 42. Fulton kept hopes alive when he completed a pass to McClain at the El Dorado 28 with 1:44 left in the game.

El Dorado's defense backed up anticipating a pass, but Hathcote ran on a draw play and was not brought down until he reached the 2. He scored on the next play and also converted the extra-point attempt in a 14-14 tie.

Photo provided by the Arkansas Democrat-Gazette
(Left to Right) Bob McWilliams, Alvin Crawford, Charles Patterson and (bottom) Charles Teague

The Tigers celebrate their victory over Hall High

El Dorado remained on top of the conference at 3-0-1, while the Tigers were in second place with at 2-1-1. For Central to win the Big 9 championship, it needed to win its remaining conference games and hope the Wildcats were beaten at least once in conference action.

The Tigers lost their third game of the season the following week when they were shut out by Central High of Memphis. The Warriors' victory was the first over Little Rock Central since 1942. After the 28-0 defeat by the Memphis team, the Tigers began to prepare for their late-season battle with North Little Rock.

For the first time, Central High School traveled across the river to play in North Little Rock's Wildcat Stadium. The game was a stalemate until midway through the second quarter. Hathcote set the stage for a score with a 19-yard punt return to give the Tigers possession on their 43. Hathcote capped a 15-play drive when he passed to Ronnie Spann for an 8-yard touchdown. Hathcote added the extra point for a 7-0 lead.

Central added another score in the fourth quarter when Fulton completed a 4-yard pass to Collier for a touchdown. The Wildcats found the end zone late in the game when Gem Mumme completed a 28-yard touchdown pass to Glenn McVey.

However, one touchdown would not be enough as the Tigers defeated North Little Rock 13-6. Hathcote finished the night with 164 yards on 36 carries.

After a 25-0 victory over Pine Bluff, Central traveled to Blytheville to take on the Chicks for its final conference game. Since El Dorado had already clinched the conference championship, the Tiger were playing for a second in the Big 9 Conference.

Central scored a dominating 20-0 victory as Hathcote rushed for 240 yards on 19 carries, scoring on runs of 88, 70 and 2 yards.

The next week, a game all of Little Rock had been awaiting, marked the first meeting between the Tigers and Little Rock Hall High School. Quigley Stadium was the site of this Thanksgiving Day game, and more than 6,000 fans were in attendance to see what was billed as the city championship.

The No. 2 Warriors, in only their second season of existence, entered 10-0-0. Third-ranked Central was 7-3-1.

Both head coaches described the game as one of the hardest hitting and best defensive battles of the season. The outcome was decided by a Hall High mistake late in the in the second quarter. The mistake occurred when a Central punt glanced off the helmet of Hall's Jim Rowland and was recovered by Collier.

The scoring drive began from the Warriors 25 and ended with an 8-yard pass from Fulton to Jim Kinderman. Hathcote converted the extra-point attempt with 50 seconds left in the first half for a 7-0 lead.

The lead held up as the Tigers allowed only 99 yards rushing and 37 yards passing. Hathcote rushed for 107 yards in Central's 7-0 holiday victory over its new city rival.

Coach Gene Hall ended his first season as head coach 8-3-1 and with a No. 2 ranking in the statewide polls. When the team's winning streak ended at 35 games early in the season, magazines such as *Sports Illustrated, Life* and *Newsweek* featured the Tigers for their achievement.

1958 TIGER SCHEDULE

West Monroe, LA 14	LRCH 20
Tilghman High of Paducah, KY 14	LRCH 25
Istrouma High of Baton Rouge, LA 42	LRCH 0
*Hot Springs 0	LRCH 6
*Fort Smith 19	LRCH 6
*Texarkana, AR 21	LRCH 38
*El Dorado 14	LRCH 14
Central High of Memphis, TN 28	LRCH 0
*North Little Rock 6	LRCH 13
*Pine Bluff 0	LRCH 25
*Blytheville 0	LRCH 20
LR Hall 0	LRCH 7

AN UNCHARACTERISTIC RECORD

1959   4-6-0

Head Coach: Gene Hall
Assistants: Ralph Holland, V.E. Baber, Clyde Hart
Team Trainer: Clyde Hart
Team Physician: Dr. John McCollough Smith

1959 LETTERMEN

Bob Brazzell	Claude Fulton	Jerry Knowles	Fred Stansberry
Richard Carpenter	Mike Hales	Jim Lea	Gayle Voth
Lee Casey	Jerrell Holloway	John McCarty	Gary Wahlquist
Darrell Collier	Ross Honea	Gary Mobley	Darrell Ward
Charles Cusick	Jim Kinderman	Gary Robinson	Jerry Welch
Charles Dodd	Tom King	Royce Rose	Fred Worthington
Larry Dum	Bill Knight	Ronnie Spann	

1959 MANAGERS

Larry Balding	Jerry McKenney
Donald Bennett	Jerry McNabb
Bill Crippen	Jon Tate

1959 ALL-STATE
Gary Robinson

1959 ALL-STAR TEAM
Gary Robinson

Photo provided by the Arkansas Democrat-Gazette
(Left to Right) Jerry Welch, Larry Dum
and Ross Honea

For the first time in two years, the Tigers were able to prepare for an upcoming season without the fear of any political repercussions resulting from actions in the school building. The Little Rock School District was in the middle of its desegregation plan, and there was no threat of protests or closings.

Central began the season with an open date, allowing the Tigers to have an additional week to prepare for powerful Tilghman High of Paducah, Ky. Quarterback Claude Fulton threw four touchdown passes and ran for another, all in the first half, in a dominating performance against Tilghman.

Central opened the road game by intercepting a Tilghman pass near midfield on the game's first play from scrimmage. The Tigers quickly drove 56 yards in six plays for their first touchdown, a 21-yard pass from Fulton to Bill Knight with 8:04 remaining in the first quarter.

Just minutes later, Central began a 77-yard march. The five-play drive was capped by a 49-yard touchdown pass from Fulton

to Jim Kinderman with 5:05 left in the first quarter.

Less than two minutes later, Fulton connected with Gary Robinson on a 40-yard scoring pass. Richard Carpenter converted the extra point for a 19-0 first-quarter lead.

The Tigers went on to score three more touchdowns, and Fulton finished with 227 yards passing in a 39-7 victory over the Tornadoes.

After another open date, Central hosted the Hot Springs Trojans at Quigley Stadium. The Tigers dominated the game, gaining 481 total yards and holding Hot Springs to only 99 total yards in a 40-0 victory.

Included in Central's six touchdowns were three scoring passes from Fulton, a 19-yard fumble return by Tom King and a 51-yard run by Robinson. The joy from the victory did not last long as the Tigers suffered their first loss of the season the following week against Fort Smith, 20-6.

A 3-yard touchdown run by Fulton ended a 77-yard drive by Central the next week against Texarkana, Ark. The second-quarter touchdown was the only time that either team came close to scoring. In a defensive battle, the Tigers celebrated homecoming with a 7-0 victory.

Another Big 9 Conference matchup the following week pitted Central against El Dorado at Little Rock's Quigley Stadium. In what Coach Gene Hall called "a sorry exhibition of football," the Tigers managed only 36 total yards in the first half. The Wildcats gained 162 yards in the first half, scoring in the second quarter on a 25-yard run by Leroy McHan.

The El Dorado defense held Central 12 times inside the Wildcats 10. Two goal-line stands enabled the Wildcats to escape 7-0, a loss that virtually eliminated the Tigers from the Big 9 Conference race.

The Central High Tigers traveled to Memphis the following week to play the Central High Warriors. Memphis media considered the game to be one most exciting played in Tennessee during the 1959 season. The Warriors led 7-6 as the fourth quarter opened. Then, the excitement began.

Jerry Knowles scored from the 1 to cap an 81-yard drive by the Tigers. The first play following the ensuing kickoff resulted in a 59-yard touchdown run by Memphis. Robinson then returned the ensuing kickoff 81 yards to the 9. Two plays later, the Tigers had another touchdown, but Memphis took the ensuing kickoff 87 yards for a touchdown. The Tigers could never regain the momentum in a 27-18 loss to the Warriors.

Central's woes continued the next week when it lost to North Little Rock High School for the first time since 1951. The Tigers struck first after Fulton completed three consecutive passes to move to the 1. Carpenter then went over for the score and a 6-0 lead.

The Wildcats answered with a 63-yard drive that ended with an 8-yard touchdown run by Don Caple. North Little Rock scored again just moments later when Gem Mumme passed to Jerry Jones for a 29-yard touchdown. Mumme's extra point gave the Wildcats a 14-6 lead.

Central's second touchdown came in the third quarter when Larry Dum picked up a Mumme fumble and returned it 65 yards for the score. The extra-point attempt failed. This incompletion, combined with the first failed conversion, would haunt the Tigers as they lost to the Wildcats 14-12.

A week later, the bitter rivalry with Pine Bluff ensued. Coach Marcus Kaufman's Zebras scored early in the first quarter following the recovery of a Fulton fumble.

John Kitchen recovered at the 30 for Pine Bluff, setting up the game's only steady drive. Charles Phillips ended the drive with a 6-yard touchdown run to put the Zebras up 6-0.

Just after Pine Bluff scored, the weather took a dramatic change for the worse. A driving rain and bitter cold winds

resulted in both a slippery field and slippery football. Twenty fumbles were recorded during the game and neither team threatened to score again.

The early touchdown proved beneficial for the Zebras in a 6-0 victory, Pine Bluff's first in the series since a 21-19 decision in 1951.

The Tigers ended their four-game losing streak the next week with a 14-0 victory over Blytheville High School. After traveling to the northeast corner of the state to battle the Chicks, Central needed only two long plays for the victory.

The first play came just after the Tigers received the second-half kickoff. Fulton passed to Kinderman for a 54-yard touchdown play.

After receiving the ensuing kickoff, Blytheville could not gain any yardage and was forced to punt. Fulton received the kick on Central's 25 and returned it 75 yards for the Tigers' second touchdown. Kinderman converted both extra points in the two-touchdown victory over the Chicks.

More than 6,500 people began their Thanksgiving by watching the second annual "Turkey Bowl" between Little Rock Central and Little Rock Hall.

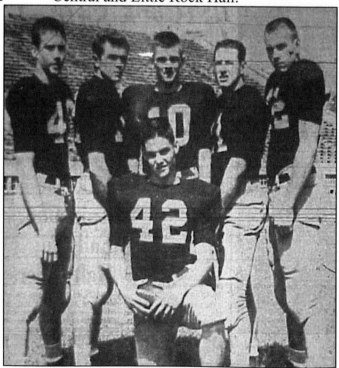

Photo provided by the Arkansas Democrat-Gazette

(Left to Right) Jim Lea, Lee Casey, Ronnie Spann, Jerry Knowles, Gary Robinson and Claude Fulton (kneeling)

The Warriors scored first after recovering a fumble deep inside Central territory. Little Rock Hall's lead, though, was short-lived as Robinson returned the ensuing kickoff 84 yards for a touchdown. Kinderman converted the extra point to make it 7-7.

Little Rock Hall quarterback Richard Massie helped the Tigers gain another score when he threw an interception to Gary Mobley, who returned it for a touchdown to give Central a 13-7 advantage. Little Rock Hall, however, grounded out an 81-yard scoring drive in 15 plays for a 13-13 tie.

Tom McKnelly provided the big play for the Warriors when he kicked a game-winning field goal with 20 seconds remaining to give Little Rock Hall its first victory over the Tigers. The Warriors finished the game with 305 yards rushing, including 119 from Chester Storthz.

Little Rock Hall's 10-1-0 season was highlighted by a Big 9 Conference title and the 1959 state championship. Little Rock Central ended the season with a 3-5-0 con-

Photo provided by the Arkansas Democrat-Gazette
Gary Robinson (22) against North Little Rock

ference record and a 4-6-0 overall record. The 1959 season was the first losing season for the Tigers since they were 4-6-1 in 1942.

1959 TIGER SCHEDULE

Tilghman High of Paducah, KY 7	LRCH 39
*Hot Springs 0	LRCH 40
*Fort Smith 20	LRCH 6
*Texarkana, AR 0	LRCH 7
*El Dorado 7	LRCH 0
Central High of Memphis, TN 27	LRCH 18
*North Little Rock 14	LRCH 12
*Pine Bluff 6	LRCH 0
*Blytheville 0	LRCH 14
*LR Hall 16	LRCH 13

UNDEFEATED, UNTIED, BIG 9 CHAMPION

1960   12-0-0

Head Coach: Gene Hall
Assistants: Ralph Holland, V.E. Baber, Clyde Hart, Clyde Horton
Team Trainer: Clyde Hart
Team Physician: Dr. John McCollough Smith

1960 LETTERMEN

Billy Ball	Mike Hales	Tommy McDermott	Fred Stausberry
Richard Britt	Jerrell Holloway	Bob McElroy	Gerry Stracener
Richard Carpenter	Ross Honea	Gary Mobley	Darrell Ward
Lee Casey	Gene Howard	Bob Moser	Jerry Welch
Bob Corley	Bill Knight	Dale Ramsey	James Wilburn
Tommy Evans	Jerry Knowles	David Sharp	Nick Williams
Claude Fulton	Tommy Maddox	Leon Sneed	Fred Worthington

1960 MANAGERS

Louis Averitt	Sammy Leath
Larry Bolding	David Shewmaker
David Dashiell	Terry Taylor
Terry Henson	

1960 ALL-AMERICAN
Mike Hales

1960 ALL-SOUTHERN
Claude Fulton
Mike Hales
Bill Knight

1960 ALL-SOUTHWEST
Bill Knight

1960 ALL-STATE

Claude Fulton   Gene Howard
Mike Hales   Bill Knight
Ross Honea   Jerry Welch

1960 ALL-STAR TEAM
Claude Fulton
Jerry Welch
Gene Hall - Coach

Photo provided by Central High School
Darrell Ward

The opener was a short trip to Benton for a game against the Class AA Benton Panthers. The contest marked the first time since 1950 that Central High competed against a school from a smaller classification.

Benton's defense held tight during the opening half, and was aided by 65 yards in penalties on the Tigers during the first 21 minutes of play. With 3:10 left in the second quarter, quarterback Claude Fulton kept on a bootleg and ran around left end for a 12-yard gain. Jerry Knowles added 12 yards and 10 yards, followed by another 3 yards from Fulton to move to the Benton 15.

Central scored on the next play when Fulton handed to Lee Casey, who ran off left tackle and into the end zone. The extra-point attempt failed, but the Tigers took a 6-0 lead.

A second-half score for Central was set up by Darrell Ward's punt return to the Benton 12. Knowles gained 7 yards before Fulton carried for the touchdown. Knowles converted the extra point for a 13-0 lead.

The Tigers held the Panthers scoreless and only allowed one first down, which wasn't converted until 30 seconds into the fourth quarter.

Following a 38-7 victory over Subiaco High School the next week, Central began preparing for its battle with Texarkana, Texas. On a hot and humid night at Quigley Stadium, Fulton bulled his way through the defense and into the end zone from the 3 for a 6-0 lead with 7:06 left in the second quarter.

One minute and 11 seconds later, the Tigers scored again as Bill Knight intercepted a pass in the flats and returned it 25 yards for a touchdown. The extra-point attempt failed after each touchdown and Central led 12-0 at halftime.

With 2:25 left in the game, Texarkana quarterback Bob White completed a 12-yard touchdown pass to E.J. Miller. The extra-point conversion cut the Tigers' lead to 12-7.

But Tommy Maddox received the ensuing kickoff at his 30 and returned it along the west sideline. After breaking one tackle at the 45, he was clear for the remaining 55 yards. His 70-yard kickoff return increased

Central's lead to 18-7 and sealed the victory.

The Tigers traveled to Hot Springs for their first Big 9 Conference battle the following week and barely survived a team that had lost 16 consecutive games. Hot Springs threatened in the first quarter when it recovered a Central fumble at the Tigers 7.

After moving to the 1, fullback Max Weehunt crossed the goal line for an apparent touchdown. However, an offside penalty nullified the score. On the next play, Central recovered a fumble to end the scoring threat.

Central's only score was set up when Mike Hales blocked a Weehunt punt early in the second quarter. Central took possession at its 35 and used seven plays to move to the 5. Fulton then passed to Gary Mobley for a touchdown, and Richard Carpenter's extra point gave the Tigers a 7-0 lead and eventually the victory.

No. 2 Central faced its toughest challenge the following week when it hosted the top-ranked Fort Smith Grizzlies.

Fort Smith had already beaten No. 3 El Dorado and No. 4 Pine Bluff, and a victory over the Tigers would give the Grizzlies a shot at their first Big 9 championship.

The homecoming crowd at Quigley Stadium was smaller than usual because of rain, but the wet field did not factor into the game. The contest was a great defensive matchup and the teams battled to a 6-0 score.

Central cornerback Gene Howard recovered a fumble at the Fort Smith 9 to set

Claude Fulton

up the game's only score. Ward, playing quarterback, scored on a 1-yard sneak with 6:25 left in the first quarter. Carpenter's extra-point attempt was blocked by Jamie Beckman and Central led 6-0.

Both defensive units were nearly flawless the remainder of the game. The Tigers stopped Fort Smith at the 20, 5 and 5 in the first half. During the second half, the Grizzlies never crossed the Central 37.

The Tigers threatened only once during the second half, but the drive ended at the 11 after Fort Smith recovered a fumble. The 6-0 score was enough for a Central victory and moved the Tigers into the top spot in the state rankings.

The Central defense scored two touchdowns the following week to highlight a 43-0 victory over Texarkana, Ark. Richard Britt recovered a blocked punt in the end zone for a touchdown in the third quarter, and Maddox recovered a Texarkana fumble in the end zone for a fourth-quarter score.

A slow start by the Tigers resulted in only a 13-0 halftime lead. That advantage was a result of a 1-yard run by Casey to cap a 63-yard drive and a 38-yard scoring pass from Ward to Knight. Central finished with 15 first downs and allowed the Razorbacks only one.

Gerry Stracener

With Little Rock Hall losing to Pine Bluff the previous week, Central traveled to El Dorado as the state's top-ranked team and in sole possession of first place in the Big 9 Conference.

The Tigers struck first during the second quarter after Fulton received a punt on his 32. Fulton cut to the east sideline and the only defender between him and the end zone was leveled with a vicious block by Knight. Fulton ran the remaining distance untouched for a 68-yard touchdown. Carpenter's extra point put Central ahead 7-0 with 8:58 left in the second quarter.

El Dorado scored midway through the third quarter after a 27-yard punt return by Jerry Mooty and a 15-yard penalty by the Tigers gave the Wildcats possession at the Central 39. Gary Elia passed 13 yards to Jimmy Faulkner to the 26. From there, Faulkner took a handoff on a trap play and easily went the distance to tie the score at 7-7.

The Tigers used their ground attack to chew up most of the fourth quarter and move 85 yards for a game-winning touchdown. Knowles, at fullback, scored from the 1 with 2:29 left in the game. Carpenter converted his second extra-point attempt for a 14-7 victory over the Wildcats.

The next week, Central used 264 yards rushing, including 118 by Knowles, and 336 total yards to dominate Central High of Memphis. The Tigers scored twice off turnovers in a 32-0 victory over the Warriors.

After squeaking by North Little Rock 22-13, Central prepared for its battle with Pine Bluff. The defense sparkled in a 7-0 victory over the Zebras.

Central's score occurred with 5:32 remaining in the third quarter after Hales recovered a Pine Bluff punt at the Zebras 24. On third down, Ward eventually connected with Knight for a short touchdown pass. Carpenter converted the extra point for the 7-0 lead.

The defense took over from there. Early in the fourth quarter, it held Pine Bluff scoreless after the Zebras converted a first down inside the Central 10. Minutes later, Pine Bluff made a first down at the Tigers 1, but was stopped on four consecutive plays.

On the Zebras' next possession, they again converted a first down inside the Central 2, but were once again held scoreless on four consecutive plays. The incredible defensive effort helped Central to its 10th consecutive victory of the season.

Central scored on four of its first six possessions the next week against Blytheville in a 39-0 victory over the Chicks. Reserve players finished the first half and added two more scores in the second half on drives of 80 and 68 yards. Late in the game, the Tigers ended possessions by punting on first or second down.

The victory over the Chicks clinched the Big 9 Conference and state championship for Central. The Tigers, however, had one more game remaining on the schedule. They faced their new Thanksgiving Day foe for only the third time, but the battle with Little Rock's Hall High School was already a fierce rivalry.

"Maul Hall" was the chant of Central students as only the Warriors stood in the way of the 11th undefeated season in school history. A Hall High School victory would place the Warriors in a three-way tie with Pine Bluff and Fort Smith for second in the conference. A loss would put the Warriors in a tie with El Dorado for the conference's fourth-place team.

Claude Fulton

251

In front of more than 10,000 fans at Quigley Stadium, Ward put the Tigers in front early when he capped a 67-yard drive with a 1-yard sneak. Carpenter converted the extra point for a 7-0 lead. Just minutes later, Hall High's Johnny Jones fumbled and Hales recovered at the Warriors 48.

Photo provided by Central High School

Coach Gene Hall and the Tigers celebrate their championship

On the first offense play, Ward pitched to Fulton, who cut back through a large hole over right tackle. He then cut outside, broke one tackle and outran the defense to the end zone. Carpenter missed the extra-point attempt, but the Tigers took a 13-0 lead into halftime.

Late in the fourth quarter, Central took over on downs at its 44. Seven plays later, Knowles took the ball from the 31 and was met by two Warriors at the 21. Before being tackled, Knowles attempted to pitch to Fulton, but a Hall High player tipped the ball and it fell to the ground. Fulton was able to scoop up the ball and run untouched over the goal line, increasing the lead with 4:12 left in the game. Carpenter's extra point finished the game's scoring and gave the Tigers a 20-0 victory over the Warriors.

The game marked the first time a Big 9 Conference member scored more than two touchdowns against Hall, and it was the largest margin of victory over the Warriors in the three-year series history.

Central finished the season with eight shutouts, equaling the school record set in 1919 and 1946, and completed its third perfect season in five years. Coach Gene Hall's 1960 state championship marked the school's 25th football title.

1960 TIGER SCHEDULE

Benton 0	LRCH 13
Subiaco 7	LRCH 38
Texarkana, TX 7	LRCH 18
*Hot Springs 0	LRCH 7
*Fort Smith 0	LRCH 6
*Texarkana, AR 0	LRCH 43
*El Dorado 7	LRCH 14
Central High of Memphis, TN 0	LRCH 32
*North Little Rock 13	LRCH 22
*Pine Bluff 0	LRCH 7
*Blytheville 0	LRCH 39
*LR Hall 0	LRCH 20

NO REPEAT

1961   5-6-0

Head Coach: Gene Hall
Assistants: Ralph Holland, V.E. Baber, Clyde Hart, Clyde Horton
Team Trainer: Clyde Hart
Team Physician: Dr. John McCollough Smith

[1961 TEAM PHOTO UNAVAILABLE]

1961 LETTERMEN

Billy Ball	James Colton	John Hoffman	Troy Rhea
Sammy Beavers	Bob Corley	Don Hollingsworth	David Sharp
Tommy Brewer	Steve Elliott	Dick King	Gerry Stracener
Jim Butler	Tommy Evans	Jerry Knowles	Robert Trammel
Mike Campbell	Gilbert Fuller	Mike Kyle	Tommy Trantham
Ronnie Cassaday	Robert Gay	George Langley	Jimmy Trudell
Gary Claude	Phil Gentry	Dennis Masters	Mike Trudell
Frank Coble	Sammy Harris	Bob McElroy	Darrell Ward
Lonnie Cole	Joe Haynes	Bob Moser	

1961 MANAGERS

Louis Averitt	Terry Henson
Larry Balding	Sammy Leath
David DeShield	David Shoemaker

1961 ALL-STATE
None

1961 ALL-STAR TEAM
None

Photo provided by the Arkansas Democrat-Gazette
Joe Haynes (83) breaks through Catholic High's line to intercept a screen pass

Photo provided by the Arkansas Democrat-Gazette
Quarterback Don Hollingsworth (42)

The 1960 state champions began defense of their title against Benton High School. The *Arkansas Democrat* labeled the game as "the most brilliant combined offensive performances seen in Quigley Stadium in many a season."

An opening-night crowd of more than 6,000 witnessed an offensive display by both teams, an outburst that Benton featured first. Late in the first quarter, Danny Harmon recovered a Central fumble at the Tigers 23.

After driving to the 9, quarterback Tim Wright scored on a keeper around left end to give Benton a 6-0 lead. The lead increased to 12-0 before Benton's offense returned to the field.

Following Benton's initial score, Central was able to drive to the Panthers 15. The possession, however, ended when quarterback Darrell Ward and halfback James Colton could not connect on a pitch. Joe Bryant scooped up the fumble and returned it 80 yards for another touchdown. The extra point gave the Panthers a 13-0 halftime advantage.

The Tigers scored early in the third quarter after taking possession of the second-half kickoff at their 35. On first down,

Ward faked to Jerry Knowles and handed off to Robert Trammel. Trammel ran 65 yards for the touchdown and narrowed the deficit to 13-6.

Benton answered just minutes later when Bryant broke two tackles to score on a 47-yard reverse. Bobby Nix converted his second extra-point attempt for a 20-6 lead with 4:15 left in the third quarter.

Central, though, scored once more before the end of the third quarter. Knowles broke for a 34-yard gain to the 4. He eventually scored from the 1, running over three Benton players to get to the end zone. Lonnie Cole missed his second extra-point attempt and the Tigers trailed 20-12.

The Panthers scored again in the fourth quarter when Nix broke free for a 42-yard touchdown run. Central immediately answered when Don Hollingsworth capped a 36-yard drive with a 2-yard touchdown run. Knowles missed the extra-point attempt and the score remained 27-18 the rest of the way. Knowles was the only Central highlight, rushing for 159 yards on 20 attempts.

This marked the first time that Benton High School had beaten the Tigers. It was the 10th meeting between the schools, the first being played in 1906. The Panthers had not scored more than seven points against Central until this 1961 matchup.

More than 5,000 fans were in War Memorial Stadium to watch the Tigers the following week against Little Rock Catholic. Little Rock end Joe Haynes returned an interception 20 yards for a touchdown and a 6-0 lead early in the first quarter.

Two more Catholic turnovers resulted in two more Central touchdowns. The Tigers recovered a fumble at the 33 and Knowles eventually scored from the 2. Another fumble, this time recovered by Central at the 34, resulted in a 6-yard touchdown pass from Ward to Haynes.

Catholic High held the Tigers scoreless in the second half, but the three first-half touchdowns were enough for Central to win 18-0. This win gave the Tigers their first victory of the season and set up a battle with Texarkana, Texas, the following week.

Texarkana halfback Donnie Richardson ran for touchdowns of 58 and 24 yards en route to 131 yards rushing. The Texas team dominated Central 31-0, its last touchdown coming on a 30-yard interception return by John Ride with 20 seconds left in the game.

The Tigers opened Big 9 Conference action the next week when they hosted winless Hot Springs. Central capitalized on a mistake early in the first quarter after the Tigers' Sammy Harris punted.

Central's Ward was down the field before the kick landed and hoped to down it inside the 10. John Beebe was back to receive the punt and planned to let the kick bounce into the end zone for a touchback.

Beebe noticed Ward and immediately tried to catch the ball, but fumbled it instead. Ward was there to recover, giving the Tigers possession inside the Trojans 10.

Knowles ran 3 yards off right tackle, and Colton covered the remaining 6 yards for the score. Cole converted his first extra-point attempt of the season for a 7-0 lead.

Central struck again in the second quarter when Trammel took a pitch around right end, cut back inside and crossed the goal line 40 yards later to increase the Tigers' lead. Cole's second extra point gave Central a 14-0 halftime advantage.

Hollingsworth, Central's backup quarterback, finished the scoring when he ran for a 41-yard touchdown late in the fourth quarter. Cole converted the extra point for a 21-0 victory.

Central took its vaunted ground game to Fort Smith the following week to battle the undefeated Grizzlies. Fort Smith's defense, though, did not allow any running backs near the goal line in a 19-0 victory.

The Grizzlies' first score occurred after an 80-yard drive was capped by a 3-yard run by Bill Cole. They scored again with six minutes left in the second quarter when Jack Thompson returned a punt 96 yards for a touchdown. Quarterback Joe Jones con-

verted the extra-point attempt for a 13-0 halftime lead.

The game's last score took place in the third quarter after Fort Smith recovered a Central fumble at the Tigers 24. Larry Stafford ended the short drive with a 6-yard touchdown run to put the Grizzlies in front 19-0. The victory kept Fort Smith's record spotless, while Central dropped to 2-3 overall and 1-1 in the Big 9 Conference.

Knowles led the Tigers to a victory the next week when Central played Texarkana, Ark., at Quigley Stadium. Knowles rushed for 206 yards on 18 attempts and scored two touchdowns in a 42-0 victory over the Razorbacks. Central reserves saw plenty of action in the second half.

Following the big victory over Texarkana, Central had more disappointment the next week when it hosted El Dorado High School for homecoming. The Wildcats' first score was set up when they recovered a fumble by the Tigers.

Ward was back to field a punt, but he fumbled as he tried to catch it. Cliff Parnell recovered for the Wildcats, giving them

Dennis Masters (left) and Jerry Knowles

255

possession on the Central 33. Facing fourth down from the 1, halfback Jerry Mooty scored and the extra point gave El Dorado a 7-0 lead.

The Wildcats' second touchdown was also set up by a turnover. Parnell intercepted a Ward pass in the third quarter to give El Dorado possession on the Central 35. A few plays later, quarterback Gary Elia kept on a sweep around the end to score from the 10. The extra-point attempt increased the lead to 14-0.

The Wildcats scored on their next possession as well. David Patterson ran down the sideline for a 36-yard touchdown. Mooty's third extra point ended the scoring at 21-0. The defeat, along with a loss to Fort Smith, ended any chance the Tigers had to repeat as Big 9 champions.

Hollingsworth took over as Central's starting quarterback and led the Tigers with 81 yards rushing the following week against North Little Rock. He scored the game's first touchdown on a 21-yard run down the sideline to give Central a lead it

Photo provided by the Arkansas Democrat-Gazette
Darrell Ward (left) and Don Hollingsworth

would never lose. The Tigers scored twice more and defeated the Wildcats 21-0 for only their third conference victory.

The Pine Bluff Zebras, Central's next opponent, put together scoring drives of 71 yards and 40 yards to defeat the Tigers 14-0. Central would take out the resulting frustration when it traveled to Blytheville the next week to battle the Chicks.

Hollingsworth again led the Tigers' attack by scoring three touchdowns. Central's first score came on the opening kickoff when Hollingsworth returned it 88 yards for a touchdown.

Blytheville answered just minutes later when Roland Warrington returned an interception 97 yards before being brought down at the 2. Barry Hughes, the Chicks' 200-pound fullback, bulled his way through the line to tie the score at 6-6.

The Tigers took the lead just before halftime when Hollingsworth scored from the 17. He increased the lead early in the third quarter when he returned a punt 72 yards for a touchdown to make it 18-6.

Backup quarterback Ward added another touchdown when he passed to Trammel for a 30-yard scoring play. Hollingsworth then scored again on a 22-yard run, and Knowles scored on a 1-yard run to help Central to a 38-6 victory over the Chicks.

Photo provided by the Arkansas Democrat-Gazette
Dennis Masters intercepts a Hot Springs pass.

256

More than 5,000 fans attended a Thanksgiving Day game between Little Rock Central and Little Rock Hall. The Warriors' only touchdown came in the first quarter following Paul Becton's interception of a Hollingsworth pass on the Tigers 31.

Seven plays after the interception, Donnie Dietz scored from the 1 for a 6-0 lead with 5:10 left in the first quarter. Hall High added to its lead with 3:55 remaining in the third quarter on a 24-yard field goal by Jerry Bass.

Knowles returned the ensuing kickoff 30 yards to the 45. This set up Central's only score of the game, a 55-yard touchdown run by Ward. The teams combined for 221 rushing yards in a defensive battle that ended with Little Rock Hall winning 9-6.

The Tigers finished the season as the fifth-place team in the Big 9 Conference and recorded only their second losing season since 1942. The Warriors finished tied for second in the conference and gave Coach Ray Peters his fifth consecutive winning season.

1961 TIGER SCHEDULE

Benton 27	LRCH 18
LR Catholic 0	LRCH 18
Texarkana, TX 31	LRCH 0
*Hot Springs 0	LRCH 21
*Fort Smith 19	LRCH 0
*Texarkana, AR 0	LRCH 42
*El Dorado 21	LRCH 0
*North Little Rock 0	LRCH 21
*Pine Bluff 14	LRCH 0
*Blytheville 6	LRCH 38
*LR Hall 9	LRCH 6

A SECOND-HALF TEAM

1962   8-2-1

Head Coach: Gene Hall
Assistants: Ralph Holland, Clyde Hart, Clyde Horton, Jim Cathcart
Team Trainer: Clyde Hart
Team Physician: Dr. John McCollough Smith

1962 LETTERMEN

Sammy Beavers	Emmett Find	Mike Kyle	Robert Teague
Tommy Brewer	Don Garrison	George Laughy	Robert Trammel
George Calhoun	Sammy Harris	Tommy Marshall	Tommy Trantham
Ronnie Cassaday	Greg Harvill	Dennis Masters	Roger Vandiver
Gary Claude	Joe Haynes	Louis Nalley	Kenneth Youngblood
Lonnie Cole	Johnny Heflin	Larry Puckett	
James Colton	John Hoffman	Jim Rath	
Steve Elliott	Don Hollingsworth	Bill Reynolds	

1962 MANAGERS
Bill Bounds
Ray Hill
Jesse Johnson
Steve McKissack
Larry Meyers

1962 ALL-STATE
Sammy Beavers
James Colton
Sammy Harris
Robert Trammel

1962 ALL-STAR TEAM
Robert Trammel
Tommy Trantham

Following a miserable 5-6-0 season in 1961, the Little Rock Central Tigers were expected to perform much better in 1962. It was up to Coach Gene Hall to mold a group of players who possessed tremendous speed, strength and talent into a championship team.

The Tigers opened with a trip to the defending Region IIIAA champion Benton High School. The Little Rock team played like the Central teams of old as it easily defeated the Panthers 41-7. More than 5,500 watched the Tigers avenge one of their previous season's losses with three touchdowns in the fourth quarter to put the game away.

After a scoreless first quarter, Central began a 37-yard scoring drive to open the second period. Quarterback Don Hollingsworth connected with Tommy Trantham for a 10-yard touchdown pass to end the short drive. Lonnie Cole's extra point gave the Tigers a 7-0 lead with 8:55 left in the first half.

Central made it 14-0 by halftime after Dennis Masters recovered a Benton fumble on the Panthers 42. After reaching the 2, Masters finished the drive with a burst up the middle for the score. Cole converted the extra-point attempt to increase the lead to 14-0.

Just prior to a 1-yard touchdown run by Benton that capped a 66-yard drive in the third quarter, Hollingsworth returned a punt 90 yards for touchdown. Central led 21-7 after Benton's extra point.

Gary Claude intercepted quarterback Calvin Jones to set up the Tigers' fourth touchdown. James Colton broke through the line for a 19-yard gain to the 4. Masters scored from there to increase Central's lead 27-7.

Central reserves added two more scores late in the game. The first score came when quarterback Tommy Brewer completed an 18-yard touchdown pass to Trantham with

Photo provided by Central High School
Robert Trammel

2:45 left. The last touchdown occurred on the last play of the game when fullback Roger Vandiver scored on a 33-yard run.

More than 5,000 fans attended Central's first home game of the season. Catholic High School visited Quigley Stadium in a nonconference battle between the two Little Rock teams. A game-time temperature of 82 degrees did not affect the Tigers as they had plenty of substitutes available. The heat, though, did quickly wear down the Rockets since most of their players were required to play both ways because of a lack of depth.

Even hot and tired, the Catholic defense played a spectacular game and only allowed Central to score once during each half of play. Central reserve quarterback Jim Rath entered the game in the second quarter on a third-down play from his 40. He passed to

Don Hollingsworth (42) and Larry Puckett (20)

Trantham, who took the reception to the 2 before being brought down by Johnny Brainerd.

Halfback Robert Trammel then broke over left tackle for a touchdown with 5:20 remaining in the half. Cole's extra-point attempt was wide, but Central was able to take a 6-0 lead into halftime.

The Tigers' last touchdown came in the third quarter when they faced fourth down from the Rockets 10. Hollingsworth passed to Trantham, who caught the ball as he fell backward into the end zone for the score. Cole converted the extra-point attempt with 2:12 left in the quarter for a 13-0 victory. The loss was the 14th consecutive for Catholic.

The Tigers enjoyed an open date and an extra week to prepare for their first Big 9 Conference game against the Hot Springs Trojans. More than 4,000 fans, the Trojans' largest home crowd in more than 10 years, filled Rix Stadium in Hot Springs.

Hollingsworth got Central on the scoreboard with 3:55 left in the first quarter. He capped an 11-play, 53-yard drive by passing to Trantham for a 10-yard touchdown. Trantham and defender Jim French both jumped for the pass in the end zone, with Trantham taking the ball away from French for the score.

The Tigers struck again after Hot Springs' first possession of the second half ended in a punt. Central took possession on its 18 and put together a 20-play, 82-yard drive that consumed most of the third quarter. Hollingsworth ended the drive with a 1-

yard dive on fourth down. Cole's extra-point conversion was good for a 13-0 lead.

Even after a late touchdown by the Trojans, the Tigers held on for a 13-7 victory. The victory was their third of the season and set up a homecoming showdown with defending Big 9 champion Fort Smith at Quigley Stadium.

With the Grizzlies leading 6-0, Central drove 54 yards in the second quarter to take the lead. Trammel scored from the 3; Cole converted the extra-point attempt with 31 seconds left in the half for a 7-6 lead.

After recovering a fumble in the third quarter, Fort Smith moved to the 26 before attempting a field goal. Tom Corbin's kick was good to give the Grizzlies a 9-7 lead with 6:23 remaining in the third period. Later in the quarter, the Grizzlies' Butch Edwards scored from the 1 to cap a 42-yard drive. Corbin converted the extra-point attempt with five seconds left to increase Fort Smith's lead to 16-7.

Fort Smith never lost the lead en route to a 23-14 victory, its fourth over Central in the last five meetings. With one conference loss, the teams were tied for second place in the state's largest classification.

After the Tigers traveled to Texarkana, Ark., and beat the Razorbacks 20-0, they

Larry Puckett (20)

traveled south again, this time to battle El Dorado. Central's special teams were the difference as they scored three of four touchdowns to overcome an offense that could only manage two first downs, 89 yards of total offense and lost six fumbles.

Central scored midway through the first quarter when linebacker Sammy Harris recovered Jay Johnston's blocked punt in the end zone for a touchdown. Just minutes later, Trammel returned a punt 85 yards for a touchdown. These scores, along with Larry Puckett's 88-yard punt return for a touchdown in the second quarter and Cole's three conversions, gave the Tigers a 21-0 lead.

Central's final score came after Steve Elliott recovered a fumble on the El Dorado 13. Trammel ended the short drive with a 2-yard run. Cole added another extra point to give the Tigers a 28-0 lead. A late El Dorado score was not enough as Central defeated the Wildcats 28-7.

The following week was a break from the Big 9 Conference when the Tigers played Region IIIAA's unbeaten Conway Wampus Cats. The Central defense, combined with an offensive spurt by Trammel, was enough to hold the high-powered Conway offense to seven first downs and 128 total yards.

The game's initial touchdown occurred with 6:44 left in the second quarter when Conway quarterback Gary Nutter connected with Luke Gordy for a 7-yard touchdown to complete a 56-yard drive. The extra-point attempt failed, but the Wampus Cats led 6-0.

The Tigers, though, answered just a few minutes later as Trammel set up a score with a 31-yard run to the Conway 23. It took six more plays, but Colton eventually broke through the middle of the defense for a touchdown to end a 57-yard drive. Cole added the extra point with 21 seconds remaining in the first half for a 7-6 lead.

Central's first possession of the fourth quarter followed a turnover that occurred when a Nutter pass was intercepted by Claude. The Tigers put together a 56-yard march that featured the running of both Trammel and Colton. Trammel finished the drive with a 4-yard touchdown run with 11:56 remaining in the game. Cole's extra-point attempt was good, helping Central to a 14-6 victory over the Region IIIAA team.

Following a 27-3 victory over last-place North Little Rock, the Tigers hosted ancient rival Pine Bluff for a conference game that would potentially decide the Big 9 championship. Quarterback Gordon Norwood led the way for Pine Bluff as he opened the game with a 2-yard run around left end for a touchdown. His extra point put the Zebras ahead 7-0 with 5:49 left in the first quarter.

Late in the second quarter, Central tied the score when Trammel broke for a 62-yard touchdown run. Cole converted the extra-point attempt to tie the score at 7-7. The deadlock lasted until the fourth quarter as a turnover allowed the Zebras another opportunity to score.

Harris intercepted one of Norwood's passes deep inside Central territory. As he began to return the interception, he fumbled and it was recovered by Pine Bluff. Four plays later from the 2, Norwood scored the

Photo provided by Central High School

Sammy Beavers (80)

Photo provided by Central High School
The 1962 Tiger cheerleaders

winning touchdown with 10:11 remaining in the game. The extra-point attempt failed, but the Zebras led 13-7.

Central was unable to move after the ensuing kickoff. Pine Bluff took possession and ran six minutes off the clock before turning the ball over to the Tigers with two minutes left. Central was unable to move and went on to lose 13-7.

The Zebras played incredible ball control, allowing the Tigers only nine offensive plays in the second half. Pine Bluff's victory in front of more than 10,000 fans at Quigley Stadium guaranteed it at least a share the Big 9 Conference championship.

Central needed a two-touchdown second half the next week to defeat the Blytheville Chicks. It needed another second-half comeback the following week when it battled Little Rock Hall on Thanksgiving Day. More than 11,000 fans at Quigley Stadium watched the Warriors take a 14-0 halftime lead.

Their first score was in the first quarter, set up by the recovery of a fumble. Tackle Ken Polk recovered the fumble at the Central 49, and 12 plays later Cloud Keyes scored from the 2. Bill Lile added the extra point with 2:42 left in the quarter to give Hall High a lead that it would hold until late in the third quarter.

The second touchdown came after the Tigers' next possession. After receiving a Central punt at its 47, Hall High drove the needed 53 yards to increase its lead to 14-0. Quarterback Johnny Darracott passed the final 20 yards to Mike Weed. Lile followed with the extra point to make it 14-0 with 10:26 left in the first half.

With 3:19 left in the third quarter, the Tigers capped a 61-yard drive with a 15-yard touchdown pass from Hollingsworth to Trantham. Cole kicked the extra point to narrow the deficit to 14-7. Central added another score in the fourth quarter when Hollingsworth passed to Sammy Beavers for a 15-yard touchdown. Cole's extra point made it 14-14. The game ended 14-14.

The Warriors finished 9-1-1 and second to undefeated Pine Bluff in the Big 9 Conference.

The Tigers finished 8-2-1 and third in the conference.

1962 TIGER SCHEDULE

Benton 7	LRCH 41
LR Catholic 0	LRCH 13
*Hot Springs 7	LRCH 13
*Fort Smith 23	LRCH 14
*Texarkana, AR 0	LRCH 20
*El Dorado 7	LRCH 28
Conway 6	LRCH 14
*North Little Rock 3	LRCH 27
*Pine Bluff 13	LRCH 7
*Blytheville 0	LRCH 13
*LR Hall 14	LRCH 14

DUELING DEFENSES

1963   6-5-1

Head Coach: Gene Hall
Assistants: Ralph Holland, Clyde Horton, Bobby Hannon, Jim Cathcart
Team Physician: Dr. John McCollough Smith

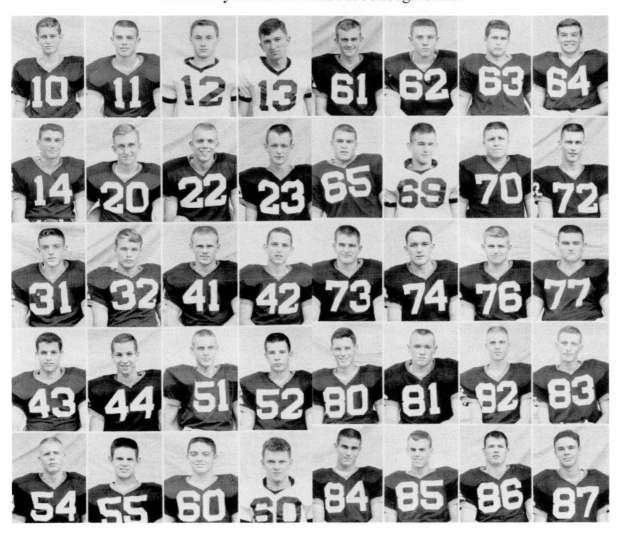

1963 LETTERMEN

Bill Baldwin	Bruce Cunningham	Mike Key	Doug Spencer
Tommy Brewer	Larry Ellis	Tommy Marshall	Gary Spears
Phillip Bryan	Carl Gachot	Ricky McBride	Robert Teague
George Calhoun	Don Garrison	Richard McCauley	Roger Vandiver
Stanley Clark	Danny Gortney	Louis Nalley	David Wagnon
Kenneth Clifton	Charles Green	Larry Puckett	Hansel Weiss
Frank Coble	Mike Greer	Jim Rath	Kenneth Youngblood
Charles Crum	Bobby Johnson	Bill Reynolds	

Coach Tom Hardin brought his Benton Panthers to Quigley Stadium to try and avenge a 41-7 loss to Central High the previous year. Benton installed a new offense, featuring split ends and a flanker.

Benton's game plan was to get around the end and outrun the defense. The two Benton running backs, however, were thrown for 39 yards in losses as the Central defense was able to catch them before they reached the line of scrimmage. The Panthers still managed a 7-6 lead late in the fourth quarter.

Benton scored first after an interception by Greg Gattin gave the Panthers possession at their 24. The big play in the 76-yard drive was a 50-yard pass from Robert Koppel to Ken Brown.

Photo provided by the Arkansas Democrat-Gazette
Tommy Brewer (41) and the Central High offense

Halfback Glen Hockersmith ended the drive with a 2-yard burst up the middle for the touchdown. Brown converted the extra point for a 7-0 lead with 7:30 remaining in the second quarter.

It wasn't until the fourth quarter that the Tigers finally scored. The touchdown came after a 66-yard drive ended with a 23-yard scoring pass from Bruce Cunningham to Larry Puckett. The extra-point attempt failed with 8:04 left in the game, leaving Central behind 7-6.

On the ensuing Benton possession, the Tigers forced a punt. The kick, though, was not caught and bounced against a Central lineman. Benton recovered at the Tigers 49 with 5:09 remaining.

Three plays later, Central's Robert Teague intercepted a Koppel pass at mid-

field and returned it 50 yards for a touchdown. Cunningham kicked the extra point to give Central a 13-7 lead with 3:45 left in the game.

The Panthers could not move on their next possession. The Tigers escaped Region IIIAA Benton High School 13-7.

The Catholic High Rockets and Coach Mike Malham hosted Central the next week at War Memorial Stadium. Coach Malham's defense held the Tigers for most of the game, but gave up one long drive that proved costly.

In the middle of a 71-yard drive, Central's Tommy Brewer passed to Ricky McBride for a 25-yard gain to the Rockets 19. Brewer then went the distance for the

Ken Clifton (left) **and Ricky McBride**

score. Cunningham's extra point gave Central a 7-0 lead early in the first quarter. The last three quarters were a defensive battle, a battle the Tigers won.

Jonesboro High School visited Quigley Stadium the following week and tied the score midway though the second quarter when Tony Snow passed to Bob McDaniel for a 9-yard touchdown. Snow's extra point made it 7-7.

An 8-yard punt by Jonesboro gave Central possession on the Hurricane 44 with 1:27 left in the opening half. A throw-back pass from Brewer to Puckett on the first play moved the ball to the 8.

Fullback Roger Vandiver bulled his way up the middle for the go-ahead touchdown. Cunningham's extra point gave the Tigers a 14-7 lead with 32 seconds left in the half.

With just a few seconds remaining in the game, Jonesboro was threatening to score at the Central 32. The threat ended, though, when Phillip Bryan intercepted a

Snow pass and returned it 68 yards for a touchdown. The extra-point attempt failed, but the score sealed a 20-7 victory.

The Tigers opened Big 9 Conference action the following week with their fourth consecutive victory of the season, a 20-0 shutout over Hot Springs. The winning streak was snapped the next week when Central traveled to Fort Smith to take on the Grizzlies.

Following a scoreless first quarter, the Tigers received a punt and took possession on their 27. Vandiver, Puckett and a penalty moved the ball to the Central 44. Vandiver gained 2 more yards for a first down, but a penalty put the Tigers in a first-and-15 situation.

Brewer attempted a pass on the next play, but was intercepted by Fort Smith's James McKinley. Two offensive plays moved Fort Smith to the Central 33. From there, quarterback Bebo Slates threw a touchdown pass to Danny Stafford. The extra-point attempt failed, but the Grizzlies took a 6-0 lead with 1:39 remaining in the half.

Central's fate was decided on the last play of the game.

From the Fort Smith 20, Cunningham threw a pass into the end zone. Before the pass could land in the arms of the intended receiver, it was intercepted by Stafford. He returned the interception to the 5 as time expired, clinching the victory for the Grizzlies.

The next game was a must-win situation for Central in order to stay in the Big 9 Conference race. The Tigers hosted Texarkana, Ark., and were able to strike first with 2:18 left in the first quarter.

A 30-yard pass from Brewer to McBride was good for the game's first score. Cunningham converted the extra-point attempt for a 7-0 lead.

On the first play of the second quarter, Texarkana's Travis Giles caught a Fred Green pass at the Central 35. He was hit hard by two defenders, but managed to escape the tackle and make his way to the 15 before being brought down.

Fullback David Cooper ran to the 7 before Green scored around left end. Duane Patterson's conversion was successful to make it 7-7 with 10:30 remaining in the half.

Late in the first half, Jerry Beckman stopped a Central threat when he intercepted a pass at his 15. The turnover led to an 85-yard drive that ended with a short touchdown run by Joe Blagg. Patterson once again added the extra point and Texarkana led 14-7 with 42 seconds left in the half.

With 3:48 remaining in the game, the Tigers scored again when Cunningham completed a pass in the end zone to McBride. Cunningham was set to tie the score with the extra-point attempt, but Jimmy Gross broke through the line and blocked the kick.

The Tigers were unable to score again and left with their second loss of the season, 14-13.

A homecoming game against El Dorado proved exciting as special teams were the key to success. The Wildcats scored before their offense took the field when Arky Floyd returned a punt 85 yards for a touchdown. Jim Barnes converted the extra-point attempt for a 7-0 lead.

With 40 seconds left in the opening quarter, Bill Baldwin returned a punt 64 yards before being brought down at the 1. Brewer, playing quarterback, scored on the next play and Cunningham converted the extra-point attempt to make it 7-7.

Central's Kenneth Youngblood set up the winning touchdown when he recovered an El Dorado fumble on the Wildcats 14. Five plays later, Baldwin scored from the 2 for a 13-7 lead. Both defenses were strong the remainder of the game as Central posted its fifth victory of the season. The victory evened its Big 9 Conference record, 2-2-0.

Playing against Region IIIAA Conway High School, the Tigers were only able to score one touchdown in a 7-6 victory. Central ended a 53-yard drive with a 20-yard touchdown pass from Cunningham to Ken Clifton. The extra point proved to be the game-winning play as the Tigers were victorious by one point.

In his first season as head coach, North Little Rock's Ken Stephens brought his Wildcats to Quigley Stadium to take on Central. Another defensive battle was highlighted by one play just as the first half was ending.

On the last play of the second quarter, North Little Rock's Joe Smelser broke free on a trap play and raced 85 yards for a touchdown. The 6-0, 180-pound halfback outran Bryan, a Central track star, for the game's only score.

The defensive battle continued during the second half and the Wildcats won 6-0.

North Little Rock improved to 6-3-0 overall and 3-3-0 in the conference. Central dropped to 6-3-0 and 2-3-0 in Big 9 Conference action.

The undefeated Pine Bluff Zebras beat Central 23-0 the following week. Pine Bluff was scheduled to play winless Hot Springs in its final game of the season. The victory over the Tigers moved the Zebras closer to their second consecutive state championship.

On Nov. 22, 1963, Central traveled to Blytheville to meet the Chicks. Both teams and fans were subdued following the news

Photo provided by the Arkansas Democrat-Gazette
Bill Baldwin (11)

266

of President John F. Kennedy's assassination. The game was solemn, but the battle was one that the Tigers were used to, a defensive struggle.

In the third quarter of a scoreless game, Blytheville held Central four consecutive downs from the 4. After taking possession, the Chicks fumbled at their 15. Carl Gachot recovered for the Tigers to give them possession deep inside Blytheville territory.

Central fullback George Calhoun went on to score from the 5 for the game's first touchdown. The extra-point kick was blocked by Butch Smotherman, but the Tigers still led 6-0.

Midway through the fourth quarter, the Chicks took possession inside Central territory when they recovered a fumble at the 3. Three plays later, quarterback Gary Elliott scored to make it 6-6.

Lark Anderson converted the extra point to give Blytheville a 7-6 victory, its first over the Tigers in 15 years.

More than 6,000 fans came to Quigley Stadium to watch the Central Tigers and Hall High Warriors battle for fourth place in the Big 9 Conference. The Thanksgiving Day game was another defensive battle for the Tigers as neither team gained more than 100 yards of total offense.

A penalty nullified a 38-yard touchdown pass from Jim Callaway to Alf Carter, and Hall missed another scoring opportunity when Jim Lorenz's 42-yard field-goal attempt fell short.

Photo provided by the Arkansas Democrat-Gazette
Roger Vandiver (left) and Larry Ellis

Central's only scoring chance was a 25-yard field-goal attempt that was wide right.

The game ended in a 0-0 tie and allowed the Warriors to take sole possession of fourth place, while the Tigers dropped to eighth place in the conference standings. The game evened the series between the two schools at 2-2-2.

1963 TIGER SCHEDULE

Benton 7	LRCH 13
LR Catholic 0	LRCH 7
Jonesboro 7	LRCH 20
*Hot Springs 0	LRCH 20
*Fort Smith 6	LRCH 6
*Texarkana, AR 14	LRCH 13
*El Dorado 7	LRCH 13
Conway 6	LRCH 7
*North Little Rock 6	LRCH 0
*Pine Bluff 23	LRCH 0
*Blytheville 7	LRCH 6
*LR Hall 0	LRCH 0

267

A TOUGH TIGER DEFENSE

1964   7-3-2

Head Coach: Gene Hall
Assistants: Bobby Hannon, Clyde Horton, Ralph Holland, Jim Cathcart
Team Physician: Dr. John McCollough Smith

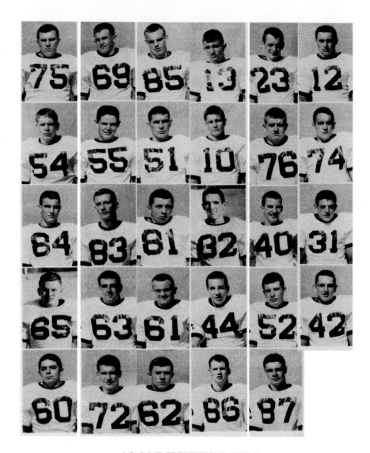

1964 LETTERMEN

Paul Babb	John Fink	Ricky Langhammer	Gary Tate
Mike Brown	Stuart Frye	Mike Manney	Ken Thomas
Phillip Bryan	Carl Gachot	Richard McCauley	David Wagnon
George Calhoun	Danny Gortney	Louis Nalley	Bob Warren
Stanley Clark	Walter Graham	Gary Russ	Cleve Warrick
Kenneth Clifton	Charles Green	Randy Spann	Hansel Weiss
Bruce Cunningham	Mike Greer	Gary Spears	Greg Wren
Larry Ellis	Mike Key	Doug Spencer	

1964 MANAGERS
David Cash
Doug Greene
Joe Hastings
Steve Kirkland
Easton Williams

1964 ALL-STATE
George Calhoun
Richard McCauley
Louis Nalley
David Wagnon

1964 ALL-STAR TEAM
Louis Nalley

The Central High Tigers opened as the team to beat in the Big 10 Conference. The first game, though, was against nonconference Class AA Benton High School.

In his first year as head coach, Winky May had his Panthers ready for their battle with Central. While his defense held the Tigers time after time, Benton was the only team that threatened to score. The first chance, though, ended with a missed 25-yard field-goal attempt by Rusty Kaufman.

Benton finally scored late in the fourth quarter after Glen Hockersmith recovered a Central fumble at the Tigers 35. Five plays later, Hockersmith took a hand-off at fullback and ran to his right.

The defense converged on the running back, but Hockersmith pulled up and threw a pass to sophomore Jackie Pelton. Pelton caught the ball in the end zone to complete a 22-yard touchdown play. Kaufman's extra point gave Benton a 7-0 lead with 5:37 left in the game.

The Tigers were unable to score and fell to the Panthers 7-0. The victory gave Benton (2-0) its second consecutive shutout of the season.

More than 5,000 fans were in Quigley Stadium the next week as Central hosted Little Rock Catholic High School. The Tigers broke loose, amassing 254 yards of total offense and scoring more points than any game the previous season.

Central's initial touchdown came on the first play of the second quarter and capped a 12-play, 53-yard drive. The score came when quarterback Bruce Cunningham snuck into the end zone from the 1.

The Tigers also ended their next series with a touchdown as Phillip Bryan scam-

Photo provided by Central High School
Jackie Pelton catches game-winning pass for Benton

pered 24 yards untouched to complete a 54-yard drive for a two-touchdown lead. The points continued to mount as Central added to its lead late in the half.

Facing first-and-37 from its 26, Central would have been content to run out the clock. But a 53-yard burst around the end by Bryan moved the Tigers to the Rockets 16. Three plays later, Cunningham scored from the 1 for a 20-0 lead with 20 seconds remaining in the half.

A 48-yard drive featured a 24-yard pass completion from Cunningham to Doug Spencer and ended the game's scoring. The touchdown occurred when Larry Ellis ran up the middle for 12 yards, helping the Tigers beat Catholic 26-0. The victory was the first of the season for Central and gave it the confidence needed for the opening of conference play the following week against the Jonesboro Hurricane.

In Jonesboro, the Tigers scored enough points to win, and the defense did its part to keep the Hurricane out of the end zone.

Central scored in the second quarter when Cunningham connected with Bryan for a 19-yard touchdown. The Tigers struck

269

Photo provided by the Arkansas Democrat-Gazette
(Left to Right) George Calhoun, Hansel Weiss, Larry Ellis and Bruce Cunningham

again in the fourth quarter when Mike Greer broke through the Jonesboro line to block Tom Tull's punt.

Defensive end Richard McCauley recovered the ball for Central and returned it 32 yards for a touchdown. George Calhoun's second extra-point conversion helped the Tigers to a 14-0 victory.

Little Rock Central traveled to Hot Springs to play a struggling team the next week. The Tigers started fast with a long scoring drive midway through the first quarter. All 91 yards were gained on the ground. The 16-play drive ended when Calhoun scored on a short run. Calhoun also added the extra point for a 7-0 lead with 10:15 remaining in the second quarter.

Hot Springs answered after Denis Bonzo returned the ensuing kickoff 40 yards to the Central 49. On the first play from scrimmage, Sandy Elliott ran 46 yards before being brought down at the 3.

Photo provided by the Arkansas Democrat-Gazette
George Calhoun (44)

He slipped through the defense again on the following play to score. Terry Quast converted the extra-point attempt for a 7-7 tie.

The Tigers answered with another long drive that covered 77 yards in 12 plays. A 26-yard pass from Cunningham to Gary Spears on first-and-25 highlighted the drive and put Central in scoring position. Ellis carried the final 15 yards before Calhoun added his second extra point for a 14-7 lead.

The Tigers scored their final touchdown with nine minutes left in the third quarter when quarterback Larry Brian made a bad pitch while being pressured by the Central defensive line. Mike Manney recovered the fumble and returned it 50 yards for the score. Calhoun's third conversion put the Tigers up 21-7.

Hot Springs, though, was not done as it put together a 78-yard scoring drive on its next possession. The series only took nine plays, with Dick Young capping it on a 3-yard run. Quast's extra-point attempt was blocked and Central led 21-13.

The Tigers controlled the ball in the final period, running 23 of the quarter's 29 offensive plays. Central ended the game on the Trojans 5 and escaped a major upset 21-13.

Bryan's 17-yard punt return against Fort Smith Northside the next week at Quigley Stadium set up the Tigers' first score. A 29-yard field goal by Calhoun ended a 49-yard drive and gave Central a 3-0 lead with 1:35 to go in the first half.

Late in the third quarter, a Bryan punt rolled out of bounds at the Grizzlies 3. Two plays later, Frank Ward was hit hard at the 9 and fumbled. Carl Gachot recovered for the Tigers and Central scored in

Photo provided by the Arkansas Democrat-Gazette
Little Rock Hall's Don Bona

two plays as Calhoun ran into the end zone on a sweep and also converted the extra point.

The Tigers' final touchdown was scored with 34 seconds left in the game. The score was set up when Central forced Fort Smith's quarterback to fumble as he tried to pass. Louis Nalley recovered at the Grizzlies 4. On first down, Randy Spann ran off left tackle for the touchdown. Gary Tate kicked the extra point in a 17-0 victory over Fort Smith Northside.

The next week in Texarkana Ark., the Tigers had a great start. Central scored in the second quarter after Greer intercepted a pass and returned it 66 yards for a touchdown. Calhoun added the extra point for a 7-0 lead.

The Tigers recovered the ensuing kickoff at the Razorbacks 34. On first down, Cunningham connected with Bryan for another score and a 13-0 halftime lead.

The Razorbacks came back, though, tying the score with a 36-yard drive in the third period. But the Tigers answered in the fourth quarter when they drove 46 yards for

the winning score, a 3-yard pass from Cunningham to Spencer.

Central's defense held tight as Texarkana reached the Tigers 8 just before the game ended. The 19-13 victory gave Central a 4-0-0 conference record and the conference lead.

After slipping past El Dorado 6-0, the Tigers hosted nonconference foe Conway High School at Quigley Stadium. The Wampus Cats were leading Region IIIAA-West at 7-0-0 and hoped a strong defense would hold Central's offense at bay.

More than 7,000 fans watched as the game's only score was set up when Conway's David Spatz recovered a Calhoun fumble at the Central 9. J.B. Pendergraft took the handoff on fourth down and fought his way into the end zone for the touchdown. Jim Wilson converted the extra-point attempt as Conway upset the top-ranked Tigers 7-0. The Wampus Cats took over the state's top ranking, while Central continued to lead the Big 10 Conference.

Following a 0-0 tie with North Little Rock, a 7-0 victory over Pine Bluff and a 20-20 tie with Blytheville, the Tigers entered their Thanksgiving Day game against Little Rock Hall. The Warriors were 7-1-0 in the conference and Central was 6-0-2. More than 10,000 fans at Quigley Stadium watched a game that decided the state championship.

Early in the first quarter, Hall High's Tommy Bullion took a snap from center and rolled to his right. As the Tigers rotated in that direction, Bullion pulled up and passed to his left toward Don Bona. Bona, all alone behind the secondary, caught the pass and raced into the end zone to complete a 47-yard pass play.

The extra-point attempt failed, but the Warriors led 6-0 just two minutes into the game. The remainder of the contest was a defensive battle, with Hall High celebrating the holiday with a 6-0 victory and the 1964 state championship.

1964 TIGER SCHEDULE

Benton 7	LRCH 0
LR Catholic 0	LRCH 26
*Jonesboro 0	LRCH 14
*Hot Springs 13	LRCH 21
*Fort Smith 0	LRCH 17
*Texarkana, AR 13	LRCH 19
*El Dorado 0	LRCH 6
Conway 7	LRCH 0
*North Little Rock 0	LRCH 0
*Pine Bluff 0	LRCH 7
*Blytheville 20	LRCH 20
*LR Hall 6	LRCH 0

TOUGH TIGERS POUND OUT VICTORIES

1965   8-3-0

Head Coach: Gene Hall
Assistants: Ralph Holland, Clyde Horton, Bobby Hannon, Jim Cathcart
Team Physician: Dr. John McCollough Smith

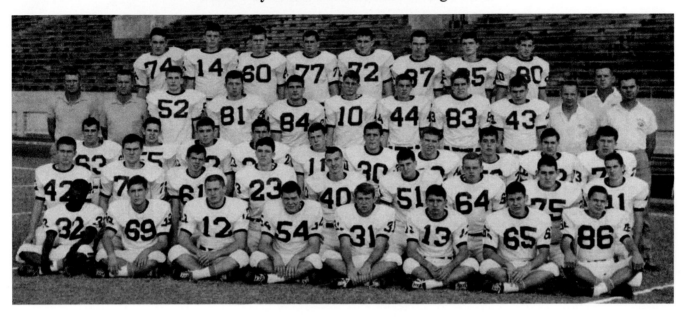

1965 LETTERMEN

Jimmy Allison	Glen Fuller	Mike Manney	Randy Spann
Paul Babb	Keith Golden	Richard McCauley	Gary Tate
Mike Beard	Phillip Grable	Mike Middleton	Bob Warren
Curtis Bradbury	Walter Graham	Mike Moore	Cleve Warrick
Jim Bradberry	David Hartman	Forrest Packard	Larry White
Mike Brown	Randall Haynes	Rodger Pavan	Billy Wood
John Buttain	Dickie Heien	Larry Proctor	Charles Wood
Stanley Clark	David Holloman	Gary Russ	Robert Young
Phillip Crouch	Willie Jones	Jerry Schmidt	
Eddie Douglas	Ricky Langhammer	Ed Smith	
Stuart Frye	Ronnie Lehman	Robert E. Smith	

1965 MANAGERS
Joe Davis
Gary Fort
Steve Kirkland
Eston Williams

1965 ALL-STATE
Stanley Clark
Richard McCauley
Randy Spann
Gary Tate

1965 ALL-STAR TEAM
Gary Tate

Coach Gene Hall entered his eighth season as head coach with high expectations for his Tigers. Coach Hall's positive outlook was based on several returning starters from a team that narrowly missed the state championship in 1964, when Hall High beat Central 6-0 in the final game of the season.

Coach Hall prepared his players for another tough schedule and began the championship campaign at Quigley Stadium against Benton High School.

Approximately 1,500 fans braved the on-shore remnants of Hurricane Betsy as sheets of rain poured into the stadium throughout the game. A muddy and flooded field caused a mistake-filled game. Three of these mistakes, however, led to Central touchdowns.

Walter Graham's opening kickoff rolled into the end zone for a touchback, giving the Panthers possession at the 20. After gaining only 8 yards in three plays, Benton's Larry Nix stepped back to punt. The snap was too far to the left of Nix and slipped through his hands. Nix recovered at the 9, but the Tigers took over on downs.

Central quarterback Gary Tate recovered his own fumble on first down for a 2-yard loss, but Ronnie Spann gained 3 yards

Photo provided by Dickie Heien
(Left to Right) Rodger Pavan, Coach Ralph Holland and Dickie Heien

on second down to the 8. On the next play, Tate faked to his fullback and sprinted around right end. Three defenders closed in, but each slipped and allowed Tate to run untouched into the end zone. Graham's extra-point attempt was wide, but Central led 6-0 with 8:40 remaining in the first quarter.

Bobby Meeks returned the ensuing kickoff to the 23, but the offense could only manage 8 yards in three plays. Nix once again lined up in punt formation and once again failed to kick the ball.

Mike Manney, Richard McCauley and Jim Bradberry broke through the line to pressure the punter. Bradberry blocked the kick and the Tigers recovered at the 2. A penalty by the Panthers gave Central possession on the 1. Tate snuck for the touchdown and Graham converted the extra point for a 13-0 lead with 5:42 left in the opening quarter.

On the last play of the third quarter, Nix's 66-yard punt pinned the Tigers at their 8. Central's offense could only move 1 yard before Phillip Grable went back to punt from his goal line. Grable could not handle a low snap, giving Phillip Ritchey and Bob Cushing time to break through the line.

Photo provided by Central High School
Keith Golden (20)

274

Photo provided by Central High School
Gary Tate (40)

Ritchey blocked the punt and Cushing recovered in the end zone for a Benton touchdown. Nix converted the extra point with 10:52 left in the game to narrow Central's lead to 13-7.

A bad punt by Nix midway through the fourth quarter gave the Tigers possession on the Panthers 42. On the first play, Tate ran over left tackle, cut to the sideline and outran the defenders to the end zone. The extra-point attempt failed, but the touchdown sealed a 19-7 season-opening victory for Central.

The next week, more than 5,000 watched Little Rock Catholic put together a 71-yard drive in the first quarter to score against the Tigers and win 7-0, the Rockets' first victory in the series.

Central finally got its offense together the following week when it hosted the Jonesboro Hurricane. The Tigers gained 388 yards, but more important, controlled the clock by running 64 offensive plays.

Leading the way was Tate, a 149-pounder who rushed for 144 yards on 15 carries, passed for 40 yards and returned kicks for 130 yards.

The Tigers' first score came after a 63-yard drive ended with a 1-yard run up the middle by Spann. Spann ended the next drive as well when he burst up the middle

for a 4-yard touchdown to end a 58-yard, four-play series.

With 1:22 remaining in the first half, Hurricane quarterback Ronnie Burnett completed a quick pass to John Rees. The split end's pattern took him inside, but when he caught the pass he cut back toward the sideline and outran the defensive backs to the end zone. Gary Quick's extra-point conversion narrowed Central's lead to 14-7.

Late in the third quarter, a snap sailed over punter Tom Tull's head into the end zone. Tull recovered but was tackled by Stanley Clark for a safety. The two points increased Central's lead to 16-7.

Manney set up the Tigers' next touchdown when he intercepted a pass. Tate eventually scored from the 8 and also converted his third extra point. The game's final touchdown occurred when Central reserves scored with only 28 seconds remaining in the game. Cleve Warrick ran off left tackle for the 17-yard touchdown to help the Tigers to a 29-7 victory.

Prior to visiting Fort Smith to battle Northside High School, Central easily defeated Hot Springs 34-0. The victory over the Trojans was a confidence builder and just what the Tigers needed before entering their game with the top-ranked and unbeaten Grizzlies.

After a touchdown run by Spann helped Central to a 7-0 halftime lead, Fort Smith answered in the third quarter when Bobby Crouch sprinted through the defense for a 57-yard gain to the 1. Halfback David Carter scored on the next play. Greg Shaks converted the extra point for a 7-7 tie.

With 8:30 remaining in the final quarter, Tate completed a 17-yard touchdown pass to Gary Russ. The play completed a 58-yard drive and the extra-point attempt by Tate gave Central a 14-7 lead. The Grizzlies never threatened to score again, and the Tigers knocked off the state's No. 1 team to continue their unbeaten streak in league play, 3-0-0.

Quigley Stadium was the site of Central's next game as it hosted Texarkana, Ark. On the game's opening drive, Texarkana was forced to punt from the Tigers 45. The kick rolled out of bounds inside the 1, forcing Central to move almost 100 yards to score.

The Tigers answered the challenge as Spann capped the 99-yard drive with a 1-yard plunge up the middle. Tate's conversion gave Central a 7-0 lead with 2:05 left in the first quarter.

Tate led the Tigers to another score on their first possession of the second half. Bradberry was the lead blocker for Tate as he scored on a short run to cap a 68-yard drive. Tate's extra point gave Central 14-0 lead. He finished the night with 130 yards on 25 carries. Central held the Razorbacks scoreless and won its fourth consecutive conference game.

After narrowly escaping El Dorado 13-7, the top-ranked Tigers enjoyed an off week to prepare for an important Class AAA Eastern Division showdown with North Little Rock. The game at Quigley Stadium was one that Central never controlled. The Wildcats dominated the Tigers 20-6, improving to 8-0-1 and clinching the Eastern Division championship.

Gary Tate (40)

No. 3 Central rebounded when it traveled to Pine Bluff to take on the No. 5 Zebras. Pine Bluff struck first with a 17-play, 80-yard drive capped by a 1-yard run from sophomore quarterback Jim Buckner. Ray Harrison missed the extra-point attempt, but the Zebras led 6-0 with 9:14 left in the first half.

With 2:32 remaining in the second quarter, Tate capped a 37-yard drive with a 10-yard run. He converted the extra point for a 7-6 halftime lead.

The Central defense shut down Pine Bluff the remainder of the game. Central took the lead when Clark recovered a fumbled snap in the end zone for a touchdown. The score midway through the fourth quarter and extra point by Tate helped the Tigers escape 14-6 and improve to 7-2-0.

Following a 27-0 victory over the 1-8-0 Blytheville Chicks, Central met Little Rock Hall in the annual season-ending holiday battle.

More than 8,000 watched the Warriors run through and around the Tigers. Don Bona set up Hall High's first score when he returned a punt to the Tigers 49. A five-play drive was highlighted by a 34-yard pass from Fred Wanger to Bona. Steve Hock-

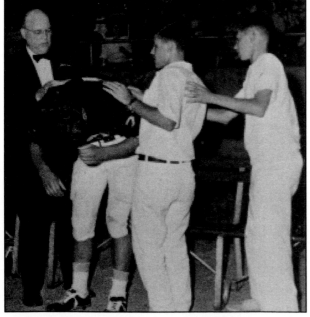

Dr. John McCollough Smith (left)
examines Paul Babb

ersmith pounded through the left side of the line for a 1-yard touchdown run. Buz McArthur converted the extra point with 8:23 remaining in the first quarter.

With 2:03 left in the first half, Hockersmith raced down the sideline for a 48-yard touchdown run to help the Warriors take a 13-0 lead. John Carter then intercepted a Tate pass on the Tigers' ensuing possession, setting up Hall High's final score.

It took three plays for the Warriors to move 34 yards. The touchdown occurred on a long pass from Wanger, giving Hall High a 20-0 halftime advantage.

Central scored early in the fourth quarter when Tate connected with Russ in the end zone. Tate converted the extra point, but it was not enough as the Warriors dominated the Tigers 20-7.

1965 TIGER SCHEDULE

Benton 7	LRCH 19
LR Catholic 7	LRCH 0
*Jonesboro 7	LRCH 29
*Hot Springs 0	LRCH 34
*Fort Smith 7	LRCH 14
*Texarkana, AR 0	LRCH 14
*El Dorado 7	LRCH 13
*North Little Rock 20	LRCH 6
*Pine Bluff 6	LRCH 14
*Blytheville 0	LRCH 27
*LR Hall 20	LRCH 7

CENTRAL AGAIN BREAKS RACIAL BARRIERS

1966   7-5-0

Head Coach: Gene Hall
Assistants: Ralph Holland, Bobby Hannon, Clyde Horton, Jim Cathcart
Team Physician: Dr. John McCollough Smith

1966 LETTERMEN

Jimmy Allison	Wayne Gills	Willie Jones	Charles Stevens
Mike Beard	Phillip Grable	Mike Middleton	Larry White
Steve Blair	Walter Graham	Tommy Miller	Billy Wood
Jim Bradberry	Dennis Greenlee	Mike Moore	Charles Wood
Bill Brooks	Keith Golden	Forrest Packard	Louis Woodson
Eddie Douglas	Edward Harris	Rodger Pavan	Robert Young
Mike Elms	Randall Haynes	Larry Proctor	
Richard Faulkner	Dickie Heien	Jerry Schmidt	
Glen Fuller	David Holloman	Ed Smith	

1966 MANAGERS

Joe Davis
Gary Forte
Gary Goff
Billy McGinley
Don Pruitt

1966 ALL-STAR TEAM
None

A letdown in the season opener against the Texarkana Razorbacks resulted in a 6-2 loss. Play didn't improve the next week as it took a long pass in the fourth quarter to defeat Benton High School.

The pass from Jerry Schmidt to Bill Brooks covered 44 yards and was the game's only touchdown. Wayne Gills converted the extra point to help Central to a 7-0 victory over the Panthers.

The Tigers were in for a hard fight the next week when Little Rock Catholic visited. Central, though, struck first on a 63-yard touchdown pass from Mike Beard to Brooks. The extra-point attempt put the Tigers up 7-0.

The Rockets scored on their first possession of the second half, driving 95 yards in 17 plays. The drive ended on a Walter Selakovich 2-yard scoring run. Robert Kershaw's conversion tied the score.

Catholic's next touchdown came after Roger Harnish recovered a fumble at the Central 1. The fumble occurred after a punt by the Rockets was downed at the 1. Beard was unable to handle the first-down snap from center and the mistake proved costly to the Tigers.

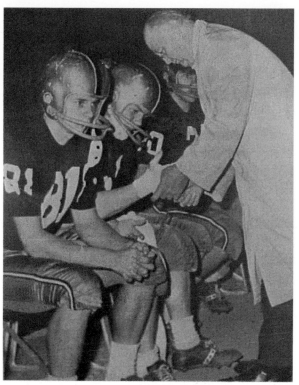

Photo provided by Central High School
Dr. John McCollough Smith evaluates a player

Selakovich scored on the first play and Kershaw's kick was perfect, giving Catholic a 14-7 lead. Central, though, took the ensuing kickoff and marched 56 yards in seven plays for its second touchdown.

The score occurred when Beard and Brooks connected again, this time for a 20-yard touchdown pass. Pat Morrison broke through the line to block the extra-point attempt, leaving the Rockets in front 14-13.

Central had a chance to win with possession on Catholic's 4 and 11 seconds left in the game. But John Claud hit Beard behind the line of scrimmage, forcing Beard to fumble. Tom Callahan recovered at the 16 as time expired.

The 14-13 outcome was the second consecutive season that Catholic beat Central and only its second victory in the series.

Photo provided by Central High School
The 1966 homecoming court

Keith Golden (20)

In Jonesboro the following week, the Hurricane scored first when Ronnie Burnett connected with tailback John Rees in the end zone for a 10-yard touchdown. The conversion attempt was wide, but Jonesboro led 6-0 with 8:23 left in the first quarter.

With 1:19 remaining in the first half, Central's Mike Moore blocked Tom Tull's punt and the ball rolled out of the end zone for a safety to make it 6-2.

Central scored again in the fourth quarter when Moore recovered a Keith Golden fumble in the end zone, a lucky break that put Tigers ahead 8-6. However, the Hurricane answered just one minute later when Burnett completed a short pass to Rees, who raced 73 yards for a go-ahead touchdown.

Central then put together a 70-yard drive that was capped by a 10-yard pass from Beard to Ed Smith. Smith jumped between two defenders to catch the pass

in the end zone with 1:10 remaining in the game.

Jonesboro was unable to put together a game-winning drive and suffered its first loss of the season, 14-12. The Tigers completed 14 of 34 passes for 188 yards and moved to 2-2-0.

Beard connected with Brooks for two touchdowns the next week against Hot Springs. The first touchdown occurred on a 48-yard pass play. The next score was a 1-yard run by Beard. After the Tigers recorded their third safety of the season, Beard hit Brooks again, this time for a 46-yard touchdown.

The 20-0 victory over the Trojans set the stage for a tough outing the next week when Central met second-ranked and undefeated Fort Smith Northside. The AAA Central Conference game was dominated by the Grizzlies as they justified their ranking by shutting down the Tigers and moving with ease against the Central defense.

Fort Smith outgained the Tigers 308 to 111 yards. Just before halftime, the Grizzlies scored first on a 23-yard pass from Lawrence Fitting to David Carter. Their second score came on a 12-yard run by Carter to cap a 77-yard drive in the third quarter. The final touchdown came on the last play of the game when Jackie Martin fumbled the snap while in punt formation. Martin scooped up the ball, cut to the left sideline and ran untouched for a 73-yard touchdown.

Jimmy Allison (74) blocks for Forrest Packard

Photo provided by Central High School
Robert Young (22)

Fort Smith remained unbeaten and improved to 6-0-0 after beating Central 21-0.

Wildcat Stadium in North Little Rock was the site of the Tigers' next conference game. The contest was played in a steady rain throughout the first half before a torrential downpour hit during the second half.

The No. 3 Wildcats used a long run in the second quarter to beat Central 7-0. Tailback Danny Duke took a sweep around right end, stiff-armed two Tigers, ran over another at the 30 and ran the final 30 yards for the game's only touchdown. Benny Davis' extra point gave North Little Rock the edge with 7:45 remaining in the half.

Duke finished with 130 yards on 20 carries to help the Wildcats earn their sixth victory of the season and second in the Central Conference.

Central rebounded the following week to win its first conference game, 32-14 over El Dorado. Robert Young starred for the Tigers, rushing for 155 yards on 20 carries. Young accounted for four of Central's touchdowns, passing for two and rushing for two.

The following week, the Tigers took a break from conference action to make Arkansas high school football history. The game marked the first time a predominately white Class AAA school competed against an all-black school. The matchup pitted Little Rock Central against Little Rock Horace Mann.

Quigley Stadium, which was full for Horace Mann's homecoming, was the site for the historic game. Dickie Heien accounted for the game's first touchdown as he recovered a Horace Mann fumble in the end zone. The fumble occurred with the Bearcats lined up in punt formation and a bad snap sailed over the head of the punter. The Tigers missed the extra-point attempt, but led 6-0 midway through the first quarter.

Central stopped a Horace Mann drive at its 23, then used 10 plays to drive the needed 77 yards for a second touchdown. Young scored on a short run and Walter Graham's extra point increased the lead to 13-0.

The Tigers regained possession at the Bearcats 48 after a Horace Mann punt. It took only four plays for Central to score. Graham went the final 2 yards and the extra point made it 20-0 at halftime.

Bruce Swinton passed Horace Mann to its only touchdown when he connected with Troy Brooks for a 12-yard score. The play ended an 80-yard drive and kept the Bearcats from being shut out. Swinton completed 14 of 19 passes for 138 yards. Troy Brooks had 114 receiving yards.

Richard Faulkner, the Tigers' sophomore quarterback, started only his third game of the season, but passed for more than 100 yards. Young finished with 124 yards rushing to lead all rushers.

A 34-7 nonconference domination of the Jacksonville Red Devils primed Central for the annual battle with rival Pine Bluff. In front of a large crowd in Quigley Stadium, Graham intercepted a Jimmy Buckner pass at the Zebras 45 and returned it to the 28.

On the following play, Faulkner connected with Brooks for a first-quarter touchdown. The extra-point attempt failed and the Tigers led 6-0.

The teams traded punts throughout the second quarter until Mike Middleton recovered a fumble for Central at the Pine Bluff 38. Faulkner completed three consecutive passes to Brooks, the last a 5-yard touchdown. The extra-point attempt again failed, but the Tigers increased their lead to 12-0.

An 11-yard touchdown run by Brooks ended the scoring and gave Central an 18-0 victory. Faulkner passed for 162 yards, including 117 yards to Brooks in the Tigers' seventh victory of the season.

The holiday classic was next on the schedule for Central as the No. 8 Tigers prepared to battle the second-ranked Hall High Warriors, who had only one loss.

Central scored midway through the second quarter when Gills capped a 71-yard drive with a 24-yard field goal for a 3-0 lead.

The advantage lasted until the end of the third quarter when Steve Hockersmith ended a 60-yard drive with a short touchdown run. Mack Shotts converted the extra-point attempt for a 7-3 Hall lead. The Tigers were unable to put together another scoring drive and were beaten on Thanksgiving Day for the third consecutive year.

1966 TIGER SCHEDULE

Texarkana, AR 6	LRCH 2
Benton 0	LRCH 7
LR Catholic 14	LRCH 13
Jonesboro 12	LRCH 14
Hot Springs 0	LRCH 20
*FS Northside 21	LRCH 0
*North Little Rock 7	LRCH 0
*El Dorado 14	LRCH 32
LR Horace Mann 7	LRCH 20
Jacksonville 7	LRCH 34
*Pine Bluff 0	LRCH 18
*LR Hall 7	LRCH 3

Photo provided by Central High School
Central vs. Hall on Thanksgiving Day, 1966

NONCONFERENCE VICTORS

1967   7-4-0

Head Coach: Gene Hall
Assistants: Ralph Holland, Bobby Hannon, Clyde Horton, Don Nixon
Team Physician: Dr. John McCollough Smith

1967 LETTERMEN

Jim Allen	Randy Diles	Randall Haynes	Rodger Pavan
Steve Blair	Mike Elms	Phil Herndon	Ed Rownd
Carl Butler	Louis Dodson	Tommy Hoffman	David Saugey
Gary Capshaw	Eddie Douglas	Johnny Johnson	Ed Smith
Walter Coleman	Richard Faulkner	Bobby Loux	Howard Thresher
Gary Cope	Dennis Greenlee	Tommy Miller	Robert Young
Art Davis	Edward Harris	James Nelson	

1967 MANAGERS
Joe Davis

1967 ALL-STATE
Rodger Pavan
Robert Young

1967 ALL-STAR TEAM
Rodger Pavan

For the sixth time in seven years, the Central High Tigers began their campaign for a championship season against Benton High School. Behind Robert Young's 157 yards rushing on 38 carries and three touchdowns, including one of 53 yards, Central defeated the Panthers 27-7.

Young led the Tigers the following week as he rushed for 204 yards and two touchdowns, one from 63 yards, to give Central an early 7-0 lead against Catholic High School. This first-quarter score was set up after Richard Faulkner fielded a punt and was downed at the Tigers 37.

Faulkner, Central's junior quarterback, pitched to Young on the next play, and the tailback sprinted around left end, cut toward the sideline and was never touched as he outran the defense for a 63-yard touchdown. Faulkner's extra-point attempt was wide, but the Tigers led 6-0 early in the first half.

Late in the second quarter, a bad snap forced Catholic's punter to retrieve the loose ball and quickly get off a kick. The kick was short and downed by a teammate before it even reached the line of scrimmage. Central benefited from this mistake by putting together a short drive, scoring on a 6-yard run by Young. Faulkner converted the extra-point attempt for a 13-0 lead with 53 seconds remaining in the half.

The Tigers were held out of the end zone during the second half, but more important, managed to keep the Rockets from crossing the goal line in a 13-0 victory.

In only their second meeting in history, the Little Rock Horace Mann Bearcats fell to the Little Rock Central Tigers. Young was held to 83 yards rushing. But he was able to break free in the final quarter for a 60-yard touchdown run in a 26-6 victory.

Photo provided by Central High School
Robert Young (22)

Photo provided by Central High School
Richard Faulkner

As in previous weeks, it was the Young and Faulkner show during Central's next game against Hot Springs High School. The two juniors each scored two touchdowns in a 27-2 victory over the Trojans, the Tigers' fourth consecutive victory.

Carl Butler was on the receiving end of two Faulkner touchdown passes, and Young rushed for 124 yards and two touchdowns. Young and Faulkner were also responsible for Hot Springs' two points in the second quarter after Central was backed up at its 5 following a punt.

The duo didn't connect on a handoff, causing the ball to roll behind the goal line. Just as Young made the recovery, he was tackled in the end zone for a safety.

The Tigers next traveled to Fort Smith for their first conference game. The unbeaten Northside Grizzlies scored three first-half touchdowns against the unbeaten Central Tigers to take a 20-0 lead at halftime.

Fort Smith's initial touchdown drive began when the Tigers turned the ball over on downs after reaching the Grizzlies 9 early in the first quarter. Northside ran to the Central 30, then surprised the Tigers with a 30-yard touchdown pass to take the lead.

Two possessions later, the Grizzlies took over at their 42 and began a second scoring march. After reaching the 35,

Carl Butler (20)

Dwight Moore passed to Robert Owens at the 20. Owens took the pass and raced the remaining distance for the touchdown. The extra point gave Fort Smith a 13-0 lead.

Central was again forced to punt on its next possession and Northside took over on its 37. Just moments into the drive, Moore passed for another touchdown and the Grizzlies took a 20-0 lead.

The Tigers' Ed Haynes set up a Central touchdown when he was able to break through the Fort Smith line to block a punt. Haynes gave the Tigers excellent field position when he recovered the ball at the Northside 16. On first down, Faulkner passed to Butler for Central's only score of the game.

The Grizzlies answered on their next possession when Moore passed to Joe Releford for a 70-yard touchdown. This ended the scoring as neither team threatened during the final quarter. Fort Smith continued its unbeaten streak by defeating the Tigers 27-7.

Coach Ken Stephens brought his North Little Rock Wildcats to Quigley Stadium for Central's next conference game. Butler highlighted the game in the second quarter after fielding a punt at his 5. Butler cut be-

hind several blocks and outran the remaining Wildcats for a 95-yard touchdown. Faulkner converted the extra-point attempt for a 7-0 lead.

North Little Rock was able to match Central's touchdown when Danny Duke capped a 30-yard drive with a short run off left tackle. The conversion attempt, however, was unsuccessful and the Tigers were able to escape with a 7-6 victory.

A 72-yard drive by El Dorado resulted in a touchdown for the Wildcats the following week. The conversion gave El Dorado a 7-0 lead with 5:38 left in the first quarter. The only success for Central was 134 yards rushing by Young. The 7-0 defeat marked the second loss for the Tigers.

Even with Faulkner and Young held out of the next game because of injuries, Central was able to rely on Butler and David Saugey to dominate North Little Rock Jones High 33-0. Another victory the next week, 14-8 over Jacksonville High School, set the stage for the Tigers' matchup with Pine Bluff.

The Zebras received the opening kickoff and took possession at their 15. An 85-yard drive ended when Jim Buckner snuck in from the 1 on the drive's 16th play. Harold Pointer added the extra point for a 7-0 lead with 4:50 remaining in the first quarter.

Central's Ray Gillespie fumbled the second-half kickoff. Pine Bluff's Griff Grif-

Central vs. Hall

fin recovered and returned it 30 yards for a touchdown. The conversion attempt failed, but the Zebras led 13-0 only 12 seconds into the third quarter.

Later in the same quarter, a 10-play, 63-yard drive by Pine Bluff was capped by David Calkins' 16-yard sweep. Pointer added his second extra point to give the Zebras a 20-0 lead.

On the first play of the fourth quarter, Buckner connected with Tim O'Connell for a 16-yard touchdown pass. Three of the Zebras' touchdowns weren't needed as the Tigers never scored. Pine Bluff defeated Central 26-0. It was the Zebras' first victory over the Tigers in four years and broke a five-game losing streak. The Thanksgiving Day game against Little Rock Hall High proved disappointing for Central. The Warriors tallied late in the second quarter for a 7-0 halftime lead. Hall High came out in the second half and scored 21 points in a 28-0 victory.

Photo provided by Central High School

Thanksgiving Day, 1967

1967 TIGER SCHEDULE

Benton 7	LRCH 27
LR Catholic 0	LRCH 13
LR Horace Mann 6	LRCH 26
Hot Springs 2	LRCH 27
*FS Northside 27	LRCH 7
*North Little Rock 6	LRCH 7
*El Dorado 7	LRCH 0
NLR Jones 0	LRCH 33
Jacksonville 8	LRCH 14
*Pine Bluff 26	LRCH 0
*LR Hall 28	LRCH 0

TOUGH YEAR FOR THE TIGERS

1968   4-6-0

Head Coach: Gene Hall
Assistants: Ralph Holland, Gary Wahlquist, Bobby Hannon, Don Nixon
Team Physician: Dr. John McCollough Smith

1968 LETTERMEN

Rick Abbott	Lee Douglas	David Jungkind	Ted Smith
Steve Allison	Dwight Duhart	Danny Korte	David Steele
Perry Black	Richard Faulkner	Larry Larkan	Richard Stinson
Johnny Blaylock	Ray Gillespie	Nathan McQuaney	Gene Tanner
Gary Capshaw	Allen Griffith	Tommy Oakley	Joe Taylor
Walter Coleman	James Hall	John Peace	Howard Thresher
Gary Cope	Robert Hallmark	John Richardson	Frank Westmoreland
Art Davis	Ben Hood	Ed Rownd	Jesse Williams
Larry Davis	Johnny Johnson	Joey Shelton	Troy Willis

1968 MANAGERS
Unknown

1968 ALL-STATE
Richard Faulkner

1968 ALL-STAR TEAM
Richard Faulkner

The 1968 season began with many question marks.

The Tigers lost several starters to graduation, and Coach Gene Hall was forced to fill the holes with young and inexperienced players. Still, one of the biggest concerns was not replacing a player who had graduated, but one who was injured.

Richard Faulkner had played quarterback almost to perfection the past two seasons, but he suffered an injured knee to-

287

ward the end of the 1967 season. The injury required surgery during the off-season and caused Faulkner lingering problems in pre-season practice. The quarterback was available to play, but he would not be 100 percent.

Coach Hall also began the season without one of his top assistants. Coach Clyde Horton, who was a member of the Air Force reserves, was called to active duty in February 1968 as the Pueblo Crisis began in North Korea. Coach Horton and many other reservists were away from their civilian jobs for approximately one year while negotiations for peace were in progress.

In Coach Horton's absence, Coach Bobby Hannon was named interim track coach and Gary Wahlquist was hired as an assistant football coach. Among Wahlquist's responsibilities was to coach the JV team.

As usual, the season began against Benton High School. The inexperienced Tigers were able to use their depth to overcome the tough Panthers. Quarterbacks David Saugey, John Peace and Faulkner each completed three passes in a 13-7 victory over the Saline County team.

Faulkner accounted for Central's first touchdown when he ran around right end for a 35-yard touchdown. The conversion attempt failed, but the Tigers took a 6-0 lead early in the first quarter.

Central's Walter Coleman set up the third-quarter score when he intercepted a pass at the Panthers 45 and returned it to the 35. Nathan McQuaney, who rushed for 100 yards, converted fourth-and-1 from the 26 to keep the short drive alive.

Saugey eventually connected with Johnny Johnson in the end zone for the second touchdown. Larry Golightly added the extra point for a 13-0 advantage.

The Panthers' next possession ended with a 25-yard touchdown run by quarterback Charlie Keene. The conversion tightened the score, 13-7. The Panthers, though, were unable to put together another drive and Central was victorious.

A 45-yard touchdown pass from David Kershaw to Dickie Selakovich and a fumble

288

Photo provided by the Arkansas Democrat-Gazette
Carl Butler (20)

recovery by Tim Brewer in the end zone were enough for Coach George Loss' Catholic High Rockets to defeat the Tigers. A short touchdown run by Carl Butler was not enough for Central as it fell 14-6.

The Tigers were the first to strike in their game against Little Rock Horace Mann the following week. After taking over at the Bearcats 45, Butler picked up a first down when he reached the 34. Several plays later, Faulkner gave to Richard Stinson on a reverse and Stinson maneuvered around left end for a 21-yard touchdown.

Horace Mann took over at its 40 following the ensuing kickoff. On first down, Charles Williams ran around left end for a 60-yard touchdown. The extra-point attempt gave the Bearcats a 7-6 lead.

Central's next score came just before the first quarter ended. A 46-yard drive was capped by a 15-yard touchdown pass from Faulkner to Butler. Golightly converted the extra-point attempt as Central regained the lead.

Late in the first half, James Hall blocked a Horace Mann punt to give the

Tigers possession at the Bearcats 22. The short drive appeared to have stalled at the 2, but McQuaney bulled his way into the end zone on third down. The conversion increased Central's lead to 20-7.

Following the kickoff, Horace Mann took over at its 42. Behind a 15-yard penalty on the Tigers and a potent running attack, the Bearcats scored on an 11-yard run from Williams with two seconds remaining in the half to narrow the deficit to 20-13.

Central sealed a victory when an Ed Rownd interception resulted in another score. The 62-yard drive ended with a 1-yard touchdown pass from Faulkner to Ray Gillespie. Central beat Horace Mann 26-13.

For homecoming the following week, the 2-1-0 Tigers hosted undefeated and top-ranked Fort Smith Northside. The Grizzlies struck first even after a Central punt backed them up to their 12.

On first down, Fort Smith quarterback Joe Releford easily made his way through the defense for an 88-yard touchdown. The extra-point kick gave the Grizzlies a 7-0 lead at halftime.

Northside scored again on its second possession of the second half when Nick Avlos capped a 38-yard drive with an 11-yard touchdown run. The conversion increased the lead to 14-0.

Photo provided by the Arkansas Democrat-Gazette
Richard Faulkner (43)

Central was able to score after the ensuing kickoff when a 23-yard touchdown pass from Faulkner to Johnson capped the short drive. Another score came after a four-play, 58-yard drive ended with a 9-yard touchdown pass from Faulkner to Gillespie. The Tigers converted only one extra-point attempt, which allowed Coach Bill Stancil's Grizzlies to escape with a 14-13 victory.

Following a 14-6 loss to North Little Rock and a 13-7 victory over El Dorado, Central faced North Little Rock's Jones High School for only the second time in history.

The Tigers scored in the first quarter after Howard Thresher recovered a fumble at the Dragons 33. On fourth-and-5, Rownd caught a pass from Faulkner to give the Tigers first-and-goal at the 5. Two plays later, Stinson ran for a touchdown, but the extra-point attempt failed.

Faulkner fumbled on Central's next possession and Jones High recovered at the Tigers 15. Stan Gulley eventually scored on a 5-yard run over right tackle. The Dragons converted the extra-point attempt to take a 7-6 lead.

Even though Faulkner completed 11 of 30 passes for 150 yards, Central was unable to score again. According to the *Arkansas Democrat*, the outcome marked the first time a black Class AAAA or AAA team defeated a predominantly white team.

Quigley Stadium was the site for the first meeting between the Tigers and Fort Smith's Southside High School. Central relied on Faulkner, who threw touchdown passes of 7, 8 and 40 yards to Johnson, in the 19-7 victory over the Rebels.

The next week, McQuaney's 102 yards rushing and two touchdowns gave the Tigers a 13-10 lead over Pine Bluff. The fourth-quarter lead, though, soon disappeared as Central's last possession ended with a punt.

The Zebras wasted no time in taking advantage of this situation. With less than a minute to play, quarterback Joe Fakouri connected with Bobby Casali for a 32-yard touchdown. The extra point gave Pine Bluff a 17-13 victory over the Tigers.

Central ended the season the next week with its Thanksgiving Day game against Hall High School. The first half belonged to the Warriors as they held the Tigers to minus-20 yards of total offense. Danny Holmes' 25-yard field goal put Hall High up 17-0 with 8:27 left in the first half.

The second half belonged to Central. After a punt was downed in the end zone, the Tigers took over on their 20. Faulkner took the first snap and connected with Gillespie, who was sprinting down the right sideline. Gillespie caught the pass at the 40 and outran the defense for an 80-yard touchdown. Rownd converted the extra-point attempt to make it 17-7.

Scotty Shipp fumbled on Hall High's next possession and Central recovered at the 37. After two incomplete passes, Faulkner connected with Johnson at the 2. On fourth down, Faulkner snuck in for the touchdown. Rownd again converted the extra-point attempt to narrow the deficit to 17-14.

The Tigers were marching toward the end zone again with under two minutes to play, but an interception by Robert Palmer ended any hope Central had for a comeback victory.

1968 TIGER SCHEDULE

Benton 7	LRCH 13
LR Catholic 14	LRCH 6
*LR Horace Mann 13	LRCH 26
*FS Northside 14	LRCH 13
*North Little Rock 14	LRCH 6
*El Dorado 7	LRCH 13
NLR Jones 7	LRCH 6
FS Southside 7	LRCH 19
*Pine Bluff 17	LRCH 13
*LR Hall 17	LRCH 14

A DEFENSIVE TEAM

1969   6-2-2

Head Coach: Gene Hall
Assistants: Clyde Horton, Gary Wahlquist, Jerry Welch, Don Nixon
Team Physician: Dr. John McCollough Smith

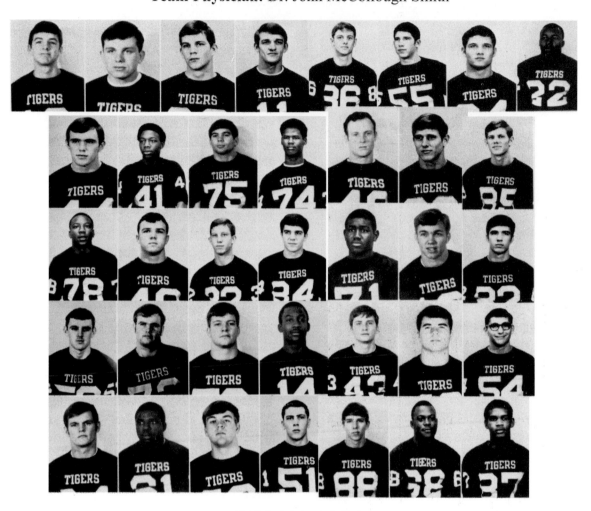

1969 LETTERMEN

Mike Abbott	Larry Davis	David Jungkind	Joey Shelton
Jon Bain	Randy Diles	Danny Korte	Ted Smith
Gary Bemberg	Lee Douglas	Tony Martin	David Steele
Perry Black	Dwight Duhart	Nathan McQuaney	Gene Tanner
Bob Bonner	Ray Gillespie	Genard Medley	Frank Westmoreland
Gary Capshaw	Larry Golightly	James Nelson	Jesse Williams
Roosevelt Clark	James Hall	Bill Norwood	Troy Willis
Walter Coleman	Robert Hallmark	Melvin Paxton	
Danny Crossett	Ed Horvath	John Peace	
Art Davis	Johnny Johnson	Ed Rownd	

1969 MANAGERS
Unknown

1969 ALL-SOUTHERN
Ed Rownd

1969 ALL-STATE
Ray Gillespie
Ed Rownd

1969 ALL-STAR TEAM
Ray Gillespie
Ed Rownd

Photo provided by Central High School
Coach Gene Hall and senior Larry Davis

Offensively and defensively, Central was in midseason form when it opened the season against Benton High School. In a game the Tigers dominated, the Panthers could not stop their opponent, nor move the ball.

Central held Benton to minus-1 yard of total offense, while the Tigers had their greatest offensive output since Billy Moore led them to a 54-13 victory over Texarkana, Texas, in 1957.

Moore's brother, Steve, led Central against Benton with 89 yards rushing and two touchdowns. Perry Black set up the first score when he ended the Panthers' opening possession with an interception at the Benton 33. Following two plays and a penalty, Moore ran off left tackle for a 5-yard touchdown. Ed Rownd converted the extra point for an early 7-0 lead.

Benton was forced to punt on its next possession, setting the stage for the Tigers' next score. A 49-yard drive ended with Moore's second touchdown, an 11-yard run. A failed extra-point attempt left the score at 13-0.

Central put the game away on its next possession when John Peace ran 45 yards for a touchdown on second down. Rownd converted the extra point just before the end of the first quarter. The high-powered offense scored four more touchdowns in a 47-0 victory over the Panthers.

The second-ranked Tigers traveled just a few blocks to War Memorial Stadium to take on No. 5 Catholic High School the following week. Central did not play quite as well as the previous week, but was able to lead in rushing yards (159) and passing yards (76). The Rockets, however, led where it mattered most, the scoreboard.

Catholic High scored three touchdowns, each set up by a Central turnover. Jim Blake intercepted a pass at the Central 19 to set up the first score. On third down, Jimmy Doolittle scored from the 1 to cap the short drive. Tim Brewer missed the extra-point attempt, but the Rockets led 6-0 with 59 seconds remaining in the first quarter.

The Tigers' ensuing possession ended on their 25 when Mike Stack recovered a Moore fumble. Three plays later, Mike Campbell caught a 4-yard touchdown pass from Doolittle to put Catholic High up 12-0 with 11:07 remaining in the first half.

After receiving a punt, Central put together a 60-yard drive that ended with an 8-

yard touchdown run by Moore. Rownd converted the extra point to narrow the third-quarter deficit to 12-7.

Blake intercepted a pass and returned it to the Tigers 30 to set up a third Catholic touchdown, a 7-yard run by Campbell.

A 13-yard touchdown run by Jon Bain in the fourth quarter would not be enough as Catholic was able to run out the clock and hand Central its first loss of the season, 20-14.

After leading only 7-0 at halftime the following week, the Tigers came out and demolished the Little Rock Horace Mann Bearcats in the final half. Central received its first AAAA Conference victory, 33-6.

The Tigers dropped two classifications the following week as they traveled to Class AA Conway High School. Neither team scored until 1:25 remained in the first half.

Rownd recovered a fumble at the Wampus Cats 40. On the next play, quarterback Tony Martin connected with Ray Gillespie, who caught the pass at the 10 and ran it into the end zone for a 6-0 halftime lead.

For the second consecutive week, the Tigers answered the call in the second half.

Central forced Conway to punt on its first possession and took over at the 44. Dwight Duhart eventually scored from the 4. A two-point conversion increased the

Photo provided by Central High School
John Peace hands off to Nathan McQuaney

lead to 14-0.

Walter Coleman set up the Tigers' final touchdown when he intercepted his second pass of the game. Coleman even tallied the score when he caught a 7-yard pass from Martin. Rownd converted the extra point for a 20-0 lead and the victory.

Next, in front of a standing-room only crowd in Fort Smith, Central met top-ranked and undefeated Fort Smith Northside. Midway though the second quarter, Northside struck first when quarterback Barry Lunney connected with Doug Moore for a 3-yard touchdown pass. Randy Walker converted the extra-point attempt with 5:26 left in the first half.

Joey Shelton intercepted a Grizzly pass to set up the Tigers' first score. The 48-yard drive was capped with a 1-yard run by Duhart. Larry Golightly's conversion made it 7-7 at halftime.

Central took the lead on its first possession of the second half when Duhart scored from the 8 to end a 64-yard drive. Golightly converted the extra-point kick for a 14-7 lead.

Photo provided by Central High School
Larry Golightly kicks off to Horace Mann

293

Photo provided by the Arkansas Democrat-Gazette
Walter Coleman vs. El Dorado

Northside answered on its next possession with a 60-yard scoring march. Joe Releford and Robert Owens combined for the yardage, with Owens scoring from the 5. Walker's extra-point kick tied the score, 14-14, with 5:37 left in the third quarter.

Northside regained the lead when an 80-yard drive was capped by Releford bulling his way into the end zone from the 8. The extra-point kick gave the Grizzlies a 21-14 lead.

The Tigers again tied the score when Martin passed to Gary Capshaw for a 50-yard touchdown. Golightly converted the extra point to make it 21-21.

One of two Lunney passes on the Grizzlies' final drive was a third-down, 8-yard completion to Gary White at the Central 45. Releford put Northside up with a 2-yard touchdown run. Walker kicked the extra point for a 28-21 lead with 2:15 left to play.

Capshaw returned the ensuing kickoff to the Grizzlies 42. Martin then connected with Gillespie to the 5. But with 58 seconds remaining, Fort Smith recovered a fumble to end any hope for Central to tie or beat the defending Class AAAA champion.

Coach Bill Stancil, who was coaching the Grizzlies for the 13th year, retired following the season. He was honored by Fort Smith fans after his team's victory over the Tigers.

After defeating North Little Rock Ole Main 14-0 and tying El Dorado 0-0, Central traveled to Fort Smith again, this time to play the Southside Rebels. The Tigers wasted no time scoring as Duhart ran 71 yards for a touchdown on the game's first play from scrimmage.

Central scored on its next possession when Bain caught a 16-yard touchdown pass from Peace to end an 11-play, 50-yard drive. Rownd's extra-point conversion extended Central's lead to 14-0.

Shelton added to the first-quarter fireworks when he intercepted a pass and returned it 24 yards for a touchdown to give the Tigers a 20-0 halftime lead. Central added to its lead in the second half when Joe Taylor scored on a 4-yard run and Duhart scored on a 67-yard run. The Tigers shut out the Fort Smith school 34-0.

While playing rival Pine Bluff the next week, Central's defense kept its offense in the game by keeping the Zebras off the field. The Tigers intercepted five passes and recovered four fumbles in a 27-0 victory.

Duhart scored the first touchdown on a 5-yard run and later reached the end zone on a 33-yard run. Peace scored on a 6-yard run and completed a 34-yard touchdown pass to Gillespie.

Central compiled 297 yards rushing, led by Duhart's 156 yards on 25 carries. The conference victory over Pine Bluff set the stage for a holiday battle with Little Rock

Photo provided by Central High School
Thanksgiving Day, 1969

Hall High, a game with the state championship on the line.

The Warriors were undefeated and a victory over the Tigers would guarantee them the state title. Central, with only one Class AAAA loss, could force a tie for the championship with a Thanksgiving Day victory.

Coleman set up the Tigers' best opportunity to score when he intercepted a pass and returned it to the Hall High 27. After the offense was unable to move, Golightly attempted a 44-yard field goal. The kick had plenty of distance, but was wide right.

Neither team came close to scoring again, resulting in a 0-0 tie. The top-ranked Warriors sealed their state championship and ended the year with the first unbeaten season in school history. Central clinched second place in Class AAAA with the tie.

One of Central High School's own received a national award following the season. Coach Clyde Horton, assistant football and head track coach, was named the "National Coach of the Year" for 1969 by the National High School Athletic Association. Coach Horton was honored for the success of his track program.

1969 TIGER SCHEUDLE

Benton 0	LRCH 47
LR Catholic 20	LRCH 14
*LR Horace Mann 6	LRCH 33
Conway 0	LRCH 20
*FS Northside 28	LRCH 21
*NLR Ole Main 0	LRCH 14
*El Dorado 0	LRCH 0
FS Southside 0	LRCH 34
*Pine Bluff 0	LRCH 27
*LR Hall 0	LRCH 0

A LOW POINT IN TIGER HISTORY
1970   1-8-1

Head Coach: Jerry Welch
Assistants: Clyde Horton, Gary Wahlquist, Bill Lawrence, Don Nixon
Team Physician: Dr. John McCollough Smith

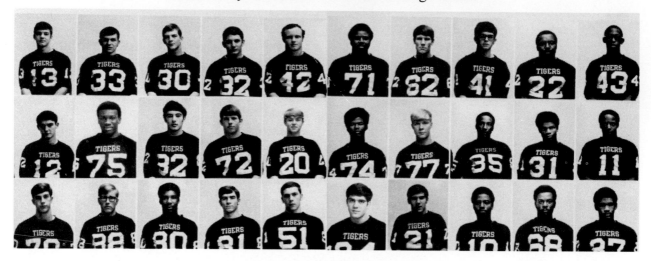

1970 LETTERMEN

Mike Abbott	Robert Clements	Randy Imbeau	Will Robinson
Jon Bain	Bob Coleman	Mike Mathes	Joey Shelton
Gary Bemberg	Ron Collar	Nathan McQuaney	Tommy Starnes
Phil Billingsley	Chester Hanson	Mike Mothershed	Vernon Wiley
Bob Bonner	Kirke Herman	Bill Norwood	Jessie Williams
Ralph Bradbury	Gary Hill	Phillip O'Dell	Troy Willis
Spencer Burroughs	Ed Horvath	Melvin Paxton	
Pete Campbell	Donald Hughes	Nathaniel Robinson	

1970 MANAGERS
Bryan Carroll
Dale Edney
Bill Humphries
Hershall Morse
David Rowe

1970 ALL-STATE
Joey Shelton

1970 ALL-STAR TEAM
Joey Shelton
Troy Willis

Following the 1969 season, Coach Gene Hall resigned as Central High's head coach to accept a sales position with Spaulding Athletics. One of Hall's former players, Jerry Welch, was promoted from assistant coach to lead Central's program.

The Tigers entered the season ranked No. 4 by the *Arkansas Democrat*. The team, though, quickly fell to No. 12 after a season-opening loss to Pine Bluff, which racked up 353 yards of total offense in a 32-0 victory.

Following a 34-6 loss to Class AAA Catholic High School, the Class AAAA Tigers dropped out of the statewide rankings. And the losses kept mounting. Central was beaten 26-6 by Little Rock Horace Mann, its first upset in the short series. The next week brought a 20-0 loss to West Memphis, leaving the Tigers 0-4-0.

Ralph Bradbury's 17 of 31 passing for 210 yards was not good enough the following week as Central was beaten 28-14 by Fort Smith Northside. Nine turnovers hurt the next week as the Tigers fell once again, this time 49-14 to North Little Rock Ole Main, the state's No. 1 team.

The six-game losing streak brought a new offense for Central. Coach Welch implemented the Shotgun formation and the change gave its next opponent, El Dorado, fits. Will Robinson completed a 35-yard touchdown pass to Gary Hill and a 40-yard touchdown pass to Pete Campbell.

The Tigers posted a 12-7 halftime lead, but a 3-yard touchdown run by Bill Johnson in the third quarter and a fourth-quarter safety sparked El Dorado to a 15-12 victory.

Central used its Shotgun offense to perfection during homecoming the next week, recording its first victory of the season against North Little Rock Northeast. Robin-son completed two touchdown passes, 35 yards to Campbell and 37 yards to Hill, in the 19-13 victory. Spencer Burroughs added to the scoring when he picked up a fumble and returned it for a touchdown.

A 14-14 tie against Little Rock Parkview allowed the Tigers to avoid another loss. However, Central couldn't escape another against Little Rock Hall High School on Thanksgiving Day. The second-ranked Warriors and the Tigers battled in front of approximately 3,400 fans in Quigley Stadium.

Alan Thompson rushed for 199 yards and four touchdowns in Hall High's 35-14 victory. The Tigers, though, were credited with maybe the most spectacular play of the year in Arkansas high school football.

Central was punting from its 8 when the ball was snapped to Joey Shelton in the end zone. Shelton's punt sailed 63 yards in the air and then proceeded to roll the remaining distance into the end zone. Shelton was credited with a 92-yard punt, the longest in state history.

Little Rock Central, a football powerhouse in the past, managed only one victory during the 1970 season. The 1-8-1 record was the school's worst mark since the Tigers and Coach O.D. Longstreth finished 0-5-0 in 1905.

1970 TIGER SCHEDULE

*Pine Bluff 32	LRCH 0
LR Catholic 34	LRCH 6
*LR Horace Mann 26	LRCH 6
West Memphis 20	LRCH 0
*Fort Smith Northside 28	LRCH 14
*NLR Ole Main 49	LRCH 14
*El Dorado 15	LRCH 12
*NLR Northeast 13	LRCH 19
LR Parkview 14	LRCH 14
*LR Hall 35	LRCH 14

SHOWING IMPROVEMENT

1971   5-6-0

Head Coach: Jerry Welch
Assistants: Clyde Horton, Gary Wahlquist, A.C. Crater, Don Nixon
Team Physician: Dr. John McCollough Smith

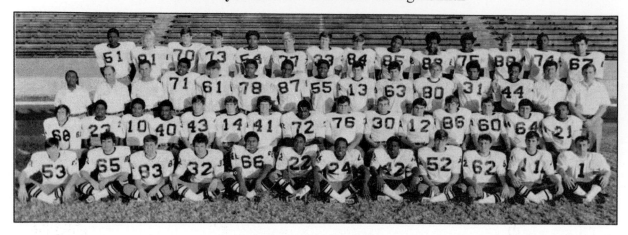

1971 LETTERMEN

Randy Abbott	Lee Cooper	Fred Moore	James Smith
Gary Bemberg	Carl Cross	Gordon Miller	John Smith
Phil Billingsley	Scott Gunn	Phillip O'Dell	Stan Turney
Ralph Bradbury	Kenneth "Muskie" Harris	Melvin Paxton	George Walker
Wayne Bradford	Jimmy Henson	Bruce Pippins	Cliff Whisnant
Danny Brown	Angelo Hronas	Greg Price	Vernon Wiley
Tommy Bryan	Allen Illing	Billy Ray Robinson	James Willbanks
Spencer Burroughs	Gary Korte	Eddie Robinson	Wayne Wilson
Paul Burton	Terry Langston	Nathaniel Robinson	Bob Worthington
Charles Cleaver	Mike Mathes	Will Robinson	
Ron Collar	Stanley McDaniel	David Rowe	

1971 MANAGERS
Pat McHughes

1971 ALL-STATE
Spencer Burroughs

1971 ALL-STAR TEAM
Spencer Burroughs

Even after a miserable 1-8-1 season in 1970, Central High School opened 1971 as the *Arkansas Democrat's* No. 9 team. Will Robinson was able to get his Top 10 team off on the right foot in the opener against Marianna High School.

Robinson received the opening kickoff and returned it 30 yards to the Tigers 47. Just a few plays later, he ran 15 yards for Central's first score. Ralph Bradbury added to this lead in the second quarter when he passed to Vernon Wiley for a 20-yard touchdown and a 12-0 advantage.

The second half opened with another touchdown by the Tigers as Robinson swept right end for a 78-yard score. Nathaniel Robinson capped a short touchdown drive in the fourth quarter with a 1-yard run.

Rodney Slater scored the lone touchdown for the Trojans on an 85-yard run. Slater finished with 153 yards rushing. Will Robinson had 154 of Central's 344 yards rushing. The season-opening victory matched Central's total for 1970.

The Tigers traveled to Pine Bluff the next week and returned home with a 21-0 victory, avenging a 32-0 loss to the Zebras the previous year.

Following a scoreless first half, Central's second possession of the third quarter ended with the game's first touchdown. Bradbury connected with Eddie Robinson for a 44-yard pass play, then Nathaniel Robinson bulled his way up the middle on the next play for a 4-yard touchdown run.

A 26-yard pass from Bradbury to Paul Burton ended with a fumble recovery in the end zone by Wiley. Another pass play late in the game, this one a 55-yarder from Bradbury to Will Robinson, set the ball at the Zebras 3. Will Robinson scored from there and David Rowe converted his third extra point of the game.

In their third consecutive road game, the No. 7 Tigers traveled across town to War Memorial Stadium to battle the No. 2 Catholic High Rockets.

Central scored first when Bradbury connected with Wiley midway through the

Photo Provided by the Arkansas Democrat-Gazette
Kenneth "Muskie" Harris

first quarter on a 40-yard touchdown. Just minutes later, the Tigers' Ron Collar recovered Phil Billingsley's fumble in the end zone for another touchdown. Rowe converted his second extra point for a 14-0 lead.

Terry Blaylock passed to Mike Duke for an 11-yard touchdown on Catholic's ensuing possession, a 10-play, 66-yard drive that narrowed Central's lead to 14-7.

The Tigers, though, had an answer. Two plays after receiving the ensuing kickoff, Kenneth "Muskie" Harris ran 68 yards for a touchdown, breaking three tackles at the line of scrimmage. Rowe's extra-point kick gave Central a 21-7 advantage.

But four minutes and 18 seconds later, the Rockets were ahead 22-21. A 16-yard pass from Blaylock to Duke ended a 72-yard drive. A two-point conversion brought Catholic High within one touchdown, 21-15. The Rockets got that touchdown just a minute later when Pat Campbell ran over right tackle from the 2. The extra point gave Catholic a one-point lead.

Coach George Loss' Rockets, who used 29 formations during the game, were able to tally two more score for a 35-21 victory.

Following an open date, Central hosted the West Memphis Blue Devils. The contest was decided in the first half since neither team scored in the second.

Photo provided by the Arkansas Democrat-Gazette
Tiger defenders hit Ole Main's David Haustein

Photo provided by the Arkansas Democrat-Gazette
Hall High's Walter Rowan eludes Tiger defenders

The Tigers opened the game by kicking off, but Central's Billy Robinson recovered a fumble at the Blue Devils 37. No time was wasted in scoring as Bradbury completed a 37-yard touchdown pass to Everette Robinson.

Central scored again on its next possession, moving 70 yards in seven plays. Will Robinson ended the drive when he scored from the 15. Bradbury then passed to Wiley for a two-point conversion to make it 14-0 with 7:23 left in the first quarter.

West Memphis was forced to punt on its next possession and the Tigers took advantage, scoring in three plays. The touchdown came on a 5-yard run by Billingsley. Rowe converted the extra point for a 21-0 advantage.

The Blue Devils answered with a 10-play, 80-yard drive capped by a 1-yard sneak from quarterback Lonnie James. Chuck Mullen kicked the extra point.

Will Robinson ended a 65-yard drive with a 13-yard touchdown run. Bradbury connected with Will Robinson for a 23-yard touchdown pass for Central's final touchdown. Rowe converted both extra points to set the final at 35-7.

Will Robinson and Rowe starred the next week for the No. 5 Tigers, combining to score every point in a 31-10 victory over the Fayetteville Bulldogs. Robinson, who rushed for 102 yards in the first quarter, scored four touchdowns, while Rowe converted four extra points and kicked a 37-yard field goal.

Fourth-ranked Central lost its second game of the season the following week when it played host to North Little Rock Ole Main. The No. 5 Wildcats passed their way to victory behind 17 of 30 completions for 225 yards by quarterbacks David Haustein and Stan McClure.

Haustein passed for two touchdowns, both to Bruce Wooldridge. Bill Bird added field goals of 37, 30 and 29 yards in the 23-14 victory over the Tigers.

Central's fortunes didn't change the next week in a 28-13 loss to fifth-ranked El Dorado. The Tigers did get back on track with a 21-0 shutout of North Little Rock Northeast, but were upset again by Fort Smith Northside.

The Grizzlies scored on plays of 90, 70 and 52 yards to highlight their 35-14 victory. The victory kept Northside in the conference's top spot and dropped Central to seventh.

The Tigers began their next game by kicking off to Class AAA Little Rock Parkview. Aaron Cook returned it 90 yards, setting the stage for a blowout.

Parkview dominated Central 38-0 and went on to share its conference championship with Hot Springs. The Trojans, though,

Photo provided by the Arkansas Democrat-Gazette
Gary Bemberg (30) and Spencer Burroughs (75) tackle Hall High's Steve Berthelson (34)

went on to represent the AAA-West Conference in the state playoffs because they defeated the Patriots in September.

Senior quarterback Walter Rowan led his Hall High Warriors with 227 total yards in a Thanksgiving Day victory over the Tigers. Rowan highlighted the game on the first play of the fourth quarter when he broke free around right end for an 86-yard touchdown. Little Rock Hall defeated Central 28-7.

Following the season, Coach Jerry Welch announced his resignation from Little Rock Central High School. He planned to attend Northwestern (La.) State University to do graduate work. In his late 20s, Coach Welch was one of the youngest head football coaches to ever lead one of Arkansas' major high school programs.

1971 TIGER SCHEDULE

Marianna 6	LRCH 24
*Pine Bluff 0	LRCH 21
*LR Catholic 35	LRCH 21
West Memphis 7	LRCH 35
Fayetteville 10	LRCH 31
*NLR Ole Main 23	LRCH 14
*El Dorado 28	LRCH 13
*NLR Northeast 0	LRCH 21
*FS Northside 35	LRCH 14
LR Parkview 38	LRCH 0
*LR Hall 28	LRCH 7

TIGERS RETURN TO WINNING WAYS

1972   5-4-2

Head Coach: Joe Fred Young
Assistants: Bernie Cox, Clyde Horton, A.C. Crater, Johnny Greenwood
Team Physician: Dr. John McCollough Smith

1972 LETTERMEN

Randy Abbott	Jerry Corrothers	Johnny Maddox	James Smith
Glen Anderson	Bruce Crabtree	Fred Moore	John Smith
Eddie Bowman	Carl Cross	Charles Patillo	Tim Stolzer
Ralph Bradbury	Vincent Freeman	Herbert Rideout	George Walker
Wayne Bradford	Thomas Halton	Billy Ray Robinson	Jimmy Walker
Danny Brown	Kenneth "Muskie" Harris	Eddie Robinson	Cliff Whisnant
Charles Cleaver	Jimmy Henson	Robin Robinson	James Willbanks
Charlie Coleman	Charles Jamison	Will Robinson	Bob Worthington
Lee Cooper	Joe Jewell	David Rowe	
Garry Corrothers	Steve Johnson	Darwin Smith	

1972 MANAGERS
Unknown

1972 ALL-STATE
Charles Cleaver
Lee Cooper
Kenneth "Muskie" Harris
Will Robinson

1972 ALL-STAR TEAM
Lee Cooper
Will Robinson

Coach Jerry Welch's departure for higher education brought about the hiring of new head coach Joe Fred Young. Coach Young came to Little Rock from Conway High School, where he was head coach for one year and an assistant coach prior to that.

Coach Young's top assistant in Conway, Bernie Cox, made the move to Little Rock as well. Coach Cox continued his role as Coach Young's assistant head coach and offensive coordinator. Also joining the coaching staff was Johnny Greenwood, who also coached the basketball team.

Coach Clyde Horton (left) and head coach
Joe Fred Young (center) talk with a Tiger player

The new head coach took the wide-open offense of the previous two years and replaced it with the more conservative Wishbone offense. The new look, though, did not surprise Central's first opponent.

Pine Bluff kept the Wishbone in check most of the night, but the seventh-ranked Tigers capitalized on three mistakes by the Zebras to score their points. The first Central touchdown came after Thomas Halton recovered a bad pitchout by Pine Bluff quarterback George Makris at the 1.

Charles Patillo ran over left tackle on the next play for the score. David Rowe converted the extra point for a 7-0 lead with 9:30 left in the first half.

On the kickoff to open the second half, the Zebras' Ricky Ferguson fumbled and Charles Jamison recovered for the Tigers at the Pine Bluff 35. Central couldn't get into the end zone, but Rowe kicked a 28-yard field goal for a 10-0 lead.

Late in the third quarter, Makris was intercepted by Jerry Corrothers. The Tigers took possession at the Zebras 38, and a 12-yard pass from Ralph Bradbury to Will Robinson was good for Central's last touchdown. Rowe missed the conversion attempt, but the Tigers had a 16-0 lead.

Pine Bluff scored late in the game on a 1-yard run by John Shiver. The run capped a 13-play, 55-yard drive, but it wouldn't be enough as Central defeated the Zebras 16-6.

After leading 10-0 at halftime the next week against Little Rock Catholic, the Tigers suddenly lost the lead in the fourth quarter. Bradbury, though, then completed a screen pass to Kenneth "Muskie" Harris, who ran 71 yards for a touchdown as Central regained the lead 17-13 following Rowe's extra point.

The Rockets answered on their next possession when John Leroux caught a short scoring pass from quarterback Rick Kyle to regain the lead for good. The play ended a 66-yard drive in Catholic's 20-17 victory over the Tigers.

Bill Reed and his Jacksonville Red Devils hosted Central the next week. The Tigers jumped ahead early as Robinson re-

Offensive coordinator Bernie Cox and quarterback
Ralph Bradbury (12)

303

turned the opening kickoff 87 yards for a touchdown. Rowe missed the extra-point attempt, but Central took a 6-0 lead just 10 seconds into the game.

The Tigers forced Jacksonville to punt on its first series and used the opportunity for their next score. Although they were unable to reach the end zone, they used a 27-yard field goal by Rowe to increase the lead to 9-0.

After an exchange of punts, Central marched 92 yards for its second touchdown. Patillo capped the drive with a 4-yard run with 1:48 remaining in the half.

A 1-yard run by Bradbury, a 6-yard run by Harris and a 34-yard screen pass from Bradbury to Patillo rounded out the scoring. The Tigers defeated the Red Devils 35-0.

Central made only one mistake the following week against West Memphis, but that one mistake cost the Tigers a chance at victory. With just 10 minutes to play in the game and Central in punt formation, Charlie Coleman's snap sailed over the head of Cliff Whisnant. The ball rolled out of the end zone and gave the Blue Devils a safety, the only score of the game.

With just seconds remaining in the next game against Forrest City, Woodson Hill missed a 25-yard field-goal attempt that would have given the Mustangs the victory. The teams settled for a 7-7 tie.

The following week, North Little Rock Ole Main's Charles Walker rushed 26 times

Photo provided by Central High School
Ralph Bradbury (12)

for 145 yards and scored on a 4-yard run with 1:34 remaining to break a 13-13 tie. Arvis Harper converted the extra point in a 20-13 victory over Central. The Tigers' two touchdowns came on a 52-yard run by Lee Cooper and a 74-yard run by Robinson. Rowe made one of the two extra-point attempts for a 13-6 third-quarter lead.

Another 7-7 tie, this time with El Dorado, sent an angry Central team into its homecoming game with North Little Rock Northeast. Pam Johnson was crowned homecoming queen, and she reigned over a game that featured the offensive power of the home team.

While only playing in the first half, Robinson highlighted the effort with 200 yards rushing on 21 carries. Robinson scored on runs of 42 and 54 yards. Corrothers scored the game's final touchdown on a 70-yard run. Rowe added the final point in a 40-7 victory over the Chargers.

In Fort Smith the next week, the Tigers needed a last-minute drive to come out ahead. To complete a 90-yard, nine-play drive, Bradbury connected with Eddie Robinson for a 24-yard touchdown

Photo provided by Central High School
Charles Patillo (14)

304

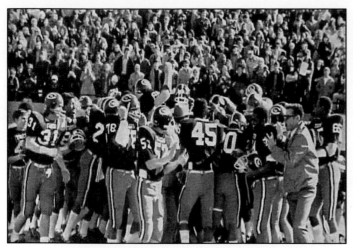

Pregame excitement on Thanksgiving Day

with one second remaining in the game. The 14-10 victory over Northside improved Central to 4-3-2.

Little Rock Parkview, playing its first Class AAAAA season, wasn't much of a match for Central. With 1:18 left in the first half, Bradbury scored on a quarterback keeper to cap a 64-yard, 11-play drive. Rowe's conversion gave the Tigers a 7-0 halftime lead.

Midway through the third quarter, Billy Ray Robinson intercepted a Bucky Layne pass and returned it 48 yards to the Patriots 44. From the 23, Will Robinson carried four consecutive times to score. Rowe missed the extra-point attempt, but Central led 13-0 with 44 seconds remaining in the quarter.

Will Robinson ended another drive in the final quarter when he ran over right tackle for a 2-yard touchdown. Rowe converted the extra point for a 20-0 lead. A Parkview touchdown late in the game was not enough as the Tigers defeated the Patriots 20-7.

The holiday tradition continued when Little Rock Hall High and Little Rock Central High battled on Thanksgiving Day at Quigley Stadium.

Central's defense controlled the first half of play, but its offense was only able to score once. Bradbury led his team on a 79-yard drive in eight plays to score in the first quarter. Will Robinson received a pitch from Bradbury, but he pulled up and threw a spiral to his brother, Eddie, for a 23-yard touchdown. Rowe's conversion gave Central a 7-0 advantage at halftime.

The Warriors took the second-half kickoff and marched 68 yards in 10 plays to tie the score, 7-7. Alfred Jones capped the drive with a 33-yard touchdown run.

Hall High dominated the second half, controlling the football for 20 of the 24 minutes. The Warriors scored again when Greg Martin kicked a 23-yard field goal in the third quarter. The kick gave Hall High a 10-7 lead and eventually the victory.

The loss dropped the Tigers to 5-4-2 overall and ninth in the conference standings. In the final statewide polls, they were ranked No. 8 by the *Arkansas Democrat* and No. 9 by The Associated Press.

1972 TIGER SCHEDULE

*Pine Bluff 6	LRCH 16
*LR Catholic 20	LRCH 17
Jacksonville 0	LRCH 35
West Memphis 2	LRCH 0
Forrest City 7	LRCH 7
*NLR Ole Main 20	LRCH 13
*El Dorado 7	LRCH 7
*NLR Northeast 7	LRCH 40
*FS Northside 10	LRCH 14
*LR Parkview 7	LRCH 20
*LR Hall 10	LRCH 7

PROVING THE POLLSTERS WRONG

1973   8-3-0

Head Coach: Joe Fred Young
Assistants: Bernie Cox, Clyde Horton, A.C. Crater, Johnny Greenwood
Team Physician: Dr. John McCollough Smith

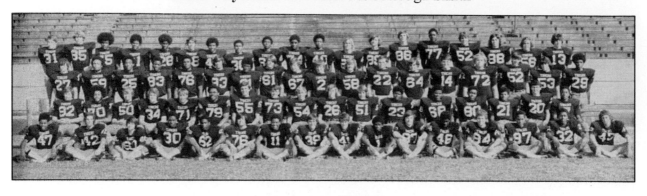

1973 LETTERMEN

Glen Anderson	Duane Heard	Stanley McDaniel	Eddie Robinson
Jeff Bemberg	Jimmy Henson	Ronald Moore	Nathaniel Robinson
Eddie Bowman	Brad Horne	Houston Nutt	Joe Shotts
Kenneth Cole	Joe Jewell	Charles Patillo	Darwin Smith
Garry Corrothers	Ruben Johnson	Tommy Pearce	Eric Thrasher
Jerry Corrothers	Mike Jones	Don Perkins	Emanuel Tolbert
Bruce Crabtree	Steve Lawson	Jay Pettit	Ezekiel Vaughn
Robert Farrell	Larry Lovelace	Troy Price	Jimmy Walker
Randy Gilbert	Mike MacDonald	Herbert Rideout	
Carl Hamilton	Randall Mack	Danny Ray Robinson	

1973 MANAGERS

Bruce Bailey	Sam Oglesby
Roy Barnhill	Richard Roller
James McHughes	Fred Smith

1973 ALL-STATE
Jimmy Henson
Houston Nutt
Herbert Rideout
Eddie Robinson
Jimmy Walker

1973 ARKANSAS SOPHOMORE OF THE YEAR
Houston Nutt

1973 ALL-STAR TEAM
Jimmy Henson

Photo provided by the Arkansas Democrat-Gazette
Eddie Robinson (7)

After a relatively successful year in 1972, the Tigers hoped to be even better in 1973. In preseason polls, Central was ranked eighth out of nine schools in the AAAAA Conference. In the state's overall polls, the Tigers were not even mentioned among the top 20 teams.

With Ralph Bradbury and Will Robinson lost to graduation, Coach Joe Fred Young had to find replacements at two critical positions. Tailback was taken over by Robinson's brother, Eddie, and the quarterback job was up for grabs between Jay Pettit and Houston Nutt.

In the season opener against Marianna High School, Pettit led the team in the first half, while Nutt ran the offense in the second half. Robinson, though, stepped right into his brother's position and didn't miss a beat, rushing for 223 yards on 38 carries.

On its first possession of the second quarter, Central capped a 75-yard scoring drive with a 2-yard run by Robinson. Duane Heard converted the extra point for a 7-0 lead with 6:22 left in the half.

The Tigers added another score on their next possession when they drove 97 yards for a touchdown. Two touchdowns were enough to defeat the Trojans 14-0.

The following week in Pine Bluff, a mistake by each punting team resulted in the game's only points.

The No. 8 Zebras scored first with 13 seconds remaining in the first quarter. Central's punter fumbled the snap, and Pine Bluff's Lee Palles returned it 27 yards for the score. The extra-point attempt was blocked.

The No. 7 Tigers had the Zebras backed up to their 22 and punting on fourth-and-3. Pine Bluff's punter shanked a kick that was fielded at the 18 by Mike MacDonald, who returned the kick for a touchdown to tie the score. Heard's extra point with 7:53 remaining in the game was enough to beat the Zebras.

Following Jimmy Henson's interception of a Catholic High pass in the third quarter the next week, Charles Patillo capped a 39-yard drive with a 14-yard touchdown run. This gave Central a 12-0 lead with 5:18 left in the third quarter.

Photo provided by the Arkansas Democrat-Gazette
Michael Hall (36) and Danny Ray Robinson (23)

The Rockets immediately answered as Mark Neihouse returned the ensuing kick-off 87 yards for a touchdown. Catholic attempted a two-point conversion, but the pass attempt was knocked down by the Tigers' Garry Corrothers.

Catholic's Andy Beavers blocked an Eric Thrasher punt and it was recovered by the Rockets, giving them possession within scoring distance. Six plays later, Pat Longinotti caught a touchdown pass with 6:42 left in the game. The extra point gave the Rockets a 13-12 lead.

In the closing minutes, Emanuel Tolbert returned a Dan Boone punt 4 yards to the Central 17. A 10-yard pass from Nutt to Bruce Crabtree and runs by Patillo and Robinson set the stage for a game-winning field goal by Heard.

With seven seconds remaining in the game, Heard's 29-yard field-goal attempt was good to give the Tigers a 15-13 victory over the Rockets.

Against Forrest City High School the next week, Robinson was out of the lineup because of an injury. This forced Patillo to move to tailback while Jeff Bemberg played fullback. The new backfield moved the 64 yards needed for Central's first score. The touchdown came on a 34-yard pass play from Nutt to Mike Jones. Heard

Photo provided by the Arkansas Democrat-Gazette
Charles Patillo scores against Catholic High

added the extra point for a 7-0 lead with 4:49 left in the first quarter.

Heard added to the lead with 4:47 left in the game when he kicked a 20-yard field goal. The Mustangs scored moments later, but it wasn't enough to defeat the Tigers.

Central, the state's new No. 2 team, hosted West Memphis the following week. Nutt, Central's sophomore quarterback, was key in this victory as he kept two drives alive with pinpoint passing.

Facing third-and-4 from the Blue Devils 47, Nutt hit Crabtree for a 20-yard completion to the 27. Three plays later, Nutt scrambled before finding Crabtree at the 10. Crabtree caught the ball, lowered his shoulder and bulled his way into the end zone.

Early in the final quarter, Nutt struck again as he connected with Jones on a 17-yard touchdown pass. Heard missed both conversion attempts, but Central won 12-0 for its fifth consecutive victory.

Sixth-ranked North Little Rock Ole Main dominated the No. 2 Tigers the following week. The Wildcats turned Central mistakes into touchdowns in a 34-7 victory, knocking the Tigers to No. 5 in the polls.

Central's first score the next week against El Dorado was set up by a 21-yard pass from Nutt to Bemberg. Several plays later, Nutt scored on a run around right end.

Photo provided by the Arkansas Democrat-Gazette
Central's defense closes in on an Ole Main back

Photo provided by the Arkansas Democrat-Gazette
Bruce Crabtree vs. Forrest City

Robert Farrell converted the extra point for a 7-0 advantage.

The Tigers struck again in the third quarter after Corrothers blocked a Scott Tanner punt. Herbert Rideout recovered and returned the blocked punt 34 yards for the touchdown. Farrell's extra point gave Central a 14-0 lead.

Later in the game, Farrell fair caught a punt at the Wildcats 44. Nutt then passed to Jones on the first play for a 34-yard gain to the 10. Michael Hall scored on the next play, and Farrell's kick completed Central's 21-0 victory.

Danny Ray Robinson, Eddie Robinson, and Hall combined for 323 rushing yards against North Little Rock Northeast the following week. The Robinson brothers each scored a touchdown, while Farrell kicked a 29-yard field goal and Corrothers picked up a fumble and returned it 19 yards for a touchdown. Central defeated the Chargers 23-12.

The top-ranked Tigers were upset the next week by Fort Smith Northside. Central held the conference lead, but the loss pushed the Tigers into a tie with Little Rock Parkview, Little Rock Hall and Ole Main.

The Grizzlies were able to score two touchdowns in a 14-0 victory over the Tigers.

A packed Quigley Stadium watched Parkview and Central battle for first place in the conference the following week. The Tigers started strong as Crabtree recovered a Parkview fumble on the game's first play from scrimmage.

It took just four plays for Central to take advantage of the turnover. From the 9, Nutt passed to Crabtree for a touchdown. Heard converted the extra point for a 7-0 lead.

Parkview answered with an eight-play, 66-yard, drive that ended with quarterback Bucky Layne's 6-yard touchdown run. David Tucker's extra point made it 7-7.

Midway through the second quarter, Layne connected with tight end Clarence Finley for a 4-yard touchdown. Layne then faked the extra-point kick and hit Finley, who was all alone in the end zone. The touchdown gave Parkview the lead for good, but the Patriots went on to score four more times in a 42-7 blowout.

In the annual Thanksgiving Day game against Little Rock Hall High, the Tigers only needed one pass to win. Nutt completed a 57-yard pass to Eddie Robinson for the game's only touchdown. Heard converted the extra point for a 7-0 first-half lead.

The Warriors could only manage a field goal after recovering a Nutt fumble at the Central 37. With four seconds remaining in the second quarter, Doug Parrish kicked a 40-yard field goal to narrow the lead to 7-3.

Neither team scored during the second half, allowing the Tigers a true holiday celebration for the first time since 1960. The victory put Central in a three-way tie with Hall and Ole Main for second in the conference.

1973 TIGER SCHEDULE

Marianna 0	LRCH 14
*Pine Bluff 6	LRCH 7
*LR Catholic 13	LRCH 15
Forrest City 6	LRCH 10
West Memphis 0	LRCH 12
*NLR Ole Main 34	LRCH 7
*El Dorado 0	LRCH 21
*NLR Northeast 12	LRCH 23
*FS Northside 14	LRCH 0
*LR Parkview 42	LRCH 7
*LR Hall 3	LRCH 7

GAME OF THE DECADE

1974   10-1-1

Head Coach: Joe Fred Young
Assistants: Bernie Cox, Clyde Horton, A.C. Crater, Eddie Boone
Team Physician: Dr. John McCollough Smith

1974 LETTERMEN

Glen Anderson	Michael Hall	Mike MacDonald	Nathaniel Robinson
Jeff Bemberg	David Hamilton	Donny McCuin	Joe Shotts
Morris Bhones	Reginald Harris	Anson Nix	Jimmy Smith
Jeff Boggess	Brad Horne	Houston Nutt	Stephen Thornhill
Anthony Brown	Eldon Jewell	Tommy Pearce	Eric Thrasher
Sylvester Chaney	Joe Jewell	Michael Perry	Emanuel Tolbert
Tony Dunnick	Steve Lancaster	Jay Pettit	Roger Varnell
Robert Farrell	Steve Lawson	Mike Pollock	Ezekiel Vaughn
Victor Gatewood	Tim Logue	Troy Price	Jimmy Walker
Scott Grable	Randall Mack	Danny Ray Robinson	Leslie Wright

1974 MANAGERS
Roy Barnhill
Fred Smith

1974 ALL-AMERICAN
Houston Nutt

1974 ALL-STATE
Robert Farrell
Houston Nutt
Jimmy Walker

1974 ALL-STAR TEAM
Jimmy Walker

Opening No. 5 in the *Arkansas Democrat* Top 10, Central High School began the season at Marianna. The game-winning play occurred early in the first quarter when Central's Marvin Davis intercepted a pass and returned it 30 yards for a touchdown. The extra point put Central ahead 7-0.

The Tigers lost four fumbles compared to Marianna's one. Central, though, took advantage of the turnover and added to its lead when Emanuel Tolbert scored from the 2. The 13-0 victory gave the Tigers momentum heading home to meet Pine Bluff.

The Zebras shocked a large Quigley Stadium crowd on the first offensive play of the game. Tailback Laydell Jordan took a delayed handoff from Scott Irwin and ran 73 yards for a touchdown. Larry Wallace converted the extra point for a 7-0 lead only 32 seconds into the game.

Central didn't answer until early in the second quarter. On first down from the Tigers 45, quarterback Houston Nutt passed to Robert Farrell for a 55-yard touchdown. Farrell's extra point made it 7-7.

Pine Bluff took a 16-7 lead with a field goal and a touchdown before Farrell added to Central's score with a field goal of his own. The 31-yard kick brought the Tigers within six points early in the third quarter.

Midway through the fourth quarter, Farrell fair caught a Pine Bluff punt at the Zebras 34. After Danny Ray Robinson carried six consecutive times, Nutt handed off to him once again. From the 3, Robinson ran around right end and dove into the corner of the end zone to tie the score. Farrell's kick proved to be the game winner, giving Central a 17-16 victory in its first conference game.

Catholic High School gave the Tigers a big scare the next week when a 25-yard field goal by Fred Meadors gave the Rockets a 22-0 lead midway through the third quarter. Central, though, answered with a four-minute, 83-yard drive that was capped by a 3-yard run by Michael

Hall. A pass from Nutt to Farrell was good for a two-point conversion.

After forcing Catholic High to punt, the Tigers took over at their 49. On second down, Nutt found Tony Dunnick open at the 4 and he jogged across the goal line for the score. Nutt passed to David Hamilton for the two-point conversion to narrow the deficit to 22-16 with 10:18 left in the game.

Central again forced the Rockets to punt on their ensuing possession and took over at the Catholic 49. The 49-yard drive was completed when Robinson crossed into the corner of the end zone to make it 22-22. Farrell, with an injured knee and broken toe, converted the game-winning extra point. Nutt completed 10 passes for 165 yards in the 23-22 comeback victory.

Forrest City High School held the Tigers at bay long enough for a scoreless tie when the final buzzer sounded. Central entered the next game with Hot Springs as the state's No. 2 team.

Dale Marlow of Hot Springs ran all over Central, carrying 21 times for 165 yards and scoring on runs of 77 and 30 yards. Steve Yearby's extra-point attempt following the second touchdown was wide, allowing the Tigers to escape with a 14-13 victory.

After a 34-6 blowout of West Memphis, Central narrowly escaped North Little Rock Ole Main. In another close call, the

Photo provided by Central High School
Houston Nutt hands off to Michael Hall

312

Photo provided by the Arkansas Democrat-Gazette
Houston Nutt (14) eludes Parkview's
Charles Clay (85)

Tigers needed a missed extra-point attempt by the Wildcats to win 7-6. Michael Perry, however, was a bright spot as he rushed for 115 yards for the second consecutive week.

In El Dorado the next week, No. 2 Central used two first-half touchdowns to overcome the 1-5-0 Wildcats.

El Dorado's Wes Haynie punted with just under a minute remaining in the first quarter, and Perry returned it 52 yards for a touchdown. Farrell's conversion gave Central a 7-0 lead.

In the second quarter, the Tigers took control at their 44 and drove for another touchdown. The drive lasted two plays. Nutt passed to Robinson on first down to reach the El Dorado 37 and then hit Dunnick in the end zone for the score. Farrell again converted the extra point and Central wasn't threatened the remainder of the game.

With less than two minutes remaining against North Little Rock Northeast the following week, the Tigers trailed 15-10. Nutt, however, led his team to a three-play, 60-yard game-winning drive.

A screen pass from Nutt to Tolbert gained 19 yards to the Chargers 41. Following an incomplete pass, Nutt connected

with Farrell at the 20. Farrell stayed on his feet after being hit by two defenders and dragged them into the end zone. The touchdown gave the Tigers a 16-15 win, their fifth one-point victory of the season.

Central's 528 total yards the next week against Fort Smith Northside was highlighted by Nutt's 202 yards passing on nine completions. Robinson rushed for 117 yards on 14 carries, and Perry rushed for 103 yards on six carries in a 34-0 victory over the Grizzlies.

The domination of Fort Smith set the stage for the state's biggest game of the season, a contest that pitted top-ranked and undefeated Little Rock Parkview against No. 2 and undefeated Little Rock Central.

The Patriots entered the game as Class AAAAA's top rushing team, averaging 297.1 yards per game, and ranked fourth in passing yardage. The Tigers entered the game as the conference's top passing team, averaging 108 yards per game, and were fifth in rushing yardage.

More than 12,000 fans were at Quigley Stadium on Nov. 14 to see what sportswriters billed as "The Game of the Decade." Parkview struck first on a first-and-10 play from the Central 49. Quarterback John Barnett rolled right and pitched to Gerald Jones, who faked out cornerback Jay Pettit and ran untouched for a 49-yard touchdown.

Photo provided by Central High School
Coach Joe Fred Young

Central responded after Brad Horne intercepted a pass on Parkview's next possession. Perry gained 9 yards and Nutt then passed to Jeff Boggess for 19 yards. After Perry gained another yard on a run, Nutt then hit Tolbert in the end zone for a touchdown. Farrell's kick made it 7-7.

Parkview recovered a fumble by Perry at the Tigers 48 and capitalized eight plays later when Jones scored his second touchdown of the game. The extra point put the Patriots in front 14-7 with 1:59 remaining in the second quarter.

With 51 seconds remaining in the half, the Patriots forced the Tigers to turn the ball over. Just a few seconds later, Barnett passed 15 yards to Charles Clay for a touchdown.

Horace Springer, Parkview's extra-point holder, pulled the ball off the tee and passed to Scott Lamb for a two-point conversion. The Patriots then led 22-7 just before the half.

Parkview, though, wasn't done adding to its lead. After using a squib kick on the ensuing kickoff, the Patriots recovered the ball after it touched a Central player. Parkview used two plays to reach the 22, and

Photo provided by Central High School
Jeff Boggess (84) vs. Little Rock Parkview

Photo provided by Central High School
Coach Bernie Cox talks with Jay Pettit

Scott Riggan kicked a 39-yard field goal to give the Patriots a 25-7 halftime lead.

Midway through the third quarter, Central took possession after a punt and followed with its second scoring drive. Hall capped the 52-yard drive with a 3-yard run.

The Tigers continued the comeback on their next series. Nutt completed six passes in the 66-yard drive, the final a touchdown to Farrell. The extra point by Farrell brought the Tigers within 25-21 with 6:37 remaining to play.

The top-ranked Patriots, however, wouldn't be denied. They put the game away when John Barron capped a 39-yard drive with a short run up the middle. Central was defeated 31-21.

One highlight in the loss for the Tigers was Nutt, who passed for 344 yards and two touchdowns. However, Central fumbled five times, twice inside the Parkview 10, and another that Parkview turned into a scoring drive. Nutt was also sacked seven times for 70 yards in losses.

Charles Stanley sacked Nutt three times and sophomore George Stewart had two sacks. Parkview's offensive line was strong, helping the Patriots rush for 244 yards on 46 carries. Among the stars on the line were Clay, Mike Meyers, Brooks Hollingsworth, Robert Jordan, Jim Kissire and Jerry Sullivan.

Two weeks later on Thanksgiving Day, the Tigers battled Little Rock Hall for second in the conference. Nutt passed for three touchdowns, two to Tolbert and another to Farrell. Tolbert also scored the game-winning touchdown on a short run around right end with 1:03 left to play in the game.

In its sixth one-point victory of the season, Central again had to come from behind to win. The 25-24 victory was only the second time the Tigers defeated the Warriors since 1960.

After completing his third season as head coach, Joe Fred Young resigned to become an assistant coach at the University of Arkansas. Coach Young's assistant head coach and offensive coordinator, Bernie Cox, was named the school's 16th head coach by the Little Rock School Board in January 1975.

1974 TIGER SCHEDULE

	Marianna 0	LRCH 13
*	Pine Bluff 16	LRCH 17
*	LR Catholic 22	LRCH 23
	Forrest City 0	LRCH 0
	Hot Springs 13	LRCH 14
	West Memphis 6	LRCH 34
*	NLR Ole Main 6	LRCH 7
*	El Dorado 0	LRCH 14
*	NLR Northeast 15	LRCH 16
*	FS Northside 0	LRCH 34
*	LR Parkview 31	LRCH 21
*	LR Hall 24	LRCH 25

THE COX ERA BEGINS WITH A CHAMPIONSHIP

1975   12-0-0

Head Coach: Bernie Cox
Assistants: Gail Mote, Clyde Horton, A.C. Crater, Eddie Boone
Team Physician: Dr. John McCollough Smith

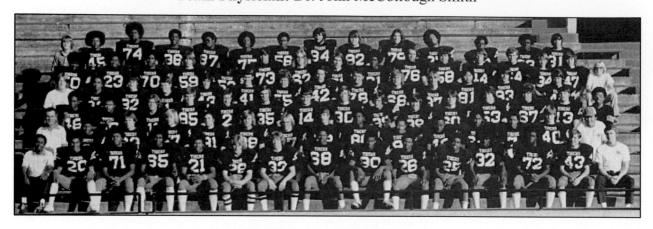

1975 LETTERMEN

Lovey Broomas	Reginald Harris	Anson Nix	Jimmy Smith
Anthony Brown	Mike Heiman	Dickey Nutt	Russell Swindell
James Campbell	Gene Heiskell	Houston Nutt	Stephen Thornhill
Sylvester Chaney	Michael Hudson	Michael Perry	Eric Thrasher
Herbert Coleman	Steve Lancaster	Mike Pollock	Emanuel Tolbert
Courtney Duhart	Allen Lockhart	Rick Pringle	Roger Varnell
Tony Dunnick	Randall Mack	Danny Ray Robinson	Ezekiel Vaughn
Robert Farrell	Joe McCraney	Scott Sanders	Reginald Woods
Michael Hall	Teddy Morris	Bob Scott	Ray Young
David Hamilton	Bryan Morrison	Joe Shotts	

1975 MANAGERS
Charlie Barnhill
Roy Barnhill
Paul Campbell
Dale Garner
Fred Smith

1975 ALL-AMERICAN
Robert Farrell
Houston Nutt

1975 ALL-STATE
Robert Farrell
Michael Hall
Houston Nutt
Stephen Thornhill
Ezekiel Vaughn

1975 ALL-STAR TEAM
Robert Farrell
Houston Nutt

1975 ARKANSAS COACH OF THE YEAR
Bernie Cox

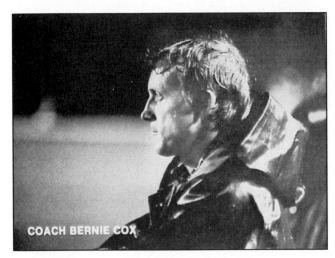

Photo provided by Central High School
Bernie Cox, Central's first-year head coach

Central's new head coach, Bernie Cox, filled a coaching position with his former college teammate and roommate at Harding University, Gail Mote. Coach Mote joined the staff from Gainesville High School in Gainesville, Texas, where he was defensive coordinator. Coach Mote had the same job at Central.

Returning the state's top offensive backfield and receivers, the Tigers were the top contender for the 1975 AAAAA state championship. Among those returning was standout quarterback Houston Nutt, who threw for 1,663 yards and 14 touchdowns as a junior, leading the conference in almost every passing category.

Central returned 21 lettermen, but a major concern was inexperience in the offensive and defensive lines. The polls, however, weren't concerned since the *Arkansas Gazette* ranked the Tigers No. 3 in its preseason poll, while Central opened No. 1 in the *Arkansas Democrat*.

The Tigers began the season with an outstanding performance against Marianna High School. Central's defense held the Trojans to minus-11 yards rushing and 18

yards passing. The Tigers finished with 322 total yards in a 39-0 victory.

Jordan Stadium in Pine Bluff was filled the following week as Central took on the Zebras. The Tigers scored on their first possession when Danny Ray Robinson took a pitchout and turned the right corner, racing untouched for a 75-yard touchdown. Robert Farrell kicked the extra point for an early 7-0 lead.

After trading punts, Central scored again. Emanuel Tolbert went around left end for a 14-yard touchdown run to cap a 43-yard drive. Farrell's extra-point attempt was wide left, but Central led 13-0.

Pine Bluff scored next when it used almost 11 minutes to drive 80 yards in 18 plays. The touchdown came on fourth down as fullback Lance Shinall scored from the 1. Scott Carter converted the extra point to make it 13-7.

Photo provided by Central High School
Danny Ray Robinson (23)

317

After a third touchdown by the Tigers, a 12-yard pass from Nutt to Robinson, the Zebras began to control the game. On the ensuing possession, Pine Bluff's Randy Curtis hit Carnell Williams for a 72-yard touchdown. Carter's extra-point conversion narrowed the deficit to 20-14.

The Zebras held Central scoreless the remainder of the game. Pine Bluff had one last chance to score when it regained possession with 3:34 left in the game. Behind Ted Palles, Andrea Jackson and Shinall, the Zebras moved 57 yards to the Tigers 2.

But Central's defense kept Pine Bluff out of the end zone four consecutive plays to secure a 20-14 conference victory. After rushing for 100 yards on his first two attempts, Robinson finished with 143 yards.

A 24-yard run by Nutt the next week highlighted a short drive that Farrell ended with a 27-yard field goal. The kick gave the Tigers a 3-0 lead over Catholic High School.

Facing third-and-13 from the Tigers 45 on their third possession, quarterback Hank Hooper faked an option pitch and kept for

Photo provided by Central High School
Michael Hall (36)

Photo provided by Central High School
Joe McCraney (50)

12 yards to the 33. A penalty on the Tigers moved the Rockets to the 19. Two plays later, Hooper gained 13 yards to the 1.

George Loftus broke through the defense for a touchdown, but a poor snap on the conversion attempt kept Catholic from adding an additional point. The Rockets took the lead, 6-3, with 4:53 left in the half.

The Tigers scored the winning touchdown with a minute remaining in the third quarter to end an 11-play, 70-yard drive.

The drive began after Ezekiel Vaughn recovered a fumble on the Central 20. Nutt passed the Tigers down the field, ending the march with a 14-yard touchdown to Farrell. Farrell converted the extra point in Central's 10-6 comeback victory.

Following another comeback victory the next week, 14-3 against Forrest City, the Tigers entered their game against Hot Springs as the state's No. 1 team in every poll. Central did not let the ranking go to its head, dominating the Trojans 31-7.

Nutt threw for 164 yards as a potent offensive attack finished with 365 total yards.

Although he didn't realize it until the next morning, Nutt was injured during the game.

Taking hit after hit on option plays, Nutt developed a deep thigh bruise and was ordered by team physician, Dr. John McCollough Smith, to miss at least one week for the area to heal.

Instead of using a young inexperienced backup quarterback, sophomore Dickey Nutt, Coach Cox decided to put one of his best athletes under the center. Farrell led Central to a 23-3 victory over West Memphis the next week and helped the Tigers to a 16-0 victory over North Little Rock Ole Main the following week. Although he passed for 66 yards against the Wildcats, Farrell's foot was the real star of the game. Farrell kicked three field goals, including a 48-yarder, while Robinson added 119 yards rushing on 17 carries.

Nutt returned the next week for a battle against El Dorado. In a light rain, Robinson and Michael Hall each scored a touchdown and Farrell kicked a 37-yard field goal. Central also added a safety after a bad snap by the punt team sailed out of the end zone. The 19-0 victory marked the Tigers' third shutout of the season.

Central needed three touchdown passes from Nutt and a 90-yard interception return by Mike Heiman to overcome a 12-0 deficit and beat North Little Rock Northeast 29-14. The next week wasn't quite as tough, though, as the Tigers won their homecoming game, 40-14, over Fort Smith Northside.

The following week, Central easily beat Little Rock Parkview 33-0. Farrell kicked field goals of 46 and 35 yards, while Hall, Robinson and Perry each rushed for a touchdown. Randall Mack and Nutt connected for a 33-yard touchdown as the Tigers handed the Patriots their first shutout in three years.

Central clinched at least a share of the AAAAA state championship with its victory over the Patriots. Little Rock Hall was the only team standing between a perfect season and outright title.

The Tigers struck quickly in the annual Thanksgiving Day game when Robinson returned a punt 60 yards for a touchdown. Farrell added the extra point for a 7-0 lead with 10:18 left in the first quarter.

Jimmy Smith recovered a fumble at the Hall 42 and returned it to the 6 to set up

Houston Nutt (14)

Robert Farrell

319

The 1975 defense allowed only 67 points in 12 games

state championship, their first since 1960. Central was the only team from a major high school in Arkansas to go undefeated in 1975. As a result, every major high school poll in the state declared the Tigers undisputed state champions.

The nucleus for the team included three seniors who were three-year starters: Nutt, Farrell and Vaughn. All three players signed scholarships with the University of Arkansas. Both Nutt and Farrell appeared on All-American teams selected by national magazines and sports organizations.

Nutt, who was considered one of the state's best quarterbacks in more than a decade, led Central to a 30-4-1 record during his three years as quarterback. He passed for more than 3,400 yards, including 1,059 yards and 15 touchdowns in 10 games during 1975.

On the receiving end of many of Nutt's touchdown passes was Farrell, who was named "Athlete of the Year" by the *Arkansas Gazette*. Farrell was one of the state's most versatile players, excelling at almost every position he played. Farrell not only led the AAAAA Conference in pass receptions, but he also was the leader in punting yardage and extra points kicked.

Vaughn, a linebacker, was the defensive leader and dubbed the "unsung hero of Central's team." Vaughn led the conference in several defensive categories, including tackles, sacks and fumble recoveries.

Central's next score. On second down, Nutt passed to Tolbert for a touchdown. Farrell converted the kick for a 14-0 lead.

Perry fumbled to set the stage for Hall's only touchdown. Greg Davis recovered the fumble at the Tigers 14 and returned it to the 4. It took three plays, but Gary Woods scored from the 1. A two-point conversion attempt was no good.

Smith recovered another fumble to set up Central's next score. A 31-yard drive ended when Nutt went in from the 1. Nutt passed for the game's last touchdown when he hit Tony Dunnick with a 23-yard pass.

A 26-6 victory over the Warriors gave the Tigers a 12-0-0 record and an outright

1975 TIGER SCHEDULE

Marianna 0	LRCH 39
* Pine Bluff 14	LRCH 20
* LR Catholic 6	LRCH 10
Forrest City 3	LRCH 14
Hot Springs 7	LRCH 31
West Memphis 3	LRCH 23
* NLR Ole Main 0	LRCH 16
* El Dorado 0	LRCH 19
* NLR Northeast 14	LRCH 29
* FS Northside 14	LRCH 40
* LR Parkview 0	LRCH 33
* LR Hall 6	LRCH 26

THE YEAR OF THE TIGER, PART II?

1976   7-4-0

Head Coach: Bernie Cox
Assistants: Gail Mote, Clyde Horton, A.C. Crater, Eddie Boone
Team Physician: Dr. John McCollough Smith

1976 LETTERMEN

Larry Baxter	James Falls	Bob McCoy	Reginald Perry
Jimmy Bennett	Roosevelt Gantt	Joe McCraney	Richard Richardson
Barry Brown	Roger Gibson	Jim McKenzie	Scott Sanders
Bill Bush	Bill Griffin	Teddy Morris	Harvey Scott
Homer Cherry	Rickey Hammond	Mike Nelson	Mike Sheppard
Robin Cline	Duke Hinerman	Mike Niggel	Bryan Smith
Ricky Cody	Michael Hudson	James Nunnley	Jimmy Smith
Jeff Connerly	John Jewell	Dickie Nutt	Wendell Smith
Marvin Davis	Roger Jolly	Donald Parker	Mike Sykes
Tony Dunnick	John Martin	Michael Perry	Ray Young

1976 MANAGERS
Charlie Barnhill
Paul Campbell
Dale Garner
Will Robinson
Mike Short

1976 ALL-STATE

Tony Dunnick	Michael Perry
Joe McCraney	Jimmy Smith
Teddy Morris	Ray Young

1976 ALL-STAR TEAM
Michael Perry
Jimmy Smith

Coming off an undefeated state championship, many in Little Rock had bumper stickers that labeled 1976 as "Year of the Tiger, Part II." Central hoped to live up to this billing when it met No. 2 Pine Bluff in the opening game.

Coach Bernie Cox and his Tigers entered their first game with only two returning lettermen on offense and a new quarterback, Roosevelt Gantt, who converted from running back. He led Central with 58 yards rushing against the Zebras.

Neither team scored during regulation (48 minutes), allowing the new overtime system to be instituted. Overtime, which began in 1976, gave each team four downs to score from the 10. If neither scored or the possessions ended in a tie, another session would be played until a winner was determined.

The Tigers won the toss in overtime and elected to play offense first. James Nunnley picked up 1 yard over right guard, and Gantt then completed a pass to Tony Dunnick for 6 yards to the 3. Gantt faked to Nunnley on the next play and ran around right end for the score. Mike Sykes converted the extra-point attempt for a 7-0 lead.

Ricky Cody and Ray Young sacked Pine Bluff's quarterback to end the game, giving unranked Central High a 7-0 victory over one of the state's top ranked teams.

The *Arkansas Democrat's* No. 5 team hosted the Catholic High Rockets the following week and found itself trailing early in the game. A muffed punt by Marvin Davis was recovered by Catholic's Steve Morris on the Tigers 21. Four plays later, Carl Easley scored on a 1-yard run for the game's first touchdown. Easley also converted the two-point conversion for an 8-0 lead with 1:03 left in the first quarter.

The lead only lasted 46 seconds, though. Catholic tried an onside kick, but Central recovered at midfield and needed only two plays to score. Tailback Michael

Photo provided by Central High School
Tony Dunnick (87)

Perry ran over right tackle and cut outside for a considerable gain. Perry then cut back inside toward the Catholic sideline and raced untouched for a 51-yard touchdown. Central attempted a two-point conversion, but Gantt was stopped just short of the goal line and the Tigers trailed 8-6 at halftime.

Central's defense dominated the game in the second half. After allowing the Rockets only 8 yards on their first possession, Cody recovered a fumble to end Catholic's next possession. Reginald Perry broke free for a 15-yard touchdown run on the next play. The conversion attempt was again unsuccessful, but Central took the lead, 12-8, with 4:15 remaining in the third quarter.

Three minutes into the fourth quarter, the Tigers scored again. Dunnick intercepted a Bobby Alexander pass and re-

Michael Perry (9)

quarter of a scoreless game, Sykes stood at his 5 in punt formation. As the ball was snapped, defensive end Carl Johnson broke through the line and blocked the kick. Donald Willis recovered at the 9, giving Hot Springs its best field position of the game.

Central's defense allowed only 3 yards in three plays, but Robert Gentry was able to kick a 21-yard field goal to beat the Tigers. The loss snapped Central's 16-game winning streak and was Cox's first loss at the school as head coach. The game also marked the first time Hot Springs Coach Bobby Hannon, a former assistant coach at Central High, beat his former team.

In West Memphis the next week, the Class AAA Blue Devils controlled the Tigers most of the game. Central, though, did score first on an 80-yard punt return by Michael Perry in the first quarter. West Memphis answered with a 60-yard drive that resulted in a 20-yard field goal by Stuart Hutchinson.

The Blue Devils later took the lead when a 70-yard drive ended in a 2-yard

turned it 48 yards for a touchdown. Sykes missed the extra-point attempt, but another score just minutes later by Donald Parker sealed the 25-8 victory for Central.

The Tigers had problems the next week when they traveled to Forrest City. Central only had 106 total yards and four first downs against a tough defense. The Mustangs struck first when Jim Abels kicked a 22-yard field goal midway through the second quarter.

It wasn't until the third quarter that the Tigers were able to score, and the points weren't produced by the offense. Michael Perry returned a punt 85 yards for the game's only touchdown and a 6-3 Central victory. Central's defense played well, holding Forrest City to only 59 yards rushing, with Mildton Norwood accounting for 57 yards.

The fourth-ranked Hot Springs Trojans traveled to Quigley Stadium to meet No. 5 Central High in what proved to be a defensive standoff that ended only after a mistake by the Tigers. Midway through the fourth

Donald Parker (45)

touchdown run by fullback Jody Looney. The conversion attempt failed and West Memphis led 9-6.

From the Blue Devils 22 with 4:15 left to play, Gantt dropped to pass. After being forced out of the pocket, he broke through the defense and ran untouched for a touchdown. Sykes converted the extra-point attempt and the Tigers escaped West Memphis 13-9.

Gantt was ill the following week and unable to play against North Little Rock Ole Main. Even with a backup quarterback, Central was still directed by a familiar name. Dickey Nutt, brother of former Central quarterback Houston Nutt, led the Tigers to a 7-0 victory over the Wildcats and won the starting job.

Ole Main's Arvis Jackson fumbled at the Central 29 after being hit hard by linebacker Jimmy Smith. Teddy Morris recovered for the Tigers, and it took nine plays for Central to score the winning touchdown.

Nutt relied on Parker for most of the drive's yardage, including the 7 yards needed for the touchdown. Sykes kicked the

Jimmy Smith (70)

Michael Perry (9)

extra point for a 7-0 lead and the victory. The game was highlighted by a Central defense that forced six turnovers.

Fourth-ranked Central traveled to El Dorado the following week where Nutt again found himself leading the offense. Having thrown for only 12 yards the previous game, Nutt passed the Tigers up and down the field against the south Arkansas team.

Central opened the game's scoring in the first quarter when Nunnley capped a short drive with a 5-yard run. Sykes converted the extra point for a 7-0 lead. El Dorado answered in the second quarter when quarterback Jerry Rushing scored from the 11. The extra-point attempt made it 7-7 before the Wildcats took the lead, 14-7, on Rushing's 33-yard run in the third quarter.

Nutt needed only 1:30 to tie the score, using his arm to take the Tigers 75 yards. More than half of the yardage came on a

44-yard touchdown pass to Dunnick. The game's winning play came next when Nutt connected with Dunnick again, this time for a two-point conversion. Central, once again coming from behind, won the conference game 15-14.

Few fans attended the Tigers' homecoming game against North Little Rock Northeast, which was played on a cold, windy and rainy night. Central's defense shined with eight sacks and four fumble recoveries. Only two of these turnovers, though, led to scores.

Cody recovered a fumble at the Northeast 33. On the Tigers' first offensive play, Nutt connected with Dunnick, who caught the pass at the 10 and was finally hit and brought down at the 2. Parker needed three attempts, but finally scored the touchdown. Sykes converted the extra point for a 7-0 lead with 43 seconds left in the first quarter.

The game's only other score was a safety, recorded when Central defensive end Larry Baxter sacked quarterback Richard Farr in the end zone. The 9-0 victory over the Chargers improved Central to 5-0-0 in the conference and 7-1-0 overall.

Mayo-Thompson Stadium in Fort Smith was the sight of the next game when the No. 3 Tigers met the No. 9 Northside Grizzlies. A 7-yard pass from Nutt to Gantt capped a 60-yard drive to begin the game's scoring. The extra-point attempt was wide, but the Tigers led 6-0 at halftime.

On their second possession of the second half, the Grizzlies fielded a punt at midfield and needed only six plays to tie the score. A 35-yard touchdown pass from Tim Bland to split end Barry East was good for six points. The extra-point attempt was blocked for a 6-6 tie.

Central answered just minutes later when Nutt passed to Dunnick for a 50-yard touchdown. A two-point conversion attempt failed when Northside forced Nutt into an incomplete pass. The Tigers, though, led 12-6.

With 4:05 left in the game, Fort Smith gained possession and drove 55 yards to tie the score. Sophomore halfback Phil Caldwell scored on his fourth try from the 1.

Norm Parrish converted the extra-point attempt with 58 seconds remaining for a 13-12 lead.

Central, though, continued to fight. After receiving the ensuing kickoff, Nutt passed the Tigers into scoring range until he was intercepted at the Northside 10. The Grizzlies ran out the clock to hand Central its first conference setback since losing to Little Rock Parkview in 1974.

The Tigers met those Parkview Patriots the following week at Quigley Stadium. The Patriots were undefeated and the state's top-ranked team, while No. 5 Central only had one league loss. The Tigers hoped to force a tie for the conference lead with a victory.

Nutt shined in the first half. He was 6 of 7 passing for 92 yards, including a 20-yard touchdown to Dunnick, and ran for a 1-yard touchdown. The defense was equally strong, helping Central to a 14-0 lead over the state's top team with just over five minutes remaining in the game.

Photo provided by Central High School
James Nunnley (32)

325

After taking over on downs at their 33, the Patriots reached the Central 29 before Jimmy Bonner connected with Don Atkins for a touchdown. There was a bad snap on the conversion attempt, but the lead was narrowed to 14-6.

Just minutes later, the Tigers were forced to punt and a 24-yard return gave Parkview possession on the Central 42. The Patriots needed only one play to score.

John Presley caught a Bonner pass at the 15 and fought off two defenders en route to the end zone. Bonner snuck his way over left tackle to score and convert the two-point conversion.

With the score 14-14 and 1:42 remaining in the game, the Patriots regained possession. Facing second-and-8 from the Tigers 37, Bonner passed to Darryl Mason for a 26-yard gain. Three running plays moved the Patriots to the 3 with only five seconds left to play. Kurt Nelson then kicked a 20-yard field for a 17-14 comeback victory.

The annual Thanksgiving Day game against Little Rock Hall High School ended on a spectacular play, only the play belonged to the Warriors.

The Tigers led 10-3 early in the fourth quarter when they faced fourth-and-19 from the Hall High 48. Bill Griffin punted to the Hall 20, but the ball bounced toward the original line of scrimmage. As the ball rolled past the 39, Griffin touched it to apparently end the play, and an official then threw his hat down on the field.

The official's action did not end the play as Hall High's Arthur Williams picked up the ball and ran full speed approximately 50 yards for a touchdown. Quarterback Greg Peters passed to Kevin Kullander for the two-point conversion and an 11-10 lead with 8:53 left in the game.

The score didn't change as the Warriors defeated Central for the first time in four years. Both teams finished the season in a tie for third place in the conference.

1976 TIGER SCHEDULE

*Pine Bluff 0	LRCH 7
*LR Catholic 8	LRCH 25
Forrest City 3	LRCH 6
Hot Springs 3	LRCH 0
West Memphis 9	LRCH 13
*NLR Ole Main 0	LRCH 7
*El Dorado 14	LRCH 15
*NLR Northeast 0	LRCH 9
*FS Northside 13	LRCH 12
*LR Parkview 17	LRCH 14
*LR Hall 11	LRCH 10

FINISHING AT .500

1977   6-6-0

Head Coach: Bernie Cox
Assistants: Mike Isom, Clyde Horton, A.C. Crater, Eddie Boone
Team Physician: Dr. John McCollough Smith

1977 LETTERMEN

George Adkins	Jackie Fells	Teddy Morris	Scott Sanders
Joe Baird	Milton Fields	Mike Nelson	Harvey Scott
J.C. Baker	Bill Griffin	Harold Noble	Robert Shephard
Charles Barfield	Steve Griffith	Allen Nooner	Chris Smith
Jeff Chatman	Rodney Hayes	Danny Nutt	Floyd Smith
Ricky Cody	Michael Hudson	John Pace	Wendell Smith
David Coleman	Roger Jolly	Donald Parker	Roger Thomas
Travis Coleman	Chi Chi Lee	Reginald Perry	Henry Topps
Jeff Connerly	Charlie Lewis	Gerald Pride	Greg Trotter
Joe Cook	James McCraney	Richard Richardson	William Walker
Keith Curry	Jerry McCraney	Vantriss Rideout	Dwain Washington
Tony Downs	Joe McCraney	Billy Ridgeway	Bert Zinamon
Sylvester Dunbar	Bruce McDaniel	Tony Ridgle	
Fred Dunnick	Jim McKenzie	Bobby Rudley	

1977 MANAGERS
Charlie Barnhill
Paul Campbell
Dale Garner
Will Robinson
Marcus Wiggins

1977 ALL-STATE
Joe McCraney
Teddy Morris

1977 ALL-STAR TEAM
Joe McCraney
Teddy Morris

Little Rock Central High School was celebrating the 50th anniversary at its present location when the Tigers hosted Forrest City at Quigley Stadium. With the score tied 7-7, Central took possession on its 38 with just over two minutes remaining in the game.

Late in the drive, Reginald Perry gained 8 yards to the Mustangs 38 with only 24 seconds remaining. On the next play, quarterback Scott Sanders rolled left and passed to John Pace. Kirk Sandifer, Forrest City's defensive back, tried for the interception by diving for the pass. Sandifer missed and Pace caught the ball near the sideline at the 18. With no other defenders around him, he easily ran into the end zone for the score.

Many of the 2,700 fans rushed the field, and because of the celebration no conversion kick was attempted. The Tigers defeated the defending AAA champion Mustangs 13-7.

An overflow crowd packed Jordan Stadium in Pine Bluff the next week as the *Arkansas Gazette's* third-ranked Zebras shut down the No. 6 Tigers in all phases of the game. A slow start in the first half ended in only a safety for the Zebras. Central's punter, Bill Griffin, recovered a wild snap before being tackled in the end zone with 7:59 left in the first quarter.

Tailback Harry Humphrey, who rushed for 146 yards on 17 carries, scored Pine Bluff's first touchdown on a 1-yard run. Quarterback David Richardson passed to Mike Johnston for a 7-yard touchdown in the fourth quarter. Both extra-point attempts were good to give the Zebras a 16-0 victory over the Tigers. The game marked the first time Coach Harold Tilley had defeated Little Rock Central in six years as Pine Bluff's head coach.

Catholic High School's Tony Paladino kicked a 30-yard field goal with seven sec-

Photo provided by Central High School
Reginald Perry (7)

onds remaining to defeat the Tigers 3-0. The second consecutive shutout loss dropped the Tigers' conference record to 0-2-0 and knocked them out of the statewide rankings.

After losing by a field goal against the Rockets, Central defeated Huntington High School of Shreveport by a field goal the following week. Jim McKenzie recovered a fumble by the Raiders at the Tigers 4 to end Shreveport's only scoring threat.

Just minutes later, Central recovered another fumble and began a 41-yard drive. Fullback Donald Parker took a pitch around right end and wasn't brought down until he

328

Photo provided by Central High School
Donald Parker (45)

reached the 11. From there, no progress was made and Coach Bernie Cox called on Greg Trotter to attempt a field goal. The 28-yard kick was good with 1:53 left in the first half and eventually led to 3-0 victory.

Even in victory, the Tigers did not play well. Central had only two first downs and 53 yards of offense. The Tigers also lost two fumbles and were penalized for 45 yards. However, they were able to score for the first time in three games.

Michael Hudson scored Central's only touchdown the next week when the Tigers traveled to Hot Springs to take on Bobby Hannon's Trojans. With 5:16 remaining in the third quarter, Hudson blocked a Hot Springs field-goal attempt and picked up the ball at the 22. He then outran the Trojans for a 78-yard touchdown. A two-point conversion attempt failed, leaving Hot Springs with a 10-6 lead. The Trojans added one more touchdown in their 16-6 victory.

The following week against West Memphis, Sanders completed a 38-yard touchdown pass to Parker and Hudson added a

safety to give the Tigers a 9-0 halftime lead. Danny Nutt debuted at quarterback during the second half, scoring on a 1-yard run and completing a 21-yard touchdown pass to Teddy Morris. Central's offense was much sharper in a 23-0 victory over the Blue Devils.

Parker began the scoring the next week against North Little Rock Ole Main, capping a two-play, 19-yard drive with a sweep around right end for a 7-yard touchdown run. Trotter converted the extra point for a 7-0 lead with 3:45 left in the first quarter.

Ole Main scored during the second quarter when Guy Sallis blocked Griffin's punt. The ball rolled into the end zone and was recovered by Greg Greer for a touchdown. A two-point conversion attempt failed when tailback Shawn Jones was hit hard at the 1.

With 6:49 left in the game, Parker received a Jones punt at the Central 39. Parker followed his blockers until he scored 61 yards later. Trotter's extra-point attempt was wide left, but the Tigers had a 13-6 lead.

Deep inside its territory, Central faced fourth down with only 43 seconds remaining. Coach Cox ordered Nutt to step out of the end zone for a safety to avoid a blocked punt.

The plan worked as the Tigers were able to hold on for a 13-8 victory over the Wildcats.

Quigley Stadium was the site of Central's next game, a battle with El Dorado. The Wildcats recovered a fumble at the Tigers 34 and were unable to move on their first three plays. On fourth down, Pete Parks dropped to punt and faked a reverse handoff. Parks then threw toward the sideline and connected with Joe Jackson for a 31-yard touchdown. Parks added the extra point for a 7-0 lead with 4:53 left in the half.

As the fourth quarter began, Joe McCraney blocked a Parks punt. Tony Downs caught the ball at the 1 and stepped into the end zone for Central's first score of the night. The extra-point attempt failed and El Dorado led 7-6.

Late in the game, the Tigers regained possession at the Wildcats 36. Nutt quickly led Central to the game-winning touchdown.

On the sixth play of the series, Nutt found Morris in the corner of the end zone for a 7-yard touchdown pass. Trotter kicked the extra point in the 13-7 victory.

Leading North Little Rock Northeast 10-8 with 4:30 remaining in the game, Central had possession at the Chargers 27. Nutt, however, was intercepted by Buford Johnson, who returned it to the Northeast 32. The Chargers only needed seven plays to cover 68 yards for the game-winning touchdown.

Dennis Whitlock passed to Chuck Boaz for a 28-yard touchdown in a 14-10 victory, Northeast's first over Central in school history.

Behind Trotter's three field goals and Perry's 146 yards on 25 carries, Central narrowly escaped the Fort Smith Grizzlies during the Tigers' homecoming game at Quigley Stadium. Travis Coleman scored from the 4 and Trotter added an extra point in a 16-14 conference victory.

Central High School was the visiting team in Quigley Stadium the following week when Little Rock Parkview celebrated homecoming by dominating the Tigers. The Patriots had touchdown drives of 80, 73, 55 and 30 yards. Darryl Mason scored on a 1-yard run and a 35-yard touchdown reception, while Mike Linebarier scored from the 1 and 7.

McKenzie was the only bright spot for Central as he recovered a fumbled option pitch and returned it 28 yards for the Tigers' only score. Parkview beat Central 30-6.

The unranked Tigers played their next game for pride when they met No. 1 Little Rock Hall High School on Thanksgiving Day. The Warriors, who were tied for the conference lead with Little Rock Parkview and Pine Bluff, needed a victory to share the conference and state championship.

Photo provided by Central High School
Danny Nutt (9)

Quarterback Greg Peters was 9 of 14 passing for 105 yards, including a 17-yard touchdown to Bobby Cummins. Peters also scored on a 1-yard run to give Hall High a 13-0 halftime lead.

Central finally scored with 1:22 left on a 10-yard pass from Nutt to Morris. Nutt then completed a two-point conversion pass to Griffin to narrow the Warriors' lead.

The holiday contest was not decided until Nutt was sacked for a 5-yard loss on the game's last play. The 13-8 victory by Coach C.W. Keopple's team gave it a share of the state championship with Pine Bluff and Parkview. The Associated Press named the Pine Bluff Zebras its No. 1 team in the final poll.

1977 TIGER SCHEDULE

Forrest City 7	LRCH 13
*Pine Bluff 16	LRCH 0
*LR Catholic 3	LRCH 0
Huntington of Shreveport, LA 0	LRCH 3
Hot Springs 16	LRCH 6
West Memphis 0	LRCH 23
*NLR Ole Main 8	LRCH 13
*El Dorado 7	LRCH 13
*NLR Northeast 14	LRCH 10
*FS Northside 14	LRCH 16
*LR Parkview 30	LRCH 6
*LR Hall 13	LRCH 8

UNRANKED TO NUMBER ONE

1978   9-0-3

Head Coach: Bernie Cox
Assistants: Mike Isom, Clyde Horton, A.C. Crater, Eddie Boone
Team Physician: Dr. John McCollough Smith

1978 LETTERMEN

Lance Alworth	Marcus Elliott	James McCraney	Bobby Rudley
J.C. Baker	Mark Fields	Jerry McCraney	Chris Smith
Charles Barfield	Milton Fields	Bruce McDaniel	Floyd Smith
David Coleman	Keith Gibson	Danny Nutt	Wendell Smith
Joe Cook	Ken Gray	John Pace	Roosevelt Thompson
Keith Curry	Steve Griffin	Donald Parker	Greg Trotter
Tony Downs	Steve Griffith	Gary Patillo	Alan Turner
John Doyle	Ruben Harris	Roland Pennington	Dishongh White
Sylvester Dunbar	Rodney Hayes	Gerald Pride	Bert Zinamon
Byron Dunnick	Mark Horton	Richard Richardson	
Fred Dunnick	Kenneth Martin	Tony Ridgle	

1978 MANAGERS
Chris Brewer
James Patton
Jeff Smith
Marcus Wiggins

1978 ALL-STATE

J.C. Baker	Sylvester Dunbar	Tony Ridgle
David Coleman	Fred Dunnick	Bobby Rudley
Keith Curry	Richard Richardson	Bert Zinamon

Coach Bernie Cox and his Tigers returned only seven starters from a team that finished 6-6-0 overall. With this in mind, Arkansas sports writers did not place Central in any preseason polls. The Tigers, though, soon worked their way into the rankings and surprised many people.

Gerald Pride rushed for 165 yards and one touchdown to go along with Tony Ridgle's two touchdowns in a 24-0 opening victory over Forrest City. The outcome gave the Tigers much needed confidence for their matchup against No. 2 Pine Bluff.

Central struck first with 5:51 left in the first half. David Coleman tackled Pine Bluff's punter, Matthew Whitner, in the end zone for a safety and a 2-0 lead.

The lead held up until Central's Donald Parker fumbled on the Zebras 24 in the third quarter. Tommy Atchley returned it 76 yards for a Pine Bluff touchdown. Jerry Owen kicked the extra point for a 7-2 lead.

Backed up at its 46, Central regained the lead when Danny Nutt passed to Fred Dunnick at the Zebras 25. Dunnick was well behind the secondary and easily made it into the end zone. Nutt's two-point conversion pass to John Pace was incomplete, but the 8-7 score lasted long enough to give the Tigers an upset victory over one of Arkansas' highly rated teams.

Central, now ranked No. 3 by the *Arkansas Gazette* and No. 4 in the *Arkansas Democrat*, needed only one of its two touchdowns the following week to defeat Catholic High School. Just after the second quarter began, the Tigers had possession on their 10. Dunnick ran a post pattern and caught a pass from Nutt at the Central 40. Dunnick had no problem outrunning the defense to complete a 90-yard touchdown play and give the Tigers a 6-0 lead.

Photo provided by Central High School
Rodney Hayes (30)

Ridgle added another touchdown with a short run into the end zone to put Central up 12-0. Dennis Nutt missed both conversion attempts, but 12 points was plenty for Central's third victory of the season.

The next week at Shreveport Huntington, Central scored on a 2-yard run by Anthony Green, a short run by Ridgle and touchdown passes of 41 and 34 yards from Danny Nutt to Dunnick. The victory gave the Tigers a 4-0-0 record and a No. 2 state ranking.

After tying the Hot Springs Trojans 0-0, Central traveled to West Memphis to take on the Blue Devils. Kenneth Martin recovered a West Memphis fumble at the Blue Devils 7 with 8:41 left in the half. Ridgle eventually scored from the 1. Greg Trotter added the extra point for a 7-0 lead.

With 7:41 left in the half, Nutt passed to Dunnick for a 25-yard touchdown. Trotter converted his second extra-point attempt for a 14-0 lead. Nutt found Dunnick again in the third quarter, this time for a 20-yard touchdown play and a 20-0 lead.

The Blue Devils capitalized on a Frank Holbrook fumble recovery at the Central 19. The West Memphis touchdown came three plays later when Tim Root dove into the end zone from the 1.

Pride completed the game's scoring with a short run from the 1. Trotter added the extra point and the Tigers won 27-6 for their fifth victory.

Following a 23-6 victory over North Little Rock Ole Main and a 14-14 tie with El Dorado, Ridgle ran Central past North Little Rock Northeast with 137 yards rushing on 23 carries and one touchdown.

Photo provided by Central High School
Tony Ridgle (49)

Coleman recovered a Northeast fumble to set up a 33-yard scoring run by Ridgle to cap a 70-yard, 13-play drive.

A 14-yard touchdown run by Pride and 1 of 2 extra-point attempts by Roland Pennington gave Central a 13-7 victory over No. 8 North Little Rock Northeast. The Chargers' only score came with 25 seconds remaining in the game when quarterback Steve Murdock passed to Brad Crow in the flats. Crow immediately pitched back to Steve Arnold, who ran into the end zone. The play covered 73 yards, but was not enough to defeat the Tigers.

In Fort Smith the next week, Central scored first when Pennington kicked a 21-yard field goal to end a 61-yard drive that stalled at the Northside 4. The Tigers increased their lead in the second quarter when Ridgle capped a 59-yard drive with a 2-yard run. Pennington added the extra point, increasing the lead to 10-0 with 1:46 left in the half.

Phil Caldwell answered on the ensuing kickoff when he ran along his left sideline for a 98-yard touchdown. The extra point narrowed Central's lead to 10-7.

The Tigers received the second-half kickoff and drove 64 yards for another touchdown. Two passes from Nutt to Pride covered most of the yardage, and Ridgle ended the drive with a 5-yard touchdown run. Pennington added the extra point for a 17-7 lead.

Mike Dickerson recovered a Central fumble at the Northside 40 with less than three minutes to play in the game. Eventually, a 16-yard pass from Ike Jackson to Cooper McCraney gave Northside its second touchdown. It converted the extra-point attempt but fell 17-14.

Quigley Stadium was full the next week when No. 1 Little Rock Parkview and No. 2 Little Rock Central battled for a possible state title. The Tigers looked in control early as they took the opening kickoff and drove 80 yards for a touchdown.

Central's yardage came on Ridgle's powerful running up the middle and Pride's quick runs around the end. Ridgle capped an 18-play drive that consumed 7:49 with a short run into the end zone. Pennington kicked the extra point for a 7-0 lead in the first quarter.

Defensive coordinator Mike Isom had his team prepared to defend the Patriots. Central's defense, led by nose guard Richard Richardson, controlled running backs Duke Scott and Jerome Sims, as well as highly regarded quarterback Drake Hawkins.

It was Central's offense that made the game's crucial mistake.

Late in the third quarter, Central took over at the Patriots 45 following a punt. On third down, Nutt passed for a first down to tight end Wendell Smith at the 33. The next play proved costly for the Tigers as Pride fumbled at the 35. Melvin Floyd scooped up the ball and returned it 65 yards for a Parkview touchdown. The extra point, by Kyle Perkins made it 7-7 with 10:28 remaining in the game.

Neither team threatened to score again, resulting in a 7-7 tie. The outcome guaran-

Photo provided by Central High School
Fred Dunnick (88)

teed Little Rock Parkview, 6-0-2 in the conference, at least a share of the league and state title. Central (5-0-2) still had another league game remaining, its championship hopes on the line during the annual Thanksgiving Day matchup with Little Rock Hall.

The first half of the holiday game was dominated by the Tigers. During the first 24 minutes, Central's defense allowed only one first down and 15 yards of total offense. An 11-yard run by Rodney Hayes, a 26-yard field goal by Pennington and a 52-yard pass from Nutt to Dunnick put the Tigers up 17-0 at halftime.

Hall High would fight back in the final half. Unable to run, Coach C.W. Keopple opened up his offense by utilizing the Shotgun. The Warriors began the fourth quarter with possession on their 23. Quarterback George Loss Jr. continued to connect with Doug Roberts, Mikel Kullander and Clay

Photo provided by Central High School
1978 varsity cheerleaders

Photo provided by Central High School
Danny Nutt

Hathorne in a 77-yard drive that ended with a short touchdown run by Bryan Salley. Alan Hope, in at quarterback, ran around right end for the two-point conversion to bring Hall High within 17-8 with 7:11 left in the game.

The Warriors forced Central to punt on its next series and regained possession at the Tigers 46. Loss again led his team down the field, passing for approximately 24 yards before Salley scored from the 1. Ricky Borkins attempted a sweep around the end for two points, but Central's Keith Curry caught him at the 2.

Down 17-14 with 2:14 left to play, Hall High attempted an onside kick. The kick was successful as Michael Cummins recovered at the Tigers 41. On first down, Loss tried to force a pass to a covered receiver. It was intercepted by Todd Vardaman to end Hall's upset bid.

Nutt and the Central offense ran out the clock and celebrated the second state title under Cox. It was Cox's second undefeated state championship team in four seasons at the school and earned him Arkansas High School Coach of the Year in 1978.

Central shared the AAAAA and state title with Little Rock Parkview. But The Associated Press named the Tigers its No. 1 team and overall state champions.

1978 TIGER SCHEDULE

Forrest City 0	LRCH 24
*Pine Bluff 7	LRCH 8
*LR Catholic 0	LRCH 12
Huntington High of Shreveport, LA 0	LRCH 27
Hot Springs 0	LRCH 0
West Memphis 6	LRCH 27
*NLR Ole Main 6	LRCH 23
*El Dorado 14	LRCH 14
*NLR Northeast 7	LRCH 13
*FS Northside 14	LRCH 17
*LR Parkview 7	LRCH 7
*LR Hall 14	LRCH 17

1979 TURKEY BOWL: WINNER TAKES ALL

1979   9-1-1

Head Coach: Bernie Cox
Assistants: Mike Isom, Clyde Horton, Ray Gillespie, Raymond Scogin, Eddie Boone
Team Physician: Dr. John McCollough Smith

1979 LETTERMEN

Kenneth Alexander	Olins Dunnick	Tracy Korte	Rob Popovitch
Alonzo Bennett	Marcus Elliott	Scott McCord	Tony Ridgle
Jeff Bizzell	Brad Ellis	Jerry McCraney	Roosevelt Thompson
Andy Bollinger	Mark Fields	Mike McGibbony	Greg Trotter
Marc Breedlove	Milton Fields	Danny Nutt	Alan Turner
Mike Breedlove	Keith Gibson	Dennis Nutt	Larry Weekley
Harry Coleman	Steve Griffith	John Palmer	Dishongh White
Robert Cortinez	Ruben Harris	Gary Patillo	Bert Zinamon
Bobby Duckworth	Rodney Hayes	Roland Pennington	
Byron Dunnick	Mark Horton	Paul Phillips	

1979 MANAGERS
Chris Brewer
Andrew Clark
James Patton
Marcus Wiggins

1979 ALL-STATE
Milton Fields
Rodney Hayes
Danny Nutt
Tony Ridgle
Bert Zinamon

1979 ALL-STAR TEAM
Milton Fields
Bert Zinamon

Coach Bernie Cox returned several starters from an undefeated state championship team. Because of this, every major high school poll in Arkansas ranked the Tigers No. 1 to open the season. The Associated Press, though, picked Pine Bluff to beat Central in the Tigers' season opener.

Unable to find an opponent for Week 1, Central used the extra time to prepare for the No. 2 Zebras. In front of a capacity crowd at Pine Bluff's Jordan Stadium, Central's defense, led by linebackers Milton Fields and Bert Zinamon, dominated early, forcing the Zebras to fumble on the game's second play. Alan Turner recovered at the Pine Bluff 22.

The Zebras would not allow Central into the end zone. Three plays after taking possession, Roland Pennington was forced to attempt a 34-yard field goal. The kick was long enough, but wide right and Pine Bluff escaped the early threat.

Photo provided by Central High School
Coach Bernie Cox and the Tigers

Central regained possession moments later when Marc Breedlove intercepted a Feryl Jordan pass at the Zebras 24. Danny Nutt passed to Byron Dunnick for 18 yards, and three plays later Tony Ridgle scored on a 3-yard run. Pennington added the extra point for a 7-0 lead with 2:09 left in the first quarter.

Greg Trotter's only bad kick of the night, a 13-yard punt, gave Pine Bluff possession at the Tigers 30. The tough Central defense held the Zebras out of the end zone for seven plays before Danny Cox kicked a 28-yard field goal with 6:46 left in the half.

Dunnick received the second-half kickoff and returned it to his 32, setting up Central's second touchdown drive. Mark Fields gained 2 yards on first down. An incomplete pass by Nutt gave the Tigers third down from the 34. On the next play, Nutt rolled right and pitched to Fields just before being tackled. Fields, who finished with 149 yards rushing, cut back inside and raced 66 yards for a touchdown. Pennington added the extra point for a 14-3 lead with 10:49 left in the third quarter.

The remainder of the game featured two great defenses keeping the opponent out of the end zone. Central's two touchdowns were more than enough for a season-opening victory over Pine Bluff.

Following a 43-6 victory over Sapulpa, Okla., the Tigers hosted Little Rock McClellan High School at Quigley Stadium. Central's defense held the Lions to minus-15 yards rushing and 66 yards of total offense in a 20-0 victory.

The offense was highlighted by Ridgle's scoring runs of 5 yards and 3 yards and Mark Fields' 78-yard scoring run. Pen-

The Tigers practice during two-a-days

nington converted 2 of 3 extra-point attempts in the conference victory.

At War Memorial Stadium the next week, Catholic High's Gene Smith burned the Central secondary by completing 13 of 25 passes for 227 yards. The Tigers, though, scored first when Ridgle ran five times for 72 yards, scoring on a 4-yard run with 10 minutes left in the half. Pennington kicked the extra point for a 7-0 lead.

After the ensuing kickoff, it only took the Rockets three plays, including two pass completions by Smith, to get into the end zone. Catholic High attempted a two-point conversion, but the pass by Smith was incomplete.

On Central's second play of the third quarter, Nutt and Ridgle fumbled a handoff and it was recovered by Catholic's Clay Patterson at the Tigers 32. Smith and Shy Anderson ended the short drive when they connected for a 17-yard touchdown with 8:08 left in the quarter. Smith attempted to pass for two points, but he was sacked by Ruben Harris before finding an open receiver.

In the fourth quarter, Nutt was hit hard by Patterson as he prepared to pass. The hit caused Nutt to fumble and Steve Gattis recovered for Catholic High at the Tigers 44. The Rockets reached the 5 before Central's Kenneth Alexander intercepted a Smith pass at the goal line and returned it 77 yards to the Catholic 23.

Nutt then passed to Dunnick in the back of the end zone for a 12-yard touchdown.

Another pass from Nutt to Dunnick was good for two points and a 15-12 lead with 3:06 left in the game. The victory kept the Tigers undefeated and the Rockets winless, 0-5-0.

Central's next game was against one of Tennessee's top teams, Washington High School of Memphis. Both schools entered 4-0-0, but the Tigers beat the Warriors 17-6. Central scored on short runs by Rodney Hayes and Keith Gibson, as well as a 19-yard field goal by Pennington. The Tigers held Washington to 15 yards rushing.

Defense was all that kept Central in its next game against North Little Rock Ole Main. An upset, of sorts, occurred when the Tigers were unable to score a touchdown. Drives stalled at the 15, 8 and 1 before Pennington attempted a 17-yard field goal with 2:07 remaining in the game.

Pennington's kick was wide left, leaving the game scoreless and keeping Central from winning its sixth game. The tie dropped the Tigers to No. 2 in the *Arkansas Gazette* poll and to 5-0-1 overall.

Central's next opponent, El Dorado, was led by first-year head coach Donnie Cox, formerly Little Rock Parkview's offensive coordinator and the younger brother of Bernie Cox. The matchup was the first

Robert Cortinez (21) and Milton Fields (45)

between the two brothers as head coaches.

Gibson led Central past the Wildcats with 117 yards rushing and two touchdowns in a 25-7 victory that moved the Tigers back to No. 1 in the *Arkansas Gazette* rankings. Gibson added another touchdown the next week, Milton Fields returned an interception 25 yards for a touchdown and Hayes had 47-yard punt return for a touchdown in a 21-3 victory over the North Little Rock Northeast Chargers.

Two touchdowns by Gibson (runs of 64 yards and 2 yards), combined with a 19-yard touchdown pass from Nutt to Olins Dunnick helped Central beat Fort Smith Northside 20-0. The Tigers dominated the Grizzlies, holding them to 49 yards of total offense and gaining 306 yards. Gibson was the leading rusher with 109 yards, followed by Ridgle with 99 yards.

The victory set the stage for an important battle the next week with No. 3 Little Rock Parkview. Played in front of a large crowd at Quigley Stadium, the game was critical for both teams to remain in contention for the league title.

The Patriots scored the game's first points after a Parkview punt bounced off Alexander and was recovered by Algray Pettus at the Tigers 46. Carnell Finley's bursts up the middle and Carl Lowe's

Photo provided by Central High School
Danny Nutt (9) and the Tiger offense

sweeps around the end moved Parkview to the 13. The Patriots were forced to attempt a 30-yard field goal. Lowe's kick was good to give Parkview a 3-0 lead with 6:22 left in the half.

Central received the ensuing kickoff and put together a 74-yard drive that was capped by a 19-yard pass from Nutt to Byron Dunnick. Pennington's kick gave the Tigers a 7-3 lead with 39 seconds left in the half.

Hayes returned a second-half punt 23 yards to the Patriots 26, setting up Central's next score. Seven plays later, Hayes took a draw play up the middle for the touchdown. Pennington failed to convert the extra-point attempt, but the Tigers were in control 13-3. Central went on to win and set up a Thanksgiving Day showdown between the state's top two teams, No. 1 Central and No. 2 Little Rock Hall High School.

The Warriors were led by a great passing quarterback, Jay Gadberry, and five dependable receivers in Reggie Watkins, Ricky Johnson, Ralph Hopes, James Smith and Benton Williams. Their running game was strong behind tailback Ricky Borkins and fullback Andre Crawford. Hall High was averaging 18.3 points per game and allowing only 6.7 points per game.

Photo provided by Central High School
Tony Ridgle (33) and the Tiger offense

Central was averaging 18.8 points per game and allowing only 5.7 points per game. The defense was one of the most feared in the state, possessing a "major college look, size, and quickness," according to the Nov. 23 edition of the *Arkansas Gazette*. The defense was led by Zinamon and Milton Fields at linebacker, Gary Patillo and Tracy Korte at end and linemen Jerry McCraney, Turner and Harris. These players prided themselves in allowing only 357 yards rushing and only one rushing touchdown in the previous 10 games.

More than 10,000 fans watched this "Turkey Bowl." Hall received an early break when Tyree Layne recovered a fumble at the Central 23. On second down, Gadberry passed to Johnson for 20 yards to the 3. But on the next play, Crawford fumbled and Harris recovered at the 1 with 2:37 left in the first quarter.

Central was then forced to punt. The Warriors took possession at the Tigers 36, setting the stage for the game's first score. Borkins broke free into the Central secondary for a 20-yard gain before being tackled by Hayes. Hall High's offense was unable to get into the end zone on the next three plays, forcing it to attempt a 25-yard field goal. Todd Vardaman's kick was perfect, giving the Warriors a 3-0 lead with 8:15 left in the half.

The Tigers received the second-half kickoff, but were again unable to move. A 25-yard punt by Trotter gave Hall High possession at its 28. Johnson ran 26 yards on a reverse. Borkins then burst up the middle for 7 yards. Crawford ran off left tackle for 10 yards to put the Warriors within scoring distance. Borkins scored just minutes later on a 10-yard run. Jim Wheeler converted the extra point for a 10-0 lead with 6:07 left in the third quarter.

On Central's next possession, Nutt was intercepted by Reginald Hood at the Tigers 48. Originally, the drive ended with a punt at midfield. However, roughing the kicker on Zinamon gave Hall High new life at the Central 35. Crawford eventually scored from the 1. Wheeler added the extra point with 4:33 remaining in the game, giving the Warriors a 17-0 victory and the state championship.

Arkansas' top-rated defense now belonged to Hall High School, which allowed only 131 total yards. Central's defense crumbled, allowing 230 rushing yards and two rushing touchdowns.

The game marked Central's first loss since a 13-8 upset by Hall High in 1977. Central finished runner-up in AAAAA and No. 3 in the state's final overall polls.

1979 TIGER SCHEDULE

*Pine Bluff 3	LRCH 14
Supulpa, Oklahoma 6	LRCH 43
*LR McClellan 0	LRCH 20
LR Catholic 12	LRCH 15
Washington High of Memphis 6	LRCH 17
*NLR Ole Main 0	LRCH 0
*El Dorado 7	LRCH 25
*NLR Northeast 3	LRCH 21
*FS Northside 0	LRCH 20
*LR Parkview 3	LRCH 13
*LR Hall 17	LRCH 0

A NEW DECADE, ANOTHER CHAMPIONSHIP

1980　　　9-0-2

Head Coach: Bernie Cox
Assistants: Mike Isom, Clyde Horton, Ray Gillespie, Raymond Scogin, Eddie Boone
Team Physician: Dr. John McCollough Smith

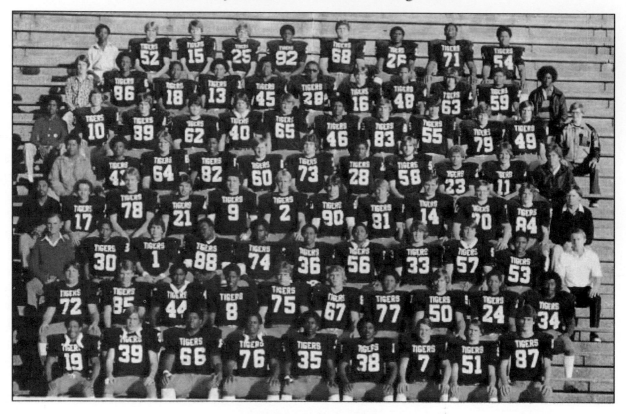

1980 LETTERMEN

Will Allen	Olins Dunnick	Chris Lane	Chris Shead
Sammy Baker	Marcus Elliott	Terry Mack	Joey Smith
Jeff Bizzell	Brad Ellis	Scott McCord	John Steed
Chip Blenden	Mark Fields	Mike McGibbony	Todd Tesney
Marc Breedlove	Michael George	David Moore	Jim VonSteen
Harry Coleman	Keith Gibson	Rich Morgan	Carl Williams
Tony Cook	Mike Hale	Jimmy Nowden	Mark Williams
Robert Cortinez	Mark Horton	Dennis Nutt	Clint Witcher
Elie Curry	Ben Hughes	John Palmer	Robert Yates
Chuck Dinger	Bennie Jackson	Gary Patillo	
Byron Dunnick	Albert James	Rob Popovitch	

1980 MANAGERS
Chris Brewer
Ricky Dowd
Anthony Downs
Thomas Stewart
Anthony Wilson

1980 ALL-AMERICAN
Marcus Elliott

1980 ALL-STATE

Will Allen	Scott McCord
Byron Dunnick	Jimmy Nowden
Marcus Elliott	Dennis Nutt
Mark Fields	Gary Patillo
Mark Horton	Rob Popovitch

1980 ALL-STAR TEAM
Byron Dunnick
Marcus Elliott

Photo provided by Central High School
Byron Dunnick (35)

Little Rock Central opened the new decade as the *Arkansas Democrat's* No. 4 team. The Tigers, who lost only one game during the 1979 season, returned two starters from the previous season's dominating defense. Coach Bernie Cox and his staff were charged with rebuilding a defensive unit that could compete in Arkansas' largest classification.

After being idle during the first playing date in 1979, Coach Cox was able to schedule a game with Texas High School from Texarkana, Texas. Central got off to a great start when it received the opening kickoff and marched 61 yards for the game's first score. The 13-play drive included a holding penalty, a delay penalty and a 7-yard scoring run from tailback Mark Fields. Chuck Dinger converted the extra-point attempt for a 7-0 lead with 5:28 left in the first quarter.

Midway through the second quarter, a Clint Witcher fumble was recovered by Texarkana's Ricky Cooks to give the Texas team possession on its 37. From the Tigers 26, fullback Randy Higgins exploded through the defense for a touchdown. The extra-point attempt was good to make the score 7-7.

The Tigers had two possessions late in the game to try and break the tie. The first ended when an incomplete pass by quarterback Dennis Nutt turned the ball over on downs. Central was given its second chance when linebacker Will Allen intercepted a pass at the Texarkana 33. On first down, however, a Nutt pass was intercepted by Troy Burkins and returned to the Tigers 40.

Nathan Jones moved Texas to the Central 23 after gaining 17 yards on a draw play. Following an incomplete pass, Texarkana was forced to attempt a 40-yard field goal with five seconds remaining in the game. The middle of Central's defense broke through to block Jerry Copeland's attempt and preserve a 7-7 tie.

Quigley Stadium was the site of Central's next game against Pine Bluff. The Zebras struck first when Danny Bradley passed to Charles McLarty for a 52-yard touchdown. Erick Grant's conversion kick gave Pine Bluff a 7-0 lead with 13 seconds left in the first half.

The Tigers were unable to score during the first half, even though they were inside the Zebras 20 three times. On their first possession of the second half, they had no problem moving 78 yards for a score. Central did receive a scare on the drive's last play when Keith Gibson took a handoff at the 4, was met hard at the line of scrimmage and fumbled into the end zone. Fortunately, Byron Dunnick was able to recover for Central's first touchdown. Dinger's extra point made it 7-7.

Pine Bluff answered with an 11-yard touchdown pass by Bradley and extra point by Grant. But Pine Bluff was stopped on its next drive when Robert Cortinez intercepted a Bradley pass to end the third quarter. Eighteen plays later, the Tigers scored when Fields went over right tackle.

With 4:31 left in the game, Coach Cox decided to go for the tie by kicking the extra point. A high snap, though, forced Nutt to abort the kick and roll to his left in an attempt for two points. Nutt found Brad Ellis in the end zone for a two-point conversion that ended up being the game-winning play. Central defeated the Zebras 15-14.

Photo provided by Central High School
Mark Fields (38)

Fields scored on a 16-yard run, a 76-yard punt return and a 94-yard kickoff return to help the Tigers escape Greenville, Miss., in Quigley Stadium the following week. Nutt completed touchdown passes of 17 yards to Olins Dunnick and 11 yards to Mark Horton. Dinger converted 4 of 5 extra-point attempts in a 34-28 victory over the Hornets.

Another offensive explosion occurred the next week as Nutt completed 11 of 16 passes for 150 yards and two touchdowns against Little Rock McClellan. Nutt connected with Byron Dunnick for touchdowns of 27 and 9 yards, and Fields, who rushed for 117 yards, capped a 61-yard drive with a 5-yard run. Chris Lane's 51-yard interception return added another touchdown. Dinger converted all four extra-point attempts. The 28-12 victory over the Lions gave the Tigers a No. 2 ranking.

Nutt passed for 195 yards, completing touchdown passes of 50 and 34 yards to Olins Dunnick and 46 and 37 yards to Byron Dunnick, the next week against Little Rock Catholic. Witcher added a 1-yard scoring run and Dinger kicked five extra points in a 35-20 victory over the Rockets.

Photo provided by Central High School
Clint Witcher (33)

A 24-0 victory over North Little Rock Ole Main gave Central the state's top ranking before traveling to El Dorado. The unranked Wildcats snapped an 18-game losing streak the previous week with an upset over Little Rock Parkview. El Dorado's second-year head coach, Donnie Cox, hoped for another major upset, this time against his older brother's top-ranked team.

The Tigers jumped to an early lead when Nutt passed to Olins Dunnick for a 38-yard touchdown with 5:39 left in the first quarter. The Wildcats answered on their next possession when they used 10 plays to drive 61 yards. Andra Bailey scored from the 11 as time expired in the first quarter. The extra point made it 7-7.

The game-winning drive covered 73 yards in 14 plays and ended with a 7-yard pass from Nutt to Horton. Witcher added another score on a 1-yard run to cap a 39-yard drive that began when Central recovered a fumble. Dinger's extra points gave the Tigers a 21-7 victory over El Dorado.

Behind two touchdown passes from Nutt to Horton, Central defeated North Little Rock Northeast 20-0 before traveling to Fort Smith for a battle of conference leaders. The Grizzlies took the opening kickoff and drove 62 yards before Tyrone Morris fumbled the ball into the end zone. John Steed recovered for the Tigers to give them possession at the 20.

Photo provided by Central High School
Olins Dunnick (88)

It took seven plays for Central to drive the needed distance, scoring on a short pass from Nutt to Byron Dunnick. Dinger added the extra point for a 7-0 lead with 2:57 left in the first quarter.

The remainder of the game was dominated by defense until a Central mistake late in the fourth quarter changed the momentum of the game. Nutt and one of his running backs fumbled on an attempted handoff and it was recovered by Robert Conine at the Northside 15.

A long pass from Ike Jackson to Herb Alston on first down moved Northside to the Central 39. Three plays later from the 28, Jackson connected with Morris, who raced down the sideline before being tackled at the 1 by Fields. Jackson then snuck behind right guard for the touchdown.

Northside Coach Ron Toothaker decided to go for the tie rather than chance a two-point conversion attempt. Randy Harriman's extra point with 1:15 left to play left the teams in a 7-7 tie.

Because of the tie, the Grizzlies earned a half-game lead over the Tigers in the conference standings. Central needed to beat its two remaining opponents to win a share of the league title. A tie or a loss to either team would give Northside an outright championship.

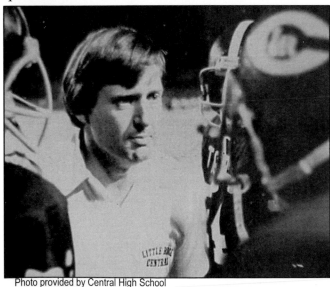

Photo provided by Central High School
Coach Mike Isom, defensive coordinator

345

The Tigers passed their first test the following week with a 13-0 victory over Little Rock Parkview. Fields rushed for 119 yards, Gibson 106 in a contest that featured Central's running attack instead of its normal passing game.

One more hurdle needed to be cleared before the Tigers could claim their 28th state title and third under Coach Cox. Fifth-ranked Little Rock Hall High School was not a contender for the conference or state title with an 8-2-0 record, but wanted nothing more than to spoil the season for the state's No. 1 team.

Fans who packed Quigley Stadium on Thanksgiving Day were met with cold temperatures and 4 inches of snow. The weather played a key factor in the game as neither team was able to move on the ground. On many occasions, the Warriors punted on third down because of the weather conditions, as well as to keep Central backed up in its territory.

With 7:57 left in the third quarter, the Tigers received a Hall High punt at their 24. Fields and Gibson each carried once to the 36. Following a motion penalty, Nutt dropped into the Shotgun formation and fired a pass to Horton for a 13-yard gain. Fields then bulled his way up the middle for another first down at the 46.

Nutt continued to stay in the Shotgun and connected with Olins Dunnick for a first down at the Warriors 37. After an incompletion on first down, Nutt passed to Byron Dunnick for a 16-yard gain. Two plays later, Nutt hit Fields for a 17-yard touchdown. Dinger converted the extra-point attempt for a 7-0 lead with 3:26 left in the quarter.

There was 3:42 remaining in the game when Hall High began its last possession.

Photo provided by Central High School
Mark Horton (87)

The Warriors put together their only drive of the game, moving 70 yards in eight plays.

The ninth play proved fatal.

Quarterback Greg Loss' pass along the sideline was intercepted by Allen at the 10 and ended any hope for a Hall High comeback. The victory provided Central High School with a share of the AAAAA-Conference championship and preserved its ranking as Arkansas' No. 1 team.

The end of the 1980 season brought an end to the Nutt era. The starting quarterback for Little Rock Central High School belonged to this family for eight consecutive years. Houston Jr. (1973-1975), Dickey (1976), Danny (1977-1979) and Dennis (1980) combined to lead Central's football team to three state championships. All four received college scholarships for their athletic ability.

1980 TIGER SCHEDULE

Texarkana, TX 7	LRCH 7
*Pine Bluff 14	LRCH 15
Greenville, MS 28	LRCH 34
*LR McClellan 12	LRCH 28
LR Catholic 20	LRCH 35
*NLR Ole Main 0	LRCH 24
*El Dorado 7	LRCH 21
*NLR Northeast 0	LRCH 20
*FS Northside 7	LRCH 7
*LR Parkview 0	LRCH 13
*LR Hall 0	LRCH 7

SECOND STRAIGHT STATE TITLE

1981   9-2-0

Head Coach: Bernie Cox
Assistants: Mike Isom, Clyde Horton, Ray Gillespie, Raymond Scogin
Team Physician: Dr. John McCollough Smith

1981 LETTERMEN

Stephen Adkins	Vincent Dunbar	Chris Lane	Lee Thompson
Will Allen	Olins Dunnick	Terry Mack	Scott Whittington
Sammy Baker	Mark Ellis	Matt McLeod	Barry Williams
John Bass	Larry Farmer	David Moore	Carl Williams
Marc Breedlove	Michael George	John Palmer	Mark Williams
Wilson Chambers	Mike Hale	Joel Pettit	Clint Witcher
Robert Cortinez	Kelly Haley	Kenneth Richardson	Robert Yates
Louis Cryer	Ben Hughes	Chris Shead	
Elie Curry	Bennie Jackson	Joey Smith	
Chuck Dinger	Ronnie Jackson	John Steed	

1981 MANAGERS

Bryan Douglas	Richard Redus
Anthony Downs	Thomas Stewart
Cedric Moore	Thomas Watson

1981 ALL-STATE

Will Allen	Terry Mack
Robert Cortinez	John Palmer
Elie Curry	Kenneth Richardson
Vincent Dunbar	Chris Shead
Olins Dunnick	John Steed
Michael George	Carl Williams
Chris Lane	

1981 ALL-STAR TEAM
Will Allen

The defending state champion Tigers began two-a-day practices Aug. 17. Central's offensive backfield returned only fullback Clint Witcher, forcing Coach Bernie Cox to find replacements at quarterback and tailback.

All-State linebacker Will Allen, the team's backup quarterback in 1980, became the offensive leader, while Olins Dunnick moved from split end to tailback. The defense returned many starters, the main reason the Tigers were the state's preseason top-ranked team by the *Arkansas Gazette*.

Central traveled to Texarkana, Texas, for the opener and hoped to avenge a 7-7 tie in 1980. The Texas team received the opening kickoff and drove 66 yards to the Tigers 2. Tracy Holmes then dove over left tackle, but fumbled. Terry Mack recovered in the end zone and Central took over at its 20.

The Tigers were forced to punt and Tony Burkins returned the kick 13 yards to Central's 48. Texarkana used 13 plays to drive into the end zone, with Irvin Atkin scoring from the 1 just as the first quarter ended. A bad snap spoiled the extra-point attempt and Texas led 6-0.

The first quarter ended with 112 yards rushing by Texarkana compared to 11 yards by the Tigers. The Texas team ran 22 plays, while the Tigers only ran three.

Central fumbled on its ensuing series, giving Texarkana possession at the Tigers 29. Jerry Copeland capped the short drive with a 6-yard run around left end. He also scored a two-point conversion for a 14-0 lead with 7:12 left in the half.

On Central's next possession, Marc Breedlove ended a 70-yard drive when he

Photo provided by Central High School
Coach Clyde Horton

took a reverse 41 yards for a touchdown. Chuck Dinger's extra-point attempt was wide left, but the touchdown narrowed the deficit to 14-6 with 6:13 left in the half.

Central's Carl Williams stopped Texas' next drive when he recovered a fumble at the Texarkana 25. Central was only able to move to the 7, forcing it to attempt a 24-yard field goal. David Moore's kick was perfect, bringing the Tigers within 14-9 with 1:03 remaining in the half.

The Tigers received the second-half kickoff and ran only five plays before Allen passed to Kenneth Richardson for a 41-yard

349

touchdown and a 15-14 lead with 10:25 left in the third quarter. Texas answered, though, as Copeland capped a drive with a 2-yard touchdown run in the third quarter. Texarkana held on during the fourth quarter, defeating Arkansas' top-ranked team 20-15.

After dropping to No. 2 in the polls, Central again went on the road and quickly fell behind against Greenville, Miss. Greenville scored on its first play from scrimmage when Carl Nichols ran 50 yards for a touchdown. Michael Brown kicked the extra point for a 7-0 lead with 9:56 left in the first quarter.

Just before halftime, Moore, who missed a 28-yard field-goal attempt on the previous possession, booted a 35-yarder to bring Central within 7-3.

With 6:11 left in the game, Robert Cortinez gave the Tigers a chance to take the lead when he intercepted a pass at his 41. Richardson and Dunnick lined up at split end, opening up the defense and allowing Witcher to break a 42-yard run to the

Photo provided by Central High School
Will Allen (14)

Photo provided by Central High School
Elie Curry (17) and Joel Pettit (11)

16. Ben Hughes added 12 yards, then Allen scored the game-winning touchdown with 3:48 left to play. A two-point conversion pass was broken up, but Central held on for a 9-7 victory.

The Tigers hosted the El Dorado Wildcats next, marking the third battle between the Cox brothers, Bernie and Donnie, as head coaches. Central quickly jumped ahead as Richardson returned the opening kickoff straight up the middle for a 90-yard touchdown. Moore converted the extra point to give the Tigers a 7-0 lead just 13 seconds into the game.

After driving 41 yards on its first possession, El Dorado fumbled. Central recovered at its 35 and scored moments later when Allen ran into the end zone from the 2. A two-point conversion attempt failed, but the Tigers had an early 13-0 lead.

Allen capped a 60-yard drive on the next possession with a touchdown pass to Richardson. Moore's kick increased the lead to 20-0 with 4:58 left in the half. One minute later, defensive end Chris Lane recovered a fumble and returned it 34 yards for a touchdown. Moore again kicked the extra point and Central led 27-0 at halftime.

A 4-yard run by Dunnick and a 10-yard run by Hughes gave the Tigers a 40-0 victory over the AAAA-South Wildcats. El Dorado dropped to 2-2-0, while the Tigers improved to 2-1-0.

After beating the Catholic High Rockets 20-0 in nonconference action, the Tigers were beaten for the second time the following week. For the first time in school history, Little Rock McClellan defeated Central High School.

A homecoming crowd at Quigley Stadium watched Scott Worthington intercept an Allen pass and return it 80 yards for the game's only touchdown. The extra-point kick gave McClellan a 7-0 lead in the second quarter. The Lions held on for the upset victory.

After dropping to No. 4 in the *Arkansas Gazette* poll, Central had no problem beating North Little Rock Ole Main 33-0. The next game against Little Rock Parkview was easy as well. Dunnick led the Tigers past the Patriots with 171 yards rushing and three touchdowns in a 28-6 victory.

The game's highlight occurred in the second quarter when Dunnick ran for his third touchdown. After receiving the handoff and running off left tackle, he cut back toward the middle of the field and outran the defense for a 74-yard score.

Central's defense allowed its first touchdown against an in-state opponent when Gregory Hayes broke free for a 65-yard touchdown run. That was all the defense allowed, however, in the easy victory.

Richardson, a sophomore split end and defensive back, starred against No. 12 North Little Rock Northeast. He caught a 15-yard touchdown pass from Allen midway through the fourth quarter and stopped two drives late in the game.

When Northeast noticed Richardson had replaced an injured Cortinez at safety, the Chargers tried to pick on the inexperienced player. Richardson, though, proved himself when he made an interception with 3:33 left in the game. He sealed the victory just three minutes later when he intercepted another Northeast pass with 33 seconds left in the game. The Tigers defeated the Chargers 7-0.

A trip to Springdale to take on Jarrell Williams' Bulldogs resulted in another victory for Central. With 10:31 left in the first quarter, Witcher capped a drive with a 1-yard scoring run. The extra point by Moore gave the Tigers a 7-0 lead.

Photo provided by Central High School

Tailback Olins Dunnick and the Tiger offense vs. Little Rock Hall High

On the last play of the quarter, Robert Yates increased the lead to 13-0 when he returned a punt 67 yards for a touchdown. Dinger added a 36-yard field goal with 2:09 remaining for a 16-0 lead.

Allen connected with Kyle Williams on an 11-yard screen pass with 6:43 left in the game for the final touchdown. Dinger's extra point gave the Tigers a 23-0 lead, helping them to a victory over the AAAA-West team.

Third-ranked Central played at Pine Bluff's Jordan Stadium against the No. 10 Zebras next. The Tigers took control after Sammy Baker struck quarterback Rodney Forte hard enough to jar the ball loose and

Thanksgiving Day, 1981

have it recovered by Cortinez.

Central capitalized on this turnover three plays later when Allen capped an 18-yard drive with a 1-yard run. The extra point by Dinger gave the Tigers a 7-0 lead with 3:47 left in the second quarter.

After being held to 0.8 yards per carry during the first half, Pine Bluff came out in the second half and drove 99 yards in 14 plays to take the lead. Forte scored from the 6 and then passed to Leonard Jackson for a two-point conversion. This allowed the Zebras to take the lead at 8-7 with 2:43 left in the third quarter.

Three possessions later, Central faced third-and-16 from its 46. An Allen pass to Richardson, who was double covered near the goal line, was tipped by a Pine Bluff defender. Richardson, though, was able to make the catch after the tip to give the Tigers possession at the 4. Hughes scored from the 3 with 19 seconds remaining in the game to give Central a 13-8 victory.

The win improved the Tigers to 4-1-0 and put them in a tie for AAAAA's top spot. The other team receiving top billing in the conference was No. 7 Little Rock Hall High School.

The two teams met on Thanksgiving Day to decide the AAAAA Conference championship and state championship. This marked the fifth consecutive season that the holiday game had a state championship on the line.

A large crowd filled Quigley Stadium and watched Lane set up the Tigers' first score when he recovered a fumble at the Hall High 23. Central, though, was unable to move past the 6 and had to settle for a 23-yard field goal by Moore. This kick gave the Tigers a 3-0 lead with 41 seconds left in the first quarter.

Another turnover resulted in Central's first touchdown. An Ivan Wilson pass intended for Willie Davis was intercepted by Elie Curry at the Central 36. The drive ended when Allen hit Richardson for a 32-yard touchdown pass with 2:46 left in the half. Keith Hill blocked Dinger's extra-point attempt, but Central led 12-0.

On Hall High's first offensive play following the ensuing kickoff, Williams intercepted another pass by Wilson. The Tigers took over at their 32 and went the distance on second down.

Allen was sacked for a 6-yard loss on first down, but pitched to Dunnick on the

352

next play. Dunnick acted like he was running a sweep, but stopped and threw a perfect spiral to Richardson, who was behind the secondary. Dinger's extra-point attempt was blocked again, but Central led 15-0 at halftime.

The Tigers allowed only 26 yards rushing, 97 yards passing and three first downs. Hall High's only scoring threat was a missed 31-yard field-goal attempt by Jim Wheeler.

Central's offense was controlled by a tough defense as well. The Tigers rushed for only 124 yards and passed for 134 yards in the 15-0 victory. Central finished with a 5-1-0 conference record and won the AAAAA Conference championship, as well as the state championship.

In the *Arkansas Gazette's* final poll, the Tigers were ranked No. 2 behind Class AAAA Jacksonville High School. The Red Devils finished 14-0-0.

1981 TIGER SCHEDULE

Texarkana, Texas 20	LRCH 15
Greenville, Mississippi 7	LRCH 9
El Dorado 0	LRCH 40
LR Catholic 0	LRCH 20
*LR McClellan 7	LRCH 0
*NLR Ole Main 0	LRCH 33
*LR Parkview 6	LRCH 28
*NLR Northeast 0	LRCH 7
Springdale 0	LRCH 23
*Pine Bluff 8	LRCH 13
*LR Hall 0	LRCH 15

END OF THE AAAAA CONFERENCE

1982   7-3-0

Head Coach: Bernie Cox
Assistants: Norman Callaway, Clyde Horton, Ray Gillespie, Eddie Boone, Raymond Scogin
Team Physician: Dr. John McCollough Smith

1982 LETTERMEN

James Alsbrook	Kelvin Edwards	Ben Hughes	Kenneth Richardson
John Arrant	Danny Ellis	Shane Hughes	Chris Rule
Geoffrey Brown	Mark Ellis	Jeff Jones	John Steed
Phillip Bryant	Steve Ensminger	Scott McGibbony	Skip Stoelzing
Elgin Clemons	Larry Farmer	Matt McLeod	Lee Thompson
Chris Connerly	David Fillmore	Tony Nesterenko	Michael Thompson
Stephen Criner	Tom Foltz	Robert Peterson	Barry Williams
Roderick Davenport	Johnny George	Joel Pettit	Kyle Williams
Charles Davis	Jeff Gingerich	Walter Porter	
Rodney DeClue	Kelly Haley	Ricky Powell	
John Delaware	Tony Holmes	Gary Pride	

1982 MANAGERS

Fred Davis	Cedric Moore
Bryan Douglas	Eddie Ridgeway
Glen Johnson	Rod Thompson

1982 ALL-STATE

Geoffrey Brown	Ben Hughes
John Delaware	Kenneth Richardson
Mark Ellis	John Steed
Tony Holmes	Michael Thompson

1982 ALL-STAR TEAM
Mark Ellis
John Steed

Mike Isom, Central's defensive coordinator since 1977, became an assistant at the University of Central Arkansas following the 1981 season. Coach Isom's replacement was Norman Callaway. Callaway, who was offensive line coach at Little Rock Hall High School for 16 years before becoming the school's offensive coordinator in 1980, joined Central's staff as assistant head coach and offensive coordinator.

With several key players returning, the two-time defending state champion Tigers were the preseason No. 1 pick by the *Arkansas Gazette*. Because of Central's recent success, Coach Bernie Cox was unable to find an opponent for the first two weeks of the season.

On the state's third playing date, Central finally opened against Memphis Carver High School at Quigley Stadium. A defensive play by the Tigers gave them the game's only scoring opportunity.

Carver quarterback Steve Jefferson passed to tight end Harold Williams for a short gain at midfield. Williams, though, fumbled after he was hit hard by James Alsbrook. Central's Michael Thompson recovered to give the Tigers possession at their 46.

On first down, quarterback Joel Pettit threw a long pass to Ben Hughes. As the ball came down, it bounced off of Hughes' shoulder pads and into the arms of Central's

Photo provided by Central High School
Joel Pettit (11)

Kenneth Richardson for first-and-goal at the 5.

It took two plays, but Larry Farmer scored on an off-tackle play. An extra-point attempt by Tom Foltz was wide left, but Central took a 6-0 lead with 3:42 left in the first quarter. The lead held up throughout the final three quarters as the Tigers came away with an unimpressive 6-0 victory over the Cobras.

The annual battle between brothers continued the next week as Bernie Cox took Central to El Dorado to play Donnie Cox's Wildcats. El Dorado, ranked No. 8, was in the AAAA-South Conference and 2-0-1. Joe Jones set up the Wildcats' first score when he recovered a fumble at the Tigers 17. Central's defense held El Dorado out of the end zone, but couldn't keep Rickey Nesbitt's field-goal attempt from splitting the uprights. The 30-yard kick gave the Wildcats a 3-0 lead with 1:22 left in the first quarter.

Darryl Sherman set up an El Dorado touchdown when he intercepted a pass at his 27. James Allen, who finished with 112 yards rushing, took a pitchout on first down and outran the defense for a 73-yard touchdown. Nesbitt converted the extra-point attempt for a 10-0 lead with 3:34 left in the half.

The only time Central threatened to score was when John Steed returned a fumble

Lee Thompson (30)

their climb back to the top against Catholic High School at Quigley Stadium. Central took the opening kickoff and drove 53 yards before being forced to settle for a 26-yard field goal by Foltz.

The Rockets took the ensuing kickoff and drove 95 yards, highlighted by an 82-yard run by Greg Hogue, for their only touchdown. Steve Parker scored from the 3 for a 6-3 lead over the Tigers.

Central regained the lead for good when Richardson returned a punt 64 yards for a touchdown, giving the Tigers a 9-6 advantage at halftime. In the third quarter, Richardson set up Farmer's 8-yard touchdown run with a 67-yard punt return. With a 15-6 lead, Pettit added another score late in the fourth quarter with a 1-yard run. Foltz added the extra point for a 22-6 victory.

After beating Little Rock McClellan (16-0) and North Little Rock Ole Main (27-7), Central celebrated homecoming against another cross-town rival. The sixth-ranked Tigers hosted No. 5 Little Rock Parkview at Quigley Stadium.

Central struck first when sophomore tailback Tony Holmes, who rushed for 132 yards on the night, took a pitchout on his 49 and ran to the right. Holmes faked a reverse to Richardson and ran 51 yards for a touchdown. Foltz kicked the extra point for a 7-0 lead with 9:25 left in the half.

The Tigers' first possession of the second half ended when Parkview's Rickey

71 yards for an apparent touchdown. The score was nullified, though, due to a clipping penalty. The Tigers were unable to score in the 10-0 loss, the Wildcats' first victory over Central since 1971 and Donnie Cox's first head coaching victory over his brother.

Following the loss, the Tigers dropped to No. 12 in the polls. They hoped to begin

Tony Holmes (87)

356

Williams recovered a fumble at the Central 22. The Tigers forced the Patriots to attempt a 33-yard field goal. The successful kick narrowed the deficit to 7-3 with 7:31 left in the third quarter.

David Fillmore stopped a Parkview scoring threat when he intercepted a pass in the end zone and returned it to the 5. Central was only able to move to the 9 and was forced to punt. Instead of risking a blocked punt, which could have easily resulted in a Parkview score, Coach Cox instructed Foltz to step out of the end zone once he received the snap. This awarded the Patriots a safety with 1:27 left in the game. The Tigers held Parkview on its next possession and escaped with a 10-5 victory.

Central then beat North Little Rock Northeast (14-6) and Springdale (25-7) before meeting its ancient rival from Pine Bluff. A victory over the Zebras would guarantee the second-ranked Tigers at least a share of the AAAAA title. Pine Bluff would remain alive for at least a share of the title with a victory.

The Zebras received the opening kickoff and drove 70 yards in six plays for the game's first score. Sophomore quarterback Eric Mitchel passed to Kenneth Brown for a 36-yard touchdown. Timothy Rivers added the extra point for a 7-0 lead with 9:03 left in the first quarter.

Alsbrook recovered a Pine Bluff fumble at the end of the third quarter to set up Central's only score of the game. The Tigers

Photo provided by Central High School
John Steed (65)

drove 36 yards in eight plays, but were forced to kick a 19-yard field goal, pulling them within 7-3 with 7:39 left in the game.

Pine Bluff's Edward Hughes intercepted a pass to end another Central drive and gave Pine Bluff possession at the Tigers 24 with 4:49 left. Seven plays later, Mitchel ran around left end for a 9-yard touchdown. Rivers converted the extra-point attempt for a 14-3 upset victory over Central.

The Tigers still had one more chance to win the league title. What stood in their way was the 25th anniversary of the "Turkey Bowl," the annual Thanksgiving Day battle with Little Rock Hall High School. The winner would be guaranteed the conference and state title.

During a pregame ceremony, Mr. Harry Coonley, accompanied by former Tigers Ben Isgrig and Vernon "Red" Felix, presented a solid brass bell, synonymous with the Warrior-Tiger series. Taken from a

Photo provided by Central High School
LRCH lettermen

357

(Left to Right) Principal Richard Maple introduces Vernon Felix, Ben Isgrig and Harry Coonley as they donate "The Bell" to the Central-Hall tradition

train, the bell is awarded to the winning team and kept as a trophy until the teams meet again the following year.

Before a crowd of more than 9,000 at Quigley Stadium, Hall High received the opening kickoff but was forced to punt. Richardson returned it 89 yards for an apparent touchdown, but a clipping penalty negated the score and halted Central's momentum.

Central's first possession ended with a punt, and Hall High drove 39 yards for the game's first score. Greg Cummins scored on a 1-yard quarterback sneak. James Alton converted the extra-point attempt for a 7-0 lead with 2:32 left in the first quarter.

The Tigers took the ensuing kickoff and drove 55 yards but were forced to attempt a 25-yard field goal. Foltz's kick was wide left with 9:56 remaining in the half. Hall led 7-0 at halftime.

Central used the last 8:23 of the third quarter to drive 64 yards in 16 plays. Although the Tigers were held out of the end zone, they did score when Foltz kicked a 32-yard field goal on the second play of the fourth quarter to narrow the Warriors' lead to 7-3.

Hall High answered on its next possession when it covered 73 yards in 10 plays. Otis Evans capped the drive when he scored on a 9-yard sweep around left end. Alton's extra point increased the lead to 14-3 with 6:24 left in the game. Central didn't threaten again, allowing Coach C.W. Keopple to win his sixth state title as Hall High School's head coach.

The 1982 season marked the last time Central and Hall scheduled a Thanksgiving Day game. The Tigers had played on the holiday for 78 recorded years, the last 25 against Hall High School. Fusion of the AAAAA and AAAA classifications by the Arkansas Activities Association was the reason for the change.

Class AAAAA was the only classification without playoffs. The team finishing with the best league record was considered both the conference and state champion. The growth of Class AAAA schools forced the Arkansas Activities Association to merge the top two classifications. It formed four conferences within the new classification and instituted the playoff system to determine a true state champion.

Central did not have a traditional Thanksgiving Day rival in the early years of its football program. In fact, some games were scheduled at the last moment when the school would invite a well-known, powerful team of the time to play in Little Rock. The Tigers were also invited to play out of town on several occasions.

In 1934, a tradition began when Little Rock High School and North Little Rock High School agreed to schedule their game on the holiday. This series lasted 23 years before Little Rock Hall High School opened in 1958. With the opening of the new Little Rock school, Central began a new tradition by playing its cross-town rival on Thanksgiving Day.

In 25 seasons, the "Turkey Bowl" decided 12 state championships. The Warriors won or shared the title in 1959, 1964, 1966, 1969, 1977, 1979 and 1982. The Tigers won or shared the title in 1960, 1975, 1978, 1980 and 1981.

Beginning in 1983, Central and Hall began meeting on the fourth playing date of the season.

1982 TIGER SCHEDULE

Carver High of Memphis, TN 0	LRCH 6
El Dorado 10	LRCH 0
LR Catholic 6	LRCH 22
*LR McClellan 0	LRCH 16
*NLR Ole Main 7	LRCH 27
*LR Parkview 5	LRCH 10
*NLR Northeast 6	LRCH 14
Springdale 7	LRCH 25
*Pine Bluff 14	LRCH 3
*LR Hall 14	LRCH 3

Photo provided by Central High School

Tiger captains on Thanksgiving Day, 1982

NEW CONFERENCE, NEW TRADITIONS
1983　　7-5-0

Head Coach: Bernie Cox
Assistants: Norman Callaway, Clyde Horton, Ray Gillespie, Eddie Boone, Raymond Scogin
Team Physician: Dr. John McCollough Smith

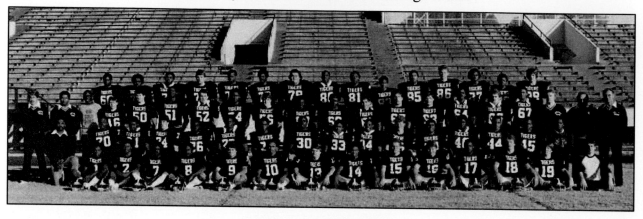

1983 LETTERMEN

Ted Adkins	Bertrand Evans	Glen Johnson	David Riesenberg
James Alsbrook	Larry Farmer	Todd Jones	Chris Rule
Walter Bell	David Fillmore	Melvin Lewis	Gerald Russell
John Brooks	Tom Foltz	Tony Nesterenko	Jerry Smith
Elgin Clemons	Johnny George	Fred Oliver	Skip Stoelzing
Roderick Davenport	Kelly Haley	Robert Peterson	Chris Thomas
Fred Davis	Tony Holmes	Walter Porter	Michael Thompson
John Delaware	Shane Hughes	Michael Powell	Earvin Walker
Kelvin Edwards	Jeff Jacob	Billy Price	Kenneth Williams
Danny Ellis	Erik Jernigan	Kenneth Richardson	

1983 MANAGERS
Cedric Moore
Eddie Ridgeway
Rod Thompson
Melvin Williams

1983 ALL-STATE
Roderick Davenport
Danny Ellis
Tony Holmes
Kenneth Richardson

1983 ALL-CONFERENCE

Fred Davis	Kelly Haley
John Delaware	Gerald Russell
Tom Foltz	Jerry Smith

1983 ALL-STAR TEAM
Fred Davis
Kenneth Richardson

The 1983 season brought an end to the AAAAA Conference, as well as Little Rock Central's traditional Thanksgiving Day game. The Tigers were now members of the new AAAA-North Conference and required to participate in the playoffs to decide the AAAA state champion. The playoffs were new only to the state's largest schools, as the smaller classifications had participated in the playoff system for many years.

Central began the season as the state's No. 2 team by the *Arkansas Democrat*. The ranking, though, may have been a bit unrealistic since the Tigers were without several starters from the previous season and planned to field only two players weighing more than 200 pounds.

Coach Bernie Cox's team had a big challenge in the opener, facing the state's No. 1 team, Little Rock Parkview, in a non-conference matchup at Quigley Stadium. Little Rock Parkview fielded what was thought to be its most powerful team in school history and was out to avenge a 1982 loss to Central that kept the Patriots from winning the AAAAA state title.

Little Rock Parkview's domination began immediately.

The Tigers ended their initial possession with a punt that was fielded by Keith Jackson at his 44. Jackson zigzagged his way through the Central's coverage team and ran the final 30 yards all alone for the game's first score. Daryl Coates converted the extra-point attempt for a 7-0 lead with 10:18 left in the first quarter.

Jackson scored again when he caught a pass from quarterback Kenneth Hayes. Jackson received the 33-yard pass just in front of the goal line and pushed his way through two defenders into the end zone. The extra-point attempt failed, but Parkview led 13-0 with 3:35 remaining in the first quarter.

Students cheer for the Tigers

The Patriots led 34-0 at halftime and backed up their No. 1 billing in a 37-7 victory.

The No. 10 Tigers entered their game against seventh-ranked Little Rock Mills with nine players out because of injury. Six of these injured players had missed the season-opening game against Little Rock Parkview, while three more were injured during the following week of practice.

The weakened Tigers were no match for the Comets as they were held to minus-13 yards rushing. Mills scored almost at will in a 35-6 victory.

The unranked Tigers traveled to No. 2 Pine Bluff the following week to continue their rivalry against the Zebras. Central's defense forced Pine Bluff to punt on its first two possessions of the game.

But the Tigers were unable to capitalize on the opportunities. On the Zebras' third possession, they drove 52 yards in four plays and scored on a 39-yard pass from Eric Mitchel to Mario Brewer. The extra-point attempt failed, but Pine Bluff took a 6-0 lead with 18 seconds left in the first quarter.

Central's Roderick Davenport intercepted a pass late in the second quarter and returned it 14 yards to the Pine Bluff 21. On third down, quarterback Chris Thomas connected with Kenneth Richardson for an 11-

361

yard touchdown pass. Tom Foltz kicked the extra point to give Central a 7-6 halftime lead.

The Zebras regained the lead on their first possession of the second half. They took possession after Victor Turner intercepted a Thomas pass at the Pine Bluff 44. Mitchel eventually threw an 8-yard touchdown pass to Chris Dixon. Mitchel's two-point conversion attempt failed, leaving the Zebras in front 12-7.

With 10:07 left in the game, the Tigers had to settle for a 24-yard field goal by Foltz to pull within 12-10.

Central had one more possession but was unable to move and forced to punt. The Zebras then converted two first downs to keep the clock running and hand the Tigers their third loss of the season.

Little Rock Central (0-3-0) and a healthy tailback, Tony Holmes, met Little Rock Hall High in a nonconference game the following week. The Warriors were 2-1-0.

The importance of having Holmes on the field was evident as he rushed for 146 yards and set up each of his team's scores. The first score, a 48-yard field goal by Foltz, put Central up 3-0 with 8:02 left in the opening quarter.

Larry Farmer (20)

With 5:55 remaining in the half, Thomas connected with Larry Farmer on a quick pass across the middle. Farmer cut back to the sideline and raced 62 yards for a touchdown. Foltz's extra point put the Tigers up 10-0.

A 12-yard run by Michael Thompson, a 50-yard run by Melvin Lewis and a 31-yard field goal by Foltz completed the scoring for Central. The Tigers defeated Hall High 26-0.

Following another loss, this time 12-3 to No. 5 Springdale, Central traveled to Conway for a AAAA-North game against the Wampus Cats.

Richardson got the Tigers started off right when he returned the game's opening kickoff 91 yards for a touchdown. Five minutes later, defensive tackle Walter Porter intercepted a Conway pass and returned it 35 yards for a touchdown. Foltz's second extra-point attempt was blocked and the Tigers had a 13-0 lead.

With 8:37 left in the second quarter, Porter intercepted another pass and returned it 41 yards for a touchdown. This score, along with a 4-yard run by Holmes earlier in the quarter, gave Central a 27-0 halftime lead.

The Tigers scored once more in the second half to beat the Wampus Cats 34-0.

Following a 24-7 homecoming victory over North Little Rock Northeast, which included another Porter interception return for a touchdown, Central battled 3-4-0 Sylvan Hills. Porter recovered a fumble at the Sylvan Hills 31 to set up the game's only touchdown.

Holmes scored the touchdown on a short run after carrying four consecutive times. Foltz added the extra point with 1:10 left in the third quarter to give the Tigers a 7-0 lead and eventually a 7-2 victory.

Central won again the next week when it scored the game's only touchdown on the last play of the first quarter against Jacksonville. Holmes capped the 13-play, 58-yard drive with a 5-yard run. Central's defense recorded its third shutout in four games in a 7-0 victory over the Red Devils.

Quarterback Chris Thomas

Central closed the regular season with a 28-12 victory over North Little Rock Ole Main the following week. The Tigers finished 1-4 in nonconference games, but captured the AAAA-North championship and a berth in the new AAAA state playoffs with a 5-0 record.

Round one of the playoffs pitted Central against Forrest City High School at Quigley Stadium. The Tigers' Gerald Russell recovered a fumble at his 4 to set up Central's first score. The 96-yard drive ended with a 69-yard touchdown pass from Thomas to Richardson. Foltz kicked the first of his four extra points to give the Tigers a 7-0 lead with 9:28 left in the first half.

Central drove 83 yards in the third quarter for its next touchdown. The score came on a 10-yard run by Holmes with 2:39 left in the quarter. The Tigers added two more scores when Thomas connected with Richardson for a 67-yard touchdown and a 1-yard run by David Riesenberg.

The victory sent Central to the second round of the playoffs for a rematch against Pine Bluff. The No. 3 Zebras (10-1-0) visited Quigley Stadium and held an 8-3 lead with 1:50 remaining in the game.

Pine Bluff was facing fourth down from its 34 when Zebras Coach Donzell Young decided to go for the first down instead of punting. Mitchel was tackled short of the first down and the Tigers took over at the Zebras 35.

Thomas passed to Richardson for a 7-yard gain, and an interference call against Pine Bluff gave Central a first down at the 20. Four plays later, the Tigers faced fourth down from the 19 with 51 seconds remaining.

Thomas was able to connect with Farmer, who got to the 11 before being pulled down by the defense. This, however, was 1 yard short of the first down. Pine Bluff regained possession and ran out the clock.

Central finished 7-5-0 and won its first AAAA-North championship.

1983 TIGER SCHEDULE

LR Parkview 37	LRCH 7
Mills 35	LRCH 6
Pine Bluff 12	LRCH 10
LR Hall 0	LRCH 26
Springdale 12	LRCH 3
*Conway 0	LRCH 34
*NLR Northeast 7	LRCH 24
*Sylvan Hills 2	LRCH 7
*Jacksonville 0	LRCH 7
*NLR Ole Main 12	LRCH 28
**Forrest City 6	LRCH 28 (state playoffs)
**Pine Bluff 8	LRCH 3 (state playoffs)

BATTLE OF THE TAILBACKS

1984   7-5-0

Head Coach: Bernie Cox
Assistants: Norman Callaway, Clyde Horton, Ray Gillespie, Raymond Scogin
Team Physician: Dr. John McCollough Smith

1984 LETTERMEN

Havard Abraham	Spencer Ellison	Shane Hughes	Clay Sanders
Ricky Anderson	Tony Eubanks	Tony Jackson	Eric Smith
Todd Auld	Bertrand Evans	Jeff Jacob	Jerry Smith
Johnny Bailey	David Falcon	Todd Jones	Todd Stanley
John Brooks	Cedric Farmer	Pepper Kesler	Forest Stolzer
Ronald Brooks	Cleo Flint	Richard Lebos	Darryl Swinton
Joey Carter	Brian Fuller	Ricky Mays	Greg Switzer
Ronnie Caveness	Kevin Garland	Michael Peoples	Chris Thomas
Elgin Clemons	Antonio Garman	Robert Peterson	Earvin Walker
Eric Clemons	Darren Hale	Michael Powell	Kevin Wright
Scott Dabbs	Kevin Harris	Gregory Ridgle	
Roderick Davenport	Mark Henry	David Riesenberg	
Tim Edggerson	Tony Holmes	Derek Russell	

1984 MANAGERS
Tony Earnest
Lamont Morgan
Gary Pride
Eric Wilborn
Fernando Wilkins

1984 ALL-STATE
Roderick Davenport
Tony Holmes
Jeff Jacob

1984 ALL-CONFERENCE

John Brooks   Robert Peterson
Tony Holmes   Jerry Smith
Todd Jones   Earvin Walker
Richard Lebos

1984 ALL-STAR TEAM
Tony Holmes

Little Rock Central opened 1984 ranked No. 5 by the *Arkansas Democrat* and again the favorite to win the AAAA-North Conference. The Tigers' season opener was against No. 3 Little Rock Parkview. The game featured two of the most highly touted running backs in the state, Tony Holmes of Central and James Rouse of Parkview.

The Tigers recovered a Parkview fumble to set up the game's first score. The 4-yard touchdown play occurred when quarterback Chris Thomas connected with Holmes in the corner of the end zone. Richard Lebos' extra-point attempt failed and Central led 6-0 with 8:03 left in the first quarter.

The Patriots took the lead as the second quarter opened when quarterback Kenneth Hayes snuck into the end zone from the 1. Aurello Scott converted the extra-point attempt to make it 7-6.

After forcing Parkview to punt out of its end zone, Holmes returned the kick 13 yards to the 19. Three plays later, Holmes went over right tackle from the 10 for the score. Thomas then connected with Ricky Mays for a two-point conversion and a 14-7 halftime lead.

Holmes and Johnny Bailey each scored on short runs during the second half. The Tigers held Rouse to only 87 yards on 19 carries and Parkview to only 164 yards of total offense. Central defeated Parkview 28-7 and replaced the Patriots as the No. 3 team in the state.

The Tigers fell behind the next week when Little Rock Mills' Marshall Malone returned Central's first punt 75 yards for a touchdown. Holmes answered with five touchdowns and 245 yards rushing in a 38-6 victory.

The No. 3 Tigers were out for revenge the following week as they hosted No. 4 Pine Bluff at Quigley Stadium. The Zebras defeated Central twice during 1983, including a playoff defeat that ended the season for the Tigers.

With Pine Bluff leading 7-0 midway through the third quarter, Forest Stolzer set up the Tigers' first score when he recovered a fumble at his 17. Two plays after a penalty moved Central back to the 14 Derek

Tony Holmes (87) and Johnny Bailey (18)

Derek Russell (2)

Springdale took its third possession into the end zone after driving 50 yards in eight plays. Allen Smith capped the drive with a 1-yard run. Phil VanHook's extra point gave the Bulldogs a 7-0 lead with 9:01 left in the first half.

After Bailey returned the ensuing kick-off 20 yards, the Tigers proceeded with a drive of their own. Holmes scored on a 1-yard run to end a 16-play, 73-yard drive that consumed 8:30 off the clock. Lebos kicked the extra point to make it 7-7.

Central was forced to punt on its first possession of the second half. Lebos kicked out of his end zone and the Bulldogs took control at the Tigers 29. Eight plays later, Mike Tubb scored from the 1 to give Springdale the lead again. VanHook increased the lead to 14-7 with the extra point midway through the third period. Springdale controlled the ball and the clock, allowing Central only three more possessions. The Tigers were unable to move and beaten for the third consecutive week.

Central hosted Conway High School in the conference opener the next week. With

Russell took a handoff from Thomas and raced 86 yards for a touchdown. Lebos' conversion was good to tie the score at 7-7 with 5:54 left in the quarter.

A missed 47-yard field-goal attempt by Lebos gave the Zebras possession at the 20 early in the final period. Pine Bluff drove 80 yards in nine plays, highlighted by a 57-yard pass from quarterback Eric Mitchel to Reginald Holt to the Tigers 1. Lugene Boyde dove over the pile for the score and a 13-7 lead.

Central was unable to score on its next three possessions, resulting in the first loss of the season. The Tigers then dropped to No. 6 in the polls as they prepared to battle another rival, Little Rock Hall High.

The unranked Warriors shocked Central 20-2. A tough defense held the Tigers to 91 yards on 46 offensive plays and limited Holmes to 35 yards rushing on 13 carries. The nonconference loss knocked Central down to No. 9 for its meeting with Springdale, the state's top-ranked team.

Johnny Bailey (18)

366

6:41 remaining in the first quarter, Holmes scored from the 7 to end a 56-yard drive and put the Tigers up 6-0.

On the first play of the fourth quarter, Central punted out of its end zone. Charlie Taylor received the kick at the Tigers 42 and returned it 20 yards to give the Wampus Cats possession at the 22.

On second down, Conway quarterback Mitchell Fusilier passed to Ernie Woodard in the end zone for a 6-6 tie. Steve Strange converted the extra-point attempt to give the Wampus Cats a 7-6 lead with 10:50 left in the fourth quarter.

Late in the game, Central put together a 55-yard drive that ended at the Conway 5. Facing fourth down and less than a minute to play, Coach Bernie Cox opted to attempt a 22-yard field goal. Lebos, who missed an extra-point attempt and a 37-yard field-goal attempt in the first half, split the uprights for a 9-7 victory.

After a 10-8 loss to conference foe North Little Rock Northeast, thc Tigers battled Sylvan Hills at rainy Quigley Stadium. The Bears struck first when Shane McGehee scored on a 3-yard run in the second quarter. Chris Cerrato, Sylvan Hills' quarterback, passed to Charles Cavin for the two-point conversion and an 8-0 lead with 9:58 left in the half.

Photo provided by Central High School
Tony Holmes (87)

It wasn't until the third quarter that Central scored. The Tigers received excellent field position after a fake punt by Sylvan Hills failed at the Bears 8. On its second play, Central scored on a 7-yard run by Holmes. Thomas then connected with Chris Sanders for the two-point conversion and an 8-8 tie.

A bad snap by the Sylvan Hills punt team gave the Tigers possession at the Bears 7. Three plays later, David Riesenberg scored from the 1. Lebos' extra point made it 15-8 with 10:57 to play.

With 4:25 remaining, Nunie Escovedo scored from the 1 for the Bears. Sylvan Hills then converted a two-point conversion when Dwight Backus scored for a 16-15 lead.

Following the ensuing kickoff, Central used 13 plays and 4:01 to drive 73 yards. Holmes concluded his 100-yard rushing performance with a 3-yard touchdown run.

Photo provided by Central High School
David Riesenberg (left) and Chris Thomas (16)

367

Lebos added the extra point to give the Tigers a 22-16 victory.

After a 16-0 victory over Jacksonville and a 14-0 victory over North Little Rock Ole Main, the conference champion Central Tigers opened the state playoffs by hosting Forrest City High School.

Following a 23-minute delay because of heavy rain and lightning midway through the first quarter, Central returned to the field and completed an 81-yard, 13-play drive. The game's only touchdown was followed by Lebos' extra point for a 7-0 lead. The Tigers held the Mustangs to 64 total yards of offense in the first-round victory.

The defeat of Forrest City set up a rematch with Hall High School. The unranked Warriors beat the previously top-ranked Springdale Bulldogs to earn a shot at the Tigers in the state quarterfinals.

Other than a 27-yard field goal by Lebos in the third quarter, the game was uneventful for Central. The Tigers could not move against the Hall High defense, which held Holmes to season-low 25 yards rushing on 14 carries. Central, as a team, could only manage 174 total yards for the game.

The Warriors were ahead 14-3 with 10:25 remaining in the game when Fred Williams intercepted a pass and returned it 64 yards for a touchdown to give Hall a 20-3 lead. Holmes scored on a 1-yard run late in the game, but the touchdown and Lebos' extra point did not help as the Tigers lost 20-10 and finished 7-5-0.

1984 TIGER SCHEDULE

LR Parkview 7	LRCH 28
Mills 6	LRCH 38
Pine Bluff 13	LRCH 7
LR Hall 20	LRCH 2
Springdale 14	LRCH 7
*Conway 7	LRCH 9
*NLR Northeast 10	LRCH 8
*Sylvan Hills 16	LRCH 22
*Jacksonville 0	LRCH 16
*Ole Main 0	LRCH 14
**Forrest City 0	LRCH 7 (state playoffs)
**LR Hall 20	LRCH 10 (state playoffs)

THREE IN A ROW

1985   11-2-0

Head Coach: Bernie Cox
Assistants: Norman Callaway, Clyde Horton, Eddie Boone
Team Physician: Dr. John McCollough Smith

1985 LETTERMEN

Ricky Anderson
Johnny Bailey
Herman Botley
Henry Berry
Ronald Brooks
Kenneth Bush
Pharoah Brown
Eric Clemons
Scott Dabbs
John Davis
Anthony Edmondson
Spencer Ellison

Tony Eubanks
Bertrand Evans
Darrin Falcon
Sedric Fillmore
Jerrod Finkston
Cleo Flint
Brian Fuller
Kevin Garland
Antonio Garman
Darren Hale
Kevin Harris
Mark Henry

Greg Jackson
Tony Jackson
David Jones
Todd Jones
Pepper Kesler
Greg Lewis
Melvin Lewis
Ricky Mays
Tommy McBrayer
Keith Morris
Tony Phillips
Jeff Price

Gregory Ridgle
Derek Russell
Eric Smith
Tommy Sproles
Todd Stanley
Seann Stewart
Keith Stinsin
Forrest Stolzer
Darryl Swinton
Greg Switzer
Kevin Wright

1985 MANAGERS
Matt Huey
Paul James
Ronnie Murphy
Myron Wright

1985 ALL-AMERICAN
Todd Jones

1985 ALL-STATE
Bertrand Evans
Todd Jones
Ricky Mays
Derek Russell

1985 ALL-CONFERENCE

Eric Clemons   Mark Henry
Kevin Garland   Greg Lewis
Darren Hale   Kevin Wright

1985 ALL-STAR TEAM
Bertrand Evans
Todd Jones

As the preseason No. 6 team by the *Arkansas Democrat*, Central opened its 1985 campaign against No. 2 Little Rock Parkview. The Patriots scored first when Gerry Rouse kicked a 29-yard field goal with 2:45 left in the first quarter.

The Tigers, though, answered early in the second quarter when Greg Jackson intercepted a Parkview pass and returned it 25 yards for a touchdown. Tommy McBrayer converted the extra-point attempt to give Central a 7-3 lead with 9:37 remaining in the half.

When the second half opened, the Tigers put together a 61-yard drive that consumed 7:02 and gave them a commanding lead over the Patriots. Central quarterback Pepper Kesler scored from the 1 and McBrayer added the extra point for a 14-3 lead.

Central added to its lead midway through the fourth quarter after Eric Clemons intercepted a pass at the Parkview 30. Backup quarterback Sedric Fillmore eventually found Derek Russell in the end zone for 27-yard touchdown pass. McBrayer converted the extra-point attempt to set the final at 21-3.

The No. 4 Tigers hosted seventh-ranked Mills High School the next week. After the opening kickoff, they moved 76 yards in 12 plays for the first half's only score. The 5:23 drive was capped by Melvin Lewis' 1-yard run. McBrayer's extra-point attempt failed and Central settled for the 6-0 lead.

Early in the fourth quarter, the Comets' Cedric McDowell fumbled on third down to give the Tigers possession at the Mills 48. On third down from the 37, Fillmore hit Russell on a fly pattern to score the game's final points. A two-point conversion failed, but Central held on for a 12-0 victory.

The Tigers met their longtime nemesis at Jordan Stadium in Pine Bluff the following week and narrowly escaped with a victory over the unranked Zebras. Ahead 16-7 with 2:12 remaining in the game, Central attempted to punt from its 30. The kick, however, was blocked by Pine Bluff's Norman Bullard.

Kenneth Nelson then recovered and returned it the necessary yardage for a Pine Bluff

Photo provided by Central High School

A Tiger pep rally

370

Coach Norman Callaway leads pregame exercises

touchdown. The extra-point kick made it 16-14, but the Tigers held the Zebras on their final possession to secure the victory.

The Tigers, ranked No. 2, played another big rival the following week. Little Rock Hall High fumbled at its 33 to give Central possession. It took five plays, but the Tigers finally scored when Fillmore completed a 27-yard pass to Eric Smith. The extra-point attempt was blocked, but Central took a 6-0 lead with 4:40 left in the first period.

The Tigers forced the Warriors to punt on their next possession, but Johnny Bailey fumbled as he attempted to field the kick. Hall High's Robert Ware recovered at the Central 6 and easily made it to the end zone to tie the score at 6-6.

With 10:04 left in the half, the Tigers struck again. They drove 56 yards in five plays, scoring on an 18-yard pass play from Kesler to Spencer Ellison. Central attempted a two-point conversion, but was unsuccessful and settled for a 12-6 lead.

The Tigers stopped the Warriors' next possession by blocking a punt and recovering at the Hall High 37. Bailey eventually scored on a 3-yard run. Kesler snuck for the two-point conversion and a 20-6 lead. Another touchdown by Hall High during the fourth quarter was not enough as Central held on 20-14.

A trip to Springdale was next for the Tigers and a battle with the seventh-ranked Bulldogs. Springdale took an early lead af-

ter a special-teams mistake lead to a score. Central attempted to punt on its first possession, but Mark Henry's snap sailed over the head of McBrayer. The ball ended up in the end zone and McBrayer fell on it, resulting in a safety for Springdale.

Clemons set the stage for the Tigers to take the lead when he intercepted a pass midway through the third quarter. Unable to push the ball into the end zone, Central relied on Erick Brown to kick a 41-yard field goal to give the Tigers a 3-2 lead with 4:49 left in the third quarter.

With 6:21 remaining in the game, Luke George answered for the Bulldogs when he kicked a 25-yard field goal. George's first career field goal was enough to defeat No. 2 Central 5-3.

Conference play began the following week with a matchup between the Tigers and Conway High School. The Wampus Cats jumped out to an early lead when Johnny Kennedy and Dave Naylor combined on a 15-yard touchdown pass to end a

Melvin Lewis (34)

55-yard drive. The extra point gave Conway a 7-0 lead.

Central, however, scored on its ensuing possession with a 58-yard pass play from Kesler to Ricky Mays. The extra-point attempt made it 7-7, a score that lasted until the third quarter.

Midway through the third quarter, Central's Tony Phillips recovered a fumble in Conway territory. On first down from the 6, Scott Dabbs ran to his right and broke two tackles to score. The extra-point attempt was good and Central took a 14-7 lead.

With just under three minutes to play in the game, Conway had a first down at the Tigers 11. Kennedy, who had dropped to pass, was heavily pressured by the defensive line and forced a pass into the end zone. Clemons was there to intercept and end the scoring threat. This allowed the Tigers to escape the Wampus Cats 14-7.

Central traveled across the river for its next contest against No. 1 North Little Rock Northeast. The Chargers scored first when they drove 61 yards in nine plays late in the first period. Ju Ju Harshaw scored the touchdown on a 1-yard run and converted the extra-point attempt with 35 seconds left in the quarter.

On their ensuing possession, the Tigers drove 71 yards to the Northeast 9. Central, though, had to settle for a 26-yard field goal by Jeff Price to cut Northeast's lead to 7-3 at halftime.

Photo provided by Central High School
Greg Lewis (83)

A Harshaw fumble was recovered by the Tigers' Cleo Flint at the Northeast 12. Central would again have to settle for a field goal by Price, this time a 20-yarder, that narrowed the deficit to 7-6 with 6:42 left in the third quarter.

A Northeast punt with 4:08 left in the game gave the Tigers one last possession to regain the lead. On first down, fullback Tony Eubanks broke through the middle of the line for a 64-yard gain. Fillmore passed to Mays for a 21-yard gain. Dabbs carried three consecutive times before scoring with 1:13 left to play. The extra-point attempt was blocked, but Central defeated the state's top-ranked team 12-7.

Now the No. 1 team in Arkansas, Central went on to defeat Sylvan Hills (28-7), Jacksonville (13-7) and North Little Rock Ole Main (23-0) before its first-round playoff matchup with Little Rock Parkview. The game was scoreless in regulation.

Each team threatened to score only once during regulation. Central's threat came on an attempted field goal in the third quarter,

Photo provided by Central High School
Ricky Mays (10)

372

Photo provided by Central High School

Ricky Mays

but the kick was wide right. The Patriots attempted a field goal in the fourth quarter, but could not field the snap.

The Tigers won the coin toss in overtime, and Coach Bernie Cox elected to play defense first. Parkview was unable to move, but the Patriots did manage a 26-yard field goal by Rouse.

On Central's first offensive play in overtime, Lewis gained 5 yards to the 5. Fillmore then took the snap and rolled to his right, stiff-armed one defender and ran into the corner of the end zone for the game-winning touchdown.

Quigley Stadium was the sight of Central's second-round playoff game against No. 4 El Dorado. A 21-13 victory over the Wildcats set up a semifinal game against Fort Smith Northside the next week.

In Fort Smith's Mayo-Thompson Stadium, the Tigers scored on their first drive of the game when they covered 59 yards in seven plays. Bailey scored from the 1 and McBrayer converted the extra-point attempt for a 7-0 lead with 7:50 left in the first quarter.

In the second quarter, Charles Fleming recovered a Central fumble at the Tigers 33. It took 10 plays for the Grizzlies to drive the needed yards, with quarterback Vincent Stevenson scoring from the 1. Bobby Morgan added the extra point to tie the score with 7:58 remaining in the second quarter.

On the ensuing kickoff, Northside recovered an on-side kick at the Central 37. The Grizzlies could not move again and were forced to settle for a 41-yard field goal by Scott Sowell. The kick put Northside ahead 10-7 with 5:30 left in the half.

On their second possession of the second half, the Grizzlies scored again. The touchdown was set up by a 57-yard run by Stevenson to the 7. Stevenson then scored three plays later to increase Northside's lead to 17-7.

The Tigers recovered another on-side kick attempt and took control at their 34. Fillmore capped an eight-play drive with a 2-yard run. McBrayer kicked the extra point to pull Central within 17-14.

Late in the game, Central regained possession at its 30. Behind the passing of Fillmore and pass interference against Northside, the Tigers drove to the Grizzlies 1. With 11 seconds remaining in the game, Fillmore threw an incomplete pass to Mays on first down. This set up the game's last play.

Fillmore took the snap from center and dropped to pass. His pocket, though, closed quickly as the defense provided pressure. He then rolled to his right and attempted to dive into the end zone from the 3.

Several defenders, however, were waiting at the 1. They were able to protect their territory by knocking Fillmore away from the goal line and forcing him to fumble. Eddie Cole recovered the fumble for Northside as time expired.

The victory sent the Fort Smith team to War Memorial Stadium to play for the AAAA state championship. The battle against Little Rock Catholic resulted in a state-record five-overtime game that the Rockets won 35-28.

Central finished 11-2-0 and won its third consecutive AAAA-North Conference championship.

1985 TIGER SCHEDULE

LR Parkview 3	LRCH 21
Mills 0	LRCH 12
Pine Bluff 14	LRCH 16
LR Hall 14	LRCH 20
Springdale 5	LRCH 3
*Conway 7	LRCH 14
*NLR Northeast 7	LRCH 12
*Sylvan Hills 7	LRCH 28
*Jacksonville 7	LRCH 13
*NLR Ole Main 0	LRCH 23
**LR Parkview 3	LRCH 6 (state playoffs)
**El Dorado 13	LRCH 21 (state playoffs)
**FS Northside 17	LRCH 14 (state playoffs)

THIRTIETH STATE CHAMPIONSHIP

1986   12-1-0

Head Coach: Bernie Cox
Assistants: Norman Callaway, Clyde Horton, Eddie Boone
Team Physician: Dr. John McCollough Smith

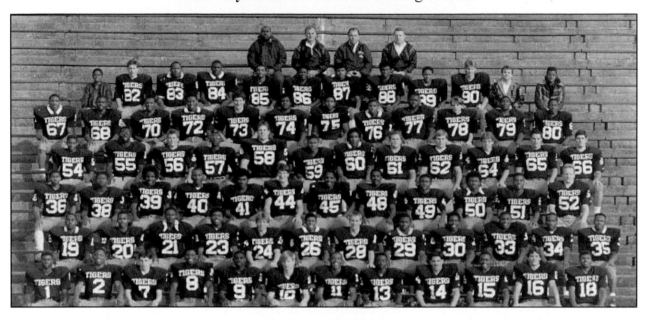

1986 LETTERMEN

Ricky Anderson	Cleo Flint	David Jones	Derek Russell
Johnny Bailey	Karl Freeman	Pepper Kesler	Warren Scott
Henry Berry	Brian Fuller	Sam Khabeer	Eric Smith
Herman Botley	Antonio Garman	Michael Levin	Tommy Sproles
Ronald Brooks	Jeff Hanson	Greg Lewis	Seann Stewart
Pharoah Brown	Kenneth Hayes	Jeff Milburn	Forrest Stolzer
Kenneth Bush	Mark Henry	Ronnie Murphy	Greg Switzer
Patrick Cameron	Melvin Hicks	Kevin Oates	Arthur Williamson
John Davis	Dexter Howard	Tony Phillips	Kevin Wright
Spencer Ellison	Kip James	Kevin Richardson	Michael Young
Darrin Falcon	Paul James	Gregory Ridgle	

1986 MANAGERS
Kenneth Dunning
Matt Huey
Kevin Walker
Wallace Webster

1986 ALL-AMERICAN
Derek Russell

1986 ALL-SOUTHERN
Derek Russell

1986 ALL-STATE
Spencer Ellison
Mark Henry
Greg Lewis
Derek Russell

1986 ALL-CONFERENCE

Ricky Anderson	Forrest Stolzer
Johnny Bailey	Greg Switzer
Eric Smith	Kevin Wright
Tommy Sproles	

1986 ALL-STAR TEAM
Greg Lewis
Derek Russell

In its preseason poll, the *Arkansas Democrat* ranked Little Rock Central No. 2. Many in the state favored the Tigers to win their fourth consecutive AAAA-North Conference title and vie for the state championship. Central returned many starters from a team that finished 11-2-0 and reached the semifinals of the state playoffs. One starter who did not return, however, was Sedric Fillmore. Already considered a major-college prospect, the talented sophomore quarterback was not eligible for his junior season because of academic problems.

For the second consecutive year, Coach Bernie Cox and his staff looked to a

Photo provided by Central High School
Herman Botley (55)

sophomore to lead the offense. Sam Khabeer made his debut midway through the second quarter of the season opener against Little Rock Parkview. The first carry of his career resulted in a touchdown as he ran a bootleg around left end from the 3. Greg Fackler converted the extra-point attempt to give Central a 7-0 lead with 7:40 left in the half.

Just before halftime, the Patriots completed an 82-yard, 15-play drive with a 1-yard sneak by quarterback Reginald Johnson. Gerry Rouse, though, missed the extra-point attempt and the Tigers used the mistake to defeat Parkview 7-6.

Central played Little Rock Mills the next week and held the Comets to only five first downs and 104 yards of total offense. Derek Russell started the scoring when he returned Mills' first punt 72 yards for a touchdown. Johnny Bailey scored from the 1, then Eric Smith caught a 38-yard touchdown pass from Khabeer to set the first-quarter score at 21-0.

Tailback Kenneth Bush then took over for the Tigers as he rushed for 91 yards and three touchdowns. Bush scored on runs of 2 yards, 10 yards and 50 yards to complete Central's 41-0 victory over the Comets.

Central hosted old rival Pine Bluff the following week and took advantage of a mistake to take the lead with 1:12 left in the opening period. Pine Bluff was punting deep in its territory when the center

Johnny Bailey

snapped the ball over the head of the punter and out of the end zone. This resulted in a safety and a 2-0 lead for the Tigers.

The ensuing kickoff gave Central possession at the Zebras 48. Eight plays later, Bailey went over left tackle to score from the 1. Bush was brought down before he could add the two-point conversion, but the Tigers led 8-0 with 8:32 remaining in the half.

Late in the third quarter, Pine Bluff's Michael James was stripped of the ball at his 3. Jeff Hanson recovered for Central and Bush scored two plays later on a 1-yard run. The extra-point kick was blocked, but the Tigers maintained the lead at 14-0.

Gregory Ridgle, Central's fullback, fumbled midway through the fourth quarter. The ball was recovered by Marcus Wallace and returned 68 yards for a Pine Bluff touchdown. James ran for two points to narrow the deficit to 14-8 with 4:43 left in the game.

With 11 seconds remaining, Tommy Sproles intercepted a desperation pass to seal a victory for the Tigers.

No. 5 Little Rock Hall High was the next opponent for Central.

The Tigers were able to take an early lead after Bailey returned a punt 41 yards to the Hall High 21. Central was unable to reach the end zone and had to settle for a 29-yard field goal by Greg Switzer with 1:53 left in the first quarter.

Central took the second-half kickoff and drove 71 yards in 10 plays for the game's final score. The drive, kept alive by a 28-yard pass from Khabeer to Spencer Ellison, ended with a 14-yard run by Russell. Switzer's extra-point attempt failed, setting the final at 9-0.

The Tigers ran 57 plays for 202 total yards, while the Warriors ran 38 plays for 68 total yards. Central's defense gave up only three first downs and did not allow Hall High to cross midfield. It also held standout tailback Al Walker to 42 yards on 13 carries.

Next up was a matchup between the top-ranked and undefeated Springdale Bulldogs and the No. 2 and undefeated Little Rock Central Tigers. The battle for No. 1 in the polls drew a crowd of more than 5,000 to Quigley Stadium.

Jamie McEvoy intercepted a Khabeer pass at the Tigers 48 to set up a Springdale touchdown in the first quarter. Mark Mhoon capped the eight-play drive with a 1-yard sneak. Todd Roblee added the extra point to give the Bulldogs a 7-0 lead with 1:20 left in the quarter.

Central received the ensuing kickoff and needed only five plays to score. Bush

Coach Norman Callaway and Mark Henry (58)

377

scored on a 21-yard run up the middle. Switzer's extra-point attempt was wide left, but Springdale's lead was cut to 7-6 in the second quarter.

After receiving the second-half kickoff, the Tigers turned the ball over to the Bulldogs when Bush fumbled at his 30. Springdale's offense could only gain 1 yard and was forced to try a 46-yard field goal. Roblee's kick fell short and the Bulldogs still led 7-6.

With 1:14 left in the game, Switzer attempted a 34-yard field goal. The kick was tipped at the line of scrimmage and fell into the hands of Springdale's Bryan Thompson at the 10. Thompson thought the ball was dead and handed it to Central's Tony Phillips, who took it into the end zone for a touchdown.

As Central fans and players were celebrating, Bulldogs Coach Jarrell Williams called a timeout to talk with the head linesman. Williams protested that the whistle had blown and an official had waved his hands above his head to signal the ball dead. The officials let the play stand and Central took the lead. Springdale stopped Russell's two-point conversion attempt, but the Tigers won the game 12-7 and received the state's top billing in every major high school poll.

After a 21-0 defeat of the Conway Wampus Cats, Central had to come from behind to beat No. 10 North Little Rock Northeast. Trailing 13-2 midway through the fourth quarter, Khabeer was intercepted by David Runsick at the Tigers 24. Runsick, though, was hit hard by Smith and fumbled back to Central to give the Tigers better field position.

Two plays later, Khabeer rolled to his right and threw a deep pass down the sideline to Russell. Once Russell caught the ball, he outran two defenders en route to a 64-yard touchdown. A two-point conversion made it 13-8 with 6:24 left in the game.

After the ensuing kickoff, the Chargers ran two plays before Joe Cyr fumbled. Ricky Anderson recovered to give the Tigers possession on the Northeast 31 with 4:40 remaining.

A 17-yard pass from Khabeer to Smith and two running plays moved Central to the 13. With 3:31 remaining, Bailey took a pitch around right end and outran the defense to the end zone. The two-point conversion again failed, but Central had a 14-13 lead.

Northeast had two final possessions, but each resulted in a turnover. The first ended with a fumble after Cyr was blindsided, and the second ended when Cyr threw an interception. The Tigers were able to hold on for their seventh consecutive victory of the season.

Central tallied another one-point victory the next week when it beat No. 3 Sylvan Hills 13-12. The Tigers finally met their match a week later when unranked Jacksonville High School defeated them on Barry Hickingbotham's 51-yard field goal with eight seconds remaining in the game.

The loss dropped Central to No. 3 in the polls, but the Tigers rebounded with a strong 21-0 win over North Little Rock Ole Main to end the regular season. For the fourth consecutive year, Cen-

Photo provided by Central High School

Kicker Michael Young (10)

tral won the AAAA-North Conference and earned a playoff appearance. This season, the Tigers received a first-round bye.

Central began the playoffs with a second-round matchup against two-time defending state champion Little Rock Catholic High School. The Rockets shocked the Tigers with a long first-quarter drive that ended with an 8-yard touchdown pass from Emmanuel McKeever to Brendan Cook. Rick Richardson converted the extra-point attempt for a 7-0 lead with 1:16 remaining in the first quarter.

Central, however, answered on its next possession when Khabeer ran an option play to the right side. After turning the corner, he pitched to Russell who ran down the sideline for a 51-yard touchdown. Michael Young kicked the extra point to make it 7-7 with 10:15 remaining in the half.

A third-quarter interception by linebacker Greg Lewis gave the Tigers possession at the Catholic High 34 and set up the game-winning touchdown. On Central's seventh play, Russell scored from the 1. Young added the extra point for a 14-7 lead and the victory.

The Class AAAA semifinal game at Quigley Stadium featured top-ranked El Dorado against the No. 2 Tigers.

In front of more than 6,000 fans, Sproles intercepted a pass for Central and returned it to the Wildcats 19. Five plays later, Russell went over right tackle for a 1-yard touchdown. Young then converted the extra-point attempt for a 7-0 lead with 1:29 left in the first quarter.

El Dorado's answer came early in the next period when it drove 67 yards in 14 plays. Terry Davis scored on a run around right end. Kevin Cottrell kicked the extra point to tie the score, 7-7, with 7:26 remaining in the half. The Tigers

regained the lead when Young kicked a 27-yard field goal just before halftime.

An interception by Ellison early in the second half set up an opportunity for Central to increase its lead. A double pass, which ended in the hands of Russell, gained 39 yards to the Wildcats 16. Bailey then went over left tackle for another touchdown. A bad snap hindered the extra-point attempt, but Central led 16-7 midway through the third quarter.

After Bush padded the lead with a 20-yard touchdown run on Central's next possession, El Dorado came back to give the Tigers a scare. Quarterback John Tubberville connected with Davis on a screen pass that resulted in a 63-yard touchdown. The two-point conversion by Davis was good to make it 22-15.

El Dorado had three more possessions, but was unable to capitalize against the strong Central defense. With this 22-15 upset victory over the Wildcats, Central earned a trip to War Memorial Stadium to play for the Class AAAA state championship.

Central, once again Arkansas' No. 1 team, faced No. 3 Fort Smith Northside. Both teams entered the title game with

1986 Tiger cheerleaders

379

similar statistics. The Tigers were averaging 16.3 points per game and allowing 6.5 points per game. The Grizzlies were scoring 15.3 points per game and allowing 8.2 points per game.

In addition to a rematch of the 1985 semifinal game, the battle for the state's official No. 1 team in the largest classification pitted two old friends against each other. Coach Cox and Northside head coach Joe Fred Young worked together for seven years prior to their professions taking them in different directions in 1975. This 1986 matchup marked only the second time that the two coaches met on the field since they parted ways.

At 7:30 p.m. Dec. 6, the Tigers kicked off to Northside to begin the game. The Grizzlies quickly jumped ahead after they put together a nine-play, 69-yard drive that took 4:21 off the clock.

The drive was highlighted by a 34-yard completion from Keith Oglesby to Pat Elam to the Central 9. The touchdown came three plays later when fullback Steve Bell bulled his way through the middle of Central's defense for 6 yards and the score. David Martin converted the extra-point attempt for a 7-0 lead with 7:25 left in the first quarter.

Photo provided by Central High School
Derek Russell (2)

The scoring drive, however, came with a price. Oglesby, Northside's senior quarterback, suffered a broken collarbone and was removed from the game.

The ensuing kickoff by Fort Smith was a high, short kick that gave the Tigers possession at their 44. Central responded with a 56-yard drive that ended after six plays when Russell scored on a 22-yard run. Young added the extra point to tie the score at 7-7 with 4:29 left in the period.

The Tigers took the lead in the second quarter when Russell capped a short drive with a 1-yard run. Young's kick set a halftime score at 14-7.

Central received the second-half kickoff and used only four plays to score. A third-down conversion highlighted the possession when Khabeer dumped a short pass to Smith in the left flat. Lorenzo Jones, the Grizzly defender covering Smith, attempted to intercept the ball, but missed. This left Smith all alone, enabling him to run uncontested for 49 yards and another Central touchdown. Young again converted the extra-point attempt and Central led 21-7 just 1:49 into the third quarter.

After the ensuing kickoff, sophomore quarterback Jay Richardson was

Photo provided by Brian Cox
Coach Bernie Cox is carried off the field following his fifth state championship and the school's 30th

moving the Grizzlies before he was intercepted by Lewis. Lewis returned the interception to the Northside 49, setting up the Tigers' next score.

The 13-play drive consumed 5:58 and produced a 22-yard field goal by Young to make it 24-7 with 1:41 left in the third period.

Central relied on its defense the remainder of the game. The Tigers allowed only 97 yards rushing and 50 yards passing for a total of 147 yards of total offense. It also limited the Grizzlies to six first downs in a 24-7 championship victory.

The Tigers finished the season with a 12-1-0 record, ranked No. 1 in all of Arkansas' major polls and 19th nationally by the National Sports News Service. The season also marked the 30th state championship won by Little Rock Central High School, second nationally to the 35 titles won by Sioux Falls, S.D.

1986 TIGER SCHEDULE

LR Parkview 6	LRCH 7
Mills 0	LRCH 41
Pine Bluff 8	LRCH 14
LR Hall 0	LRCH 9
Springdale 7	LRCH 12
*Conway 0	LRCH 21
*NLR Northeast 13	LRCH 14
*Sylvan Hills 12	LRCH 13
*Jacksonville 10	LRCH 7
*NLR Ole Main 0	LRCH 21
**LR Catholic 7	LRCH 14 (state playoffs)
**El Dorado 15	LRCH 22 (state playoffs)
**FS Northside 7	LRCH 24 (state playoff final)

DEFENDING THE CHAMPIONSHIP

1987   9-1-1

Head Coach: Bernie Cox
Assistants: Norman Callaway, Eddie Boone
Team Physician: Dr. Jim McKenzie

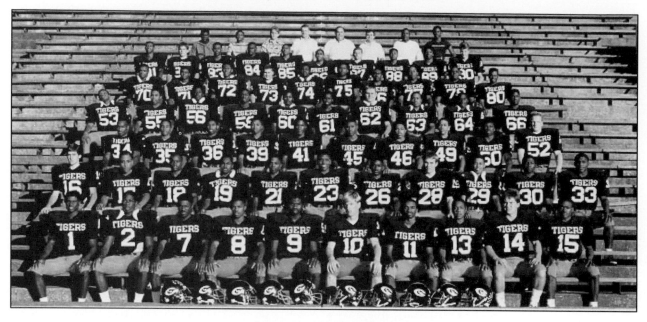

1987 LETTERMEN

Patrick Adams	Chris Gregory	Kurt Johnson	Ronnie Sanders
Henry Berry	Chris Gunn	Kayward Jolly	Fabian Scott
Isaac Brown	Jeff Hanson	Sam Khabeer	Kenneth Smith
Pharoah Brown	William Hargro	Tony Lawson	Patrick Stribling
Kenneth Bush	Kenneth Hayes	Damian McNeal	Keith Trotter
Khayyam Eddings	James Hicks	Jeff Milburn	Kendrick Turner
Anthony Edmondson	Melvin Hicks	Chuck Mitchell	Doug Wallace
Darrin Falcon	Dexter Howard	Mark Persley	Myrick Ware
Chris Fields	Kyle Howard	Tony Phillips	Michael Young
Sedric Fillmore	Kip James	Keith Pride	
Craig Foster	Paul James	Kevin Richardson	
Karl Freeman	Isaac Jenkins	Keith Saine	

1987 MANAGERS

Donnie Craig	Matt Huey
Shawn Davis	Marvin Richardson
Carlos East	James Smith

1987 ALL-AMERICAN
Tony Phillips

1987 ALL-SOUTHERN
Sedric Fillmore

1987 ALL-STATE
Henry Berry
Sedric Fillmore
Tony Phillips

1987 ALL-CONFERENCE
Henry Berry
Kenneth Bush
Sedric Fillmore

1987 ALL-STAR TEAM
Henry Berry
Kenneth Bush

When the 1987 season opened, Central High School was without Dr. John McCollough Smith and Coach Clyde Horton, who both retired after the 1986-87 school year. Both served Tiger athletics for more than half their lives.

Dr. Smith, who played football under Coach Earl Quigley, graduated from Little Rock High School in 1924. In 1944, after his return from World War II where he served as a field surgeon, he became Little Rock's team physician. He spent 43 years taking care of athletes and was affectionately known as "Mr. Tiger."

Coach Horton, who played football under Coach Raymond Burnett, graduated from Little Rock High School in 1947. He returned to Central in 1960 as an assistant football and track coach. He was promoted to head track and cross country coach in 1962, leading the Tigers to eight state championships in track and 14 state championships in cross country.

The retirement of Coach Horton put the Central coaching staff in a predicament. While some football programs in the state had as many as seven coaches, the Tigers had only two full-time assistants.

One of these assistants, Coach Eddie Boone, was an invaluable member of the coaching staff during two-a-day practices and early in the season. However, his time

Photo provided by Central High School

Coach Bernie Cox talks with the defense during a timeout

383

Photo provided by Central High School

Quarterback Sedric Fillmore

with the football team was cut short each year because he was also boys head basketball coach. This thinned the coaching staff to two by the third playing date of the season.

The Little Rock School District turned its head when this issue arose and would not allow Coach Bernie Cox to hire any other coaches until a suitable teaching position became available.

This situation forced assistant coach Norman Callaway to take charge of the entire offense, while Coach Cox handled the defense. There was little time to work on individual positions, or to give any attention to the junior-varsity team. In addition, nobody was available to scout or be in the press box during games.

Even though Coach Cox expected 1987 to be a rebuilding year, the *Arkansas Democrat* ranked Central No. 4 in its preseason poll. The Tigers did prove they could still win as the defense held Little Rock Parkview to 50 yards of total offense in the season-opening game.

Sedric Fillmore, Central's 1985 quarterback who was ineligible in 1986 because of grade problems, was back and led the Tigers to two quick touchdowns. The first score occurred with the help of a little luck and capped a 77-yard drive.

From the Patriots 46, fullback Kurt Johnson burst up the middle and into the Parkview secondary. Johnson, though, fumbled as he was hit by a defender at the 15. Central's Tony Phillips was there to recover and run it into the end zone for the touchdown. Michael Young's conversion attempt was kicked into the line, but Central led 6-0 with 9:38 left in the first quarter.

On their next possession, the Tigers needed only three plays to score. Following an incomplete pass and a penalty, Fillmore connected with Kayward Jolly across the middle. Once Jolly caught the pass, he headed for the sideline and outran the defense for a 69-yard touchdown. Kyle Howard's extra-point attempt was wide, but Central led 12-0 with 6:41 left in the period.

Kenneth Bush scored on a 5-yard run and Kip James scored on a 24-yard interception return in the fourth quarter to put the game away for the Tigers. The game marked the 17th consecutive victory for Central at Quigley Stadium.

A battle with unranked Little Rock Hall ended in a tie game after a special-teams mistake by the Tigers ended in a touchdown for the Warriors. Midway through the first quarter, Phillips fumbled a punt and Hall High's Robert Adams returned it 6 yards for a touchdown. Jason Thompson then added the extra point and the Warriors led 7-0.

It was a big play that got Central on the scoreboard as well. The play came on the Tigers' first possession of the second half when Bush broke free for a 59-yard touchdown run. Young's extra-point attempt tied the score at 7-7.

Central fumbled three times and was intercepted once during the remainder of the third quarter to end any scoring threats.

Young missed a 28-yard field-goal attempt in the fourth quarter, forcing the Tigers to settle for a tie. The tie dropped Central one spot in the poll to No. 5.

The Tigers traveled to Pine Bluff to play the No. 3 Zebras the next week. Central's defense held Pine Bluff to 152 yards of total offense. Bush gave the Tigers a 6-0 lead on a 54-yard run in the second quarter. The defensive effort by Central was good enough for the victory and a 2-0-1 record heading into conference action.

After the second-ranked Tigers won their first two conference games, 21-6 over North Little Rock Ole Main and 29-0 over North Pulaski, they faced No. 4 North Little Rock Northeast.

With 1:11 left in the scoreless first half, Anthony Hubbard intercepted Fillmore at the North Little Rock 4. Three plays moved the Chargers to the 12. Just prior to a Northeast punt, Coach Cox called timeout.

As play resumed, Jolly received the punt at the North Little Rock 45, where he called for a fair catch with 18 seconds left in the half. Coach Cox immediately sent his kicking team in the game and Young proceeded with a free kick that ended in a state-record 55-yard field goal.

Northeast began passing as the second half opened, but it quickly ended as Jolly intercepted Jon Beavers and returned it to the Chargers 38. Seven plays later, it was Bush rushing for a Central touchdown as he went up the middle 14 yards. The snap for the extra-point attempt was dropped by holder Khayyam Eddings, but the Tigers increased their lead to 9-0.

The ensuing possession by North Little Rock was the first scoring drive the Central defense gave up during the season. The 17-play, 80-yard drive took almost nine minutes off the clock and ended when Beavers passed to Anthony Rossini for a 15-yard touchdown. Jay Harbour converted the extra-point attempt to bring Northeast within 9-7 with 11:44 left in the game.

Another touchdown by Bush, this time on a 19-yard run, and an extra point by Young in the fourth quarter sealed the victory for the Tigers, 16-7. The victory

Photo provided by Central High School
Sam Khabeer

moved Central up another spot in the *Arkansas Democrat* poll. The Tigers were now the state's No. 1 team.

The only loss of 1986 was avenged the following week when Central defeated Jacksonville High School 16-7. Young began the scoring with a 42-yard field goal in the second quarter. Just moments later, Sam Khabeer caught a 44-yard touchdown pass from Fillmore for a 9-0 halftime lead.

Bush added a 7-yard touchdown run in the third quarter, but it was unnecessary as the Tigers went on to defeat the Red Devils and remain unbeaten in their last 19 games in Quigley Stadium.

Central traveled to Conway for a game with the Wampus Cats next, a matchup dominated by the Tigers.

One of Conway's first possessions ended with an interception by Jolly, who returned it 35 yards for a touchdown. Another early possession was halted when Central recovered a fumble. The Tigers turned this turnover into a 37-yard field goal by Young for a 10-0 first-quarter lead.

Kenneth Bush (34)

After stopping Conway on fourth-and-goal from the 2, Khabeer led Central on a 13-play, 98-yard drive. The drive was capped by a 21-yard touchdown pass from Khabeer to Jeff Milburn.

Bush added to the lead on the Tigers' first possession of the second half when he broke loose for a 67-yard touchdown run. He scored again on a 19-yard run in the fourth quarter to help the Tigers beat the Wampus Cats 31-0.

Following a 24-3 victory over Sylvan Hills, Central ended the regular season against Cabot High School. On the line for the Tigers was an unbeaten regular season and an outright AAAA-North Conference championship.

Central entered the regular-season finale with five starters out with injuries. The Tigers, though, managed to score three touchdowns to beat the Panthers 21-7.

Keith Pride scored on a 3-yard run, Jolly scored on a 6-yard run and Fillmore highlighted the game with a 66-yard touchdown run. Young converted all three extra-point attempts in helping Central to its ninth victory of the season and its fifth consecutive AAAA-North Conference title.

As a result of their conference championship, the Tigers earned the right to play the first round of the AAAA state playoffs at Quigley Stadium. Central, which was unbeaten and ranked No. 1 in the state, met Benton High School, a team that was unranked and 5-5-0.

Early in the first quarter, a personal-foul penalty was called against the Tigers when a Panther was hit while making a fair catch. This gave Benton possession on the Central 48 and set the stage for the game's first score.

Facing third down from the 24, quarterback Tommy Jumper rolled to his left and found Monty Cornwell alone in the end zone for a touchdown. The extra-point attempt was converted by Randy Russell for a 7-0 lead with 1:32 left in the first quarter.

In the fourth quarter, linebacker Kirk Shelnut intercepted a Fillmore pass at the Benton 49. On first down, Greg Holmes burst through the middle of the defense for a 23-yard gain. A few plays later, a 9-yard pass from Jumper to Scott Long moved Benton to the 14.

Benton eventually ended the series with a 37-yard field goal by Russell to take a 10-0

Coach Norman Callaway and
Sedric Fillmore (9)

lead with 7:22 remaining in the game. Central could not overcome the penalties it continued to tally and eventually succumbed to the Panthers.

The Tigers hadn't been beaten in 20 consecutive games played at Quigley Stadium until this loss against Benton. The last time Central tasted defeat on its home field was during a second-round playoff game against Little Rock Hall School on Nov. 15, 1984.

1987 TIGER SCHEDULE

LR Parkview 0	LRCH 25
LR Hall 7	LRCH 7
Pine Bluff 0	LRCH 6
*NLR Ole Main 6	LRCH 21
*North Pulaski 0	LRCH 29
*NLR Northeast 7	LRCH 16
*Jacksonville 7	LRCH 16
*Conway 0	LRCH 31
*Sylvan Hills 3	LRCH 24
*Cabot 7	LRCH 21
**Benton 10	LRCH 0 (state playoffs)

SIXTH CONSECUTIVE CONFERENCE TITLE

1988   11-2-0

Head Coach: Bernie Cox
Assistants: Norman Callaway, Larry Siegel, Eddie Boone
Team Physician: Dr. Jim McKenzie

1988 LETTERMEN

Marvin Allen	Karl Freeman	Kayward Jolly	Andrew Shelby
Sidney Allen	Chris Gunn	Jeff Jones	Andre Smith
Derrick Anderson	Patrick Hannah	Jabbar Joshua	Doug Switzer
Greg Brown	Kenneth Hayes	Sam Khabeer	Rodney Thompson
Isaac Brown	James Hicks	Damian McNeal	Keith Trotter
Brian Bruso	Melvin Hicks	Chris Moore	Kendrick Turner
Bobby Campbell	Dexter Howard	Jeffrey O'Donald	Doug Wallace
Michael Cunning	Kyle Howard	Mark Persley	Brad Williams
Shawn Davis	Kevin Jacob	Keith Pride	Michael Young
Khayyam Eddings	Isaac Jenkins	Reid Robinson	
Tino Fletcher	Kurt Johnson	Ronnie Sanders	

1988 MANAGERS

Tony Ashley	William Hargro
Grady Bradford	John Hill
Gino Davis	Marvin Richardson

1988 ALL-STATE
Kenneth Hayes
Melvin Hicks
Dexter Howard
Kendrick Turner

1988 ALL-CONFERENCE

Karl Freeman	Damian McNeal
Kurt Johnson	Ronnie Sanders
Kayward Jolly	Andre Smith
Sam Khabeer	

1988 ALL-STAR TEAM
Kenneth Hayes
Dexter Howard

Mrs. Helena K. Quigley, who taught speech at Central High until her retirement in 1951 and wife of the late Earl F. Quigley, left $100,000 to Quigley Stadium after her death in the fall of 1987. The money donated went to the renovation of press boxes, lobbies and rest rooms. The donation also purchased new goal posts, field markers, a sprinkler system, sideline benches, dressing room lockers and a memorial plaque honoring Coach Quigley.

After an unbeaten regular season in 1987 and the loss of few starters to graduation, the Tigers were ranked the state's top team by the *Arkansas Democrat*. The No. 1 team began its campaign with a game against Little Rock Parkview.

The Patriots jumped to an early lead when Roslyn Tensley scored on a 1-yard run to end a short drive. Jeff Hunter converted the extra-point attempt for a 7-0 lead with 4:13 left in the second quarter. Within the next 1:18, though, Central would take total control of the game.

On their ensuing possession, the Tigers scored on a 72-yard pass from Chris Gunn to Kendrick Turner. Michael Young added the extra point to tie the score, 7-7. Parkview's ensuing possession ended on third down when Ronnie Sanders intercepted a Chris Jones pass and returned it 20 yards for a touchdown. Young's extra-point conversion was good for a 14-7 lead with 2:54 left in the half.

Central opened the second half with a 57-yard drive that ended with a 35-yard field goal by Young. The defense then forced the Patriots to end their ensuing possession with a punt. Kayward Jolly received the kick at his 20 and returned it 80 yards for a touchdown. Young's conversion ended the game's scoring and helped Central to a 24-7 season-opening victory.

The Tigers allowed their next opponent, Little Rock Hall High School, only two first downs and an average of 0.6 yards per play. Gunn and Keith Pride both scored on short runs, enabling Central to defeat the Warriors 13-0.

No. 7 Pine Bluff visited Quigley Stadium the next week and once again gave Central a hard-fought battle. The Tigers scored first when Young kicked a 33-yard field goal with 3:09 left in the first quarter. The Zebras tied the score just before half-

Photo provided by Central High School
Kurt Johnson (35)

389

Kayward Jolly

time when Carlos James completed an 11-play drive with a 37-yard field goal.

In the third quarter, Gunn completed a 26-yard pass to Turner to set up a 1-yard scoring run by Jolly. Young's extra-point attempt failed, but he later kicked a 37-yard field goal with 7:10 to play in the game. Central ended up defeating Pine Bluff 12-3 and opened conference play the next week against North Little Rock Ole Main.

Following a 28-0 victory over the Wildcats, a 37-0 victory over North Pulaski and a 23-7 victory over North Little Rock Northeast, the Tigers traveled to Jan Crow Stadium in Jacksonville to play the Red Devils.

When Jacksonville's initial possession ended with a punt, the kick was partially blocked and Central took over at the Red Devils 34. Quarterback Sam Khabeer rolled to his left to score from the 9. Young's conversion attempt was wide, but the Tigers took a 6-0 lead with 6:30 left in the first quarter.

Jacksonville tailback Derrick Taylor attempted to pass on the Red Devils' next possession, but was hit from behind and fumbled. Sanders recovered at the Jackson-

ville 18. It took five plays, but the Tigers scored when Khabeer found Jolly in the end zone for a 4-yard touchdown pass. The two-point conversion attempt failed, but Central took a 12-0 lead into halftime.

The Red Devils scored in the third period when Brian Weber recovered a fumble by Jolly on the second-half kickoff. Two plays after taking over at the 27, Taylor scored on a 21-yard run. The conversion attempt was wide, but the Tigers' lead was cut to 12-6.

With two minutes remaining in the game, Jacksonville had first down on the Central 38. Two plays later, however, Central's Isaac Jenkins intercepted a screen pass to end the scoring threat. Khabeer took a knee three times to end the game and the Tigers escaped with a 12-6 victory.

Unranked Conway High School (3-4-0) visited Quigley Stadium the next week to take on top-ranked Central.

Greg Brown (18)

The Tigers controlled the first half and even opened the third quarter with a 74-yard drive that ended with a 1-yard touchdown run by Greg Brown. Kyle Howard missed the extra-point attempt, but Central led 16-0 with 7:57 left in the quarter.

The Wampus Cats finally scored on their next possession when Mark Griffin took an option pitch and raced 74 yards for a touchdown. Lance Ellison converted the extra-point attempt to pull Conway within 16-7.

The Tigers received the ensuing kickoff and drove 52 yards to the Conway 12. Khabeer, however, fumbled at the 15 and it was recovered by the Wampus Cats' Jamie McDougal.

Conway put together a 15-play, 86-yard drive and scored on a 10-yard slant pass form Michael Wiley to Tom Fisher. Ellison's conversion attempt was good to bring the Wampus Cats within 16-14 with 9:25 remaining in the game.

On Central's next possession, it again drove into Conway territory and again ended the drive with a turnover. The Wampus Cats took control with 5:12 left after Bobby Campbell caught a pass from Khabeer and fumbled at the 30.

After Conway had driven to the Tigers 22, Ellison entered the game to attempt a 39-yard field goal with 35 second left. The

Photo provided by Central High School
Keith Pride (30)

Photo provided by Central High School
Jabbar Joshua

kick sailed over the crossbar with plenty of room to spare to give the Wampus Cats a 17-16 victory over Central. The game, which marked only the Tigers' second loss in Quigley Stadium since Nov. 15, 1984, knocked them to No. 4 in the statewide rankings.

With 22 seconds left in its next game, Central needed a 51-yard touchdown run by Khabeer to beat Sylvan Hills. Young's extra point set the final at 16-12. The victory guaranteed the Tigers at least a share of their sixth consecutive AAAA-North Conference title.

Following a 20-3 victory over Cabot in the regular-season finale, Central opened the playoffs with a 41-0 victory over Helena-West Helena Central to set up a rematch with Pine Bluff High School in the quarterfinals of the playoffs.

Field goals of 35 and 23 yards by Young, along with Pride's 3-yard touchdown run, were enough to defeat the Zebras 13-3. Pride rushed for 144 yards and was

391

involved in 29 of Central's 42 offensive plays during the victory.

The No. 3 Tigers hosted No. 4 Fort Smith Southside in the semifinals of the state playoffs the following week.

The Rebels held Pride to 45 yards rushing and limited Central's offense to only one scoring threat, a 26-yard field goal attempt that was missed by Young. The game was highlighted by Eric Botsch's 67-yard punt return that helped Southside to a 17-0 upset victory over the Tigers.

1988 TIGER SCHEDULE

LR Parkview 7	LRCH 24
LR Hall 0	LRCH 13
Pine Bluff 3	LRCH 12
*NLR Ole Main 0	LRCH 28
*North Pulaski 0	LRCH 37
*NLR Northeast 7	LRCH 23
*Jacksonville 6	LRCH 12
*Conway 17	LRCH 16
*Sylvan Hills 12	LRCH 16
*Cabot 3	LRCH 20
**Helena-West Helena 0	LRCH 41 (state playoffs)
**Pine Bluff 3	LRCH 13 (state playoffs)
**FS Southside 17	LRCH 0 (state playoffs)

THE AAAA-NORTH DOMINATION ENDS

1989   6-5-0

Head Coach: Bernie Cox
Assistants: Norman Callaway, Larry Siegel, Eddie Boone
Team Physician: Dr. Jim McKenzie

1989 LETTERMEN

Sidney Allen	Brian Cox	James Hicks	David Peevy
Eric Barnes	Bob Davenport	Kyle Howard	Carlton Peoples
Marc Bridges	Kelly Eddings	Isaac Jenkins	Mark Persley
Calvin Brown	Khayyam Eddings	James Johnson	Reid Robinson
Isaac Brown	Nathan Freeman	Jabbar Joshua	Jason Starling
Charlie Bruce	Chris Gregory	Earl Lyons	Doug Switzer
Brian Bruso	Jay Griffin	Chris Moore	Keith Trotter
Bobby Campbell	Chris Gunn	Jason Moore	Steve Warren
Michael Cunning	Derrick Hampton	Dorrian Myles	Brad Williams

1989 MANAGERS
Tony Ashley
Marvin Richardson
Charles Walker

1989 ALL-STATE
James Hicks
Jabbar Joshua

1989 ALL-CONFERENCE

Marc Bridges   Jabbar Joshua
Chris Gregory   Doug Switzer
James Hicks   Steve Warren
Isaac Jenkins

1989 ALL-STAR TEAM
Jabbar Joshua

Graduation took with it many of the starters from the 1988 lineup. Because of this, Central High School entered the new season unranked for the first time in several years.

The Tigers dressed 64 players in their season-opening game against Little Rock Parkview. After holding the Patriots on their first possession, Central's Doug Switzer fielded a Parkview punt and returned it 58 yards for a touchdown. A bad snap on the extra-point attempt forced holder Chris Gunn to roll out and attempt a two-point conversion. Gunn found Brad Williams in the end zone to put the Tigers up 8-0 with 8:45 left in the first quarter.

Gunn also passed for two touchdowns, 9 yards to Switzer and 24 yards to Williams, and Charlie Bruce scored on a 5-yard run to help defeat the Patriots 29-14. The game ended early because of severe light-ning, which caused the lights to go out with 4:13 remaining.

For Central's next game against Little Rock Hall High, the starting time and date of the game were changed. To try and stir memories of the Thanksgiving Day rivalry, tradition and atmosphere, the game was moved to Saturday morning at 10.

The Warriors scored on their first possession of the game after driving 60 yards in nine plays. From the Tigers 28, Hall High quarterback Siegfried Ward rolled to his left and was hit hard by Steve Warren. Just before hitting the ground, though, Ward pitched to tailback Aaron Gardner, who took it into the end zone. Jason Gillen's extra-point attempt hit the upright, but the Warriors took a 6-0 lead.

In the second quarter, a 42-yard pass from Gunn to Switzer gave Central first down at the Hall High 11. On fourth down from the 2, however, tailback Marc Bridges was stopped for no gain and the Warriors took possession.

On Hall High's first play, James Hicks recovered a fumble by Gardner. This set up a 3-yard touchdown pass from Gunn to Switzer. Kyle Howard's extra-point attempt was wide, but the Tigers had tied the score, 6-6.

After recovering the second-half kickoff, the Warriors put together a 12-play, 69-yard drive. Billy Sliger scored from the 2, but Ward passed incomplete for the two-point conversion.

Photo provided by Central High School
Tailback Marc Bridges (2) vs. Little Rock Hall

394

Isaac Jenkins (46) and Brad Williams (13)

Hall High had a 12-6 lead with 5:56 left in the third quarter, but Central would answer only seconds later.

On their ensuing possession, the Tigers again tied the score when Gunn passed to Bridges for a 75-yard touchdown. Gunn's two-point conversion pass to Williams was incomplete to set the score at 12-12.

Midway through the fourth quarter, the Warriors drove deep into Central territory and faced fourth down at the 2. Ward took the snap, faked to Sliger, ran to his right and pitched to Gardner while being hit. Gardner ran around the cornerback to score the game-winning touchdown. Gillen converted the extra-point attempt and Hall High held on for a 19-12. The game marked the first time in six years that the Tigers were defeated by the Warriors.

Jordan Stadium in Pine Bluff was the site of Central's next game.

As the Zebras' Basil Shabazz fielded a Howard punt in the second quarter, he received a block from Tracy Caldwell, cut toward his left sideline and outran the punt coverage team en route to an 86-yard touchdown. Mike Meroney's extra point gave Pine Bluff a 7-0 lead.

With 12 seconds remaining in the half, Pine Bluff added to its lead. Quarterback Keith Campbell rolled to his right and passed to Dennis Johnson. Johnson weaved his way through the Central secondary for a 58-yard touchdown play. Meroney converted the extra-point attempt and the Zebras went on to defeat the Tigers 14-0.

AAAA-North Conference play began the following week against North Little Rock Ole Main. Central struck first with a 14-play, 56-yard drive that was capped by a 4-yard run by Bridges. Bridges added the two-point conversion to give the Tigers an 8-0 advantage with 1:38 left in the second quarter.

The Wildcats took the ensuing kickoff and drove to the Central 40. But quarterback Demetris Chism was then intercepted by Warren at the 27 with 1:20 left in the half. The Tigers, though, were unable to run out the clock and were forced to punt with seven seconds remaining.

The snap by Brian Cox, Coach Bernie Cox's son, sailed over the head of Howard and into the end zone. Ole Main's Mark Jones recovered to give the Wildcats a touchdown with no time left. Chism con-

Dorrian Myles (48) blocks a punt

verted the two-point conversion to make it 8-8 at halftime.

Central opened the second half and controlled the clock during a 13-play, 67-yard drive that consumed 6:13 of the third quarter. Bridges ended the drive with a 3-yard touchdown run. Howard added the extra point to give the Tigers a 15-8 victory over Ole Main.

A 21-0 victory over North Pulaski and a 13-2 defeat of North Little Rock Northeast, which featured an 81-yard touchdown run by Bruce, set up a homecoming battle against Jacksonville High School.

On Wednesday prior to the game, a homecoming pep rally took place in the courtyard of Central High School. The fun and spirited event, however, soon turned ugly.

A fight broke out among a few students and soon escalated into a free-for-all race riot. Numerous fights took place on the front lawn and on every floor of the five-story school.

With the world's eyes continually watching Little Rock and Central High following the integration crisis of 1957, only 32 years earlier, news of the racial situation quickly made its way around the globe. Increased security and increased absences were normal for several days following the event.

The game, however, went on as scheduled and homecoming continued to get worse as the Red Devils defeated Central 3-0. The game-winning play occurred in second quarter when Jody Urquhart kicked a 25-yard field goal.

Bridges, the Tigers' sophomore tailback, led Central past Conway High School the next week. Bridges rushed for 152 yards on 23 carries and scored three touchdowns, including a 43-yarder, in a 27-7 victory over the Wampus Cats.

Photo provided by Central High School

Marc Bridges (2)

No. 8 Sylvan Hills was next on the schedule for the Tigers. Bears quarterback Rufus Pearson put his team on the scoreboard first when he turned a broken play into a 43-yard touchdown run.

Central, though, answered on its next possession when Bridges capped an 80-yard drive with a 1-yard touchdown run. Howard converted the extra-point attempt to make it 7-7 with one second left in the opening quarter.

With 49 seconds remaining in the half, Sylvan Hills again took the lead when Chad Allen ended a 10-play drive with a 40-yard field goal. The kick would prove to be the game-winning play, but the Bears added another score in the fourth quarter when Pearson connected with John Dippel for a 7-yard touchdown pass. Allen's extra-point conversion gave Sylvan Hills a 17-7 victory and guaranteed the Bears the AAAA-North Conference championship.

Following a convincing 27-0 victory over Cabot High School to end the regular season, the Tigers opened postseason play with a trip to C.W. Lewis Stadium to take on Benton High School. The Panthers, AAAA-South Conference champions, totaled 375 yards of offense against Central, while the Tigers finished with 66 yards passing and only 8 yards rushing.

Central punted to end its first possession and then quickly fell behind. After receiving the kick, Benton put together a 61-yard drive and scored on a 3-yard run by Jamie Jones. John Graves added the extra point and the Panthers led 7-0 with 4:02 left in the first quarter.

The Tigers punted again on their next possession, and Benton again took advantage. On the Panthers' first play, quarterback Brad Collatt connected with Rick Daniel on a short slant pass. Daniel outran the defense for a 65-yard touchdown.

Graves' extra point gave Benton a 14-0 lead with 1:32 remaining in the first quarter.

The Panthers opened the second half with an 18-play, 81-yard drive that consumed 9:29 off the clock. Greg Mundy bulled his way up the middle for a 2-yard touchdown run. Graves converted the extra-point attempt to give Benton a 21-0 victory over the Tigers.

The first-round playoff loss ended Central's season at 6-5-0. It also marked the first time in six years that the Tigers had not won the AAAA-North Conference. Central finished tied for second in the conference with Jacksonville High School.

1989 TIGER SCHEDULE

LR Parkview 14	LRCH 29
LR Hall 19	LRCH 12
Pine Bluff 14	LRCH 0
*Ole Main 8	LRCH 15
*North Pulaski 0	LRCH 21
*NLR Northeast 2	LRCH 13
*Jacksonville 3	LRCH 0
*Conway 7	LRCH 27
*Sylvan Hills 17	LRCH 7
*Cabot 0	LRCH 27
**Benton 21	LRCH 0 (state playoffs)

BERNIE COX WINS MORE THAN ANY OTHER

1990   8-5-0

Head Coach: Bernie Cox
Assistants: Norman Callaway, Larry Siegel, Eddie Boone
Team Physician: Dr. Jim McKenzie

1990 LETTERMEN

Eric Barnes	Derrick Harris	Shaun Molden	Allen Rose
Marc Bridges	Leotis Harris	Jason Moore	Kipkeno Saine
Brian Bruso	Tate Heuer	Allen Morton	Michael Sanders
Bob Davenport	Calvin Jefferson	Dorrian Myles	Ray Sessions
Marcus Day	James Johnson	Ray Nealy	Jason Starling
Mark Dickerson	Bobby Khabeer	David Peevy	Doug Switzer
Kelly Eddings	Reginald Killingsworth	Carlton Peoples	Steve Warren
Nathan Freeman	Earl Lyons	Albert Peterson	Brad Williams

1990 MANAGERS
John Milligan
Chris Windsor

1990 ALL-STATE
Marc Bridges
Doug Switzer
Brad Williams

1990 ALL-CONFERENCE
Eric Barnes
Leotis Harris
Dorrian Myles
David Peevy

1990 ALL-STAR TEAM
Doug Switzer

The Tigers opened the new decade with a 40-0 domination of Little Rock Parkview. Marc Bridges highlighted the game with 107 yards rushing and four touchdowns. Brad Williams scored for the defense when he returned an interception 40 yards for a touchdown. Ray Nealy also returned a punt 67 yards for a touchdown.

Eight days later on Saturday morning, the Tigers met Little Rock Hall High School. Central took the opening kickoff and put together a six-play, 70-yard drive that ended with a 48-yard touchdown run by Bridges. The extra-point attempt was blocked, but the Tigers led 6-0.

Hall, though, answered on its first possession when it also drove 70 yards for a touchdown. Quarterback Delando Mack completed a 16-yard pass to Aaron Gardner for the score with 1:20 left in the quarter.

Hall's Chris Hayes intercepted Central quarterback Doug Switzer in the second quarter to give the Warriors possession at their 40. Hall quickly scored when Mack passed to Russell Watson for a 35-yard touchdown. A two-point conversion attempt failed, but Hall led 12-6 at halftime.

The Tigers turned a fourth-quarter interception into points. Just minutes after the first turnover, Switzer passed to Nealy for a 35-yard touchdown. Only three plays into the Warriors' next possession, Mack was intercepted by Albert Peterson, who returned it 52 yards for a touchdown to give Central an 18-12 lead.

The final touchdown by the Tigers occurred with 23 seconds remaining in the game. Bridges took a handoff from Switzer and raced 47 yards for the score. Jason Moore's extra point set the final at 25-12.

Bridges led all rushers with 144 yards on 16 carries. The victory avenged a 19-12 loss to Hall in 1989 and also brought the bell back to Central High School.

Photo provided by Central High School

Tiger fans vs. Little Rock Hall

The unranked Tigers hosted third-ranked Pine Bluff the following week. With Bridges sidelined by an injury, sophomore Bobby Khabeer got the start at tailback. On Central's third possession, Khabeer ran 15 yards around left end for a touchdown. Moore's extra point gave Central a 7-0 lead in the first quarter.

The Zebras' Basil Shabazz returned the ensuing kickoff 43 yards, and his team then put together a 54-yard drive that lasted only seven plays. Quarterback Bradley Benton followed Shabazz over right tackle from the 2 for the score. Chris Anderson converted the extra-point attempt to make it 7-7.

In the third quarter, Pine Bluff took the lead when Benton capped a 56-yard drive with a 36-yard scoring pass to Shabazz. The extra-point attempt was blocked and the Zebras led 13-7. The Tigers, though, took the ensuing possession and drove 65 yards in nine plays to regain the lead.

Bridges entered the game and carried five times to set up a 10-yard pass from Switzer to Williams for a touchdown. Moore's kick gave Central a 14-13 lead. The lead increased just before the game

Photo provided by Central High School
Doug Switzer (8)

ended when Switzer passed to Nealy for a 16-yard touchdown. Moore's extra point gave Central a 21-13 victory.

Safety Steve Warren led Central's defense with three interceptions and several pass breakups. Bridges led the offense with 102 yards rushing in the second half. Following the victory over Pine Bluff, the Tigers entered the *Arkansas Gazette* poll at No. 8.

The victory was Coach Bernie Cox's 134th at Central, tying the school record set by Earl Quigley. Quigley coached Central for 19 seasons and amassed a record of 134-52-9.

North Little Rock Ole Main and North Little Rock Northeast merged following the 1989 season, resulting in the rebirth of North Little Rock High School. The North Little Rock Charging Wildcats marked the conference opener for the Tigers.

A record-setting victory for Cox did not come the following week as unranked North Little Rock scored a 38-13 upset. The Charging Wildcats held Central to three first downs and only 87 yards rushing. The

Tigers' only touchdowns came on a 42-yard run by Bridges and a 74-yard pass from Switzer to Peterson. The game marked the first loss of the season for Central and dropped it to No. 9 in the *Arkansas Gazette* poll.

North Pulaski was the site of the Tigers' next game. The Falcons jumped ahead early when they took the opening kickoff and drove 76 yards in seven plays. Welton Walker scored on a 12-yard run; Thomas Hudson converted the extra-point attempt for a 7-0 lead with 9:10 left in the initial quarter.

It wasn't until late in the quarter that Central answered. A 19-yard pass from Switzer to Nealy was good for a touchdown. Moore's kick tied the score at 7-7. With 6:15 left in the half, the two connected again, this time on a 15-yard touchdown pass. Moore's kick gave the Tigers a 14-7 lead.

Leotis Harris recovered a Michael Nunnerly fumble on North Pulaski's next offensive play to give Central possession at the Falcons 30. On fourth down from the 5, Bridges scored on a sweep. Moore's kick increased the lead to 21-7.

With the Tigers leading 21-14, North Pulaski was at the Central 1 with 5:37 remaining in the game. Carlton Peoples inter-

Photo provided by Central High School
Marc Bridges (2)

cepted a fourth-down pass and returned it 49 yards to end the Falcons' scoring threat. Bridges, who finished with 183 yards on 29 carries, ran 11 yards for a touchdown with 2:19 left to seal the victory.

The victory over North Pulaski finally gave Coach Cox his 135th victory and made him the winningest coach in Central High School history.

Seventh-ranked Benton High School defeated the No. 8 Tigers 10-6 in a nonconference game at C.W. Lewis Stadium in Benton. Bridges rushed for 107 yards, but Central's offense could only manage two field goals by Moore.

The Tigers fell to Jacksonville High School 14-12 in their next game. Down 14-6 with 3:46 left in the game, Central's Eric Barnes recovered a fumble in the end zone to narrow the score to 14-12. Bridges then attempted a two-point conversion, but was stopped by the Red Devils' Eric Williams.

After falling out of the *Arkansas Gazette's* prep poll, the Tigers tried to regain respect when they hosted Conway High School. After being held to 59 yards rushing against Jacksonville, Bridges gained 186 yards on 18 carries and scored one touchdown against the Wampus Cats.

The scoring didn't begin until the second quarter when Switzer hit Nealy for a 44-yard touchdown pass. Harris then intercepted a Conway pass and returned it 34

Photo provided by Central High School
Bobby Khabeer

yards for a touchdown.

In the third quarter, Nealy caught another touchdown pass from Switzer, this one a 24-yard reception. Bridges scored from the 1 in the fourth quarter, and Moore converted his fourth extra-point attempt of the game in a 28-9 victory.

Following a 30-10 loss to Sylvan Hills, the Tigers defeated Cabot High School and guaranteed themselves a spot in the AAAA state playoffs. Central finished fourth in the AAAA-North Conference and entered the playoffs as a No. 4 seed. The Tigers opened the playoffs at West Memphis, No. 1 seed from the AAAA-East Conference.

Switzer led his team past the Blue Devils by completing 8 of 13 passes for 121 yards. After a 21-yard scoring run by Bridges, Central almost immediately struck again when a Switzer to Bridges pass ended in a 63-yard touchdown completion. Moore added the game's final points when he kicked a 29-yard field goal. The Tigers defeated West Memphis 17-0.

In a quarterfinal playoff game, Central hosted No. 5 Little Rock Catholic. The Tigers, now ranked No. 12, controlled the game early as their defense held the Rockets to nine offensive plays, 36 yards of of-

Photo provided by Central High School
Albert Peterson

401

fense and one first down during the first half.

Central took the lead in the first quarter after driving 80 yards in 17 plays. Bridges carried 13 times for 62 yards during the drive and capped it with a 2-yard scoring run. Moore's extra-point attempt failed, but he made up for it in the second quarter when he kicked a 34-yard field goal to give the Tigers a 9-0 lead with 9:30 left in the half.

An 88-yard drive by Catholic ended only 32 seconds into the fourth quarter when Chris Flis scored on a 5-yard run. Spencer Davies added the extra point to narrow the score to 9-7.

Quarterback Q. Perna went down with an injury on Catholic's next possession, and his replacement, sophomore Rustin Glover, threw an interception on the next play. Peo-

ples returned the interception 17 yards for a touchdown. Moore's extra point increased Central's lead to 16-7.

Gary Hogue brought the Rockets to within three points, 16-13, after a 1-yard touchdown run ended a short drive in the fourth quarter. The Tigers, though, put the game away just 32 seconds later when Bridges scampered 53 yards for a touchdown in a 22-13 victory. Bridges finished with 167 yards on 37 carries.

This victory set up a semifinal game between No. 5 Central and No. 3 Texarkana. The 12-0-0 Razorbacks, though, would not allow the contest to be interesting.

Texarkana dominated the game, holding the Tigers to only 26 yards rushing and 56 yards of total offense. After taking a 20-0 halftime lead, the Razorbacks ended Central's season 30-0.

1990 TIGER SCHEDULE

LR Parkview 0	LRCH 40
LR Hall 12	LRCH 25
Pine Bluff 13	LRCH 21
*North Little Rock 38	LRCH 13
*North Pulaski 14	LRCH 28
Benton 10	LRCH 6
*Jacksonville 14	LRCH 12
*Conway 9	LRCH 28
*Sylvan Hills 30	LRCH 10
*Cabot 13	LRCH 27
**West Memphis 0	LRCH 17 (state playoffs)
**LR Catholic 13	LRCH 22 (state playoffs)
**Texarkana 30	LRCH 0 (state playoffs)

A NEW CONFERENCE, A NEW CHAMPIONSHIP

1991   9-4-0

Head Coach: Bernie Cox
Assistants: Norman Callaway, Larry Siegel, Eddie Boone
Team Trainer: Ricky Yamin
Team Physician: Dr. Roger Clark

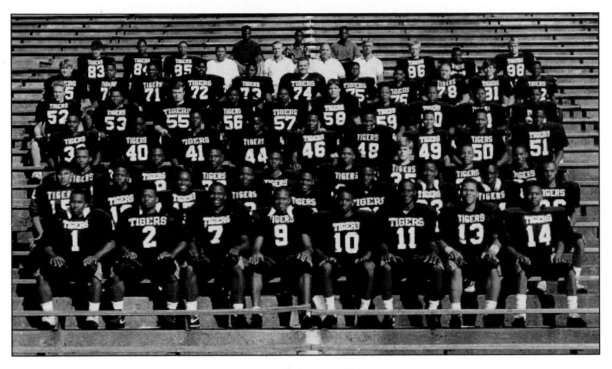

1991 LETTERMEN

Corry Adams	Leodis Gupton	Bobby Khabeer	David Peevy
Eric Barnes	Moses Hall	Reginald Killingsworth	Carlton Peoples
Marc Bridges	Derrick Harris	Jason Lilly	Albert Peterson
Damon Coleman	Leotis Harris	Darryl Lunon	Allen Ross
Marlon Coleman	Tate Heuer	Earl Lyons	Kenon Saine
Dwan Cribbs	Byron Hilliard	Jason Moore	Kenoris Saine
Mark Dickerson	Bion James	Mellow Moore	Kipkeno Saine
Bryan Dorathy	Calvin Jefferson	Allen Morton	Michael Sanders
Marcus Eubanks	James Johnson	Dorrian Myles	Ray Sessions
Nathan Freeman	Eric Jones	Ray Nealy	Reggie Swinton

1991 MANAGERS
Nathaniel Austin
Cory Smith
Gary Ticey

1991 ALL-STATE
Eric Barnes
Marc Bridges
Leotis Harris
David Peevy

1991 ALL-CONFERENCE

Corry Adams   Earl Lyons
Mark Dickerson   Allen Morton
Tate Heuer   Dorrian Myles
James Johnson

1991 ALL-STAR TEAM
Marc Bridges
David Peevy

Central welcomed a transfer from Sylvan Hills High School for the 1991 season. Corry Adams rushed for more than 1,000 yards as a sophomore at Sylvan Hills and now, as a junior, gave the Tigers a much more explosive backfield. Adams and senior Marc Bridges split time at tailback and shared the field in a split-back formation to give Central a double threat against opposing defenses.

The season opened with a game against defending state champion Pine Bluff. A large crowd turned out at Quigley Stadium to watch the *Arkansas Democrat's* No. 2 Zebras and the No. 10 Tigers battle in a game of ball control.

Following a scoreless first half, Central finally scored when Jason Moore kicked a 27-yard field goal with 4:54 left in the third quarter. Pine Bluff answered with seven seconds remaining in the quarter when quarterback Bradley Benton ended a 12-play, 67-yard drive with a 4-yard touchdown run. Ronnie Adams converted the extra-point attempt for a 7-3 lead.

The fourth quarter was scoreless and the Zebras held on to defeat the Tigers. Bridges finished with 108 yards rushing, but could not find the end zone. The Tigers did, however, move up to No. 7 in the polls.

The competition only got tougher as they hosted top-ranked Fort Smith Southside the next week. A passing team, the Rebels were led by Coach Barry Lunney's son, quarterback Barry Lunney Jr.

A fumble by Lunney Jr. led to a Central touchdown in the first quarter. Mark

Photo provided by Central High School
Corry Adams

Dickerson recovered at the Southside 45. The Tigers scored five plays later when quarterback Leotis Harris Jr. completed a 25-yard pass to Ray Nealy. Moore added the extra point for a 7-0 lead with 4:53 left in the opening quarter.

Central struck again on its next possession when Adams capped a 72-yard drive with a 6-yard touchdown run. Moore converted the extra-point attempt and the Tigers took a 14-0 lead.

Central's Joseph McCardell recovered a fumble on the ensuing kickoff and the Tigers took control on the Rebels 30. As Central was driving in for another score, Harris fumbled at the 9. Jamie Mackey recovered for Southside and ended a serious scoring threat by the Tigers.

Lunney took his team down the field and threw a 27-yard touchdown pass to Donnie Knotts with 3:57 left in the half. Louie Castenada converted the extra-point attempt and Central's lead was narrowed to 14-7.

The Rebels tied the score with 59 second left in the third quarter when Lunney found Justin Forsgren for a 46-yard touchdown pass. Castenada added the extra point to make it 14-14.

The Tigers answered immediately. Adams, who finished with 206 yards rushing, broke through the line for a 63-yard touchdown run. The conversion attempt failed, however, leaving Southside an opportunity to take the lead if it could score and convert the extra-point attempt.

Lunney needed only 1:32 to do just that. He led his Rebels to the end zone using only three plays. Pass plays of 16 yards and 31 yards to Forsgren and a 48-yard touchdown pass to Knotts was all it took to tie the score, 20-20. Castenada gave Southside the lead when his extra-point kick cleared the uprights with 5:23 left in the game.

Central was able to move against a tired defense, but was forced to attempt a 23-yard field goal. The kick, which would have won the game, was blocked by Knotts and Derrick Arter with 1:28 to play. The Tigers remained winless, but dropped only one spot in the polls to No. 8.

Photo provided by Central High School
Reggie Swinton

After opening the season with losses against the state's top two teams, Central won its first game, 21-0, over Little Rock Fair High School. The game, which was the first meeting between the schools, featured a 56-yard touchdown pass from Harris to Nealy, a 29-yard touchdown pass from Harris to Bridges, a 3-yard touchdown run by Bridges and a stout defense that allowed the War Eagles only 141 total yards of offense.

Sophomore Reggie Swinton helped Central beat Little Rock Hall the next week when he scored on punt returns of 67 and 63 yards. The Tigers easily defeated the Warriors 34-6 to win the annual "Battle for the Bell."

Things were not as easy the following week at Lion Stadium, where Central took on Little Rock McClellan. The Tigers needed a 75-yard kickoff return by Nealy and a 76-yard touchdown run by Adams to defeat the Lions. Adams rushed for 150 yards in the 20-16 conference victory.

No. 5 Central hosted North Little Rock the next week and relied on size and strength to bull its

Photo provided by Central High School
Corry Adams (8) and Marc Bridges (2)

405

way past the Charging Wildcats. Trailing 10-6, the Tigers' Allen Morton recovered a fumble at the North Little Rock 8. Adams broke through the defense on the next play for a touchdown; Moore's extra point put Central in front 12-10.

The Charging Wildcats had a short drive stall at their 34 with 2:12 left in the game. The Tigers took possession and attempted to run out the clock, but Adams popped through the middle of the line for a 16-yard touchdown run with 1:03 left. Moore's extra point ended Central's 19-10 victory.

After moving up to No. 4, Central traveled to Conway for a conference battle with the No. 10 Wampus Cats.

With the score tied 7-7 in the fourth quarter, the Tigers were held on downs at the Conway 27. On the first play from scrimmage, quarterback Reuel Shepherd ran 70 yards before being brought down at the 3. Three plays later, Shepherd crossed the goal line to take the lead. Blake Merritt added the extra point with 6:27 left in the game in Conway's 14-7 victory.

Central had a chance for a final possession with approximately a minute remaining. But two return men could not field a punt cleanly and Conway recovered to end any last-minute hopes for the Tigers.

After falling to No. 9 in the polls, Central used the next two games to regain its confidence. The Tigers dominated Little Rock Parkview 53-7, and then beat Sylvan Hills 55-14.

Harris completed three touchdown passes in the victory over the Patriots, while Dickerson added a touchdown on a 52-yard interception return. Against the Sylvan Hills Bears, Central's backfield accounted for 275 yards and seven touchdowns.

The Tigers needed this confidence boost going into their final game of the regular season, a matchup against No. 5 Little Rock Catholic. The winner would be guaranteed at least a share of the AAAA-Central Conference title. The Tigers had been a member of AAAA-North from 1983-1990.

Down 7-6 in the fourth quarter, Central defensive lineman James Johnson intercepted quarterback Josh Wilson's batted down pass to give the Tigers possession with 7:45 left in the game. A 32-yard drive ended when Adams scored his second touchdown of the night on a 1-yard run. Harris passed to Nealy for a two-point conversion to give the Tigers a 14-7 lead with 4:07 remaining.

The Rockets, however, put together a 76-yard drive after receiving the ensuing kickoff. Wilson completed two passes to Pat Longworth, the last a 2-yard touchdown. Catholic received a motion penalty during the extra-point attempt and the ball was moved back 5 yards to the 8. John Watts' kick was no good and Central remained ahead 14-13. Morton recovered an onside kick and the Tigers ran out the 11 seconds left on the clock to win a share of the conference championship.

Central shared the title with North Little Rock, which also had a 6-1 record. But Central's victory over the Charging Wildcats earlier in the season gave the Tigers the conference's No. 1 playoff seed.

After playoff victories over Jonesboro (34-0) and Benton (35-0), Central traveled to Northwest Arkansas to take on No. 1 Springdale. Prior to the game, a torrential downpour caused the field to turn into a muddy nightmare for both teams. The game

Marc Bridges (2)

immediately became a battle of the defenses.

The No. 4 Tigers held the Bulldogs to 123 yards of total offense, five first downs and six points. These points occurred on a 12-yard pass from Shane Beyer to Casey McMillan with 11:55 left in the first half. The 11-play, 49-yard drive was the only offensive flurry Springdale put together all night.

It turned out to be enough.

Central's only score occurred after a nine-play, 69-yard drive ended when Moore kicked a 32-yard field goal as the first half expired.

The 6-3 loss to the Bulldogs ended the season for the Tigers and brought an end to the career of another outstanding tailback at Little Rock Central. Bridges finished his junior and senior seasons with more than 1,000 yards rushing and finished his career with 3,299 yards.

Bernie Cox was named Metro Coach of the Year by the *Arkansas Democrat* following the season. Coach Cox ended the season with a career record of 148-46-7.

1991 TIGER SCHEDULE

Pine Bluff 7	LRCH 3
FS Southside 21	LRCH 20
LR Fair 0	LRCH 21
LR Hall 6	LRCH 34
*LR McClellan 16	LRCH 20
*North Little Rock 10	LRCH 19
*Conway 14	LRCH 7
*LR Parkview 7	LRCH 53
*Sylvan Hills 14	LRCH 55
*LR Catholic 13	LRCH 14
**Jonesboro 0	LRCH 34 (state playoffs)
**Benton 0	LRCH 35 (state playoffs)
**Springdale 6	LRCH 3 (state playoffs)

CONFERENCE CHAMPS AGAIN

1992   8-3-0

Head Coach: Bernie Cox
Assistants: Norman Callaway, Larry Siegel,
Team Trainer: Rick Yamin
Team Physician: Dr. Roger Clark

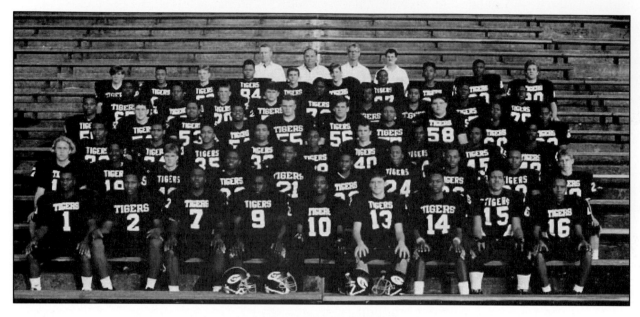

1992 LETTERMEN

Corry Adams	Mark Dickerson	Bobby Khabeer	Bill Ruth
Keith Adams	Travis Gamble	Chris Killingsworth	Kenon Saine
Tony Baker	Robert Gray	Brad Kusturin	Kenoris Saine
Rory Bernard	Brian Harris	Ryan McElroy	John Sartin
Thomas Blake	Derrick Harris	Mellow Moore	Ray Sessions
Fuller Bumpers	Tate Heuer	Davin Moorman	Jhmichea Snyder
Drew Cates	Bion James	Ray Nealy	Reggie Swinton
Derrick Coleman	Byron Jenkins	Brant Owens	Will Thurmond
Dwan Cribbs	Kevin Jenkins	Gary Pighee	Bobby Torrence
Marcus Day	Kevin Jones	Ryan Rusinko	Dustin Turner

1992 MANAGERS
None

1992 ALL-STATE
Corry Adams
Derrick Harris
Tate Heuer
Ray Nealy

1992 ALL-CONFERENCE
Mark Dickerson
Bobby Khabeer
Bill Ruth
Ray Sessions

1992 ALL-STAR TEAM
Derrick Harris

After sharing the conference championship with North Little Rock the previous year, Central entered 1992 hoping to win its first outright title in the AAAA-Central Conference. The schedule, though, began with nonconference foe Pine Bluff.

The fifth-ranked Tigers traveled to Jordan Stadium in Pine Bluff, where the No. 9 Zebras posed no threat throughout the game. Central's defense held Pine Bluff scoreless as the offense, led by Corry Adams' 123 yards rushing, posted 14 points in the victory.

The first score occurred midway through the first quarter when a 64-yard drive ended with a 28-yard touchdown pass from Ray Nealy to Adams. The extra-point attempt failed, but Central led 6-0. The final score occurred in the third quarter after the Tigers recovered a Pine Bluff fumble at the Zebras 20.

It took three plays to go the distance, with Adams scoring on a 3-yard run. He also added the two-point conversion to set the final at 14-0.

The Tigers traveled the next week as well when they took on No. 2 Southside High School in Fort Smith. The defending state champion Rebels dominated Central in the second half en route to a 28-14 victory. The loss dropped the Tigers to No. 7 in the *Arkansas Democrat-Gazette* poll.

Unranked Little Rock Fair was next for the Tigers in a game played on a water-logged field at Quigley Stadium. The soggy turf resulted in 10 fumbles between the two teams and a scoreless game until late in the fourth quarter.

With 2:04 remaining to play, Nealy scrambled 34 yards on a broken play to cap a 75-yard drive. After a failed extra-point attempt, the Tigers sealed the victory when they recovered a fumble on the ensuing kickoff. With Adams sitting out of the game for disciplinary reasons, Bobby Khabeer led Central's ground attack with 83

Photo provided by Central High School
Corry Adams (2)

yards on 23 carries, helping the Tigers to a 6-0 victory.

Central, 2-1-0, entered its conference schedule the next week with the annual "Battle for the Bell" against Little Rock Hall High School. Played on Saturday morning, the game featured two touchdowns by the Tigers in the first half. Adams scored the first touchdown on a 23-yard run. Reggie Swinton scored the second when he caught a 28-yard pass from Nealy with 1:51 left in the half. Khabeer converted a two-point conversion after the first touchdown for a 14-0 lead.

The Warriors, though, struck early in the second half after gaining possession on the Central 30 following a 10-yard punt by the Tigers.

On third down, Hall High quarterback Roosevelt Simmons lobbed a 28-yard touchdown pass to Steve Foley. Fullback Anthony Ransom converted the two-point conversion and the Warriors narrowed the deficit to 14-8.

Central took control of the game midway through the fourth quarter. Adams broke free for a 38-yard touchdown run, ending a five-play, 73-yard drive. He ran for two points to increase the lead to 22-8.

The Tigers weren't done, though, as Kenoris Saine scampered 49 yards to the Hall High 1 on Central's next possession. Saine scored on the next play. Adams finished with a career-high 214 yards on 27 carries and scored two touchdowns in the 28-8 victory over the Warriors.

The following week, the Tigers hosted Little Rock McClellan. The Lions pulled within 24-23 when Kevin Williams scored on a 2-yard run with 2:27 left in the game. McClellan lined up to tie the score with its extra-point attempt, but Central jumped offside.

With the ball placed 1½ yards from the goal line, Lions Coach Ellis Register decided to go for the two-point conversion and the victory. Once McClellan's Kevin Bufford took the ball toward the goal line, he was hit by Khabeer and kept out of the end zone. This defensive play and Adams' 208 yards rushing gave the Tigers their fourth victory of the season.

Following a 14-9 victory over North Little Rock the next week, No. 5 Central hosted unranked Conway High School. The Wampus Cats struck on their first possession when Reuel Shepherd broke several tackles on a 47-yard touchdown run. Kevin Leach added the extra point to give Conway a 7-0 lead.

The Wampus Cats added to their lead just before halftime when Tony Turner broke free for a 46-yard touchdown run. Leach's extra point gave Conway a 14-0 lead with 2:29 left in the half.

The Tigers, though, were able to use that time to march 65 yards before Nealy capped the drive with a 12-yard touchdown run. Nealy also added a two-point conversion to make it 14-8 at halftime.

Photo provided by Central High School
Ray Nealy (7)

Early in the fourth quarter, Trey Tyler intercepted a Central pass to give Conway possession at the Tigers 36. Five plays later, Turner scored from the 11 and the Wampus Cats led 20-8. They increased that lead to 23-8 on their next possession with a 34-yard field goal.

Central scored late in the game when Nealy passed to Bill Ruth for a 59-yard touchdown. Adams converted the two-point conversion to pull Central within 23-16. The Tigers had one more opportunity before time expired, but it ended when Nealy was intercepted by Justin Hargis. The loss marked Central's second of the season and first in conference action.

Following impressive victories the next two weeks against Little Rock Parkview (25-0) and Sylvan Hills (29-16), the Tigers dominated Little Rock Catholic in the regular-season finale. Third-ranked Central finished with 500 yards of total offense, including 402 yards rushing.

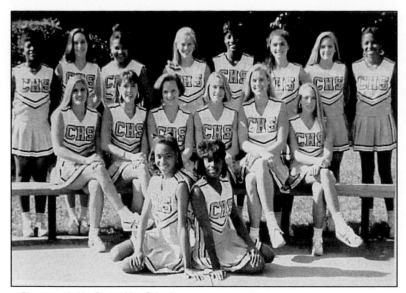

Photo provided by Central High School
The 1992 Tiger cheerleaders

A great performance by Central's offensive line allowed Adams and Nealy to both rush for new career highs. Adams rushed for 222 yards on 44 carries; Nealy rushed for 100 yards in a 35-21 victory over the Rockets. The victory put Central in a three-way tie with Little Rock McClellan and Conway for the conference's top team.

Because of the loss to Conway, the Tigers entered the state playoffs as the conference's No. 3 seed and traveled to Jan Crow Stadium in Jacksonville to take on the No. 10 Red Devils in the first round.

Jacksonville struck first with 3:34 left in the opening quarter when quarterback David Monsrud passed to Joe Bolden for 23 yards and a touchdown. Kendall Mills added the extra point for a 7-0 lead and the first half's only score.

Just 1:14 into the second half, Robert Thomas ended a 57-yard drive with a 24-yard touchdown run. Mills again added the extra point to give the Red Devils a 14-0 lead.

Just as the fourth quarter opened, Adams capped an 83-yard, 15-play drive with a 1-yard scoring run. The two-point conversion attempt by Nealy failed, leaving it 14-6.

With 4:28 left in the game, Mills kicked an 18-yard field goal to increase Jacksonville's lead to 17-8. This would eventually become the play of the game.

Just three minutes later, the Tigers scored on a 25-yard pass play from Nealy to Adams. Adams converted the two-point conversion to set the final at 17-14. Central finished the season 8-3-0.

1992 TIGER SCHEDULE

Pine Bluff 0	LRCH 14
FS Southside 28	LRCH 14
LR Fair 0	LRCH 6
*LR Hall 8	LRCH 28
*LR McClellan 23	LRCH 24
*North Little Rock 9	LRCH 14
*Conway 23	LRCH 16
*LR Parkview 0	LRCH 25
*Sylvan Hills 16	LRCH 29
*LR Catholic 21	LRCH 35
**Jacksonville 17	LRCH 14 (state playoffs)

ANOTHER LOW POINT IN TIGER HISTORY

1993   1-9-0

Head Coach: Bernie Cox
Assistants: Norman Callaway, Larry Siegel
Team Trainer: Mayfield Armstrong
Team Physician: Dr. Roger Clark

1993 LETTERMEN

Keith Adams	Dwan Cribbs	Brad Kusturin	Stervin Smith
Antonio Austin	Joseph Davis	Matthew Mittelstaedt	Reggie Swinton
John Batson	Earnest Dukes	Mellow Moore	Aaron Waddell
Rory Bernard	Robert Gray	Davin Moorman	Ernest Waddell
Roland Brown	Robert Guinn	Brant Owens	Learrie White
Chablis Carroll	Jay Hardin	Gary Pighee	Lowrekus Wordlaw
Khalil Carter	Joe Hill	Clay Rowe	Kevin Wright
Drew Cates	Bion James	Ryan Rusinko	Seth Young
Tyrone Christian	Bilal Johns	Kenoris Saine	
Reginald Collins	Chris Killingsworth	Kevan Smith	

1993 MANAGERS
None

1993 ALL-STATE
Reggie Swinton

1993 ALL-CONFERENCE
Robert Gray
Ryan Rusinko
Kenoris Saine

Photo provided by Central High School
Matthew Mittelstaedt (15)

and also kicked a 23-yard field goal just as time ran out in the first half. The Rebels, though, scored twice between Central's touchdown and field goal.

Southside's Clay York scored on a 17-yard run and threw a 1-yard touchdown pass to Mike Wilson. Clay Redding converted 1 of 2 extra-point attempts points as the Rebels led 13-10 at halftime.

Central's defense did step up in the second half to hold Southside to two field goals. The offense, though, could not score again and the Tigers dropped their second game of the season.

After another defeat, this one 13-6 to Little Rock McClellan, Central battled Little Rock Hall in the annual "Bell Bowl" the following Saturday morning.

The Tigers jumped out to an early lead after a 31-yard field goal by Mittelstaedt in the first quarter and a 1-yard touchdown run by Bilal Johns in the second quarter. Central added to the lead with 2:57 remaining in the third quarter when Dwan Cribbs blocked a punt out of the end zone for a

Central, which graduated many starters from the 1992 team, opened the season against top-ranked Pine Bluff. The Zebras took the opening kickoff and set the tone for the game when they drove 79 yards in 14 plays to score their first of four touchdowns. Otis Steen scored on a 2-yard run and James Welch added the extra point for a 7-0 lead with 5:49 left in the first quarter.

The Tigers were stagnant on offense, finishing with only 161 yards in a 28-0 loss. Unranked Central did not fare much better the next week when it hosted No. 7 Fort Smith Southside.

The Tigers, however, did score the game's first points when Drew Cates found an opening in the line for an 18-yard touchdown run in the first quarter. Matthew Mittelstaedt converted the extra-point attempt

Photo provided by Central High School
Bilal Johns (8)

413

safety. The 12-0 lead, though, did not last for long.

Two plays after the ensuing kickoff, an option pitch by quarterback Joe Hill was intercepted by Hall High's Patrick Gordon and returned 52 yards for a touchdown. Jason Stewart converted the extra-point attempt to bring the score to 12-7.

On the ensuing kickoff, Reggie Swinton fumbled the catch. The ball was scooped up by Barsha Fields, who ran 23 yards for another Hall touchdown. A two-point conversion attempt failed, but in a matter of 58 seconds the Warriors took a 13-12 lead.

Neither team threatened to score during the fourth quarter, giving Central its fourth loss of the season. It marked the first time Coach Bernie Cox had lost his first four games in 22 years as coach.

It took an overtime period, but Central finally won the next week when it traveled to Mountain Home to take on the Bombers. Hill sent the game into overtime, 7-7, after he scored on a 31-yard quarterback keeper.

The Tigers' overtime score occurred when Joseph Davis completed a short pass to Johns for a touchdown. Mittelstaedt's extra-point attempt proved the difference as Mountain Home failed to convert its extra-point attempt following its overtime touchdown. Central escaped with a 14-13 victory.

Photo provided by Central High School
Kenoris Saine (left) and Cupid Jackson (46)

The Tigers would not win again, though. They were beaten by North Little Rock (21-7), Conway (10-0), Little Rock Parkview (14-7), Sylvan Hills (21-6) and Little Rock Catholic (14-7).

Little Rock Central and Coach Cox experienced a rare losing season.

Central posted its second-worst record in program history. The 1970 team finished 1-8-1, while the 1905 team recorded the school's worst record (0-5-0). This was Coach Cox's first losing season since he became head coach in 1975.

After winning a share of the conference championship the past two years, the Tigers were at the bottom. The 1993 season was the first time that Central did not make the playoffs since the fusion of the state's two largest classifications following the 1982 season.

Photo provided by Central High School
Coach Norman Callaway and the Tiger offense

1993 TIGER SCHEDULE

Pine Bluff 28	LRCH 0
FS Southside 19	LRCH 10
LR McClellan 13	LRCH 6
*LR Hall 13	LRCH 12
*Mountain Home 13	LRCH 14
*North Little Rock 21	LRCH 7
*Conway 10	LRCH 0
*LR Parkview 14	LRCH 7
*Sylvan Hills 21	LRCH 6
*LR Catholic 14	LRCH 7

REBUILDING THE WINNING TRADITION

1994   4-6-0

Head Coach: Bernie Cox
Assistants: Norman Callaway, Larry Siegel, Travis Mann
Team Trainer: Mayfield Armstrong
Team Physician: Dr. Roger Clark

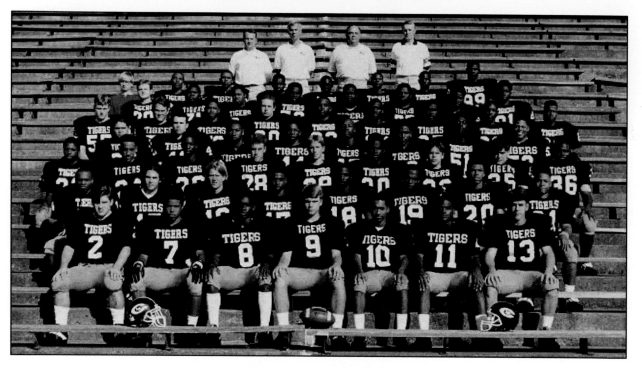

1994 LETTERMEN

Keith Adams	Reginald Collins	Joseph McCraney	Blake Rutherford
Antonio Austin	Brandon Copeland	Davin Moorman	Kenric Saine
Elisha Barnum	Joseph Davis	Chris Moses	Kevan Smith
John Batson	Jerry Franklin	Orlando Newburn	Robby Sullenger
Errick Berry	Travis Gamble	Brant Owens	Aaron Waddell
Billy Brooks	Alpha Gaston	Brian Piggee	Kevin Wright
Brian Bunche	Joe Goods	Donnie Rayford	Marcus Yarbrough
Chablis Carroll	Robert Gray	Keenan Richardson	Seth Young
Drew Cates	Cupid Jackson	Kelton Roach	
Tyrone Christian	Virgil Jones	Clay Rowe	

1994 MANAGER
Erick Beulah

1994 ALL-STATE
Drew Cates
Robert Gray

1994 ALL-CONFERENCE
Keith Adams
Antonio Austin
Davin Moorman
Brant Owens

1994 ALL-STAR TEAM
Drew Cates

Following a miserable 1993 season in which Central finished 1-9-0, Central's coaching staff hoped to rebuild the program into the dominant force it once was. The 1994 squad included 23 sophomores, 15 of whom lettered, giving Central a solid foundation for the future.

The season began with a road trip to No. 1 Pine Bluff and a nonconference battle against the defending state champion Zebras. Pine Bluff dominated every aspect of the game, especially special teams. Dedetron Parks returned two punts and a kickoff for touchdowns. The offense was highlighted by a 52-yard touchdown pass from Tommy Wofford to Randy Walters, helping Pine Bluff to a 45-0 victory over the Tigers.

The nonconference schedule did not get any easier for Central as it was beaten twice more, 31-6 by No. 3 Fort Smith Southside and 33-0 by No. 9 Little Rock McClellan.

Little Rock Hall High (1-2-0) and the Tigers (0-3-0) fought on the fourth playing date in the annual "Battle for the Bell." The game was expected to be a low-scoring affair since neither team displayed much offense during past weeks. The Warriors, though, finished the game with 293 total yards and three touchdowns.

Just before halftime, Hall High scored the game's first touchdown with an 11-play, 97-yard drive. William Wade ran 16 yards for a touchdown; Akil Herbert added the two-point conversion for an 8-0 lead.

Central's ensuing possession ended when Darrell Brown intercepted a pass and returned it to the Tigers 43. A pass from Herbert to Chris Akins moved Hall to the 1, and then Herbert scored with 23 seconds left in the half. Jason Stewart added the extra point for a 15-0 lead.

The Warriors scored again late in the fourth quarter when Akins returned a punt 60 yards for a touchdown. Akins also converted the two-point conversion to give his team a 23-0 lead with 2:50 left in the game.

Central avoided the shutout with 25 seconds remaining when Robby Sullenger completed a 19-yard touchdown pass to Marcus Yarbrough. Kevin Wright added the two-point conversion to set the final at 23-8.

Winless Mountain Home and the winless Tigers battled at Quigley Stadium the next week. The Bombers struck first when Nathan Winham kicked a 20-yard field goal with 51 seconds left in the first quarter.

Central took its ensuing possession and drove 69 yards in 13 plays for its first touchdown. After the Tigers completed three third-down conversions, Drew Cates ran over right tackle to score from the 16. Chris Moses converted the extra-point attempt for a 7-3 lead with 8:11 left in the half.

On its next possession, Central drove 52 yards to score again. Yarbrough began the drive with a 38-yard reverse and Sullenger ended the drive with an 11-yard option keeper around left end. Moses' extra-point kick gave the Tigers a 14-3 lead with 3:57 remaining in the half.

Central added to its lead in the second half.

Chablis Carroll scored on a 20-yard run in the third quarter and Virgil Jones scored on a 5-yard run in the fourth quarter. Moses converted both extra-point attempts in the 28-3 victory. The homecoming victory ended the Tigers' nine-game losing streak.

North Little Rock High School celebrated homecoming the following week

417

against Central. The Charging Wildcats scored first when Geary Allmon capped a seven-play, 46-yard drive with a 1-yard run. Mike Mayeux converted the extra-point attempt for a 7-0 lead with 5:49 left in the half. The Tigers, though, struck just minutes later when Wright ended a 62-yard drive with a 1-yard run. Wright's extra-point attempt was perfect and tied the score, 7-7, with 30 seconds left in the half.

With 52 seconds left in the game, Mayeux kicked a 45-yard field goal for a 10-7 lead.

After the ensuing kickoff, Central took control at its 48. With 26 seconds remaining in the game, Sullenger took the snap, rolled to his right and passed to Keenan Richardson at the 30. After the ball had been tipped twice by the Charging Wildcats, it fell into the hands of Richardson, who raced to the end zone to complete a 52-yard touchdown. The extra-point attempt failed, but the touchdown gave the Tigers a 13-10 victory over North Little Rock.

Following a close loss to No. 7 Conway, 14-7, Central was forced into overtime by Little Rock Parkview the next week. With the score 7-7, the Tigers won the overtime coin toss and elected to play offense first.

After a 4-yard run by Jones on first down, Central was penalized 10 yards for holding. The penalty gave the Tigers second down from the 13. Out of the Power-I formation, Sullenger rolled to his right and passed to his left, connecting with Cates for a touchdown. Moses missed the extra-point attempt, leaving the score 13-7.

The Patriots were penalized for holding on first down, and then quarterback Kevin Montgomery was sacked for a 10-yard loss at the 30. Three plays later on fourth down, Montgomery attempted a pass to Willie Robinson. Cates, though, was there to knock down the pass and preserve the victory for Central.

Cates also highlighted the Tigers' next game against Sylvan Hills. The end result,

though, was not as favorable. Cates returned a kickoff 84 yards for a touchdown, scored on a 3-yard run and converted a two-point conversion to provide Central with 14 of its 15 points.

The Bears, down one point with six seconds left in the game, attempted a 39-yard field goal. Bart Gann's kick failed, but a roughing-the-kicker penalty gave him another chance. This time, from 27 yards out and one second remaining, his kick split the uprights and gave Sylvan Hills a victory over the Tigers.

Central, which did not make the play-offs for only the second time in school history, played its final game of the season against Little Rock Catholic. The game took place at War Memorial Stadium and was played in a tremendous downpour of rain.

The Rockets scored first when they blocked a punt. It was recovered by Catholic's Lance Matlock and returned 14 yards for a touchdown. Mike Zehr converted the extra-point attempt for a 7-0 lead with 8:08 left in the first quarter. Zehr added to the lead in the second quarter when he kicked a 39-yard field goal with four seconds left in the half.

Central received the second-half kickoff and returned it to the 27, but a face-mask penalty gave the Tigers possession at the 42. Cates carried six consecutive times and was able to reach the 8 with the help of another face-mask penalty. Sullenger eventually scored from the 1. Moses converted the extra-point attempt to narrow the deficit to 10-7.

With 4:43 left in the game, Central took possession at its 29 and needed only one play to score. On first down, Sullenger handed to Cates, and the speedy tailback broke free up the middle before cutting to the outside and outrunning defenders for a 71-yard touchdown. Moses converted the extra-point attempt and the Tigers won their fourth game of the season.

1994 TIGER SCHEDULE

Pine Bluff 45	LRCH 0
FS Southside 31	LRCH 6
LR McClellan 33	LRCH 0
*LR Hall 23	LRCH 8
*Mountain Home 3	LRCH 28
*North Little Rock 10	LRCH 13
*Conway 14	LRCH 7
*LR Parkview 7	LRCH 13
*Sylvan Hills 17	LRCH 15
*LR Catholic 10	LRCH 14

THE IMPROVEMENT CONTINUES

1995   5-6-0

Head Coach: Bernie Cox
Assistants: Norman Callaway, Larry Siegel, Travis Mann
Team Trainer: Cody Martin
Team Physician: Dr. Roger Clark

1995 LETTERMEN

John Batson	Donald Floyd	Leonard McDonald	Kenric Saine
Errick Berry	Jerry Franklin	Ahmad McMullen	Kevan Smith
Andre Bolton	Alpha Gaston	Joshua Neal	Zach Steadman
Anthony Britton	Jeff Grimmett	Orlando Newburn	Robby Sullenger
Billy Brooks	Clarence Guy	Clay Packard	Brian Thomas
Michael Brown	Joseph Guy	Erick Patrick	Aaron Waddell
Chablis Carroll	David Honorable	Rob Pearson	Ben Walters
Tyrone Christian	Chris Johnson	Brian Piggee	Josh Webb
Terrence Clark	Virgil Jones	Kelton Roach	Mark Williams
Montreal Cobb	Keith Lilly	Chester Robinson	Kevin Wright
Reginald Collins	Frederick Marks	Nikarlo Rogers	Marcus Yarbrough
Derrick Floyd	Joseph McCraney	Blake Rutherford	

1995 MANAGERS
Erick Beulah
Joseph Guy
Seth Young

1995 ALL-STATE
John Batson
Tyrone Christian
Virgil Jones

1995 ALL-CONFERENCE

Errick Berry	Kelton Roach
Keith Lilly	Kevan Smith
Frederick Marks	Kevin Wright
Ahmad McMullen	Marcus Yarbrough

1995 ALL-STAR TEAM
None

With 15 sophomores lettering in 1994, Central entered its new season young, but with slightly more experience. The rebuilding evident, the Tigers hoped to challenge for the conference title and make the playoffs for the first time in three years.

Because the Pine Bluff and Central game had become such a mismatch in recent years, Coach Bernie Cox replaced the ancient rival with Fayetteville High School for the season opener. The 1995 season marked only the seventh time in 90 years that the Zebras and Tigers had not battled.

Central did not benefit from the change, however, as the Bulldogs defeated the Tigers 23-15. The losses continued in the weeks to come. Central was beaten by Little Rock Fair (32-14), Little Rock McClellan (24-0) and Little Rock Hall (14-8).

Central's only score during the "Battle for the Bell" occurred when Ahmad McMullen picked up a fumble and returned it 81 yards for a touchdown. Virgil Jones converted the two-point conversion, but it wasn't enough to overcome scoring drives of 75 yards and 65 yards by the Warriors.

After starting the season 0-4-0 for the third consecutive year, Central traveled to Mountain Home the next week hoping to begin a winning streak. The Tigers did end their four-game skid with the help of Jones' 94 yards rushing and two touchdowns. Central defeated the Bombers 27-7 for the first victory of the season.

A 5-yard touchdown pass from Derrick Floyd to Marcus Yarbrough with seven seconds left in the first half was all that was needed to beat North Little Rock the next week. The touchdown gave the Tigers the lead after the Charging Wildcats kicked a 30-yard field goal early in the first quarter. Jones rushed 23 times for 100 yards and the defense held North Little Rock each time it threatened to score a touchdown.

After being beaten by Conway (10-0), the Tigers once again played a close game against Little Rock Parkview. Central scored early with a 9-yard touchdown run by Jones and an 81-yard interception return by Kevin Wright.

Jones added another score on a 1-yard run with 8:36 left in the game to give Central a 22-7 lead. Both the Tiger players and fans believed the game was over. The Patriots, however, were not finished fighting and needed only 1:49 and seven plays to narrow the score.

Photo provided by Central High School
Derrick Floyd (15)

421

Ahmad McMullen (17)

Parkview put together a 57-yard drive, scoring after Willie Robinson received a lateral from Kevin Montgomery and threw to Timothy Piggee for a 46-yard touchdown. Robinson faked the extra-point attempt and ran into the end zone for a two-point conversion and a 22-15 score.

Central only gained 3 yards on its next possession and punted for a net of 13 yards, giving the Patriots control at the Tigers 32. Following a 2-yard loss, Harry Winkler scrambled in the backfield on third down before passing to Gary Godley for a 34-yard touchdown.

With the Tigers leading 22-21, Parkview again faked the extra-point attempt. Trying for the two-point conversion, Robinson, though, could not handle a high snap from center and was tackled in the backfield with 3:36 remaining in the game.

The Patriots had one last chance to win the game when they faced fourth down from the Tigers 15 with 16 seconds remaining. Robinson attempted a 32-yard field goal, but the kick was short and the Tigers escaped with a 22-21 victory.

Central played one of its best games of the season the following week when it defeated Sylvan Hills 26-14. Jones rushed for 164 yards and two touchdowns on 26 carries, while Yarbrough rushed for 96 yards on 12 carries. Aaron Waddell returned an interception 42 yards for a touchdown in the second quarter, and Chablis Carroll returned an interception 50 yards for a touchdown in the fourth quarter to help the Tigers beat the Bears.

With a victory the next week against Little Rock Catholic, Central would clinch its first playoff berth in three years. The contest would take two overtimes in order to decide the fate of the Tigers.

Down 14-0 at halftime, the Tigers finally scored with 3:24 left in the third quarter when Robby Sullenger completed a 9-yard touchdown pass to McMullen. With place-kicker Blake Rutherford out of the game because of mononucleosis, Central was forced to attempt a two-point conversion. Yarbrough, though, could not cross the goal line and the Tigers trailed 14-6.

Just as the fourth quarter began, Donnie Rayford recovered a Catholic fumble at the Rockets 31. It took seven plays, but Central scored on a 4-yard run by Yarbrough. He also completed the two-point conversion to make it 14-14 at the end of regulation.

Catholic was on offense first during the initial overtime period and scored on a 6-yard pass play. The Tigers held the Rockets on the conversion attempt and matched their score when Jones burst up the middle on a 1-yard run. The two-point conversion attempt failed and a second overtime period was played.

On offense first in the second overtime, Central faced fourth down from the 1. But the Tigers scored easily when Sullenger faked a handoff to Jones and hit McMullen with a pass. Jones converted the two-point conversion for a 28-20 lead. Catholic then took its turn on offense.

The Rockets eventually faced fourth down from the 1 and scored when quarterback Matt Miller snuck up the middle for the touchdown.

However, Miller's two-point conversion pass was intercepted by Kevan Smith to give Central the victory and a trip to the state playoffs.

As the No. 3 seed from the AAAA-Central Conference, the Tigers earned a trip to Cabot to take on the Panthers. Cabot was the No. 2 seed from the AAAA-East Conference. The Panthers struck first midway through the opening quarter when Jason Eddy scored on a 34-yard run. Jeremy Smith added the extra point for a 7-0 lead.

Central answered with 1:16 left in the quarter. The drive began after a Cabot punt stalled in the wind and netted only 21 yards, giving the Tigers possession on the Cabot 33. Seven plays later, Jones scored on a 1-yard run and Rutherford's extra-point attempt tied the score at 7-7.

With 7:16 left in the first half, Danny Farrar capped a short drive with a 2-yard scoring run. Smith's extra-point attempt was blocked by Tyrone Christian and the Panthers led 13-7. Cabot increased the lead on its next possession when Smith kicked a 52-yard field goal with 1:15 left in the half for a 16-7 lead.

Central answered just after the ensuing kickoff. On first down from the 20, Sul-

Photo provided by Central High School

A school pep rally prior to the battle against Hall High School

lenger passed to Floyd. The end result was an 80-yard touchdown to pull Central within 16-13 at halftime.

The second half was dominated by the Cabot offense. Farrar, who finished with 188 yards rushing, scored three second-half touchdowns to lead Cabot over the Tigers 37-13.

The loss dropped Central to 5-6-0, only the third losing season in Coach Cox's 21 seasons at the school.

1995 TIGER SCHEDULE

Fayetteville 23	LRCH 15
LR Fair 32	LRCH 14
LR McClellan 24	LRCH 0
*LR Hall 14	LRCH 8
*Mountain Home 7	LRCH 27
*North Little Rock 3	LRCH 6
*Conway 10	LRCH 0
*LR Parkview 21	LRCH 22
*Sylvan Hills 14	LRCH 26
*LR Catholic 26	LRCH 28
**Cabot 37	LRCH 13 (state playoffs)

BACK IN CHAMPIONSHIP FORM

1996   8-4-0

Head Coach: Bernie Cox
Assistants: Norman Callaway, Larry Siegel, Travis Mann, Ken Davis
Team Trainer: Keith Shireman
Team Physician: Dr. Roger Clark

1996 LETTERMEN

Chris Adams
Quincy Anderson
William Bennett
Chris Benson
Errick Berry
Romar Blackmon
Michael Block
Kelsey Bobo
Anthony Britton
Billy Brooks
Michael Brown
Scottie Burnett
Montreal Cobb
Andre Covington
Joseph Davis
Kelley Davis

Wade Davis
Lewis Dillahunty
Jonathan Findlay
Derrick Floyd
Ryan Goins
Derrick Goodman
Jeff Grimmett
Clarence Guy
Nicholas Guy
David Honorable
Darius Hunter
Ralph Jackson
Wa-Li Johnson
Virgil Jones
Keith Lilly
Mark Magee

Frederick Marks
Jerome Marshall
Joseph McCraney
Leonard McDonald
Ahmad McMullen
Joshua Neal
Orlando Newburn
Victor Okoye
Eric Patrick
Rob Pearson
Brian Piggee
Keenan Richardson
Kelton Roach
Chester Robinson
Nikarlo Rogers
Kenric Saine

Rodney Savage
Sidney Small
Erick Smith
Ray Smith
Patrick Sullenger
Robby Sullenger
Tim Talley
Brian Thomas
Ben Walters
Josh Webb
Andre Williams
Mark Williams
Marcus Yarbrough

1996 MANAGERS
Eric Beulah
Joseph Guy
Leslie Harmon
James Williams

1996 ALL-STATE
Virgil Jones
Joseph McCraney
Kenric Saine
Marcus Yarbrough

1996 ALL-CONFERENCE

Errick Berry	Kelton Roach
Keith Lilly	Nikarlo Rogers
Ahmad McMullen	Robby Sullenger
Brian Piggee	Brian Thomas

1996 ALL-STAR TEAM
Virgil Jones
Joseph McCraney

Little Rock Central High School entered 1996 on the heels of three consecutive losing seasons, something never experienced by the tradition-rich program. With several returning starters and talent at both the line and skill positions, Central hoped it could return to its winning ways.

The opener, though, set the Tigers back to 0-1-0 when thcy lost to Fayetteville High School 31-6. Central was limited to only 100 yards of total offense in the loss.

The offense made up for its poor performance the following week against Sylvan Hills as tailback Virgil Jones rushed for 181 yards. Marcus Yarbrough put Central ahead with a 4-yard scoring run in the third quarter. The defense helped secure the first victory of the season by allowing the Bears only 11 yards rushing in the final quarter. Central defeated the Bears 33-24.

The Tigers traveled to West Memphis the next week, but were demolished by the Blue Devils. Tailback Charles Stackhouse rushed for four touchdowns and 339 yards. West Memphis finished with 710 yards of total offense in a 55-34 victory over Central.

Conference play began six days later when the Tigers and Little Rock Hall High met on Thursday night in the annual "Battle for the Bell."

Already leading 7-0, Central took possession in the third quarter and put together an 18-play, 89-yard drive that consumed

Photo provided by Central High School
Central High students cheer on the Tigers

8:18 off the clock. The drive ended on the first play of the fourth quarter with a 6-yard scoring run by Jones. The Tigers also controlled the clock in the fourth quarter, driving 94 yards in 13 plays. Yarbrough ended the march with a 7-yard scoring run off tackle with 3:57 left in the game. The extra-point attempt failed, but Central won its AAAA-Central opener 20-0.

After being upset 14-7 by North Little Rock, the Tigers played host to No. 10 Conway High School.

425

Robby Sullenger (9)

Central took the lead on its second possession of the game, moving 94 yards in 16 plays. Jones rushed for 69 yards on 13 carries during the drive and scored on fourth down from the 4 with a run up the middle. Kenric Saine's extra-point attempt was wide right, but the Tigers had a 6-0 lead with 11:21 left in the first half.

Central held the 6-0 lead until Yarbrough intercepted a Conway pass at his goal line and returned it to the Tigers 29. Central then put together a 71-yard drive, which included a 39-yard run by Brian Piggee and a 14-yard pass play from Robby Sullenger to Joseph McCraney, to reach the 5. Jones eventually scored from the 4 and also added the two-point conversion for a 14-0 lead with 10:21 left in the game.

The Wampus Cats scored late in the game when Michael Allen capped a 10-play, 69-yard drive with an 8-yard touchdown run with 6:39 to play. Terrence Fuller converted the two-point conversion to narrow the score to 14-8, but it was not enough as the Tigers won their second conference game and evened their overall record at 3-3-0.

Central recorded its second shutout of the season the following week, 28-0 over Little Rock Catholic. Jones rushed for 136 yards in the first quarter, including a 77-yard touchdown run.

The Tigers took advantage of two defensive plays to score two of their four touchdowns. McCraney blocked a punt at the Rockets 11. Four plays later, Jones scored from the 2 with 9:39 left in the half.

With 11:44 left in the game, Nikarlo Rogers recovered a fumble and returned it 76 yards for a touchdown. Saine converted his fourth extra point in the 28-0 victory.

Ahmad McMullen was the difference in the next game against Little Rock Parkview.

The Tigers were trailing 7-6 in the third quarter when McMullen intercepted a pass at the Parkview 25 and returned it to the 8. Two plays later, Jones scored on a 6-yard run and also converted the two-point conversion for a 14-7 lead with 5:26 left in the quarter.

With 6:51 left in the game, McMullen intercepted another pass, this time taking it 39 yards for a touchdown. Yarbrough added the two-point conversion to increase the lead to 22-7.

Parkview answered when Fred Leonard passed to Kelton Lyons for an 8-yard touchdown, capping a 65-yard drive. The two

Marcus Yarbrough (20)

players connected again for a two-point conversion, but it wouldn't be enough as Central beat the Patriots 22-15.

The Tigers were victorious over Mountain Home (32-6) the next week and Little Rock Fair (31-14) the following week. The victories gave Central a share of the AAAA-Central Conference title and a trip to the state playoffs following a three-year absence.

Springdale High School, the third seed from the AAAA-West Conference, visited Quigley Stadium for a first-round postseason battle with Central.

On their opening possession of the game, the Tigers marched 77 yards in 13 plays before being held on downs at the Bulldogs 2. On the next possession, though, Jones scored on a 41-yard run. Saine converted the extra-point attempt for a 7-0 lead with 10:49 left in the first half.

An interception by Derrick Floyd set up Central's next score. Floyd returned it 42 yards to the Springdale 8, leading to a 6-yard touchdown run by Jones. The extra-point attempt was blocked, but the Tigers extended their lead to 13-0.

The Bulldogs scored with 8:17 to play in the game when Brian Stewart passed to Michael Walton for a 30-yard touchdown. The extra point made it 13-7.

Central answered on its ensuing possession when Jones ran 74 yards for a touchdown. Yarbrough then added the two-point conversion to seal a 21-7 defeat of Springdale.

After the victory, the Tigers entered the *Arkansas Democrat-Gazette* Top 10 as the state's No. 9 team. Central would battle an-

Photo provided by Central High School
Virgil Jones

other Top 10 team the next week when it traveled to No. 3 El Dorado.

El Dorado is where the season ended for the Tigers.

The Wildcats dominated the game, holding Central to only 88 yards of total offense and controlling both the ball and the clock en route to a 27-7 victory.

Jones ended the season with 1,989 yards rushing and Central ended its three year losing skid with an 8-4-0 record, a conference championship and a trip to the second round of the playoffs.

1996 TIGER SCHEDULE

Fayetteville 31	LRCH 6
Sylvan Hills 24	LRCH 33
West Memphis 55	LRCH 34
*LR Hall 0	LRCH 20
*North Little Rock 14	LRCH 7
*Conway 8	LRCH 14
*LR Catholic 0	LRCH 28
*LR Parkview 15	LRCH 22
*Mountain Home 6	LRCH 32
*LR Fair 14	LRCH 31
**Springdale 7	LRCH 21 (state playoffs)
**El Dorado 27	LRCH 7 (state playoffs)

LONG DRIVES AND CLOCK CONTROL

1997   6-5-0

Head Coach: Bernie Cox
Assistants: Norman Callaway, Larry Siegel, Travis Mann, Darrell Seward
Team Trainer: B.J. Maack
Team Physician: Dr. Ken Martin

1997 LETTERMEN

Adam Acklin	Joseph Davis	Antijuan Jackson	Eric Patrick
Chris Adams	Wade Davis	Antonio Johnson	Rob Pearson
Quincy Anderson	Tyrone Eason	Wa-Li Johnson	Harold Phillips
Matthew Atobe	Breck Enoch	Orlando Jones	Arturo Rodriguez
Romar Blackmon	Reginald Fossette	Willie Leggs	Zach Steadman
Michael Block	Ryan Goins	Keith Lilly	Lakeem Staggers
Anthony Britton	John Goss	Mark Magee	Kevin Stolzer
Michael Brown	Jeff Grimmett	Frederick Marks	Tim Talley
Patrick Bynum	Clarence Guy	Jerome Marshall	Brian Thomas
Brandon Campbell	Nicholas Guy	Ahmad McMullen	Ben Walters
Paul Chester	Meidro Hemphill	Freeman McKindra	Josh Webb
Montreal Cobb	Marcus Hill	Joshua Neal	Bryan Williams
Andre Covington	Rodney Hood	Victor Okoye	
Eric Cross	Darius Hunter	Chris Parker	

1997 MANAGERS
None

1997 ALL-STATE
Andre Covington
Keith Lilly
Brian Thomas

1997 ALL-CONFERENCE

Romar Blackmon	Frederick Marks
Anthony Britton	Jerome Marshall
Michael Brown	Ahmad McMullen
Jeff Grimmett	

Keith Lilly

After a successful 1996 campaign that included an 8-4-0 record and a conference championship, the Tigers entered the new season with a suspect defense. Central, though, hoped ball control could shorten the game and keep opponents from having too many possessions.

With a nine-play, 47-yard drive on their first possession against No. 6 Fayetteville, the season began just as planned for the Tigers. The possession ended at the Bulldogs 33, but Central regained possession just five plays later when Ahmad McMullen returned an interception 32 yards to the Fayetteville 23.

It took the Tigers nine plays to cover the needed distance. Tailback Andre Covington put Central on top with a 2-yard touchdown run over left tackle. Arturo Rodriguez kicked the extra point to give the Tigers a 7-0 lead with 1:23 left in the first quarter.

The good start, however, ended sour for Central as the Bulldogs went on to score a 24-7 victory.

Covington was the star for Central the following week when he helped the Tigers defeat Sylvan Hills. Covington rushed 44 times for 251 yards and scored three touchdowns and two two-point conversions in the 29-25 victory.

John Goss returned the opening kickoff 45 yards to set up the game's first score. Covington alone covered the 33 yards needed with runs of 5, 6, 11, 7 and 4 yards. Rodriquez converted the extra-point attempt for a 7-0 lead with 9:52 left in the first quarter.

The Bears answered on their ensuing possession when they put together a seven-play, 63-yard drive that was capped by Herman Harris' 17-yard touchdown run with 6:22 remaining in the first quarter.

The extra-point attempt was blocked, leaving Central ahead 7-6.

Sylvan Hills took the lead on its next possession with a four-play, 75-yard drive that ended when Blake Martin passed to Mark Luther for a 45-yard touchdown. Brandon Owens kicked the extra point to give the Bears a 13-7 advantage with 45 seconds left in the quarter.

A 3-yard touchdown run by Covington capped a 10-play, 56-yard drive that tied the score, 13-13, with 3:09 remaining in the half. A two-point conversion attempt by Covington failed and the score was tied at halftime.

The Tigers took a 21-13 lead with 11:32 left in the game when Ryan Goins scored on a 13-yard run. Covington added a two-point conversion. Sylvan Hills, though, answered just 20 seconds later when Martin scored on a 47-yard quarterback sneak around left end make it 21-19.

With 2:58 remaining in the game, the Bears faced fourth-and-3 from their 47. Harris ran around right end and didn't stop until he crossed the goal line 53 yards later to give Sylvan Hills a 25-21 lead.

Central had time for one last possession after returning the ensuing kickoff to its 39. The Tigers ended the contest with a 61-yard drive that was capped by Covington's 5-yard run with 38 seconds remaining in the

Photo provided by Central High School

Tailback Andre Covington (30)

Coach Darrell Seward and the Tiger offense

game. Covington also converted the two-point conversion to seal the victory.

Central leaned again on Covington the next week when it hosted West Memphis High School. The tailback rushed 27 times for 182 yards and scored three touchdowns in a 28-20 victory over the Blue Devils. Charles Stackhouse, who rushed for 339 yards and four touchdowns against the Tigers in 1996, was limited to 107 yards and one touchdown.

The following week marked the season's first conference game, the annual "Battle for the Bell" against Little Rock Hall High School.

The Warriors trailed 14-12 at halftime, but came out in the third quarter and put together a short drive before being forced to punt. The kick, however, set Central back at its 1.

Hall High's defense held strong and forced the Tigers to punt. The kick, only 21 yards, gave the Warriors possession at the Central 21. Five plays later, John Burkhong scored from the 1 with 1:20 left in the quarter for an 18-14 lead.

The Tigers fumbled the ensuing kickoff, but Hall High fumbled four plays later and Central took possession on its 9 to began the game-winning drive.

A 20-play, 91-yard march, which consumed more than 10 minutes, ended when

Covington scored on a 2-yard run with 48 seconds remaining in the game. Covington, who accounted for 75 yards on the final drive, ended the night with 165 yards rushing in a 21-18 victory.

Two consecutive losses, 38-14 to North Little Rock and 28-0 to No. 4 Conway, set the stage for a conference matchup between the 1-2-0 Tigers and 1-2-0 Little Rock Catholic.

Covington scored on runs of 45, 8 and 4 yards to lead Central past the Rockets. The Tigers were able record their first shutout of the season, 21-0.

The next week against Little Rock Parkview, Central held a comfortable 25-7 lead late in the fourth quarter. While substitutes were entering the game for the Tigers, the Patriots scored two unanswered touchdowns in less than one minute.

An onside kick by Parkview was recovered by the Patriots' Glean Finley, but the officials needed more than three minutes to discuss the situation before awarding Parkview possession at the Central 49 with 2:29 left in the game.

Nicholas Guy (2)

431

The Patriots crumbled during the possession, succumbing to a holding penalty, two sacks and two incomplete passes before turning the ball over on downs. The Tigers ran out the clock to record their fifth victory of the season.

After Covington rushed for 119 yards and two touchdowns to defeat Mountain Home 34-0, Central met a tough Little Rock Fair team in the regular-season finale. The War Eagles began their domination on the game's opening kickoff. Fa'Quan Harris received the ball at his 12 and then broke several arm tackles en route to an 88-yard return for a touchdown.

Little Rock Fair easily defeated Central 27-6. The loss sent the Tigers to the state playoffs as the fourth seed from the AAAA-Central Conference.

As the fourth seed, the Tigers were pitted against the top seed from the AAAA-East Conference. This happened to be No. 1 and undefeated Cabot High School. The Panthers showed no mercy in the first round as they demolished the Tigers 35-8.

Photo provided by Central High School

Central High student section

With a 6-5-0 overall record and a 4-3-0 conference record, Central was unable to capture the coveted conference crown. However, the Tigers avoided a losing season that had haunted them earlier in the decade.

1997 TIGER SCHEDULE

Fayetteville 24	LRCH 7
Sylvan Hills 25	LRCH 29
West Memphis 20	LRCH 28
*LR Hall 18	LRCH 21
*North Little Rock 38	LRCH 14
*Conway 28	LRCH 0
*LR Catholic 0	LRCH 21
*LR Parkview 21	LRCH 25
*Mountain Home 0	LRCH 34
*LR Fair 27	LRCH 6
**Cabot 35	LRCH 8 (state playoffs)

YOUNG TIGERS KNOW HOW TO WIN

1998   7-3-1

Head Coach: Bernie Cox
Assistants: Norman Callaway, Larry Siegel, Darrell Seward, Travis Mann
Team Trainer: B.J. Maack
Team Physician: Dr. Ken Martin

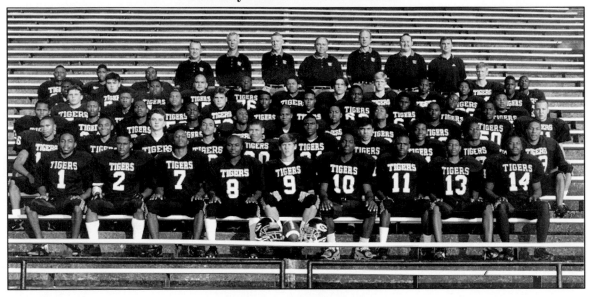

1998 LETTERMEN

Adam Acklin	Joseph Davis	Antijuan Jackson	Michael Pleasant
Matthew Atobe	Kyle Davis	Antonio Johnson	Eddie Robinson
Demetrius Baker	Wade Davis	Willie Leggs	Arturo Rodriguez
Charles Blake	Breck Enoch	Mark Magee	Lakeem Staggers
Patrick Bynum	Reginald Fossette	Derrick Mason	Kevin Stolzer
Brandon Campbell	John Goss	Justin Massie	Tim Talley
Paul Chester	Nicholas Guy	Freeman McKindra	Bryan Williams
Matthew Clark	Meidro Hemphill	Michael Mothershed	Ronnie Williams
Andre Covington	Marcus Hill	Victor Okoye	Ryan Williams
Lawrence Dade	Darius Hunter	Richard Parker	Shawn Williams

1998 MANAGERS
None

1998 ALL-STATE
Andre Covington
Nicholas Guy
Mark Magee

1998 ALL-CONFERENCE

Paul Chester	Justin Massie
Reginald Fossette	Richard Parker
Willie Leggs	Arturo Rodriquez
Derrick Mason	

1998 ALL-STAR TEAM
Andre Covington
Mark Magee

With the retirement of Little Rock Hall Coach Roy Wade and Little Rock Parkview Coach John Kelley following the 1997 season, Tigers Coach Bernie Cox was asked numerous times about his plans to stay at Little Rock Central. Coach Cox, Central's head coach for the past 23 seasons, stated that he had no plans to retire in the near future. With this in mind, the Tigers prepared for their season.

Andre Covington

With only seven returning starters and no experienced quarterback, Central traveled to West Memphis to open against the Blue Devils. Andre Covington scored from the 5 in the second quarter to give the Tigers an early lead. West Memphis then answered with a 79-yard touchdown pass from Brandon Drossett to Lyndell Buckingham. The two-point conversion failed and Central led 7-6.

Arturo Rodriguez (23)

Nicholas Guy returned the ensuing kickoff 80 yards for a touchdown, putting Central up 14-6. Just before halftime, though, De'Arrius Howard ran for a 72-yard touchdown. The two-point conversion again failed, but Central's lead was cut to 14-12.

Late in the fourth quarter, Andrew Tacito returned a Central fumble 22 yards to the 1. Howard then scored his second touchdown, giving West Memphis an 18-14 lead and eventually the victory.

Central dominated the first half against Sylvan Hills the following week. Covington rushed for 107 yards and two touchdowns during the opening 24 minutes, but the Bears took over in the second half.

Sylvan Hills stopped the Tigers on their first possession of the third quarter, then drove 62 yards in five plays to score. Cedric Shaw ended the drive with a 34-yard touchdown run. Two possessions later, Sylvan Hills began a game-tying drive from its 30.

During the series, Mike Bredensteiner picked up 15 yards to give the Bears a first down at the Central 47. Josh Hum then connected with Levi Roy for a 31-yard pass completion to the 16. Three plays later, Hum passed to Roy in the right corner of the end zone for a touchdown and a 14-14 tie.

Central barely escaped Little Rock McClellan the next week. The Lions fumbled on their first possession of the game, giving the Tigers control on their 26. Central quarterback John Goss scored on a 1-yard keeper. Arturo Rodriguez's extra point put the Tigers in front 7-0.

McClellan, which suffered five turnovers, began a drive at its 24 with 51 seconds left in the game. It only took the Lions six plays to cover the 76 yards needed. Brandon Bonds capped the drive with an 8-yard touchdown run. McClellan then chose to go for the win with a two-point conversion. Central's defense, though, stopped Reuben Shakur at the 1 to secure a 7-6 victory. Covington finished with 125 yards rushing on 39 carries.

The annual "Bell Bowl" against Little Rock Hall opened the conference season for the Tigers. Central took a punt by Hall High and drove 50 yards in five plays for its first touchdown. Covington carried all five times and scored from the 5.

During the next possession, Covington rushed seven consecutive times to the Warriors 26. From there, Derrick Mason connected with Tim Talley for a 14-0 lead.

Photo provided by the Arkansas Democrat-Gazette
Reginald Fossette (55)

Central's Eddie Robinson intercepted a Hall High pass on its next possession and returned it to the Warriors 21. After a 5-yard penalty on the Tigers, Mason passed to Guy for a 26-yard touchdown. Central took a 21-0 lead into halftime.

Hall High's Brandon Muldrow returned the second-half kickoff to the Tigers 25, giving the Warriors their first scoring opportunity. After a 24-yard run by Kendrain Cane, Donnell Montgomery went in from the 1 for Hall High's first touchdown.

Central answered when it drove to the Hall High 18, where Mason again connected with Guy. The pass completion was good for an 18-yard touchdown. The Warriors, however, were not finished scoring. Muldrow capped an 80-yard drive with a 2-yard run to make it 28-12 at the end of the third quarter.

The Tigers controlled the rest of the game, especially after Robinson's 5-yard touchdown run increased the lead to 35-12, where it remained until the final buzzer.

The season's first big victory came the next week against the North Little Rock Charging Wildcats. Trailing 7-6 with just under nine minutes left in the game, Central used eight minutes to drive 70 yards for the game-winning touchdown.

Covington carried nine consecutive times from the Charging Wildcats 40 to the end zone. His shortest carry of the game was a 2-yard touchdown run that put the Tigers on top for good. Covington finished with 165 yards on 34 carries.

The following week, unranked Central hosted the No. 4 Conway Wampus Cats. Conway missed a 47-yard field-goal attempt on its opening possession of the game. The Tigers never looked back. Central took possession at the 20 and used 6:26 of clock before the drive ended with a 37-yard field goal by Rodriguez.

Leading 3-0 in the third quarter, the Tigers added to their lead with a nine-play, 56-yard drive. A 25-yard pass from Mason to Paul Chester kept the drive alive. It ended with a 1-yard, off-tackle run by Covington for the score. The Wampus Cats answered on their next possession when Brent

Photo provided by the Arkansas Democrat-Gazette
Andre Covington (30)

Salter went in from the 1 to narrow the score to 9-7.

Central iced the victory when Mason went 1 yard to cap a 61-yard drive with 26 seconds remaining in the game. The Tigers converted the two-point conversion to take a 16-7 victory. Covington finished with 166 yards on 33 carries. After this game, Central entered the polls as the No. 10 team in the state.

After victories over Little Rock Catholic (41-7) and Little Rock Parkview (31-6), the Tigers narrowly escaped winless Mountain Home 15-12. Central scored on its opening possession with a 44-yard pass from Mason to Guy. Rodriguez added the extra point for a 7-0 lead.

The Bombers scored with 9:35 left in the second quarter after a 3-yard run by Shane Collins capped a 70-yard drive.

The Tigers fumbled on their next possession, giving Mountain Home possession at the 49. A 20-yard pass from Adam Fisher to Joe Fremion and a 31-yard run by Paul Simmons was all it took for the Bombers to go 51 yards and take a 12-7 lead.

Central opened the fourth quarter with a 14-play, 86-yard drive to regain the lead. Covington scored from the 1 for the go-ahead touchdown and on a sweep to convert the two-point conversion. The Tigers were able to hold on for a 15-12 victory to remain undefeated in conference play.

No. 8 Central met No. 2 Little Rock Fair for its final regular-season game. The matchup not only had city bragging rights on the line, it decided the AAAAA-Central Conference championship.

Cedric Cobbs, Fair's highly regarded halfback, rushed 12 times for 155 yards and one touchdown. Fair's defense played outstanding, limiting Covington to a season-low 87 yards rushing. The War Eagles accounted for 505 yards of total offense in a 39-16 domination of Central.

The No. 8 Tigers hosted the unranked Sylvan Hills Bears for their first-round game of the state playoffs. The game would be a rematch of the 14-14 tie in Week 2 of the season.

Sylvan Hills controlled the game from the start and easily defeated Central. William Farmer ran for a 63-yard touchdown on the game's second play to give the Bears a 7-0 lead. Sylvan Hills added another score on its next possession when Hum connected with Nathan Ramsey for a 46-yard touchdown pass. A 19-yard run by Kuji Wright put the Bears in front 20-7 late in the first quarter.

Two turnovers by Sylvan Hills led to two touchdowns by the Tigers. Mason's 2-yard pass to Guy and Covington's 15-yard run gave Central its only lead, 21-20.

The second half belonged to the Bears. Hum passed for 182 yards in a 42-28 victory..

Covington rushed for 132 yards on 27 carries, his ninth 100-yard game of the season. The Tigers finished 7-3-1 and Covington ended a stellar career at Central with 3,083 yards rushing.

1998 TIGER SCHEDULE

West Memphis 18	LRCH 14
Sylvan Hills 14	LRCH 14
LR McClellan 6	LRCH 7
*LR Hall 12	LRCH 35
*North Little Rock 7	LRCH 12
*Conway 7	LRCH 16
*LR Catholic 7	LRCH 41
*LR Parkview 6	LRCH 31
*Mountain Home 12	LRCH 15
*LR Fair 39	LRCH 16
**Sylvan Hills 42	LRCH 28 (state playoffs)

YEAR OF THE SUPER SOPHOMORE

1999   10-2-0

Head Coach: Bernie Cox
Assistants: Norman Callaway, Larry Siegel, Ken Davis, Darrell Seward,
Stan Williams, Frank Troutman
Team Trainer: B.J. Maack
Team Physician: Dr. Ken Martin

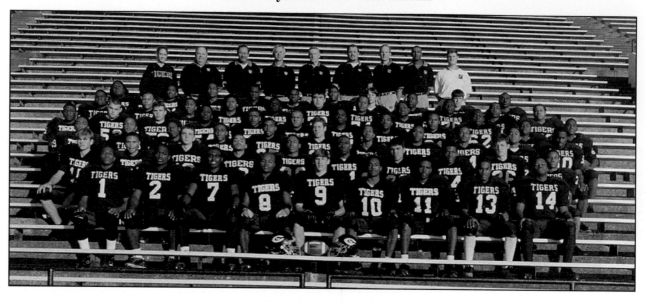

1999 LETTERMEN

Adam Acklin	John Goss	Justin Massie	Arturo Rodriguez
Matthew Atobe	Allen Harris	Nick McGee	Lakeem Staggers
Demetrius Baker	Meidro Hemphill	Ronnie Moreland	Kevin Stolzer
Charles Blake	Ronald Hendrix	Michael Mothershed	Josh Sullivan
Patrick Bynum	Marcus Hill	James Muhammad	Walter Wakwe
Brandon Campbell	Jeffrey Johnson	Anthony Nichols	Bryan Williams
Matthew Clark	Sean Jones	Daryl Parker	Keith Williams
Lawrence Dade	Arthur Jordan	Richard Parker	Ronnie Williams
Michael Ewings	Andre Luckey	Michael Pleasant	Ryan Williams
Reginald Fossette	Derrick Mason	Dedrick Poole	

1999 MANAGER
Christal Ransom

1999 ALL-AMERICAN
Dedrick Poole

1999 NATIONAL SOPHOMORE OF THE YEAR
Dedrick Poole

1999 ALL-STATE
Marcus Hill
Justin Massie
Dedrick Poole
Arturo Rodriguez

1999 ALL-CONFERENCE

Patrick Bynum   Lakeem Staggers
John Goss   Bryan Williams
Derrick Mason   Ronnie Williams

1999 ALL-STAR TEAM
Marcus Hill
Arturo Rodriguez

Photo provided by Brian Cox

Derrick Mason

Central, which returned 13 starters, entered as the state's No. 9 team in the preseason polls. The Tigers opened their last season of the century by hosting West Memphis High School.

Sophomore tailback Dedrick Poole began his high school career by rushing for 222 yards, scoring three touchdowns and a two-point conversion. Quarterback Derrick Mason scored on a 12-yard run and fullback Ronnie Williams also scored.

Kicker Arturo Rodriguez made four extra-point attempts to give Central a 34-20 victory over the Blue Devils.

Moving up one spot in the polls to No. 8, Central faced No. 3 Sylvan Hills the next week. Central took a 17-7 lead into halftime, but the Bears scored on their first possession of the second half to cut the lead to 17-14. Sylvan Hills scored that touchdown four plays after recovering a Central fumble on the Tigers 27.

With 6:45 left to play in the game, the Tigers were backed up to their 8. Poole answered the call when he carried on 11 of 13 plays to cover the 92 yards needed. He scored on a 5-yard run with 54 seconds left to play in the game to give Central a 24-14 victory.

Poole rushed for 251 yards on 28 carries and scored three touchdowns, including runs of 20 yards and 7 yards in the first half.

The Tigers narrowly escaped Little Rock McClellan the following week. Central, which jumped to No. 5 after defeating Sylvan Hills, trailed the unranked Lions 27-24 in the fourth quarter.

Late in the game, Central's Ronald Hendrix intercepted a pass by Terrell Hammonds and returned it to the Lions 30. Poole went 25 yards on first down and then ran into the end zone on the next play to give Central a 31-27 lead. The Tigers held the Lions the remaining minutes of the game to move to 3-0.

Photo provided by Brian Cox

Coach Norman Callaway

439

Poole's ground game was too much for McClellan as he rushed for 261 yards on 27 carries and scored four touchdowns, including an 80-yard run on Central's first possession.

More than 10,000 fans at Quigley Stadium the next week watched the No. 4 Tigers host longtime rival Little Rock Hall High.

Hendrix, at defensive back, almost single-handedly shut down the Warriors' passing attack when he ended three consecutive scoring threats. Hendrix broke up two Hall High passes in the end zone and intercepted another at the Central 13 to hold the Warriors to just two scores.

Poole rushed for 126 yards on 17 carries and three touchdowns (50, 28 and 25 yards). Williams scored the Tigers' other touchdown on an 8-yard run. Central beat Hall High 26-14, but still trailed in the series 20-19-4.

Following a 31-13 victory over North Little Rock, a 21-6 victory over Conway and a 33-14 victory over Little Rock Catholic, the Tigers went for their sixth consecutive victory over Little Rock Parkview.

The Patriots were no match for the No. 3 Tigers, who scored a 61-16 victory. Poole rushed for 219 yards on 17 carries and scored on runs of 26, 8 and 2 yards.

Backup tailback Ramone Fossette rushed for 136 yards on 10 carries and three touchdowns. Fossette scored on runs of 20,

Photo provided by Brian Cox
Dedrick Poole (30)

15 and 11 yards. Mason scored on a 14-yard run and connected with Lawrence Dade for a 25-yard touchdown pass. The victory over the Patriots marked the first time Central had won its first eight games since 1986.

Against Mountain Home the following week, Poole rushed for a school-record 308 yards. He also scored three touchdowns in a 28-12 victory over the Bombers.

Poole scored on runs of 80, 77 and 53 yards. Nick McGee scored the Tigers' last touchdown on an 8-yard run.

The final regular-season game put undefeated Central against Little Rock Fair. The War Eagles were undefeated in conference play and the game would decide both the conference championship and bragging rights within the city of Little Rock.

The game was a defensive battle, with the score tied 3-3 at halftime. With 9:37 left to play in the game, Fair quarterback Zac Bradley threw a short pass to Davin Washington that ended in a touchdown 67 yards later.

The Tigers were unable to score as the War Eagles won the game and the conference championship 10-3.

Photo provided by Brian Cox
Head Coach Bernie Cox

440

Photo provided by Brian Cox

Tiger Fans vs. Little Rock Fair

Central ended its regular season 9-1-0.

The Tigers hosted their first-round play-off game against the Pine Bluff Zebras. Central advanced 31-27 as Poole rushed for 173 yards on 26 carries and scored on a 2-yard run.

Other scores came on a 13-yard touchdown pass from Mason to Keith Williams, runs of 1 and 2 yards by McGee and a 37-yard field goal by Rodriguez.

Third-ranked Central traveled to Fayetteville for a second-round playoff game and found itself trailing the Bulldogs 24-0 going into the fourth quarter. The Tigers, though, came alive when Mason moved to receiver and sophomore Josh Sullivan entered the game at quarterback.

Sullivan immediately got Central on the scoreboard when he hit Poole for a 15-yard touchdown pass. Sullivan then converted the two-point conversion to make it 24-8.

On the Tigers' next possession, Sullivan connected with Keith Williams for a 77-yard touchdown pass. The two-point conversion failed but the deficit was narrowed to 24-14.

Central recovered a fumble at the Bulldogs 12 to set up its next score. On second down, Sullivan completed a 15-yard touchdown pass to Mason. The extra-point attempt failed, but Central only trailed 24-20 with 3:33 left to play in the game. Fayetteville received the ensuing kickoff and converted three first downs to run out the clock.

The Tigers ended the season 10-2-0, their best record since an 11-2-0 mark in 1988. They finished the season ranked No. 8 in the state.

The 1999 season brought many new and skilled sophomore players to Little Rock Central High School, including tailback Dedrick Poole, fullback Nick McGee, safety Ronald Hendrix, receiver Keith Williams and quarterback Josh Sullivan.

Poole rushed for over 100 yards in 10 of 12 games and finished with a single-season school-record 2,211 yards on 247 carries. It was also a new single-season rushing record for a sophomore in the state's largest classification.

1999 TIGER SCHEDULE

West Memphis 20	LRCH 34
Sylvan Hills 14	LRCH 24
LR McClellan 27	LRCH 31
*LR Hall 14	LRCH 26
*North Little Rock 13	LRCH 31
*Conway 6	LRCH 21
*LR Catholic 14	LRCH 33
*LR Parkview 16	LRCH 61
*Mountain Home 12	LRCH 28
*LR Fair 10	LRCH 3
**Pine Bluff 27	LRCH 31 (state playoffs)
**Fayetteville 24	LRCH 20 (state playoffs)

COACH BERNIE COX WINS HIS 200th GAME

2000   10-2-0

Head Coach: Bernie Cox
Assistants: Norman Callaway, Larry Siegel, Ken Davis, Darrell Seward,
Stan Williams, Frank Troutman
Team Trainer: Brian Cox
Team Physicians: Dr. Wesley Burks, Dr. Elton Cleveland, Dr. Brian Hardin

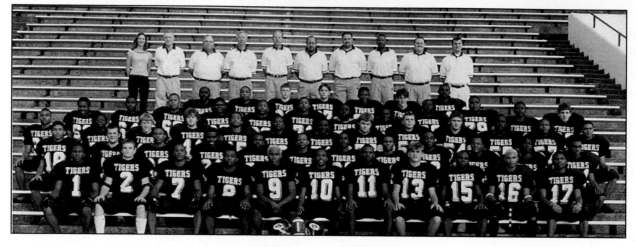

2000 LETTERMEN

Stephen Agnew	Reginald Harris	Will McClinton	Eddie Robinson
Greg Baber	Ronald Hendrix	Nick McGee	Larry Sanders
Demetrius Baker	DeShawn Jackson	Jeffrey Moore	Emanuel Savage
Charles Blake	Jeffrey Johnson	Michael Mothershed	Blaine Siegel
Chris Burks	Marcus Johnson	Evan Nichols	Josh Sullivan
Mac Compton	Sean Jones	Brandon Nunnley	Richard Townsend
Seth Cooper	Arthur Jordan	Daryl Parker	Kenneth Wakwe
Antwan Dickson	Andre Luckey	Michael Pleasant	Walter Wakwe
John Ekenseair	Chris Mahone	Dedrick Poole	Keith Williams
John Embry	Derrick Mason	George Pree	
Ramone Fossette	Rodney Mathews	Shaan Rahmaan	

2000 MANAGERS
Molly Beuerman
James Marshall

2000 ALL-SOUTHERN
Dedrick Poole

2000 ALL-STATE
Derrick Mason
Jeffery Moore
Dedrick Poole
Josh Sullivan

442

2000 ALL-CONFERENCE

Charles Blake   Andre Luckey
Mac Compton   Nick McGee
Ramone Fossette   Michael Pleasant
Arthur Jordan

2000 ALL-STAR TEAM
None

Photo provided by Brian Cox

Quarterback Josh Sullivan and Mac Compton

After a successful 1999 campaign, Little Rock Central hoped to finish with a championship in 2000. The Tigers opened the season No. 5 in Arkansas and ranked No. 27 nationally in one poll. Central returned all its skill players, including tailback sensation Dedrick Poole. The Tigers, though, entered the season with only two experienced offensive linemen and one experienced defensive lineman.

The first game of the season pitted No. 5 Little Rock Central against No. 9 West Memphis. The game was billed as a showcase of stars, pitting Poole against West Memphis senior fullback De'Arrius Howard.

Howard rushed for 310 yards and two touchdowns. Poole rushed for 113 yards and three touchdowns. Poole lost the rushing battle but the Tigers won 35-21. With 30 seconds left in the game, backup tail-

back Michael Pleasant iced Central's victory with a 49-yard touchdown run.

After defeating Sylvan Hills 13-7, the Tigers hosted the No. 10 El Dorado Wildcats. In a defensive battle, Central led 7-3 after three quarters. On the first play of the fourth quarter, El Dorado quarterback Elliot Jacobs faked a punt and ran 34 yards for a touchdown. The Tigers were unable to score again and lost 10-7, falling to No. 6 in the state poll and dropping out of the national poll.

The Conway Wampus Cats traveled to Quigley Stadium for the opening of the Central's conference schedule. The Tigers' first score came when quarterback Derrick Mason completed a pass to Devin Morris, who sprinted 76 yards for a touchdown. Poole scored on Central's next two possessions when he crossed the goal line from the 10 and 50, respectively. Pleasant intercepted two passes in the fourth quarter to stop any threat by Conway to score. The

Photo provided by Brian Cox

Keith Williams (10) vs. Forrest City

443

18-10 victory gave Coach Bernie Cox his 200th career victory.

During the next five weeks, Central defeated its opponents by a combined score of 180-50.

"Maul Hall" was the cry during the 10th and final week of the regular season. Little Rock Hall High, whose home stadium was Scott Field, moved the game to War Memorial Stadium in order to play on a neutral site and to have enough room for the spectators.

The Tigers needed a victory to finish unbeaten in the conference and secure an outright conference championship.

Central quarterback Josh Sullivan completed a 33-yard touchdown pass to Mason and a 14-yard touchdown pass to Keith Williams. The Warriors, though, gave the Tigers a good battle, taking a 16-14 lead late in the game.

Poole, however, was too much for Hall High to handle. After the Warriors took the lead with 7:34 left in the game, Poole returned the ensuing kickoff 77 yards for the game-winning touchdown. In this 44th meeting between the schools, Central evened the series at 20-20-4. The victory gave the Tigers their first conference title since 1996.

Photo provided by the Arkansas Democrat-Gazette
Dedrick Poole (30)

With home-field advantage during the state playoffs, Central hosted the Forrest City Mustangs during the first round. Mason returned a punt 45 yards for the Tigers' first touchdown. Central scored again on its next possession when Poole faked a sweep and passed to Mason for a 73-yard touchdown. The Tigers scored again on their first three possessions of the second half and never looked back in a 35-14 victory over the Mustangs.

The following week, the Fort Smith Southside Rebels traveled to Little Rock for a quarterfinal playoff game. Rebels quarterback Josh Driscoll picked apart the Central defense by passing for 343 yards on 23 completions. Driscoll threw touchdown passes of 94, 30, 13, 13 and 2 yards. The Tigers scored on a 76-yard run by Poole and a 77-yard pass from Sullivan to Mason.

With 10 minutes to play in the game, Southside led 20-14. Unable to capitalize on two fourth-quarter interceptions by Pleasant, Central gave up two more touchdowns. For the second consecutive year, the Tigers were defeated in the second round of the playoffs, this time 33-14.

The 2000 season brought three milestones to Little Rock Central High School.

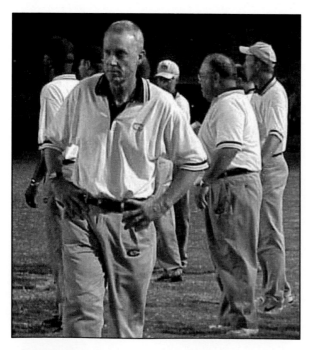

Photo provided by Brian Cox
Coach Bernie Cox

Coach Bernie Cox won his 200th career game, Little Rock Central earned its 700th recorded victory and junior tailback Dedrick Poole broke the school's career rushing record. Poole finished the season with 4,199 yards. He rushed for 1,988 yards in 2000 and 2,211 yards in 1999. The previous school record holder was Virgil Jones (3,365 yards).

2000 TIGER SCHEDULE

West Memphis 21	LRCH 35
Sylvan Hills 7	LRCH 13
El Dorado 10	LRCH 7
*Conway 10	LRCH 18
*LR Catholic 6	LRCH 35
*Mountain Home 9	LRCH 49
*LR Parkview 14	LRCH 41
*North Little Rock 6	LRCH 21
*LR McClellan 15	LRCH 34
*LR Hall 16	LRCH 20
**Forrest City 14	LRCH 35 (state playoffs)
**FS Southside 33	LRCH 14 (state playoffs)

Photo provided by Brian Cox
Kristin Kitterman
2000 homecoming queen

A RECORD NARROWLY MISSED

2001   9-2-0

Head Coach: Bernie Cox
Assistants: Norman Callaway, Larry Siegel, Darrell Seward, David Peevy,
Frank Troutman, Keith Richardson
Team Trainer: Brian Cox
Team Physicians: Dr. Wesley Burks, Dr. Elton Cleveland, Dr. Brian Hardin

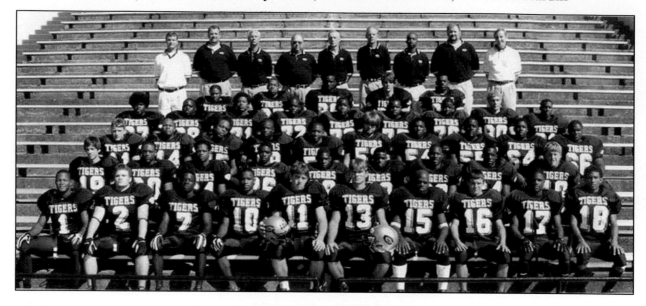

2001 LETTERMEN

Kevin Abrams	Drew Cronkhite	Chris Mahone	Blaine Siegel
Aaron Acklin	Ramone Fossette	James Marshall	Josh Sullivan
Stephen Agnew	Ronald Hendrix	Rodney Mathews	Hiram Sumlin
Dwane Barbee	Kerry Hervey	Will McClinton	A.J. Thomas
Greg Baber	Phillip Horton	Nick McGee	Richard Townsend
Fred Bledsoe	DeShawn Jackson	Adam Page	Kenneth Wakwe
Maurice Burns	Marcus Johnson	Daryl Parker	Keith Williams
Chris Burks	Sean Jones	Dedrick Poole	
Raney Cain	LeMarkus Jordan	George Pree	
Mac Compton	Andre Luckey	Shaan Rahmaan	

2001 MANAGERS
Jacob Sullivan
Victor Wynn

2001 GATORADE ARKANSAS PLAYER OF THE YEAR
Dedrick Poole

2001 ALL-STATE
Nick McGee
Dedrick Poole
Josh Sullivan
Keith Williams

2001 ALL-CONFERENCE
Stephen Agnew   Blaine Siegel
Fred Bledsoe   Hiram Sumlin
Kerry Hervey   Kenneth Wakwe

2001 ALL-STAR TEAM
Dedrick Poole
Josh Sullivan

On Sept. 1, Quigley Stadium was the site for the second annual Alltel/Hooten's Kickoff Classic. No. 3 Little Rock Central and West Memphis began the Saturday tripleheader with a noon kickoff.

Central had switched from gold helmets to black in 1970, and 31 years later it donned gold helmets once again.

Tailback Dedrick Poole opened his senior season by rushing for 204 yards on 18 carries and recording his 22nd career game with at least 100 yards rushing. The Tigers scored first when Poole fumbled into the end zone after a 16-yard run. But offensive tackle Andre Luckey recovered for a touchdown.

Quarterback Josh Sullivan scored Central's second touchdown on a 12-yard run. Poole also scored on a 2-yard run and a 35-yard run in the 27-7 victory.

The next week, Central defeated the Sylvan Hills Bears 21-12 behind Poole's 301 yards rushing and touchdowns of 64, 58 and 40 yards.

The following Tuesday, Sept. 11, the United States was attacked on its soil for the first time since Pearl Harbor was bombed Dec. 7, 1941.

Out of respect for the thousands who lost their lives as a result of terrorism in New York, Washington D.C. and Pennsylvania, the Little Rock School District cancelled all extra-curricular activities.

Practice did resume the next day as the Tigers prepared for their trip to El Dorado and a battle with the Wildcats. Central trailed 17-7 at halftime, but came out in the second half to take control of the game.

Photo provided by the Arkansas Democrat-Gazette

Josh Sullivan (13)

The Tigers were able to capitalize on two turnovers late in the game, including a fumble recovery at the El Dorado 38. When Central took possession, Sullivan connected with Poole for a 31-yard pass play. Poole then ran the remaining 7 yards to cut El Dorado's lead to 17-13.

Midway through the fourth quarter, sophomore defensive tackle Fred Bledsoe intercepted a pass and returned it 37 yards to the El Dorado 35. The Tigers then took the lead when Poole scored on a short run in the 19-17 victory.

Central played its first conference game the following week against the Conway Wampus Cats. Conway set the tone for the game on its opening possession when it moved 69 yards in 59 seconds to take a 7-0 lead.

The Wampus Cats never looked back as they rushed for 439 yards. John Duhart ran for six touchdowns in the 47-21 victory over the Tigers, a loss that

The 2001 Tiger offense

dropped Central from No. 3 to No. 9 in the *Arkansas Democrat-Gazette* poll.

The Tigers rebounded to beat Little Rock Catholic 41-6 the following week. Poole rushed for 157 yards and two touchdowns on only seven carries.

Central scored its first touchdown when linebacker Stephen Agnew intercepted a pass and returned it 90 yards. LeMarkus Jordan scored on a short run late in the first quarter, and Poole scored on a 29-yard run just before halftime to put the Tigers up 21-0.

Central would dominate the second half as well. On its first possession of the second half, Keith Williams scored on a 32-yard reverse for a 28-0 lead.

The Rockets scored on a 30-yard pass from Mark Ewersmann to Noel Hugg. The Tigers, however, scored twice more during the third quarter.

Poole scored on a 38-yard run; Nick McGee scored on a 3-yard run to put them up 41-6.

The Mountain Home Bombers traveled to Little Rock the following week. The Bombers started out strong, returning the opening kickoff 76 yards and scoring three plays later to take a 6-0 lead.

Central, though, scored the next 43 points. Sullivan began the scoring when he connected with Richard Townsend for a 26-yard touchdown pass. Poole then scored the next five touchdowns.

In the first half, Poole scored on runs of 25, 3 and 3 yards. He only touched the ball twice in the second half and scored each time.

He ran for a 25-yard touchdown on the Tigers' first possession of the second half. On the next possession, Poole, who rushed 17 times for 270 yards, scored on a 68-yard run.

Jordan, Greg Baber and Maurice Burns each had short touchdown runs in the fourth quarter to give Central a 61-20 victory over Mountain Home.

After victories over Little Rock Parkview (23-14), North Little Rock (26-14) and Little Rock McClellan (14-6), the Tigers faced Little Rock Hall in the annual "Battle for the Bell."

The game would prove to be one of the best performances by Central's offense during the year.

Poole rushed for 162 yards on 21 carries and scored two touchdowns. Jordan rushed for 111 yards on 13 carries and scored two touchdowns. McGee rushed for 120 yards on 10 carries and scored one touchdown.

The Tigers finished with 503 total yards, including 451 rushing. Their defense held the Warriors to 107 total yards of offense. With a 42-0 victory, Central took the lead in the series 21-20-4.

Dedrick Poole

The No. 5 Tigers hosted the unranked West Memphis Blue Devils for the first round of the AAAAA state playoffs.

After having no problems with the Blue Devils during the regular season, Central was highly favored to win and move on to the second round of the playoffs.

Central's defense delivered a goal-line stand just as time ran out in the first half to secure a 6-0 halftime lead. The Tigers wasted no time in the third quarter by taking a 14-0 lead after Sullivan passed to Williams for a 33-yard touchdown.

West Memphis, though, tied the score after both Kyle Payne and Taurus Gilliam scored on short runs. With 4:17 left in the game, Poole fumbled at the Central 29 and the Blue Devils' Josh Stokes recovered. West Memphis scored four plays later when Payne ran in from the 11 for a 21-14 lead.

Williams returned the ensuing kickoff to the Tigers 45, where Central began running its two-minute offense. With 32 seconds remain-ing in the game, Poole scored on a 14-yard run to pull the Tigers within 21-20.

Tigers Coach Bernie Cox elected to go for the two-point conversion and the victory, but Poole was stopped well short of the goal line. It was Central's second loss of the season and eliminated the Tigers from the playoffs.

Poole finished the season with 1,860 yards and 6,059 for his career, only 8 yards short of breaking the state record of 6,066 yards set by De'Arrius Howard of West Memphis.

Poole also set school records for rushing yards in one season (2,211), touchdowns in a career (71) and number of games with at least 100 yards rushing (30).

His 2,211 yards in 1999 was also a state record for a sophomore in the state's largest classification.

2001 TIGER SCHEDULE

West Memphis 7	LRCH 27
Sylvan Hills 12	LRCH 21
El Dorado 17	LRCH 19
*Conway 47	LRCH 21
*LR Catholic 6	LRCH 41
*Mountain Home 20	LRCH 61
*LR Parkview 14	LRCH 23
*North Little Rock 14	LRCH 26
*LR McClellan 6	LRCH 14
*LR Hall 0	LRCH 42
**West Memphis 21	LRCH 20 (state playoffs)

Photo provided by Central High School

2001 LRCH cheerleading squad, ASC national champion

450

SOPHOMORES DELIVER SUCCESS

2002   7-4-0

Head Coach: Bernie Cox
Assistants: Normal Callaway, Larry Siegel, Darrell Seward, David Peevy, Clarence Finley, Frank Troutman, Stan Williams
Team Trainer: Brian Cox
Team Physicians: Dr. Wesley Burks, Dr. Elton Cleveland, Dr. Brian Hardin

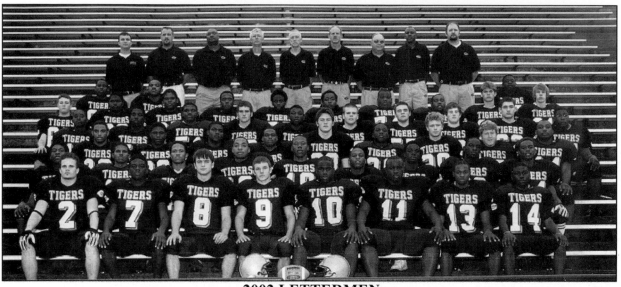

2002 LETTERMEN

Kevin Abrams	Stewart Franks	Rodney Mathews	Ryan Taylor
Charles Alexander	Kerry Hervey	Gene Moore	A.J. Thomas
James Bass	Clark Irwin	Adam Page	Kevin Thornton
Patrick Beavers	Greg Jackson	Thomas Paige	Kenneth Wakwe
Fred Bledsoe	Joseph Jackson	Rudy Patrick	Stanley Wakwe
Chris Burks	Marcus Johnson	George Pree	Tristan Wilkerson
Raney Cain	Jericho Jones	Antwain Robinson	Anton Williams
Mickey Dean	LeMarkus Jordan	Blaine Siegel	
Freddie Fairchild	William Lefear	Jake Sullivan	
Jack Fowler	James Marshall	Hiram Sumlin	

2002 MANAGER
Victor Wynn

2002 ALL-STATE
Marcus Johnson
George Pree
Blaine Siegel
Kenneth Wakwe

2002 ALL-CONFERENCE

Mickey Dean   Adam Page
Kerry Hervey   Antwain Robinson
Clark Irwin   Kevin Thornton
LeMarkus Jordan   Anton Williams
James Marshall

2002 ALL-STAR TEAM
Kenneth Wakwe

With the loss of two-time All-American tailback Dedrick Poole and 12 other starters to graduation, Coach Bernie Cox entered his 28th season as head coach with several holes to fill.

Eight seniors reported for practice and only five of these players were expected to contribute. This forced the coaching staff to play many inexperienced players, mainly sophomores. Eight of these sophomores would become starters and prove they were capable of competing against the state's best teams.

This highly regarded sophomore class was undefeated during its ninth-grade season in 2001. Central was considered home to the city's premier ninth-grade football program since its inception in 1999.

The unranked Tigers traveled to West Memphis for the season opener and took on a tough Blue Devils team. Central struck first midway through the first quarter when sophomore Clark Irwin passed to sopho-

more Kevin Thornton for a 7-yard touchdown.

Later in the quarter, Irwin kept on an option play and ran 57 yards for a touchdown. Irwin struck again early in the second quarter when he passed to Adam Page for a 15-yard touchdown.

Kyle Payne scored late in the second quarter for West Memphis, but Irwin answered with a 25-yard touchdown pass to Rodney Mathews for a 28-7 halftime lead.

The Blue Devils came out in the third quarter and cut the lead to 28-21, but the Tigers scored twice more in the fourth quarter, including a 56-yard touchdown pass from Irwin to Thornton. Chris Burks converted six extra points, helping Central to a 42-21 victory.

In his first high school football game, Irwin passed for 115 yards and accounted for five touchdowns.

After a 17-6 loss to No. 4 El Dorado, the Tigers traveled to Panther Stadium to take on Mike Malham's Cabot Panthers.

Central received the opening kickoff and sophomore Mickey Dean returned it to midfield. Irwin passed to sophomore Stewart Franks for a 37-yard gain, and then Irwin connected with Franks again for a 24-yard touchdown pass with 9:40 left in the first quarter. Burks' extra-point attempt was blocked and the Tigers led 6-0.

The No. 8 Panthers took the ensuing kickoff and used a little more

Photo provided by Brian Cox
Mickey Dean (23) and Kenneth Wakwe (67)

452

than eight minutes to drive 65 yards and tie score on a 6-yard run by Adam Baker. Brad Shirley's extra point gave Cabot a 7-6 lead.

The Panthers received the ball to open the second half and sustained a 69-yard drive that ended with Chris Robertson's 8-yard run for a touchdown. The extra point gave Cabot a 14-6 lead.

The Tigers, however, responded on their next possession when Irwin scored on a 1-yard run. LeMarkus Jordan went around left end for the two-point conversion attempt, but was met by David Rogers. Rogers downed Jordan just short of the goal line and it proved to be the game-saving play for Cabot as it held on for a 14-12 victory.

Central opened conference play the following week when the undefeated and second-ranked Conway Wampus Cats visited Quigley Stadium.

After kicking off to Conway to begin the game, the Tigers blocked a field-goal attempt and took over at their 20. Central drove 80 yards in 15 plays to score the game's first touchdown, a 5-yard run by Irwin.

After trailing 14-13 at halftime, the Tigers came out in the third quarter and drove 74 yards in 13 plays to take a 19-14 lead after Dean's 16-yard run on fourth down.

Thornton stopped the next drive by intercepting a pass and giving Central possession deep inside Conway territory.

Photo provided by Brian Cox
Kevin Thornton vs. LR McClellan

The Tigers drove to the Conway 13 with 10:31 left in the fourth quarter, but turned the ball over on downs.

Central held Conway to three plays and a punt, giving the Tigers possession at the Wampus Cats 46 with 7:49 left to play.

Central drove to the Conway 38, but had to punt back to the Wampus Cats, giving them possession inside their 15 with 5:26 left.

The Wampus Cats had used fullback Peyton Hillis the entire game, pounding the the middle for gains of 3 and 4 yards a carry. The Tigers controlled this offensive philosophy in the second half and hoped to hold Conway here to seal a victory.

But from his 33, Hillis found a hole in the right side of the line and raced 67 yards for a touchdown. The Wampus Cats converted the two-point conversion and took the lead, 22-19, with 3:41 left to play in the game.

Central took the ensuing kickoff and threatened to score, but all hope ended when Irwin was intercepted at the Conway 25.

New to the AAAAA-Central Conference was Bryant High School. Bryant took the place of Mountain Home High School, which moved into the AAAAA-East Conference.

The first-ever meeting between the schools proved to be an exciting one. The

Photo provided by Brian Cox
Sejames Humphrey (28) vs. LR Catholic

453

Fred Bledsoe (left) vs. LR McClellan

Hornets struck first on a 4-yard touchdown pass from Lance Parker to Zac Cardinal midway through the first quarter. The extra-point attempt was wide left, but Bryant was in the lead 6-0.

The Tigers took the ensuing kickoff and drove 80 yards to take the lead, 7-6, on a 1-yard run by Dean and an extra point by Burks. Central forced Bryant to punt on its next possession, but Dean fumbled the catch and Travis Wood recovered for the Hornets at the Tigers 25.

Bryant took advantage of the turnover when Parker handed off to Brandon St. Pierre, who ran around left end for a 17-yard touchdown. A two-point conversion attempt failed when Parker's pass fell incomplete.

After recovering an Irwin fumble with 1:26 left in the half, Bryant drove 38 yards to the Central 37 where Todd Bryan attempted a 47-yard field goal.

The attempt fell short with 13 seconds remaining in the half, but the Hornets still had a 12-7 lead at the break.

The Tigers were forced to punt on their first possession of the third quarter, but Wood fumbled back to Central on the return. A 52-yard drive ended with Dean's 5-yard touchdown run to put the Tigers in front 13-12.

Bryant was forced to punt on its first two possessions of the fourth quarter. Cen-

tral's Tristan Wilkerson and Blaine Siegel each had an interception to end the Hornets' final two possessions and help the Tigers hang on for a 13-12 victory.

After Anton Williams returned an interception 53 yards to seal a victory over Little Rock Parkview, Central took on North Little Rock High School.

The defense shined against the Charging Wildcats with five interceptions, including a 47-yard return for a touchdown by Thornton.

Central's defense also recorded a safety in the 36-0 defeat of North Little Rock. After the victory, Central entered the polls at No. 10.

No. 10 Little Rock Central hosted No. 8 Little Rock McClellan the following week. Each team had only one conference loss, and the winner would become the conference's second seed in the playoffs.

Coach Norman Callaway and Clark Irwin

Midway through the first quarter, the Tigers drove 53 yards in five plays. A 30-yard pass from Irwin to Mathews set up a 4-yard scoring run by Dean. Irwin fumbled on the two-point conversion attempt, but Central led 6-0.

After holding the Lions to minus-3 yards on their first two possessions, the Tigers regained possession.

With two seconds left in the first quarter, a 38-yard touchdown pass from Irwin to Thornton capped a 63-yard, seven-play drive. The two-point conversion was good to give Central a 14-0 lead.

After a scoreless second quarter, McClellan came out in the second half and scored twice in a 1:14 time span. Terrell Sims broke free for a 79-yard touchdown run, but the Tigers held Tyler Knight short of the goal line on the two-point conversion attempt.

Central's next possession ended when Mike Ross intercepted Irwin and returned it 19 yards to the Tigers 16. Knight would score from the 5, but the Tigers again kept the Lions out of the end zone on the two-point conversion attempt and held on for a 14-12 victory.

This proved to be a huge victory for Central. The same night, Bryant High School defeated Conway to give the Wampus Cats one loss in the conference. Therefore, the No. 8 Tigers needed to defeat their old rival, Little Rock Hall High, to secure a share of the conference championship and a second seed in the playoffs.

After a slow 8-0 first half, Central's second-half domination began when defensive lineman Kerry Hervey intercepted a pass at the Warriors 12. This set up Dean's 1-yard run on fourth down to increase the lead to 14-0.

Thornton ended Hall High's next possession when he made a spectacular leaping interception at the Tigers 15. On Central's first play, Dean went over right tackle and ran 84 yards to the Warriors 1. Dean scored on the next play to put the Tigers up 21-0 with 8:27 left in the game.

A fumbled option pitch on Hall High's next possession was scooped up by sophomore Antwain Robinson, who ran 6 yards for Central's final touchdown.

A 28-0 defeat of the Warriors gave the Tigers their sixth consecutive victory and Coach Cox his 15th career conference championship.

The state playoffs began the following week with unranked Jonesboro visiting Quigley Stadium. No. 8 Central held the Hurricane on its first possession and forced a punt. Jordan, though, muffed the punt and Jonesboro recovered at the Central 8.

The Hurricane lost yardage and settled for a 33-yard field-goal attempt. The kick, though, was blocked by Hervey and the Tigers took over on their 20.

On Central's first offensive play, Irwin attempted a dump pass to Fred Bledsoe. The ball sailed through the hands of Bledsoe and into the hands of Jonesboro's Darius Young, who returned it 19 yards to the Tigers 24.

This Hurricane possession resulted in a turnover when Jordan intercepted a Jim Harris pass and returned it 85 yards to the

Photo provided by Brian Cox

Tiger two-a-days

Jonesboro 11. On first down, Dean ran off right tackle for an 11-yard touchdown. The two-point conversion failed and Central led 6-0 with 7:02 left in the first quarter.

On their next possession, the Tigers turned the ball over on downs at the Hurricane 10. Harris lost 9 yards on first down, putting the ball at the 1. Jonesboro fullback Wilford Vincent was then driven back into his end zone by Hervey for a safety and an 8-0 Central lead.

The Tigers received the ensuing kickoff and drove 48 yards, but Dean fumbled an option pitch at the 18. Johnny Hutson recovered for the Hurricane to end the scoring threat.

After Central took an 8-0 lead into halftime, the third quarter opened with a series of punts by both teams. Harris was removed from the game due to a concussion, but backup quarterback Jimmy Tollison guided the Hurricane to the Tigers 10.

Central's defense held Jonesboro on three downs, but Matt Miller kicked a field goal on fourth down to narrow the score with 3:30 left in the third quarter.

On the Tigers' next possession, Irwin again threw an interception to Young, who returned it 20 yards to the Central 8.

An offside penalty on the next play moved the ball to the 3. Tollison then faked to his fullback and kept for a short scoring run. The two-point conversion attempt failed, but the Hurricane took the lead at 9-8.

The Tigers had three possessions in the closing minutes, but could not get their passing game in sync. Their last play was a 60-yard "Hail Mary" pass into the end zone that fell through the hands of Thornton.

The game marked only the second time that Jonesboro High School had defeated Little Rock Central. The series dates back to 1930, with 16 meetings between the schools. The Tigers held the Hurricane to 75 yards total yards in a 9-8 season-ending loss.

A few of Little Rock Central's outstanding sophomores included Dean (1,073 yards rushing), Irwin (570 yards passing), Robinson (54 tackles and eight quarterback sacks) and Thornton (51 tackles and five interceptions).

2002 TIGER SCHEDULE

West Memphis 21	LRCH 42
El Dorado 17	LRCH 6
Cabot 14	LRCH 12
*Conway 22	LRCH 19
*LR Catholic 13	LRCH 20
*Bryant 12	LRCH 13
*LR Parkview 6	LRCH 22
*North Little Rock 0	LRCH 36
*LR McClellan 12	LRCH 14
*LR Hall 0	LRCH 28
**Jonesboro 9	LRCH 8 (state playoffs)

DEFENSE WINS CHAMPIONSHIPS

2003   14-0-0

Head Coach: Bernie Cox
Assistants: Norman Callaway, Larry Siegel, Darrell Seward, Clarence Finley,
Frank Troutman, Stan Williams, Clyde Horton
Team Trainer: Brian Cox
Team Physicians: Dr. Elton Cleveland, Dr. Brian Hardin

2003 LETTERMEN

Kevin Abrams	Jack Fowler	LeMarkus Jordon	Ryan Taylor
Charles Alexander	Stewart Franks	Kevin Luneau	A.J. Thomas
Chris Allen	Brad Gordon	James Marshall	James Thomas
Chris Arnold	Joseph Henry	Steven McKee	Kevin Thornton
James Bass	Kerry Hervey	Marquise Merriweather	Anton Williams
Patrick Beavers	Sejames Humphrey	Gene Moore	Stanley Wakwe
Clay Bemberg	Clark Irwin	Adam Page	Antonio West
Fred Bledsoe	Andre Jackson	Thomas Paige	Tristan Wilkerson
Adam Childers	Greg Jackson	Rudy Patrick	
Mickey Dean	Joseph Jackson	Antwain Robinson	
Freddie Fairchild	Jericho Jones	Bernard Roseby	

2003 MANAGERS
Andrew Ensminger
Quadel Foreman

2003 ALL-AMERICAN
Fred Bledsoe
Antwain Robinson

2003 ALL-SOUTHERN
Fred Bledsoe
Freddie Fairchild
Antwain Robinson
Kevin Thornton

2003 ALL-STATE
Freddie Fairchild
Clark Irwin
Antwain Robinson
Kevin Thornton
Anton Williams

2003 ALL-CONFERENCE

Charles Alexander   Kerry Hervey
Fred Bledsoe   Sejames Humphrey
Mickey Dean   LeMarkus Jordan
Jack Fowler   Adam Page
Stewart Franks   Stanley Wakwe
Brad Gordon

2003 STATE CHAMPIONSHIP - MVP
Stewart Franks

2003 STATE CHAMPIONSHIP – BURLSWORTH AWARD
Antwain Robinson

2003 ALL-STAR TEAM
Fred Bledsoe
Anton Williams
Bernie Cox – Head Coach
Norman Callaway – Assistant Coach

2003 ARKANSAS COACH OF THE YEAR
Bernie Cox

Following an unbeaten run through the summer's Region 6 7-on-7 Tournament, Little Rock Central tried to carry its championship form into the regular season. The junior-laden team opened the season ranked No. 2 by the *Arkansas Democrat-Gazette*.

When two-a-day practices began July 28, the Tigers were met with a new 2,500 square-foot weight room. Space for the new facility was possible after a wall that separated the visitor's dressing room from the old track dressing room was removed. Money for the renovation and new weights was donated by parents, Central alumni and fans throughout the state.

After six weeks of practice, the Tigers opened against No. 8 West Memphis at Quigley Stadium.

Central took a 14-0 lead into halftime, but the Blue Devils opened the third quarter with a drive that lasted 7:30. The Tigers ended the scoring threat at their 1 by forcing and recovering a fumble.

Mickey Dean, however, fumbled on Central's next play. Dennis Parker recovered for West Memphis to once again give

Photo provided by DeWain Duncan
Mickey Dean (23)

458

Clark Irwin (left) and Thomas Paige (20)

the Blue Devils possession at the Tigers 1. Kyle Payne scored easily and the two-point conversion attempt, a pass from Corey Davis to Eugene Edwards, narrowed Central's lead to 14-8.

The Tigers clinched the victory with a 65-yard drive that ended with a 5-yard touchdown run by Dean. Kevin Luneau converted his third extra-point attempt to end the game's scoring at 21-8.

Central traveled to Memorial Stadium in El Dorado the next week to take on the No. 7 Wildcats. The Tigers really began to flex their defensive muscle, limiting El Dorado to only 41 yards of total offense, which included only 18 yards rushing.

Central's offense struck first when Luneau kicked a 20-yard field goal in the second quarter for a 3-0 lead. Its defense scored just moments later when Antwain

Robinson returned a fumble 20 yards for a touchdown.

The touchdown occurred when Robinson tipped an option pitch by El Dorado quarterback John Thomas Shepherd. Robinson recovered and returned it for a touchdown with 7:55 left in the third quarter. Luneau converted the extra-point attempt for a 10-0 lead. The Wildcats never threatened to score as the Tigers posted their first shutout of the season.

Central continued its tough non-conference schedule the following week at Cabot High School to take on the No. 5 Panthers.

Tristan Wilkerson set up the Tigers' first touchdown when he intercepted a pass early in the second quarter. Stewart Franks, Central's wide receiver, then scored on a 22-yard reverse with 8:46 remaining in the second quarter. Luneau's extra-point attempt was wide left, but the Tigers took a 6-0 lead.

On the first offensive play of Cabot's ensuing possession, quarterback Ryan Cotroneo was stripped of the football. Central's LeMarkus Jordan recovered at the Panthers 42 with 8:33 remaining in the first half.

On second down, Thomas Paige went around left end on a sweep and ran untouched for a 40-yard touchdown. Quarterback Clark Irwin ran for the two-point conversion, giving the Tigers a 14-0 lead.

Cabot answered with a 15-play, seven-minute drive. However, the offensive execution ended when the Panthers faced fourth-and-4 from the Central 21. Cabot's Brandon Wade was stopped for no gain, and the Tigers took their lead into halftime.

Both defenses kept the second half scoreless, giving the Central its second consecutive shutout.

A record crowd of more than 11,000 packed Conway's John McConnell Stadium for Central's first conference game. The matchup pitted the No. 2 Tigers (3-0-0) against the No. 4 Wampus Cats (3-0-0).

Conway boasted a strong running game behind fullback Peyton Hillis and halfback Kevin Wardlow. In three games, the 244-

459

The 2003 LRCH cheerleading squad, Cheersport national champion

pound Hillis had rushed for 833 yards and 11 touchdowns. The Wampus Cats were averaging 426 total yards per game.

Central, though, boasted a strong defense. It had allowed only 336 total yards and one touchdown in the three games leading up to the conference opener. However, Central's offense was the key factor during this battle.

Early in the first quarter Hillis bulled his way for a first down, but fumbled while trying to stretch for additional yardage. Central's Stanley Wakwe recovered at the Conway 37.

The Tigers needed only six plays to take advantage of the turnover as Dean weaved his way through the defense for a 10-yard touchdown. Luneau converted the extra-point attempt for a 7-0 lead with 8:46 remaining in the quarter.

Central's defense forced a punt to set up the game's second score. After receiving this punt, a short scoring drive was capped by Irwin's 1-yard plunge. Luneau's extra-

point kick increased the lead to 14-0 with 4:54 left in the first half.

Wardlow returned the ensuing kickoff 93 yards for a touchdown. The extra-point conversion failed, leaving the Tigers ahead 14-6 with 4:40 remaining in the half.

Central quickly answered, taking the ensuing kickoff and moving 71 yards in five plays to take a 21-6 lead. A 44-yard pass completion from Irwin to Franks set up Dean's 4-yard scoring burst up the middle with 2:35 left in the half.

Conway would again match the touchdown.

After the ensuing kickoff, an 18-yard pass from Brandon Solberg to Wardlow set up an 18-yard touchdown pass from Solberg to Nick Smith. Smith caught the pass in the back of the end zone to narrow Central's halftime lead to 21-13.

Hillis scored with 5:05 left in the third quarter to bring the Wampus Cats within 21-19. Just minutes later, Hillis was again closing in on the goal line, but was stripped of the ball by Wakwe and Adam Page. De-

Thomas Paige (right) vs. Cabot

fensive tackle Kerry Hervey recovered at his 16 with 7:20 remaining in the game.

Central's offense then shined as it put together a 14-play, six-minute drive. The drive, though, ended on downs at the Conway 17 and gave the Wampus Cats one last chance to score.

Conway's final series ended four plays later when Solberg was intercepted by linebacker Freddie Fairchild at the Wampus Cats 38 with 41 seconds left to play in the game.

Hillis finished with 150 yards rushing and a touchdown on 23 carries. He also broke Conway High School's career rushing record in the second half. The Central defense held the Wampus Cats to 227 yards of total offense in the 21-19 victory. The offense was led by Irwin, who threw for 139 yards.

Following an impressive four-game winning streak against Top 10 opponents, Central moved into the No. 1 spot after previously top-ranked Springdale fell to Fort Smith Southside. The Tigers received top billing by both the *Arkansas Democrat-Gazette* and The Associated Press.

A 78-yard punt return by Franks and a 41-yard touchdown run by Paige highlighted a 21-9 victory over Catholic High School the next week. The game ended with 36 seconds remaining in the fourth quarter after Wilkerson, a junior cornerback, suffered a right hip dislocation.

Wilkerson was removed from the field by ambulance and taken to Arkansas Children's Hospital where the dislocation was reduced.

No. 10 Bryant High School arrived at Quigley Stadium hoping to continue its offensive dominance by using its Spread attack against the stout Central defense. Quarterback Scott Peeler and the Hornets were averaging 411.8 yards per game and hoped to dismantle Central's defense with an offense the Tigers had not defended during the season.

Touchdown runs of 30, 6 and 2 yards by Dean and a 24-yard field goal by Luneau were enough to give Central a 24-7 victory over Bryant. The Hornets' lone touchdown came on a 4-yard pass from Peeler to Dustin Holland with 5:38 remaining in the game.

Peeler, who averaged 315.4 yards passing per game, was held to 108 yards on 15 completions. The Bryant offense netted minus-22 yards rushing on 21 attempts, due in large part to eight quarterback sacks totaling 65 yards in losses.

Following a 48-27 victory over Little Rock Parkview and a 40-17 domination of North Little Rock, Central played Little Rock McClellan with a share of the conference championship at stake.

Irwin, Central's junior quarterback, completed 8 of 12 passes for 158 yards, highlighted by a 38-yard touchdown pass to Dean with 5:01 left in the third quarter. Irwin ended Central's first possession of the game when he ran into the end zone from the 1 with 6:47 remaining in the first quarter.

Page's 9-yard interception return for a touchdown in the third quarter invoked the mercy rule and a continuously running clock throughout the remainder of the game. The Tigers finished with 200 yards of total offense and held the Lions to two first downs and 7 total yards for three quarters before taking a 38-0 victory.

Already owning at least a share of the conference title and No. 1 playoff seed, the Tigers were now playing for their first unbeaten regular season since going 9-0-1 in 1987. The opponent for the 10th playing date was Little Rock Hall High School, the annual "Battle for the Bell."

Dean began the scoring for Central when he went 53 yards for a touchdown with 8:57 left in the first quarter. Just four minutes later, Irwin faked a sweep to Dean and threw a 19-yard touchdown pass to Franks.

With 10:29 left in the first half, the Tigers struck again when Franks completed a 28-yard double pass to Kevin Thornton. Paige added another score three minutes later with a 40-yard run.

Two minutes later, with 5:22 left in the half, Thornton ran 30 yards for a touchdown. At 2:48 the score increased again, this time with Paige scoring on a 20-yard run. Luneau converted 5 of 6 extra-point attempts in a 41-8 victory over the Warriors.

Central's defense continued its dominance as it allowed Hall High only 28 total yards and one first down. The game marked the Warriors' 17th consecutive loss, and the eighth consecutive loss to the Tigers. Central increased its lead in the series to 23-20-4.

The Little Rock Central Tigers began postseason play the next week when they hosted the Searcy Lions at Quigley Stadium. The Tigers started the scoring with 7:17 left in the first quarter when Irwin passed to Franks for a 33-yard touchdown play. With 1:07 remaining in the quarter, the two players connected again, this time for a 56-yard touchdown completion.

Irwin struck again with 5:59 left in the first half when he hit Dean with a 27-yard touchdown pass.

Midway through the third quarter, Dean added to the score with a 3-yard touchdown run. He finished the scoring on the third

462

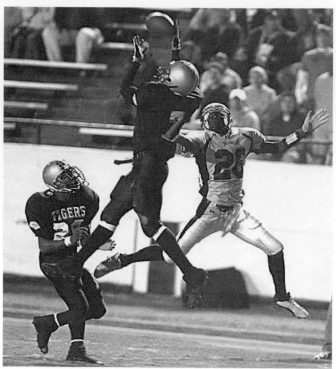

Photo provided by the Arkansas Democrat-Gazette
Kevin Thornton intercepts a pass against Springdale

play of the fourth quarter when he crossed the goal line from the 20. Luneau's fifth extra point made it 35-0 and invoked the mercy rule for the third consecutive week. Irwin completed five passes for 153 yards and three touchdowns. The Central defense held the Lions to 53 total yards and four first downs. Searcy fullback Weston Dacus, who entered the game with six consecutive 100-yard rushing games, was held to 28 yards.

The following week, approximately 10,000 fans at Quigley Stadium watched as No. 3 Springdale brought its high-powered West Coast offense to central Arkansas. Springdale, the 2002 state runner-up, was coming off a 562-yard performance in a 41-0 first-round playoff victory at Benton.

Late in the first quarter, Anton Williams set up the Tigers' first score when he intercepted a Brandon Martinez pass at the Bulldogs 30 and returned it 25 yards to the 5. A penalty moved the Tigers to the 10, but Dean got to the 2, then Irwin slipped in for the first score. Luneau converted the extra-point attempt for a 7-0 lead with 4:41 left in the quarter.

Springdale struck next with an 11-play, 88-yard drive that was capped by an 18-yard pass completion from Martinez to Andrew Norman. The extra-point attempt was good and tied the score at 7-7, where it remained until the fourth quarter.

Late in the third quarter, the Bulldogs forced Central to punt out of its end zone and then took possession at the Tigers 35. On first down, however, Thornton intercepted a Martinez pass at the 7 and returned it to the 15. Central then drove 85 yards in nine plays for the go-ahead touchdown, a 2-yard run by Dean with 8:36 remaining in the game.

The Tigers forced Springdale to punt on its next possession and took over at the Bulldogs 46. It only took four plays to drive the needed distance, with Dean dashing around right end for the score with 4:48 remaining. Luneau's third consecutive extra point increased the lead and helped Central to a 21-7 victory over Springdale.

Photo provided by DeWain Duncan
Coach Bernie Cox and Fred Bledsoe

Martinez completed 11 of 21 passes for 141 yards. Springdale totaled only 218 yards, considerably less than its 371.5 per-game average.

Central finished with 325 total yards. Dean posted a career-high 222 yards rushing on 31 carries. During the game, the junior tailback surpassed 1,000 yards rushing for the second time in his career.

A semifinal playoff game against Pine Bluff renewed an ancient rivalry dating back to 1906. The game featured the No. 1 Tigers and the No. 4 Zebras at Jordan Stadium in Pine Bluff.

Approximately 10,000 fans watched Central take control of the game on the first play from scrimmage.

Following Luneau's opening kickoff that sailed into the end zone, the game was delayed almost 15 minutes because of a tangled first-down chain.

The interruption only postponed the inevitable.

On the game's first offensive play, Robinson hit Pine Bluff's Nicholas Makris as he was preparing to pass. The ball went straight up into the air and lingered there until defensive tackle Fred Bledsoe picked it off and returned it 7 yards to the Zebras 13.

It took five plays for Central to move the 13 yards, but Dean ended the short drive with a 2-yard touchdown run. Luneau's extra point gave the Tigers a 7-0 lead with 8:52 remaining in the first quarter.

Central then took advantage of a short punt by Pine Bluff and put together a 29-yard drive that ended in five plays when Irwin scored on a 1-yard run. Luneau increased the lead to 14-0 with 10:47 left in the second quarter.

With 12 seconds left in the first half, Franks set up the next score when he returned an interception 40 yards to the Zebras 32. Two plays later, on the last play of the half, Luneau split the uprights for a 26-yard field goal. The kick gave the Tigers a 17-0 halftime lead.

An uneventful third quarter was followed by two more scores for Central in the game's final period.

On the first play of the fourth quarter, Pine Bluff was set to punt from deep inside its territory. The snap from center sailed over the head of the punter and out of the end zone, resulting in a safety and a 19-0 lead for the Tigers.

Jordan returned the ensuing kickoff to the Pine Bluff 38 to set up the next Central touchdown. The score occurred when Dean kept on a fake reverse and ran untouched for a 38-yard touchdown. Luneau's extra point gave Central a 26-0 victory.

Pine Bluff's heralded tailback, Martell Mallett, who had rushed for more than 1,700 yards during the season, was held in check by the tough defense. Mallett finished with a season-low 27 yards rushing on 14 carries.

The Central defense also posted its fifth shutout of the season and set up a rematch with West Memphis to determine the Class AAAAA state championship.

For the first time in 17 years, Little Rock Central High School played at War Memorial Stadium in Little Rock for the Arkansas state championship. The playoff bracket pitted it against a familiar foe in West Memphis, a team that the Tigers had played six times during the past five years.

The Blue Devils eliminated Central in the first round of the 2001 playoffs after falling to the Tigers in the season opener. Central prepared for a hard-fought battle, hoping that history would not repeat itself.

The Tigers won the opening coin toss. But as he normally does, Coach Bernie Cox elected to defer to the second half in order to put his talented and punishing defense on the field first. The decision proved wise as Central's defense stuffed West Memphis' Payne short of a first down when the Blue Devils gambled on fourth-and-1 from the Tigers 31.

In front of approximately 10,000 fans, Central gained the momentum on its first play from scrimmage when Irwin dropped back and delivered a perfect spiral to Franks at the West

Memphis 40. Franks outran the single-man coverage the remaining 40 yards to complete a 69-yard touchdown play. Luneau's extra point gave Central a 7-0 lead with 8:54 left in the first quarter.

B.J. Hauswirth returned the ensuing kickoff 19 yards to the Blue Devils 20, but Fairchild recovered a Vick Brown fumble on the next play to set up another threat by Central.

Three consecutive carries by Dean netted only 2 yards, forcing the Tigers to attempt a 34-yard field goal. Luneau's attempt failed and the Blue Devils took over once again at their 20.

After each team was forced to punt on its next possession, Central once again took advantage of a West Memphis mistake. The mistake was a fumble by Hauswirth that was recovered by Thornton at the Blue Devils 19 with 11:51 left in the first half.

Paige picked up 5 yards on two plays, and Irwin then passed to Rudy Patrick, who reached the 1 before being pulled down. After Dean was stopped for no gain, Irwin

Photo provided by DeWain Duncan
Stewart Franks scores against West Memphis

464

snuck up the middle on second down for a 1-yard touchdown. Luneau's kick increased the lead to 14-0, where it remained for the rest of the half.

Jordan received the second-half kickoff and returned it 15 yards to the Tigers 17. Irwin dropped to pass on first down, but was forced to scramble out the pocket and was met by Bennie Mosley, who caused Irwin to fumble. Cody Donnerson recovered for West Memphis at the Central 17.

The Tigers held strong for three plays, forcing the Blue Devils to attempt a 27-yard field goal. Xavier Murry's kick was good and narrowed the deficit to 14-3.

Central was forced to punt on its next possession, giving West Memphis possession on the Tigers 46. Payne rushed for 18 yards and Brown covered 28 yards in a drive that resulted in a 1-yard touchdown run by Payne. Brown passed to Davis for the two-point conversion to make it 14-11.

With 10:42 left in the game the Blue Devils attempted to punt. But a bad snap was recovered by Central at the 50. This set up the Tigers' next scoring drive, which was highlighted by a 30-yard halfback pass from Dean to Franks.

A 5-yard face-mask penalty was added to this second-down pass play, giving the Tigers possession at the 14. Dean rushed five times during the six-play drive, finally scoring from the 1. Luneau kicked the extra point to increase the lead to 21-11.

After a punt by West Memphis and a missed 32-yard field-goal attempt by Luneau, the Blue Devils took possession on their 20. Wakwe, Central's right defensive end, sacked Brown for a 6-yard loss on first down. An incomplete pass on second down brought third-and-16 from the West Memphis 14.

Brown dropped back and attempted a screen pass, but it was intercepted by Bledsoe at the 10, who scored his only touchdown of the season. Luneau's extra point made it 28-11.

As Davis returned the ensuing kickoff 19 yards to give the Blue Devils possession at their 28, Central was celebrating the victory by dousing Coach Cox with Gatorade.

Central's second-team defense then entered the game, and Brown connected with Davis for a 72-yard touchdown play. The two-point conversion failed with 1:08 remaining in the game and the Tigers led 28-17.

Central then recovered an onside kick and ran out the clock with three consecutive dive plays by Paige. The victory gave the

Coach Bernie Cox gets a victory ride after his sixth state championship

Tigers their first state championship since 1986, their first unbeaten season since going 9-0-2 in 1980 and their first perfect season since a 12-0-0 finish in 1975.

The 14-0-0 record marked only the second time that Central High School had won 14 games. The Tigers were also 14-0-0 in 1946 when they were named state and national champions.

Dean ended the season with 1,252 yards rushing on 224 carries, including five 100-yard games, and a career-high 222 yards against Springdale. He caught six passes for 101 yards and two touchdowns.

Franks led the Tigers in receiving with 721 yards on 36 receptions, including six touchdowns.

Robinson, at end, paced the defensive line with 21 tackles, 29 assists, one tackle for loss, 12 sacks, four forced fumbles, three recovered fumbles, two pass breakups and one blocked punt.

Fairchild finished with 77 tackles, 79 assists, five tackles for a loss, one caused fumble, two recovered fumbles, two interceptions and five pass breakups.

Thornton led the defensive backs with 29 tackles, 24 assists, one tackle for a loss, one caused fumble, two recovered fumbles, 10 interceptions and five pass breakups at safety.

In addition to leadership, Irwin completed 67 of 135 passes for 1,132 yards and 11 touchdowns. He also rushed for 147 yards and six touchdowns.

The story of the 2003 season, however, was the ability of the defense to control and dominate most games.

The Tigers allowed 1,904 yards in 14 games and an average of 3.1 yards per play. They allowed only 822 yards rushing (2.1 yards per carry) and 1,082 yards passing (11 yards per completion).

Only four rushing touchdowns and seven passing touchdowns were scored against the Tigers. This tough unit forced 21 fumbles and recovered 14, while intercepting 28 passes en route to the school's 31st state title.

2003 TIGER SCHEDULE

West Memphis 8	LRCH 21
El Dorado 0	LRCH 10
Cabot 0	LRCH 14
*Conway 19	LRCH 21
*LR Catholic 9	LRCH 21
*Bryant 7	LRCH 24
*LR Parkview 27	LRCH 48
*North Little Rock 17	LRCH 40
*LR McClellan 0	LRCH 38
*LR Hall 8	LRCH 41
**Searcy 0	LRCH 35 (state playoffs)
**Springdale 7	LRCH 21 (state playoffs)
**Pine Bluff 0	LRCH 26 (state playoffs)
**West Memphis 17	LRCH 28 (state playoff final)

TIGERS CONTINUE TO DOMINATE ARKANSAS

2004   13-1-0

Head Coach: Bernie Cox
Assistants: Norman Callaway, Larry Siegel, Darrell Seward, Clarence Finley, Stan Williams,
Keith Richardson, Clyde Horton
Team Trainer: Brian Cox
Team Physicians: Dr. Elton Cleveland, Dr. Brian Hardin

2004 LETTERMEN

Charles Alexander	Mickey Dean	Joseph Jackson	Rudy Patrick
Chris Arnold	Quadel Foreman	Rob James	Antwain Robinson
Patrick Beavers	Jack Fowler	Fernando Jenkins	Bernard Roseby
Clay Bemberg	Stewart Franks	Jericho Jones	Nic Russell
Charles Bennett	Brad Gordon	Brint Marks	Kevin Thornton
Alex Blake	Trumiel Hawkins	Drew Matlock	Stanley Wakwe
Bert Butler	Joseph Henry	Steven McKee	Tristan Wilkerson
Carlos Collier	Matt Holmes	Marquise Merriweather	Michael Witherspoon
Will Crass	Clark Irwin	Gene Moore	Kenneth Woods
David Daniels	Andre Jackson	Thomas Paige	

2004 MANAGERS
Quinton Cohen
Andrew Ensminger
James Alan Woods

2004 ALL-AMERICAN BOWL
Clark Irwin
Kevin Thornton

2004 ALL-SOUTHERN
Kevin Thornton

2004 ALL-STATE
Mickey Dean
Stewart Franks
Brad Gordon
Clark Irwin
Kevin Thornton

2004 ALL-CONFERENCE

Charles Alexander	Jack Fowler	Rudy Patrick
Chris Arnold	Joseph Henry	Bernard Roseby
Patrick Beavers	Joe Jackson	Stanley Wakwe
Bert Butler	Thomas Paige	

2004 STATE CHAMPIONSHIP – MVP
Mickey Dean

2004 STATE CHAMPIONSHIP – BURLSWORTH AWARD
Brad Gordon

2004 ALL-STAR TEAM
Brad Gordon
Clark Irwin

2004 NFHS ARKANSAS COACH OF THE YEAR
Bernie Cox

2004 CLASS AAAAA COACH OF THE YEAR
Bernie Cox

2004/2005 LOWELL MANNING AWARD (OUTSTANDING COACH IN ARKANSAS)
Bernie Cox

Photo provided by DeWain Duncan
Quarterback Clark Irwin

The defending AAAAA state champion Tigers were dealt a huge blow prior to the season as All-American defensive end Antwain Robinson was lost for the year. Surgery was needed to repair a knee condition known as osteochondritis dissecans. Following a lengthy rehabilitation process, Robinson's knee was expected to be strong enough to play at the collegiate level.

The rehabilitation outlook was good news because Robinson was offered a scholarship by the University of Arkansas following his junior season. Just days after his surgery, Robinson was notified by Coach Houston Nutt and his Arkansas staff that the scholarship offer would be honored.

Quarterback Clark Irwin competed in the inaugural Top Gun Quarterback Challenge during the summer, a three-day competition held at Springdale High School.

The top 10 quarterbacks from the state competed in five categories: Long Ball Challenge, Speed and Mobility Test, On-the-Move Targets, Stationary Targets and a 50-question multiple-choice quiz to determine mental makeup. Irwin did not win any of the categories, but a top three finish in each allowed him to total enough points to win the overall contest.

Irwin also led his team to its first state championship in the Fellowship of Christian Athletes 7-on-7 State Tournament. After breezing through the Region 6 Tournament, as it had the previous summer, Central entered the state tournament as the No. 1 seed. The Tigers played two games before losing to Warren 30-26 in the final of the winner's bracket. Central immediately played Rogers in the loser's bracket final and defeated the Mounties 19-6 to advance to the championship round.

The Tigers defeated Warren 18-8 in the first game and 27-21 in the final to win the third annual FCA state championship tournament. This championship gave them a taste of what they really wanted, a second consecutive AAAAA state title.

Photo provided by DeWain Duncan
Coach Bernie Cox (left) and
Coach Norman Callaway

Photo provided by DeWain Duncan
Mickey Dean (23)

Central returned many starters from its 2003 undefeated team. Some made the preseason All-Arkansas Team, including tailback Mickey Dean, receiver Stewart Franks, safety Kevin Thornton and defensive linemen Charles Alexander and Stanley Wakwe. Thornton was also selected preseason Defensive Player of the Year.

Because of all the returning players, every major poll in Arkansas ranked the Tigers as the preseason No. 1 team. The *Student Sports* FAB 50 poll ranked Central No. 14 nationally and No. 4 in the Southwest Region.

Defense of their state championship began Sept. 4 as the Tigers traveled to Hamilton-Schultz Stadium in West Memphis for a rematch of the 2003 state championship game. The No. 4 Blue Devils, who were hoping to avenge three consecutive losses to Central, were no match for the Tigers.

On the first offensive snap of the game, Central's Joseph Jackson stripped the ball from West Memphis quarterback Vick Brown and took it 15 yards for a touchdown. The scores kept coming as Irwin completed touchdown passes to Dean,

469

Franks and Joseph Henry. Thornton ended the scoring when he intercepted a Brown pass and returned it 57 yards for a touchdown, helping the Tigers to a 38-0 season-opening victory.

One of the oldest rivalries in the state resumed the next week when Pine Bluff replaced El Dorado on the nonconference schedule. This marked the first regular-season game between the schools since 1994 and the 90th meeting overall. Central's defense once again dominated its opponent, forcing eight turnovers in a 35-0 victory over the Zebras.

The Tigers had no problems with their second highly rated team the following week when they defeated No. 4 Cabot 35-0. Central struck first with 6:58 left in the first quarter when Thomas Paige fielded a punt at the Panthers 45. He ran to his right, broke four tackles, reversed his field and then ran untouched into the end zone. Rob James converted the extra-point attempt for a 7-0 lead.

Cabot took the ensuing kickoff and drove to the 19 before James Fortner was tackled for a 5-yard loss. Brandon Shiell missed a 42-yard field-goal attempt on fourth down to give the Tigers possession on their 20.

With 7:12 left in the half, Dean capped a 13-play, 80-yard drive with a 16-yard run. James' kick made it 14-0.

Cabot again drove deep inside Central territory, but this time ran out of downs at the 22 with 1:34 remaining in the half. It only took five plays for the Tigers to score again. Irwin passed to Franks for a 45-yard touchdown. The extra point by James made it 21-0 at halftime.

After forcing the Panthers to punt on their first possession of the second half, Central scored again when Irwin connected with Thornton for a 22-yard touchdown pass. James converted the extra-point attempt for a 28-0 lead with 7:30 left in the third quarter.

The Tigers began their next possession when Cabot again turned the ball over on downs, this time at the Central 24. Three plays later, Franks was streaking across the middle when he caught a short pass from Irwin. Franks never broke stride as he took the pass 73 yards for Central's final touchdown with 1:28 left in the third quarter.

James' extra-point attempt was good to give the Tigers a 35-0 lead and invoke the mercy rule. This marked the first time Cabot had fallen victim to the mercy rule since the rule began in 2002. The rule keeps the game clock running continuously in the second half if there is a 35-point difference in the score.

Behind Dean's 125 yards rushing, Irwin's 108 yards passing and a stifling defense, Central defeated the rebuilding Conway Wampus Cats 21-0. With the victory the Tigers posted their 18th consecutive victory, fourth consecutive shutout and moved to No. 13 in the national poll.

Photo provided by DeWain Duncan

Tiger fans cheer at a home game

Irwin's 167 yards passing the next week helped extend the consecutive victory streak to 19, but a 38-yard field goal by Catholic High's Walker Lusk ended the shutout streak. The Rockets recovered a fumble by Central's second-team offense at the Tigers 38 just as the fourth quarter opened. They were forced to settle for the field goal when they could not get the ball in the end zone.

The kicking of both James and Henry highlighted the game for the Tigers. James, a sophomore, converted 4 of 4 extra-point attempts and kicked his first career field goal, a 35-yarder. Henry, a senior, had one punt of 57 yards downed at the Catholic High 2 and another punt of 45 yards downed at the Rockets 10.

Top-ranked Central traveled to No. 6 Bryant High School hoping to breeze through the game as it had the previous five weeks. Tremendous rain poured throughout the day and during pregame warm-ups. The rain, though, ended just prior to the opening kickoff.

The Hornets kicked off to open the game and the Tigers returned it to the 37. Dean picked up 5 yards on the first play from scrimmage, then Irwin hit Franks for a 55-yard gain to reach the 3. It took three plays to get into the end zone, but Irwin finally snuck over center for the score. James' extra-point attempt was good to give Central a 7-0 lead.

Both teams traded punts before Bryant took possession and drove to the Tigers 20. Chris Arnold, though, ended the scoring threat when he intercepted an Anthony Mask pass at the 17 and returned it to the 27. Central, however, was unable to move

Photo provided by DeWain Duncan

Clark Irwin (left) and Coach Bernie Cox

and forced to punt as the second quarter opened.

The Hornets converted three first downs, one on an offside penalty by the Tigers on third-and-4, to move to the Central 29. Two short passes set up a 15-yard fade route from Mask to Richie Wood for a touchdown. The extra-point attempt was unsuccessful, but the Tigers' lead was narrowed to 7-6.

After receiving the ensuing kickoff, Irwin was picked off by Bryan Griffith at the Central 45. Griffith was hit hard by Henry, which caused the ball to pop loose. Bryant, though, recovered and took possession at the Tigers 47.

Central's Patrick Beavers was penalized for pass interference on the third play from scrimmage, setting the Hornets up with a first down at the 20. The Tigers held Bryant out of the end zone and forced a 35-yard field-goal attempt. Todd Bryan's kick was wide right, but Central's Bert Butler was penalized for jumping over the deep snapper and the Hornets received a first down at the 10.

The Tigers held tight and again forced a field-goal attempt. The 23-yard attempt by Bryan was perfect to give Bryant a 9-7 lead with 2:20 left in the half.

On Central's ensuing possession, Thornton, a standout receiver and safety, sprained his right ankle and was removed

Photo provided by DeWain Duncan

Thomas Paige

471

from the game. The Tigers were forced to punt, but the Hornets were able to run only three plays before the clock ran out in the first half.

On the third play of the second half, Wakwe forced a Bryant fumble and it was recovered by Beavers at the 50. Irwin, though, was intercepted on second down and the Hornets took over at their 40.

Facing fourth-and-5 at the 45, Mask completed a pass for a first down at the 25. On the next play, Mask found Wood all alone on a post route. Wood made a great one-handed catch as he crossed into the end zone for a touchdown. Central jumped off-side on the extra-point attempt, and Bryant then decided to go for a two-point conversion. The short run up the middle was stuffed by the Tigers, but the Hornets increased their lead to 15-7.

Late in the third quarter, Central took over after Alexander recovered a fumble at the Bryant 30. A 3-yard gain by Rudy Patrick and an incomplete pass ended the quarter, but a screen pass to Dean gave the Tigers a first down. Four plays later, Irwin snuck up the middle for a touchdown. On the two-point conversion attempt, Irwin kept on an option play, but tripped over Franks before reaching the end zone. The Hornets retained the lead at 15-13 with 9:43 left in the game.

Following a punt with 3:11 remaining, Central took possession at the Bryant 45. After a 4-yard loss by Dean and an incomplete pass, Irwin connected with Franks for a 38-yard pass play to the 11.

On first down, Dean ran around right end and then cut back inside to reach the end zone. A pass for the two-point conversion attempt fell incomplete, but the Tigers led 19-15 with 1:46 left in the game.

The Hornets took possession at their 27 after the ensuing kickoff. They picked up a first down on a pass to Wood, but then faced fourth-and-10 after three consecutive incomplete passes.

472

Mask converted the fourth-down play with a pass to Wood for a first down at the Central 49. Following two incomplete passes, Mask found Dustin Holland for a first down at the 32. Three plays later, the Hornets had another first down after Mask completed a pass to Brandon Butler at the 16.

On first down, Mask spiked the ball to stop the clock with 16 seconds. He found himself under heavy pressure on the next play and was forced to scramble to his right before throwing to a receiver in the end zone. Nic Russell, though, was there to knock the pass away. Mask, on third down, was again faced with heavy pressure before being forced to throw the ball out of bounds.

With 10 seconds left in the game, Bryant faced fourth down on the Tigers 16. Mask took the snap, ignored the pressure and fired a perfect spiral to Holland, who caught the pass 1-yard deep in the end zone. The extra point gave the Hornets a 22-19 victory over No. 1 Little Rock Central. With the loss, the Tigers fell to No. 3 in the *Arkansas Democrat-Gazette* Top 10 and completely out of the national poll.

Following a rebound victory over Little Rock Parkview (41-0), Central went across the river to battle North Little Rock. The game's first score did not occur until 1:39 remaining in the half when Irwin went in from the 5 on an option keeper. James converted the extra-point attempt for a 7-0 lead.

Clark Irwin (8) scores for the Tigers

Mickey Dean vs. Springdale

The ensuing kickoff landed in the arms of Fred McElwee at the Charging Wildcats 1. McElwee immediately ran to his right, cut up the North Little Rock sideline and ran untouched for a 99-yard touchdown.

In their two-minute offense, the Tigers reached the Charging Wildcats 30 before Irwin was intercepted by Brian Stickney, who returned it 75 yards for another North Little Rock touchdown. The extra-point attempt was wide right, but the Charging Wildcats took a 13-7 halftime lead.

The second half, however, was a different story as Central shut down every aspect of North Little Rock's game and scored 28 points for a 35-13 victory. Dean scored on runs of 1, 18 and 62 yards, while Patrick ended the scoring with a 2-yard run. Dean finished with 167 yards rushing. Franks finished with 132 yards receiving. Irwin passed for a career-high 212 yards, surpassing 1,000 yards for the season. The Tigers finished with 528 yards of total offense.

After a 49-14 blowout victory over Little Rock McClellan the next week, Central was the visiting team in its home stadium in the annual "Battle for the Bell" against Little Rock Hall High School. The Tigers invoked the mercy rule in a 43-0 victory over the Warriors.

The victory in the regular-season finale guaranteed Central a share of the AAAAA-Central Conference championship. Dean rushed 12 times for 147 yards and 1 touchdown, his 16th career 100-yard rushing game. The Tigers scored on their first four possessions en route to a 29-0 halftime lead. The victory secured Central a No. 2 seed in the state playoffs and a first-round home game against Fayetteville High School, a No. 3 seed.

The Tigers allowed only 129 yards of total offense against the Spread attack. More important, Central kept Fayetteville out of the end zone to record its seventh shutout of the season.

The Tigers put up 30 points. with touchdown runs of 5 and 2 yards by Dean, a 44-yard double pass from Irwin to Franks to Thornton, a 7-yard run by Arnold and a safety. The safety occurred when Wakwe, a defensive end, overpowered a running back to sack Hayden Sherman in the end zone. The 30-0 victory sent Central on the road the next week to battle El Dorado in the second round of the state playoffs.

The Tigers again jumped out to an early lead when they scored on five of their first seven possessions. This 35-14 victory over the Wildcats, coupled with Bryant's loss to Fort Smith Northside, allowed Central to move up one spot in the polls to No. 2. This set the stage for a game that Arkansas had been waiting on the entire season.

Springdale High School, undefeated and ranked No. 1, traveled to Quigley Stadium to take on No. 2 Little Rock Central in a semifinal playoff game. In what some media outlets labeled as the "Game of the Century," approximately 15,000 fans gathered to watch the two teams battle for the right to play in the state championship game.

The Bulldogs, ranked No. 18 in the nation by *Students Sports,* entered the matchup with the state's top offense.

473

Springdale was averaging 204.8 yards passing per game, 171.3 yards rushing, 376.1 total yards and 39.3 points. The Bulldogs had also invoked the 35-point mercy rule on 10 of its 12 opponents.

The Tigers, on the other hand, entered the matchup with the state's top defense. Central was allowing an average of only 85.7 yards passing, 53.7 yards rushing, 139.4 total yards and 5.5 points. The Tigers had also shut out seven of 12 opponents.

The game began when James' kickoff was fielded at the Springdale 7 by Aaron Davis. A message was sent to the Bulldogs when Davis was met hard by Bernard Roseby and body slammed at the Springdale 21.

On first down, highly touted quarterback Mitch Mustain connected with Andrew Norman at the line of scrimmage. Arnold immediately hit Norman and brought him down for a 2-yard loss. Damian Williams received an option pitch on the next play and was tackled by Wakwe for a 3-yard loss. Mustain was forced out of the pocket on third down and threw the ball out of bounds to avoid a sack. A bad punt gave Central possession at the Springdale 41.

The Tigers, though, were unable to move and their punt rolled into the end zone, allowing the Bulldogs to take over at the 20. On second down, Mustain was intercepted at the 45 by Thornton, who returned it to the 12.

Dean gained 4 yards, Irwin gained 1 yard on an option keeper to get to the 1 and then snuck up the middle for the score. James added the extra point for a 7-0 lead with 6:29 left in the opening quarter. This marked the first time Springdale had trailed since the third week of the season.

James' kickoff went into the end zone to set the Bulldogs up at the 20. On second down, Mustain was sacked by Andre Jackson and Joseph Jackson. This marked only

474

the third time a Springdale quarterback had been sacked all season. The Bulldogs were forced to punt after their next play and another bad kick gave Central possession at the 44.

Patrick, Dean and Irwin worked to get the ball to the 25, where the Tigers faced fourth down. Irwin rolled to his left and found Thornton for a 25-yard touchdown pass. The extra point set the score at 14-0 with 1:53 left in the first quarter.

Springdale once again began its next possession from the 20. A direct snap to the fullback gained 4 yards, while a Mustain pass to Davis picked up a first down at the 41. Two plays later, pass interference on Butler gave the Bulldogs a first down at the Tigers 44. Four plays gained 24 yards to give Springdale second down at the 20.

On the first play of the second quarter, Mustain threw into the end zone for Norman. Franks, though, was standing at the 1 and was able to make the interception. He returned the ball 92 yards before being tackled at the 7. On second down, Paige ran over left tackle for the touchdown. The extra-point attempt by James was wide right, but Central led 20-0 with 10:56 left in the half.

On the first play of the Bulldogs' next possession, Mustain was sacked for a 13-

Jack Fowler (56) and Will Crass (61) block for the Tiger offense

yard loss by Wakwe and Joseph Jackson. Unfortunately, Mustain suffered a fracture in both the radius and ulna bones in his right arm. Mustain's backup, Dylan Adams, stepped in and immediately completed two passes. They weren't enough for a first down, though, and Springdale was forced to punt.

The Tigers were also forced to punt on their next possession, giving the Bulldogs control at the Central 42. On second down, Adams connected with Davis for a 39-yard gain to the 3. A reverse to Williams lost 1 yard and a quarterback draw gained 3 yards to the 1. It took two more plays for Adams to sneak into the end zone. The extra-point attempt was good with 3:48 left in the second quarter to make it 20-7 at halftime.

Both teams traded punts to open the second half before Irwin was intercepted by Davis at the 41. Springdale put together a 10-play drive, converting one first down on fourth down and one on third down, to score on a reverse by Norman. The extra-point attempt was good to narrow the Tigers' lead to 20-14 with 4:31 left in the third quarter.

The Bulldogs kicked off into the end zone. Central began its ensuing possession at the 20. In the Power-I formation, the Tigers dominated the line of scrimmage, driving 80 yards in 14 plays. The 7:35 drive was capped by an amazing 13-yard touchdown run by Dean. The scoring play began when Irwin faked to Patrick up the middle and then pitched to Dean for a sweep around right end. Once Dean got to the line of scrimmage, he spun out of one tackle, bounced off a tackler at the 7 and hit another head on at the 3 as two more grabbed him from behind. Dean continued to drive his legs and carried three defenders into the end zone. James' extra-point attempt was good to give Central a 27-14 lead.

Springdale's ensuing possession ended at the Tigers 7 when Franks intercepted an Adams pass and returned it to the 16. Once again from the Power-I formation, Central dominated the line of scrimmage with Paige and Dean gaining 3 to 4 yards per carry. Paige, though, fumbled as he was tackled at

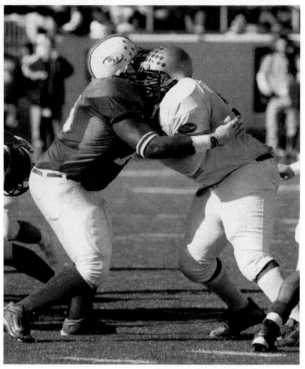

Photo provided by DeWain Duncan
Defensive lineman Andre Jackson (right)

the Bulldogs 47. Russ Greenlee scooped up the ball and returned it 53 yards for a touchdown. The extra point narrowed the score to 27-21 with 4:22 left in the game.

Dean received the ensuing kickoff and returned it to the 29. Along with a 46-yard run by Dean, the Tigers used eight plays and 4:04 to set up a 27-yard, game-sealing field goal by James. The kick gave Central a 30-21 lead with 18 second remaining in the game.

After the kickoff, Springdale began its possession at the 20 and attempted to run a hook-and-lateral play. Norman received the lateral, but fumbled when he was hit by Wakwe. Beavers recovered for the Tigers at the 29.

Irwin took a knee on first down to end the game and give Central an upset victory over the No. 1 Bulldogs. The victory sent the Tigers to the state final for the second consecutive season. There, they would once again battle West Memphis for the Class AAAAA state title.

On Dec. 6, a mild 53 degrees greeted more than 8,000 fans at War Memorial Stadium for a noon kickoff. The game began after Central won the ceremonial coin toss and elected to defer until the second half.

James' kick was caught at the Blue Devils 1 and returned 14 yards to the 15. Three offensive plays netted only 7 yards and West Memphis was forced to punt on its first possession. A 26-yard kick by Justin Conway gave the Tigers excellent field position at the Blue Devils 48.

Dean found a seam up the middle to gain 11 yards on the first play from scrimmage, but was stopped for no gain and thrown for a 2-yard loss on the following two plays. Irwin was sacked for a loss of 4 yards on third down and Henry was called on to punt.

The tough Central defense forced another West Memphis punt after the Blue Devils lost 6 yards on their second possession. Conway's punt netted only 7 yards and gave the Tigers control at the West Memphis 20.

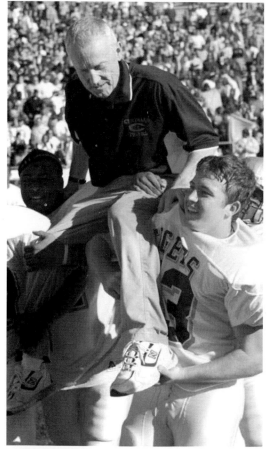

Photo provided by DeWain Duncan

Coach Bernie Cox gets a victory ride after his seventh state title at Central

On first down, Dean took a pitch around left end for a 15-yard gain to reach the 5. He then added a 3-yard run and a 2-yard run to get into the end zone for the game's first score. James added the extra point for a 7-0 lead with 5:51 left in the first quarter.

After forcing another punt, Central took possession at the 50 and drove the distance in eight plays and 4:25. Facing fourth-and-3 at the 25, Irwin kept the drive alive when he connected with tight end Michael Witherspoon for a 14-yard pass play. Irwin kept on the next play, running around the end for another touchdown. James converted the extra-point attempt to increase Central's lead to 14-0 with 11:50 remaining in the half.

Both teams traded punts on their next possession, but the Tigers' punt team came up with a big play after Arnold forced Brown to fumble just as he caught the kick. Arnold also recovered to give Central possession at the 9.

On first down, Dean found a seam over left guard to easily reach the end zone. James then converted his third extra-point attempt for a 21-0 lead with 6:29 left in the half. Just 3:08 later, Franks intercepted a pass by Brown and returned it 35 yards to the West Memphis 5. Dean easily scored again and James' extra point extended the lead to 28-0.

With 1:25 remaining in the half, the Tigers took over on downs at the Blue Devils 34. Irwin passed to Thornton on first down to cover the 34 yards for the touchdown. James' extra point made it 35-0 at halftime, invoking the mercy rule for the second half.

Central scored only once during the second half as Paige capped a seven-play, 58-yard drive with a 2-yard burst up the middle. The Tigers ended the contest with 265 yards of total offense and their second consecutive state title.

The story of the day, though, was defense. For the game, Central allowed only 126 yards of total offense (an average of 3.4 yards per play), while giving up only one score. That occurred with 50 seconds remaining in the game.

The 41-7 victory over West Memphis gave Little Rock Central its 32nd state championship and 749th victory since 1904. Coach Cox ended his 30th season as head coach with his 250th victory and seventh state championship.

Dean completed his third consecutive 1,000-yard rushing season with 1,352 yards on 200 carries. He averaged 6.8 yards per carry and scored a team-high 21 rushing touchdowns. He scored two more on pass receptions. Irwin completed 88 of 179 passes for 1,487 yards and 16 touchdowns.

Central's defense ended the 14-game season with seven shutouts and gave up only 716 yards rushing and 1,276 yards passing. Opponents scored only four rushing and five passing touchdowns and averaged only 3.1 yards per play.

The defensive unit was not highlighted by just one player, but several. Among those to strike fear in opposing offenses were Alexander and Wakwe. Alexander recorded 36 tackles, four sacks and three pass breakups at nose guard, while Wakwe posted 25 tackles, seven sacks and two caused fumbles at end.

In the secondary, Franks intercepted eight passes and made 25 tackles. Thornton had 24 tackles, intercepted eight passes and broke up six more. These two also starred at receiver. Franks caught 33 passes for 634 yards and four touchdowns to go along with

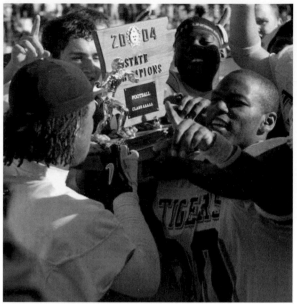

Photo provided by DeWain Duncan

**Players celebrate the school's
32nd state championship**

Thornton's 17 catches for 343 yards and five touchdowns.

Irwin ended his career with 3,189 yards passing. Dean finished with 4,677 yards rushing. Thornton ended his time at Central with the All-Arkansas Defensive Player of the Year honor and 23 career interceptions. Both Irwin and Thornton were invited to the Max Emfinger All-American Bowl in Shreveport.

The 2005 graduating class posted a record of 34-5-0, winning three conference championships and two state championships.

2004 TIGER SCHEDULE

West Memphis 0	LRCH 38
Pine Bluff 0	LRCH 35
Cabot 0	LRCH 35
*Conway 0	LRCH 21
*LR Catholic 3	LRCH 31
*Bryant 21	LRCH 19
*LR Parkview 0	LRCH 41
*North Little Rock 13	LRCH 35
*LR McClellan 14	LRCH 49
*LR Hall 0	LRCH 43
**Fayetteville 0	LRCH 30 (state playoffs)
**El Dorado 14	LRCH 35 (state playoffs)
**Springdale 21	LRCH 30 (state playoffs)
**West Memphis 7	LRCH 41 (state playoff final)

FOOTBALL RECORDS – YEAR BY YEAR

Year	Record		Year	Record
1904	0 – 1 – 1		1955	9 – 3 – 0 *
1905	0 – 5 – 0		1956	12 – 0 – 0 *
1906	4 – 3 – 0		1957	12 – 0 – 0 **
1907	7 – 2 – 0 *		1958	8 – 3 – 1
1908	8 – 0 – 0 *		1959	4 – 6 – 0
1909	7 – 0 – 0 *		1960	12 – 0 – 0 *
1910	3 – 2 – 2		1961	5 – 6 – 0
1911	5 – 2 – 0		1962	8 – 2 – 1
1912	3 – 3 – 0		1963	6 – 5 – 1
1913	4 – 2 – 1		1964	7 – 3 – 2
1914	8 – 1 – 0 *		1965	8 – 3 – 0
1915	5 – 1 – 2 *		1966	7 – 5 – 0
1916	2 – 5 – 2		1967	7 – 4 – 0
1917	7 – 2 – 0 *		1968	4 – 6 – 0
1918	1 – 2 – 0 *		1969	6 – 2 – 2
1919	9 – 0 – 1 *		1970	1 – 8 – 1
1920	8 – 1 – 0 *		1971	5 – 6 – 0
1921	8 – 0 – 1 *		1972	5 – 4 – 2
1922	8 – 2 – 0		1973	8 – 3 – 0
1923	11 – 0 – 0 *		1974	10 – 1 – 1
1924	5 – 5 – 0		1975	12 – 0 – 0 *
1925	5 – 5 – 0		1976	7 – 4 – 0
1926	7 – 2 – 1		1977	6 – 6 – 0
1927	7 – 2 – 1		1978	9 – 0 – 3 *
1928	7 – 3 – 1		1979	9 – 1 – 1
1929	5 – 5 – 1		1980	9 – 0 – 2 *
1930	9 – 2 – 0		1981	9 – 2 – 0 *
1931	8 – 3 – 0		1982	7 – 3 – 0
1932	7 – 4 – 0		1983	7 – 5 – 0
1933	9 – 2 – 0		1984	7 – 5 – 0
1934	7 – 4 – 0		1985	11 – 2 – 0
1935	5 – 5 – 1		1986	12 – 1 – 0 *
1936	6 – 3 – 2		1987	9 – 1 – 1
1937	9 – 1 – 1		1988	11 – 2 – 0
1938	10 – 0 – 1 *		1989	6 – 5 – 0
1939	9 – 1 – 1		1990	8 – 5 – 0
1940	7 – 4 – 0		1991	9 – 4 – 0
1941	5 – 5 – 1		1992	8 – 3 – 0
1942	4 – 6 – 1		1993	1 – 9 – 0
1943	8 – 1 – 2		1994	4 – 6 – 0
1944	10 – 1 – 0 *		1995	5 – 6 – 0
1945	8 – 1 – 2		1996	8 – 4 – 0
1946	14 – 0 – 0 **		1997	6 – 5 – 0
1947	12 – 0 – 1 *		1998	7 – 3 – 1
1948	9 – 1 – 1 *		1999	10 – 2 – 0
1949	10 – 1 – 0 *		2000	10 – 2 – 0
1950	10 – 2 – 0 *		2001	9 – 2 – 0
1951	9 – 3 – 0		2002	7 – 4 – 0
1952	9 – 2 – 0 *		2003	14 – 0 – 0 *
1953	8 – 2 – 1 *		2004	13 – 1 – 0 *
1954	9 – 3 – 0 *			

* State championship
** State and national championship

UNDEFEATED TEAMS

YEAR	RECORD	COACH
1908 *	8 – 0 – 0	H.J. Bischoff
1909 *	7 – 0 – 0	G.J. Van Buren
1919 *	9 – 0 – 1	Earl Quigley
1921 *	8 – 0 – 1	Earl Quigley
1923 *	11 – 0 – 0	Earl Quigley
1938 *	10 – 0 – 1	Clyde Van Sickle
1946 **	14 – 0 – 0	Raymond Burnett
1947 *	12 – 0 – 1	Wilson Matthews
1956 *	12 – 0 – 0	Wilson Matthews
1957 **	12 – 0 – 0	Wilson Matthews
1960 *	12 – 0 – 0	Gene Hall
1975 *	12 – 0 – 0	Bernie Cox
1978 *	9 – 0 – 3	Bernie Cox
1980 *	9 – 0 – 2	Bernie Cox
2003 *	14 – 0 – 0	Bernie Cox

* State championship
** State and national championship

HIGH SCORES

174 vs Russellville (0), 1919
137 vs Augusta (6), 1913
111 vs Stuttgart (0), 1917
110 vs England (0), 1926
107 vs. Texarkana, AR (0), 1933
105 vs Arkadelphia (0), 1933
90 vs Paragould (0), 1919
85 vs. Memphis Central (6), 1937
80 vs State Normal (UCA) (0), 1909

77 vs McGehee (0), 1928
76 vs Hot Springs (0), 1928
75 vs Camden (0), 1921
74 vs Lonoke (6), 1920
73 vs Springfield Central (0), 1923
73 vs Van Buren (0), 1933
70 vs El Dorado (0), 1920
70 vs Memphis Univ. High (0), 1927

CENTRAL HIGH SCHOOL VS. THE NATION

117-52-6

ALABAMA (5-2-0)
Bessemer	1-1-0
Birmingham Ensley	2-1-0
Gadsden	2-0-0

GEORGIA (0-1-0)
Atlanta Tech	0-1-0

ILLINOIS (3-1-0)
Chicago Lindblom	2-1-0
East St. Louis	1-0-0

KANSAS (1-2-0)
Wichita Central	1-2-0

KENTUCKY (9-5-0)
Louisville DuPont Manual	0-2-0
Louisville Male	1-1-0
Paducah Tilghman	8-2-0

LOUISIANA (17-9-1)
Baton Rouge Istrouma	4-4-0
New Orleans Warren Easton	6-0-0
Shreveport Byrd	4-5-1
Shreveport Huntington	2-0-0
West Monroe	1-0-0

MISSISSIPPI (7-0-0)
Clarksdale	2-0-0
Greenville	3-0-0
Tupelo	1-0-0
Tupelo Military Institute	1-0-0

MISSOURI (13-0-0)
Joplin Central	3-0-0
Poplar Bluff	2-0-0
Springfield Central	6-0-0
St. Louis Grover Cleveland	1-0-0
St. Louis Soldan	1-0-0

OKLAHOMA (16-5-1)
Muskogee Central	5-0-0
Norman	2-0-0
Oklahoma City Capitol Hill	1-1-0
Oklahoma City Central	0-2-0
Oklahoma City Classen	4-0-0
Sapulpa	1-0-0
Tulsa Central	3-2-1

TENNESSEE (35-18-3)
Chattanooga Central	0-1-0
Christian Brothers College	0-3-0
Knoxville Central	1-0-0
Memphis Carver	1-0-0
Memphis Central	27-13-3
Memphis Christian Brothers	2-0-0
Memphis Southside	1-0-0
Memphis Treadwell	1-1-0
Memphis University High	1-0-0
Memphis Washington	1-0-0

TEXAS (11-9-1)
Dallas Adamson	1-0-0
Dallas Bryan Street	2-0-0
Dallas Woodrow Wilson	1-0-0
Texarkana	7-9-1

CENTRAL HIGH SCHOOL VS. THE STATE

632-224-42

Arkadelphia	9-1-3	Little Rock McClellan	12-4-0
Arkansas Military Academy	0-3-0	Little Rock Mills	3-1-0
Augusta	2-0-0	Little Rock Parkview	28-7-2
Batesville	3-0-0	Lonoke	4-1-0
Benton	19-6-0	Magnolia	1-0-0
Blytheville	18-5-1	Malvern	4-1-0
Bryant	2-1-0	Marianna	4-0-0
Cabot	6-3-0	McGehee	1-0-0
Camden	8-0-0	Morrilton	4-0-0
Clarksville	3-1-0	Mountain Home	9-0-0
Clary Training School	3-1-0	North Little Rock	38-14-2
Conway	17-10-0	North Little Rock Jones	1-1-0
Dermott	1-0-0	North Little Rock Northeast	18-2-0
El Dorado	37-12-6	North Little Rock Ole Main	16-4-1
England	2-1-0	North Pulaski	4-0-0
Fayetteville	2-4-0	Ouachita College	1-0-0
Fordyce	19-3-2	Paragould	1-0-0
Forrest City	9-0-2	Physicians and Surgeons College	0-0-1
Fort Smith Northside	46-26-3	Pine Bluff	50-35-5
Fort Smith Southside	2-6-0	Portland	1-0-0
Helena-West Helena Central	3-0-0	Prescott	3-2-0
Henderson College	5-1-0	Russellville	11-1-1
Hendrix College	1-3-1	Searcy	3-0-0
Hope	3-0-0	Springdale	6-4-0
Hot Springs	40-6-5	State Normal School	3-0-0
Jacksonville	8-4-0	Stuttgart	2-0-0
Jonesboro	14-2-1	Subiaco Academy	3-0-0
Little Rock Catholic	33-9-0	Sylvan Hills	14-5-1
Little Rock College	2-0-1	Texarkana	20-3-0
Little Rock Fair	3-4-0	Training Battalion of Camp Pike	0-1-0
Little Rock Hall	24-20-4	Van Buren	2-0-0
Little Rock Horace Mann	4-1-0	West Memphis	17-5-0

ALL-AMERICAN

Henry Fitzgibbons, 1948
Wigwam Wiseman
of America

Eddie Bradford, 1950
Wigwam Wiseman
of America

Stuart Perry, 1953
Publication unknown

Frank Plegge, 1955
Publication unknown

Bruce Fullerton, 1957
The Sporting News magazine

Bill Hicks, 1957
Teen magazine

Mike Hales, 1960
Publication unknown

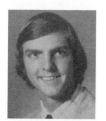
Robert Farrell, 1975
Parade magazine

Houston Nutt, 1974, 1975
Scholastic Coach magazine

Marcus Elliott, 1980
National High School
Athletic Coaches Association

Todd Jones, 1985
National High School
Athletic Coaches Association

Derek Russell, 1986
National High School
Athletic Coaches Association

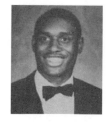
Tony Phillips, 1987
National High School
Athletic Coaches Association

Dedrick Poole, 1999, 2001
Student Sports, SuperPrep

Fred Bledsoe, 2003
SuperPrep

Antwain Robinson, 2003
Student Sports
Jr. All-America

ALL-SOUTHERN

John Hoffman, 1944	Henry Moore, 1951	Ed Rownd, 1969
Billy Woodiel, 1944	Bobby Hannon, 1952	Derek Russell, 1986
Jimmy Albright, 1946	Stuart Perry, 1953	Sedric Fillmore, 1987
Bucky Carson, 1946	Jimmy Clark, 1953	Dedrick Poole, 2000
Jack Rushing, 1946	Richard Bennett, 1953	Fred Bledsoe, 2003
Louie Schaufele, 1946	Bill Hicks, 1956	Freddie Fairchild, 2003
Henry Fitzgibbons, 1948	Bill Knight, 1960	Antwain Robinson, 2003
Kenneth Carter, 1949	Mike Hales, 1960	Kevin Thornton, 2003, 2004
Eddie Bradford, 1950	Claude Fulton, 1960	

ALL-TIME TEAMS

1904 – 1914 OFFENSE

POSITION	NAME
END	Billy Letson
END	Robert Doyle
HALFBACK	Sibley Ward
HALFBACK	Walter Terry
FULLBACK	Ludovic Alexander
QUARTERBACK	Miller Silliman
CENTER	Fred Hoeltzel
GUARD	Lee Hampel
GUARD	Harper Harb
TACKLE	Jesse Weidemeyer
TACKLE	Harold Young
KICKER – (General)	Thomas Doyle
ATHLETE	Robert Martin
ATHLETE	Russell May

1915 – 1929 OFFENSE

POSITION	NAME
END	Ben Isgrig
END	Mackey Whitten
HALFBACK	Ivan Williams
HALFBACK	Clifford Shaw
FULLBACK	Dick Bright
QUARTERBACK	Alvin Bell
CENTER	Corbin Neblett
GUARD	Harry Coonley
GUARD	Orval Williams
TACKLE	Homer Stalnaker
TACKLE	Nate Ginsberg
KICKER – (General)	Robert Avinger
ATHLETE	Vernon Felix
ATHLETE	Douglas Wycoff

1930 – 1944 OFFENSE

POSITION	NAME
END	Kenneth Kavanaugh
END	Billy Maack
HALFBACK	Ralph LaForge
HALFBACK	John Hoffman
FULLBACK	Lowell Martindale
QUARTERBACK	Harry Carter
CENTER	Leo Ambort
GUARD	John Donaldson
GUARD	Clyde Williams
TACKLE	Neill Robins
TACKLE	Melville Gamblin
KICKER – (General)	Clifford Stalnaker
ATHLETE	Howard Hughes
ATHLETE	Arnold Castleberry

1945 – 1959 OFFENSE

POSITION	NAME
END	Jimmy Clark
END	Bill Hicks
HALFBACK	Kenneth Carter
HALFBACK	Bruce Fullerton
FULLBACK	Henry Moore
QUARTERBACK	Billy Moore
CENTER	Henry Fitzgibbons
GUARD	Stuart Perry
GUARD	Fred Williams
TACKLE	Frank Plegge
TACKLE	Eddie Bradford
KICKER – (General)	Louie Schaufele
ATHLETE	Jimmy Albright
ATHLETE	Gene Hall

1960 – 1974 OFFENSE

POSITION	NAME
END	Bill Knight
RECEIVER	Ray Gillespie
RECEIVER	Bill Brooks
TAILBACK	Keith Golden
FULLBACK	Jerry Knowles
QUARTERBACK	Richard Faulkner
CENTER	Louis Nalley
GUARD	Richard McCauley
GUARD	Robert Hallmark
TACKLE	Jerry Welch
TACKLE	Gary Capshaw
KICKER – (General)	Lonnie Cole
ATHLETE	Gary Tate
ATHLETE	Claude Fulton

1960 – 1974 DEFENSE

POSITION	NAME
SAFETY	Walter Coleman
SAFETY	George Calhoun
CORNERBACK	Jerry Corrothers
CORNERBACK	Gene Howard
LINEBACKER	Joey Shelton
LINEBACKER	Ed Rownd
NOSE MAN	Mike Hales
DEFENSIVE TACKLE	Jimmy Walker
DEFENSIVE TACKLE	Ross Honea
DEFENSIVE END	Ricky McBride
DEFENSIVE END	David Wagnon
KICK RETURNER	Don Hollingsworth
ATHLETE	Kenneth "Muskie" Harris
ATHLETE	Will Robinson

1975 – 1989 OFFENSE

POSITION	NAME
END	Tony Dunnick
RECEIVER	Derek Russell
RECEIVER	Robert Farrell
TAILBACK	Tony Holmes
FULLBACK	Tony Ridgle
QUARTERBACK	Houston Nutt
CENTER	Mark Henry
GUARD	Forrest Stolzer
GUARD	Marcus Elliott
TACKLE	Todd Jones
TACKLE	John Palmer
KICKER – (General)	Michael Young
ATHLETE	Eddie Robinson
ATHLETE	Danny Ray Robinson

1975 – 1989 DEFENSE

POSITION	NAME
SAFETY	Kendrick Turner
SAFETY	Robert Cortinez
CORNERBACK	Rodney Hayes
CORNERBACK	Floyd Smith
LINEBACKER	Bert Zinamon
LINEBACKER	Milton Fields
NOSE MAN	Richard Richardson
DEFENSIVE TACKLE	John Steed
DEFENSIVE TACKLE	Dexter Howard
DEFENSIVE END	Tony Phillips
DEFENSIVE END	Stephen Thornhill
KICK RETURNER	Kenneth Richardson
ATHLETE	Ricky Mays
ATHLETE	Spencer Ellison

1990 – 2004 OFFENSE

POSITION	NAME
END	Joseph Henry
RECEIVER	Ray Nealy
RECEIVER	Stewart Franks
TAILBACK	Mickey Dean
FULLBACK	George Pree
QUARTERBACK	Clark Irwin
CENTER	Jack Fowler
GUARD	Mark Magee
GUARD	Keith Lilly
TACKLE	Brad Gordon
TACKLE	David Peevy
KICKER – (General)	Kevin Luneau
ATHLETE	Dedrick Poole
ATHLETE	Derrick Mason

1990 – 2004 DEFENSE

POSITION	NAME
SAFETY	Kevin Thornton
SAFETY	Michael Pleasant
CORNERBACK	Adam Page
CORNERBACK	Sejames Humphrey
LINEBACKER	Dorrian Myles
LINEBACKER	Freddie Fairchild
NOSE MAN	Charles Alexander
DEFENSIVE TACKLE	Fred Bledsoe
DEFENSIVE TACKLE	James Johnson
DEFENSIVE END	Antwain Robinson
DEFENSIVE END	Stanley Wakwe
KICK RETURNER	Reggie Swinton
ATHLETE	Albert Peterson
ATHLETE	LeMarkus Jordan

1904 – 1954 OFFENSE

POSITION	NAME
END	Ben Isgrig
END	Billy Maack
HALFBACK	Ivan Williams
HALFBACK	John Hoffman
FULLBACK	Henry Moore
QUARTERBACK	Alvin Bell
CENTER	Henry Fitzgibbons
GUARD	Stuart Perry
GUARD	Fred Williams
TACKLE	Eddie Bradford
TACKLE	Neill Robins
KICKER – (General)	Louie Schaufele
ATHLETE	Howard Hughes
ATHLETE	Douglas Wycoff

1904 – 1954 DEFENSE (Not Applicable)

POSITION	NAME

1955 – 2004 OFFENSE

POSITION	NAME
END	Bill Hicks
RECEIVER	Robert Farrell
RECEIVER	Derek Russell
TAILBACK	Mickey Dean
FULLBACK	Bruce Fullerton
QUARTERBACK	Houston Nutt
CENTER	Mark Henry
GUARD	Frank Plegge
GUARD	Marcus Elliott
TACKLE	Todd Jones
TACKLE	Brad Gordon
KICKER – (General)	Michael Young
ATHLETE	Danny Robinson
ATHLETE	Dedrick Poole

1955 – 2004 - DEFENSE

POSITION	NAME
SAFETY	Kevin Thornton
SAFETY	Robert Cortinez
CORNERBACK	Floyd Smith
CORNERBACK	Gene Howard
LINEBACKER	Bert Zinamon
LINEBACKER	Milton Fields
NOSE MAN	Richard Richardson
DEFENSIVE TACKLE	John Steed
DEFENSIVE TACKLE	Mike Hales
DEFENSIVE END	Tony Phillips
DEFENSIVE END	Antwain Robinson
KICK RETURNER	Kenneth Richardson
ATHLETE	Spencer Ellison
ATHLETE	Will Robinson

NOTE: The above teams are the opinion of the author. Players were selected on high school performance only. Those with honors of All-American, All-Southern, All-State and those who helped lead their team to championships were given extra consideration. Due to lack of defensive records between 1904 and 1959, all-time defensive teams were not feasible.

FOOTBALL LETTERMEN
1904 - 2004

Abbott – 1905
Abbott, Mike – 1969, 1970
Abbott, Randy – 1971, 1972
Abbott, Rick – 1968
Abraham, Havard – 1984
Abrams, Kevin – 2001, 2002, 2003
Acklin, Aaron – 2001
Acklin, Adam – 1997, 1998, 1999
Adams, Chris – 1996, 1997
Adams, Corry – 1991, 1992
Adams, Coy – 1929, 1930, 1931
Adams, Julian – 1917, 1918
Adams, Keith – 1992, 1993, 1994
Adams, Patrick – 1987
Adkins, George – 1977
Adkins, Hubert – 1918
Adkins, Stephen – 1981
Adkins, Ted – 1983
Agnew, Stephen – 2000, 2001
Albright, Jimmy – 1944, 1945, 1946
Alexander, Charles – 2002, 2003, 2004
Alexander, Kenneth – 1979
Alexander, Ludovic – 1911, 1912
Allen, Chris – 2003
Allen, Elbert – 1920
Allen, Jim – 1967
Allen, Joe – 1951, 1952
Allen, Marvin – 1988
Allen, Sidney – 1988, 1989
Allen, Will – 1980, 1981
Allison, Jimmy – 1965, 1966
Allison, Steve – 1968
Almond, Chester – 1943
Almond, Floyd – 1947
Almond, Richard – 1956
Alsbrook, James – 1982, 1983
Alworth, Lance – 1978
Ambort, Leo – 1935, 1936, 1937, 1938
Anderson, Derrick – 1988
Anderson, Glen – 1972, 1973, 1974
Anderson, Quincy – 1996, 1997
Anderson, Ricky – 1984, 1985, 1986
Anderson, Shy – 1919
Anderson, Tom – 1930
Anderson, William – 1913, 1914
Anderson, William – 1934, 1935

Arendt, George – 1923, 1924
Arendt, John – 1920
Argo, Warren – 1956
Armstrong, John – 1948
Arnold, Chris – 2003, 2004
Arnold, Gilbert – 1956, 1957
Arrant, John – 1982
Atkinson, Bill – 1938
Atkinson, Drexel – 1942, 1943
Atkinson, Randall – 1940
Atobe, Matthew – 1997, 1998, 1999
Auld, Todd – 1984
Austin, Antonio – 1993, 1994
Avinger, Allan – 1927, 1928
Avinger, Charles – 1926, 1927, 1928
Avinger, Robert – 1922, 1923
Babb, Paul – 1964, 1965
Baber, Greg – 2000, 2001
Bacon, Henry – 1904
Baer, Carl – 1938
Bagby, Harold – 1952
Bailey, George – 1942
Bailey, Johnny – 1984, 1985, 1986
Baily, Tilburn – 1929
Bain, Jon – 1969, 1970
Baird, Joe – 1977
Baird, Percy – 1924
Baker, Demetrius – 1998, 1999, 2000
Baker, J.C. – 1977, 1978
Baker, Sammy – 1980, 1981
Baker, Tony – 1992
Baldwin, Bill – 1963
Bale, Eugene – 1920, 1921, 1922
Ball, Billy – 1960, 1961
Barbee, Dwane – 2001
Barbee, Edward – 1918, 1919
Barfield, Charles – 1977, 1978
Barksdale, Thomas – 1940
Barksdale, Walter – 1942, 1943
Barnard, Bill – 1947, 1948, 1949
Barnard, Lewis – 1954, 1955
Barnes, Eric – 1989, 1990, 1991
Barnett, Gene – 1954, 1955
Barnhouse, Bill – 1951
Barnum, Elisha – 1994
Barron, Jay – 1950

Bass, James – 2002, 2003
Bass, John – 1981
Bates, Joe – 1949
Batson, John – 1993, 1994, 1995
Baxter, Larry – 1976
Beach – 1905
Beals, Burdette – 1916, 1917
Beard, Mike – 1965, 1966
Beavers, Bill – 1949
Beavers, Clark – 1934
Beavers, Patrick – 2002, 2003, 2004
Beavers, Sammy – 1961, 1962
Bell, Alvin – 1916, 1917, 1918, 1919
Bell, John – 1930
Bell, Richard – 1953, 1954
Bell, Walter – 1983
Bellingrath, Ted – 1950, 1951
Bemberg, Clay – 2003, 2004
Bemberg, Gary – 1969, 1970, 1971
Bemberg, Jeff – 1973, 1974
Benard, Bill – 1927
Benight, Albert – 1943, 1946
Bennett, Alonzo – 1979
Bennett, Charles – 2004
Bennett, Francis – 1927, 1928
Bennett, Jimmy – 1976
Bennett, Richard – 1952, 1953
Bennett, William – 1996
Benson, Chris – 1996
Bernard, Rory – 1992, 1993
Bernard, Wesley – 1938
Berry, Errick – 1994, 1995, 1996
Berry, Henry – 1985, 1986, 1987
Berry, Wayne – 1943, 1944, 1945
Bhones, Morris – 1974
Biddle, James – 1935
Biddle, Joe – 1928, 1929
Biggadike, Roy – 1918, 1920
Billingsley, Phil – 1970, 1971
Birch, Frankie – 1941
Bizzell, Jeff – 1979, 1980
Black, Perry – 1968, 1969
Blackmon, Romar – 1996, 1997
Blackwell, Buford – 1957, 1958
Blagg, Ted – 1956, 1957
Blagg, Thomas – 1950, 1951
Blair, Steve – 1966, 1967
Blake, Alex – 2004
Blake, Charles – 1998, 1999, 2000

Blake, Thomas – 1992
Blass, Alvin – 1912
Blass, Noland – 1904, 1905
Blaylock, Johnny – 1968
Bledsoe, Fred – 2001, 2002, 2003
Bledsoe, Page – 1924, 1925
Blenden, Chip – 1980
Block, Michael – 1996, 1997
Bobo, Kelsey – 1996
Boggess, Jeff – 1974
Bollinger, Andy – 1979
Bolton, Andre – 1995
Bonner, Bob – 1969, 1970
Botley, Herman – 1985, 1986
Bowman, Earl – 1941
Bowman, Earle – 1913
Bowman, Eddie – 1972, 1973
Boyd, Haco – 1920
Boydston, Curtis – 1908
Bracy, Alfred – 1944
Bradberry, Jim – 1965, 1966
Bradbury, Curtis – 1965
Bradbury, Ralph – 1970, 1971, 1972
Bradford, Eddie – 1949, 1950
Bradford, Wayne – 1971, 1972
Bradley, Allen – 1926
Brasher, Bill – 1922, 1923
Bratton, Ulysses – 1917
Brazzell, Bob – 1958, 1959
Breedlove, Marc – 1979, 1980, 1981
Breedlove, Mike – 1979
Brewer, Tommy – 1961, 1962, 1963
Brickhouse, Linwood – 1914, 1915
Bridges, Marc – 1989, 1990, 1991
Bright, Miles – 1923
Bright, Richard – 1921, 1922
Brinkley, Leroy – 1928
Britt, Richard – 1960
Britton, Anthony – 1995, 1996, 1997
Brodie, Ralph – 1956, 1957
Brooks, Bill – 1966
Brooks, Billy – 1994, 1995, 1996
Brooks, John – 1983, 1984
Brooks, Ronald – 1984, 1985, 1986
Brooks, S.M. – 1949
Broomas, Lovey – 1975
Brown, Anthony – 1974, 1975
Brown, Barry – 1976
Brown, Calvin – 1989

Brown, Danny – 1971, 1972
Brown, Geoffrey – 1982
Brown, Greg – 1988
Brown, Isaac – 1987, 1988, 1989
Brown, Kelton – 1938, 1939
Brown, Kenneth – 1953
Brown, Kuhl – 1911
Brown, Michael – 1995, 1996, 1997
Brown, Mike – 1964, 1965
Brown, Pharoah – 1985, 1986, 1987
Brown, Robert – 1909
Brown, Robert – 1953
Brown, Roland – 1993
Bruce, Charlie – 1989
Bruso, Brian – 1988, 1989, 1990
Bryan, Phillip – 1963, 1964
Bryan, Tommy - 1971
Bryant, Phillip – 1982
Buchanan, Clyde – 1928
Bumpers, Fuller – 1992
Bunche, Brian – 1994
Burks, Chris – 2000, 2001, 2002
Burnett, Don – 1942
Burnett, Scottie – 1996
Burns, Maurice – 2001
Burroughs, Asa – 1917
Burroughs, Spencer – 1970, 1971
Burrows, Tom – 1937
Burton, Paul – 1971
Bush, Bill – 1976
Bush, Kenneth – 1985, 1986, 1987
Bushmaier, Binks – 1937
Butler, Bert – 2004
Butler, Carl – 1967
Butler, Jim – 1961
Buttain, John – 1965
Bynum, Patrick – 1997, 1998, 1999
Cain, Raney – 2001, 2002
Calhoun, George – 1962, 1963, 1964
Cameron, Patrick – 1986
Campbell, Bobby – 1988, 1989
Campbell, Brandon – 1997, 1998, 1999
Campbell, James – 1975
Campbell, Marshall – 1915
Campbell, Mike – 1961
Campbell, Pete – 1970
Capel, Archie – 1915
Caple, Frank – 1951
Capshaw, Gary – 1967, 1968, 1969

Carpenter, Richard – 1958, 1959, 1960
Carpenter, Warren – 1948
Carroll, Chablis – 1993, 1994, 1995
Carson, Bucky – 1946
Carson, Kit – 1944, 1945
Carter, Charles – 1954, 1955
Carter, Harry – 1937, 1938, 1939
Carter, Joey – 1984
Carter, Kenneth – 1947, 1948, 1949
Carter, Khalil – 1993
Casey, Lee – 1959, 1960
Cassaday, Ronnie – 1961, 1962
Castleberry, Arnold – 1927, 1928, 1929, 1930
Castleberry, Robert – 1954
Cate, George – 1951
Cates, Drew – 1992, 1993, 1994
Cathey, Otis – 1941, 1942
Cauthron, Jim – 1949, 1950
Caveness, Ronnie – 1984
Chambers, Wilson – 1981
Chaney, Jack – 1939
Chaney, Sylvester – 1974, 1975
Chatman, Jeff – 1977
Cherry, Homer – 1976
Chester, Paul – 1997, 1998
Childers, Adam – 2003
Christian, Tyrone – 1993, 1994, 1995
Christian, William – 1909
Clark, Edward – 1926
Clark, Fred – 1948, 1949
Clark, George – 1955, 1956
Clark, Jimmy – 1952, 1953
Clark, Matthew – 1998, 1999
Clark, O.B. – 1924, 1926
Clark, Roosevelt – 1969
Clark, Stanley – 1963, 1964, 1965
Clark, Terrence – 1995
Claude, Gary – 1961, 1962
Cleaver, Charles – 1971, 1972
Clements, Drew – 1949, 1950
Clements, Robert – 1970
Clemons, Elgin – 1982, 1983, 1984
Clemons, Eric – 1984, 1985
Clifton, Kenneth – 1963, 1964
Cline, Robin – 1976
Cobb, Montreal – 1995, 1996, 1997
Coble, Frank – 1961, 1963
Cochran, John – 1951
Cockrill, Ashley – 1921

Cody, Ricky – 1976, 1977
Coggins, John – 1958
Cole, Kenneth – 1973
Cole, Lonnie – 1961, 1962
Coleman, Bob – 1970
Coleman, Buddy – 1943, 1944, 1945
Coleman, Charlie – 1972
Coleman, Damon – 1991
Coleman, David – 1977, 1978
Coleman, Derrick – 1992
Coleman, Harry – 1979, 1980
Coleman, Herbert – 1975
Coleman, Marlon – 1991
Coleman, Travis – 1977
Coleman, Walter – 1967, 1968, 1969
Collar, Ron – 1970, 1971
Collier, Bill – 1956, 1957, 1958
Collier, Carlos – 2004
Collier, Darrell – 1958, 1959
Collins, Charles – 1904, 1905
Collins, Reginald – 1993, 1994, 1995
Colton, James – 1961, 1962
Compton, Mac – 2000, 2001
Connerly, Chris – 1982
Connerly, Jeff – 1976, 1977
Conrad, David – 1947
Cook, Bobby – 1943
Cook, Joe – 1977, 1978
Cook, Tony – 1980
Coonley, Harry – 1925, 1926
Cooper, Lee – 1971, 1972
Cooper, Seth – 2000
Coots, Sam – 1940, 1941, 1942
Cope, Gary – 1967, 1968
Copeland, Brandon – 1994
Copeland, Eddie – 1953, 1954
Cork, Gene – 1941
Corley, Bob – 1960, 1961
Corrothers, Garry – 1972, 1973
Corrothers, Jerry – 1972, 1973
Cortinez, Robert – 1979, 1980, 1981
Couch, Pat – 1923
Countryman, Don – 1947, 1948
Covington, Andre – 1996, 1997, 1998
Cox, Brian – 1989
Cox, J. Gilroy – 1910
Crabtree, Bruce – 1972, 1973
Crafton, Gene – 1943
Crafton, Jimmy – 1940, 1941

Craig, Alfred – 1911
Craig, Alfred – 1941
Crass, Will – 2004
Crawford, Alvin – 1957, 1958
Cribbs, Dwan – 1991, 1992, 1993
Criner, Stephen – 1982
Crist, Clarence – 1956, 1957
Cronkhite, Drew – 2001
Crook, Darrell – 1918, 1919
Cross, Carl – 1971, 1972
Cross, Eric – 1997
Crossett, Danny – 1969
Crouch, Phillip – 1965
Crowson, Walter – 1937, 1938, 1939
Crum, Charles – 1963
Cryer, Louis – 1981
Cunning, Michael – 1988, 1989
Cunningham, Bruce – 1963, 1964
Curran, John – 1911
Curry, Elie – 1980, 1981
Curry, Keith – 1977, 1978
Curry, Lee – 1952
Cusick, Charles – 1959
Cusick, John – 1952
Dabbs – 1905
Dabbs, Scott – 1984, 1985
Dade, Lawrence – 1998, 1999
Dalrymple, Bill – 1931, 1934
Dangston, Joe – 1933
Daniels, David – 2004
Danner, Leroy – 1955
Darling, Bob – 1954, 1955
Davenport, Bob – 1989, 1990
Davenport, Roderick – 1982, 1983, 1984
Davidson, Percy – 1930
Davies, Ladd – 1956, 1957
Davis, Andy – 1952
Davis, Art – 1967, 1968, 1969
Davis, Charles – 1982
Davis, Fallon – 1957
Davis, Fred - 1983
Davis, Jim – 1957
Davis, John – 1985, 1986
Davis, Joseph – 1993, 1994
Davis, Joseph – 1996, 1997, 1998
Davis, Kelley – 1996
Davis, Kyle – 1998
Davis, Larry – 1968, 1969
Davis, Marvin – 1976

Davis, Shawn – 1988
Davis, Wade – 1996, 1997, 1998
Day, Joe – 1954, 1955
Day, Marcus – 1990, 1992
Dean, Mickey – 2002, 2003, 2004
DeClue, Rodney – 1982
Delaware, John – 1982, 1983
Deloney, Lawson – 1907, 1908
DeMent, James – 1916, 1917
Demmer, Bill – 1948
DeViney, Charles – 1948, 1949
Dickerson, Mark – 1990, 1991, 1992
Dickey, Williard – 1932
Dickinson, John – 1908
Dickson, Antwan – 2000
Diles, Randy – 1967, 1969
Dillahunty, Lewis – 1996
Dillon, Charles – 1941, 1942
Dinger, Chuck – 1980, 1981
Dixon, Phil – 1949
Dodd, Charles – 1958, 1959
Dodson, Louis – 1967
Donaldson, Harry – 1939, 1940
Donaldson, John – 1932, 1933
Donham, Bill – 1937
Donoho, David – 1947, 1948
Dorathy, Bryan – 1991
Douglas, Eddie – 1965, 1966, 1967
Douglas, Lee – 1968, 1969
Dowell, Elbert – 1915
Downs, Tony – 1977, 1978
Doyle, John – 1978
Doyle, Robert – 1906, 1908
Doyle, Thomas – 1906, 1907
Doyne, Russell – 1904, 1906
Driver, Charles – 1934
Duckworth, Bobby – 1979
Dugan, Charles – 1948
Duggar, Daney – 1957
Dugger, Bob – 1953
Duhart, Courtney – 1975
Duhart, Dwight – 1968, 1969
Dukes, Earnest – 1993
Dum, Larry – 1958, 1959
Dunaway, Tommy – 1947, 1948
Dunbar, Sylvester – 1977, 1978
Dunbar, Vincent – 1981
Duncan, Bob – 1950
Dunnick, Byron – 1978, 1979, 1980

Dunnick, Fred – 1977, 1978
Dunnick, Olins – 1979, 1980, 1981
Dunnick, Tony – 1974, 1975, 1976
Eason, Tyrone – 1997
Eberle, Gene – 1945, 1946
Eberts, Jimmy – 1945
Eddings, Kelly – 1989, 1990
Eddings, Khayyam – 1987, 1988, 1989
Edggerson, Tim – 1984
Edgin, Marlin – 1948
Edmondson, Anthony – 1985, 1987
Edwards, Billy – 1935, 1936, 1937, 1938
Edwards, George – 1955, 1956
Edwards, Kelvin – 1982, 1983
Ekenseair, John – 2000
Elkins, Don – 1953
Ellington, Kelly – 1931, 1932
Elliott, Choice – 1922, 1923
Elliott, Marcus – 1978, 1979, 1980
Elliott, Steve – 1961, 1962
Ellis, Brad – 1979, 1980
Ellis, Danny – 1982, 1983
Ellis, Larry – 1963, 1964
Ellis, Mark – 1981, 1982
Ellison, Spencer – 1984, 1985, 1986
Elms, Mike – 1966, 1967
Elrod, Earle – 1917, 1919
Embry, John – 2000
England, Callan – 1913
Enoch, Breck – 1997, 1998
Ensminger, Steve – 1982
Eschweiler, Edward – 1947
Estrada, John – 1926, 1927
Eubanks, Marcus – 1991
Eubanks, Tony – 1984, 1985
Evans, Bertrand – 1983, 1984, 1985
Evans, Glen – 1947
Evans, J.B. – 1935, 1936
Evans, Tommy – 1960, 1961
Ewings, Michael – 1999
Fairchild, Freddie – 2002, 2003
Faisst, Harold – 1925
Falcon, Darrin – 1985, 1986, 1987
Falcon, David – 1984
Falk, Randall – 1911
Falls, James – 1976
Farmer, Cedric – 1984
Farmer, Larry – 1981, 1982, 1983
Farrell, Morris – 1904

Farrell, Phillip – 1933
Farrell, Robert – 1973, 1974, 1975
Faulkner, Richard – 1966, 1967, 1968
Fausette, Alton – 1957
Felix, Vernon – 1920, 1921, 1922
Fells, Jackie – 1977
Ferriter, Charles – 1956
Fields, Chris – 1987
Fields, Mark – 1978, 1979, 1980
Fields, Milton – 1977, 1978, 1979
Fields, Russell – 1905
Fields, Terry – 1937
Fillmore, David – 1982, 1983
Fillmore, Sedric – 1985, 1987
Finch, Dick – 1945, 1946
Find, Emmett – 1962
Findlay, Jonathan – 1996
Fink, John – 1964
Finkston, Jerrod – 1985
Fitzgibbons, Bill – 1940
Fitzgibbons, Henry – 1947, 1948
Fletcher, Tino – 1988
Flint, Cleo – 1984, 1985, 1986
Floyd, Derrick – 1995, 1996
Floyd, Donald – 1995
Floyd, Tom – 1945
Foltz, Tom – 1982, 1983
Foreman, Quadel – 2004
Fossette, Ramone – 2000, 2001
Fossette, Reginald – 1997, 1998, 1999
Foster, Craig – 1987
Fowler, Jack – 2002, 2003, 2004
Fraiser, Lacy – 1952
Francisco, Doug – 1954, 1955
Franklin, Jerry – 1994, 1995
Franks, Stewart – 2002, 2003, 2004
Frazer, Lacy – 1951
Freeland, Byron – 1963
Freeland, Estes – 1937, 1938, 1939
Freeman McKindra – 1997
Freeman, Karl – 1986, 1987, 1988
Freeman, Nathan – 1989, 1990, 1991
Freeman, Vincent – 1972
Fritts, Clinton – 1940, 1941
Frye, Stuart – 1964, 1965
Fulford, Clay – 1931
Fuller, Brian – 1984, 1985, 1986
Fuller, Gilbert – 1961
Fuller, Glen – 1965, 1966

Fullerton, Bruce – 1955, 1956, 1957
Fulton, Claude – 1958, 1959, 1960
Fulton, John – 1928
Fuqua, Don – 1945, 1946, 1947
Futrell, Dan – 1933
Gachot, Carl – 1963, 1964
Galloway, Rench – 1923
Gamble, Travis – 1992, 1994
Gamblin, Melville – 1931, 1932, 1933
Gantt, Roosevelt – 1976
Gardiol, Richard – 1936, 1937, 1938, 1939
Garland, Kevin – 1984, 1985
Garman, Antonio – 1984, 1985, 1986
Garner, Don – 1950
Garner, Gilroy – 1956
Garrison, Don – 1962, 1963
Gaston, Alpha – 1994, 1995
Gatewood, Victor – 1974
Gay, Robert – 1961
Gentry, Phil – 1961
George, Johnny – 1982, 1983
George, Michael – 1980, 1981
Gibson, Keith – 1978, 1979, 1980
Gibson, Roger – 1976
Gilbert, Randy – 1973
Gildehaus, Charles – 1947, 1948
Gill, Sam – 1957
Gillespie, Ray – 1968, 1969
Gills, Wayne – 1966
Gingerich, Jeff – 1982
Ginsberg, Nate – 1921, 1923
Glasscock, Bill – 1955
Glover, Billy – 1933, 1934, 1935
Glover, Bobby – 1950, 1951
Goad, Paul – 1950, 1951
Goins, Ryan – 1996, 1997
Goldberg, Stanley – 1946
Golden, Keith – 1965, 1966
Goldman, Ed – 1950
Goldman, Ralph – 1952, 1953, 1954
Golightly, Larry – 1969
Goodman, Derrick – 1996
Goods, Joe – 1994
Gordon, Brad – 2003, 2004
Gortney, Danny – 1963, 1964
Goss, John – 1997, 1998, 1999
Gosser, Bob – 1949, 1950
Grable, Phillip – 1965, 1966
Grable, Scott – 1974

Graham, Walter – 1964, 1965, 1966
Grant, Frank – 1956
Gray, Ken – 1978
Gray, Robert – 1992, 1993, 1994
Graydon, Douglas – 1926, 1927
Green, Charles – 1963, 1964
Green, Joe – 1936, 1937, 1938
Green, Troy – 1953, 1954
Greenlee, Dennis – 1966, 1967
Greer, Mike – 1963, 1964
Gregory, Chris – 1987, 1989
Griffin, Bill – 1976, 1977
Griffin, Jay – 1989
Griffin, Steve – 1978
Griffith, Allen – 1968
Griffith, Steve – 1977, 1978, 1979
Grimmett, Jeff – 1995, 1996, 1997
Grimmett, Randall – 1927
Guinn, Robert – 1993
Gunn, Chris – 1987, 1988, 1989
Gunn, Guy – 1925, 1926
Gunn, Hamilton – 1936
Gunn, Scott – 1971
Gupton, Leodis – 1991
Gutheridge, Bob – 1956
Guthrie – 1905
Guy, Clarence – 1995, 1996, 1997
Guy, Joseph – 1995
Guy, Nicholas – 1996, 1997, 1998
Habig, Carl – 1952
Hackney, Gary – 1958
Hale, Darren – 1984, 1985
Hale, Mike – 1980, 1981
Hales, Mike – 1959, 1960
Haley, Kelly – 1981, 1982, 1983
Hall, Carl – 1922, 1923, 1924
Hall, Gene – 1944, 1945, 1946
Hall, Hampton – 1928, 1929
Hall, James – 1968, 1969
Hall, Michael – 1974, 1975
Hall, Moses – 1991
Hall, Norman – 1915, 1916
Hallmark, Robert – 1968, 1969
Halton, Thomas – 1972
Hamilton, Carl – 1973
Hamilton, David – 1974, 1975
Hammer, Lee – 1952, 1953
Hammonds, Jerry – 1956
Hammond, Rickey – 1976

Hammonds, Homer – 1910
Hammons, Foy – 1911
Hampel, Lee – 1913
Hampton, Derrick – 1989
Hannah, Patrick – 1988
Hannon, Bobby – 1951, 1952
Hanson, Chester – 1970
Hanson, Jeff – 1986, 1987
Harb, Harper – 1909, 1910, 1911
Harb, Joe – 1915
Harb, Winnifred – 1910
Hardin, Jay – 1993
Hargro, William – 1987
Harlan, Joe – 1929
Harmon, Bill – 1954, 1955
Harris, Allen – 1999
Harris, Brian – 1992
Harris, Carl – 1955
Harris, Derrick – 1990, 1991, 1992
Harris, Edward – 1966, 1967
Harris, Frank – 1943
Harris, Harold – 1914, 1916, 1917
Harris, Kenneth "Muskie" – 1971, 1972
Harris, Kevin – 1984, 1985
Harris, Leotis – 1990, 1991
Harris, Reginald – 1974, 1975
Harris, Reginald – 2000
Harris, Ruben – 1978, 1979
Harris, Sammy – 1961, 1962
Harris, Todd – 1915
Harris, Tom – 1913, 1914
Harris, W. D. – 1926
Hartman, David – 1965
Harvey, Earl – 1944, 1945, 1946
Harvill, Greg – 1962
Hastings, Bill – 1950, 1951
Hathcote, Bill – 1957
Hathcote, Steve – 1956, 1957, 1958
Hawkins, Trumiel – 2004
Hawn, Russell – 1926, 1927
Hayes, Kenneth – 1986, 1987, 1988
Hayes, Rodney – 1977, 1978, 1979
Haynes, Harry – 1930
Haynes, Joe – 1961, 1962
Haynes, Randall – 1965, 1966, 1967
Haynes, William – 1928
Head, Bob – 1958
Heard, Duane – 1973
Heath, Claude – 1927

Heflin, Johnny – 1962
Heien, Dickie – 1965, 1966
Heiman, Mike – 1975
Heiskell, Gene – 1975
Heitman, Lloyd – 1935, 1936, 1937
Hemphill, Meidro – 1997, 1998, 1999
Hendrix, Ronald – 1999, 2000, 2001,
Henry, Carol – 1950
Henry, Joseph – 2003, 2004
Henry, Mark – 1984, 1985, 1986
Henson, Jimmy – 1971, 1972, 1973
Herbert, Darryl – 1952, 1953, 1954
Herbert, Jack – 1931
Herman, Kirke – 1970
Herndon, Phil – 1967
Hervey, Kerry – 2001, 2002, 2003
Hestir, Johnny – 1944, 1946
Heuer, Tate – 1990, 1991, 1992
Hicks, Bill – 1955, 1956, 1957
Hicks, James – 1987, 1988, 1989
Hicks, Melvin – 1986, 1987, 1988
Hill, Gary – 1970
Hill, Joe – 1993
Hill, Marcus – 1997, 1998, 1999
Hilliard, Byron – 1991
Himsteadt, Hickey – 1911
Hinerman, Duke – 1976
Hinton, A.C. – 1938, 1939
Hinton, Charles – 1934
Hodges, Basil – 1943
Hodges, J.H. – 1922
Hodgins, Will – 1908
Hoeltzel, Fred – 1912, 1913, 1914
Hoffman, Emmett – 1917, 1919
Hoffman, John – 1942, 1943, 1944
Hoffman, John – 1961, 1962
Hoffman, Leon – 1935, 1936, 1937
Hoffman, Tommy – 1967
Hogshed, George – 1922
Holcomb, Robert – 1931
Holiman, Max – 1935
Hollaway, Bob - 1955
Hollingsworth, Don – 1961, 1962
Hollis, Bill – 1947
Holloman, David – 1965, 1966
Holloway, Jerrell – 1959, 1960
Holman, Danny – 1950
Holmes, Harry – 1906, 1909
Holmes, Matt – 2004

Holmes, Ronnie – 1958
Holmes, Tony – 1982, 1983, 1984
Holt, B. – 1906
Holt, Cecil– 1906
Holt, Fred – 1925, 1926
Honea, Ross – 1959, 1960
Honorable, David – 1995, 1996
Hood, Ben – 1968
Hood, Rodney – 1997
Hooper, Edward – 1927, 1928
Horne, Brad – 1973, 1974
Horton, Clyde – 1944, 1946
Horton, Mark – 1978, 1979, 1980
Horton, Paul – 1942
Horton, Phillip – 2001
Horvath, Ed – 1969, 1970
Howard, Clarence – 1918
Howard, Dexter – 1986, 1987, 1988
Howard, Gene – 1960
Howard, Kearnes – 1924
Howard, Kyle – 1987, 1988, 1989
Hronas, Angelo - 1971
Hudson, Don – 1940, 1941, 1942
Hudson, Michael – 1975, 1976, 1977
Huff, P.D. – 1934, 1935
Hughes, Ben – 1980, 1981, 1982
Hughes, Donald – 1970
Hughes, Howard – 1937, 1938, 1939
Hughes, Shane – 1982, 1983, 1984
Hull, Hugh – 1904, 1905
Humphrey, Sejames – 2003
Hunt, John – 1947
Hunter, Billy – 1933
Hunter, Darius – 1996, 1997, 1998
Hunter, David – 1947
Hutchins – 1905
Illing, Allen – 1971
Imbeau, Randy – 1970
Irwin, Clark – 2002, 2003, 2004
Irwin, Robey – 1948, 1949
Isgrig, Allen – 1918, 1919
Isgrig, Ben – 1915, 1916, 1917
Jackson, Andre – 2003, 2004
Jackson, Antijuan – 1997, 1998
Jackson, Bennie – 1980, 1981
Jackson, Cupid – 1994
Jackson, DeShawn – 2000, 2001
Jackson, Greg – 1985
Jackson, Greg – 2002, 2003

Jackson, Joseph – 2002, 2003, 2004
Jackson, Ralph – 1996
Jackson, Ronnie – 1981
Jackson, Tony – 1984, 1985
Jackson, Walter – 1912, 1913
Jacob, Jeff – 1983, 1984
Jacob, Kevin – 1988
James, Albert – 1980
James, Bion – 1991, 1992, 1993
James, Kip – 1986, 1987
James, Paul – 1986, 1987
James, Rob – 2004
Jamison, Charles – 1972
Jefferson, Calvin – 1990, 1991
Jenkins, Byron – 1992
Jenkins, Fernando – 2004
Jenkins, Isaac – 1987, 1988, 1989
Jenkins, Kevin – 1992
Jernigan, Erik – 1983
Jewell, Eldon – 1974
Jewell, Joe – 1972, 1973, 1974
Jewell, John – 1976
Johns, Bilal – 1993
Johns, Michael – 1954, 1955
Johnson, Antonio – 1997, 1998
Johnson, Bob – 1931, 1932, 1933
Johnson, Bobby – 1963
Johnson, Chris – 1995
Johnson, Dub – 1950, 1951
Johnson, Glen – 1983
Johnson, Henry – 1947
Johnson, James – 1989, 1990, 1991
Johnson, Jeffrey – 1999, 2000
Johnson, Johnny – 1967, 1968, 1969
Johnson, Kurt – 1987, 1988
Johnson, Marcus – 2000, 2001, 2002
Johnson, Marvin – 1922, 1923, 1924
Johnson, Oliver – 1912
Johnson, Ruben – 1973
Johnson, Steve – 1972
Johnson, Wa-Li – 1996, 1997
Jolly, Don – 1952
Jolly, Kayward – 1987, 1988
Jolly, Roger – 1976, 1977
Jones, Bill – 1932
Jones, Bill – 1951, 1952, 1954
Jones, Curtis – 1904, 1907
Jones, David – 1985, 1986
Jones, Dudley – 1910, 1912

Jones, Eric – 1991
Jones, Jeff – 1982
Jones, Jeff – 1988
Jones, Jericho – 2002, 2003, 2004
Jones, Kevin – 1992
Jones, Larry – 1949, 1950
Jones, Mike – 1973
Jones, Orlando – 1997
Jones, Sean – 1999, 2000, 2001
Jones, Todd – 1983, 1984, 1985
Jones, Virgil – 1994, 1995, 1996
Jones, Willie – 1965, 1966
Jordan, Arthur – 1999, 2000
Jordan, LeMarkus – 2001, 2002, 2003
Joshua, Jabbar – 1988, 1989
Julian, Charles – 1916
Julian, Scott – 1913
Jungkind, David – 1968, 1969
Kavanaugh, Floyd – 1914
Kavanaugh, Frank – 1911
Kavanaugh, Kenneth – 1933, 1934, 1935
Keith, Roy – 1929
Keith, Troy – 1929
Keopple, C.W. – 1943, 1946
Keopple, George – 1912
Kesler, Pepper - 1984, 1985, 1986
Key, Mike – 1963, 1964
Khabeer, Bobby – 1990, 1991, 1992
Khabeer, Sam – 1986, 1987, 1988
Killingsworth, Chris – 1992, 1993
Killingsworth, Reginald – 1990, 1991
Kinderman, Jim – 1958, 1959
King, Dick – 1961
King, Lorayne – 1931
King, Tom – 1958, 1959
King, Warren – 1906
Kinney, Homer – 1939
Kirby, Kent – 1924
Kirkpatrick, Frank – 1921
Knight, Bill – 1959, 1960
Knight, Roger – 1947
Knowles, Jerry – 1959, 1960, 1961
Kopert, Albert – 1936, 1937, 1938
Korte, Danny – 1968, 1969
Korte, Gary – 1971
Korte, Tracy – 1979
Kruger, Edward – 1917, 1918, 1919
Kumpuris, Billy – 1951
Kumpuris, Mike – 1943, 1944

Kupferle, Nick – 1911
Kusturin, Brad – 1992, 1993
Kyle, Mike – 1961, 1962
Lackey, G.H. – 1943
Lacky, Joe – 1925
Ladd, George – 1921
LaForge, Charles – 1927
LaForge, Ralph – 1928, 1929, 1930
Laing, Nelson – 1956
Lancaster - 1929
Lancaster, Steve – 1974, 1975
Lane, Chris – 1980, 1981
Lane, Tom – 1949
Langhammer, Ricky – 1964, 1965
Langley, George – 1961
Langston, Joe – 1934
Langston, Terry – 1971
Larkan, Larry – 1968
Laughy, George – 1962
Lawson, Steve – 1973, 1974
Lawson, Tony – 1987
Lea, Jim – 1959
Lebos, Richard – 1984
Lee, Chi Chi – 1977
Lefear, William – 2002
Leggs, Willie – 1997, 1998
Lehman, Ronnie – 1965
Lemmer, Robert - 1953
Lenow, Harrell – 1912, 1913
Letson, Billy – 1906, 1908
Levin, Michael – 1986
Lewis, Charlie – 1977
Lewis, Gaughan – 1933, 1934, 1935, 1936
Lewis, Greg – 1985, 1986
Lewis, Melvin - 1983, 1985
Lilly, Jason – 1991
Lilly, Keith – 1995, 1996, 1997
Lindsey, Lee – 1915
Link, Howard – 1932, 1933
Lipe, J.T. – 1924, 1925
Lipe, Steele – 1928
Lockhart, Allen – 1975
Logue, Tim – 1974
Long, J.T. – 1942, 1943
Loux, Bobby – 1967
Lovelace, Larry – 1973
Luckey, Andre – 1999, 2000, 2001
Luneau, Kevin – 2003
Lunon, Darryl – 1991

Lyons, Earl – 1989, 1990, 1991
Maack, Billy – 1937, 1938, 1939
Mabbitt, Harold – 1920
MacDonald, Mike – 1973, 1974
Mack, Randall – 1973, 1974, 1975
Mack, Terry – 1980, 1981
Maddox, Johnny – 1972
Maddox, Tommy – 1960
Magee, Mark – 1996, 1997, 1998
Mahone, Chris – 2000, 2001
Majors, Robert – 1935, 1936
Malczycki, Boris – 1955
Malczycki, Igor – 1953
Maley, Frank – 1949
Manes, Don – 1952, 1953
Manney, Mike – 1964, 1965
Manning, Van – 1915, 1916
Marks, Brint – 2004
Marks, Frederick – 1995, 1996, 1997
Marlin, Bob – 1949
Marrow, Owen – 1935
Marshall, Campbell – 1914
Marshall, James – 2001, 2002, 2003
Marshall, Jerome – 1996, 1997
Marshall, Tommy – 1962, 1963
Marshall, Wayne – 1939, 1940
Martin, Clay – 1906
Martin, Jimmy – 1954, 1955
Martin, John – 1976
Martin, Kenneth – 1978
Martin, Robert – 1910, 1911, 1912
Martin, Tony – 1969
Martindale, Lowell – 1935, 1936, 1937
Mashburn, Lewis – 1920
Mason, Derrick – 1998, 1999, 2000
Massie, Justin – 1998, 1999
Masters, Dennis – 1961, 1962
Masters, Julian – 1924, 1925
Mathes, Mike – 1970, 1971
Mathews, Rodney – 2000, 2001, 2002
Matlock, Drew – 2004
Matthews, Joe – 1956, 1957
Maxwell, Richard – 1954
May, Bill – 1956, 1957
May, Russell – 1908, 1909
Mays, Ricky – 1984, 1985
McBrayer, Tommy - 1985
McBride, Ricky – 1963
McCarthy, Lewis – 1921

McCarty, John – 1958, 1959
McCauley, Richard – 1963, 1964, 1965
McClain, Jack – 1957, 1958
McClinton, Will – 2000, 2001
McConnell, Carl – 1930
McConnell, Don – 1936, 1937
McCord, Scott – 1979, 1980
McCowan, Mitchell – 1925, 1926
McCoy, Bob – 1976
McCraney, James - 1977, 1978
McCraney, Jerry – 1977, 1978, 1979
McCraney, Joe – 1975, 1976, 1977
McCraney, Joseph – 1994, 1995, 1996
McCuin, Donny – 1974
McCully, Ed – 1934
McDaniel, Bruce – 1977, 1978
McDaniel, Stanley – 1971, 1973
McDermott, Neal – 1916, 1917, 1918, 1919
McDermott, Tommy – 1960
McDonald, Donald – 1963
McDonald, Leonard – 1995, 1996
McElroy, Bob – 1960, 1961
McElroy, Ryan – 1992
McElvaney, Seth – 1935, 1936
McFarlin, Bob – 1951
McGee, Nick – 1999, 2000, 2001
McGehee, Scott – 1904, 1905
McGibbony, Mike – 1956
McGibbony, Mike – 1979, 1980
McGibbony, Scott – 1982
McKee, Steven – 2003, 2004
McKenzie, Jim – 1976, 1977
McKindra, Freeman – 1997, 1998
McKinney, Gerald – 1940
McLeod, J.J. – 1928
McLeod, Matt – 1981, 1982
McMullen, Ahmad – 1995, 1996, 1997
McMurray, Bill – 1955
McMurray, Woodrow – 1931, 1932
McMurry, Osborne – 1939
McNeal, Damian – 1987, 1988
McNemer, Philip – 1904, 1905
McQuaney, Nathan – 1968, 1969, 1970
McVay, G.W. – 1948, 1949
McWilliams, Bob – 1956
Means, H.N. – 1953
Medley, Genard – 1969
Medlin, Earnest – 1942
Meeks, Harold – 1950, 1951

Melton, Ray – 1946
Merriweather, Marquise – 2003, 2004
Middleton, Mike – 1965, 1966
Milburn, Jeff – 1986, 1987
Miller, Ernest – 1932
Miller, Gordon – 1971
Miller, Melvin – 1925
Miller, Sterling – 1930, 1931
Miller, Tommy – 1966, 1967
Milligan, Buddy – 1953, 1954, 1955
Milliken, James – 1915, 1916, 1917
Mills, Dawson – 1921, 1923
Mills, James – 1919
Milner, Elbert – 1934
Miracle, Marvin – 1950
Mitchell, Chuck – 1987
Mitchell, Jack – 1945, 1946
Mitchell, Willie – 1917
Mittelstaedt, Matthew – 1993
Mize, Rex – 1937, 1938
Mobley, Gary – 1959, 1960
Molden, Shaun – 1990
Moore, Billy – 1955, 1956, 1957
Moore, Calvin – 1954, 1955, 1956
Moore, Chris – 1988, 1989
Moore, David – 1980, 1981
Moore, Fred – 1971, 1972
Moore, Gene – 2002, 2003, 2004
Moore, Henry – 1950, 1951
Moore, Jason – 1989, 1990, 1991
Moore, Jeffrey – 2000
Moore, Mellow – 1991, 1992, 1993
Moore, Mike – 1965, 1966
Moore, Ronald – 1973
Moore, William – 1910, 1911
Moorman, Davin – 1992, 1993, 1994
Moose, Menefee – 1910
Moreland, Ronnie – 1999
Morgan, Fred – 1954, 1955
Morgan, Jimmy – 1940
Morgan, Rich – 1980
Morley, Dean – 1904
Morris, Bruce – 1922
Morris, Keith – 1985
Morris, Teddy – 1975, 1976, 1977
Morrison, Bryan – 1975
Morton, Allen – 1990, 1991
Moser, Bob – 1960, 1961
Moses, Chris – 1994

Mosley, Elwood – 1952
Mothershed, Michael – 1998, 1999, 2000
Mothershed, Mike – 1970
Moult, Vernon – 1922, 1923
Muhammad, James – 1999
Mullens, Larry – 1950
Muller - 1910
Mullins, Larry – 1951
Murphy, Ronnie – 1986
Murray, Gordon – 1915
Murrey, James – 1911, 1912
Murrey, Joe - 1911
Myles, Dorrian – 1989, 1990, 1991
Nahlen, Larry – 1954
Nalley, Louis – 1962, 1963, 1964
Nalls, Reggie – 1952
Naylor, George – 1906, 1908
Neal, Joshua – 1995, 1996, 1997
Nealy, Ray – 1990, 1991, 1992
Neblett, Corbin – 1926, 1927, 1928
Neely, Bill – 1945
Nelson, James – 1967, 1969
Nelson, Mike – 1976, 1977
Nesterenko, Tony – 1982, 1983
Newburn, Orlando – 1994, 1995, 1996
Newby, Jack – 1931
Nicholas, Billy – 1941
Nichols, Anthony – 1999
Nichols, Bill – 1941, 1942
Nichols, Evan – 2000
Nicholson, Nick – 1920
Nickell, Louie – 1938
Nickelson, S.B. – 1921
Niggel, Mike – 1976
Nix, Anson – 1974, 1975
Noble, Harold – 1977
Nooner, Allen – 1977
Norwood, Bill – 1969, 1970
Nowden, Jimmy – 1980
Nunnley, Brandon – 2000
Nunnley, James – 1976
Nutt, Danny – 1977, 1978, 1979
Nutt, Dennis – 1979, 1980
Nutt, Dickey – 1975, 1976
Nutt, Houston – 1973, 1974, 1975
Nutt, John – 1951, 1952
O'Dell, Phillip – 1970, 1971
O'Donald, Jeffrey – 1988
O'Neal, Rex – 1912, 1913

Oakley, Tommy – 1968
Oates, Kevin – 1986
Oberle, Bob – 1951
Okoye, Victor – 1996, 1997, 1998
Oliver, Fred – 1983
Oliver, George – 1947, 1948
Owens, Brant – 1992, 1993, 1994
Pace, John – 1977, 1978
Packard, Clay – 1995
Packard, Forrest – 1965, 1966
Page, Adam – 2001, 2002, 2003
Paige, Thomas – 2002, 2003, 2004
Palmer, John – 1979, 1980, 1981
Parker – 1905
Parker, Charles – 1943, 1946
Parker, Chris – 1997
Parker, Daryl – 1999, 2000, 2001
Parker, Donald – 1976, 1977, 1978
Parker, Jodie – 1950, 1951
Parker, Richard – 1998, 1999
Parks, Paul – 1926, 1928
Patillo, Charles – 1972, 1973
Patillo, Gary – 1978, 1979, 1980
Patrick, Eric – 1995, 1996, 1997
Patrick, Rudy – 2002, 2003, 2004
Patterson, Charles – 1953
Patterson, Charles – 1957, 1958
Patterson, Jack – 1920
Patterson, John – 1930
Pavan, Rodger – 1965, 1966, 1967
Paxton, Melvin – 1969, 1970, 1971
Peace, John – 1968, 1969
Pearce, Howard – 1935
Pearce, Tommy – 1973, 1974
Pearrow, Arthur – 1956, 1957
Pearson, Rob – 1995, 1996, 1997
Peckham, Earnest – 1914, 1915
Peevy, David – 1989, 1990, 1991
Penick, Graham – 1904, 1906
Penn, Jim - 1957
Pennington, Roland – 1978, 1979
Peoples, Carlton – 1989, 1990, 1991
Peoples, Michael – 1984
Perkins, Don – 1973
Perry, Michael – 1974, 1975, 1976
Perry, Reginald – 1976, 1977
Perry, Stuart – 1952, 1953
Persley, Mark – 1987, 1988, 1989
Peters, Sammy – 1956, 1957

Peterson, Albert – 1990, 1991
Peterson, Joe – 1948
Peterson, Robert – 1982, 1983, 1984
Pettit, Jay – 1973, 1974,
Pettit, Joe – 1981, 1982
Pevia, Harold – 1941, 1942, 1943
Pfaff, Terrence – 1913, 1914, 1915
Phillips, Harold – 1997
Phillips, James – 1932
Phillips, Paul – 1979
Phillips, Tony – 1985, 1986, 1987
Pickens, Jerry – 1957
Piggee, Brian – 1994, 1995, 1996
Pighee, Gary – 1992, 1993
Pippins, Bruce – 1971
Pitcock, Jack – 1914, 1915
Plaster, George – 1949
Pleasant, Michael – 1998, 1999, 2000
Plegge, Frank – 1953, 1954, 1955
Pollock, Mike – 1974, 1975
Pool, Eugene – 1931, 1932
Poole, Dedrick – 1999, 2000, 2001
Popovitch, Rob – 1979, 1980
Poppenheimer, William – 1925
Porter, Walter – 1982, 1983
Porter, Winston – 1950, 1951
Powell, Bill – 1945
Powell, Michael – 1983, 1984
Powell, Ricky – 1982
Powell, Robert – 1918, 1919
Powell, William – 1916, 1917
Pree, George – 2000, 2001, 2002
Price, Albert – 1904
Price, Billy – 1983
Price, Greg – 1971
Price, Jeff – 1985
Price, Troy – 1973, 1974
Pride, Gary – 1982
Pride, Gerald – 1977, 1978
Pride, Keith – 1987, 1988
Pringle, Rick – 1975
Pritchard, Leland – 1937
Proctor, Larry – 1965, 1966
Puckett, Larry – 1962, 1963
Rahmaan, Shaan – 2000, 2001
Ramoly, Brinton – 1953, 1954
Ramsey, Dale – 1960
Rath, Jim – 1962, 1963
Rath, John – 1956, 1957, 1958

Ray, Herman – 1931
Rayford, Donnie – 1994
Reagan, Roy – 1942
Reed, Charles – 1951
Reese, Joe – 1952, 1953
Reynolds, Bill – 1962, 1963
Reynolds, Joe – 1950
Rhea, Troy – 1961
Richardson, John – 1968
Richardson, Keenan – 1994, 1996
Richardson, Kenneth – 1981, 1982, 1983
Richardson, Kevin – 1986, 1987
Richardson, Richard – 1976, 1977, 1978
Rideout, Herbert – 1972, 1973
Rideout, Vantriss – 1977
Ridgeway, Billy – 1977
Ridgle, Gregory – 1984, 1985, 1986
Ridgle, Tony – 1977, 1978, 1979
Riesenberg, David – 1983, 1984
Riffel, Hershell - 1918
Riggs, Lamar – 1955
Riley, Howard – 1956
Roach, Kelton – 1994, 1995, 1996
Robbins, Jack – 1932, 1933
Robbins, Leo – 1912, 1913
Roberts, Bert – 1934
Roberts, Wayland – 1949, 1950
Robertson, Gregory – 1956
Robins, Neill – 1942, 1943, 1944
Robinson, Antwain – 2002, 2003, 2004
Robinson, Billy Ray – 1971, 1972
Robinson, Brooks – 1933
Robinson, Chester – 1995, 1996
Robinson, Danny Ray – 1973, 1974, 1975
Robinson, Eddie – 1971, 1972, 1973
Robinson, Eddie – 1998, 2000
Robinson, Gary – 1958, 1959
Robinson, Nathaniel – 1970, 1971
Robinson, Nathaniel – 1973, 1974
Robinson, Reid – 1988, 1989
Robinson, Robin – 1972
Robinson, Will – 1970, 1971, 1972
Rodriguez, Arturo – 1997, 1998, 1999
Rogers, Nikarlo – 1995, 1996
Rogoski, Alex – 1911, 1912
Rolf, Raymond – 1939, 1940
Rooker, Oley – 1948, 1949
Rose, Allen – 1990
Rose, Royce – 1959

Roseby, Bernard – 2003, 2004
Ross, Allen – 1991
Roth, Bill – 1955
Rowe, Clay – 1993, 1994
Rowe, David – 1971, 1972
Rowe, Edgar – 1947
Rownd, Ed – 1967, 1968, 1969
Rudisill, Clare – 1916
Rudley, Bobby – 1977, 1978
Rule, Bill – 1945
Rule, Chris – 1982, 1983
Rule, Herb – 1953, 1954
Rule, Herbert – 1920, 1921
Rushing, Jack – 1944, 1945, 1946
Rusinko, Ryan – 1992, 1993
Russ, Gary – 1964, 1965
Russell, Ben – 1933, 1934
Russell, Derek – 1984, 1985, 1986
Russell, Gerald – 1983
Russell, John – 1936, 1937, 1938
Russell, Nic – 2004
Ruth, Bill – 1992
Rutherford, Blake – 1994, 1995
Saine, Keith – 1987
Saine, Kenon – 1991, 1992
Saine, Kenoris – 1991, 1992, 1993
Saine, Kenric – 1994, 1995, 1996
Saine, Kipkeno – 1990, 1991
Salley, Bert – 1921, 1922, 1923
Sanders, Clay – 1984
Sanders, Larry – 2000
Sanders, Michael – 1990, 1991
Sanders, Ronnie – 1987, 1988
Sanders, Sammy – 1943, 1944
Sanders, Scott – 1975, 1976, 1977
Sartin, John - 1992
Satterfield, Hammond – 1954, 1955
Satterwhite, Robert – 1927, 1928
Saugey, David – 1967
Saunders, Preston – 1948
Savage, Emanuel – 2000
Savage, Rodney – 1996
Schaufele, Louie – 1946
Schmidt, Jerry – 1965, 1966
Schmuck, Norman – 1936, 1937
Scott, Bob – 1975
Scott, Fabian – 1987
Scott, Harvey – 1976, 1977
Scott, Ray – 1916

Scott, Warren – 1986
Scroggins, Benny – 1953
Scroggins, Jesse – 1913
Sessions, Ray – 1990, 1991, 1992
Sewell, James – 1949, 1950
Sewell, Ralph – 1953
Shackleford, Marshall – 1912, 1913, 1914
Sharp, David – 1960, 1961
Sharp, James – 1923, 1924
Shaw, Clifford – 1924, 1925, 1926
Shead, Chris – 1980, 1981
Shelby, Andrew – 1988
Shell, Richard – 1946
Shelton, Clark – 1950
Shelton, Joey – 1968, 1969, 1970
Shephard, Robert – 1977
Shepherd, Bob – 1957
Sheppard, Mike – 1976
Sherrill, John – 1904, 1905
Shotts, Joe – 1973, 1974, 1975
Siegel, Blaine – 2000, 2001, 2002
Silliman, Miller – 1911, 1912, 1914
Sims, Bill – 1956
Sims, Billy – 1940, 1941
Slaughter, Carl – 1950
Sloan, Bob – 1915
Small, Sidney – 1996
Smith, Andre – 1988
Smith, Ardis – 1915, 1916
Smith, Beford – 1939
Smith, Billy – 1930
Smith, Bryan – 1976
Smith, Charles – 1954, 1955
Smith, Chris – 1977, 1978
Smith, Darwin – 1972, 1973
Smith, Ed – 1965, 1966, 1967
Smith, Eric – 1984, 1985, 1986
Smith, Erick – 1996
Smith, Eugene – 1932, 1933
Smith, Floyd – 1977, 1978
Smith, Harry – 1925, 1926
Smith, James – 1971, 1972
Smith, Jerry – 1983, 1984
Smith, Jimmy – 1974, 1975, 1976
Smith, Joey – 1980, 1981
Smith, John – 1922
Smith, John – 1971, 1972
Smith, Kenneth – 1987
Smith, Kevan – 1993, 1994, 1995

Smith, Ray – 1996
Smith, Robert E. – 1965
Smith, Stervin – 1993
Smith, Ted – 1968, 1969
Smith, Tucker – 1946
Smith, Wendell – 1976, 1977, 1978
Sneed, Leon – 1960
Snow, Armil – 1925
Snyder, Jhmichea – 1992
Sommers, Charles – 1912
Spann, Bobby – 1948, 1949
Spann, Randy – 1964, 1965
Spann, Ronnie – 1958, 1959
Spatz, Arthur – 1924
Spaulding, Byron – 1938
Spaulding, Tom – 1937, 1938
Speaker, Edwin – 1924
Spears, Gary – 1963, 1964
Spencer, Doug – 1963, 1964
Sprick, George – 1922, 1923
Sproles, Tommy – 1985, 1986
St. John, Warner – 1954, 1955
Stafford, Ned – 1929, 1930
Staggers, Lakeem – 1997, 1998, 1999
Stalnaker, Clifford – 1930, 1931
Stalnaker, Homer – 1927, 1928,
Stalnaker, Wallace – 1937
Stanley, Todd – 1984, 1985
Stansberry, Fred – 1959
Stansbury, Ernest – 1910
Stanton, Jimmy – 1941
Starling, Jason – 1989, 1990
Starnes, Bowman – 1940
Starnes, Tommy – 1970
Stathakis, Sam – 1942
Stausberry, Fred – 1960
Steadman, Zach – 1995, 1997
Steed, Charles – 1939
Steed, John – 1980, 1981, 1982
Steele, David – 1968, 1969
Steele, Mack – 1911
Stevens, Charles – 1966
Stevens, M.L. – 1951
Stevenson, Alan – 1941
Stewart, Carl – 1930
Stewart, Charles – 1918, 1919
Stewart, Seann – 1985, 1986
Stillman, John – 1933, 1934
Stinsin, Keith – 1985

Stinson, Richard – 1968
Stoelzing, Skip – 1982, 1983
Stolzer, Forest – 1984, 1985, 1986
Stolzer, Kevin – 1997, 1998, 1999
Stolzer, Tim – 1972
Stone, Harold – 1952
Stracener, Gerry – 1960, 1961
Stribling, Patrick – 1987
Sullards, Fletcher – 1943
Sullenger, Patrick – 1996
Sullenger, Robby – 1994, 1995, 1996
Sullivan, Jake – 2002
Sullivan, Josh – 1999, 2000, 2001
Sumlin, Hiram – 2001, 2002
Swindell, Russell – 1975
Swinton, Darryl – 1984, 1985
Swinton, Reggie – 1991, 1992, 1993
Switzer, Doug - 1988, 1989, 1990
Switzer, Greg – 1984, 1985, 1986
Sykes, Mike – 1976
Tackett, Buddy – 1957, 1958
Tackett, Cecil – 1956
Talley, Tim – 1996, 1997, 1998
Tanner, Gene – 1968, 1969
Tate, Gary – 1964, 1965
Taylor, Joe – 1968
Taylor, Ryan – 2002, 2003
Taylor, Tommy – 1953
Teague, Charles – 1957
Teague, Robert – 1962, 1963
Teddar, Sonny – 1952, 1953
Terry, Walter – 1909, 1910
Tesney, Todd - 1980
Thomas, A.J. – 2001, 2002, 2003
Thomas, Brian – 1995, 1996, 1997
Thomas, Chris – 1983, 1984
Thomas, James – 2003
Thomas, Ken – 1964
Thomas, Robert – 1937, 1938, 1939
Thomas, Roger – 1977
Thompson, Henry – 1924
Thompson, Lee – 1981, 1982
Thompson, Michael – 1982, 1983
Thompson, Rodney – 1988
Thompson, Roosevelt – 1978, 1979
Thorne, Edward – 1957
Thornhill, Stephen – 1974, 1975
Thornton, Kevin – 2002, 2003, 2004
Thorpe, Clifford – 1931

Thorpe, Wilfred – 1934, 1935
Thrasher, Eric – 1973, 1974, 1975
Thresher, Howard – 1967, 1968
Thurmond, Will – 1992
Tilley, Harold – 1949
Tolbert, Emanuel – 1973, 1974, 1975
Topps, Henry – 1977
Torrence, Bobby – 1992
Townsend, Richard – 2000, 2001
Tracy, Clyde – 1949
Tracy, Kermit – 1946, 1947
Trammel, Robert – 1961, 1962
Trantham, Tommy – 1961, 1962
Trieschmann, John – 1953
Trotter, Greg – 1977, 1978, 1979
Trotter, Keith – 1987, 1988, 1989
Trudell, Jimmy – 1961
Trudell, Mike – 1961
Tubb, Ben – 1953
Tubbs, Freddie – 1953
Tubbs, Robert – 1927, 1928
Tucker, Jack – 1947
Tucker, Jack – 1956
Turner, Alan – 1978, 1979
Turner, Dustin – 1992
Turner, J.D. – 1932
Turner, Kendrick – 1987, 1988
Turney, Stan – 1971
Underwood, Ronald – 1951, 1952
Updegraff, Bob – 1948
Vandiver, Roger – 1962, 1963
Varnell, Roger – 1974, 1975
Vaughn, Ezekiel – 1973, 1974, 1975
Venable, John – 1952
Venner, Allen – 1948, 1949
Vestal, Charles – 1940
Vinsant, Gerald – 1922, 1923
VonSteen, Jim – 1980
Voth, Gayle – 1958, 1959
Waddell, Aaron – 1993, 1994, 1995
Waddell, Ernest – 1993
Waddle, Benjy – 1939
Wage, Paul – 1925, 1926
Wagnon, David – 1963, 1964
Wahlquist, Gary – 1958, 1959
Wakwe, Kenneth – 2000, 2001, 2002
Wakwe, Stanley – 2002, 2003, 2004
Wakwe, Walter – 1999, 2000
Walden, Gene – 1931, 1932, 1933

Walden, Harry – 1930, 1932, 1933
Waldron, Louis – 1945, 1946
Walker, Earvin – 1983, 1984
Walker, George – 1971, 1972
Walker, Jimmy – 1972, 1973, 1974
Walker, Johnny – 1948, 1949
Walker, William – 1977
Wallace, Doug – 1987, 1988
Wallace, Jim – 1951
Walters, Ben – 1995, 1996, 1997
Walters, Louis – 1937, 1938
Walthall, Billy – 1948, 1949
Ward, Darrell – 1959, 1960, 1961
Ward, John – 1918
Ward, Sibley – 1906, 1907, 1908
Wardlaw, Don – 1949
Ware, Halliburton – 1934, 1935
Ware, Myrick – 1987
Warren, Bob – 1964, 1965
Warren, Steve – 1989, 1990
Warrick, Cleve – 1964, 1965
Washington, Dwain – 1977
Wassell, Lynn – 1907
Wayman, Armour – 1946
Wayman, Eugene – 1935, 1936
Webb, John – 1946, 1947
Webb, Josh – 1995, 1996, 1997
Weekley, Larry – 1979
Weeks, Ronnie – 1952, 1953
Weidemeyer, Harry – 1909
Weidemeyer, Jesse – 1909, 1910, 1911
Weiss, Hansel – 1963, 1964
Weist, Edwin – 1913, 1914, 1915
Welch, Charles – 1918, 1919, 1920
Welch, Jerry – 1959, 1960
Wells, Otto – 1914
West, Antonio – 2003
Westmoreland, Frank – 1968, 1969
Wetherington, Jim - 1952, 1953, 1954
Whisnant, Cliff – 1971, 1972
White, Dishongh – 1978, 1979
White, Larry – 1965, 1966
White, Learrie – 1993
White, Melvin – 1937, 1938
Whitten, Mackey – 1925, 1926
Whittington, Scott – 1981
Wilburn, James – 1960
Wiley, Vernon – 1970, 1971
Wilkerson, Tristan – 2002, 2003, 2004

Wilkins, Jack – 1946, 1947
Willbanks, James – 1971, 1972
Williams, Andre – 1996
Williams, Anton – 2002, 2003
Williams, Barry – 1981, 1982
Williams, Brad – 1988, 1989, 1990
Williams, Bryan – 1997, 1998, 1999
Williams, Carl – 1945, 1946
Williams, Carl – 1980, 1981
Williams, Clyde – 1927, 1928, 1929, 1930
Williams, Fred – 1945, 1946, 1947
Williams, Ivan – 1919, 1920, 1921
Williams, Jesse – 1968, 1969
Williams, Jessie – 1970
Williams, Keith – 1999, 2000, 2001
Williams, Kenneth – 1983
Williams, Kyle – 1982
Williams, Mark – 1980, 1981
Williams, Mark – 1995, 1996
Williams, Milton – 1951
Williams, Morris – 1942
Williams, Nick – 1960
Williams, Orval – 1919, 1920
Williams, Ronnie – 1998, 1999
Williams, Ryan – 1998, 1999
Williams, Shawn – 1998
Williams, Stuart – 1925
Williamson, Arthur – 1986
Willis, Troy – 1968, 1969, 1970
Wilson, Wayne – 1971
Winburn, Hardy – 1949
Witcher, Clint – 1980, 1981
Withee, Norman – 1929, 1930
Withers, Art - 1934

Witherspoon, Michael – 2004
Wittenberg, G.H. – 1909
Wood, Billy – 1965, 1966
Wood, Charles – 1965, 1966
Wood, Jimmy – 1954, 1955, 1956
Woodiel, Billy – 1943, 1944
Woodmansee, Scott – 1952, 1953, 1954
Woods, Kenneth – 2004
Woods, Reginald – 1975
Woodsmall, Otis – 1924
Woodson, Louis – 1966
Wordlaw, Lowrekus – 1993
Worthington, Bob – 1971, 1972
Worthington, Fred – 1959, 1960
Wren, Greg – 1964
Wright, Bill – 1945, 1946, 1947
Wright, Kevin – 1984, 1985, 1986
Wright, Kevin – 1993, 1994, 1995
Wright, Leslie – 1974
Wycoff, Douglas – 1920, 1921
Yarbrough, Marcus – 1994, 1995, 1996
Yates, Robert – 1980, 1981
Young, Harold – 1905, 1908, 1909
Young, Luther – 1947, 1948
Young, Michael – 1986, 1987, 1988
Young, Ray – 1975, 1976
Young, Robert – 1965, 1966, 1967
Young, Seth – 1993, 1994
Youngblood, Kenneth – 1962, 1963
Zinamon, Bert – 1977, 1978, 1979
Zini, Kenneth – 1956, 1957, 1958

NOTE: Letters were not officially awarded until 1907. However, those who played between 1904 and 1906 are listed as letterman, due in large part to their help in creating a lasting history for the city of Little Rock and Central High School.

ARKANSAS STATE CHAMPIONS
Largest Classification

1904	Unknown	1936	Blytheville	1972	NLR (Ole Main)
1905	Fort Smith	1937	Pine Bluff	1973	LR Parkview
1906	Unknown	1938	LR Central	1974	LR Parkview
1907	LR Central	1939	Pine Bluff	1975	LR Central
1908	LR Central	1940	Blytheville	1976	LR Parkview
1909	LR Central	1941	Blytheville	1977	LR Parkview
1910	Fort Smith	1942	El Dorado		LR Hall
1911	Fordyce Clary Training	1943	Pine Bluff		Pine Bluff
1912	Van Buren	1944	LR Central	1978	LR Central
1913	Fort Smith	1945	El Dorado		LR Parkview
1914	LR Central		Fort Smith	1979	LR Hall
1915	LR Central		Texarkana	1980	LR Central
1916	Pine Bluff	1946	LR Central		FS Northside
1917	LR Central	1947	LR Central	1981	LR Central
1918	LR Central	1948	LR Central	1982	LR Hall
1919	LR Central	1949	LR Central	1983	FS Southside
1920	LR Central	1950	LR Central	1984	LR Catholic
1921	LR Central	1951	Pine Bluff	1985	LR Catholic
	Pine Bluff	1952	LR Central	1986	LR Central
1922	Pine Bluff	1953	LR Central	1987	FS Northside
1923	LR Central	1954	LR Central	1988	FS Southside
1924	El Dorado	1955	LR Central	1989	Springdale
1925	Pine Bluff	1956	LR Central	1990	Pine Bluff
1926	Pine Bluff	1957	LR Central	1991	FS Southside
1927	Pine Bluff	1958	El Dorado	1992	FS Southside
1928	Pine Bluff	1959	LR Hall	1993	Pine Bluff
1929	Pine Bluff	1960	LR Central	1994	Pine Bluff
1930	Van Buren	1961	FS Northside	1995	Pine Bluff
1931	Fort Smith	1962	Pine Bluff	1996	Van Buren
	Camden	1963	Pine Bluff	1997	FS Southside
1932	Pine Bluff	1964	LR Hall	1998	LR Fair
	Fort Smith	1965	North Little Rock	1999	FS Northside
	El Dorado	1966	LR Hall	2000	Cabot
1933	El Dorado		North Little Rock	2001	Bentonville
	Russellville		FS Northside	2002	FS Southside
	Searcy	1967	FS Northside	2003	LR Central
1934	Hot Springs	1968	FS Northside	2004	LR Central
	Blytheville	1969	LR Hall		
	DeQueen	1970	NLR (Ole Main)		
1935	Pine Bluff	1971	LR Catholic		
	Blytheville		FS Northside		

LITTLE ROCK CENTRAL HIGH
ALMA MATER

HAIL TO THE OLD GOLD,

HAIL TO THE BLACK.

HAIL ALMA MATER,

NAUGHT DOES SHE LACK.

WE LOVE NO OTHER,

SO LET OUR MOTTO BE-

VICTORY

LITTLE ROCK CENTRAL HIGH!!

LITTLE ROCK CENTRAL HIGH
"FIGHT SONG"

Fight 'em Tigers,

Fight 'em Tigers,

Run right through that line,

Run the ball clear down the field boys,

Touchdown sure this time- rah rah rah!

Fight 'em Tigers,

Fight 'em Tigers,

Fight on for your fame

Fight Tigers, Fight, Fight, Fight

To win this game! Hey!

Chi cha ha ha Tigers, Tigers Rah Rah Rah

Chi cha ha ha Tigers, Tigers Rah Rah Rah

TIGERS TIGERS

Yeah Tigers!